SCOTT FORESMAN

SOCIAL STUDIES

Grade 1
Teacher's Edition

All Together

Editorial Offices: Glenview, Illinois • Parsippany, New Jersey • New York, New York
Sales Offices: Parsippany, New Jersey • Duluth, Georgia • Glenview, Illinois
Coppell, Texas • Ontario, California

ISBN: 0-328-01886-4

1 2 3 4 5 6 7 8 9 10 V064 11 10 09 08 07 06 05 04 03 02

What makes this program different and better?

People make the difference. The people behind Scott Foresman Social Studies share a personal commitment to this program. They believe it can change students' lives and help build a better future.

PROGRAM AUTHORS

Dr. Candy Dawson Boyd
Professor, School of Education
Director of Reading Programs
St. Mary's College
Moraga, California

Dr. C. Frederick Risinger
Director, Professional Development and Social Studies Education
Indiana University
Bloomington, Indiana

Dr. Allen D. Glenn
Professor and Dean Emeritus
College of Education
Curriculum and Instructio
University of Washington
Seattle, Washington

Dr. Geneva Gay
Professor of Education
University of Washington
Seattle, Washington

Sara Miranda Sanchez
Elementary and Early Childhood Curriculum Coordinator
Albuquerque Public Schools
Albuquerque, New Mexico

Dr. Carole L. Hahn
Professor, Educational Studies
Emory University
Atlanta, Georgia

Rita Geiger
Director of Social Studies and Foreign Languages
Norman Public Schools
Norman, Oklahoma

Dr. James B. Kracht
Associate Dean for Undergraduate Programs and Teacher Education
College of Education
Texas A & M University
College Station, Texas

Dr. Valerie Ooka Pang
Professor of Teacher Education
San Diego State University
San Diego, California

CONTRIBUTING AUTHORS

Dr. Carol Berkin
Professor of History
Baruch College and the Graduate Center,
The City University of New York
New York, New York

Dr. M. Gail Hickey
Professor of Education
Indiana University-Purdue University
Ft. Wayne, Indiana

Lee A. Chase
Staff Development Specialist
Chesterfield County Public Schools
Chesterfield County, Virginia

Dr. Bonnie Meszaros
Associate Director
Center for Economic Education and Entrepreneurship
University of Delaware
Newark, Delaware

Dr. Jim Cummins
Professor of Curriculum
Ontario Institute for Studies in Education
University of Toronto
Toronto, Canada

CONTENT CONSULTANTS

Dr. Michael Frassetto
Studies in Religions
Independent Scholar
Chicago, Illinois

Dr. Gerald Greenfield
Hispanic-Latino Studies
History Department
University of Wisconsin, Parkside
Kenosha, Wisconsin

Dr. Frederick Hoxie
Native American Studies
University of Illinois
Urbana, Illinois

Dr. Michael Khodarkovsky
Eastern European Studies
University of Chicago
Chicago, Illinois

Dr. Cheryl Johnson-Odim
Dean of Liberal Arts and Sciences
and Professor of History
African American History Specialist
Columbia College
Chicago, Illinois

CLASSROOM REVIEWERS

Diana Vicknair Ard
Woodlake Elementary School
St. Tammany Parish
Mandeville, Louisiana

Dr. Charlotte R. Bennett
St. John School
Newburgh, Indiana

Sharon Berenson
Freehold Learning Center
Freehold, New Jersey

Betsy Blanford
Pocahontas Elementary School
Powhatan, Virginia

Gloria Cantatore
Public School Number Five
West New York, New Jersey

LuAnn Curran
Westgate Elementary School
St. Petersburg, Florida

Louis De Angelo
Office of Catholic Education
Archdiocese of Philadelphia
Philadelphia, Pennsylvania

Dr. Trish Dolansinski
Paradise Valley
Arrowhead Elementary School
Phoenix, Arizona

Dr. John R. Doyle
Social Studies Coordinator
Miami-Dade County Schools
Miami, Florida

Roceal Duke
District of Columbia Public Schools
Washington, D.C.

Peggy Flanagan
Community Consolidated School
District #64
Roosevelt Elementary
Park Ridge, Illinois

Mary Flynn
Arrowhead Elementary School
Glendale, Arizona

Sue Gendon
Spring Branch I. S. D.
Houston, Texas

Su Hickenbottom
Totem Falls Elementary School
Snohomish School District
Snohomish, Washington

Sally Hunter
Highland Park Elementary School
Austin I. S. D.
Austin, Texas

Allan Jones
North Branch Public Schools
North Branch, Minnesota

Brandy Bowers Kerbow
Bettye Haun Elementary School
Plano I. S. D.
Plano, Texas

Sandra López
PSJA Service Center
San Juan, Texas

Martha Sutton Maple
Shreve Island School
Shreveport, Louisiana

Lyn Metzger
Community Consolidated School
District #64
Carpenter School
Park Ridge, Illinois

Marsha Musey
Riverbend Elementary School
West Monroe, Louisiana

Christine Nixon
Warrington Elementary School
Escambia County School District
Pensacola, Florida

Liz Salinas
Supervisor
Edgewood I. S. D.
San Antonio, Texas

Beverly Scaling
Desert Hills Elementary
Las Cruces, New Mexico

Madeleine Schmitt
St. Louis Public Schools
St. Louis, Missouri

Barbara Schwartz
Central Square
Intermediate School
Central Square, New York

Dr. Thad Sitton
St. Edwards University
Austin, Texas

Ronald Snapp
North Lawrence
Community Schools
Bedford, Indiana

Lesley Ann Stahl
Westside Catholic
Consolidated School
Evansville, Indiana

Carolyn Moss Woodall
Loudoun County of Virginia
Public Schools
Leesburg, Virginia

Suzanne Zeremba
J B Fisher Model School
Richmond Public Schools
Richmond, Virginia

How do I teach my students key content?

Children need to explore their world and see how they can contribute as individuals.
Scott Foresman Social Studies helps every child become an active, involved, and informed citizen.

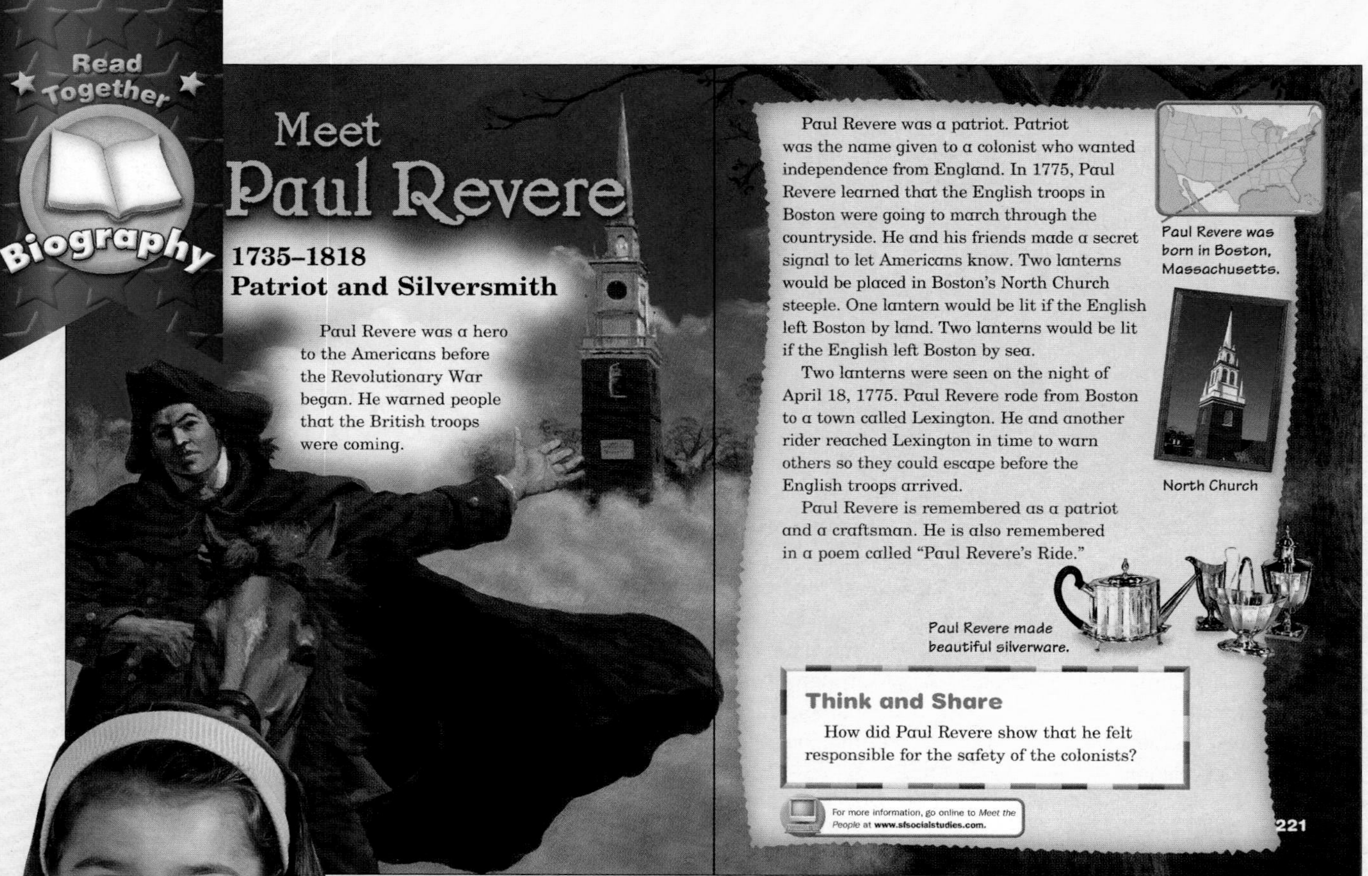

Read Together
Biography
Meet Paul Revere
1735–1818
Patriot and Silversmith
Paul Revere was a hero to the Americans before the Revolutionary War began. He warned people that the British troops were coming.
Paul Revere was a patriot. Patriot was the name given to a colonist who wanted independence from England. In 1775, Paul Revere learned that the English troops in Boston were going to march through the countryside. He and his friends made a secret signal to let Americans know. Two lanterns would be placed in Boston's North Church steeple. One lantern would be lit if the English left Boston by land. Two lanterns would be lit if the English left Boston by sea.
Two lanterns were seen on the night of April 18, 1775. Paul Revere rode from Boston to a town called Lexington. He and another rider reached Lexington in time to warn others so they could escape before the English troops arrived.
Paul Revere is remembered as a patriot and a craftsman. He is also remembered in a poem called "Paul Revere's Ride."
Paul Revere was born in Boston, Massachusetts.
North Church
Paul Revere made beautiful silverware.
Think and Share
How did Paul Revere show that he felt responsible for the safety of the colonists?
For more information, go online to Meet the People at www.sfsocialstudies.com.
221

HISTORY TO ENGAGE AND INSPIRE

- ★ Up-to-date, accurate, and comprehensive
- ★ Fully aligned to curriculum standards
- ★ Biographies that bring key figures to life
- ★ Museum-quality artwork, photographs, and diagrams
- ★ Web-based updates and activities
- ★ Interactive multimedia

GEOGRAPHY TO LINK PEOPLE AND PLACES

- ★ Exclusive maps that are custom built for Scott Foresman by MapQuest™
- ★ Maps that show change and movement
- ★ Beautifully illustrated map adventures
- ★ Lessons to help children read maps and understand directional terms
- ★ Online atlas with up-to-the-minute maps and current information

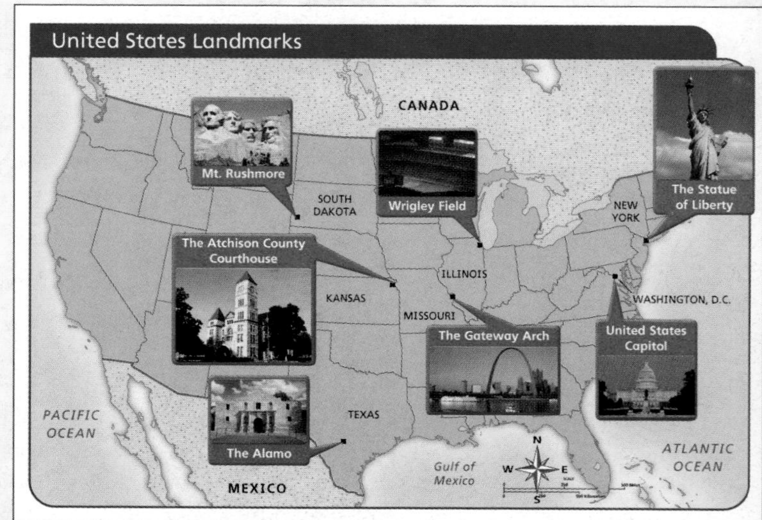

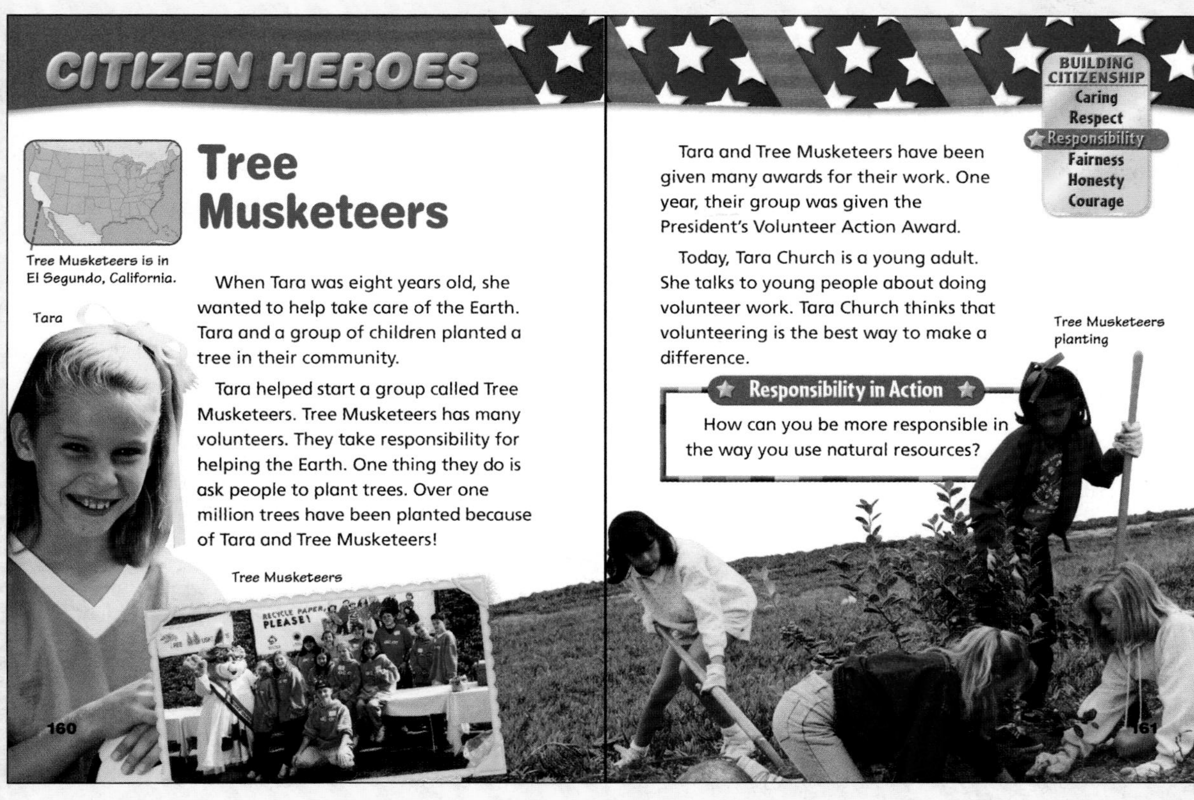

CITIZEN HEROES

Tree Musketeers

Tree Musketeers is in El Segundo, California.

Tara

When Tara was eight years old, she wanted to help take care of the Earth. Tara and a group of children planted a tree in their community.

Tara helped start a group called Tree Musketeers. Tree Musketeers has many volunteers. They take responsibility for helping the Earth. One thing they do is ask people to plant trees. Over one million trees have been planted because of Tara and Tree Musketeers!

Tree Musketeers

160

BUILDING CITIZENSHIP
Caring
Respect
Responsibility
Fairness
Honesty
Courage

Tara and Tree Musketeers have been given many awards for their work. One year, their group was given the President's Volunteer Action Award.

Today, Tara Church is a young adult. She talks to young people about doing volunteer work. Tara Church thinks that volunteering is the best way to make a difference.

Tree Musketeers planting

Responsibility in Action

How can you be more responsible in the way you use natural resources?

161

CITIZENSHIP LESSONS TO HELP CHILDREN MAKE A DIFFERENCE

- Built-in lessons in the student book teach good citizenship skills and a positive self concept: Caring, Respect, Responsibility, Fairness, Courage, and Honesty.
- Historic figures and everyday citizen heroes inspire students.
- Engaging, real-life applications

Content that covers the key social studies strands

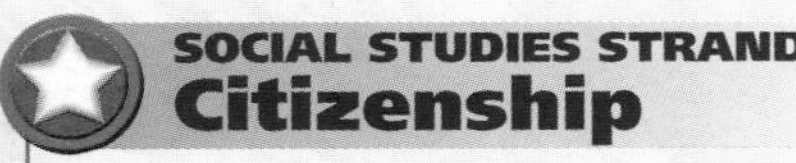

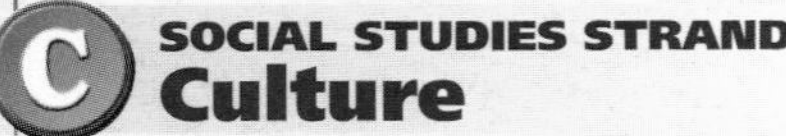

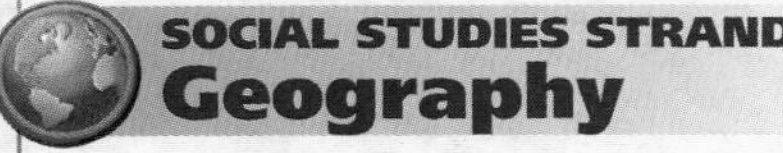

SOCIAL STUDIES STRAND
Government

SOCIAL STUDIES STRAND
History

SOCIAL STUDIES STRAND
Science • Technology

Content organized for the way you teach

If time is short, use the Quick Teaching Plan to cover the core content and skills.

If time is short, write the vocabulary words on the board.

- Have volunteers suggest words related to each vocabulary word.
- List the responses on the board.

OR

To add depth and richer enjoyment, use the wealth of information in each lesson.

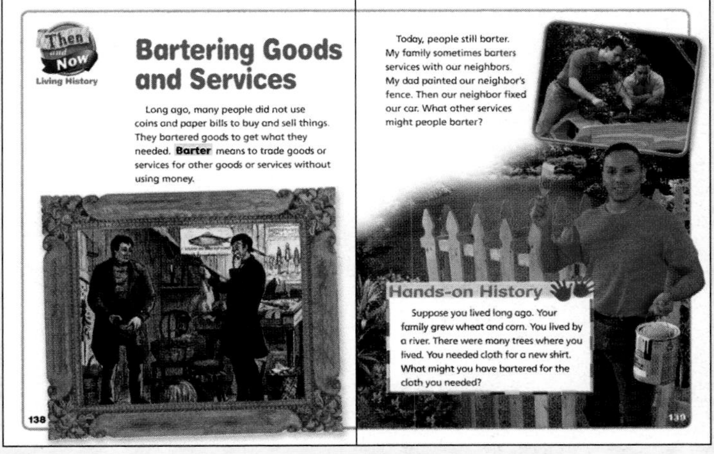

Then and Now
Living History

Bartering Goods and Services

Long ago, many people did not use coins and paper bills to buy and sell things. They bartered goods to get what they needed. **Barter** means to trade goods or services for other goods or services without using money.

138

Today, people still barter. My family sometimes barters services with our neighbors. My dad painted our neighbor's fence. Then our neighbor fixed our car. What other services might people barter?

Hands-on History

Suppose you lived long ago. Your family grew wheat and corn. You lived by a river. There were many trees where you lived. You needed cloth for a new shirt. What might you have bartered for the cloth you needed?

139

What can I do to reach all my students?

If children are going to be successful, they need to practice and apply effective reading strategies. Scott Foresman Social Studies provides systematic instruction to improve comprehension and to reach out to all learners.

UNIT 3

Reading Social Studies

Ben at Work

Put Things in Order

Target Skill

Hi! I'm Ben. Someday I want to own a pizza shop.

Saturday I had a lemonade stand. These pictures show the order in which things happened. Use your own words to tell what I did.

First

Next

92

Did you use words like **first, next,** and **last?** Those words tell the order in which things happened.

First, I made the lemonade.

Next, I set up my stand.

Last, I sold a cup to my friend.

Look for **first, next,** and **last** as you learn more about people at work.

10¢ Lemonade 10¢

Last

Try it!

Tell or write about how Ben could make a pizza. Use the words **first, next,** and **last.** Draw pictures to show the order in which things happen.

93

DEVELOPING READING SKILLS WITH SOCIAL STUDIES

- ★ Built-in comprehension skill lessons in every unit
- ★ Preteach a target comprehension skill, then apply the same skill throughout the unit for sustained practice
- ★ Graphic organizers provide support for every skill.

Target Skill

LOOK FOR THE TARGET SKILL ICON!

- ★ At the beginning of lesson
- ★ In Lesson Reviews
- ★ Throughout the units
- ★ In Unit Reviews

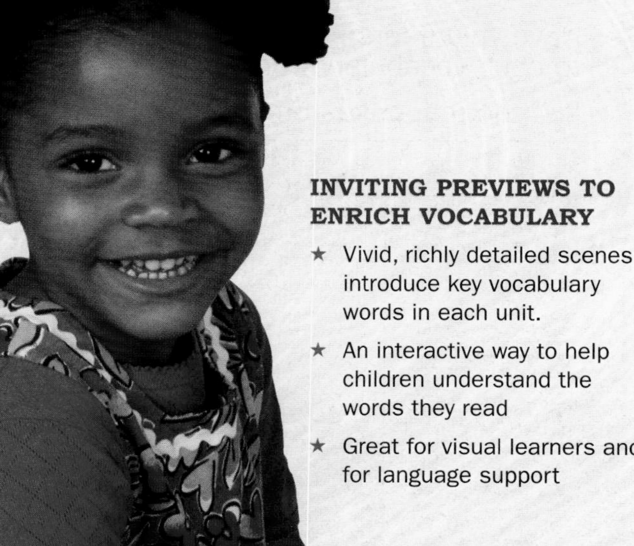

INVITING PREVIEWS TO ENRICH VOCABULARY

- ★ Vivid, richly detailed scenes introduce key vocabulary words in each unit.
- ★ An interactive way to help children understand the words they read
- ★ Great for visual learners and for language support

UNIT 3

Vocabulary Preview

100

101

MEETING INDIVIDUAL NEEDS
Leveled Practice

Interviews

Children choose a service worker they want to find out more about by writing interview questions.

Easy Have children write one interview question they would like to ask a service worker. **Reteach**

On-Level Children write three or four questions for an interview. Questions can be about the duties performed, how the worker uses tools to perform his or her job, who pays the worker, and the challenges the worker faces every day. **Extend**

Challenge Have pairs of children take turns interviewing and being interviewed, using their questions. Encourage children to preview the questions they will be asked and find answers as needed. **Enrich**

LEVELED PRACTICE TO MATCH CHILDREN'S ABILITIES

- ★ The same activity at three instructional levels to reach all learners
- ★ Specific strategies for various learning styles
- ★ Promotes active participation and learning in every lesson

service
A job a person does to help others. As a firefighter, my mom provides a service to our neighborhood.

ESL ESL Support

Using Pictures Show children pictures of modern-day soup kitchens or other places people can go for help in the community.

Beginning Ask children to point to the pictures as they repeat the names of jobs of the workers pictured on pp. 108–111. Then show other job pictures and help children brainstorm a list of other jobs.

Intermediate Have children follow along as you read the sentences in speech balloons on pp. 108–110. Then have children name the workers pictured on p. 111 and dictate sentences the workers might say.

Advanced After children identify the workers pictured in the book, they can find pictures of other workers and use them to talk about the jobs these people do and the goods or services they provide.

For additional ESL support, use Every Student Learns Guide, pp. 50–53.

LANGUAGE STRATEGIES AT POINT OF USE

- ★ Effective strategies for Beginning, Intermediate, and Advanced language learners in every lesson
- ★ Explore word meanings, usage, and form as well as cognates, etymologies, and more

AUDIO TEXT AND VOCABULARY CARDS TO HELP ALL STUDENTS ACCESS CONTENT

- ★ All lessons are recorded so students can listen and read along.
- ★ Vocabulary cards for all key terms include picture and definition.

Every Student Learns

- ★ Access prior knowledge/build background: poster discussions, read alouds, word banks, word webs, and activity ideas
- ★ Access content: lesson summaries, graphic organizers, and blackline practice worksheets
- ★ Extend language: activities that use the language and content of the lesson

How can I engage and motivate my students?

Scott Foresman Social Studies is brimming with compelling visuals, intriguing facts, and exciting real-world learning. It makes every child an interested social studies student who feels, knows, and thinks.

SMITHSONIAN VISUAL LESSONS

- ★ Developed exclusively for Scott Foresman in cooperation with the Smithsonian Institution
- ★ Brilliant visual lessons that bring children up close to national treasures and fascinating artifacts
- ★ A museum in every student book

DORLING KINDERSLEY VISUAL LESSONS

- ★ Recognized around the world for its visually stunning informational books and resources
- ★ Bold, large-as-life photographs with interesting, easy-to-read expository captions
- ★ Helps children visualize their world and its past

DORLING KINDERSLEY

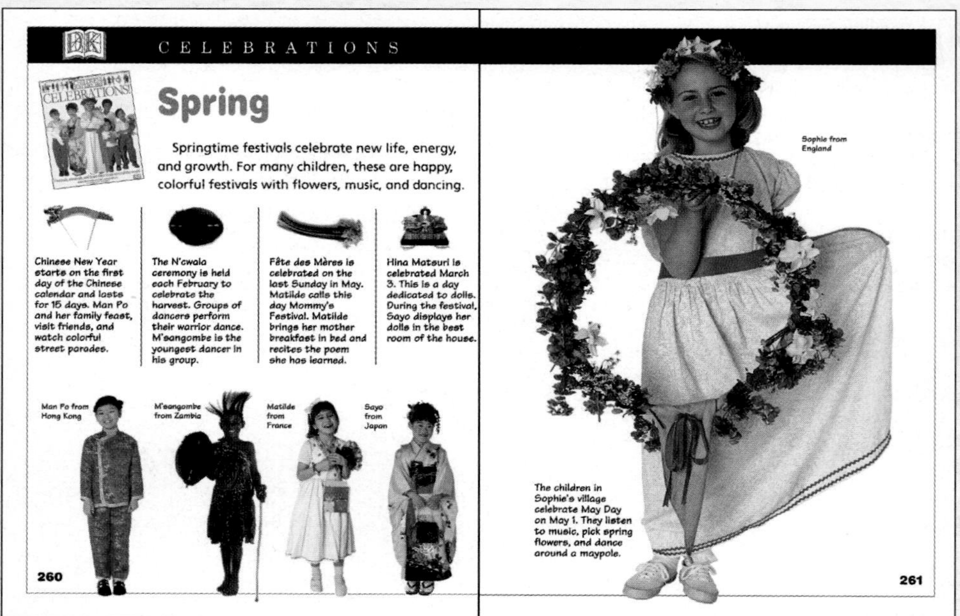

A Note from the Smithsonian

Viewing treasures of the past

What makes us want to see the flag that inspired the national anthem? Why do we stand in awe before George Washington's historic uniform?

These are treasured icons of our nation. They tell the story of America, our story. It is a story filled with great courage and sacrifice, with heartfelt convictions and a lasting belief in liberty and justice for all. These treasured icons, these priceless relics, bring us closer to who we are and what we believe as a nation.

The mission of the Smithsonian Institution is "the increase and diffusion of knowledge." Nowhere is the knowledge of our past more useful than in the minds and hearts of our children. Museum objects and their unique stories bring history alive and make it more exciting for children to learn. It is an honor to fulfill our mission this way by sharing these objects with a new generation of students.

UNIT
3
Begin with a Song
Ben's Pizza
Lots of Jobs
by Latrice Butler
Sung to the tune of "Skip to My Lou"
Baker, teacher, doctor, too.
Lots of jobs I'd like to do.
Care for animals in the zoo.
What kinds of work would you do?
88
89

BEGIN WITH A SONG FOR LIVELY ENGAGING LEARNING

- ★ Introduce important concepts and vocabulary in each unit with fun rhymes and rhythms
- ★ Promote interaction and social participation
- ★ Delightful recordings of each song on audio

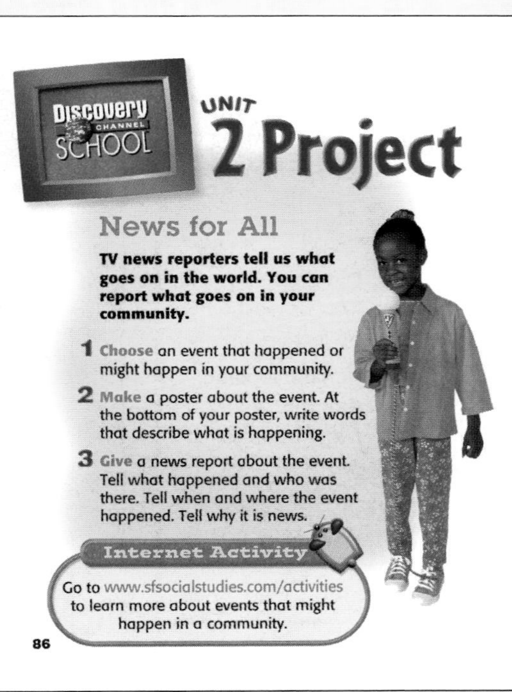

Discovery Channel School
UNIT 2 Project
News for All
TV news reporters tell us what goes on in the world. You can report what goes on in your community.
1 Choose an event that happened or might happen in your community.
2 Make a poster about the event. At the bottom of your poster, write words that describe what is happening.
3 Give a news report about the event. Tell what happened and who was there. Tell when and where the event happened. Tell why it is news.
Internet Activity
Go to www.sfsocialstudies.com/activities to learn more about events that might happen in a community.
86

DISCOVERY CHANNEL SCHOOL PROJECTS

- ★ From one of the world's leading providers of educational multimedia
- ★ Exclusive, hands-on unit projects synthesize and enhance learning.
- ★ Exciting Web-based activities extend lessons.

Social Studies Plus!

A HANDS-ON APPROACH

- ★ Long-term and short-term projects and activities to extend lessons
- ★ Social Studies Fair ideas, Readers Theater, learning center themes, holiday celebrations, writing and research activities, and more
- ★ Inspires hands-on, mind-on learning

WEB-BASED INFORMATION CENTER

- ★ **Continually updated information, maps, and biographies**
- ★ Exclusive, customized **Factmonster**™ from **Infoplease**®
- ★ Motivating, interactive learning games

How will I know my students are successful?

Children need to become critical thinkers who can solve problems, work together, and make decisions. Scott Foresman Social Studies provides built-in skill lessons and multiple assessment tools to develop thinking citizens.

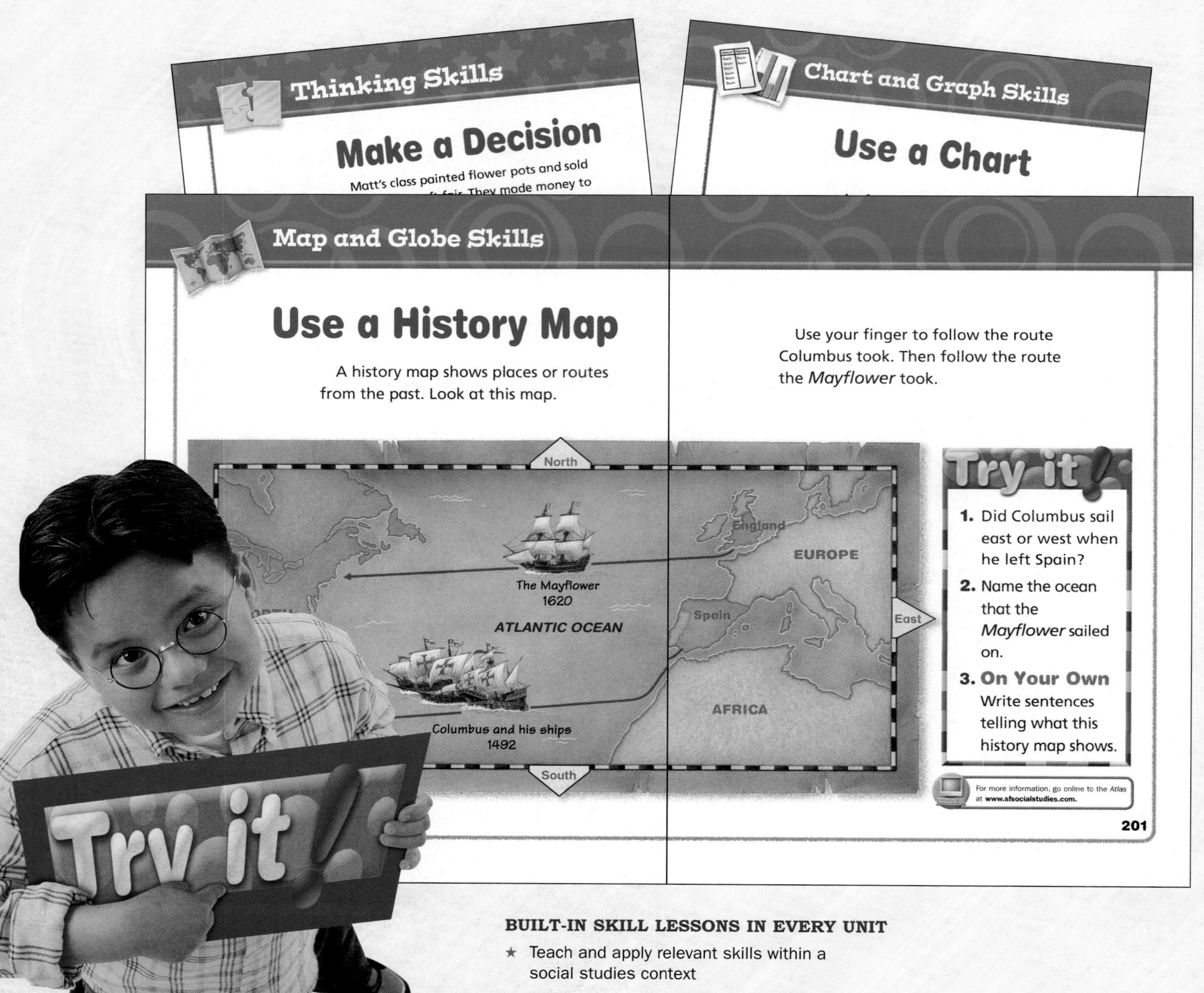

Thinking Skills
Make a Decision
Matt's class painted flower pots and sold
Chart and Graph Skills
Use a Chart
Map and Globe Skills
Use a History Map
A history map shows places or routes from the past. Look at this map.
Use your finger to follow the route Columbus took. Then follow the route the *Mayflower* took.
North
England
EUROPE
The Mayflower
1620
ATLANTIC OCEAN
Spain
East
AFRICA
Columbus and his ships
1492
South
Try it!
1. Did Columbus sail east or west when he left Spain?
2. Name the ocean that the *Mayflower* sailed on.
3. On Your Own Write sentences telling what this history map shows.
For more information, go online to the Atlas at www.sfsocialstudies.com.
201
Try it!

BUILT-IN SKILL LESSONS IN EVERY UNIT

- ★ Teach and apply relevant skills within a social studies context
- ★ Graphics that support the content

Ongoing Assessment

If... children do not know if what a particular worker provides is a good or a service,

then... remind them that goods are what workers make or grow and services are what workers do to help others.

INFORMAL ASSESSMENT OPPORTUNITIES

- ★ Monitor children's learning as you teach
- ★ If/then guidelines with specific reteaching strategies and effective practice
- ★ Assess instruction and make adjustments

TEST-TAKING STRATEGY LESSONS

- ★ Develop test-taking strategies right in the student book
- ★ Test preparation for national and state tests
- ★ Transparencies and worksheets to support instruction

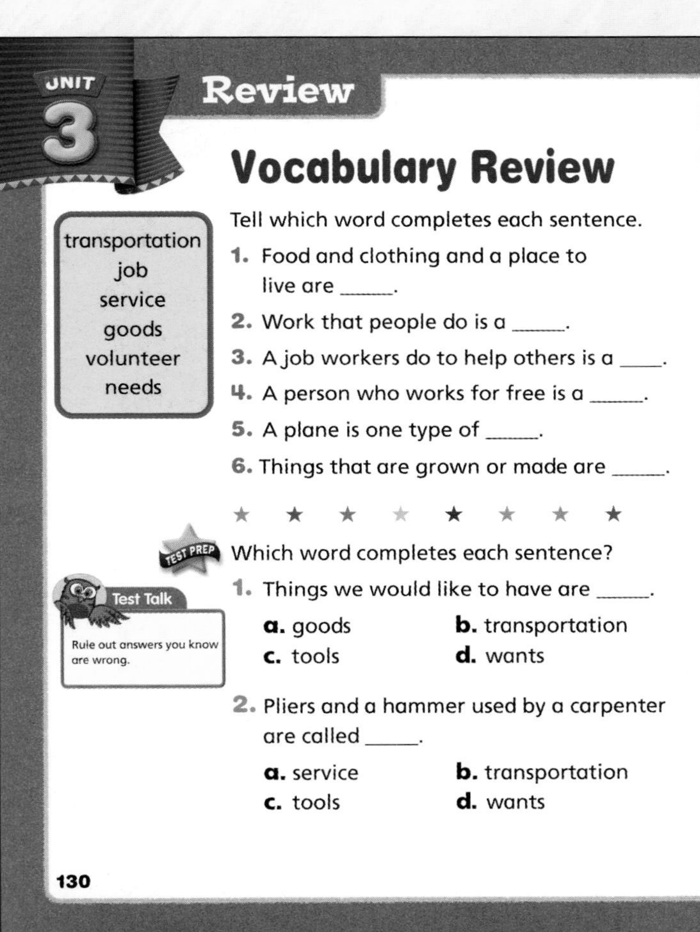
UNIT 3 Review

Vocabulary Review

transportation
job
service
goods
volunteer
needs

Tell which word completes each sentence.

1. Food and clothing and a place to live are ____.
2. Work that people do is a ____.
3. A job workers do to help others is a ____.
4. A person who works for free is a ____.
5. A plane is one type of ____.
6. Things that are grown or made are ____.

★ ★ ★ ★ ★ ★ ★ ★

TEST PREP

Test Talk

Rule out answers you know are wrong.

Which word completes each sentence?

1. Things we would like to have are ____.
   a. goods **b.** transportation
   c. tools **d.** wants
2. Pliers and a hammer used by a carpenter are called ____.
   a. service **b.** transportation
   c. tools **d.** wants

130

Skills Review

Put Things in Order

Write about a job you want to do some day. Tell what you would do **first, next,** and **last.**

★ ★ ★ ★ ★ ★ ★ ★ ★

Follow a Route

1. What buildings are east of the store?
2. Follow the route with your finger. Whe
   does Pat's route begin?
3. Tell what direction Pat goes on each

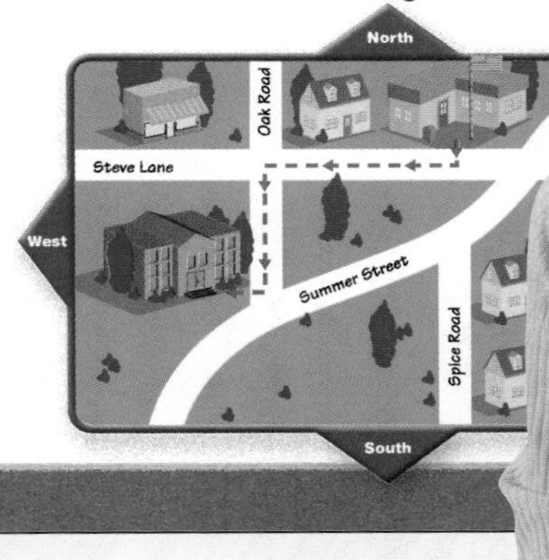

FORMAL ASSESSMENT OPPORTUNITIES

- ★ Assess children's learning and provide practice for key test-taking skills
- ★ Built-in Lesson, Chapter, and Unit Reviews in the student book
- ★ Chapter Tests and Unit Tests in the Assessment Handbook
- ★ Standardized test format with multiple-choice, open-ended, and written responses
- ★ Performance-based assessments

All Together

Teacher's Edition Table of Contents

Table of Contents iii
Social Studies Handbook H2
Unit 1 *Time for School* 1a
Unit 2 *In My Community* 43a
Unit 3 *Work! Work! Work!* 87a
Unit 4 *Our Earth, Our Resources* 135a
Unit 5 *This Is Our Country* 183a
Unit 6 *Our Country, Our World* 231a
Reference Guide R1–R28

Teacher Resources

Facing Fear: Helping Students Cope with Tragic Events TR1–TR2
Graphic Organizers TR3–TR14
Vocabulary Words TR15–TR20
Family Activities TR21–TR32
Scope and Sequence TR33–TR40
Unit Bibliographies TR41–TR46
Index TR47–TR50

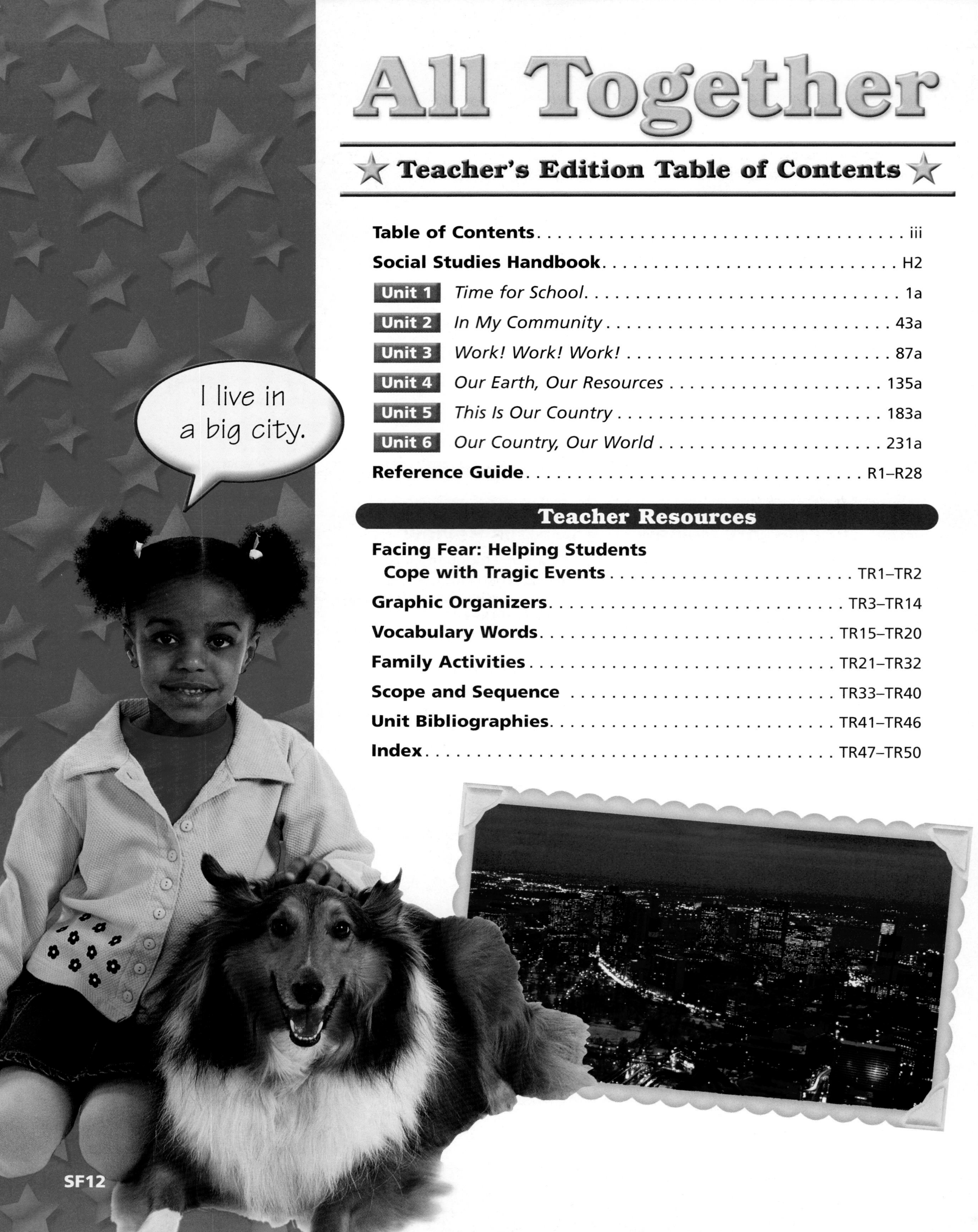

★ SCOTT FORESMAN ★
SOCIAL STUDIES
All Together

Program Authors

Dr. Candy Dawson Boyd
Professor, School of Education
Director of Reading Programs
St. Mary's College
Moraga, California

Dr. Geneva Gay
Professor of Education
University of Washington
Seattle, Washington

Rita Geiger
Director of Social Studies and Foreign Languages
Norman Public Schools
Norman, Oklahoma

Dr. James B. Kracht
Associate Dean for Undergraduate Programs and Teacher Education
College of Education
Texas A & M University
College Station, Texas

Dr. Valerie Ooka Pang
Professor of Teacher Education
San Diego State University
San Diego, California

Dr. C. Frederick Risinger
Director, Professional Development and Social Studies Education
Indiana University
Bloomington, Indiana

Sara Miranda Sanchez
Elementary and Early Childhood Curriculum Coordinator
Albuquerque Public Schools
Albuquerque, New Mexico

Contributing Authors

Dr. Carol Berkin
Professor of History
Baruch College and the Graduate Center
The City University of New York
New York, New York

Lee A. Chase
Staff Development Specialist
Chesterfield County Public Schools
Chesterfield County, Virginia

Dr. James Cummins
Professor of Curriculum
Ontario Institute for Studies in Education
University of Toronto
Toronto, Canada

Dr. Allen D. Glenn
Professor and Dean Emeritus
College of Education
Curriculum and Instruction
University of Washington
Seattle, Washington

Dr. Carole L. Hahn
Professor, Educational Studies
Emory University
Atlanta, Georgia

Dr. M. Gail Hickey
Professor of Education
Indiana University-Purdue University
Ft. Wayne, Indiana

Dr. Bonnie Meszaros
Associate Director
Center for Economic Education and Entrepreneurship
University of Delaware
Newark, Delaware

Editorial Offices: Glenview, Illinois • Parsippany, New Jersey • New York, New York
Sales Offices: Parsippany, New Jersey • Duluth, Georgia • Glenview, Illinois • Coppell, Texas • Ontario, California
www.sfsocialstudies.com

Content Consultants

Dr. Michael Frassetto
Studies in Religions
Independent scholar
Chicago, Illinois

Dr. Gerald Greenfield
Hispanic-Latino Studies
History Department
University of Wisconsin, Parkside
Kenosha, Wisconsin

Dr. Frederick Hoxie
Native American Studies
University of Illinois
Urbana, Illinois

Dr. Michael Khodarkovsky
Eastern European Studies
University of Chicago
Chicago, Illinois

Dr. Ralph Nichols
East Asian History
University of Chicago
Chicago, Illinois

Cheryl Johnson-Odim Ph.D.
Dean of Liberal Arts and Sciences and Professor of History
African American History Specialist
Columbia College
Chicago, Illinois

Classroom Reviewers

Diana Vicknair Ard
Woodlake Elementary School
St. Tammany Parish
Mandeville, LA

Dr. Charlotte R. Bennett
St. John School
Newburgh, IN

Sharon Berenson
Freehold Learning Center
Freehold, NJ

Betsy Blanford
Pocahontas Elementary School
Powhatan, VA

Gloria Cantatore
Public School Number Five
West New York, NJ

LuAnn Curran
Westgate Elementary School
St. Petersburg, FL

Louis De Angelo
Office of Catholic Education
Archdiocese of Philadelphia
Philadelphia, PA

Dr. Trish Dolansinski
Paradise Valley
Arrowhead Elementary School
Phoenix, AZ

Dr. John R. Doyle
Social Studies Coordinator
Miami-Dade County Schools
Miami, FL

Roceal Duke
District of Columbia Public Schools
Washington, D.C.

Peggy Flanagan
Community Consolidated School District #64
Roosevelt Elementary
Park Ridge, IL

Mary Flynn
Arrowhead Elementary School
Glendale, AZ

Sue Gendon
Spring Branch I. S. D.
Houston, TX

Su Hickenbottom
Totem Falls Elementary School
Snohomish School District
Snohomish, WA

Sally Hunter
Highland Park Elementary School
Austin I. S. D.
Austin, TX

Allan Jones
North Branch Public Schools
North Branch, MN

Brandy Bowers Kerbow
Bettye Haun Elementary School
Plano I. S. D.
Plano, TX

Sandra López
PSJA Service Center
San Juan, TX

Martha Sutton Maple
Shreve Island School
Shreveport, LA

Lyn Metzger
Community Consolidated School District #64
Carpenter School
Park Ridge, IL

Marsha Musey
Riverbend Elementry School
West Monroe, LA

Christine Nixon
Warrington Elementary School
Escambia County School District
Pensacola, FL

Liz Salinas
Supervisor
Edgewood I. S. D.
San Antonio, TX

Beverly Scaling
Desert Hills Elementary
Las Cruces, NM

Madeleine Schmitt
St. Louis Public Schools
St. Louis, MO

Barbara Schwartz
Central Square Intermediate School
Central Square, NY

Dr. Thad Sitton
St. Edward's University
Austin, TX

Ronald Snapp
North Lawrence Community Schools
Bedford, IN

Lesley Ann Stahl
Westside Catholic Consolidated School
Evansville, IN

Carolyn Moss Woodall
Loudoun County of Virginia Public Schools
Leesburg, VA

Suzanne Zeremba
J B Fisher Model School
Richmond Public Schools
Richmond, VA

1 2 3 4 5 6 7 8 9 10 V057 11 10 09 08 07 06 05 04 03 02

Contents

Social Studies Handbook

Welcome to Social Studies H2

Building Citizenship Skills H4

Building Geography Skills H8

Unit 1

Time for School

Begin with a Song *We Go to School* 2

Vocabulary Preview 4

Reading Social Studies *Use Picture Clues* 6

Lesson 1 • Getting to Know Andrew **8**

BIOGRAPHY *Carl Stotz* 10

Smithsonian Play Ball! 12

Lesson 2 • Home and School **14**

Citizen Heroes Ruby Bridges Hall 18

Chart and Graph Skills *Read a Calendar* 20

Lesson 3 • Rules We Follow **22**

Thinking Skills *Problem on the Playground* 26

Lesson 4 • Learning About My School **28**

BIOGRAPHY Mary McLeod Bethune 32

Then and Now Things We Use 34

End with a Poem *School Today* 36

Unit 1 Review 38

Discovery Channel School Follow Me! 42

Unit 2

In My Community

My name is Kim!

Begin with a Song *This Is My Community* 44
Vocabulary Preview 46
Reading Social Studies *Alike and Different* 48

Lesson 1 • Welcome to My Neighborhood **50**
Map and Globe Skills *Use a Map Key* 54

Lesson 2 • Different Kinds of Communities **56**
Then and Now *How a Community Changed* 58
Map and Globe Skills *Use Four Directions* 60

Lesson 3 • Special Things We Do **62**
Dorling Kindersley *Chinese New Year* 66
Citizen Heroes *Learning About Each Other* 68

Lesson 4 • Community Laws and Leaders **70**
BIOGRAPHY *Jane Addams* 72

Lesson 5 • Where in the World Do I Live? **74**
BIOGRAPHY *Sam Houston* 78

End with a Poem *One Great Big Community* 80
Unit 2 Review 82
Discovery Channel School *News for All* 86

Unit 3

Work! Work! Work!

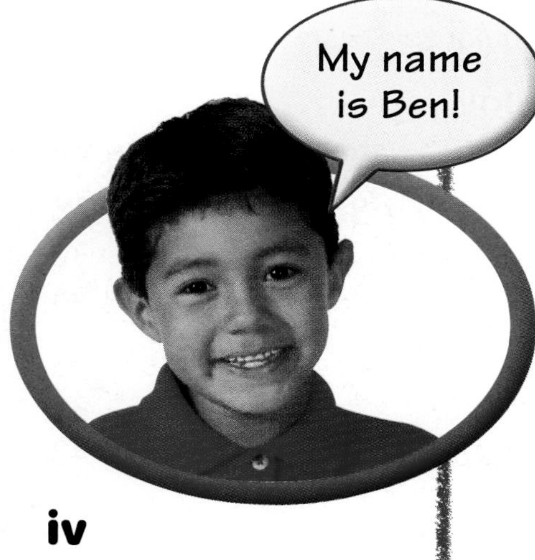

My name is Ben!

Begin with a Song *Lots of Jobs* 88
Vocabulary Preview 90
Reading Social Studies *Put Things in Order* 92

Lesson 1 • Ben's Jobs **94**
Chart and Graph Skills *Use a Chart* 98

Lesson 2 • Needs and Wants **100**
Then and Now *Changing Toys* 102

Lesson 3 • Spending and Saving **104**
Here and There *Money Around the World* 106

Lesson 4 • Welcome to Job Day! **108**
Citizen Heroes *Kid's Kitchen* 112
BIOGRAPHY *Clara Barton* 114

Lesson 5 • Interview with a Farmer **116**
Map and Globe Skills *Follow a Route* 120
BIOGRAPHY *George Washington Carver* 122

Lesson 6 • From Place to Place **124**
Dorling Kindersley *Big Wheels* 126

End with a Poem *Work Day* 128
Unit 3 Review 130
Discovery Channel School *Jobs in Your Community* 134

Unit 4

Our Earth, Our Resources

My name is Debby!

Begin with a Song *Show You Care* 136
Vocabulary Preview 138
Reading Social Studies *Find the Main Idea* 140

Lesson 1 • Different Kinds of Weather **142**
Chart and Graph Skills *Read a Time Line* 146
Smithsonian *Weather and Fun* 148

Lesson 2 • Looking at Our Land and Water **150**
Map and Globe Skills *Locate Land and Water* 154

Lesson 3 • Our Earth's Resources **156**
Citizen Heroes *Tree Musketeers* 160
BIOGRAPHY Elvia Niebla 162

Lesson 4 • Interview About Farm History **164**
BIOGRAPHY *Sacagawea* 168

Lesson 5 • Caring for Our Resources **170**
Here and There *Endangered Animals* 174

End with a Legend *Johnny Appleseed* 176
Unit 4 Review 178
Discovery Channel School *Weather Report* 182

Unit 5

This Is Our Country

My name is James!

Begin with a Song *Holidays are Special Days* 184
Vocabulary Preview 186
Reading Social Studies *Recall and Retell* 188

Lesson 1 • Native Americans **190**
Chart and Graph Skills *Read a Diagram* 192
Smithsonian *Native American Objects* 194

Lesson 2 • Early Travelers to America **196**
Map and Globe Skills *Use a History Map* 200

Lesson 3 • The Colonies Become Free **202**
BIOGRAPHY Benjamin Franklin 206

Lesson 4 • Symbols in Our Country **208**
Then and Now *Our Country's Flag* 210

Lesson 5 • We Celebrate Holidays **212**
BIOGRAPHY Abraham Lincoln 216

Lesson 6 • Choosing Our Country's Leaders **218**
Citizen Heroes *Eleanor Roosevelt* 222

End with a Song *The Star-Spangled Banner* 224
Unit 5 Review 226
Discovery Channel School *History on Parade* 230

Unit 6

Our Country, Our World

My name is Kay!

Begin with a Song *Explore with Me!* 232
Vocabulary Preview 234
Reading Social Studies *Predict* 236

Lesson 1 • Visiting the Market **238**
Thinking Skills *Make a Decision* 240

Lesson 2 • How Things Have Changed **242**
Citizen Heroes *Joseph Bruchac* 244

Lesson 3 • Inventors and Inventions **246**
Dorling Kindersley *Telephones* 250

Lesson 4 • How Travel Has Changed **252**
Chart and Graph Skills *Read a Bar Graph* 254
BIOGRAPHY Mae Jemison 256

Lesson 5 • Life Around the World **258**
BIOGRAPHY Laurence Yep 262
Here and There *It is Time to Leave* 264
End with a Folktale *The Farmer's Little Girl* 266
Unit 6 Review 268
Discovery Channel School *Future World* 272

Reference Guide

Atlas R2
Geography Terms R10
Picture Glossary R12
Index R24

Read Together
Biography

Biographies

Carl Stotz 10
Mary McLeod Bethune 32
Jane Addams 72
Sam Houston 78
Clara Barton 114
George Washington Carver 122
Elvia Niebla 162
Sacagawea 168
Benjamin Franklin 206
Abraham Lincoln 216
Mae Jemison 256
Laurence Yep 262

Maps

Williamsport, Pennsylvania 11
New Orleans, Louisiana 18
Boston, Massachusetts 28
Mayesville, South Carolina 33
Locating an Address 51
Use a Map Key 54
Use Four Directions 60
Boston, Massachusetts 68, 207
Cedarville, Illinois 73
The United States 75
Continents and Oceans 76
Lexington, Virginia 79
Money Around the World 106
Warner Robins, Georgia 112
Oxford, Massachusetts 115
Diamond Grove, Missouri 123
San Diego, California 144
Detroit, Michigan 145
Locate Land and Water 155
El Segundo, California 160
Nogales, Mexico 163
Bitterroot Mountains 169
Endangered Animals 174
Native Americans 190
Use a History Map 200
Hodgenville, Kentucky 217
Washington, D.C. 221
New York City, New York 222
Saratoga Springs, New York 244
Decatur, Alabama 257
San Francisco, California 263
Satellite Photograph of the Earth R2
Photograph of the United States R3
Map of the World R4
Map of the United States of America R6
Map of Our Fifty States R8

Skills

Reading Social Studies

Use Picture Clues 6
Alike and Different 48
Put Things in Order 92
Find the Main Idea 140
Recall and Retell 188
Predict 236

Map and Globe Skills

Use a Map Key 54
Use Four Directions 60
Follow a Route 120
Locate Land and Water 154
Use a History Map 200

Chart and Graph Skills

Read a Calendar 20
Use a Chart 98
Read a Time Line 146
Time Line: Farming 166
Read A Diagram 192
Diagram of the Liberty Bell 208
Time Line: How Travel Has Changed 252
Read a Bar Graph 254

Thinking Skills

Solve a Problem 26
Make a Decision 240

Then and Now

Things We Use 34
How A Community Changed 56
Changing Toys 102
Our Country's Flag 210

Here and There

Money Around the World 106
Endangered Animals 174
It Is Time to Leave 264

Citizen Heroes

Ruby Bridges Hall 18
CAPAY 68
Kid's Kitchen 112
Tree Musketeers 160
Eleanor Roosevelt 222
Joseph Bruchac 244

Let the Discovery Begin

Firefighters

After reading the text, invite children to talk about the picture of the firefighters.

To begin discussion, you may want to ask questions similar to the following:

- What do you think of when you look at the picture?
- Why are firefighters so important to our communities?
- Have you ever had a firefighter come to your house?
- How do firefighters help us in ways other than fighting fires?
- What do you think it would be like to be a firefighter?
- Does anyone know a firefighter or has anyone seen one on TV?
- How can we help firefighters?

Hands-on Unit Projects

The Hands-on Unit Projects at the end of each unit provide you with ongoing performance assessment projects to enrich students' learning throughout Grade 1. You can find Hands-on Unit Projects at the end of each unit in this book on the following pages:

- **Unit 1**: ***Follow Me,*** p. 42
- **Unit 2**: ***News for All,*** p. 86
- **Unit 3**: ***Jobs in Your Community,*** p. 134
- **Unit 4**: ***Weather Report,*** p. 182
- **Unit 5**: ***History on Parade,*** p. 230
- **Unit 6**: ***Future World,*** p. 272

Let the Discovery Begin

Many people live and work in communities. Some of these people help keep us safe. Firefighters help keep us safe by putting out fires. Who else in your community helps keep you safe?

Turn the pages and discover more about people everywhere!

Practice and Extend

FAST FACTS

About Firefighters and Fire Departments

- Why don't we call firefighters "firemen" any more? Although women have worked as volunteer firefighters for almost 200 years, women were first hired as official firefighters in 1974. The first woman hired as a full-time firefighter was Judith Livers in Arlington County, Virginia. In 2001, more than 5,000 women worked as career firefighters in the United States.
- Most fire departments are actually Fire and Rescue Departments. They provide emergency and non-emergency services to protect the lives and property of families in their communities. Their services can include natural disaster search and rescue, water rescue, first aid and paramedic services, ambulances with life support equipment, hazardous material removal, and arson investigation. Most firefighters also provide public education for fire prevention and child safety in homes and automobiles.

Discovery Channel School

Discovery Channel School educational products include award-winning videos, CD-ROMs, and print resources covering curriculum topics in science, social studies, literature, and more. They are created specifically for use in the classroom and are correlated to National Education Standards.

Web Site

- Discovery Channel Education's online service, **DiscoverySchool.com**, provides cutting-edge resources for teachers and students, featuring a lesson plan library, teacher's guide, and a variety of tools—*Puzzlemaker, Worksheet Generator, Quiz Center, Lesson Planner, Glossary Builder*—that allow teachers to create customized resources.
- The site remains one of the Top 10 Web sites used by teachers.

Videos

- Certain units in this book contain suggestions for using videos from Discovery Channel School.
- Please check the teacher's page containing bibliography suggestions at the beginning of each unit. If a Discovery Channel School video is suggested for the unit, it will be listed there.
- To order Discovery Channel School videos, please call the following toll-free number: 1-888-892-3484.

CURRICULUM CONNECTION
Writing

Write a Letter

- Have children write a letter to the local fire department. Encourage them to ask questions.
- If children need assistance, suggest that they ask about the fire station, what a typical day is like, and how the men and women decided to become firefighters.
- Encourage children to illustrate their letters with drawings.

Building Citizenship Skills

Read the introductory text to children as they follow along. Then read aloud the definitions of the six citizenship characteristics and talk briefly about the photographs.

Use the following questions to guide children to understand that they can demonstrate each of the characteristics in their own daily lives.

Respect

1 What is a way you can show respect to others? Possible answer: You can show consideration for what they think and feel. **Apply Information**

Caring

2 What ways can you show you care about a person? Possible answer: You can help and support a person. **Generalize**

Responsibility

3 How is the boy in the picture showing he is responsible? He is feeding the dog. **Analyze Pictures**

Fairness

4 Why is it more important to play a game by the rules than it is to win? Possible answer: A game is something people do together for fun. **Express Ideas**

Honesty

5 What might be the best time for family members to tell each other the truth about their feelings? Possible answer: The best time might be when they can sit down and quietly talk to each other. **Express Ideas**

Courage

6 Do you think a person who has courage is never afraid? Possible answer: Sometimes people are afraid but still do the right thing. **Express Ideas**

Building Citizenship Skills

There are many ways to show good citizenship. In your textbook, you will learn about people who are good citizens in their community, state, and country.

Respect means treating others as you want to be treated. 1

Caring means thinking about how someone feels and doing something to show you care. 2

Responsibility means doing the things you should do. 3

Fairness means taking turns and playing by the rules. 4

Honesty means telling the truth. 5

Courage means doing what is right even when it is hard. 6

Practice and Extend

CURRICULUM CONNECTION
Drama

Visiting the Park

- Have small groups of children take turns dramatizing going to a park, coming upon beautiful flowers, and taking responsibility for the common good.
- When one child says that he or she is going to pick a flower, the others explain that people should not pick the flowers because they are for everyone. The one child then volunteers to help water the flowers.

★Citizenship in Action★

Good citizens make careful decisions. They learn to solve problems. Help these children act like good citizens. Here are the steps they follow.

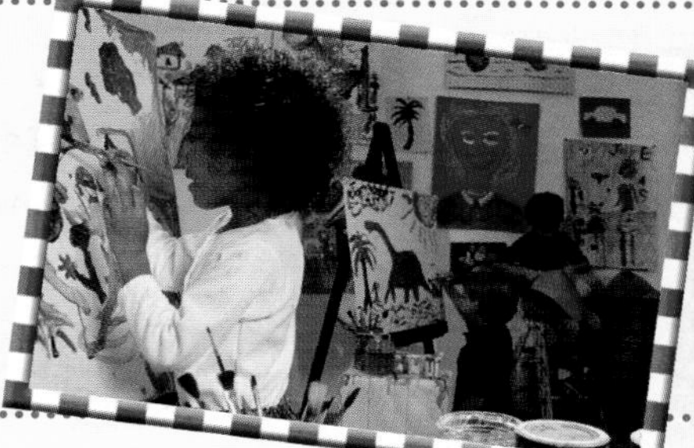

Problem Solving

The Art Center is messy. What can they do?

1. Name the problem.
2. Find out more about the problem.
3. List ways to solve the problem.
4. Talk about the best way to solve the problem.
5. Solve the problem.
6. How well is the problem solved?

Decision Making

Open House is tonight. The children want to make a sign to welcome their parents.

1. Tell what decision you need to make.
2. Gather information.
3. List your choices.
4. Tell what might happen with each choice.
5. Make a decision.

SOCIAL STUDIES STRAND
Citizenship

Citizen Heroes

In Grade 1, children will read about the following Citizen Heroes:

- Ruby Bridges Hall: Courage
- CAPAY: Fairness
- Kid's Kitchen: Caring
- Tree Musketeers: Responsibility
- Eleanor Roosevelt: Honesty
- Joseph Bruchac: Respect

★Citizenship in Action★

Read aloud the introductory paragraph and then focus children's attention on the two activities. Have children listen and follow along as you read each numbered step in each process.

As you discuss each step individually, encourage children to express a range of ideas they may have. Aside from identifying the problem or decision to be made, make it clear that there is no one correct response to each step.

Problem Solving

Discuss the problem-solving scenario. Help children solve the problem in a logical way.

1. The problem is that the Art Center is messy.
2. Identify the ways the Art Center is messy, such as crayons aren't in their boxes, and drawing paper is scattered about.
3. Possible solutions: one child or a small group could clean up.
4. One child would not get in people's way. A small group would not be overworked.
5. Children should chose the solution they feel is best.
6. Have children evaluate their solution.

Decision Making

Discuss the decision-making scenario. Help children make a careful decision.

1. A decision must be made about what greeting to put on a sign welcoming parents at Open House.
2. Children might brainstorm possible greetings.
3. The choices might include such greetings as "Welcome Parents," "Welcome to Our Class," "Our House is Your House."
4. Have children discuss their responses to different greetings.
5. Have children vote for their favorite greeting.

The United States

About "America the Beautiful"

- Read the title of the song—"America the Beautiful." Tell children that this song is one of America's most loved patriotic songs.
- Read the songwriter's name—Katharine Lee Bates. Tell children that she was a teacher.
- Tell the following about the history of the song. One day Bates went on a trip to Pikes Peak, a mountain in Colorado. The beautiful view from the top inspired her to write the song. She wrote the original version in 1893, a second version in 1904, and the final version in 1913.
- Read the words to "America the Beautiful" before singing it with children. Explain any words or phrases children may not understand, such as *spacious* and *amber waves of grain*, and *brotherhood*.

Building Citizenship Skills
The United States

America the Beautiful

by Katherine Lee Bates and Samuel A. Ward

O beautiful for spacious skies,
For amber waves of grain,
For purple mountains majesties
Above the fruited plain!
America! America!
God shed his grace on thee,
And crown thy good with brotherhood
From sea to shining sea!

H6 Social Studies Handbook

Practice and Extend

AUDIO CD Technology

Play the CD, *Songs and Music*, to listen to "America the Beautiful."

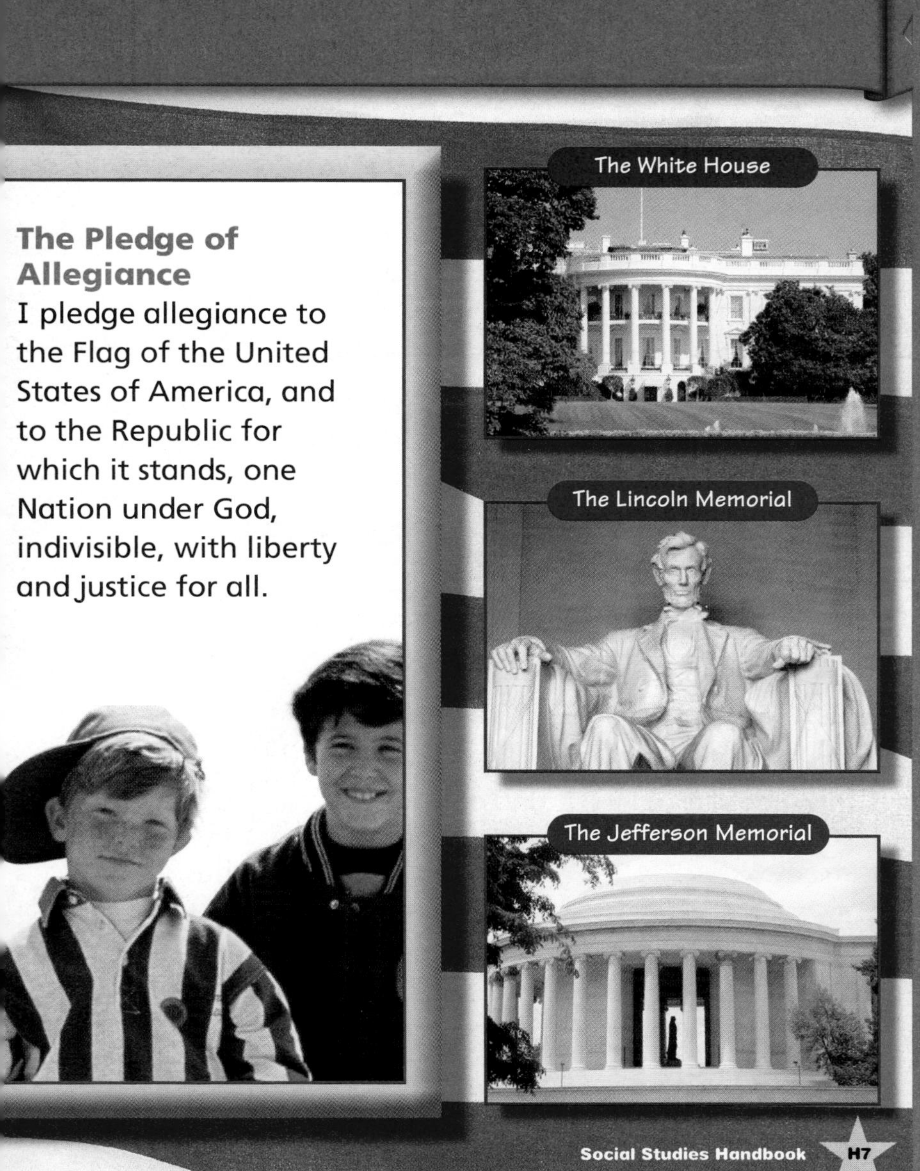

The Pledge of Allegiance
I pledge allegiance to the Flag of the United States of America, and to the Republic for which it stands, one Nation under God, indivisible, with liberty and justice for all.
The White House
The Lincoln Memorial
The Jefferson Memorial
Social Studies Handbook
H7

Taking Care of Our Flag

Point to the America flag in the classroom. Explain to children that this flag is a symbol of our country.

- Tell children that the number of stripes stands for the number of states when the country first began. Have children count the stripes with you.
- Tell children there are fifty stars—one star for each of the fifty states.

Tell children the following rules about displaying the flag:

- No other flag should be placed above the American flag.
- The flag should be displayed during school days in or near every school.
- When a flag passes in a parade, you should stand and put your hand over your heart.

Saying the Pledge of Allegiance

- Recite the Pledge of Allegiance to the United States Flag. Explain any words or phrases children may not understand, such as *allegiance*, *to the Republic for which it stands*, and *indivisible*.
- On a second reading have children echo each line.
- Encourage children to be attentive and show their respect and thanks to the United States by standing, removing their hat, facing and looking at the flag, placing their right hand over their heart, and avoiding fidgeting.

SOCIAL STUDIES Background

About the White House, Lincoln Memorial, and Jefferson Memorial

- The White House, located at 1600 Pennsylvania Avenue in Washington, D.C., is the official home of the President of the United States.
- The 132-room mansion not only contains living quarters for the President's family but also offices where the President conducts business.
- The Lincoln Memorial is a massive marble monument in Washington, D.C., that honors Abraham Lincoln, the sixteenth President of the United States. It stands at the end of the National Mall.
- The Jefferson Memorial, also in Washington , D.C., is a beautiful monument to Thomas Jefferson, the third President of the United States. It was dedicated in 1943, the 200th anniversary of Jefferson's birth.

The Five Themes of Geography

From "*Guidelines for Geographic Education: Elementary and Secondary Skills,*" prepared by the Joint Committee on Geographic Education of the National Council for Geographic Education and the Association of American Geographers.

Location

Explain to children that *location* is the place where you find something. You may wish to have children use the Big Book Atlas to complete the following.

- Explain to children their school is in a community, and their community is in a city. Help children find the exact or approximate location of their city on a map of their state.
- Have children locate their state on a map of the United States.

Place

Place is what makes one location different from another. Place can be described by telling about people or things at a location. Sometimes it is helpful to locate a place by describing how near or far it is to another place.

1 Where are the trees, grass, and other plants? They are near the school. **Analyze Pictures**

Movement

Movement is going from one place to another. It includes ways people travel.

2 How have buses and cars made it easier for some children to go to school? Possible answer: Children who live so far away from school that they can't walk can now ride to school. **Make Inferences**

Building Geography Skills

The Five Themes of Geography

Five Things to Think About

Geography is the study of Earth. This study sometimes looks at the earth in five different ways. These ways are called the five themes of geography. Each theme is another way of thinking about a place. Look at the examples of the school below.

Location

200 Melrose Street

The location of this school is at 200 Melrose Street.

Place

Trees, grass, and other plants grow near this school. 1

Movement

Some people walk to school. Others ride to the school in a bus or a car. 2

H8 Social Studies Handbook

Practice and Extend

SOCIAL STUDIES **Background**

The Essential Elements of Geography
From the National Council of Geographic Education

- **The World in Spatial Terms** Geography studies the spatial relationships between people, places, and environments.
- **Places and Regions** The identities of individuals and cultures can be found in particular places and regions.
- **Physical Systems** Physical processes shape Earth's surface and create, sustain, and change ecosystems.
- **Humans Systems** Human activities help shape Earth's surface.
- **Environment and Society** The physical environment is modified by human activities. Human activities are also influenced by Earth.
- **The Uses of Geography** Knowledge of geography enables people to understand the relationships between people, places, and environments over time.

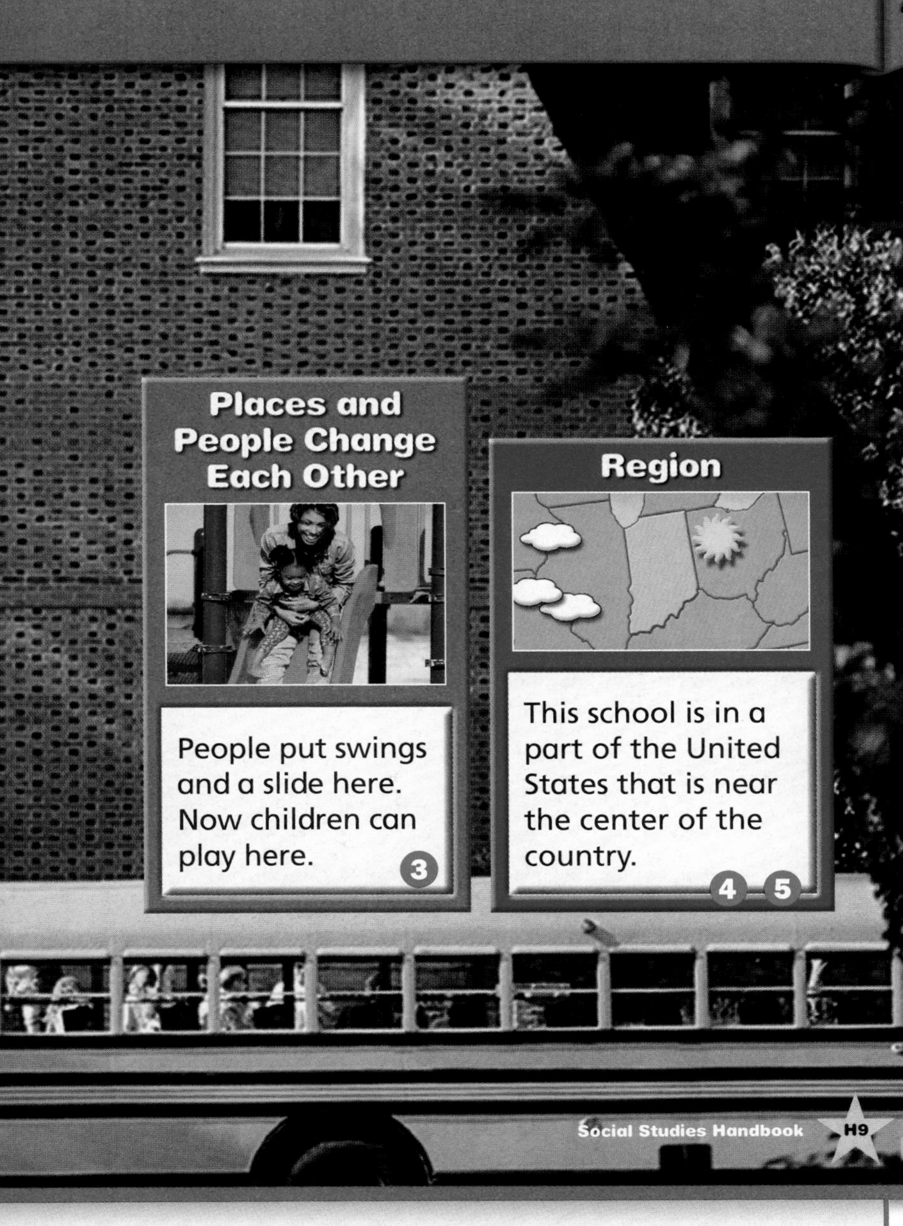

Places and People Change Each Other
People put swings and a slide here. Now children can play here.
3
Region
This school is in a part of the United States that is near the center of the country.
4
5
Social Studies Handbook
H9

Places and People Change Each Other

People can make places different. For example, people cut down trees, build houses, and farm land. *Places* can make people different. For example, people who live in cold climates must dress warmly.

3 **What might the school yard have looked like before people put swings and a slide there?** Possible answer: Rocks and grass might have been there. **Make Inferences**

Region

A *region* is a large area that is different from other large areas. A region can be described by features such as landforms and climate.

4 **What do the states in this region have in common?** They are in the center of the country. **Apply Information**

5 **What bodies of water might be near this school—lake, river, or ocean?** Lake and river **Analyze Pictures**

Additional Resources

The following resources can be used throughout Grade 1 to teach and reinforce geography skills.

- Big book Atlas
- Outline Maps
- Desk Maps
- Map Resources CD-ROM

CURRICULUM CONNECTION
Drama

Travelling to School by Bus

- Have children dramatize going to school by bus.
- Have children play the roles of bus driver, parents accompanying children to a bus stop, and children boarding the bus.
- The bus driver winds his or her way around the classroom picking up children, who follow behind. Meanwhile, the parents return to their seats,
- The final destination of the bus is the teacher's desk, where children, one-by-one, get out of the bus and return to their seats.

Building Geography Skills

Map and Globe Skills Review

Talk About the Picture of Earth

- Have children tell whether they see more land or bodies of water on this picture of Earth.
- Ask children to locate oceans and lakes.

Building Geography Skills

Map and Globe Skills Review

From the Earth to a Globe

This is a picture that looks down at our Earth. It is a picture taken from space. Earth looks round like a ball.

The smooth blue part of Earth are water. The other parts with green on them are land. It is very excitin to see Earth this way.

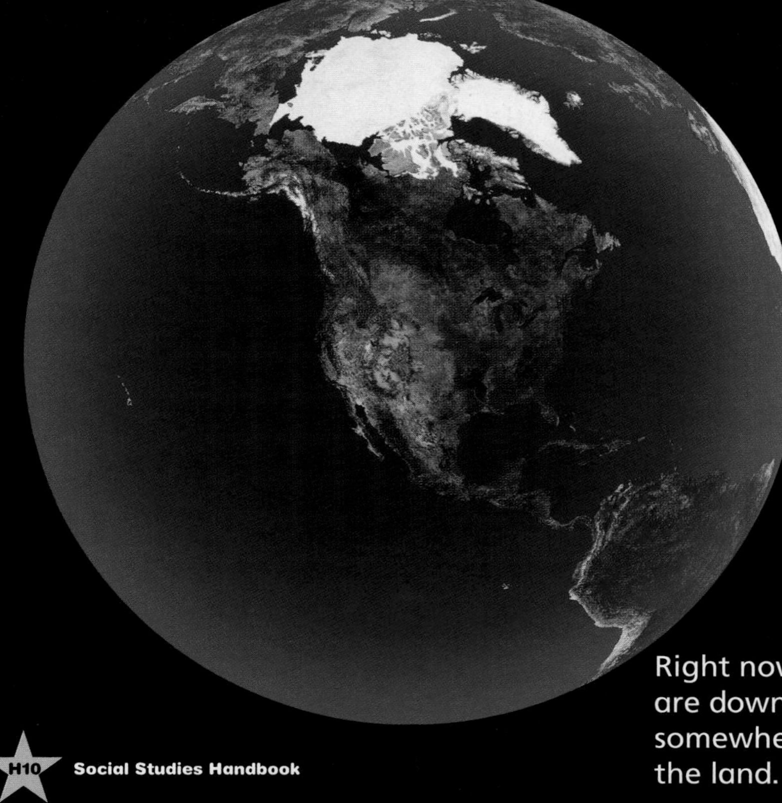

Right now you are down there somewhere on the land.

H10 Social Studies Handbook

Practice and Extend

FYI SOCIAL STUDIES Background

About Globes

- One of the first globes was made by Martin Behaim in Germany in 1492.
- Most globes are 22 inches in diameter. Some globes are so big that you can stand inside them.
- At the Dynamic Earth Globe at the American Museum of Natural History in New York, visitors seated below the globe are able to watch a special film that makes it appear that they're seeing Earth rotating from outer space.

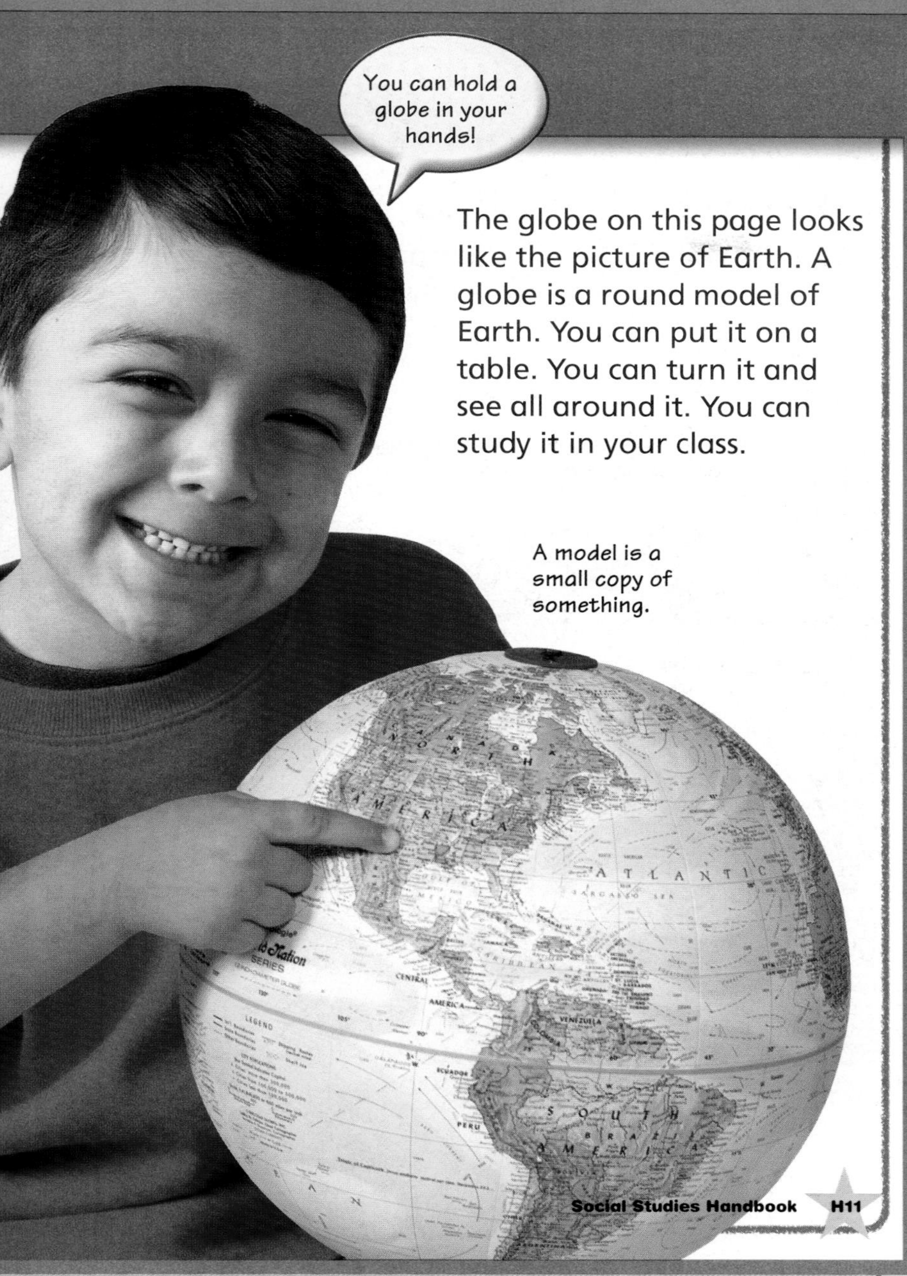

You can hold a globe in your hands!
The globe on this page looks like the picture of Earth. A globe is a round model of Earth. You can put it on a table. You can turn it and see all around it. You can study it in your class.
A model is a small copy of something.
NORTH AMERICA
ATLANTIC
SOUTH AMERICA
Social Studies Handbook H11

CURRICULUM CONNECTION Math

Measure Distances

Have children use linked paper clips to measure the shortest distance between two points on the globe.

- Europe to North America
- Africa to North America

Use a Globe

- Discuss with children that a model is a small 3-dimentional copy of something. Ask for examples of a model (a model of ship, house, or car). Then ask children to identify the similarities and differences between actual Earth pictured on p. H11 and the globe pictured on p. H12.
- Tell children that a continent is a very large body of land. Point out North America and South America on the picture of the globe. Ask children which continent the boy in the picture is pointing to (North America). Tell children that the United States is part of North America.
- Help children locate the United States on a globe. Then ask them to locate their state.

Map and Globe Skills Review

Talk About the Picture

Read p. H12 to children.

- Ask children whether the photograph of the area was taken from below, the side, or above (above).
- Ask children if the area in the photograph is a local community, state, or nation (local community).
- Have children identify things in the picture that were made by people (houses, streets).
- Have children locate the straight street and the curving street.
- Ask children if they think this is an area where people live or work (live). Why? (It has many houses and no stores.)

Point out to children that the photograph is not looking straight down. It both looks down and into the distance.

- Ask children if the buildings at the top or the bottom of the photograph are nearer to us or farther away.

From a Picture to a Map

Maybe you do not want to study the whole Earth. Maybe you want to look down only at the area where you live. Your area might look something like this.

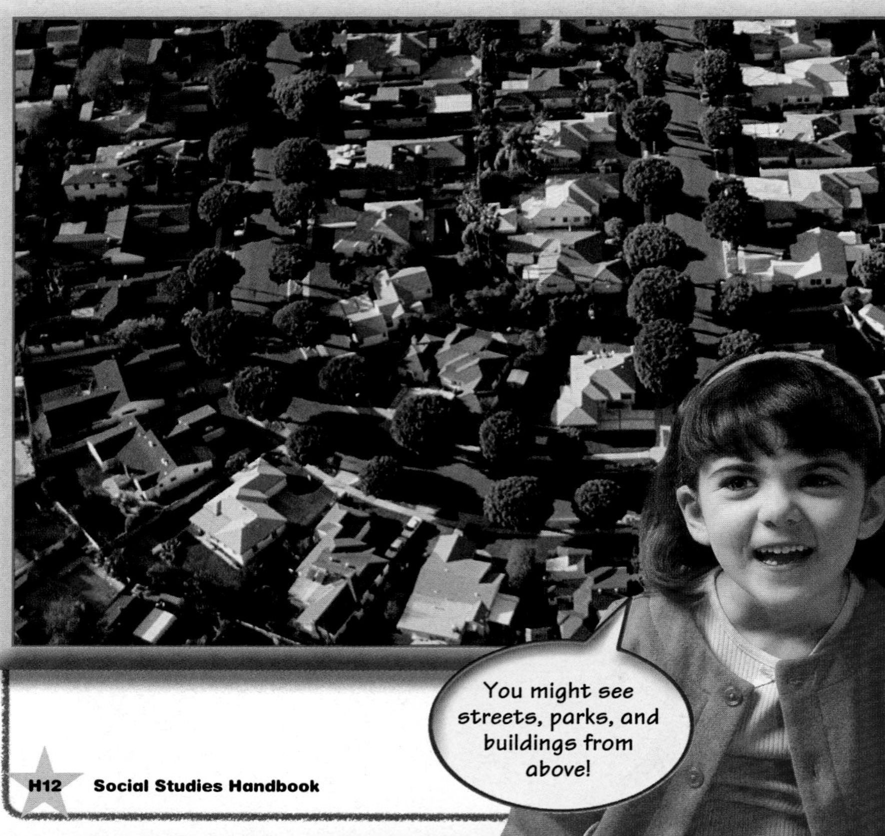

You might see streets, parks, and buildings from above!

Practice and Extend

SOCIAL STUDIES
Background

Taking Pictures of Earth from Above

- The primary task in creating a map is to accurately represent an area on a much smaller surface.
- To make a map of Earth, the size and shape of landforms and bodies of water must be carefully measured. Photographs of areas can greatly help in making these measurements.
- Airplanes are commonly used to take pictures of large areas of Earth. They can provide information more accurately and easily than ground measurements, especially when the land is rough and the climate extreme.
- Satellites and spacecraft are used to take photographs of Earth from space.

EXTEND LANGUAGE
ESL Support

Make a Map Draw a map of the classroom using shapes and colors to identify the location of places in the classroom. Point to places on the map.

Beginning Have children copy the map. Then have them point to the shapes and name what they stand for.

Intermediate Have children copy the map and name the shapes. Then have them write a title for the map: "Classroom Map."

Advanced Have children copy the map, name the shapes, and write a title for the map: "Classroom Map." Then have them include a map key to explain the shapes.

You can look down at the same area in another way. You can look at a map. A map is a drawing of an area as it is seen from above. A map of the same part of town might look like this.

How is the map the same as the picture? How is the map different from the picture?

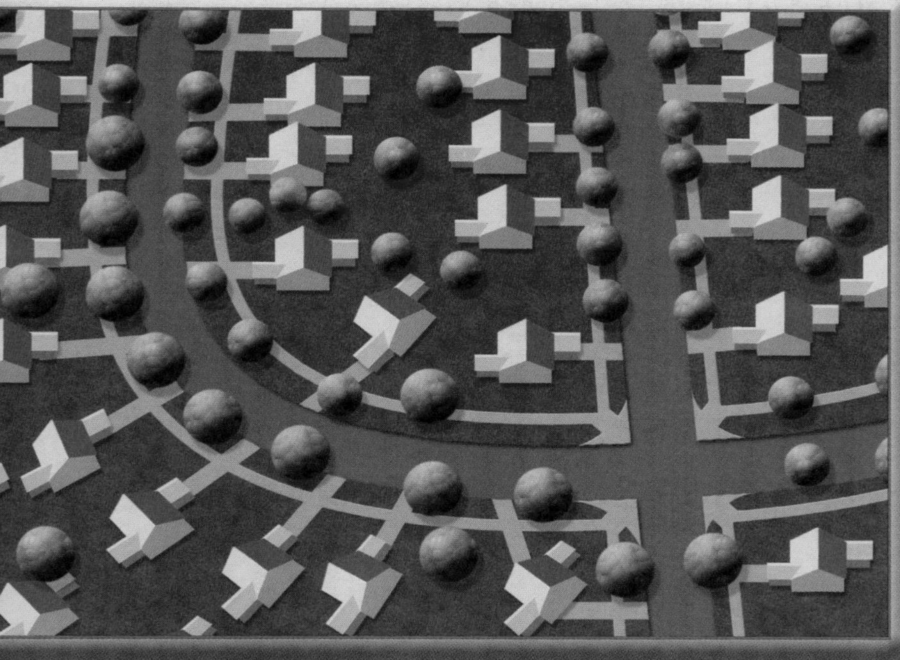

Talk About the Map

- Ask children how the map on p. H13 is similar to the picture on p. H12. (They both show the same area; are much smaller than the real area; are flat.)
- Ask children how the map is different from the picture. (The map is a drawing of the area. The picture is an actual photograph of the area.)

Tell children that the shapes on the map stand for something else.

- Have children point to the different shapes on the map. Ask them what the shapes stand for. (trees, houses, streets)
- Ask children how the shapes of trees on the map are different from the trees in the picture. (The shapes of the trees are all the same size and color. They don't have details.)
- Have children compare a map to a globe. (A map is on a page. It is flat. A globe is a rounded model of Earth.)

CURRICULUM CONNECTION
Art

Create and Use Classroom, School, Community, and State Maps

- Help children create a map of the classroom, including the location of the entrance and the place where they are sitting. Have children trace the way from the entrance to the place where they are sitting.
- Help children create a map of the hallways between the school entrance and classroom entrance. Ask them to trace the way from the entrance to their classroom.
- Help children create a map of the community showing their school and nearby streets. Have children trace the way they travel along a nearby street to the school entrance.
- Give children a map of their state. Help children locate and label their town or city on the map.

Map and Globe Skills Review

Use Directions

Explain to children that a map can be used for directions. Directions can tell you where to go.

- To activate prior knowledge, ask children to tell about when a map was used for directions at a zoo, park, shopping mall, or some other place.
- Ask children for directions to the school entrance and other school locations.

Tell children to look at the map of a zoo on p. H14.

- Ask children what animal is farthest away from the elephants (snakes).
- Ask children what animal is between the lions and the snakes (turtles).

Answers

1. Giraffes
2. Lions

Use Directions

A map helps you know where things are. Things can be near or far away. They can be between or behind other things. Look at this map of a zoo.

What animal is near the snakes?

What animal is between the lions and elephants? What animal is farthest away from the monkeys?

Practice and Extend

CURRICULUM CONNECTION
Drama

Giving Directions

Have children describe the location of self and objects using directions words such as *near, far away from, in front of, next to, between,* and *behind*. First model each activity.

- Have children describe their location relative to the classroom bulletin board.
- List classroom objects. Have children describe the location of the objects relative to the classroom bulletin board.
- Ask children to pretend that have just entered school through the main entrance. Have them describe their location relative to the school bulletin board.

★ Unit 1 ★

Time for School

Time for School

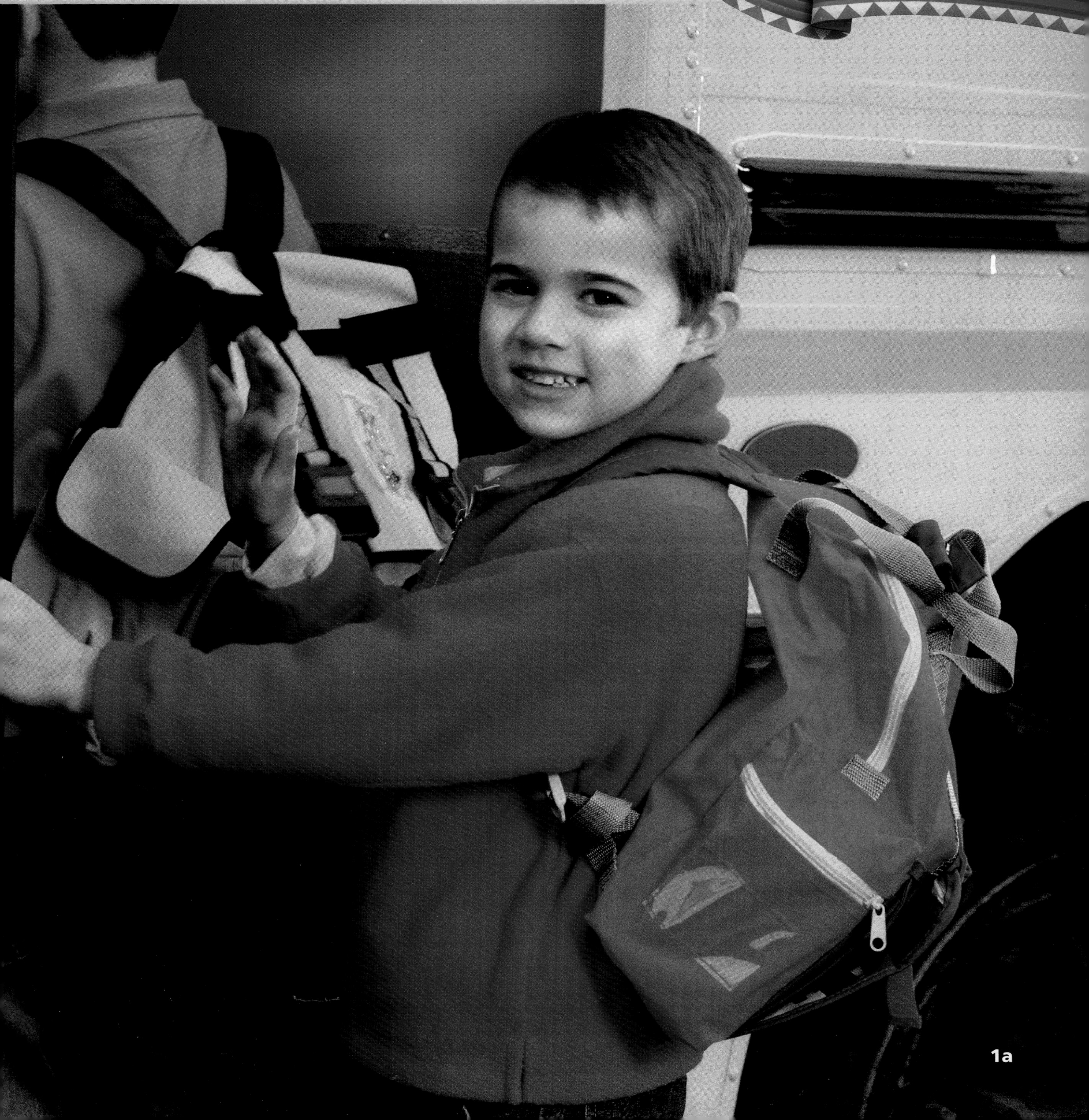

UNIT 1

Unit 1 Planning Guide

Time for School

Begin with a Song pp. 2–3 **Vocabulary Preview** pp. 4–5

Reading Social Studies, Use Picture Clues pp. 6–7

Lesson Titles	Pacing	Main Ideas
Lesson 1 **Getting to Know Andrew** pp. 8–9 **Biography: Carl Stotz** pp. 10–11 **Smithsonian Institution: Play Ball!** pp. 12–13	2 days	• A person can belong to many groups. • Carl Stotz founded Little League so that children could enjoy playing baseball. • Baseball artifacts show how the game has changed.
Lesson 2 **Home and School** pp. 14–17 **Citizen Heroes: Courage Ruby Bridges Hall** pp. 18–19 **Chart and Graph Skills: Read a Calendar** pp. 20–21	3 days	• A typical school day includes routines, one of which is pledging allegiance to the flag. • Ruby Bridges Hall showed courage by attending a school in which she was—for her first year there— the only African American student. • A calendar is a special kind of chart that shows days, weeks, and months.
Lesson 3 **Rules We Follow** pp. 22–25 **Thinking Skills: Problem on the Playground** pp. 26–27	2 days	• It is important to know the rules at school and at home—and to follow those rules. • People such as principals and teachers help us to understand the rules. • Solving a problem involves following certain steps: name the problem, investigate it, list solutions, choose and execute a good one, and evaluate the results.
Lesson 4 **Learning About My School** pp. 28–31 **Biography: Mary McLeod Bethune** pp. 32–33 **Then and Now: Things We Use** pp. 34–35	3 days	• Schools, like other things, change over time. • Mary McLeod Bethune, an educator and public speaker, started a school for African American girls. • Tools children use at school have changed over time.

✓ **End with a Poem** pp. 36–37 ✓ **Unit 1 Review** pp. 38–41 ✓ **Unit 1 Project** p. 42

✓ = Assessment Options

Vocabulary	Resources	Meeting Individual Needs
school **group**	• Workbook, pp. 3–4 • Vocabulary Cards: school, group • Every Student Learns Guide, pp. 2–5	• Leveled Practice, TE p. 13a
flag **country**	• Workbook, pp. 5–6 • Vocabulary Cards: flag, country • Every Student Learns Guide, pp. 6–9	• ESL Support, TE p. 15 • Leveled Practice, TE pp. 16, 21a
rule	• Workbook, pp. 7–8 • Vocabulary Card: rule • Every Student Learns Guide, pp. 10–13	• ESL Support, TE p. 23 • Leveled Practice, TE p. 27a
	• Workbook, p. 9 • Every Student Learns Guide, pp. 14–17	• ESL Support, TE p. 29 • Leveled Practice, TE pp. 35, 35a

Providing More Depth

Multimedia Library

- ***Sports*** **by Tim Hammond**
- ***Timothy Goes to School*** **by Rosemary Wells**
- **Songs and Music**
- **Video Field Trips**
- **Software**

Additional Resources

- Family Activities
- Vocabulary Cards
- Daily Activity Bank
- Social Studies Plus!
- Big Book Atlas
- Outline Maps
- Desk Maps

ADDITIONAL Technology

- AudioText
- TestWorks
- Teacher Resources CD-ROM
- Map Resources CD-ROM
- **www.sfsocialstudies.com**

To establish guidelines for children's safe and responsible use of the Internet, use the **Scott Foresman Internet Guide.**

Additional Internet Links
To find out more about:

- Smithsonian Institution, visit **www.si.edu**

Key Internet Search Terms

- American symbols
- School calendars

Unit 1 Objectives

Beginning of Unit 1

- **Learn why children attend school.** (pp. 2–3)
- **Determine the meanings of words.** (pp. 4–5)
- **Obtain information about a topic using pictures.** (pp. 6–7)

Lesson 1
Getting to Know Andrew
pp. 8–9

- **Understand that people belong to many different groups.**
- **Obtain information about a topic using pictures.**
- **Identify contributions of historical figures who have influenced the community, state, and nation.** (pp. 10–11)
- **Obtain information about a topic using a variety of visual sources, such as photographs of artifacts.** (pp. 12–13)

Lesson 2
Home and School
pp. 14–17

- **Explain how selected symbols reflect an American love of individualism and freedom.**
- **Explain how routines are part of our daily life at home and at school.**
- **Identify characteristics of good citizenship, such as a belief in equality.** (pp. 18–19)
- **Read and create a calendar.** (pp. 20–21)
- **Obtain information about a topic using visual sources, such as graphics and pictures.** (pp. 20–21)

Lesson 3
Rules We Follow
pp. 22–25

- **Give examples of rules.**
- **Identify the responsibilities of authority figures in the school and home.**
- **Explain the need for rules and laws in the home, school, and community.**
- **Use a problem-solving process.** (pp. 26–27)

Lesson 4
Learning About My School
pp. 28–31

- **Obtain information about a topic using a variety of oral sources, such as interviews.**
- **Compare past and present.**
- **Identify characteristics of good citizenship, such as belief in equality.** (pp. 32–33)
- **Identify the contributions of historical figures who have influenced the nation.** (pp. 32–33)
- **Recognize that things change over time.** (pp. 34–35)

End of Unit 1

- **Obtain information about a topic using literature.** (pp. 36–37)

Assessment Options

✓ Formal Assessment

- **What did you learn?** PE/TE pp. 9, 17, 25, 31, 41
- **Unit Review,** PE/TE pp. 38–41
- **Unit 1 Test,** Assessment Book pp. 1–4
- **Test Works,** (test generator software)

✓ Informal Assessment

- **Teacher's Edition Questions,** throughout Lessons and Features
- **Close and Assess,** TE pp. 9, 11, 13, 17, 19, 21, 25, 27, 31, 33, 35, 37
- **Try it!** PE/TE pp. 7, 27
- **Think and Share,** PE/TE pp. 9, 11, 17, 25, 31, 33, 41
- **Courage in Action,** PE/TE p. 19
- **Hands-on History,** PE/TE p. 35

Ongoing Assessment

Ongoing Assessment is found throughout the Teacher's Edition lessons using an **If...then** model.

If = students' observable behavior,	**then** = reteaching and enrichment suggestions

✓ Portfolio Assessment

- **Portfolio Assessment,** TE pp. 1
- **Leveled Practice,** TE pp. 4, 13a, 16, 21a, 27a, 35, 35a
- **Workbook Pages,** pp. 1–11
- **Unit Review: Skills on Your Own,** PE/TE p. 40
- **Curriculum Connection: Writing,** TE pp. 13a, 21a, 27a, 33

✓ Performance Assessment

- **Hands-on Unit Project** (Unit 1 Performance Assessment), PE/TE pp. 1, 42
- **Internet Activity,** PE p. 42
- **Unit Review: Think and Share,** PE/TE p. 41
- **Scoring Guides,** TE pp. 36a, 39, 40, 42

Test Talk

Test-Taking Strategies

Understand the Question

- **Locate Key Words in the Question,** TE p. 41
- **Locate Key Words in the Text,** TE p. 11

Understand the Answer

- **Choose the Right Answer**
- **Use Information from the Text,** TE p. 19
- **Use Information from Graphics,** TE p. 21
- **Write Your Answer,** TE p. 31

For additional practice, use the Test Talk Practice Book.

Featured Strategy

Locate Key Words in the Question

Children will:

– Find the key words in the question.

– Turn the key words into a statement that begins "I need to find out...."

PE/TE p. 41

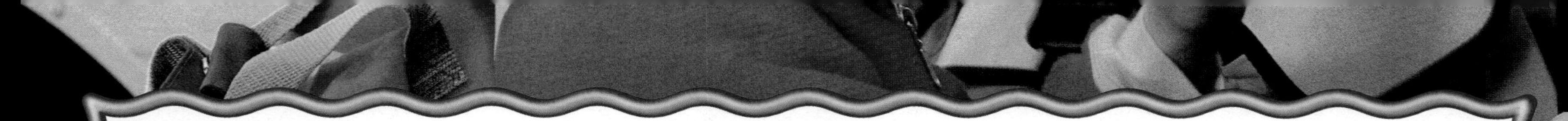

Curriculum Connections

Integrating Your Day

The lessons, skills, and features of Unit 1 provide many opportunities to make connections between social studies and other areas of the elementary curriculum.

Reading

Biographies, p. 11

Reading Skill—Use Picture Clues, pp. 8, 28

Reading Skill—Put Things in Order, p. 14

Learn a Calendar Rhyme, p. 20

Reading Skill—Classify/Categorize, p. 22

Writing

Make a Picture Glossary, p. 5

Make a Book, p. 13a

My Country, My Flag, p. 21a

Rules on Rules, p. 27a

Sharing Time, p. 33

Math

School "Counts," p. 7

Special Days, p. 21a

Tools, p. 35a

Social Studies

Literature

The Story of Ruby Bridges, p. 19

Books About School, p. 37

Science

Snack Survey, p. 16

Reducing Trash, p. 26

Music/Drama

Games We Play, p. 13a

"This Is the Way," p. 36

Art

This Is How We Work and Play! p. 3

Things I Like, p. 13a

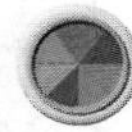
Look for this symbol throughout the Teacher's Edition to find **Curriculum Connections.**

Professional Development

Teaching Social Studies to Young Children

by Sara Miranda Sanchez
Albuquerque Public Schools

Early childhood pedagogy has long recognized that young children under the age of eight do not learn isolated facts with much success; neither are they passive learners. We know that allowing children to address academic goals that represent specific knowledge and skills in interactive, child-centered experiences will promote greater depth of learning. Yet, a common struggle in the primary classroom is finding the balance between covering predetermined content and developing multifaceted critical thinkers and learners.

My most successful practices set up experiences for children to be active participants in their own learning. The key is to find the experiences that meet the learning needs of all children. With a classroom of children each coming to school from unique situations and varying experiences, my teacher role was to create a learning environment to facilitate learning at multiple levels.

The following activities in the Teacher's Edition are designed to meet children's individual needs by suggesting variations at three levels of difficulty.

- ***Explore the School,*** *p. 4*
- ***Find Pictures of Groups,*** *p. 13a*
- ***The United States,*** *p. 16*
- ***Hooray for Me!*** *p. 21a*
- ***Wall Mural,*** *p. 27a*
- ***Guess the Time,*** *p. 35*
- ***Then or Now,*** *p. 35a*

ESL Support

by Jim Cummins, Ph. D.
University of Toronto

Activate Prior Knowledge/ Build Background

In Unit 1, you can use the following fundamental strategy to help ESL students expand their language abilities.

There is general agreement among cognitive psychologists that we learn by integrating new input into our existing cognitive structures. Our prior experience provides the foundation for interpreting new information. No learner is a blank slate. In reading, for example, we construct meaning by bringing our prior knowledge of language and of the world to the text. For example, a child who knows a lot about baseball will find it much easier to understand a story about baseball than a child who has very little prior knowledge about the game. The same holds true for social studies. The more a child already knows about a particular topic in the text, the more of the text he/she is likely to understand. And, the more of the text a child understands, the more new knowledge he/she can acquire.

The following example in the Teacher's Edition will help you to activate students' prior knowledge and build background for the concepts developed in the lesson.

- ***Finding Clues*** *on p. 6 helps English Language Learners learn how to use picture clues.*

Read Aloud

The Wheels on the Bus

**The wheels on the bus go round and round,
Round and round, round and round,
The wheels on the bus go round and round,
As off to school we go.**

**The driver on the bus says buckle up,
Buckle up, buckle up,
The driver on the bus says buckle up,
As off to school we go.**

**The children on the bus sing a song,
Sing a song, sing a song,
The children on the bus sing a song,
As off to school we go.**

**The wheels on the bus go round and round,
Round and round, round and round,
The wheels on the bus go round and round,
As off to school we go.**

Build Background

- Ask children how they get to school each day.
- Ask children to tell about rules they obey while coming to school.
- Ask children what they learn in school.

Read-Alouds and Primary Sources

Read-Alouds and Primary Sources contains additional selections to be used with Unit 1.

Bibliography

Froggy Goes to School, by Jonathan London and Frank Remkiewicz (Illustrator), (Puffin, ISBN 0-14-056247-8, 1998) **Easy**

My First Day of School, by Patrick K. Hallinan (Hambleton-Hill; ISBN 1-57102-154-X, 2000) **Easy**

My Teacher Sleeps in School, by Leatie Weiss and Ellen Weiss (Illustrator), (Econo-Clad Books, ISBN 0-808-57413-2, 1999) **Easy**

AWARD ***Owen,*** by Kevin Henkes (Greenwillow, ISBN 0-688-11449-0, 1993) **Easy** ***Caldecott Honor Book, 1994***

Double Trouble in Walla Walla, by Andrew Clements and Sal Murdocca (Illustrator), (Millbrook Press, ISBN 0-7613-0275-1, 1997) **On-Level**

AWARD ***Lilly's Purple Plastic Purse,*** by Kevin Henkes (Greenwillow, ISBN 0-688-12897-1, 1996) **On-Level** ***ALA Notable Book, 1997***

No Good in Art, by Miriam Cohen and Lillian Hoban (Illustrator), (Morrow, ISBN 0-688-84234-8, 1980) **On-Level**

Rex and Lilly Schooltime, by Laurene Krasny Brown and Marc Brown (Illustrator), (Little Brown, ISBN 0-316-10920-7, 1997) **On-Level**

Marianthe's Story: Painted Words, Spoken Memories, by Aliki (Greenwillow, ISBN 0-688-15661-4, 1998) **Challenge**

More Than Anything Else, by Marie Bradby and Chris Soentpiet (Illustrator), (Orchard Books, ISBN 0-531-09464-2, 1995) **Challenge**

Nobody's Mother Is in Second Grade, by Robin Pulver and G. Brian Karas (Illustrator), (Dial Books for Young Readers, ISBN 0-8037-1210-3, 1992) **Challenge**

AWARD ***Virgie Goes to School with Us Boys,*** by Elizabeth Fitzgerald Howard and E. B. Lewis (Illustrator), (Simon & Schuster, ISBN 0-689-80076-2, 2000) **Challenge** ***ALA Notable Book, 2001***

Bringing History Home, by M. Gail Hickey (Allyn & Bacon, ISBN 0-205-28169-9, 1998) **Teacher Reference**

Hands Around the World, by Susan Milord (Williamson, ISBN 0-913-58965-9, 1992) **Teacher Reference**

AWARD Look for this symbol throughout the Teacher's Edition to find **Award-Winning Selections**. Additional book references are suggested throughout this unit.

Time for School
UNIT 1
Why do we go to school?
1

Hands-on Unit Project

✓ Unit 1 Performance Assessment

- The Unit 1 Project, *Follow Me!* found on p. 42, is an ongoing performance assessment project to enrich children's learning throughout the unit.
- This project, which has children making a model of a video camera and then giving a video tour of their school, may be started now or at any time during this unit of study.
- A performance assessment scoring guide is located on p. 42.

Time for School

Unit Overview

This unit introduces children to aspects of life at school, such as daily routines, rules, school history, and individuals who have contributed to education.

Introduce Andrew

Read the unit title and then introduce the featured child for this unit as a first-grader named Andrew. Talk about where Andrew is going and why.

Unit Question

- Ask children the question on this page.
- Initiate a discussion of what children hope to learn at school. Encourage them to talk about things that might help them to learn, such as a quiet place, trying hard, asking questions, practicing self-control, and working with others.
- To activate prior knowledge, make a list on chart paper of children's responses to the unit question: Why do we go to school?

✓ **Portfolio Assessment** Keep the list for the Portfolio Assessment at the end of the unit.

We Go to School

Objective

- Learn why children attend school.

Resources

- *Songs and Music* CD "We Go to School"
- Poster 1
- Social Studies Plus!

Introduce the Song

Preview Tell children that they will be singing a song about school. Focus on the picture of Andrew, and review where Andrew is going.

Warm Up To activate prior knowledge, use the list generated during the Portfolio Assessment activity (p. 1). Ask each child to tell what he or she most wants to learn at school this year.

Sing the Song

- Have children sing the song "We Go to School."
- Have children pantomime the activities named in the song.
- Have children act out other things they want to learn to do at school.
- Ask children to help rewrite the third sentence of the song to reflect their own answers to the question: Why do we go to school? Then sing the song with the new lines.

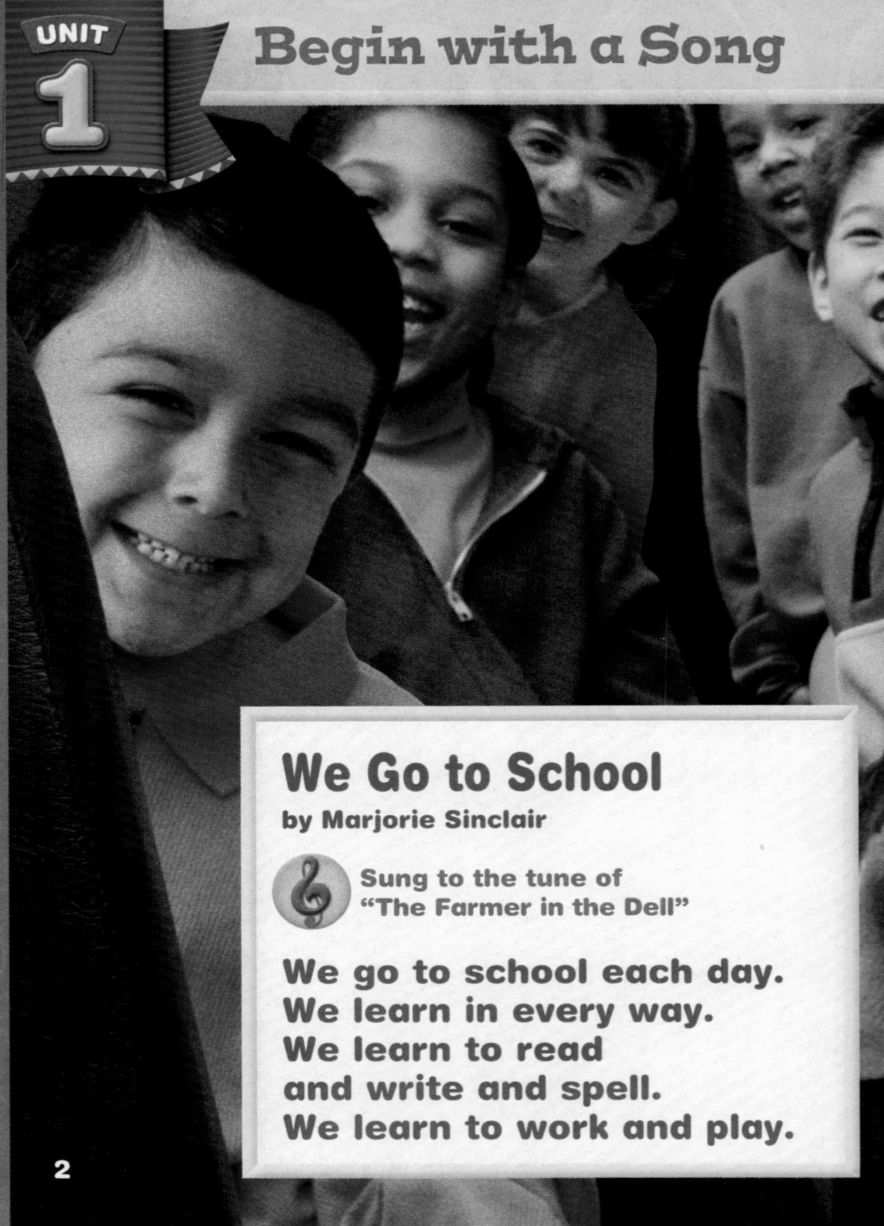

UNIT 1
Begin with a Song
We Go to School
by Marjorie Sinclair
Sung to the tune of "The Farmer in the Dell"
We go to school each day.
We learn in every way.
We learn to read
and write and spell.
We learn to work and play.
2

Practice and Extend

FAST FACTS

Learning Long Ago

You may want to mention a few of the schoolbooks that American children used long ago.

- To learn to read, they used "McGuffey's Readers," which taught patriotism as well as reading.
- To learn spelling, children used Noah Webster's "Blue-Backed Speller."

If possible, share with children an example of an old textbook, such as a McGuffey Reader.

AUDIO CD Technology

Play the CD, *Songs and Music,* to listen to "We Go to School."

CURRICULUM CONNECTION
Art

This Is How We Work and Play!

- Direct children's attention to the last sentence of the song. Ask them to name ways they learn to work and play in school.
- Have children draw a picture to illustrate their favorite work or play activity. Help them write captions for their pictures.
- Provide time for children to share their drawings with the class.

Talk About the Photograph

Direct attention to the photograph on these two pages. Point out that the children in the picture are on a school bus. Ask children if any of them take a bus to school. Then point out Andrew in the photo.

1 **Why do you think Andrew looks happy?** He may be excited about going to school; he may be eager to meet new friends and learn to do new things. **Make Inferences**

2 **Who do you think the other children on the bus are?** Possible answers: Andrew's classmates, children who go to Andrew's school. **Make Inferences**

Big Book/Pupil Book pp. 4–5

Vocabulary Preview

Objective

- Determine the meanings of words.

Resources

- Workbook, p. 1
- Vocabulary Cards
- Poster 2

Introduce the Vocabulary

Read aloud and spell each vocabulary word as you point to it and the photograph illustrating it. Ask children to repeat each word and its spelling. Have volunteers give the meanings of the words. Then have children find several examples of the vocabulary words in the illustration. Write these examples on the board.

Vocabulary Word	Illustrated Examples
school	school building, music school
group	ball team, children in classrooms
flag	flag outside school, flags in second-floor classrooms
country	two United States maps in second-floor classrooms
rule	crossing guards with stop signs, rules posted on bulletin board in second-floor left classroom

SOCIAL STUDIES STRAND

Citizenship

Listed below are some basic ideas of citizenship for young children. Direct your discussion of the illustration toward the development of these concepts.

- playing fairly
- exhibiting good sportsmanship
- helping others
- love of country
- treating others with respect
- rules to keep us safe
- taking responsibility for one's actions
- identifying compassion as a trait of a good citizen

school

group

flag

4

MEETING INDIVIDUAL NEEDS

Leveled Practice

Explore the School

Invite children to explore the school shown on pp. 4–5 with you.

Easy Begin outside the school, and name things you see. Each time you name a vocabulary word, have children repeat it after you. Continue to explore inside the school with children. **Reteach**

On-Level Have children take turns guiding a "new student" around the school. Encourage them to use vocabulary words to describe what they see. **Extend**

Challenge Invite children to describe something in the picture—without naming it. Have others try to name the item being described. **Enrich**

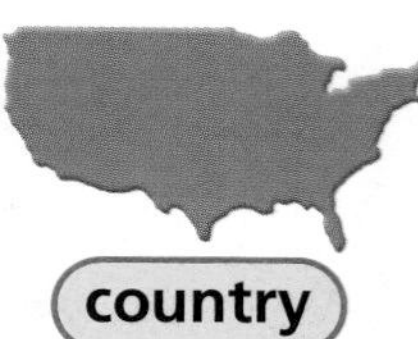

country

rule

5

Talk About the Picture

Point out that the picture shows several aspects of life at school. Then, to help children relate the picture to their own experiences, ask questions such as: *How close to the board are you? How far is the teacher's desk from the bookcase? Which way would you walk to go to the cafeteria? How close is the principal's office to the front door?*

1 **What country do you think this school is in? How do you know?** Children may assume that the school is in the United States because the setting seems familiar. Some children may use the picture clues of the United States flags and the United States maps. **Draw Conclusions**

2 **What are the children in the classrooms doing?** In one classroom, children are working at tables and putting a map puzzle together. In another classroom, children are pledging allegiance to the flag of the United States. **Analyze Pictures**

Look Ahead

Tell children that they will learn more about each of the vocabulary words as they study Unit 1.

You may want to revisit the picture with children to review the concepts and vocabulary in the unit.

3 **What do you think would happen if children didn't follow the rules of the crossing guard?** Children might get hurt crossing the street. **Hypothesize**

4 **What do you think the children pledging the flag are saying?** The Pledge of Allegiance **Draw Conclusions**

CURRICULUM CONNECTION Writing

Make a Picture Glossary

Children can add the vocabulary for Unit 1 to "My Word Book." Words may be entered at the beginning of the unit or added as they are introduced in the specific lessons.

WEB SITE Technology

You can look up vocabulary words online. Click on *Social Studies Library* and select the dictionary at **www.sfsocialstudies.com.**

Workbook, p. 1

Draw a picture for each word. Drawings will vary.
school
group
flag
rule
country

Also on Teacher Resources CD-ROM.

Andrew at School

Use Picture Clues

Objective

Obtain information about a topic using pictures.

Vocabulary

school a place where children learn (p. 6)

Resource

- Workbook, p. 2

About the Unit Target Skill

- The target reading skill for this unit is Use Picture Clues.
- Children are introduced to the unit target skill here and are given an opportunity to practice it.
- Further opportunities to use picture clues are found throughout Unit 1.

1 Introduce and Motivate

Preview Display the Vocabulary Card **school**, and ask children to name their school. Share the meaning of *school* as a place where people learn. Then, to determine if children understand the concept of using picture clues, show 2–3 photos of yourself or of others doing activities in various settings. Ask children to tell you what each picture shows. Help them identify who is in the picture and what the actions are. You might ask: *Where was the photo taken? What is this person doing? Is he/she having fun?*

Warm Up To activate prior knowledge, show children a picture book with which they are familiar. Encourage them to point out picture clues that help tell the story.

UNIT 1
Reading Social Studies

Andrew at School

Use Picture Clues

Hi. My name is Andrew. I am in first grade. The pictures show some things I do in school. **School** is the place where I learn. Look at the pictures. Then tell about my busy day.

Practice and Extend

BUILD BACKGROUND ESL Support

Finding Clues Draw a picture of a child next to a house. Include a sun and flowers. Ask children: *Is it daytime or night? How do you know?* Write the word *clue* on the board. Then point to the sun in the picture. Explain that the sun is a picture clue telling that it is daytime.

Beginning Ask children to point to various objects in the picture as you narrate. For example: *It's morning. How do we know? There's a sun. Point to the sun.*

Intermediate As you look at the picture, ask questions that elicit one-word answers or phrases. For example: *Is this the sun or the moon?*

Advanced Ask children to describe what they see. Point to various items in the picture and ask questions to elicit more language.

You can learn a lot from pictures. Pictures even help you learn about words. Where do I eat my lunch? What is the name of the place where I go to get a book?

Cafeteria

Library

Try it!

Make a picture book. Draw pictures to show what you do each day. Give the book to your partner. Have your partner get clues from your pictures to tell about your day.

7

2 Teach and Discuss

Read p. 6 and point out the pictures on pp. 6–7. Have children identify Andrew and tell what each picture shows him doing.

Read p. 7, pausing after each question. Ask children to point to the picture that shows where Andrew eats lunch. Point out the picture caption, and read the word *Cafeteria* for children. Ask if that's what they call the place where they eat lunch. Ask children to find the picture that shows where Andrew goes to get a book. Point out the picture caption, and read the word *Library* for children.

Ongoing Assessment

If... children do not understand how to use picture clues,	**then...** have them choose their favorite picture book and tell the story by looking only at the pictures. Explain that they used picture clues to tell the story.

Tell children that looking for clues in pictures can help them better understand what they read.

3 Close and Assess

Try it!

Review with children what they do each day (get ready for school, go to school, do class work, have lunch, play, and so on). Have each child select 4–5 such activities to illustrate. Help children staple sheets of drawing paper together to make a book. Tell children to draw one activity on each page. As children share their books with partners, they can use picture clues to describe events in each other's days.

CURRICULUM CONNECTION
Math

School "Counts"

Have children work in small groups to count sets of things in your classroom. They might count the number of students in your class, the number of desks in your classroom, the number of tables in the library or cafeteria. Have children use *more* and *less* to compare the size of the sets they count.

Workbook, p. 2

Use Picture Clues
Circle where each child is going.
Draw where each child is going. Drawings will vary.

Also on Teacher Resources CD-ROM.

Workbook Support

Use the following Workbook pages to support content and skills development as you teach Unit 1. You can also view and print Workbook pages from the Teacher Resources CD-ROM.

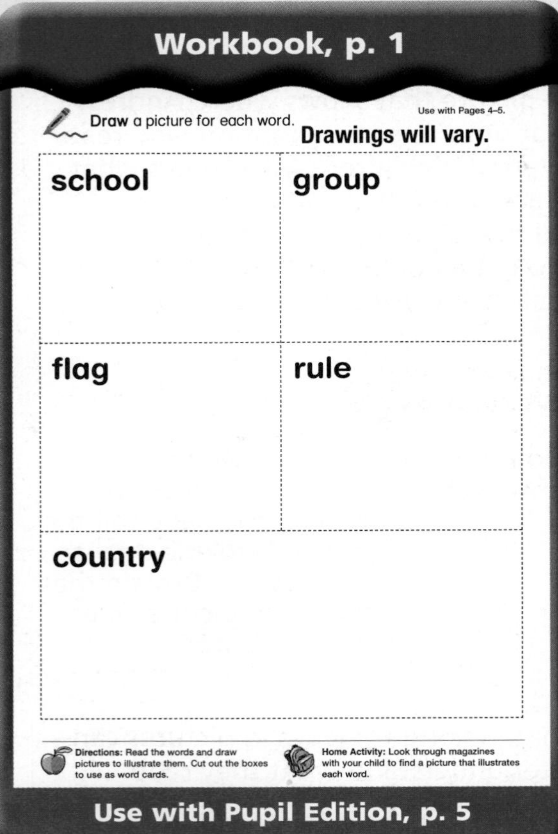

Workbook, p. 1

Use with Pages 4–5.

Draw a picture for each word. **Drawings will vary.**

school	group
flag	rule
country	

Directions: Read the words and draw pictures to illustrate them. Cut out the boxes to use as word cards.

Home Activity: Look through magazines with your child to find a picture that illustrates each word.

Use with Pupil Edition, p. 5

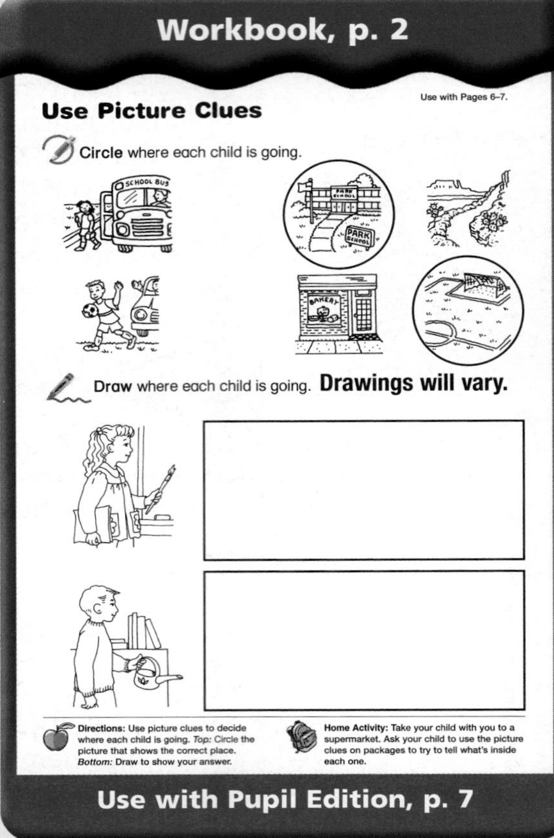

Workbook, p. 2

Use with Pages 6–7.

Use Picture Clues

Circle where each child is going.

Draw where each child is going. **Drawings will vary.**

Directions: Use picture clues to decide where each child is going. *Top:* Circle the picture that shows the correct place. *Bottom:* Draw to show your answer.

Home Activity: Take your child with you to a supermarket. Ask your child to use the picture clues on packages to try to tell what's inside each one.

Use with Pupil Edition, p. 7

Workbook, p. 3

Use with Pages 8–9.

Getting to Know Andrew

Color two pictures that show groups. **Color pictures 1 and 3.**

Draw a picture of a group. **Drawings will vary.**

Directions: *Top:* Color the two pictures that show groups. *Bottom:* Draw a picture of a group.

Home Activity: Ask your child to help you find pictures of groups at play or at work. Have your child describe what the people are doing.

Use with Pupil Edition, p. 9

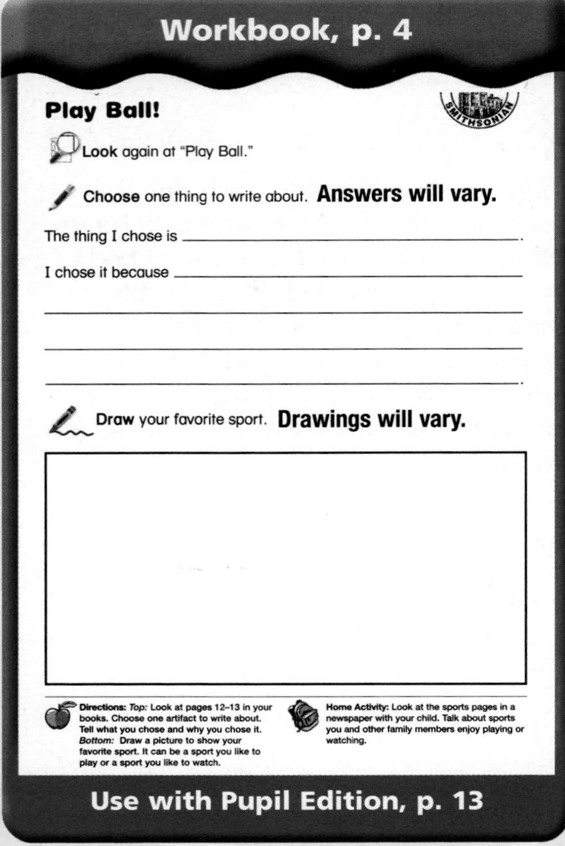

Workbook, p. 4

Play Ball!

Look again at "Play Ball."

Choose one thing to write about. **Answers will vary.**

The thing I chose is __________

I chose it because __________

Draw your favorite sport. **Drawings will vary.**

Directions: *Top:* Look at pages 12–13 in your books. Choose one artifact to write about. Tell what you chose and why you chose it. *Bottom:* Draw a picture to show your favorite sport. It can be a sport you like to play or a sport you like to watch.

Home Activity: Look at the sports pages in a newspaper with your child. Talk about sports you and other family members enjoy playing or watching.

Use with Pupil Edition, p. 13

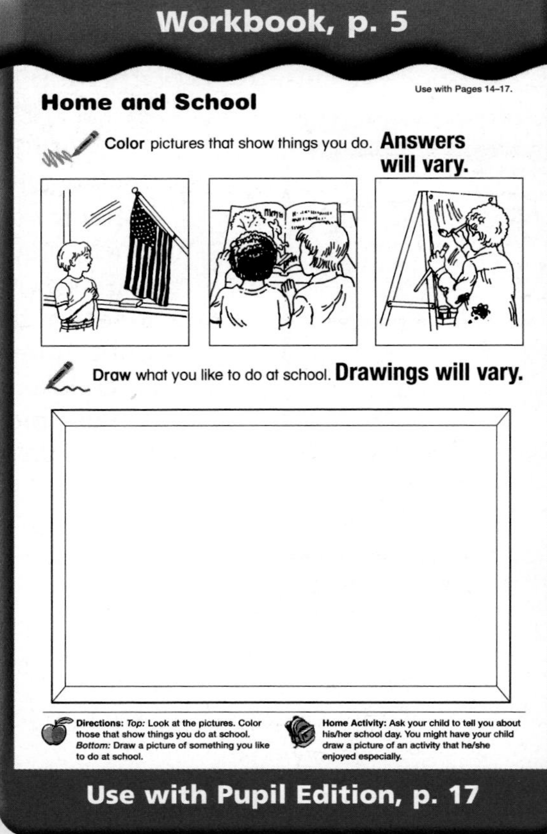

Workbook, p. 5

Use with Pages 14–17.

Home and School

Color pictures that show things you do. **Answers will vary.**

Draw what you like to do at school. **Drawings will vary.**

Directions: *Top:* Look at the pictures. Color those that show things you do at school. *Bottom:* Draw a picture of something you like to do at school.

Home Activity: Ask your child to tell you about his/her school day. You might have your child draw a picture of an activity that he/she enjoyed especially.

Use with Pupil Edition, p. 17

Workbook, p. 6

Use with Pages 20–21.

Read a Calendar

Write the numbers.

Draw a flag for July 4th.
Draw to show what you might do. **Drawings will vary.**

JULY

Sunday	Monday	Tuesday	Wednesday	Thursday	Friday	Saturday
1	2	3	4	5	6	7
8	9	10	11	12	13	14
15	16	17	18	19	20	21
22	23	24	25	26	27	28
29	30	31				

Directions: Write numbers *1–31* to show days in July. Draw a U. S. flag in the box for July 4th. Draw to show things you might do in July.

Home Activity: Have your child help you mark special days on a monthly calendar. Ask your child to check off each day of the month as it goes by.

Use with Pupil Edition, p. 21

Workbook Support

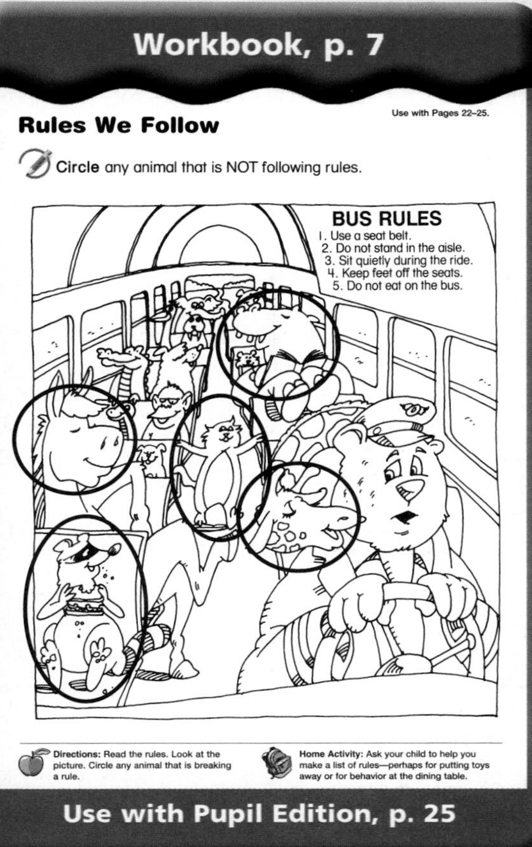
Workbook, p. 7

Use with Pages 22–25.

Rules We Follow

Circle any animal that is NOT following rules.

BUS RULES
1. Use a seat belt.
2. Do not stand in the aisle.
3. Sit quietly during the ride.
4. Keep feet off the seats.
5. Do not eat on the bus.

Directions: Read the rules. Look at the picture. Circle any animal that is breaking a rule.

Home Activity: Ask your child to help you make a list of rules—perhaps for putting toys away or for behavior at the dining table.

Use with Pupil Edition, p. 25

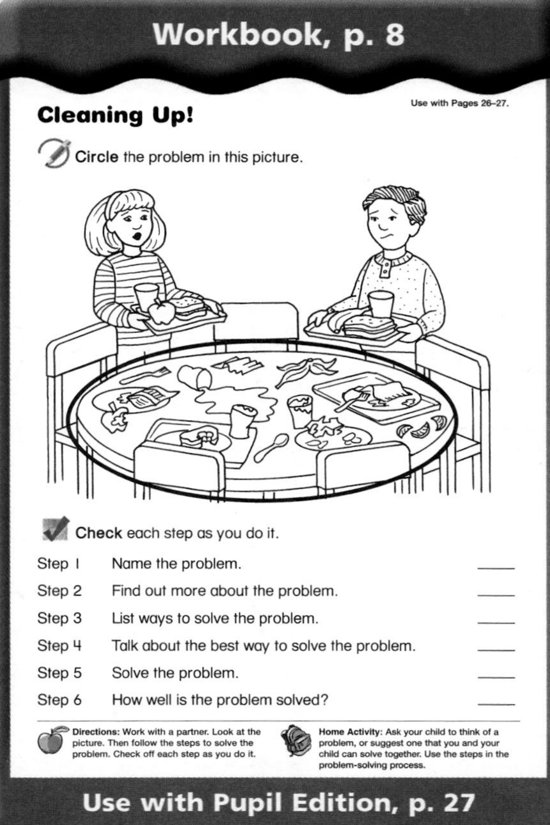
Workbook, p. 8

Use with Pages 26–27.

Cleaning Up!

Circle the problem in this picture.

Check each step as you do it.

Step 1	Name the problem.	____
Step 2	Find out more about the problem.	____
Step 3	List ways to solve the problem.	____
Step 4	Talk about the best way to solve the problem.	____
Step 5	Solve the problem.	____
Step 6	How well is the problem solved?	____

Directions: Work with a partner. Look at the picture. Then follow the steps to solve the problem. Check off each step as you do it.

Home Activity: Ask your child to think of a problem, or suggest one that you and your child can solve together. Use the steps in the problem-solving process.

Use with Pupil Edition, p. 27

Workbook, p. 9

Use with Pages 28–31.

Learning About My School

Color the picture from long ago. **Color picture 2.**

Draw your school. **Drawings will vary.**

Directions: Look at each picture. *Top:* Color the one that shows a school from the past. *Bottom:* Draw your school.

Home Activity: Share with your child photos of yourself as a youngster. Talk about how things have changed and/or stayed the same.

Use with Pupil Edition, p. 31

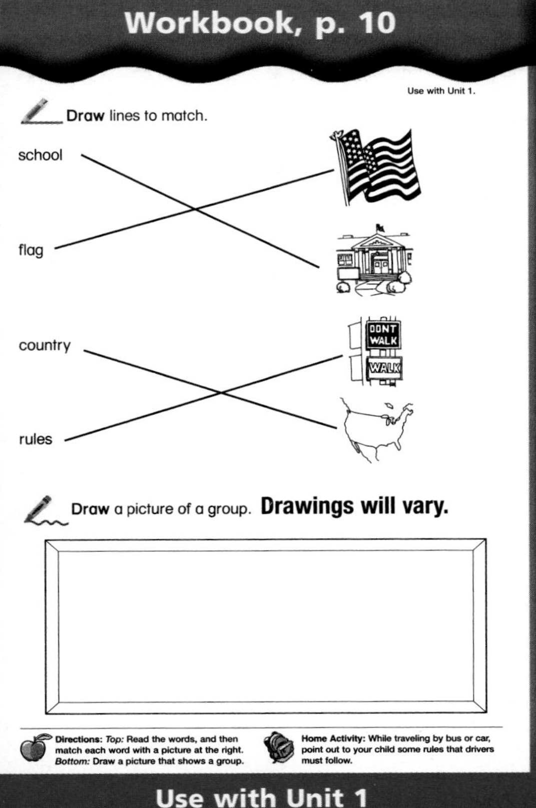
Workbook, p. 10

Use with Unit 1.

Draw lines to match.

school

flag

country

rules

Draw a picture of a group. **Drawings will vary.**

Directions: *Top:* Read the words, and then match each word with a picture at the right. *Bottom:* Draw a picture that shows a group.

Home Activity: While traveling by bus or car, point out to your child some rules that drivers must follow.

Use with Unit 1

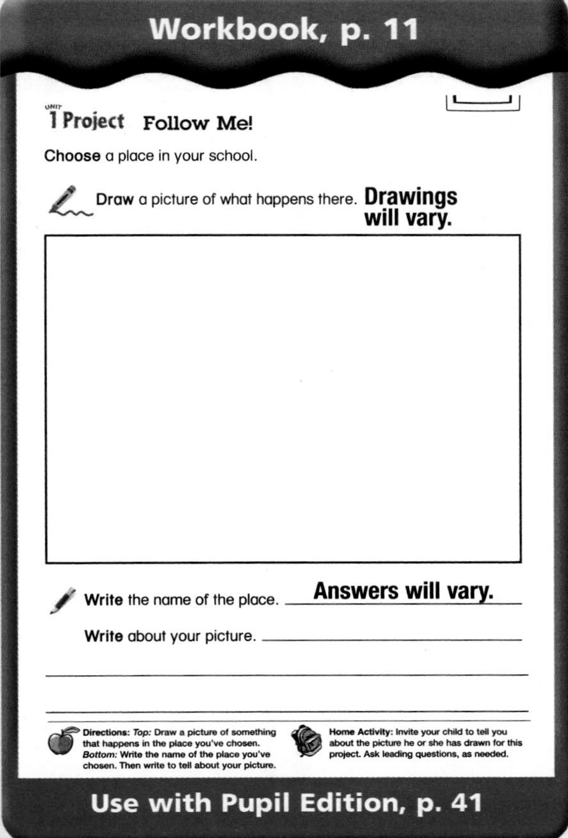
Workbook, p. 11

Unit 1 Project **Follow Me!**

Choose a place in your school.

Draw a picture of what happens there. **Drawings will vary.**

Write the name of the place. **Answers will vary.**

Write about your picture. ____________

Directions: *Top:* Draw a picture of something that happens in the place you've chosen. *Bottom:* Write the name of the place you've chosen. Then write to tell about your picture.

Home Activity: Invite your child to tell you about the picture he or she has drawn for this project. Ask leading questions, as needed.

Use with Pupil Edition, p. 41

Assessment Support

Use the following Assessment Book pages to assess content and skills in Unit 1. You can also view and print Assessment Book pages from the Teacher Resources CD-ROM.

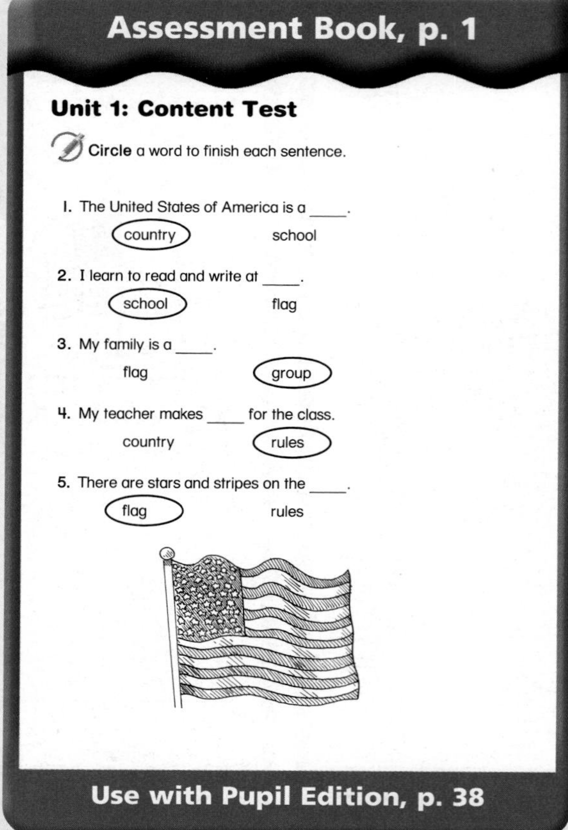

Assessment Book, p. 1

Unit 1: Content Test

Circle a word to finish each sentence.

1. The United States of America is a ____.
   (country) school
2. I learn to read and write at ____.
   (school) flag
3. My family is a ____.
   flag (group)
4. My teacher makes ____ for the class.
   country (rules)
5. There are stars and stripes on the ____.
   (flag) rules

Use with Pupil Edition, p. 38

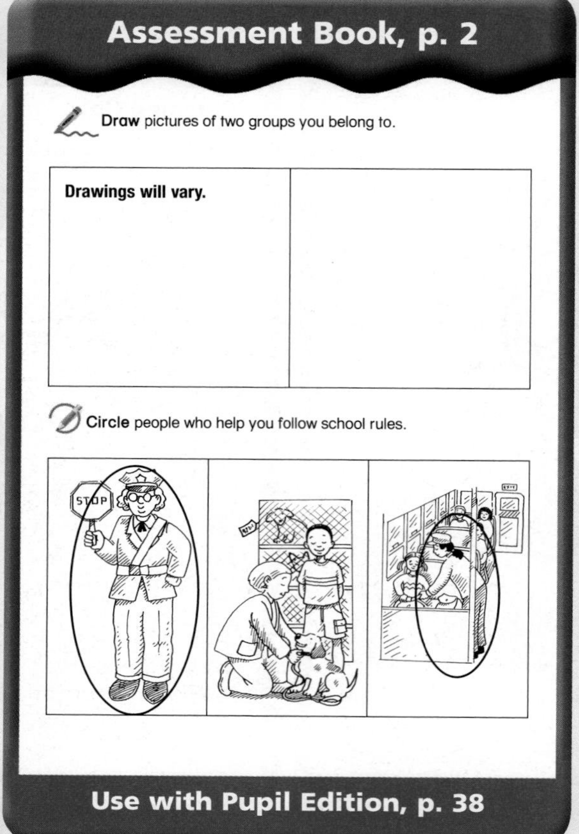

Assessment Book, p. 2

Draw pictures of two groups you belong to.

Drawings will vary.

Circle people who help you follow school rules.

Use with Pupil Edition, p. 38

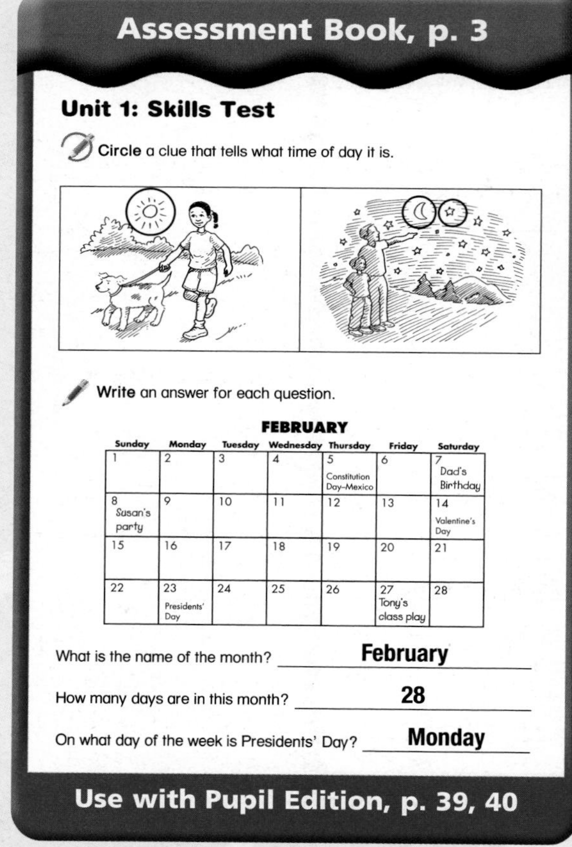

Assessment Book, p. 3

Unit 1: Skills Test

Circle a clue that tells what time of day it is.

Write an answer for each question.

FEBRUARY

Sunday	Monday	Tuesday	Wednesday	Thursday	Friday	Saturday
1	2	3	4	5 Constitution Day-Mexico	6	7 Dad's Birthday
8 Susan's party	9	10	11	12	13	14 Valentine's Day
15	16	17	18	19	20	21
22	23 Presidents' Day	24	25	26	27 Tony's class play	28

What is the name of the month? **February**

How many days are in this month? **28**

On what day of the week is Presidents' Day? **Monday**

Use with Pupil Edition, p. 39, 40

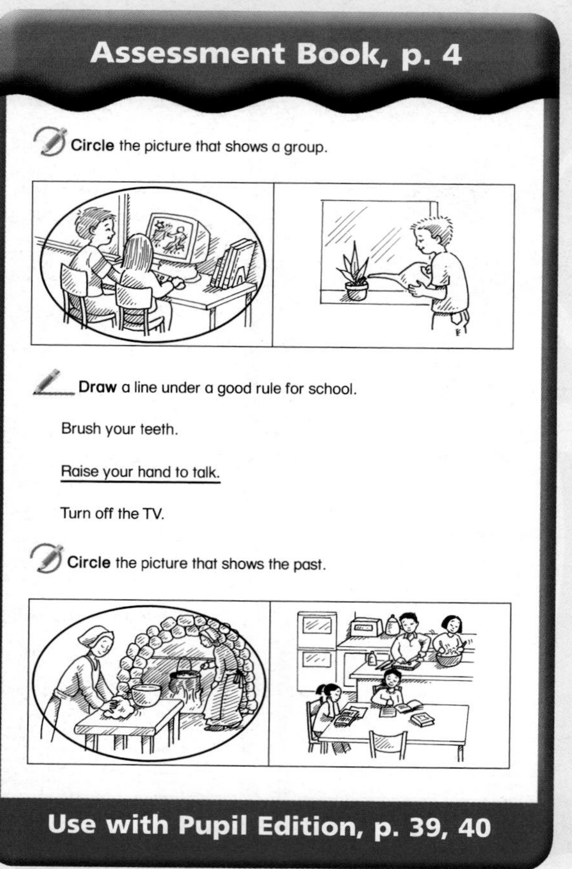

Assessment Book, p. 4

Circle the picture that shows a group.

Draw a line under a good rule for school.

Brush your teeth.

Raise your hand to talk.

Turn off the TV.

Circle the picture that shows the past.

Use with Pupil Edition, p. 39, 40

Lesson 1 Overview

Lesson	Objectives	Time and Resources
Getting to Know Andrew **pages 8–9**	Children will learn the meaning of the word *group* and explore the concept that people belong to many different groups. They will identify main ideas and obtain information from oral, visual, and print sources. 	Time 20 minutes Resources • Workbook, p. 3 • Vocabulary Card **group** • Every Student Learns Guide, pp. 2–5
Meet Carl Stotz **pages 10–11**	Children will identify contributions of figures who have influenced the community, state, and nation.	 Time 15–20 minutes
Play Ball! **pages 12–13**	Children will obtain information about baseball, using photographs of artifacts.	 Time 15–20 minutes Resource • Workbook, p. 4

Build Background

Activity

Getting to Know You

 **Time** 15–20 minutes

Ask each child to draw a picture that tells something about himself or herself. Help children put their initials, but not their names, on their pictures.

Use clothespins to suspend children's pictures from a length of twine. Then have children use their pictures to get to know each other better. Point to a picture, and ask if children can figure out who the artist is from the picture. If children don't quickly identify the artist, have him or her tell what the picture shows—and why it's important to the child.

If time is short, children can take turns introducing themselves to classmates and telling something they like or like to do.

Read Aloud

Groups

by Peri Jones

My pals and I
Like to play.
We bike or blade
Most every day.

We're quite a group—
Jed, Jan, and me—
Even though
We're only three.

My dad and I
Do things, too.
A group can be
Just us two.

Lesson 1 Getting to Know Andrew

Objectives

- Understand that people belong to many different groups.
- Obtain information about a topic using pictures.

Vocabulary

group a set of people or things (p. 9)

QUICK Teaching Plan

If time is short, have children look at the pictures and brainstorm a list of groups.

- Have each child draw a quick sketch of a group to which he or she belongs.

1 Introduce and Motivate

Preview Display the Vocabulary Card **group**, and ask children to name the group to which they *all* belong. (Children might name their room, class, or school.) Share the meaning of *group* as a "set of people or things." Have children locate the term as they preview the lesson.

Warm Up To activate prior knowledge, explain to children the difference between doing something alone and as a part of a group. Then ask children to name some interests or hobbies they have and whether they practice their interest and hobbies alone or with friends. Children may enjoy acting out games and/or activities that they and their friends do together.

Lesson 1 Getting to Know Andrew

I have so much to tell you! Look at my pictures. They will help you learn about me. Many of my friends like the same things.

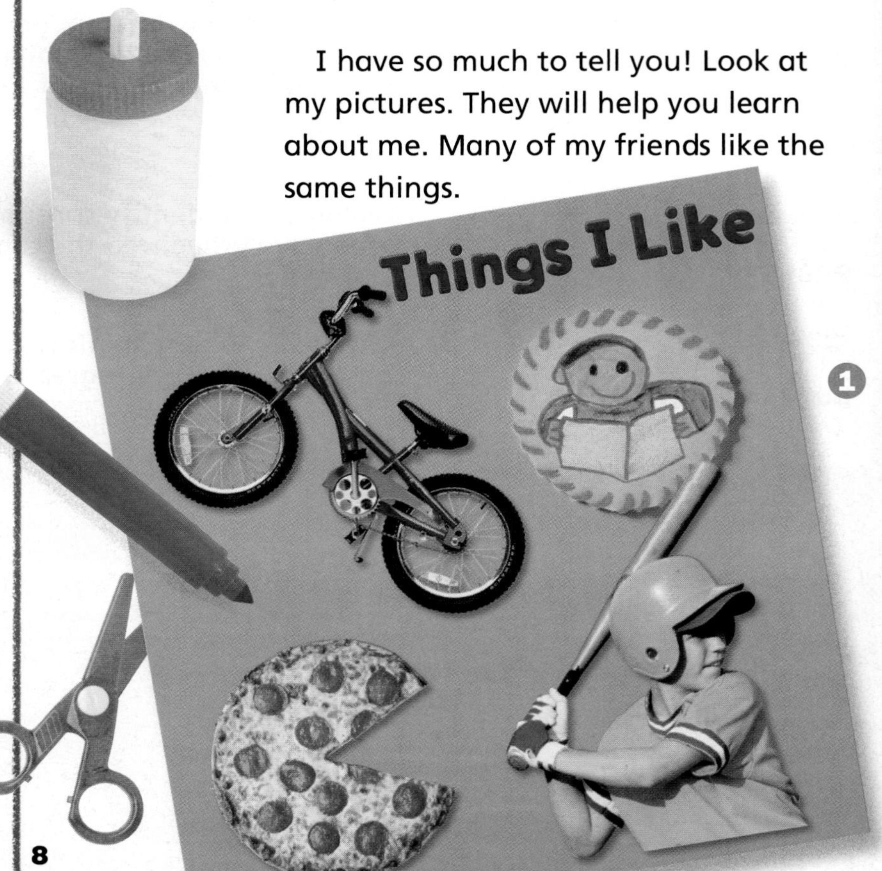

1

8

Practice and Extend

READING SKILL Use Picture Clues

Target Skill

Look! Tell children that they can learn a lot about Andrew by looking at the pictures on these pages.

- For each picture on p. 8, have children point to a picture and name the item shown to complete this sentence: *Andrew likes* ______.
- For the pictures on p. 9, have children complete this sentence: *Two groups that Andrew belongs to are* _____ *and* _____.

WEB SITE Technology

You can look up vocabulary words online. Click on *Social Studies Library* and select the dictionary at **www.sfsocialstudies.com.**

I belong to many groups. A **group** is made up of people or things. People in a group can do things together. Look at the pictures of me in different groups.

My Team
My Family

What did you learn?

1. Name three things that Andrew likes.
2. Look at the pictures of groups. Tell about each group.
3. **Think and Share** Name other groups. Tell who is in each group.

9

FYI SOCIAL STUDIES Background

Possible Misconceptions

- Help children see that groups can and do change. Show this by having children form groups (as for a game) and then form other groups (as for center activities).
- Discuss how people in a group must act responsibly and work together to accomplish a goal.

Workbook, p. 3

Getting to Know Andrew
Color two pictures that show groups. Color pictures 1 and 3.
Draw a picture of a group. Drawings will vary.

Also on Teacher Resources CD-ROM.

ESL Support

For ESL support, use Every Student Learns Guide, pp. 2–5.

2 Teach and Discuss

Page 8

Point out that Andrew made the poster shown on p. 8. Ask children to name the things that he likes.

1 **What things that Andrew likes do you like? What different things do you like?** Answers will vary but might include: alike—pizza, reading; different—bike, baseball. **Compare and Contrast**

Page 9

Help children find Andrew in each of the photographs. Then read the page with them.

2 **What groups does Andrew belong to?** A ball team, a family **Analyze Pictures**

3 **What groups do you belong to?** Answers will vary but may include a class, a team, a family, and so on. **Apply Information**

3 Close and Assess

Have children brainstorm a class list of groups they belong to. Encourage children to think of groups both inside and outside school.

✓ What did you learn?

1. Answers should include one or more of the things shown.
2. Answers should include name of group and who is in the group.
3. **Think and Share** Answers will vary but should include type of group and group members.

Carl Stotz

Objective

- Identify contributions of historical figures who have influenced the community, state, and nation.

1 Introduce and Motivate

Preview Ask children to name games or sports they enjoy playing or watching. Use their suggestions to make a word web. Write *games and sports* in the center cell.

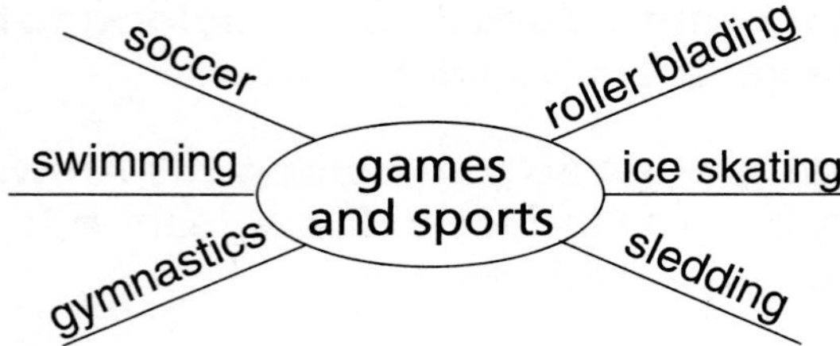

Warm Up To activate prior knowledge, ask children which of these activities they participate in—and which they like to watch. Ask if there is an activity they would like to do but are not old enough to do yet. Mark these on the web with an asterisk, or star.

Have children look at the pictures on pp. 10–11. Identify the man as Carl Stotz, and ask children what they think he is doing. Ask children who play on teams to name the people who coach those teams.

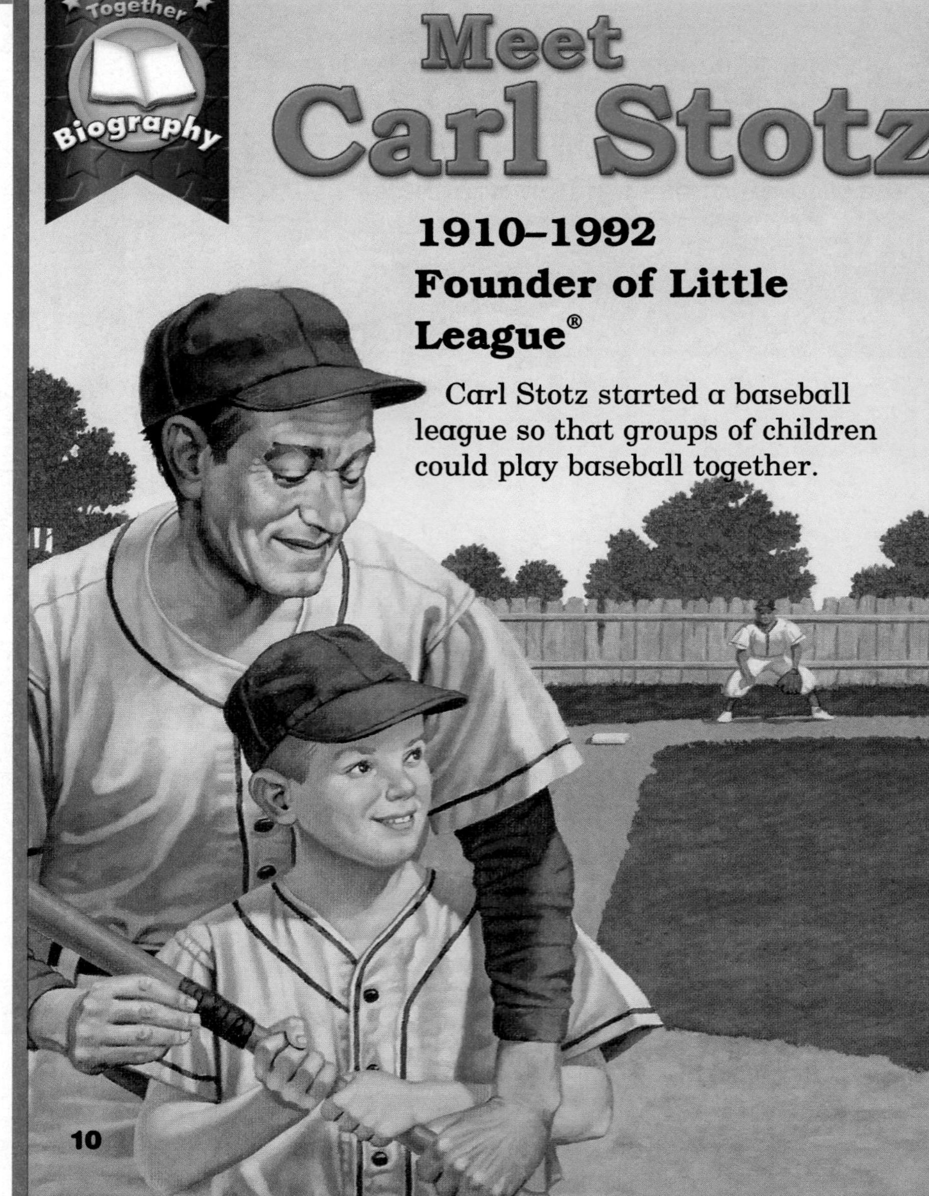

Read Together
Biography
Meet Carl Stotz
1910–1992
Founder of Little League®
Carl Stotz started a baseball league so that groups of children could play baseball together.
10

Practice and Extend

SOCIAL STUDIES Background

About Carl Stotz

- Carl Stotz, who worked by day as a clerk, founded Little League® Baseball. He was also the league's first commissioner.
- The first Little League game was played on June 6, 1939, in Williamsport. In that game, Lundy Lumber beat Lycoming Dairy 23–8.
- Williamsport is the permanent home of the annual Little League Baseball World Series.

WEB SITE Technology

You may help children find out more about Carl Stotz by clicking on *Meet the People* at **www.sfsocialstudies.com.**

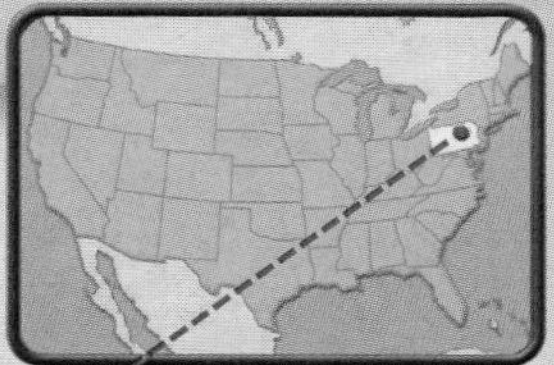

1 Carl played baseball as a boy. The games were not fun. The field was very big. The bats were too heavy. Rules were not followed. Carl wanted to make baseball fun.

Later, Carl Stotz made a baseball field for children. His field looked like a field for adults, but it was smaller. 2 He made the bats smaller and lighter. He made rules for Little League. Today, many children from around the world enjoy playing in Little League!

The first Little League game was played in Williamsport, Pennsylvania.

Carl Stotz with one of the first Little League teams

Think and Share

How did Carl Stotz make baseball fun for children to play?

For more information, go online to *Meet the People* at **www.sfsocialstudies.com.**

CURRICULUM CONNECTION
Reading

Biographies

Display examples of picture-book biographies of historical figures from your school library.

- Tell children that a biography is the true story of someone's life.
- Point out the covers on the books, and read aloud the titles. Point out that the title usually tells who the biography is about.
- Have partners select a book, look through it, and use picture clues to get a sense of subject's story.
- Ask children to select a biography for you to read aloud to them. As you share the book, point out how picture clues help readers understand a story. Also use the book to identify similarities and differences in daily life in the past and present.

2 Teach and Discuss

Read the biography together. Help children locate Pennsylvania on a map of the United States. Tell them that the Little League Baseball World Series is still held every year in Williamsport, PA.

Test Talk

Locate Key Words in the Text

1 **Why didn't Carl Stotz think it was fun to play baseball?** Answers include the field was too big, the bats were too heavy, and rules were not followed. After children respond, help them find details in the first paragraph on p. 11 to support their answers. **Cause and Effect**

2 **What changes did Carl Stotz make in the game?** He made the field smaller and the bats smaller and lighter. He made rules for young players. **Apply Information**

3 Close and Assess

Think and Share

Using their own words, children should be able to tell three ways in which Carl Stotz made baseball fun for children. (He made the playing field smaller; he made bats smaller and lighter; he made new rules.)

Play Ball!

Objective

- Obtain information about a topic using a variety of visual sources, such as photographs of artifacts.

Resource

- Workbook, p.4

1 Introduce and Motivate

Preview Ask children to name some games played with balls. Ask if they've ever heard the expression "Play ball!" Elicit that people often say "Play ball!" at the start of a ball game, especially a game of baseball.

Warm Up To activate prior knowledge, remind children that in "Meet Carl Stotz" they read about the game of baseball. Ask volunteers to share what they know about baseball, such as the equipment used, names of teams, names of positions, how runs are scored, and so on. Ask if any children collect baseball cards. If possible, show them examples of a few baseball cards.

Read the introduction with children. Then read aloud the question that Andrew asks. Tell children to keep this question in mind as they look at the pictures and read the captions.

2 Teach and Discuss

Direct attention to the old baseball card shown at the upper left. Compare and contrast this with any baseball cards that you or children may have. Talk about how baseball cards have changed over the years. Then move clockwise around the two-page spread, reading the captions and asking for children's comments.

1 Why do you think a museum would want to have a shirt worn by Jackie Robinson?
He was the first African American to play on an all-white team. **Draw Conclusions**

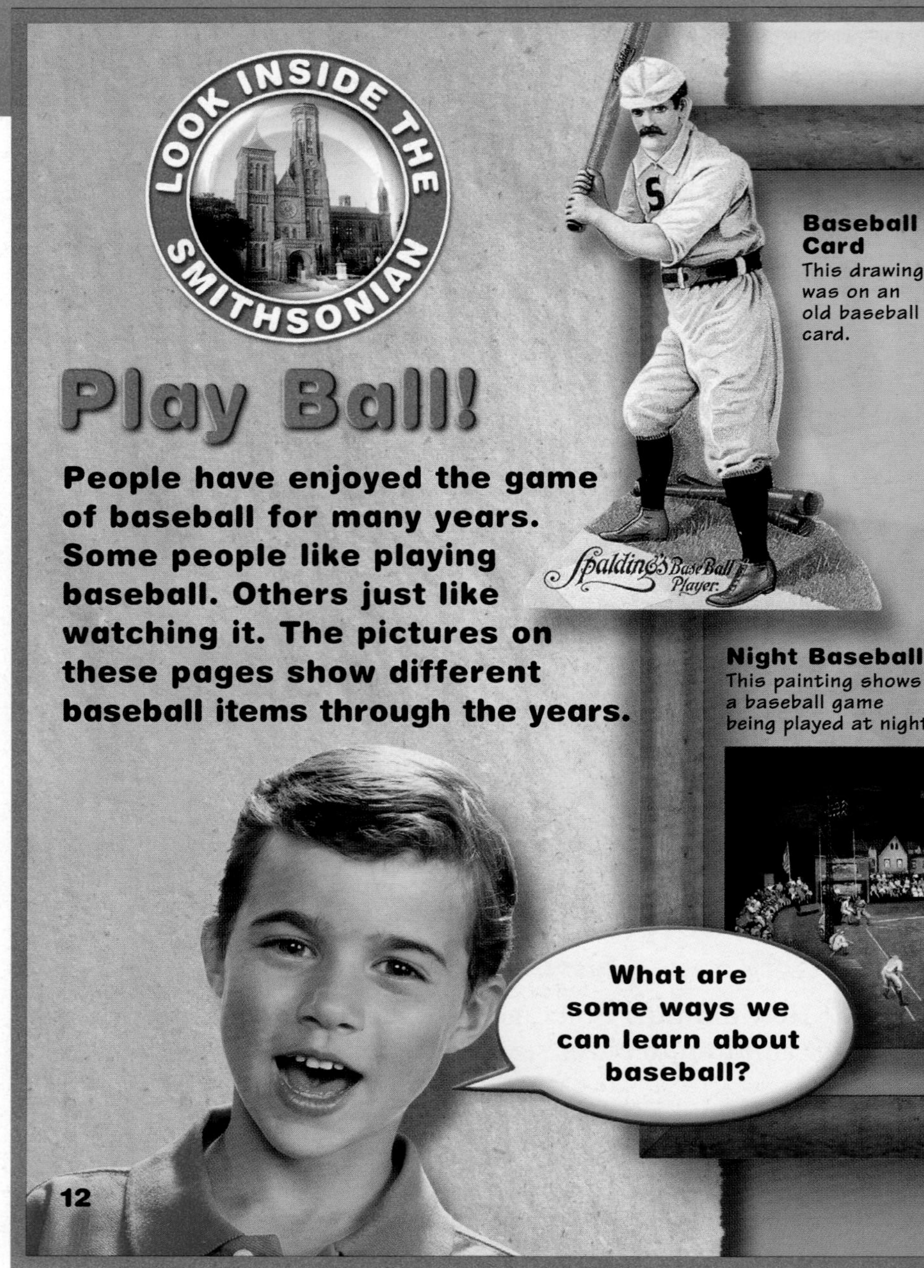

LOOK INSIDE THE SMITHSONIAN
Play Ball!
People have enjoyed the game of baseball for many years. Some people like playing baseball. Others just like watching it. The pictures on these pages show different baseball items through the years.
Baseball Card
This drawing was on an old baseball card.
Spalding's Base Ball Player
Night Baseball
This painting shows a baseball game being played at night.
What are some ways we can learn about baseball?
12

Practice and Extend

CURRICULUM CONNECTIONS
Literature

Jackie Robinson, Baseball's Legend

- Display the cover of the book *Teammates* by Peter Golenbock (Harcourt, ISBN 0-15-200603-6, 1990). Identify both Jackie Robinson and Pee Wee Reese for children.
- Explain that *Teammates* is a true story about two baseball players who showed a lot of courage. Read the book, pausing occasionally to discuss the feelings of the two main characters.
- Ask children to tell how Jackie Robinson and Pee Wee Reese each showed courage. Ask how they think these two teammates changed the game of baseball.

Jackie Robinson's Shirt
This shirt was worn by Jackie Robinson. He was the first African American to play on an all-white team.
1
Dodgers
42
Girls' Baseball League
This is a baseball uniform from a girls' baseball team called the South Bend Blue Sox from South Bend, Indiana.
2
1869-1969
UNITED STATES 6c
PROFESSIONAL BASEBALL
UNITED STATES POSTAGE
Baseball Stamps
The stamp on the left shows people playing baseball long ago. The stamp on the right celebrates the first professional baseball team, the Cincinnati Red Stockings.
3
Yankees
Artifacts are from the Smithsonian Institution.
13

2 What do girls wear today when they play baseball? How have girls' uniforms changed? Today, girls and boys wear the same kinds of uniforms. This old uniform looks more like a dress. **Compare and Contrast**

3 Which of the two stamps do you think is older? How can you tell? The stamp on the left is older. The postage is less. The uniforms look older. **Draw Conclusions**

3 Close and Assess

- Ask children why they think it's important to have artifacts like the ones shown here in museums. Ask if they would like to visit a museum in which there were baseball items like these.
- Invite children to design stamps of their own to honor a favorite baseball player.
- Encourage children who have baseball card collections to share them with classmates. Talk about why people like to collect such things as baseball cards.
- Ask children how they think baseball might change in the future.

WEB SITE Technology

You can visit the Smithsonian Institution online. Click on Smithsonian at **www.sfsocialstudies.com** or go to **www.si.edu.**

Workbook, p. 4

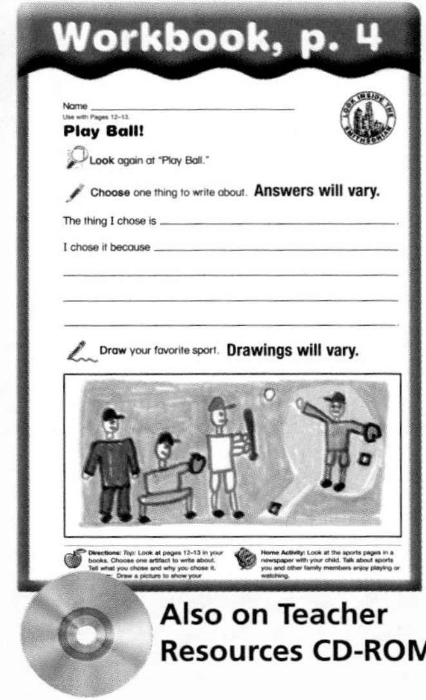

Name
Use with Pages 12–13.
Play Ball!

Look again at "Play Ball."

Choose one thing to write about. **Answers will vary.**

The thing I chose is ____

I chose it because ____

Draw your favorite sport. **Drawings will vary.**

Also on Teacher Resources CD-ROM.

Use with pages 8–13

Lesson 1 Wrap-Up

MEETING INDIVIDUAL NEEDS

Leveled Practice

Find Pictures of Groups

Ask children to cut out magazine pictures that show people in identifiable groups. Use the pictures to make a classroom bulletin board.

Easy Have each child tell about one group. **Reteach**

On-Level Help children make labels (*a family, a soccer team, a book club*, and so on) to attach to the different groups. **Extend**

Challenge Help children write captions for the pictures. Each caption should tell something about what the people in the group are doing. **Enrich**

Hands-on Activities

CURRICULUM CONNECTION

Writing

Make a Book

Objective Define and illustrate the word *group*.

Resources Vocabulary Card: **group**

Materials stiff paper, drawing paper, crayons, pencils, yarn, scissors, two-hole punch

Learning Style Visual

Individual

 **Time** 20–25 minutes

1. Using stiff paper, have children write *My Word Book* and their names.

2. Have children write the letters *Gg* at the top of a page, followed by *group*. Children then draw pictures of groups.

3. Punch holes in the pages. Tie their pages with yarn.

CURRICULUM CONNECTION

Art

Things I Like

Objective Share interests with others; obtain information using visual sources.

Materials drawing paper, crayons, glue, scissors, old magazines

Learning Style Visual/Verbal

Individual

 **Time** 20 minutes

1. Have children make posters to tell about themselves.

2. Tell children to write *Things I Like* at the top of a sheet of drawing paper.

3. Have children cut out three or four pictures of things they like and paste their pictures onto their posters.

4. As children display their posters, they should ask: "What can you learn about me from my pictures?"

CURRICULUM CONNECTION

Music/Drama

Games We Play

Objective Role-play how people interact in groups; obtain information using oral sources.

Learning Style Verbal/Visual

Group

 **Time** 15–20 minutes

1. Have small groups take turns showing how to play a favorite singing game, such as "Farmer in the Dell" or "London Bridge."

2. After children play a game, have them invite a classmate who doesn't know the game to join them. Children can explain the rules of the game to the newcomer.

Lesson 2 Overview

Home and School **pages 14–17**	Children will learn the meanings for the words *flag* and *country*, and explain how selected symbols reflect an American love of individualism and freedom.	 Time 20 minutes Resources • Workbook, p. 5 • Vocabulary Cards **flag** **country** • Every Student Learns Guide, pp. 6–9
Ruby Bridges Hall **pages 18–19**	Children will identify characteristics of good citizenship, such as a belief in equality.	Time 15 minutes
Read a Calendar **pages 20–21**	Children will explore the concept that calendars show the passing of time and identify special days. They will read and create a calendar.	Time 15–20 minutes Resource • Workbook, p. 6

Build Background

Activity

The Way We Do It

 **Time** 15–20 minutes

Create an oversized two-column chart, with the title "The Way We Do It." Label one column *School* and the other *Home*. Then have children draw pictures and/or describe in words how they do one thing every day at school and one thing every day at home.

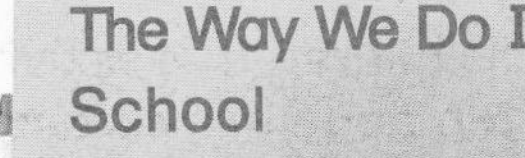

If time is short, have children contribute their ideas orally as you list them on the chart.

Read Aloud

My Busy Day

by Jane Holland

I make my bed so it's nice and flat.
I clean my room and feed the cat.
I brush my teeth, I use my comb.
These are things I do at home.

I see my friends, we all play tag.
I stand in class and salute the flag.
I work and play and follow each rule.
These are things I do at school.

Home and School

Objectives

- Explain how selected symbols reflect an American love of individualism and freedom.
- Explain how routines are part of our daily life at home and at school.

Vocabulary

flag a symbol that stands for a country or state (p. 16)

country land where a group of people live (p. 16)

QUICK Teaching Plan

If time is short, have children stand, put their hands over their hearts, and recite the Pledge of Allegiance.

- Ask why we put our hands over our hearts when we say the Pledge.

1 Introduce and Motivate

Preview Display the Vocabulary Cards for **flag** and **country**. Ask children to point out any flags on display in your room. Ask if they know the name of the country in which they live. Have children locate the words *flag* and *country* as they preview the lesson. Ask volunteers to tell the meaning of the word *loyalty*. Discuss this idea, then explain that *allegiance* means "loyalty, especially to one's country or government." Also tell them that *pledge* means "promise."

Warm Up To activate prior knowledge, ask children to tell what they do before they come to school each day. Ask what they do once they get to school. Have a child pantomime an early-morning activity; have other children try to name the activity. Then face the American flag and place your hand over your heart. Ask children if they know what you are about to do and why.

Home and Schoo

Every morning I eat breakfast. Then I brush my teeth and make my bed. What do you do every morning? 1

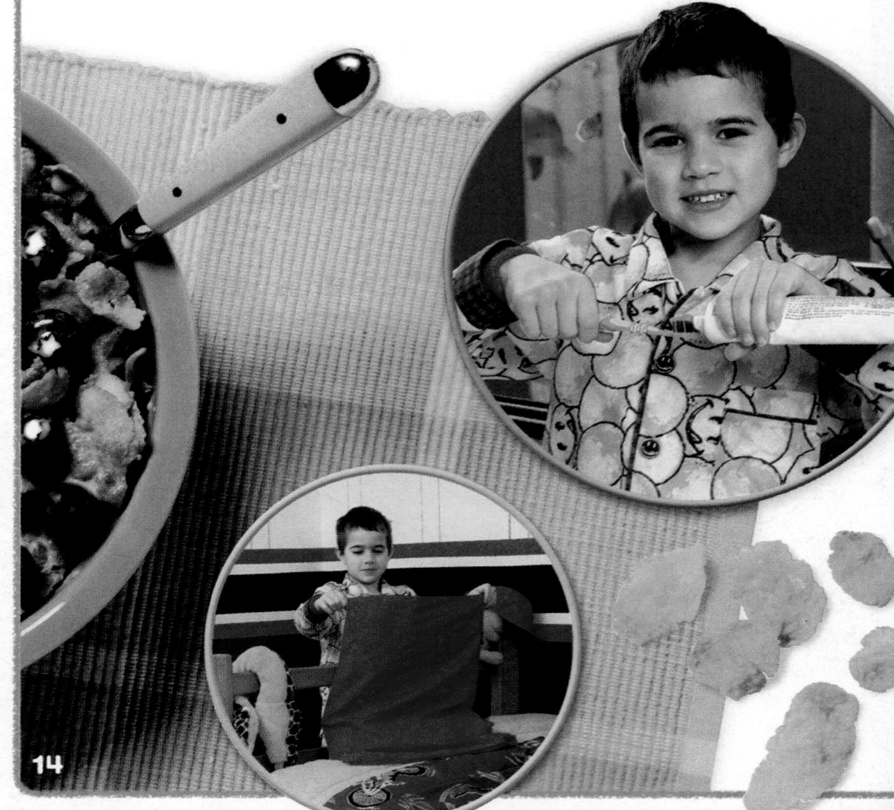

14

Practice and Extend

READING SKILL
Put Things in Order

Draw to Order

- Tell children that activities at home and school are often done in a certain order. For example, at school they may say the Pledge of Allegiance first, and then listen to school announcements.
- Discuss the order of things that children do from the time they wake up until the time they leave for school.
- Have children draw three pictures of things they do each morning before going to school.
- Have children number their pictures *1, 2, 3* to show the order in which they are done.

My class at school does the same things every morning. We hang up our coats and put our snacks away. Then we sit in our seats.

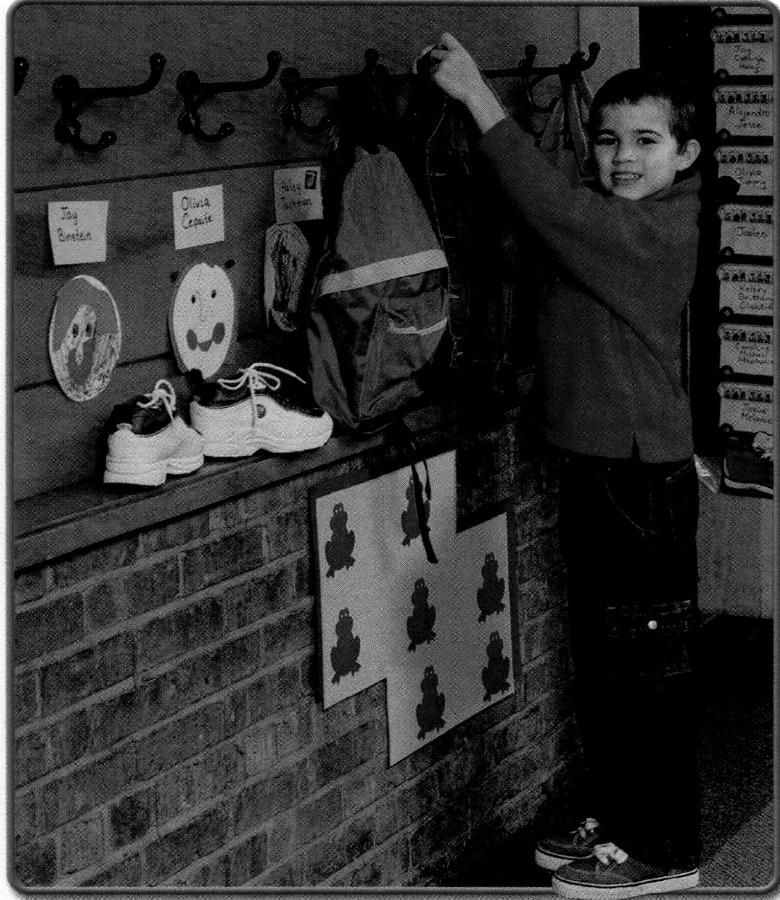

15

2 Teach and Discuss

Page 14

Ask a volunteer to identify Andrew in the pictures. Have children tell what Andrew is doing. Then read p. 14 with children.

1 **What does Andrew do first in the morning?** Eats breakfast **Does he brush his teeth before or after he eats breakfast?** After **Sequence**

2 **What else do you think Andrew does each morning?** Answers will vary but should include such tasks as gathering materials for school, feeding pets, and so on. **Make Inferences**

Page 15

3 **What does Andrew's class do every morning?** Hang up coats, put snacks away, sit down **Main Idea and Details**

4 **What does your class do each morning at school?** Possible answers: Put coats/snacks away, take attendance, say Pledge of Allegiance **Apply Information**

ESL

ACCESS CONTENT

ESL Support

Analyze Pictures The pictures in Lesson 2 show tasks that form part of Andrew's routine at home and school.

Beginning Model pointing to each picture while telling each thing that Andrew does. Then have children point to the pictures and name the activity.

Intermediate Pantomime some of the activities pictured and invite children to name them. Ask children to take turns acting out classroom routines for others to identify.

Advanced Have children point out routines Andrew does that your class does also. Have children dictate a list of routines in your class. Use the chart on p. 17 as a model.

For additional ESL support, use Every Student Learns Guide pp. 6-9.

continued

Page 16

Have children recite the Pledge of Allegiance. Explain to children that the Pledge also honors people who have sacrificed to keep our country free. Then read pp. 16–17.

Pledge of Allegiance
I pledge allegiance to the flag of the United States of America and to the Republic for which it stands, one Nation, under God, indivisible, with liberty and justice for all.

 **Why do we put our hands over our hearts when we say the Pledge of Allegiance?** To honor the flag; to show respect for our flag and country **Draw Conclusions**

SOCIAL STUDIES STRAND
Citizenship

Tell children that when we say the pledge, we are promising to be loyal to the United States. Explain that *indivisible* means "cannot be divided." Discuss the meaning of the words *liberty* and *justice*. Explain that all citizens are guaranteed liberty and justice. The flag represents these things.

Every morning, we stand and face the flag. The **flag** stands for our country. A **country** is a land where a group of people live. Our country is the United States of America. We honor our country when we face the flag. Today it is my turn to lead the class. Hooray! 5

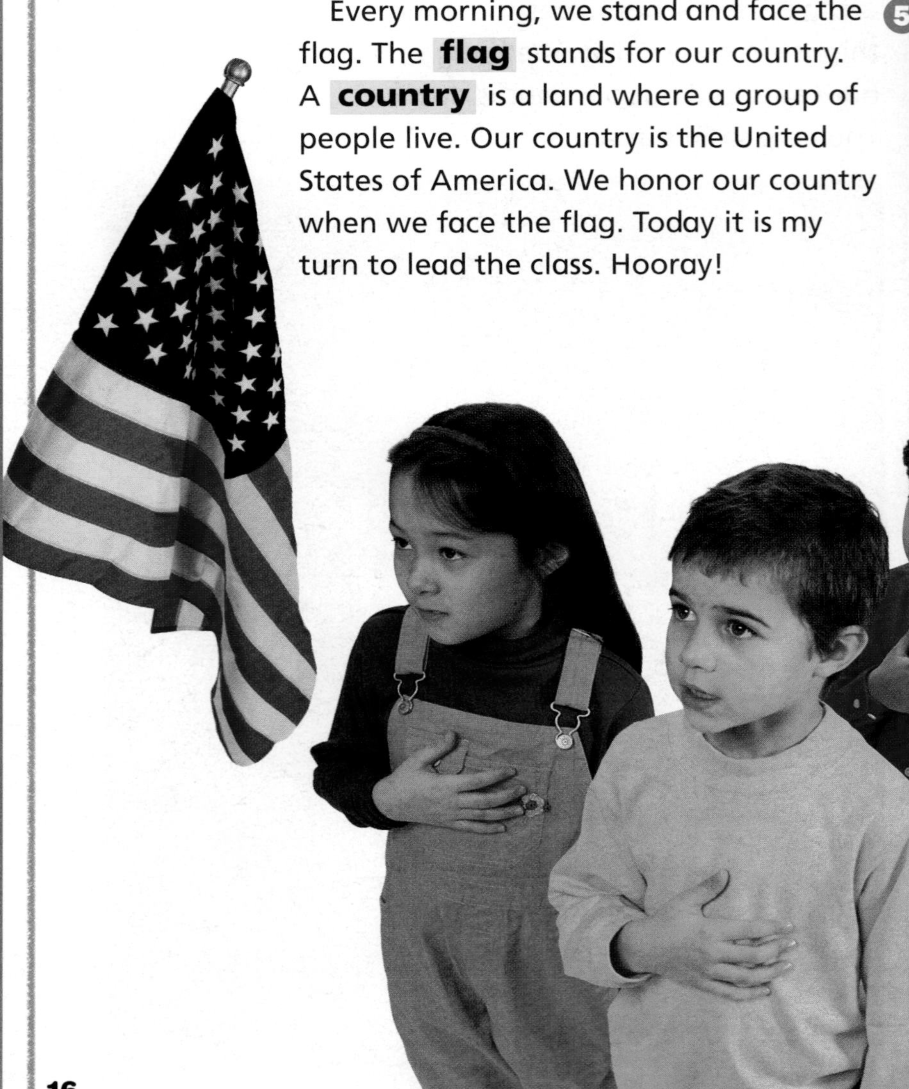

16

Practice and Extend

CURRICULUM CONNECTION
Science

Snack Survey

- Ask children to tell about snacks they often have in school. Include snacks provided by the school, and use sensitivity if children get food assistance.
- Help children categorize the foods: cereals, fruits and vegetables, breads, dairy, and meats.

WEB SITE
Technology

You can look up vocabulary words online. Click on *Social Studies Library* and select the dictionary at **www.sfsocialstudies.com.**

MEETING INDIVIDUAL NEEDS
Leveled Practice

The United States

Show children the United States on a wall map or globe.

Easy Trace your finger along the borders of the United States, and ask children to do the same. Emphasize that everything inside these lines is part of the United States. **Reteach**

On-Level Help children identify the country to the north of the United States as Canada, and the country to the south as Mexico. Ask children to trace the lines that separate the United States from Canada and Mexico. **Extend**

Challenge Help children locate Alaska and Hawaii. Explain how these two states are separated from the rest of the United States. Alaska is separated by Canada; Hawaii, by the Pacific Ocean. **Enrich**

Our Day

Say the Pledge of Allegiance.
Read the calendar.
Work on the computer.
Read a story.
Go outside.

6 7

Look at the other things we will do today. We will have a very busy day at school!

What did you learn?

1. What does Andrew do each morning at home? What does he do each morning at school?
2. Why does Andrew's class stand and face the flag each day?
3. **Think and Share** Make a list of things that you do each morning. Tell what you do at home. Tell what you do at school.

17

SOCIAL STUDIES STRAND Science/Technology

Using the Computer

- Talk with children about ways in which they will use a computer in school this year. If possible, have them help you compose an e-mail message to send to a nearby classroom.
- Discuss ways in which people communicated before they had computers. Ask a volunteer to deliver the same message by hand.
- Encourage children to ask family members about how computers have changed the way they work.

Workbook, p. 5

Home and School

Color pictures that show things you do. **Answers will vary.**

Draw what you like to do at school. **Drawings will vary.**

Also on Teacher Resources CD-ROM.

Page 17

6 Which activity on the "Our Day" list do you think will take the most time? Children may suggest that working on the computer, reading a story, and going outside will take longer than saying the Pledge of Allegiance and reading the calendar. **Evaluate**

7 Which activity on the "Our Day" list do you think would be the most fun? Why? Accept all reasonable answers. **Point of View**

3 Close and Assess

Have each child draw one thing he/she did at home and one thing he/she did at school today. Have children compare and contrast their pictures.

✓ What did you learn?

1. At home, he eats breakfast, brushes his teeth, and makes his bed. At school, he hangs up his coat, puts away his snack, takes his seat, says the Pledge of Allegiance.
2. They face the flag to honor it as they say the Pledge of Allegiance.
3. **Think and Share** Answers should reflect typical morning activities for a first grader.

CITIZEN HEROES

Ruby Bridges Hall

Objective

- Identify characteristics of good citizenship, such as a belief in equality.

1 Introduce and Motivate

Preview Ask children what they think the word *courage* means. Have volunteers share stories of things they have done themselves or seen others do that took courage. Help children understand that having courage usually means doing something you know should be done, even if it scares you.

Warm Up To activate prior knowledge, ask children why they go to school. Ask children how they would feel if they weren't allowed to go to school.

Introduce Ruby Bridges Hall. Point out the photo of Ruby as a child. Tell children that they will learn why Ruby Bridges Hall is a citizen hero.

2 Teach and Discuss

Orient children to where Ruby went to school by reviewing the small map and caption on p. 18. Use a wall map to show children where New Orleans is in relation to your state. Then read the text on p. 18 with children.

1 **How do you think Ruby felt about being the only African American child in her whole school?** Possible answer: She may have felt lonely or frightened. **Make Inferences**

2 **Why did some people not want Ruby to go to their school?** She was African American. **Cause and Effect**

3 **How did Ruby show she had courage or that she was brave?** Children should recognize that Ruby kept going to school every day. **Make Inferences**

CITIZEN HEROES

Ruby went to school in New Orleans, Louisiana.

Ruby Bridges Hall

Ruby was six years old when she began first grade. She was the only African American child in her whole school. 1 African American children had never been allowed to go to that school before. At 2 that time, people were often kept apart because of the color of their skin. Many people in the town did not want Ruby to go to their school. She was very brave. Being brave means having courage.

Ruby as a child

Mrs. Henry and Ruby Bridges Ha

18

Practice and Extend

SOCIAL STUDIES

Background

About Separate Schools

- Segregation by race was an accepted practice in American schools for almost 200 years. African American children and white children, with few exceptions, did not attend the same schools.
- In 1954, in a landmark decision known as *Brown* v. *Board of Education of Topeka*, the United States Supreme Court ruled that public schools could not separate children by race.
- While many communities moved to integrate the public schools, others resisted. In 1957 Federal troops were used to protect African American students at Central High School in Little Rock, Arkansas.

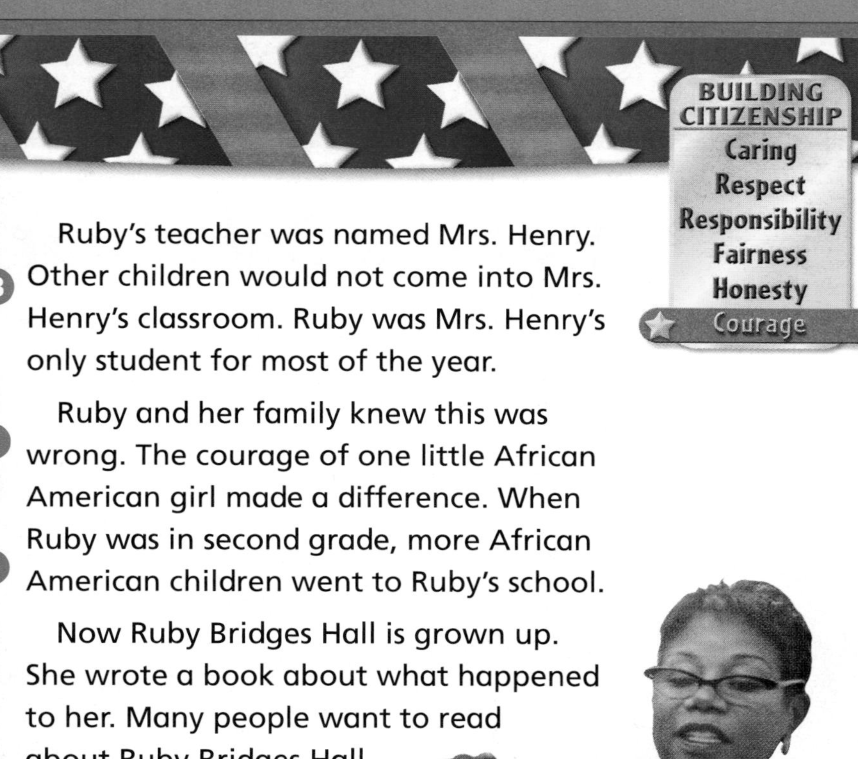

Ruby's teacher was named Mrs. Henry. Other children would not come into Mrs. Henry's classroom. Ruby was Mrs. Henry's only student for most of the year.

Ruby and her family knew this was wrong. The courage of one little African American girl made a difference. When Ruby was in second grade, more African American children went to Ruby's school.

Now Ruby Bridges Hall is grown up. She wrote a book about what happened to her. Many people want to read about Ruby Bridges Hall.

Courage in Action

What is one way to show that you are brave, or that you have courage?

19

CURRICULUM CONNECTION
Literature

The Story of Ruby Bridges

- Share with children this biography by Robert Coles (Scholastic; ISBN: 0-590-57281-4). Pause occasionally, asking children to tell how they think Ruby must have felt. Ask how they would have felt, if they had been Ruby Bridges.
- Afterwards, you may also want to read aloud selected passages from *Through My Eyes* by Ruby Bridges (Scholastic; ISBN 0-590-18923-9). Help children compare and contrast the two accounts.

4 Why was Ruby the only child in Mrs. Henry's class? Other children would not come into Mrs. Henry's room. They might not have understood the importance of treating people equally. **Draw Conclusions**

Test Talk

Use Information from the Text

5 How was Ruby's second year at school better than her first year? She wasn't the only African American at the school. Also, she began to make some friends. Point out the paragraph that begins "In second grade." Help children understand that second grade was Ruby's second year at school. Have them find details in this paragraph that support their answers. **Compare and Contrast**

SOCIAL STUDIES STRAND
Citizenship

Point out that both Ruby and Mrs. Henry showed great courage as citizens. Both believed that all children should have the same education. They believed in justice and equality. Both acted bravely when they stood up for what they believed. Ask children to name real people or story characters who have acted bravely and stood up for their beliefs.

3 Close and Assess

Courage in Action

Read the question and have children discuss possible answers. Responses may include: standing up for a friend, making a phone call in an emergency, and so on.

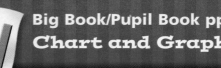

Read a Calendar

Objectives

- Read and create a calendar.
- Obtain information about a topic using visual sources, such as graphics and pictures.

Vocabulary

calendar a chart that show the days, weeks, and months of the year (p. 20)

1 Introduce and Motivate

Preview Write the word *calendar* on the board. Read the word, and ask children to point out any calendars on display in your classroom. Have children locate the term as they preview the lesson.

Warm Up To activate prior knowledge, ask children to tell what day of the week it is. Ask if anyone knows the *date*. Write the date on the board, and help children read it. Then guide children in locating the date on the classroom calendar. Confirm the name of the day of the week by pointing it out on the calendar.

Page 20

Read the introduction. Before children respond to the questions below the calendar, have them point to September 1 and name the day of the week on which it falls. Repeat for a few other dates. Then have children answer the bulleted questions.

1. **What holiday is on September 1?** Labor Day. Labor day is a day we honor people who work. **Interpret Charts**

2. **What holiday is on September 17?** Citizenship Day **Interpret Charts**

SOCIAL STUDIES STRAND
Citizenship

Tell children that Citizenship Day honors citizens who have reached voting age. It is celebrated on September 17 because that is the date on which the U.S. Constitution was signed.

Read a Calendar

Every day Andrew's class reads the calendar. A **calendar** is a chart that shows the days, weeks, and months of the year. A calendar helps us remember important days.

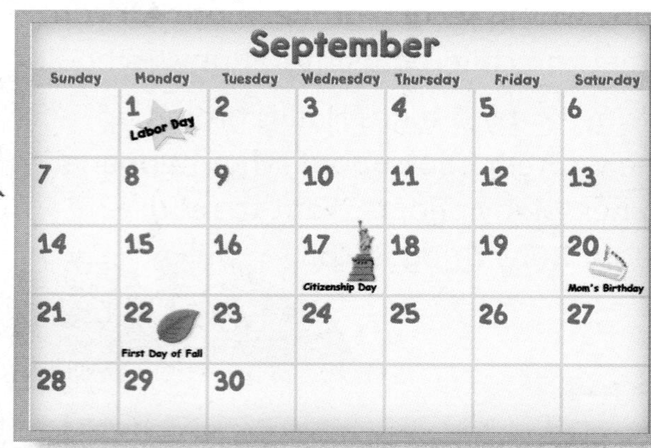

September

Sunday	Monday	Tuesday	Wednesday	Thursday	Friday	Saturday
	1 Labor Day	2	3	4	5	6
7	8	9	10	11	12	13
14	15	16	17 Citizenship Day	18	19	20 Mom's Birthday
21	22 First Day of Fall	23	24	25	26	27
28	29	30				

- The name of the month is at the top of the calendar. What month is it?
- Each square is one day. How many days are on this calendar?
- Look at the box that has the number 1 in it. Why is that day important?

Practice and Extend

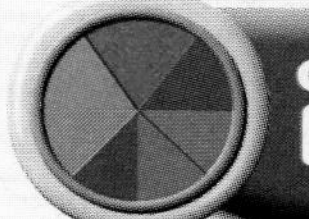

CURRICULUM CONNECTION
Reading

Learn a Calendar Rhyme

- Tell children that every four years an extra day is added to February, giving it 29 days instead of 28.
- Display the following rhyme, and have children recite it with you.

30 days has September,
April, June, and November.
All the rest have 31,
All the rest, that is, but one.
February has 28!
Except in Leap Year, that's the time
When February has 29!

Andrew likes the month of February best. This calendar shows special days in February.

Happy Valentine

February						
Sunday	Monday	Tuesday	Wednesday	Thursday	Friday	Saturday
				1	2 Groundhog Day	3
4	5	6	7	8	9	10
11	12 Lincoln's Birthday	13	14 Valentine's Day	15	16	17
18	19 President's Day	20	21	22 Washington's Birthday	23	24
25 Andrew's Birthday	26	27	28			

What did you learn?

1. What is one reason we use a calendar?
2. Why do you think that Andrew likes the month of February the best?
3. **On Your Own** Make a calendar for this month. Label the important days. Why are these days important?

21

Workbook, p. 6

Read a Calendar

Write the numbers.

Draw a flag for July 4th. Draw to show what you might do. **Drawings will vary.**

JULY

Also on Teacher Resources CD-ROM.

3 What season of the year begins toward the end of September? Fall or autumn **Interpret Charts**

Page 21

Read p. 21. Point out that Andrew's birthday is in February. Then ask:

4 Which Presidents' birthdays do we also celebrate in February? Lincoln's and Washington's birthdays **Interpret Charts**

Use Information from Graphics

5 How is the calendar for February different from the one for September? It has fewer days. It shows different special days. Be sure children understand that they need to use *both* calendars to answer the question. **Compare and Contrast**

Encourage children to bring in samples of different kinds of calendars. If possible, show them examples of appointment books, desk calendars, and so on. Guide children in finding today's date on each calendar.

✓ What did you learn?

1. Possible answer: We use a calendar to help us remember important days.
2. Possible answer: His birthday is in February.
3. **On Your Own** Calendars should show the current month with days and dates labeled. They should also show the important days in the month. Children should be able to explain why the days are important.

Use with pages 14–21

Lesson 2 Wrap-Up

MEETING INDIVIDUAL NEEDS
Leveled Practice

Hooray for Me!

Have each child draw pictures of two things he/she has learned at school so far this year. Have children take turns displaying their pictures.

Easy Ask a volunteer to put his/her pictures in order to show what was learned first. Name the two activities shown. Have all children in the group repeat. **Reteach**

On-Level Have children order their pictures and then tell what they learned *first* and *next.* **Extend**

Challenge Have children order their pictures and identify the activities. Then have them dictate captions for you to write under each picture. **Enrich**

Hands-on Activities

CURRICULUM CONNECTION
Writing

My Country, My Flag

Objective Demonstrate an understanding of the words *flag* and *country*.

Resources Vocabulary Cards: **flag, country**

Materials crayons, drawing paper

Learning Style Visual/Verbal

Individual

 **Time** 10–15 minutes

1. Write the following on the board:

The United States is our ___.

Our ___ is red, white, and blue.

2. Display the Vocabulary Cards, and have children use the words to complete the sentences.

3. Have children copy the sentences and draw pictures to illustrate them.

4. Have children add the new words to their "My Word Book."

CURRICULUM CONNECTION
Math

Special Days

Objective Make a calendar for a given month.

Materials calendar for current month, blank calendar grids, markers or crayons, self-stick notes

Learning Style Visual/Kinesthetic

Group

 **Time** 15–20 minutes

1. Help children use the classroom calendar to identify important days (holidays) in this month.

2. Invite children to draw pictures on self-stick notes to represent the holidays they have identified.

3. Have children copy the dates onto a blank calendar and then attach their pictures in appropriate places.

February

Sunday	Monday	Tuesday	Wednesday	Thursday	Friday	Saturday
1	2	3	4	5	6	7
8	9	10	11	12	13	
15	16	17	18	19	20	21
22	23	24	25	26	27	28

SOCIAL STUDIES STRAND
Citizenship

Citizen Heroes

Objective Identify good citizenship qualities in people they know.

Materials markers, bulletin board, paper

Learning Style Verbal

Individual

 **Time** 10–15 minutes

1. Have each child identify someone who shows good citizenship.

2. Give children paper and markers. Invite them to make a border of words, such as "kind to new children," describing the good citizenship.

3. Ask children to draw pictures of their citizenship heroes inside the word borders.

4. Post all the heroes on the bulletin board.

kind to new children

Lesson 3 Overview

Rules We Follow

pages 22–25

Children will learn the meaning of the word *rules* and some reasons why rules are necessary. They will also identify authority figures who help people follow the rules.

Time 20–30 minutes

Resources

- Workbook, p. 7
- Vocabulary Card 
- Every Student Learns Guide, pp. 10–13

Problem on the Playground

pages 26–27

Children will learn how to use problem-solving strategies, such as those needed to keep the schoolyard clean.

Time 15 minutes

Resource

- Workbook, p. 8

Build Background

Activity

Rules of the Game

 **Time** 15–20 minutes

Ask children to name their favorite game or sport. Write children's suggestions on the board. Then, have children make a drawing showing something about their favorite game or sport. Have a sports section of a newspaper or magazine available for reference. Ask children if there are rules for playing their game or sport.

If time is short, ask children to explain some of the rules in a game such as tag, jacks, or baseball.

Read Aloud

The Rules

by Ben Farhi

I can cross a busy street
If a grown-up is around.
This rule keeps me safe
and sound.

I wait my turn when we play,
And so does everyone.
This rule makes our play more fun!

Lesson 3 Rules We Follow

Objectives

- Give examples of rules.
- Identify the responsibilities of authority figures in the school and home.
- Explain the need for rules and laws in the home, school, and community.

Vocabulary

rule what we can do and what we should not do (p. 22)

QUICK Teaching Plan

If time is short, have children choose one picture from pp. 22–23 and tell what would happen if people didn't follow this rule.

1 Introduce and Motivate

Preview Display the Vocabulary Card **rule** and invite children to help you write a definition for it. Ask children to tell you why they think people make rules. Then ask who helps us follow the rules at home, at school, and in the community.

Warm Up To activate prior knowledge, direct children's attention to any posted lists of class or school rules. Have volunteers read these rules aloud.

Lesson 3 Rules We Follow

We learn many rules in school. A **rule** tells us what to do and what not to do. Our class thought of some rules to follow. Look at the pictures. Tell what rules the children are following. 1

Raise your hand to talk.

Sit quietly.

3

Do not run in the hallways.

22

Practice and Extend

READING SKILL Classify/Categorize

Sorting Rules

- Help children categorize the rules shown on pp. 22–23. Ask a child to point to a rule. Ask: *Is this a rule for home or for school? Is this a rule to keep you safe? Is this a rule to help people work together?*
- Have children sort the rules by labeling each as *safety, home, school,* or *working together*. Explain that some rules will be in more than one category.

WEB SITE Technology

You can look up vocabulary words online. Click on *Social Studies Library* and select the dictionary at **www.sfsocialstudies.com.**

What other rules do you follow at school? What are some rules you follow at home?

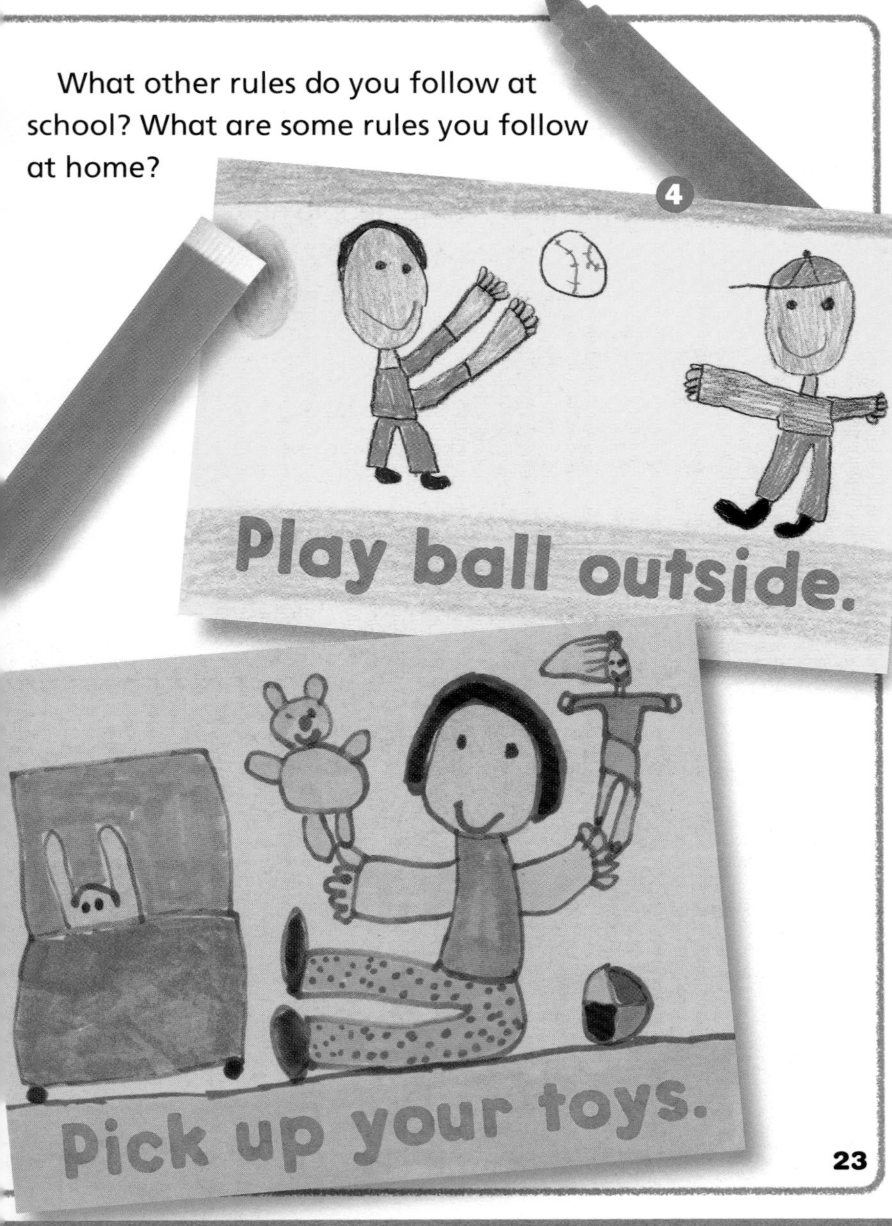
4
Play ball outside.
Pick up your toys.
23

2 Teach and Discuss

Page 22

Have children describe the rules Andrew is following.

1 **Which of these rules do you have in your class?** Children will most likely suggest that all three are rules in their school. **Compare and Contrast**

2 **Why is raising your hand to talk a good rule?** Possible answers: So everyone doesn't talk at once, so everyone gets a turn **Evaluate**

3 **What could happen if there wasn't a rule for walking in the halls?** Children could run into each other and get hurt. **Predict**

Page 23

4 **Do you think there should be a rule for playing ball outside? Why or why not?** Children may realize the danger of breaking things with balls, but some may think that ball play can be done safely in a basement or with an adult. **Point of View**

SOCIAL STUDIES STRAND
Economics

Tell children that adults have rules too. They follow rules in many places, including places they work and places they shop. Ask children to think of times they've seen their parents or other adults work or shop. What are some rules they must follow at these times? Possible answers: Stop at red lights, get places on time, pay for the things bought, wait one's turn, follow rules at work, obey people in authority, and so on.

EXTEND LANGUAGE
ESL Support

Add a Rule Review the rules already in place in your classroom. Then have children add their own rules to the list.

Beginning Invite children to pantomime the rule they would like to add to the list. Write a rule for children that reflects their pantomime.

Intermediate Pair children to develop a rule. Have them draw the rule and then write a brief caption, such as "No hitting."

Advanced Invite children to write their rules in both English and their home language. Ask them to explain why each rule is important.

For additional ESL support, use Every Student Learns Guide, pp. 10–13.

continued

Page 24

Have children identify the people (a bus driver and a crossing guard) shown in the photo. Discuss what rules they might help us follow.

5 **What are some rules that help us work together in school?** Possible answers: Taking turns, raising hands before speaking, sharing materials **Categorize**

6 **Who else helps you follow rules at school? At home?** Possible answers: Teacher aides, school custodian, cafeteria workers, guards, parents, babysitters, other family members
Apply Information

Ongoing Assessment

If... children cannot name people who help them follow school rules,	**then...** remind them of people who work or help out at your school.

SOCIAL STUDIES STRAND
Science/Technology

Point out that people use technology to help keep themselves and others safe. For example, the bus driver may have a radio, cell phone, or locating device in the bus. This enables the driver to call for help or to get information about road problems. Ask children how people they know use technology when they travel.

7 **What can Andrew do to make sure he understands the rules?** He can listen carefully, ask questions to make sure he understands the rules, and ask for help in following the rules.
Apply Information

We have rules at school and at home. Some rules help us work together. Some 5 rules help us stay safe. Look at the pictures. These people help us follow 6 rules at school. Who helps us follow rules at home?

SCHOOL BUS
Children must wait until I lead them across the street.
I am a bus driver. Children mu sit in their seats wh drive them to scho
STOP
24

SOCIAL STUDIES Background

Playing by the Rules

- Some children may think that rules spoil their fun. Ask if a game such as soccer would be more or less fun if it had no rules. Help children conclude that rules not only help a game go smoothly but also make it more fun to play.
- Young children may notice that rules sometimes vary, depending on one's age. Point out that a six-year-old may need to hold an adult's hand to cross a street, while a twelve-year-old can probably safely cross alone.

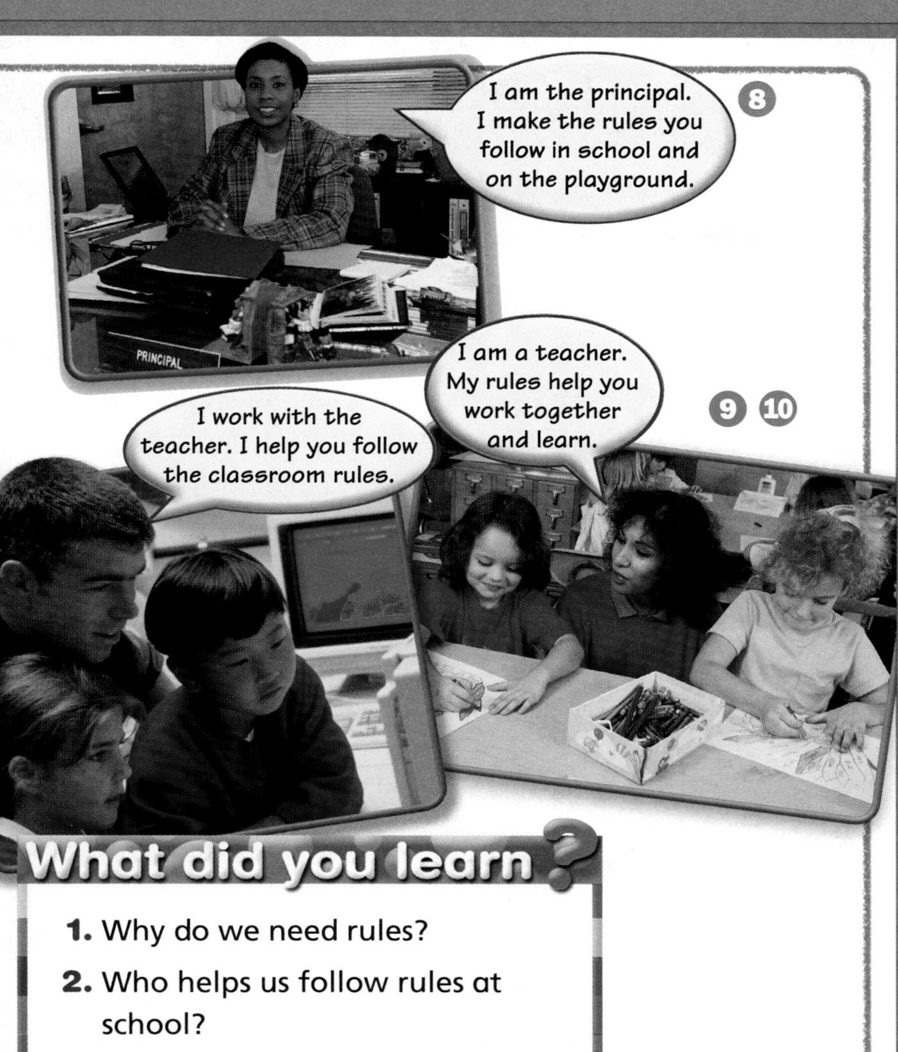

I am the principal. I make the rules you follow in school and on the playground.
8
PRINCIPAL
I am a teacher. My rules help you work together and learn.
I work with the teacher. I help you follow the classroom rules.
9 10

What did you learn?

1. Why do we need rules?
2. Who helps us follow rules at school?
3. **Think and Share** What might happen if we did not follow rules?

25

Also on Teacher Resources CD-ROM.

Page 25

Have children identify the people shown on p. 25 and tell how each person helps us follow rules.

8 **What are some rules a principal might ask children to follow?** Answers should reflect children's knowledge of school-wide rules such as for conduct in the auditorium, the cafeteria, on the playground, and in hallways. **Apply Information**

9 **How might grown-ups in Andrew's classroom help him follow the rules?** Possible answers: by posting the rules, by explaining them, by reminding him of the rules if he breaks one, by having a consequence for breaking rules **Hypothesize**

10 **How do you feel about the rules you have to follow at home and school?** Children may express sadness, anger, and/or pride in being able to follow rules or understanding the need for rules. **Express Ideas**

3 Close and Assess

To check children's understanding of rules, have them work in small teams to identify the three rules they think are most important at home, school, and in the community. After the groups exchange ideas, take a poll to choose three "high priority" rules for the class. Write these three rules on chart paper, and save for use in the Lesson 3 Wrap-Up.

✓ What did you learn?

1. We need rules to keep us safe and to help us work together.
2. Answers may include teachers, principals, aides, crossing guards, and bus drivers.
3. **Think and Share** Possible answers: People could get hurt, people might not be able to learn or do the jobs they need to do, people couldn't find things when they needed them.

Problem on the Playground

Objective

- Use a problem-solving process.

1 Introduce and Motivate

Preview Ask children to tell what they think a problem is. Then have them explain what they think it means to solve a problem.

Warm Up To activate prior knowledge, ask children to name some problems the class has solved in the last few days. If necessary, prompt children with an example, such as the class's group effort to find a missing book.

2 Teach and Discuss

Page 26

Discuss the photo with children. Ask what they think the problem is on this playground. (trash on the ground)

1 **What is the first step the children use to solve the problem?** They name the problem. **Sequence**

2 **Why do you think it is so important to start by naming the problem?** Possible answer: You need to understand what the problem is before you can pick the best way to solve it. **Solve Problems**

3 **What can Andrew and his friends do to find out more about their problem?** Possible answers: Look at the trash to see where it comes from, find out where on the playground there is trash, notice whether the trash is worse at certain times of day **Solve Problems**

Thinking Skills

Problem on the Playground

Andrew's class saw a problem. They saw trash on the playground. These are the steps Andrew's class used to solve the problem.

Step 1 Name the problem. 1 2

Step 2 Find out more about the problem. 3

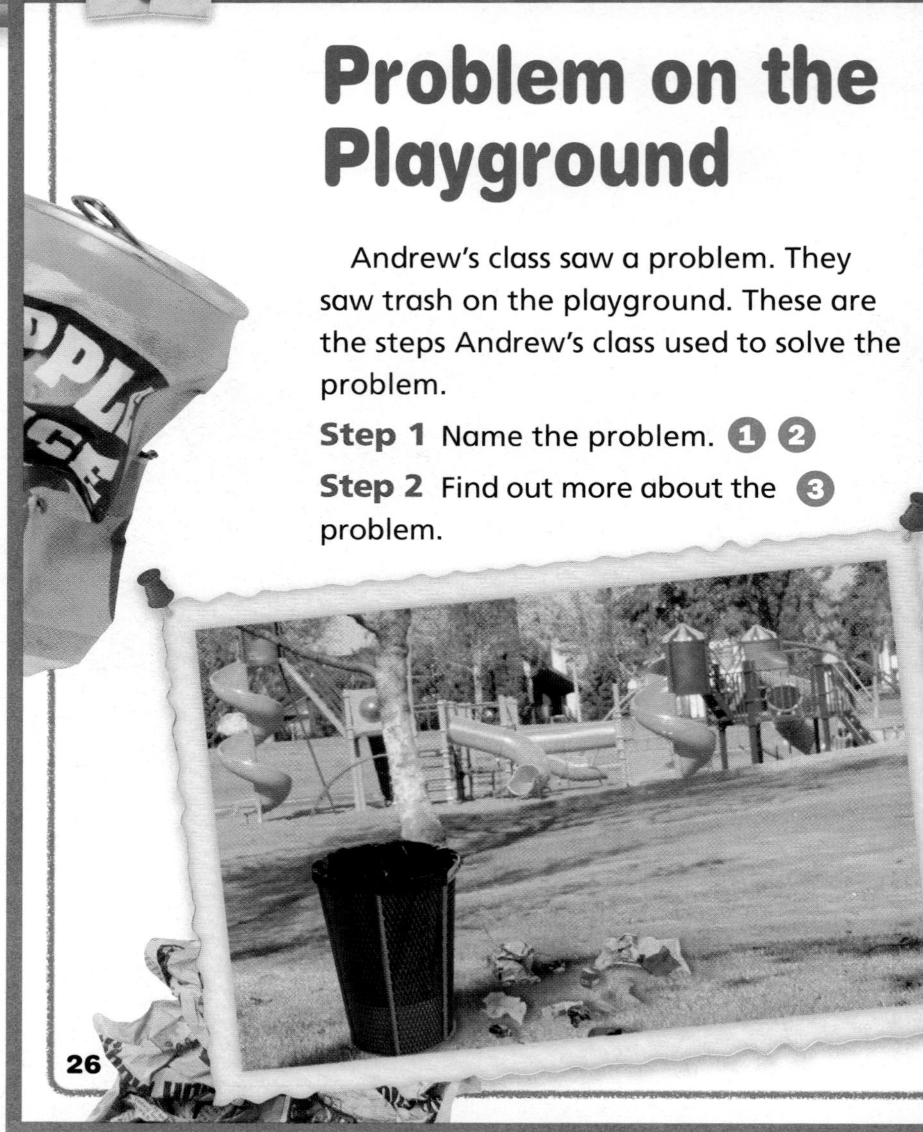

26

Practice and Extend

CURRICULUM CONNECTION
Science

Reducing Trash

- Tell children that each person in the United States produces more than four pounds of trash a day. Explain that this enormous amount of trash is a threat to our environment.
- Encourage children to examine a sample of classroom trash. Use proper precautions, such as wearing latex gloves.
- Ask children if they think some of the trash could have been recycled or reused. Work with children to generate a list of ideas for reducing trash.

Step 3 List ways to solve the problem.

Step 4 Is one way more useful than another? Talk about the best way to solve the problem. 4 5

Step 5 Solve the problem.

Step 6 How well is the problem solved?

Now we have a nice, clean playground!

1. What problem did Andrew's class see?
2. What steps did Andrew's class take to solve the problem?
3. **On Your Own** Think of a problem. Tell how you would solve it. Use the steps Andrew's class used.

PROBLEM SOLVING

Select one of the problems children identified during their walk through school and review it with the class. Help children use the following process to solve the problem.

1. Identify a problem.
2. Gather information.
3. List and consider options.
4. Consider advantages and disadvantages.
5. Choose and implement a decision.
6. Evaluate the effectiveness of the solution.

Workbook, p. 8

Cleaning Up!
Circle the problem in this picture.
Check each step as you do it.
Step 1 Name the problem.
Step 2 Find out more about the problem.
Step 3 List ways to solve the problem.
Step 4 Talk about the best way to solve the problem.
Step 5 Solve the problem.
Step 6 How well is the problem solved?

Also on Teacher Resources CD-ROM.

Page 27

Have children recount the steps Andrew and his class take to solve their problem. Remind them to keep the steps in order.

4 **How does talking about the best way to solve a problem help?** People can share ideas for how to solve the problem. This helps everyone see which ideas work and which do not.
Make Inferences

GEOGRAPHY
People and Places Change Each Other

5 **How do Andrew and his friends solve their problem?** They clean up the playground. They put trash in a trash can and recycling in a recycling bin.
Analyze Pictures

3 Close and Assess

Give children clipboards, paper, and pencils. Lead the class on a tour of the school and its grounds. Each time a child spots a problem, tell all the children to record it. When you return to the classroom, have children suggest ways each problem can be solved.

Try it!

1. They saw trash on the playground.
2. First they named the problem. Then they learned more about the problem. Next they listed ways to solve the problem. Then they talked about the best way to solve the problem. Next they put their ideas into action. Finally, they thought about how well they had solved the problem.
3. **On Your Own** Problems should be clearly named. Solutions should include the general goal, as well as each of the six problem-solving steps from the lesson.

Use with pages 22–27

Lesson 3 Wrap-Up

MEETING INDIVIDUAL NEEDS

Leveled Practice

Wall Mural
Have children draw or find pictures of people who make and enforce the rules in the home, school, and community. Use the pictures to create a wall mural.

Easy Have children identify each authority figure and give an example of a rule that the person might help them follow. **Reteach**

On-Level Next to each picture, children can write *safety* or *working together* to tell the kind of rules the pictured person makes. **Extend**

Challenge Have children make handouts to introduce others to the people shown. Handouts should tell the kind of rules each person makes and why those rules are important. **Enrich**

Hands-on Activities

CURRICULUM CONNECTION
Writing

Rules on Rules

Objective Define and illustrate the word *rule*.

Resources Vocabulary Card: **rule**

Materials ruled chart paper

Learning Style Verbal/Visual

Individual

Time 15–20 minutes

1. Using chart paper, write the word *RULES* in a vertical column.
2. For each letter, ask children to suggest a classroom rule beginning with the letter. For *R*, they may say: *Running in halls—NO!*
3. Continue for each letter. Then display the completed chart in the classroom.
4. Have children add *rule* to their "My Word Book."

Running in the halls – NO!
U
L
E
S

SOCIAL STUDIES STRAND
Government

Rule-Making

Objective Understand the rules made by the school principal.

Learning Style Verbal

Group

Time 15–20 minutes

1. Invite the school principal to visit the class for a discussion about rule-making.
2. Help children prepare questions to ask the principal about the rules he or she makes. Children might ask: *What do you think is the most important rule? Which rule gets broken the most?*
3. After the interview, have children describe what the principal's job is. Talk with them about where people such as the principal get their authority.

• What is the most important school rule?
• Which rule gets broken the most?

SOCIAL STUDIES STRAND
Citizenship

Our Rules

Objective Express a rule through a simple drawing.

Materials chart paper

Learning Style Verbal

Group

Time 10–15 minutes

1. Sign the book out.
2. Take care of the b

1. Review with children any rules you have already established for your classroom.
2. Brainstorm with children other rules that might be added to your list. Alternatively, have children create and adopt a set of rules for a specific area of your room, such as the classroom library.
3. Have children draw a picture of one of the rules they have added to the list.

Lesson 4 Overview

Learning About My School pages 28–31	Through an interview, children will learn how a school has changed and reasons for the changes. They will learn to distinguish between past, present, and future.	 Time 20–30 minutes Resources • Workbook, p. 9 • Every Student Learns Guide, pp. 14–17
Mary McLeod Bethune pages 32–33	Children will learn about Mary McLeod Bethune and how her efforts brought about important changes in education.	 Time 15 minutes
Things We Use pages 34–35	Children will learn how to use visual sources, such as pictures, to compare and contrast objects from different time periods.	Time 15 minutes

Build Background

Activity

Time Capsules

 **Time** 20–30 minutes

Ask children to imagine that they are trying to describe their school to people in the future. Have them work in groups of three or four to create time capsules. Give each group a large envelope to decorate and label "_________ School in the year 200_." Have each child draw a picture and/or dictate a sentence telling one thing about the school. Place each group's entries in its envelope and exchange the envelopes. Ask children if they were surprised to learn what other groups thought.

If time is short, make one time capsule for the whole class. Use slips of paper you complete from children's oral suggestions.

Read Aloud

School History

by Steve Lopez

Before I was born, I'm sure as can be
Other children walked these halls—
just like me
What did they learn? What did they wear?
Did their teacher sit in my teacher's chair?
It's fun to think about this little mystery.
My school has seen a lot of
things. It has
a history.

Learning About My School

Objectives

- Obtain information about a topic using a variety of oral sources, such as interviews.
- Compare past and present.

QUICK Teaching Plan

If time is short, have children use the photos on p. 29 to compare and contrast Andrew's school then and now.

1 Introduce and Motivate

Preview As you preview the lesson, point out the interview and scrapbook formats. Ask children if they keep family pictures in a scrapbook. Explain that scrapbooks are one way to preserve memories of events from the past. Tell children that in this lesson, Andrew learns about some pictures by asking questions. Explain that learning information by asking questions is called an interview. Encourage children to ask you questions about your school. Then tell them they just interviewed you!

Warm Up To activate prior knowledge, take children on a quick tour of their school. Ask children to describe different parts of the school.

2 Teach and Discuss

Page 28

Tell children that in this lesson, Andrew is talking with Mr. Jones, the principal of his school.

1 What are Andrew and Mr. Jones doing?
Looking at an old scrapbook **Analyze Pictures**

Learning About My School

Andrew Our school is so big!

Mr. Jones Yes, it is. Let me tell you a story about our school.

28

Practice and Extend

Target Skill READING SKILL
Use Picture Clues

Photo Clues

- Direct children's attention to the two photos on p. 29. Ask them to describe the photos.
- Ask children how the photos look the same and different. Answers might include that one photo is in color and one is a black-and-white photo. Both photos show a building and people.
- Tell children that they can learn a lot by looking for clues about when something happened in pictures and photographs.

Mr. Jones Look at these pictures. They give clues about how our school has changed.

Andrew Long ago, our school was in a small building. Why?

3 4 5

29

Page 29

2 Is the school in a bigger or smaller building now than it used to be? A bigger building **Apply Information**

3 Why might Andrew's school have been in a smaller building many years ago? Possible answers: Not as many children lived in the neighborhood then; perhaps they didn't need as many classrooms. **Hypothesize**

4 Which picture shows how the school looked in the *past*? The top picture **Analyze Pictures**

Ongoing Assessment

If... children cannot identify the historical picture, **then...** point out the visual clues that suggest it is from the past.

5 What other ways are the schools in the two pictures different? Possible answers: One is brick; one is wood; one has a bus in front; the people are dressed differently. **Compare and Contrast**

SOCIAL STUDIES STRAND

Geography

Tell children that schools vary not just from past to present but also from place to place. Schools reflect the culture of the people who build them and the geography of places where they are found. In cold climates, schools are often brick buildings; in hotter climates, they are often long, low, and open.

ESL

ACCESS CONTENT

ESL Support

Dialogue Explain that Mr. Jones and Andrew are having a conversation about the school. Reread pp. 28–29. Change your voice for the two characters, and point to each as you read their lines.

Beginning Ask children to point to Andrew and then to his lines. Repeat for Mr. Jones. Ask children to point to the old school and then to the new school.

Intermediate Ask simple questions about the page. For example, *Is this the school now? Is it big or small?*

Advanced Simplify part of the dialogue, and ask two children to act out a short exchange. For example:

Andrew: *Our school is big!*

Mr. Jones: *Yes, it is. Let me tell you a story about our school.*

For additional ESL support, use Every Student Learns Guide, pp. 14–17.

continued

Page 30

Have children tell what they see in the photos.

6 **How are the children in the two pictures the same? How are they different?** Possible answers: They are about the same age; their clothes are different. **Compare and Contrast**

7 **How are the classrooms different?** Children's responses may indicate that the classroom of the past looks very plain compared with the one from the present. **Compare and Contrast**

8 **What do you think a classroom of the future might look like?** Possible answers: children in very different clothing, robots in the classroom, the classroom looking like a spaceship **Hypothesize**

Mr. Jones Fewer people lived in this area in the past. We did not have as many children coming to our school then.

Mr. Jones Many people have moved here. Now we have more children. We had to build a bigger school.

6 8

30

Practice and Extend

SOCIAL STUDIES History

"Then-and-Now" Reports

Help children find out what your own school looked like in the past.

- If your building is quite old, invite a member of your local historical society to share pictures of your school as it looked in the past.
- If your building is relatively new, try to obtain pictures that show it during construction.
- Guide children in writing short "Then-and-Now" reports about your school.

MEETING INDIVIDUAL NEEDS Learning Styles

Making Room Have children demonstrate and explain how Andrew's school has changed.

Kinesthetic Designate several distinct areas in the room as "classrooms." Start with just a few children in each "classroom." As the "school" gets bigger, put more children into each "classroom." As the "classrooms" get crowded, add a new "classroom" and redistribute the children to show the effect.

Auditory Divide children into "Then" and "Now" groups. Have the groups take turns saying something they learned about Andrew's school from their time period.

Andrew The old school used to be small. Now our school is much bigger. I wonder if my ⑨ school will get even bigger in the future!

What did you learn?

1. **Use the pictures** to tell how Andrew's school changed.
2. Why did Andrew's school change in size?
3. **Think and Share** Why might your school change in the future? List ways your school might change.

31

Workbook, p. 9

Learning About My School

Color the picture from long ago. Color picture 2.

Draw your school. Drawings will vary.

Also on Teacher Resources CD-ROM.

Page 31

⑨ **What would happen if more and more children started going to Andrew's school?** Possible answers: The school would need more classrooms, class sizes might get bigger, and so on. **Hypothesize**

3 Close and Assess

To check what children have learned in this lesson, do the following activity.

- Have each child ask an older family member to tell about something that is different now from the way it was when that person was young. If possible, have children bring in visual materials that show the changes.
- Have children take turns telling what they learned.

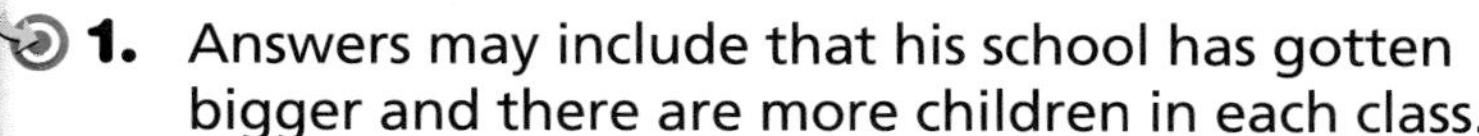

1. Answers may include that his school has gotten bigger and there are more children in each class.
2. More children attend the school.

Test Talk

Write Your Answer

3. **Think and Share** Answers will vary but may include that it will get bigger and have more students. Before children share their lists, they should ask themselves, "Do the ideas on my list make sense?"

Mary McLeod Bethune

Objectives

- Identify characteristics of good citizenship, such as belief in equality.
- Identify the contributions of historical figures who have influenced the nation.

1 Introduce and Motivate

Preview On the board, begin a word web with *Education* in the center cell. In the outer cells, write *People, Places,* and *Tools.*

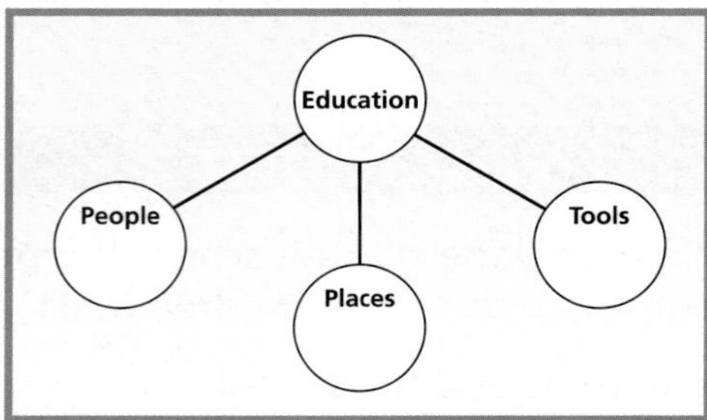

Tell children that people go to school to learn—or to get an education. Write the word *educator* under *People.* Explain that an educator is a person who helps others learn. Ask children to help fill in the word web.

Warm Up To activate prior knowledge, remind children of Ruby Bridges Hall and ask them to tell about her experience when she went to school. Tell children that they are going to read about another woman and the things she did for education.

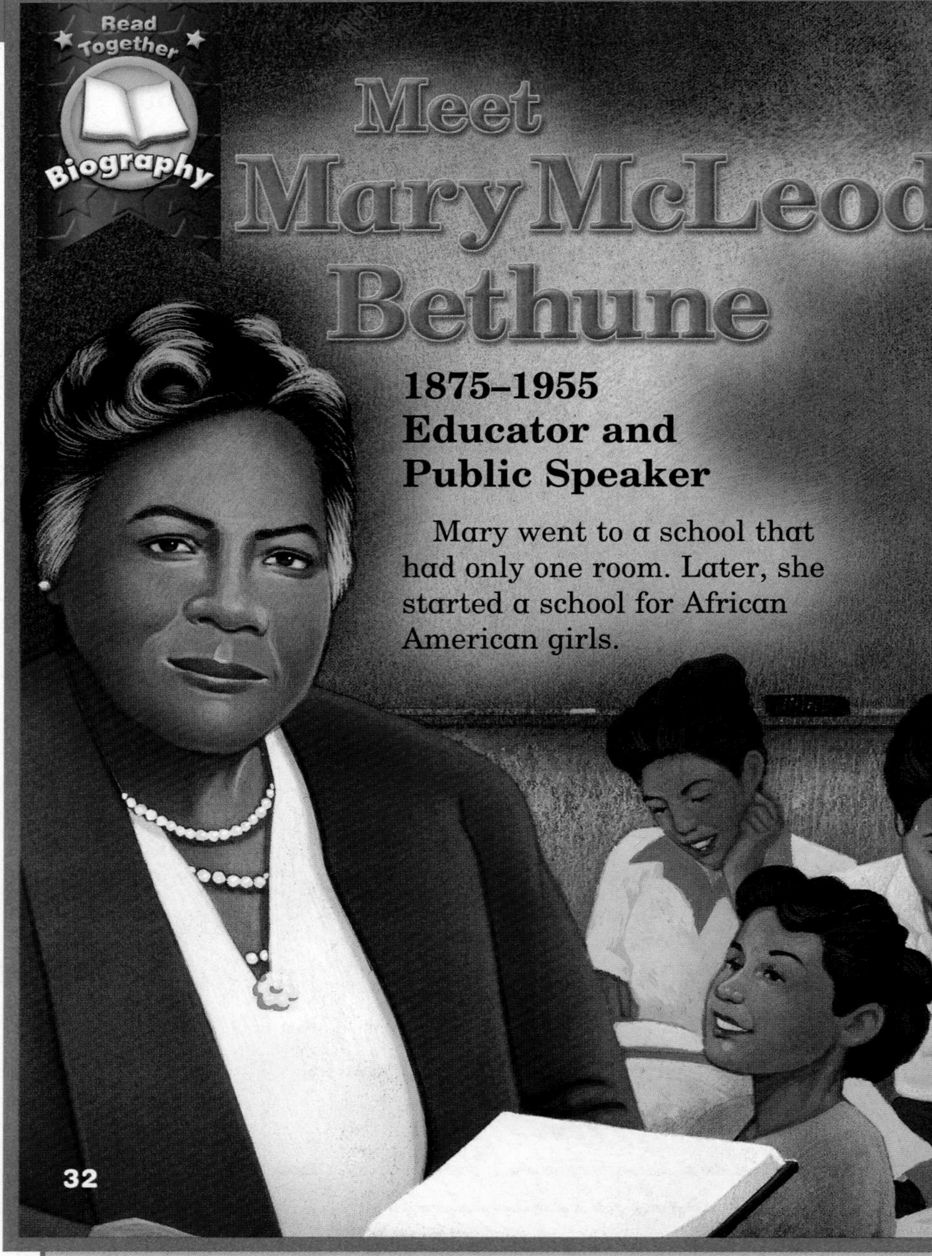

Read Together
Biography
Meet Mary McLeod Bethune
1875–1955
Educator and
Public Speaker
Mary went to a school that had only one room. Later, she started a school for African American girls.
32

Practice and Extend

SOCIAL STUDIES Background

About Mary McLeod Bethune

- After finally getting some education in the one-room school, Bethune went on to learn at a seminary and at the Moody Bible Institute in Chicago.
- Bethune represented African American women as president of organizations such as the National Association of Colored Women and by founding the National Council of Negro Women.
- In 1936, she became the first African American woman to head a federal agency. President Franklin D. Roosevelt had appointed her director of the Division of Negro Affairs of the National Youth Administration. She also served Presidents Coolidge and Truman, providing her expertise about minority affairs and education.

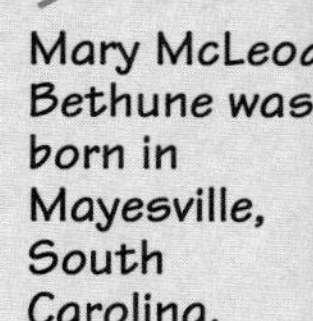

When Mary was a girl, she wanted to learn how to read. Mary could not go to school because there were no schools for African Americans. No one in her family had ever been to school. ❶ ❷

When Mary was about nine, she started going to a tiny, one room school. She came home and taught her family what she learned. ❸

When Mary McLeod Bethune became an adult, she started her own school for African American girls. She spoke to groups all around the country. ❹ She wanted to help other African Americans. She helped people understand how important it is to have good schools.

Mary McLeod Bethune was born in Mayesville, South Carolina.

Mary McLeod Bethune and a group of students

Think and Share

How did Mary McLeod Bethune help others?

For more information, go online to *Meet the People* at **www.sfsocialstudies.com.**

33

2 Teach and Discuss

Read the biography for children. Remind children that there used to be separate schools for African American children.

❶ **Why didn't Mary McLeod Bethune go to school when she was a little girl?** There were no schools for African Americans **Cause and Effect**

❷ **How old was Mary when she finally started school?** Nine **Main Idea and Details**

❸ **Why do you think Mary wanted to teach her family the things she learned at school?** Children may suggest that Mary was very excited to be learning and wanted to share her knowledge. **Make Inferences**

Ongoing Assessment

If... children have difficulty understanding why Mary wanted to teach her family and others,

then... ask them what they tell their family members or friends when something very exciting happens to them.

❹ **What did Mary McLeod Bethune do to help African American children?** She started a school for African American girls. She showed people the importance of school. **Draw Conclusions**

3 Close and Assess

Think and Share

Children may suggest that she helped African American children by starting a school and that she helped people understand the importance of good schools.

CURRICULUM CONNECTION
Writing

Sharing Time

- Review with children how Mary took what she learned in school home to teach her family. Tell children that they, too, are learning things they can share.
- Have children make four-page booklets to take home. On each page, they should draw and/or write about something they have learned at school.
- Have them take their booklets home to share with—or teach to—their families.

WEB SITE
Technology

You may help children find out more about Mary McLeod Bethune by clicking on *Meet the People* at **www.sfsocialstudies.com.**

Living History

Things We Use

Objective

- Recognize that things change over time.

1 Introduce and Motivate

Preview Have children scan pp. 34–35 and name those things that are familiar to them. Then point out the Then and Now icon, and explain that this lesson is about things children used in school in the past and things they use now.

Warm Up To activate prior knowledge, ask children to list objects they use in school. Suggest that they look around the classroom and in their desks. Record children's ideas on the board.

2 Teach and Discuss

Page 34

Help children identify any items pictured on p. 34 that may be unfamiliar to them, such as the metal lunch pail. Explain that these are items used in schools in the past.

1 **What do the pictures on p. 34 show?** Things children used in school in the past **Analyze Pictures**

2 **How do you think children used each of these things?** Possible answers: The pencil was used for writing; the pail, to carry lunch; the slate and chalk, for writing; the bookstrap, instead of a backpack; the scissors, for cutting. **Make Inferences**

3 **How do you or other children you know carry books to school today?** Possible answer: In a backpack **Apply Information**

Living History

Things We Use

These pictures show some things children used at school in the past. What did they use then?

1 2 3

34

Practice and Extend

FYI Fast Facts

School in History

- In ancient Egypt, only boys had writing tools. At first they practiced writing on pieces of broken pottery. Then, once they were good at it, they were given a few sheets of paper called papyrus.
- For a long time, children had no books. They learned by listening to the teacher. Around the Fifteenth Century, children in Europe began to get books of Latin grammar.
- In the middle of the Nineteenth Century, Louis Braille developed a reading system for the blind. After that blind people could "read" their school books too.

Some things children use at school have changed. Look at the pictures. What do you use today?

Hands-on History

Draw a picture of something you might use in a school of the future. Tell about it.

4 5 6

35

Page 35

Have volunteers identify the school tools pictured on this page. Ask children which they use at school.

4 **How do children use the calculator? the notebook? the lunch box?** The calculator is for math; the notebook, for writing; the lunch box, for carrying food. **Analyze Pictures**

5 **How are things we use in school today different from those used in the past?** Possible answer: Today we can use calculators to do math, and we write on paper instead of on a slate. **Compare and Contrast**

6 **Why can the kinds of tools we use at school change?** Answers should reflect some understanding of changing times and technologies. **Cause and Effect**

3 Close and Assess

Hands-on History

Have children brainstorm ideas for future school tools before they make their drawings. As a follow-up activity, have volunteers describe their future tools.

MEETING INDIVIDUAL NEEDS
Leveled Practice

Guess the Time Show children "Then and Now" photographs of your community, or of other subjects for which such photographs are available. Have children group the pictures into "Then" and "Now."

Easy Choose two pictures in which the time period is clearly different. Ask children leading questions, such as *Does this look like the town you live in today?* **Reteach**

On-Level Have children choose a picture and explain what picture clues they used to determine whether it was a "Then" or "Now" picture. **Extend**

Challenge Invite children to look at several pictures from the "Then" group. Ask them to suggest a possible time order for the pictures, using clues to decide which images come from farthest in the past. **Enrich**

Use with pages 28–35

Lesson 4 Wrap-Up

MEETING INDIVIDUAL NEEDS

Leveled Practice

Then or Now

Tell children that they will use objects (such as blocks) and/or pantomime to show how Andrew's school has changed.

Easy Have children show how Andrew's school has changed in size. As they point to objects or present pantomimes, other children can identify the time period by saying "Then" or "Now." **Reteach**

On-Level Remind children that there are reasons why Andrew's school has changed. Ask children to show a change—with objects or pantomime—and then tell what caused it. **Extend**

Challenge After their demonstration, children can dictate one or two sentences about how Andrew's school has changed. Then ask how the school might change if a lot of children moved from the area. **Enrich**

Hands-on Activities

SOCIAL STUDIES STRAND

Economics

Who Does What?

Objective Describe the jobs of teachers and other school workers.

Learning Style Verbal/Kinesthetic

Group

Time 20–25 minutes

1. Name some familiar school staff, such as the gym teacher, art teacher, or principal.

2. Have volunteers role-play what each worker does. If necessary, prompt children with questions about the staff member's role at school.

3. Make a list on the board of teachers in your school and what they do.

CURRICULUM CONNECTION

Math

Tools

Objective Compare school tools from different times.

Materials pencils and paper; calculators

Learning Style Kinesthetic

Partners

Time 5–10 minutes

1. Give children a grade-level appropriate math problem such as 2 + 2 = ?.

2. Show one child in each pair how to use a calculator to compute the answer. Direct the other child to find the answer using pencil and paper. Then have children exchange roles.

3. Discuss how tools have made some school tasks go more quickly for children today.

SOCIAL STUDIES STRAND

Culture

Listen Up!

Objective Learn about schools in other countries.

Learning Style Auditory/Verbal

Individual

Time 20–25 minutes

1. Arrange for an older student who has attended school in another country to visit your class. Have the student share his or her experiences. Encourage the student to tell what things are the same in both places and what things are different.

2. After the visit, help children compose a class thank-you letter to the student. Children can dictate sentences that tell what they learned.

Ending Unit 1

End with a Poem **pages 36–37**	Children will listen to and talk about a poem—"School Today" by Herbert Thomas—that answers the question: "What do I do at school?"	
Unit 1 Review **pages 38–41**	Children will review unit vocabulary words and the unit skills of using picture clues, problem solving, and reading a calendar. Children will answer questions about what they learned in the unit. Children will learn about several books about going to school.	Resources • Workbook, p. 10 ✓ • Assessment Book, pp. 1-4
Unit 1 Project **page 42**	Children will create and present a mock video tour of their school. They will also be directed to a Web site where they can learn more about schools.	Resource • Workbook, p. 11

Wrap-up

Activity

School Days

Have children make accordion picture books of things they do at school. Cut sheets of 11" x 17" paper in half lengthwise. Then, holding the paper the long way, show children how make accordion folds so there are four panels.

- On the front, children should draw a picture of something they do in school in each panel.
- On the back, children should write their names and then copy and complete this sentence: *At school I learn to* __. Allow them to complete the sentence with words or pictures.

Performance Assessment

You can use the activity on this page as a performance assessment.

✓ Assessment Scoring Guide

Make an Accordion Book About School	
4	Draws four different school activities and completes the sentence appropriately
3	Draws four activities but not all are clearly school-related. Completes the sentence appropriately.
2	Draws two or three school activities and fails to complete the sentence appropriately.
1	Draws one or two school activities and fails to complete the sentence appropriately.

School Today

Objective

- Obtain information about a topic using literature.

1 Introduce and Motivate

Preview Point to and read the title of the poem and the poet's name. Ask children what they think this poem is about. Suggest that they think about the title and look at the pictures for ideas.

Tell children that a poem is a kind of writing that often has rhyming words. Mention that this poem has many rhyming words.

Warm Up Ask children to name things they do at school each day. Ask them to tell about some things they have learned to do—and to suggest things they would like to learn before the end of the year.

2 Teach and Discuss

Explain to children that the poet is writing as if he were a child in school. Have children listen and look at the pictures as you read the poem.

1 **What are some things these children do at school?** Possible answers: Sing, play with friends, learn to read, plant seeds **Main Idea and Details**

2 **Do you do these same things at school?** Children may say that they do all or most of the things mentioned in the poem. **Compare and Contrast**

3 **Do you think the children in the pictures like going to school? Why or why not?** Possible answer: Yes, because the poem is a happy one, and because the pictures show happy children **Make Inferences**

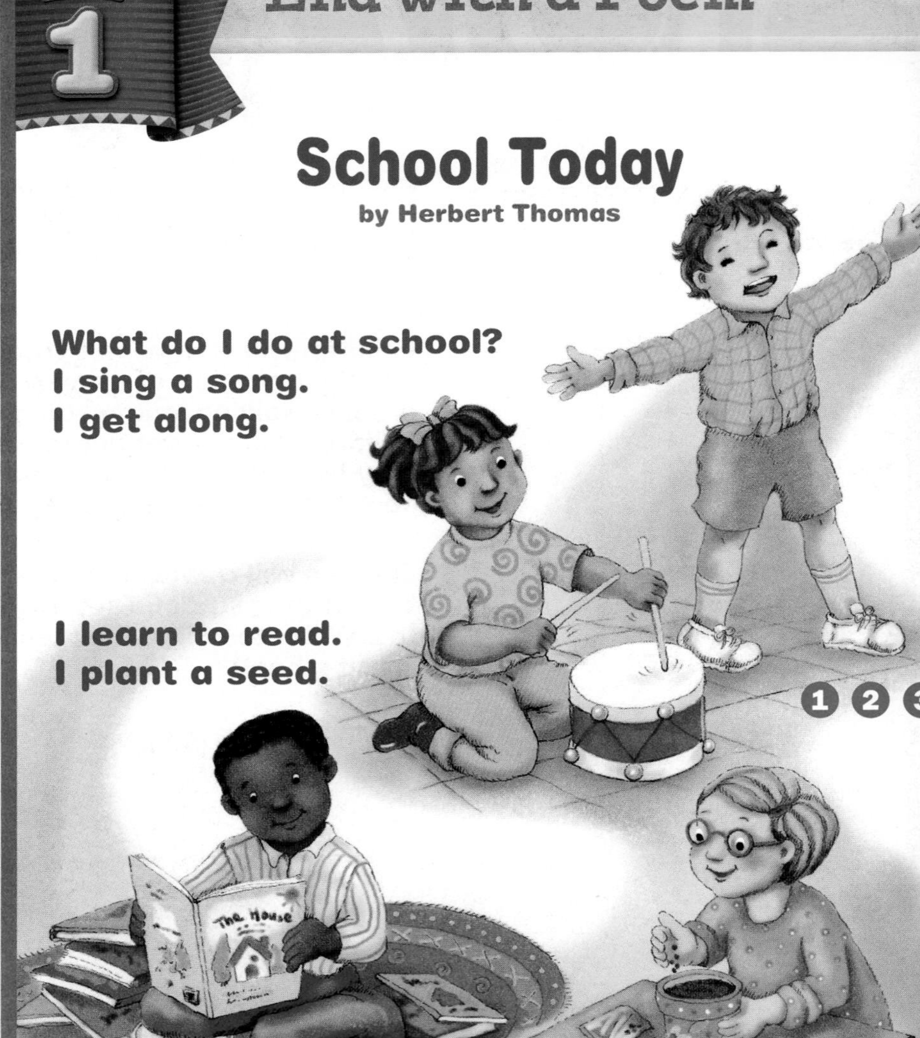
UNIT 1
End with a Poem

School Today
by Herbert Thomas

What do I do at school?
I sing a song.
I get along.

I learn to read.
I plant a seed.

1 2 3

36

Practice and Extend

CURRICULUM CONNECTION
Music

"This Is the Way"

- Teach children new words (and actions!) to the old singing game, "This Is the Way We Wash Our Clothes."

  This is the way we read our books,
  Read our books, read our books.
  This is the way we read our books,
  Each and every school day.

- Invite children to suggest their own words and actions for the words *read our books*. Use ideas from the poem on pp. 36–37, or draw from children's favorite class activities.

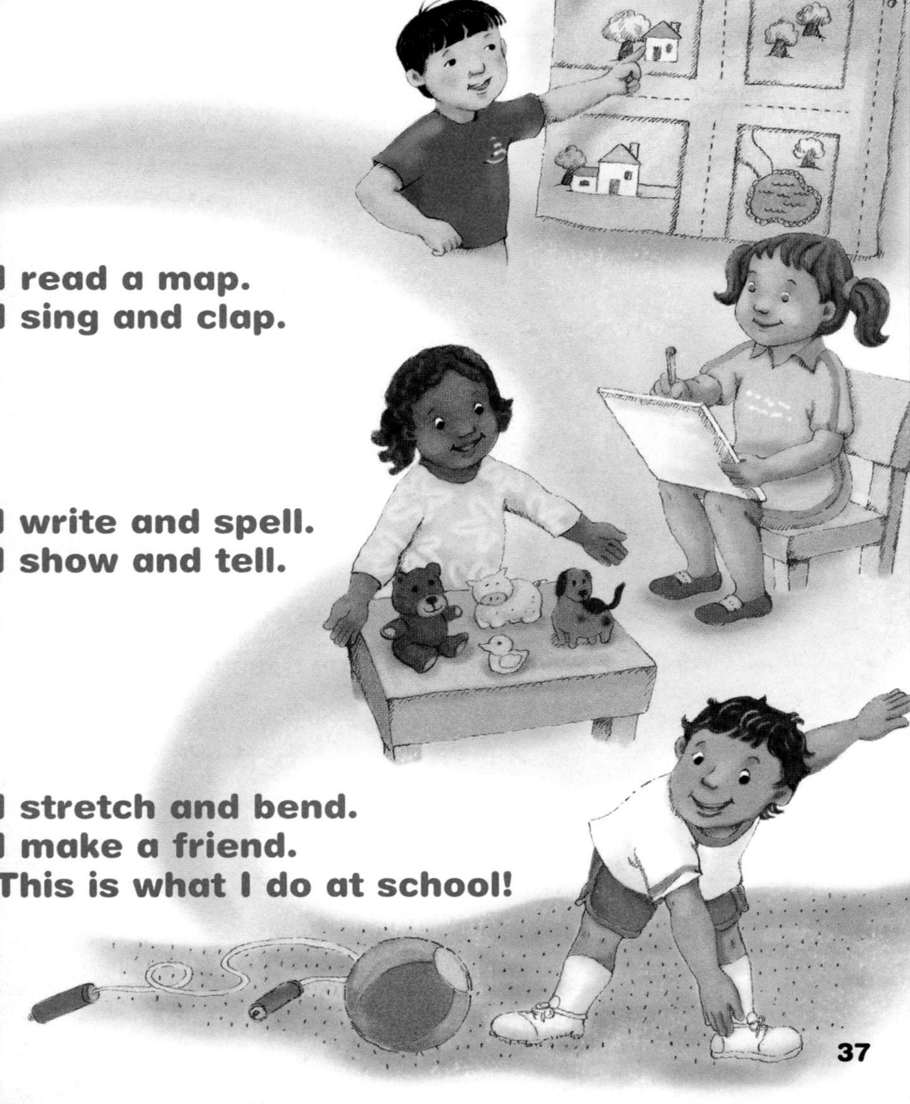

read a map.
sing and clap.
write and spell.
show and tell.
stretch and bend.
make a friend.
This is what I do at school!
37

3 Close and Assess

- Divide the class into two groups. Read the first three lines of the poem. Have one group create a pantomime for the first action: *sing a song*. Have the other group create a pantomime for the second action: *get along*.
- Reread the lines, having groups perform their pantomimes at the appropriate times.
- Continue for the remaining lines of the poem.
- Discuss with children which parts of the school day they like most. Ask if their favorite parts are mentioned in the poem.

CURRICULUM CONNECTION
Literature

Books About School

Children might enjoy reading these books related to school.

See You Tomorrow, Charles, by Miriam Cohen and Lillian Hoban (Illustrator), (Bantam Books, ISBN 0-440-41151-3, 1997) Charles is blind but he proves that he can take charge in certain situations. **Easy**

When Jo Louis Won the Title, by Belinda Rochelle and Larry Johnson (Illustrator), (Houghton Mifflin, ISBN: 0-395-81657-2, 1996) A young African American girl is afraid of being teased about her name—until her grandfather tells her the story behind that name. **On-Level**

The Toll-Bridge Troll, by Patricia Rae Wolff, Kimberly Bulcken Root (Illustrator), (Voyager Picture Book, ISBN 0152021051, 2000) When the troll who lives under the bridge demands the customary toll, Trigg decides to outwit him by using riddles and logic. **Challenge** ALA Notable Book, 1996

Review

Resources

- Assessment Book, pp. 1–4
- Workbook, p. 10: Vocabulary Review

Vocabulary Review

1. school
2. flag
3. rule
4. country

Answers to Test Prep

1. c. group
2. a. rule

UNIT 1

Review

Vocabulary Review

Match each word to its picture.

flag
school
rule
country

1. 

2. 

3.

4. 

★ ★ ★ ★ ★ ★ ★ ★

Which word completes each sentence?

1. When you play on a team, you are part of a _______.

   a. rule **b.** map

   c. group **d.** country

2. We learn to work together and stay safe when we follow a _______.

   a. rule **b.** flag

   c. map **d.** country

Practice and Extend

Assessment Options

✓ Unit 1 Assessment

- Unit 1 Content Test: Use Assessment Book, pp. 1–2
- Unit 1 Skills Test: Use Assessment Book, pp. 3–4

Standardized Test Prep

- Unit 1 tests contain standardized test formats.

✓ Unit 1 Performance Assessment

- See p. 42 for information about using the Unit 1 Project as a means of performance assessment.
- A scoring guide for the Unit 1 Project is provided in the teacher's notes on p. 42.

Test Talk

- Test Talk Practice Book

Skills Review

Use Picture Clues

Look at these pictures. Tell what is happening.

★ ★ ★ ★ ★ ★ ★ ★

Problem Solving

Your cafeteria is too noisy. Tell steps you would take to solve the problem.

39

WEB SITE
Technology

For more information, you can select the dictionary or encyclopedia from *Social Studies Library at* **www.sfsocialstudies.com.**

Workbook, p. 10

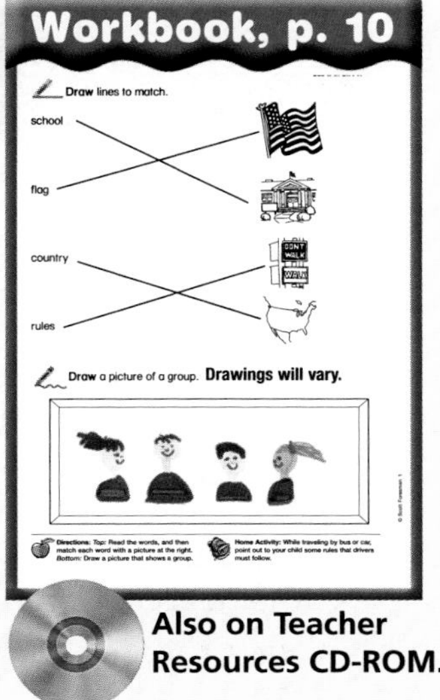

Draw lines to match.

school
flag
country
rules

Draw a picture of a group. **Drawings will vary.**

Also on Teacher Resources CD-ROM.

Skills Review

Use Picture Clues

- A girl is swinging.
- A boy is playing with his pet.
- Children are saying the Pledge of Allegiance.

✓ Assessment Scoring Guide

Picture Clues	
4	Uses precise details to describe the activity shown in each picture.
3	Describes each picture adequately and shows understanding of the activity shown in the pictures.
2	Describes each picture with few details, but is unable to identify each activity shown in the pictures.
1	Unable to use picture clues to identify details or the activity shown in each picture.

Problem Solving

Answers will vary but should include steps presented in a logical sequence according to the process taught in Problem on the Playground. Answers should identify the problem (the cafeteria is too noisy) and then describe the child's efforts to find out more about the problem, list ways to solve the problem, review possible solutions, implement the solutions, and review the impact of solutions.

Review

continued

Skills Review

Read a Calendar

- 30
- November 11th
- Wednesday

Skills on Your Own

- Children's calendars should be in the format shown for November and should include accurate labels for month and days of the week. Be sure to show children on which day the month they have chosen begins.

Use the following scoring guide.

✓ Assessment Scoring Guide

Make a Calendar	
4	Shows an accurate calendar for the chosen month, including the correct number of days and at least one special day.
3	Shows an accurate calendar format, with the correct number of days.
2	Shows a calendar for the chosen month in a format with a few errors such as the incorrect number of days or incorrect order in days of the week.
1	Shows a calendar containing many errors in information or labeling.

Review

Skills Review

Read a Calendar

1. How many days are in this month?
2. When is Veterans Day?
3. What day of the week is November 16?

November						
Sunday	Monday	Tuesday	Wednesday	Thursday	Friday	Saturday
		1	2	3	4	5
6	7	8 VOTE! Election Day	9	10	11 Veterans Day	12
13	14	15	16	17	18	19
20	21	22	23	24 Thanksgiving Day	25	26
27	28	29	30			

Skills On Your Own

Draw a calendar of your favorite month. Mark the important days.

40

Practice and Extend

Revisit the Unit Question

✓ Unit 1 Portfolio Assessment

- Have children look back at the reasons for going to school that they suggested on p. 1.
- Ask children if they wish to add any new reasons to that list now.
- Have children explain each reason they have supplied, telling why it made going to school sensible.
- Ask children to help prioritize the list in order of importance. Use *1* for the most important reason, *2* for the next most important reason, and so on.
- Have children copy the list and add it to their Social Studies Portfolio.

What did you learn?

1. Name two different groups.
2. What are two rules that help you work together? What are two rules that keep you safe?
3. Why is it important to follow rules?
4. **Think and Share** Think of rules for your class. Make a list of your rules. Share your rules with the class.

Test Talk

Look for key words in the question.

Read About School

Look for books like these in the library.

What did you learn?

1. Possible answers: Family, class, friends, team
2. Possible answers: To raise your hand before speaking, to sit quietly in class; to sit on the bus, to cross only when the guard tells you to
3. Answers may include to keep us safe, so we can work together.
4. **Think and Share** List of rules should show that children need to get along and respect others in a group situation.

Test Talk

Locate Key Words in the Question
Use Question 3 to model the strategy.

Find the key words in the question.
Remind children that a question beginning with *Why* is asking for a reason.

Turn the question into a statement.
Say: "It is important to follow rules because. . . ."
Ask children to complete the statement.

Read About School

Make books about school available to children. Have them read the books and tell about them.

Yoko by Rosemary Wells (Hyperion Press, ISBN: 0-7868-0395-9, 1998) When Yoko brings an unusual lunch to school, her teacher concocts a delicious plan to stop the teasing.

School from A to Z by Bobbie Kalman (Crabtree Publishing, ISBN: 0-86505-418-5, 1999) Tells children's experiences in school, from *A* to *Z*.

Mary McLeod Bethune by Eloise Greenfield (Harper Trophy, ISBN: 0-064-46168-8, 1994) This biography of the educator is simply told and beautifully illustrated.

Unit 1 Project

Follow Me!

Objective

- Dramatize a video tour that describes different parts of the school and explains what happens in each part.

Resource

- Workbook, p.11

Materials

paper, crayons or colored markers, small boxes, paper towel tubes, other classroom objects that can be used to make a model video camera

Follow This Procedure

- Have children use simple classroom materials to construct a model of a video camera.
- Review with children different places in and around your school, including classrooms, media center, cafeteria, and so on. Have each child choose a place.
- Explain that people who make videos first draw pictures before they begin filming. Tell children that these pictures are sometimes called storyboards. Have each child draw a picture of the place he or she has chosen.
- Divide the class into small groups. Put each group's pictures together so that they form a storyboard. Have children use their model cameras to present a video tour.

✓Assessment Scoring Guide

	Follow Me!
4	Describes and illustrates different parts of the school, using elaborate details and precise language.
3	Describes and illustrates different parts of the school, using several details and clear language.
2	Describes and illustrates different parts of the school, using few details and vague language.
1	Describes and illustrates different parts of the school, using limited details and incorrect word choices.

Follow Me!

Give a video tour of your school.

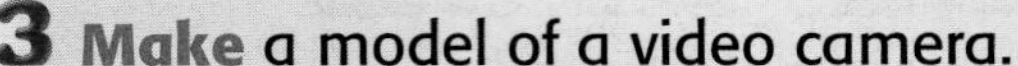

1 **Think** about what some important places are in your school. What happens in each place?

2 **Draw** a picture that shows what happens in one of the important places.

3 **Make** a model of a video camera.

4 **Use** your model camera to give a video tour. Describe the place you drew in your picture. Tell what visitors would need to know about your important place.

Internet Activity

Go to www.sfsocialstudies.com/activities to learn more about schools.

42

Practice and Extend

Hands-on Unit Project

✓Performance Assessment

- The Unit Project can also be used as a performance assessment activity.
- Use the scoring guide to assess each group's work.

WEB SITE Technology

Children can launch the activity by clicking on *Grade 1, Unit 1* at **www.sfsocialstudies.com/activities.**

Workbook, p. 11

1 Project Follow Me!

Choose a place in your school.

Draw a picture of what happens there. **Drawings will vary.**

Write the name of the place. **Answers will vary.**

Write about your picture.

Also on Teacher Resources CD-ROM.

★ Unit 2 ★

In My Community

In My Community

UNIT 2

Unit 2 Planning Guide

In My Community

Begin with a Song pp. 44–45 **Vocabulary Preview** pp. 46–47

Reading Social Studies, Alike and Different pp. 48–49

Lesson Titles	Pacing	Main Ideas
Lesson 1 Welcome to My Neighborhood pp. 50–53 **Map and Globe Skills: Use a Map Key** pp. 54–55	2 days	• A neighborhood is a place where people live, work, and play. • Neighborhoods can be alike in some ways and different in other ways. • A map key tells what the symbols used on a map stand for.
Lesson 2 Different Kinds of Communities pp. 56–57 **Then and Now: How a Community Changed** pp. 58–59 **Map and Globe Skills: Use Four Directions** pp 60–61	2 days	• A neighborhood is part of a larger community. • Cities, towns, and farms are kinds of communities. • A community may change over time. • A map includes cardinal directions: north, south, east, west.
Lesson 3 Special Things We Do pp. 62–65 DK **Chinese New Year** pp. 66–67 **Citizen Heroes: Fairness Learning About Each Other** pp. 68–69	3 days	• People in a community share many customs. • Celebrations of the Chinese New Year are a custom from another country. • Members of CAPAY help others learn what it means to be Asian Pacific Americans.
Lesson 4 Community Laws and Leaders pp. 70–71 **Biography: Jane Addams** pp. 72–73	2 days	• People must obey the laws of a community. • A mayor and other leaders work for the common good of the community. • Jane Addams started Hull House to help the people of Chicago.
Lesson 5 Where in the World Do I Live? pp. 74–77 **Biography: Sam Houston** pp. 78–79	2 days	• The United States is a country made up of fifty states. • The United States is on the continent of North America. • A continent is a large piece of land; an ocean is a large body of salt water. • Sam Houston helped Texas win its independence from Mexico and become a state in the United States.

✓ **End with a Poem** pp. 80–81 ✓ **Unit 2 Review** pp. 82–85 ✓ **Unit 2 Project** p. 86

✓ = Assessment Options

Vocabulary	Resources	Meeting Individual Needs
neighborhood	• Workbook, pp. 14–15 • Vocabulary Card: neighborhood • Every Student Learns Guide, pp. 18–21	• ESL Support, TE p. 52 • Leveled Practice, TE p. 55a
community	• Workbook, pp. 16–17 • Vocabulary Card: community • Every Student Learns Guide, pp. 22–25	• ESL Support, TE pp. 58, 61 • Leveled Practice, TE p. 61a
	• Workbook, p. 18 • Every Student Learns Guide, pp. 26–29	• ESL Support, TE p. 64 • Leveled Practice, TE p. 69a
law **leader**	• Workbook, p. 19 • Transparency 15 • Vocabulary Cards: law, leader • Every Student Learns Guide, pp. 30–33	• Leveled Practice, TE pp. 73, 73a
state **continent** **ocean**	• Workbook, p. 20 • Vocabulary Cards: state, continent, ocean • Every Student Learns Guide, pp. 34–37	• ESL Support, TE p. 76 • Leveled Practice, TE p. 79a

Providing More Depth

Multimedia Library

- ***Building*** **by Philip Wilkinson**
- ***The Little Skyscraper*** **by Paulette Bogan**
- **Songs and Music**
- **Video Field Trips**
- **Software**

Additional Resources

- Family Activities
- Vocabulary Cards
- Daily Activity Bank
- Social Studies Plus!
- Big Book Atlas
- Outline Maps
- Desk Maps

ADDITIONAL Technology

- AudioText
- TestWorks
- Teacher Resources CD-ROM
- Map Resources CD-ROM
- **www.sfsocialstudies.com**

To establish guidelines for children's safe and responsible use of the Internet, use the **Scott Foresman Internet Guide.**

Additional Internet Links
To find out more about:

- your own community, visit the Web site for your village, town, or city
- Sam Houston Memorial Museum, visit **www.shsu.edu**

Key Internet Search Terms

- maps
- Chinese New Year

Unit 2 Objectives

Beginning of Unit 2

- **Obtain information using oral sources, such as conversations, interviews, and music.** (pp. 44–45)
- **Determine the meanings of words.** (pp. 46–47)
- **Compare and contrast by telling about likenesses and differences.** (pp. 48–49)
- **Identify and describe the human characteristics of places, such as types of houses.** (pp. 48–49)
- **Express ideas orally, based on knowledge and experiences.** (pp. 48–49)

Lesson 1
Welcome to My Neighborhood
pp. 50–53

- **Identify buildings in relation to the school and neighborhood.**
- **Recognize that communities include people who have diverse ethnic origins, customs, and traditions and who make contributions to their communities.**
- **Create and use simple maps to identify the location of places in the classroom.** (pp. 54–55)
- **Construct a map using basic map symbols.** (pp. 54–55)

Lesson 2
Different Kinds of Communities
pp. 56–57

- **Explain similarities and differences between life in city, town, and farm communities.**
- **Distinguish among past, present, and future and identify changes in the community.** (pp. 58–59)
- **Locate places using the four cardinal directions.** (pp. 60–61)

Lesson 3
Special Things We Do
pp. 62–65

- **Describe various customs and traditions and explain their importance.**
- **Obtain information about a topic using a variety of sources, such as interviews.**
- **Describe selected customs.**
- **Describe community celebrations.** (pp. 66–67)
- **Describe various customs of families.** (pp. 66–67)
- **Obtain information about a topic using a variety of visual sources, such as pictures.** (pp. 66–67)
- **Identify characteristics of good citizenship, such as belief in equality.** (pp. 68–69)

Lesson 4
Community Laws and Leaders
pp. 70-71

- **Explain the need for laws in the community.**
- **Identify responsibilities of authority figures in the community.**
- **Describe the role of public officials including mayor.**
- **Identify contributions of historical figures.** (pp. 72–73)

Lesson 5
Where in the World Do I Live?
pp. 74–77

- **Locate places of significance on maps.**
- **Identify contributions of historical figures.** (pp. 78–79)

End of Unit 2
pp. 80–81

- **Obtain information about a topic using a variety of visual sources, such as pictures and literature.**
- **Identify main ideas from oral, visual, and print sources.**

Assessment Options

✓ Formal Assessment

- **What did you learn?** PE/TE pp. 53, 57, 65, 71, 77
- **Unit Review,** PE/TE pp. 82–85
- **Unit 2 Test,** Assessment Book pp. 5–8
- **TestWorks,** (test generator software)

✓ Informal Assessment

- **Teacher's Edition Questions,** throughout Lessons and Features
- **Close and Assess,** TE pp. 49, 53, 55, 57, 61, 65, 71, 73, 77, 79, 81
- **Try it!** PE/TE pp. 49, 55, 61
- **Think and Share,** PE/TE pp. 53, 57, 65, 71, 73, 77, 79
- **Fairness in Action,** PE/TE p. 69
- **Hands-on History,** PE/TE p. 59

Ongoing Assessment

Ongoing Assessment is found throughout the Teacher's Edition lessons using an **If...then** model.

If = students' observable behavior,	**then =** reteaching and enrichment suggestions

✓ Portfolio Assessment

- **Portfolio Assessment,** TE p. 43
- **Leveled Practice,** TE pp. 55a, 61a, 69a, 73a, 79a
- **Workbook,** pp. 12–22
- **Unit Review: Skills on Your Own,** PE/TE p. 84
- **Curriculum Connection: Writing,** TE pp. 45, 55a, 69a, 73a

✓ Performance Assessment

- **Hands-on Unit Project** (Unit 2 Performance Assessment), PE/TE pp. 43, 86
- **Internet Activity,** PE p. 86
- **Scoring Guides,** TE pp. 80a, 83, 84, 86

Test Talk

Test-Taking Strategies

Understand the Question

- **Locate Key Words in the Question,** TE p. 52
- **Locate Key Words in the Text,** TE p. 85

Understand the Answer

- **Choose the Right Answer,** *Test Talk Practice Book*
- **Use Information from the Text,** TE p. 67
- **Use Information from Graphics,** TE p. 47
- **Write Your Answer,** TE p. 53

For additional practice, use the Test Talk Practice Book.

Featured Strategy

Locate Key Words in the Text

Children will:

– Make sure that they understand the key words in the question.

– Find key words in the text that match key words in the question.

PE/TE p. 85

Curriculum Connections

Integrating Your Day

The lessons, skills, and features of Unit 2 provide many opportunities to make connections between social studies and other areas of the elementary curriculum.

Reading

Reading Skill—Compare and Contrast (Alike and Different), p. 50

Creating Symbols, p. 54

Reading Skill—Make Word Webs (Alike and Different), p. 56

Reading Skill—Common Customs (Alike and Different), p. 62

Reading Skill—Telling Why, p. 70

Reading Skill—Venn Diagram (Alike and Different), p. 74

Name Game, p. 79a

Math

Simon Says, p. 61a

Writing

Interview, p. 45

Add to "My Word Book," p. 55a

Customs, p. 69a

Class Letter, p. 73a

Social Studies

Literature

***Read* My New York,** p. 57

Smoky Night, p. 59

City, Country, p. 61a

Routes, p. 79a

Books About Community, p. 81

Read About Community, p. 85

Science

Wood, Stone, or Brick? p. 49

Draw to Show Weather Changes, p. 60

Where's North? p. 61a

Music/Drama

Plan a Street, p. 55a

Sing Out! p. 69a

Art

Draw Your Community, p. 47

Design a Street Sign, p. 51

Make a "Customs" Calendar, p. 64

Make a State Puzzle, p. 75

Look for this symbol throughout the Teacher's Edition to find **Curriculum Connections.**

Professional Development

Multicultural Education in a Democracy

by Geneva Gay
University of Washington, Seattle

Three essential concepts of democracy are embedded within the major concerns of multicultural education. These are equality, social justice, and interdependence. These principles suggest that:

(1) people from different ethnic groups and cultural backgrounds have the right to be treated fairly in schools and society;

(2) the contributions of diverse ethnic groups and individuals need to be known and respected;

(3) the lives of individuals and groups are interwoven; they are nourished and flourish because of people helping each other.

Here is how you can incorporate these democratic ideals as you teach *Scott Foresman Social Studies.*

Use Lesson 3 (pp. 62–65) and pp. 66–67 to explore the different customs that people in a community share. Invite culturally diverse people from your community to visit your classroom to share their customs and traditions. Go beyond the borders of your own community, as necessary.

Use "Learning About Each Other" (pp. 68–69) and "Jane Addams" (pp. 72–73) to familiarize children with citizens who have fought for the right to be treated fairly and who worked for the common good of their communities.

ESL Support

by Jim Cummins, Ph. D.
University of Toronto

In order to understand how to extend students' grasp of academic language and how to use language powerfully, it is important to distinguish the following three very different aspects of proficiency in a language:

Conversational fluency is the ability to carry on a conversation in familiar face-to-face situations.

Discrete language skills reflect specific phonological, literacy, and grammatical knowledge that students acquire as a result of direct instruction and both formal and informal practice (e.g., reading).

Academic language proficiency includes knowledge of the less frequent vocabulary of English as well as the ability to interpret and produce increasingly complex written language.

The learning of discrete language skills does not generalize automatically to academic language proficiency. ESL students who can "read" English fluently may have only a very limited understanding of the words they can decode. The development of reading comprehension ability in the content areas, and academic language proficiency generally, requires very different forms of instruction than the forms that are successful in teaching discrete language skills.

The following examples in the Teacher's Edition will help you to enable ESL students to extend language:

- ***Telling About Neighborhoods*** *on p. 52 helps English Language Learners learn and use words that describe neighborhoods.*
- ***Work with New Words*** *on p. 58 has children work with words used to talk about past, present, and future events.*
- ***A Spinning Game*** *on p. 76 involves children in playing a game that uses vocabulary relating to maps and globes.*

Read Aloud

Where I Live
by Lou Myers

I live in a house
That's painted white.
It's cozy; it's small;
For me, just right.

I live on a street
With lots of trees.
I like my neighbors
And they like me.

I live in a town
That's not very old.
It was once a farm—
Or so I am told.

Build Background
- Ask children to tell about the places where they live.
- Ask children if they would like to live in the place described in the poem. Encourage them to give reasons for their answers.

Read Alouds and Primary Sources
Read Alouds and Primary Sources contains additional selections to be used with Unit 2.

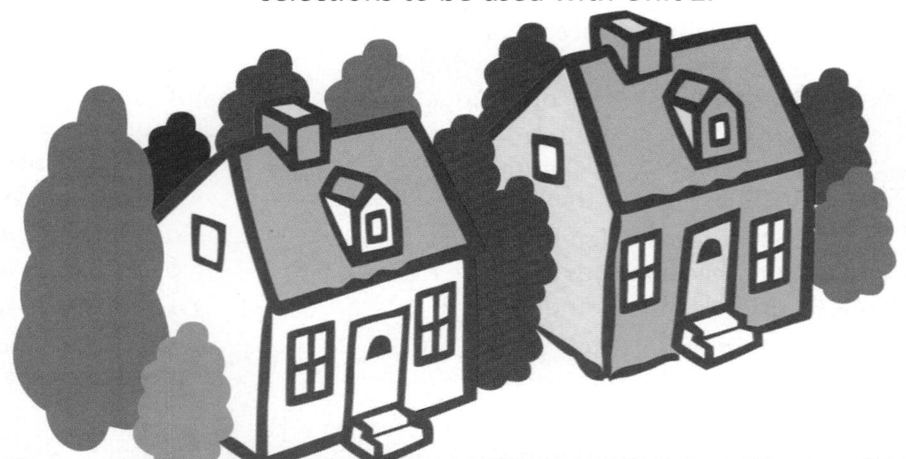

Bibliography

Carpenters, by Vicky Franchino (Compass Point Books, ISBN 0-756-50006-0, 2000) **Easy**

Fire Fighters, by Lucia Raatma (Compass Point Books, ISBN 0-756-50009-5, 2000) **Easy**

Letter Carriers, by Alice K. Flanagan (Compass Point Books, ISBN 0-756-50010-9, 2000) **Easy**

Mayors, by Alice K. Flanagan (Compass Point Books, ISBN 0-756-50064-8, 2001) **Easy**

My Town, by Rebecca Treays (EDC, ISBN 0-746-03079-7, 1998) **Easy** ***Notable Social Studies Book, 1999***

Police Officers, by Alice K. Flanagan (Compass Point Books, ISBN 0-756-50011-7, 2000) **Easy**

Aurora Means Dawn, by Scott Russell Sanders and Jill Kastner (illustrator), (Aladdin, ISBN 0-689-81907-2, 1998) **On-Level**

Little House, The by Virginia Lee Burton (Turtleback, ISBN 0-606-01531-0, 1969) ***Caldecott Medal, 1943*** **On-Level**

Philharmonic Gets Dressed, The by Karla Kuskin (HarperCollins, ISBN 0-06-443124-X, 1986) **On-Level**

Raising Yoder's Barn, by Jane Yolen and Bernie Fuchs (illustrator), (Little Brown, ISBN 0-316-96887-0, 1998) **On-Level**

Uptown, by Bryan Collier (Henry Holt, ISBN 0-805-05721-8, 2000) **On-Level** ***Coretta Scott King Award***

Journey, The by Sarah Stewart and David Small (illustrator), (Farrar Straus & Giroux, ISBN 0-374-33905-8, 2001) **Challenge**

New Coat for Anna, A by Harriet Ziefert and Anita Lobel (illustrator), (Econo-Clad Books, ISBN 0-833-51245-5, 1999) **Challenge**

Urban Roosts: Where Birds Nest in the City, by Barbara Bash (Little Brown, ISBN 0-316-08312-7, 1992) **Challenge**

Window, by Jeannie Baker (Greenwillow, ISBN 0-688-08918-6, 1991) **Challenge**

Mapmaking with Children, by David Sobel (Heinemann, ISBN 0-325-00042-5, 1998) **Teacher Reference**

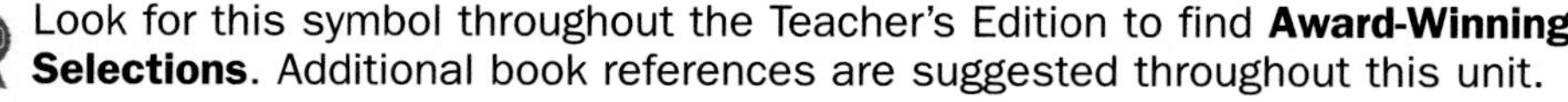

Look for this symbol throughout the Teacher's Edition to find **Award-Winning Selections**. Additional book references are suggested throughout this unit.

In My Community
UNIT
2
What do you like best about where you live? Why?
43

Unit Overview

This unit introduces children to aspects of life in a community and helps children learn about their relationship to home, neighborhood, community, and state.

Introduce Kim

Read the unit title and then introduce the featured child for this unit as a first grader named Kim. Talk about what Kim might like best about her community.

Unit Question

- Ask children the questions on this page.
- Initiate a discussion of what children like about their own community.
- To activate prior knowledge, make a list on the board of what children like about their own community.

✓ **Portfolio Assessment** Keep a copy of this list for the Portfolio Assessment at the end of the unit on p. 84.

Practice and Extend

Hands-on Unit Project

✓ **Unit 2 Performance Assessment**

- The Unit 2 Project, News for All, found on p. 86, is an ongoing performance assessment project to enrich children's learning throughout the unit.
- This project, which has children make a poster and give a news report about a community event, may be started now or at any time during this unit of study.
- A performance assessment scoring guide is on p. 86.

This Is My Community

Objective

- Obtain information using oral sources, such as conversations, interviews, and music.

Resources

- *Songs and Music* CD "This Is My Community"
- Poster 3
- Social Studies Plus!

Introduce the Song

Preview Tell children that they will be singing a song about a community. Focus attention on the urban aspects of Kim's community.

Warm Up To activate prior knowledge, refer to the list of things children like about their community. Ask if they think other communities also have these things. Ask them to share what they know about other communities. This will help you evaluate children's knowledge of communities.

Sing the Song

- Have children sing the song "This Is My Community."
- Ask children what they think Kim's day is like—based on the words of the song.
- Invite children to tell what they learned about Kim's community from singing the song.

UNIT 2
Begin with a Song

This Is My Community
by Carlos Elliot

Sung to the tune of "Twinkle, Twinkle, Little Star"

This is where I live and play,
Work and shop most every day.

Here's my home and here's my street.
This is where my neighbors meet.

Lots of people live near me.
This is my community!

44

Practice and Extend

Possible Misconceptions

Children living in suburban or rural areas may be surprised to learn that urban families can often walk to shops and offices. Conversely, children living in cities may not know that suburban and rural families often have to drive to stores and places of business. Discuss such differences among suburban, rural, and urban areas.

Play the CD, *Songs and Music*, to listen to "This Is My Community."

CURRICULUM CONNECTION
Writing

Interview

- Have each child ask an older person about the community in which he or she grew up.
- Have children draw pictures to show the communities their interviewees tell them about. Children can write or dictate captions for their pictures.
- Have children show their drawings and share what they have learned with classmates.

Talk About the Picture

Direct children's attention to the picture. Ask them to name some things in Kim's community.

1 **The song says that Kim lives and plays in her community. What else does she do there?** She works and shops. **Main Idea and Details**

2 **What does the picture show Kim doing?** Walking her dog **Analyze Pictures**

3 **Who do you think the woman in the picture is? How do you know?** She is Kim's neighbor. The song says that neighbors meet on Kim's street. **Make Inferences**

Vocabulary Preview

Objective

- Determine the meanings of words.

Resources

- Workbook, p. 12
- Vocabulary Cards
- Poster 4

Introduce the Vocabulary

Read aloud and point to each vocabulary word and the photograph illustrating it. Have volunteers give the meanings of the words. Then have children find examples of vocabulary words in the illustration. Write these examples on the board:

Vocabulary Word	Illustrated Examples
neighborhood	school neighborhood
community	city (tall buildings in distance)
law	street signs (one way, no parking), traffic lights
leader	governor, mayor
state	Florida map, Virginia map
continent	South America (on globe)
ocean	pictures (on billboard and in window) on globe

In addition, for *leader*, identify local and state leaders, as well as the leaders of our country.

SOCIAL STUDIES STRAND
Geography

Listed below are some basic principles of geography for young children. Direct your discussion of the illustration toward the development of these concepts.

- similarities and differences
- neighborhood features
- ways people use maps to locate places
- role of location and physical surroundings in people's lives
- ways communities change over time
- four cardinal directions
- community customs and celebrations

UNIT 2

Vocabulary Preview

neighborhood

community

law

leader

46

MEETING INDIVIDUAL NEEDS
Leveled Practice

Here Comes the Welcome Wagon!

Ask children to imagine that they are newcomers to this community—and that you are the welcoming committee. Tell children that you will show them around.

Easy Guide children into finding illustrations of each vocabulary word. Have children repeat the vocabulary words as you point to the illustrations. **Reteach**

On-Level Have children use picture clues to tell you more about the people and places illustrated. Encourage children to use the vocabulary words in their descriptions. **Extend**

Challenge Have children select a location in the picture (such as the travel agency or city hall) and have them find the addresses for these things in their community. If necessary, show them how to use the phone book. Then discuss what happens in these places. **Enrich**

state

continent

ocean

47

Talk About the Illustration

Allow children time to study the illustration. Encourage children to talk about what the other people in the picture are doing.

Test Talk

Use Information from Graphics

1 Which signs are telling people what to do? Possible answers: One Way sign tells drivers that cars can only go in one direction. The sign with a circle and a bar over a car means "No Parking." Traffic lights tell drivers when to stop and go. Tell children to use details from the picture to support their answers. **Analyze Pictures**

2 Ask children what special event is happening in the picture. How can they tell? Possible answer: The leader of the state, Governor Smith, is visiting. There is a welcome sign and decorations. **Analyze Pictures**

Look Ahead

Tell children that they will learn more about each of these words as they study Unit 2.

You may want to revisit the picture with children to review the concepts and vocabulary in the unit.

3 How is a community like a neighborhood? How is a community different from a neighborhood? Both are places where people live and work. A community is bigger than a neighborhood. A community has many neighborhoods. **Compare and Contrast**

CURRICULUM CONNECTION
Art

Draw *Your* Community

- Have children draw the community in which they live.
- As children share their pictures, they can point out things that make their community special.

WEB SITE
Technology

You can look up vocabulary words online. Click on *Social Studies Library* and select the dictionary at **www.sfsocialstudies.com.**

Workbook, p. 12

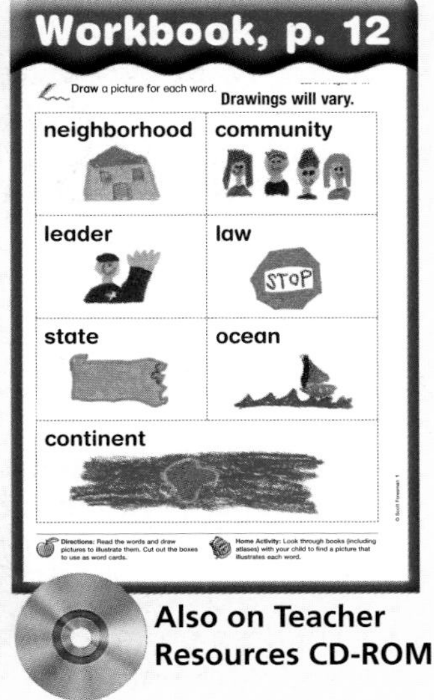
Draw a picture for each word.

Drawings will vary.

neighborhood	community
leader	law
state	ocean
continent	

Also on Teacher Resources CD-ROM.

Where Kim Lives

Alike and Different

Target Skill

Objectives

- Compare and contrast by telling about likenesses and differences.
- Identify and describe the human characteristics of places such as types of houses.
- Express ideas orally, based on knowledge and experiences.

Resource

- Workbook, p. 13

About the Unit Target Skill

- The target reading skill for this unit is Alike and Different. Children are introduced to the unit target skill here and are given an opportunity to practice it.
- Further opportunities to practice comparing and contrasting are found throughout Unit 2.

1 Introduce and Motivate

Preview Display two balls of different sizes and colors. Ask children to tell how the two objects are alike. (Both are balls; both are round spheres.) Then ask them to tell how they are different. (in size, in color) Write *alike* and *different* on the board. Relate *alike* to "same" and *different* to "not the same."

Warm Up To activate prior knowledge, remind children about the story of Andrew's school from Mr. Jones's scrapbook (Unit 1). Ask children to tell one thing about the school from long ago; for example, "It was small." Then ask them to tell if the school is still like that now. (No, it is much bigger now.)

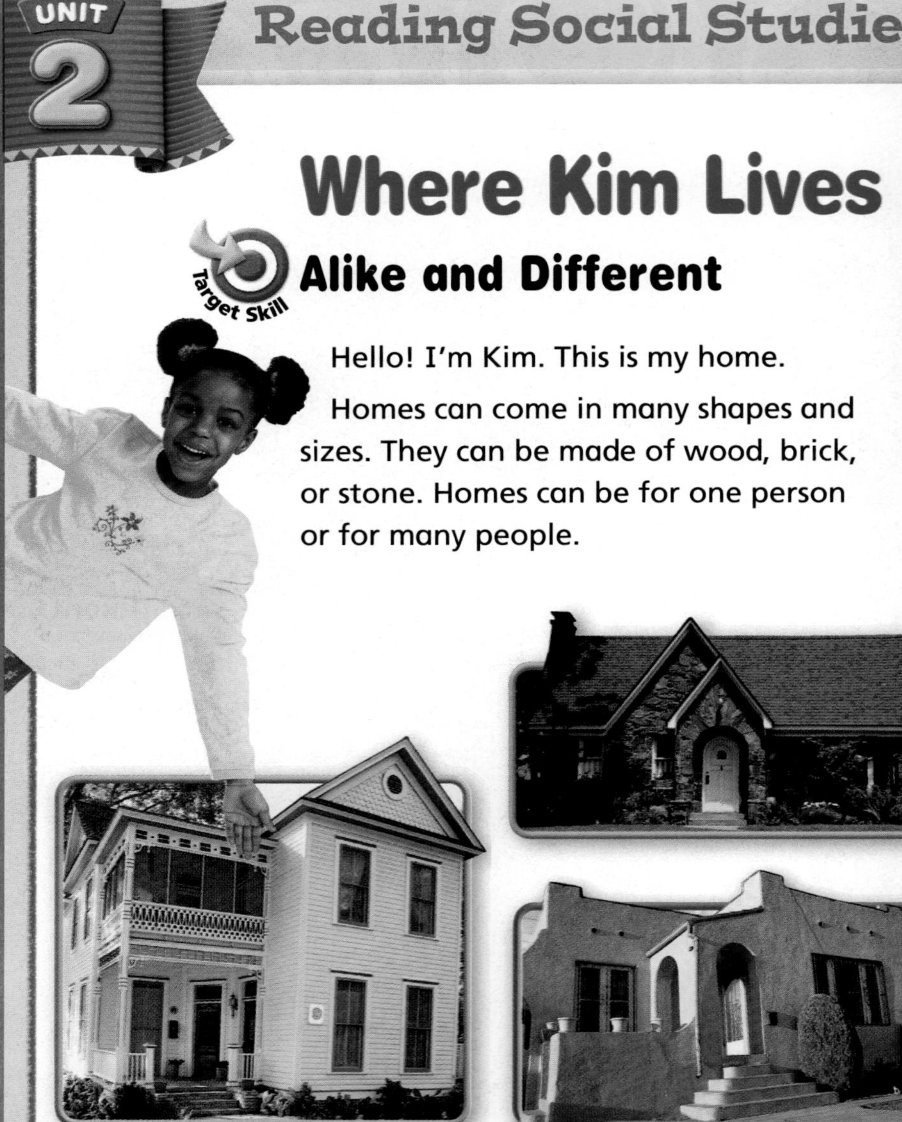
UNIT 2

Reading Social Studie

Where Kim Lives

Target Skill

Alike and Different

Hello! I'm Kim. This is my home.

Homes can come in many shapes and sizes. They can be made of wood, brick, or stone. Homes can be for one person or for many people.

48

Practice and Extend

ESL

ACCESS CONTENT

ESL Support

Work with New Words Discuss the meanings of the words *alike* and *different*. Have children write the words on cards and then draw pictures that remind them of the English meanings.

Beginning Show children two similar picture books. Have children display their *alike* or *different* cards to respond to statements you make, such as: *Both are storybooks.* (alike) *The stories are not the same.* (different)

Intermediate Show a pair of similar items, and have children prompt each other to tell how the items are alike and different.

Advanced Have children locate their own paired items, hold up their cards, and explain how the items are alike or different.

Homes can look alike. **Alike** means how things are the same. Homes can also look different from each other. **Different** means how things are not the same. Look at these pictures. How are the homes alike? How are they different?

Try it!

Draw pictures of two homes. Tell how they are **alike** and **different.**

49

2 Teach and Discuss

Read p. 48 and have children look at the pictures on pp. 48–49. Ask children to point out Kim's house. Then have them describe each of the other homes pictured.

Read p. 49 and focus on the terms *alike* and *different.* Ask children to tell one way in which the pictured homes are all alike. Then ask them to tell how the homes are different. Explain that homes have many characteristics in common because they are built for humans. Ask children why they think all the homes have windows. Discuss what this tells us about what people need. Ask why they all have doors.

Explain that we can use the word *compare* to tell how things are alike and the word *contrast* to tell how things are different.

Ongoing Assessment

If... children do not understand how to use the words *alike* and *different* to compare and contrast, **then...** display two identical items, and tell how they are alike. Then replace one with a similar but not identical item. Discuss how the two items are alike but also different.

3 Close and Assess

Try it!

Tell children that they may draw any kind of homes they like. Use the pictures on pp. 48–49 to review some possible choices. Children's drawings should show two homes. Their oral statements should include at least one point of comparison and one point of contrast.

CURRICULUM CONNECTION Science

Climate and Homes

- Tell children that climate is the kind of weather a place usually has. Show pictures of homes in several different climates, including from other countries.
- Have children find pictures that show a variety of climates. Help them observe factors that might make a difference when people decide to build a home.
- Discuss how different materials and styles can help make people more comfortable in different climates.

Workbook, p. 13

Alike and Different

Circle two houses that are alike.

Color these houses so they are different. Color the cars so they are different, too. **Answers will vary.**

Also on Teacher Resources CD-ROM.

Workbook Support

Use the following Workbook pages to support content and skills development as you teach Unit 2. You can also view and print Workbook pages from the Teacher Resources CD-ROM.

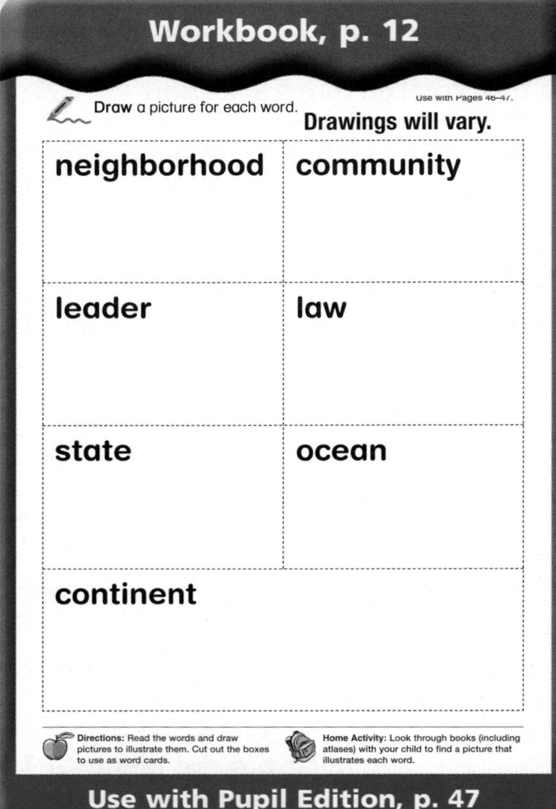

Workbook, p. 12

Use with Pages 46–47.

Draw a picture for each word. **Drawings will vary.**

neighborhood	community
leader	law
state	ocean
continent	

Directions: Read the words and draw pictures to illustrate them. Cut out the boxes to use as word cards.

Home Activity: Look through books (including atlases) with your child to find a picture that illustrates each word.

Use with Pupil Edition, p. 47

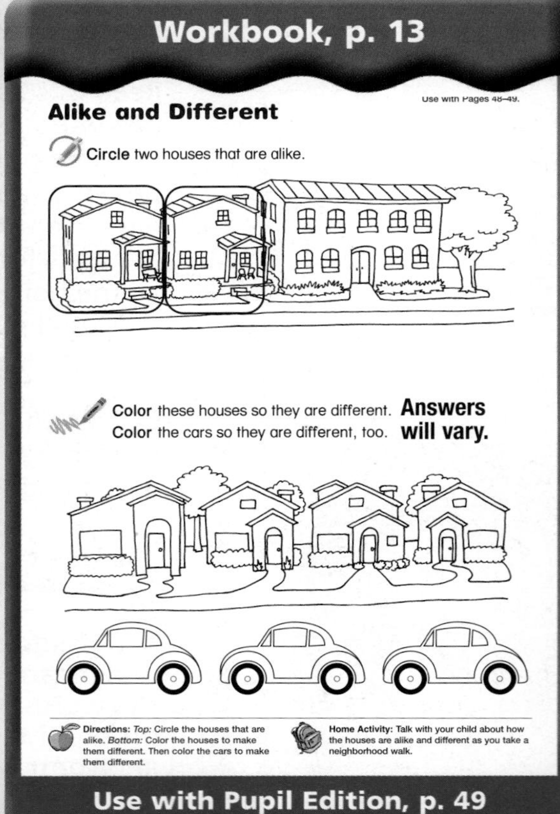

Workbook, p. 13

Use with Pages 48–49.

Alike and Different

Circle two houses that are alike.

Color these houses so they are different. **Answers will vary.**
Color the cars so they are different, too.

Directions: *Top:* Circle the houses that are alike. *Bottom:* Color the houses to make them different. Then color the cars to make them different.

Home Activity: Talk with your child about how the houses are alike and different as you take a neighborhood walk.

Use with Pupil Edition, p. 49

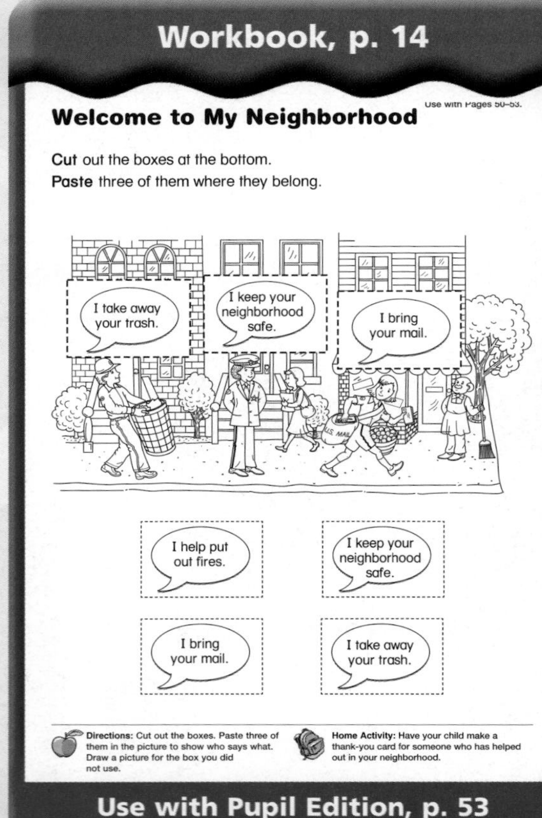

Workbook, p. 14

Use with Pages 50–53.

Welcome to My Neighborhood

Cut out the boxes at the bottom.
Paste three of them where they belong.

Directions: Cut out the boxes. Paste three of them in the picture to show who says what. Draw a picture for the box you did not use.

Home Activity: Have your child make a thank-you card for someone who has helped out in your neighborhood.

Use with Pupil Edition, p. 53

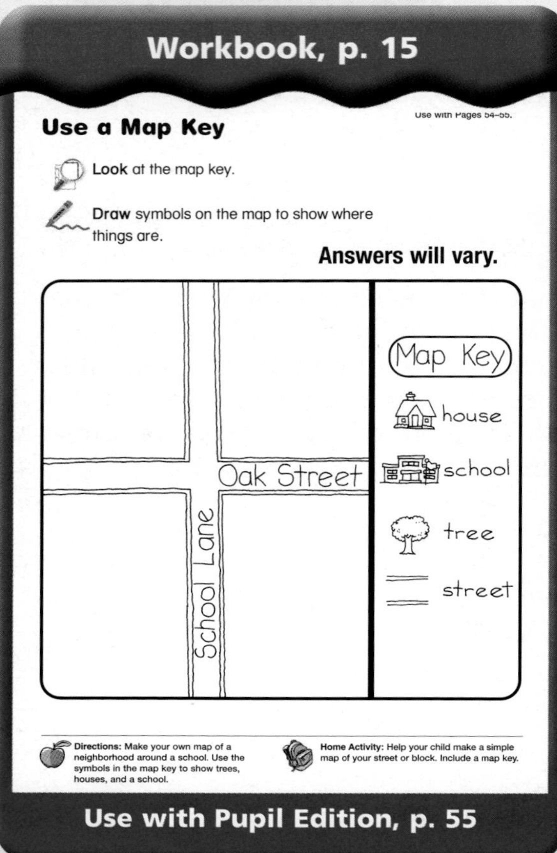

Workbook, p. 15

Use with Pages 54–55.

Use a Map Key

Look at the map key.

Draw symbols on the map to show where things are.

Answers will vary.

Directions: Make your own map of a neighborhood around a school. Use the symbols in the map key to show trees, houses, and a school.

Home Activity: Help your child make a simple map of your street or block. Include a map key.

Use with Pupil Edition, p. 55

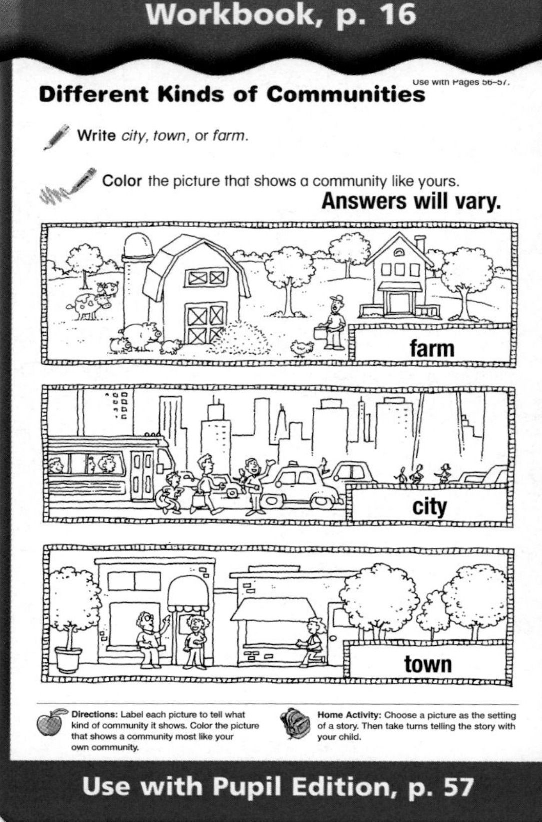

Workbook, p. 16

Use with Pages 56–57.

Different Kinds of Communities

Write *city*, *town*, or *farm*.

Color the picture that shows a community like yours.

Answers will vary.

Directions: Label each picture to tell what kind of community it shows. Color the picture that shows a community most like your own community.

Home Activity: Choose a picture as the setting of a story. Then take turns telling the story with your child.

Use with Pupil Edition, p. 57

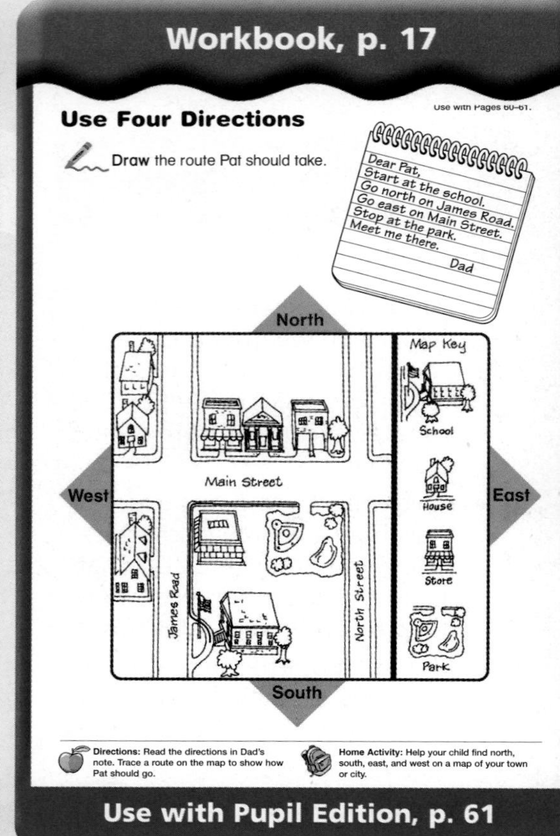

Workbook, p. 17

Use with Pages 60–61.

Use Four Directions

Draw the route Pat should take.

Dear Pat,
Start at the school.
Go north on James Road.
Go east on Main Street.
Stop at the park.
Meet me there.
Dad

Directions: Read the directions in Dad's note. Trace a route on the map to show how Pat should go.

Home Activity: Help your child find north, south, east, and west on a map of your town or city.

Use with Pupil Edition, p. 61

Workbook Support

Workbook, p. 18

Use with Pages 62–65.

Special Things We Do

Draw to show what you might do on July 4th. **Drawings will vary.**

Directions: Draw a picture to show how you would like to celebrate the 4th of July, Independence Day.

Home Activity: Tell your child about a family custom or tradition you celebrated when you were growing up.

Use with Pupil Edition, p. 65

Workbook, p. 19

Use with Pages 70–71.

Community Laws and Leaders

Circle the picture that goes with the sentence.

It is safe to cross.

Keep our park clean.

Walk your dog on a leash.

Directions: Read each sentence. Circle the picture that shows who is obeying the law.

Home Activity: Point out signs in your own community that tell people what they may and may not do.

Use with Pupil Edition, p. 71

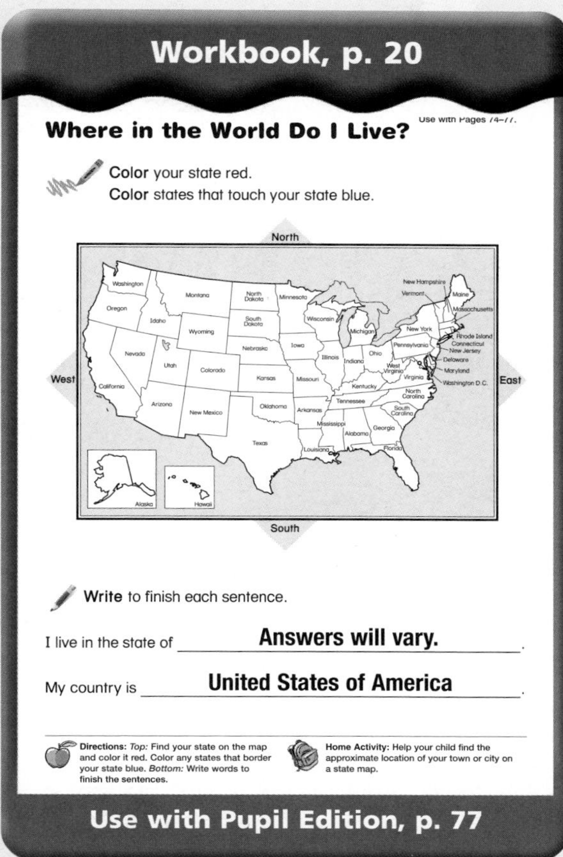

Workbook, p. 20

Use with Pages 74–77.

Where in the World Do I Live?

Color your state red.
Color states that touch your state blue.

Write to finish each sentence.

I live in the state of **Answers will vary.**

My country is **United States of America**.

Directions: *Top:* Find your state on the map and color it red. Color any states that border your state blue. *Bottom:* Write words to finish the sentences.

Home Activity: Help your child find the approximate location of your town or city on a state map.

Use with Pupil Edition, p. 77

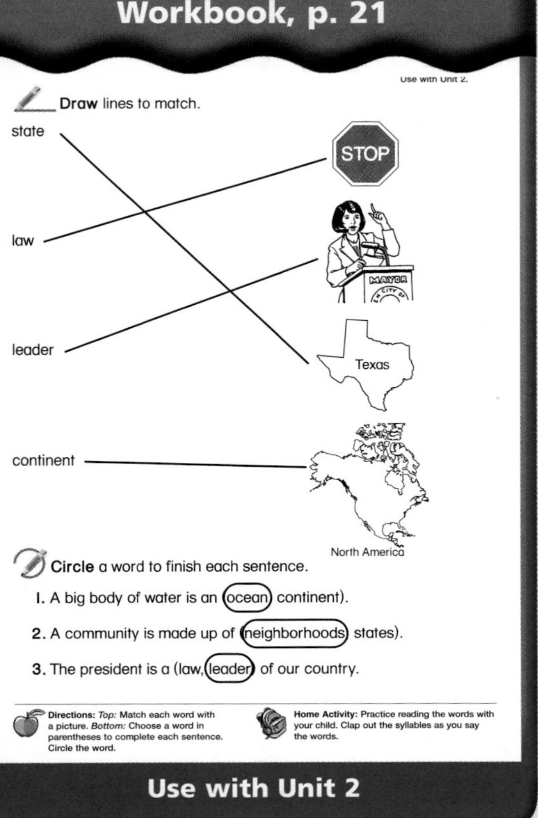

Workbook, p. 21

Use with Unit 2.

Draw lines to match.

state

law

leader

continent

Circle a word to finish each sentence.

1. A big body of water is an (ocean) continent).
2. A community is made up of (neighborhoods) states).
3. The president is a (law, (leader) of our country.

Directions: *Top:* Match each word with a picture. *Bottom:* Choose a word in parentheses to complete each sentence. Circle the word.

Home Activity: Practice reading the words with your child. Clap out the syllables as you say the words.

Use with Unit 2

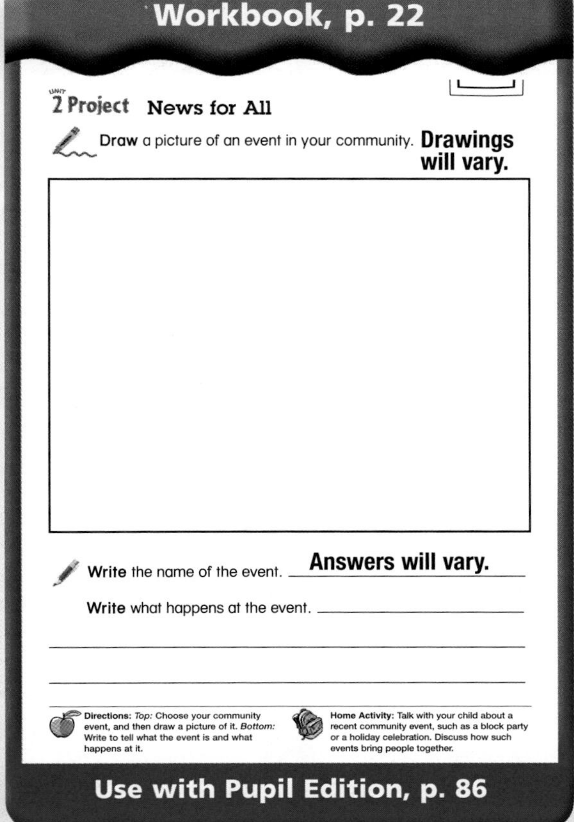

Workbook, p. 22

Unit 2 Project **News for All**

Draw a picture of an event in your community. **Drawings will vary.**

Write the name of the event. **Answers will vary.**

Write what happens at the event.

Directions: *Top:* Choose your community event, and then draw a picture of it. *Bottom:* Write to tell what the event is and what happens at it.

Home Activity: Talk with your child about a recent community event, such as a block party or a holiday celebration. Discuss how such events bring people together.

Use with Pupil Edition, p. 86

Assessment Support

Use the following Assessment Book pages and TestWorks to assess content and skills in Unit 2. You can also view and print Assessment Book pages from the Teacher Resources CD-ROM.

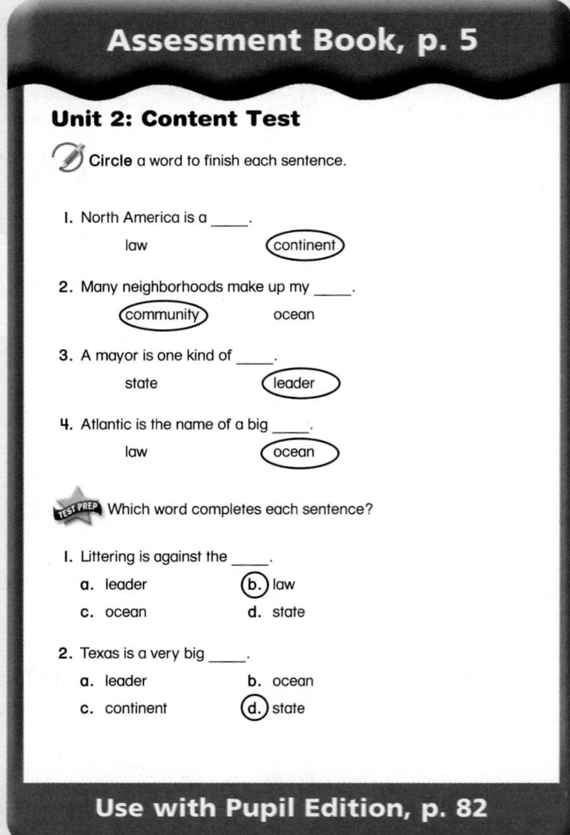

Assessment Book, p. 5

Unit 2: Content Test

Circle a word to finish each sentence.

1. North America is a ____.
   law — (continent)
2. Many neighborhoods make up my ____.
   (community) — ocean
3. A mayor is one kind of ____.
   state — (leader)
4. Atlantic is the name of a big ____.
   law — (ocean)

Which word completes each sentence?

1. Littering is against the ____.
   a. leader — (b.) law — c. ocean — d. state
2. Texas is a very big ____.
   a. leader — b. ocean — c. continent — (d.) state

Use with Pupil Edition, p. 82

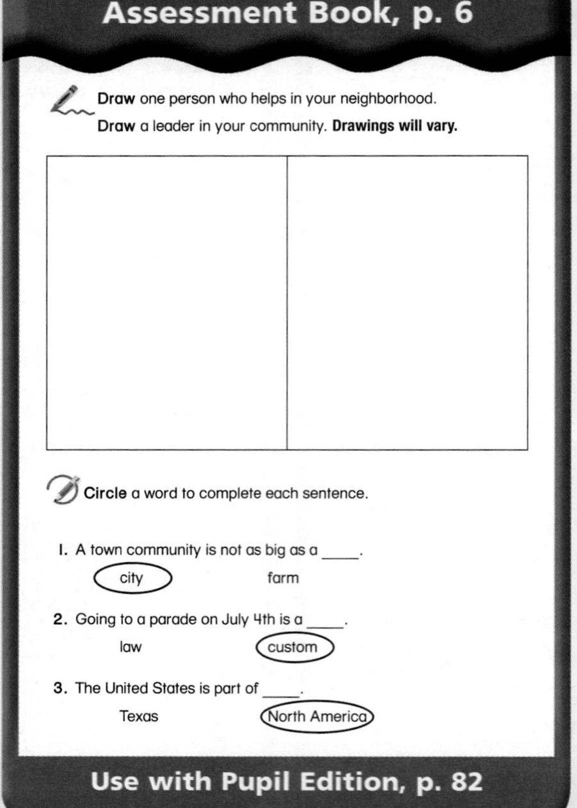

Assessment Book, p. 6

Draw one person who helps in your neighborhood.
Draw a leader in your community. **Drawings will vary.**

Circle a word to complete each sentence.

1. A town community is not as big as a ____.
   (city) — farm
2. Going to a parade on July 4th is a ____.
   law — (custom)
3. The United States is part of ____.
   Texas — (North America)

Use with Pupil Edition, p. 82

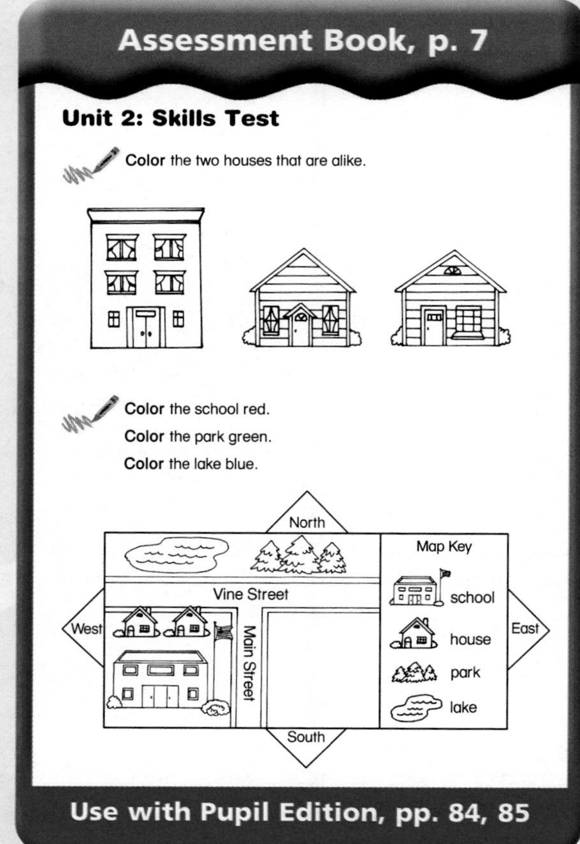

Assessment Book, p. 7

Unit 2: Skills Test

Color the two houses that are alike.

Color the school red.
Color the park green.
Color the lake blue.

Use with Pupil Edition, pp. 84, 85

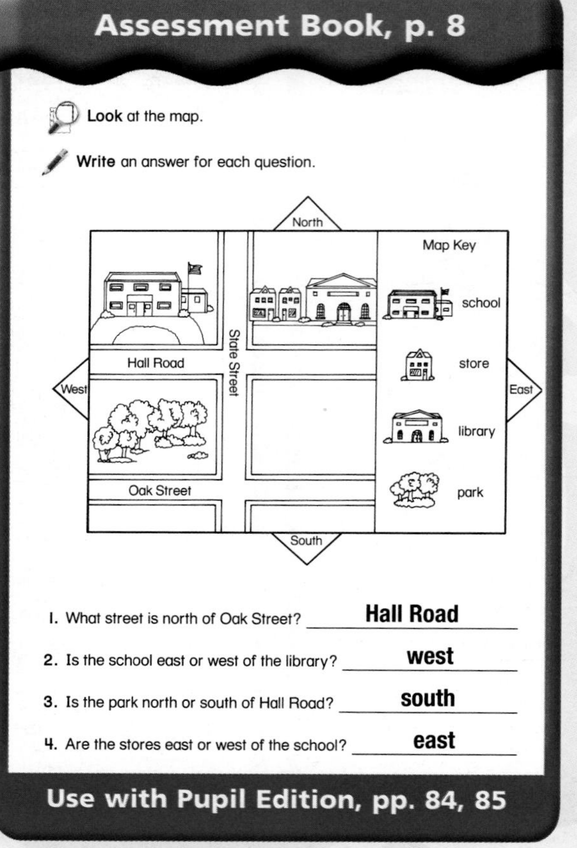

Assessment Book, p. 8

Look at the map.

Write an answer for each question.

1. What street is north of Oak Street? **Hall Road**
2. Is the school east or west of the library? **west**
3. Is the park north or south of Hall Road? **south**
4. Are the stores east or west of the school? **east**

Use with Pupil Edition, pp. 84, 85

Lesson 1 Overview

Welcome to My Neighborhood **pages 50-53**	Children will learn the meaning of the word *neighborhood*. They will explore features of a neighborhood and learn how to use a street address to locate places.	 Time 20–30 minutes Resources • Workbook, p. 14 • Vocabulary Card **neighborhood** • Every Student Learns Guide, pp. 18–21
Use a Map Key **pages 54–55**	Children will learn to use map keys, including those containing symbols.	Time 15–20 minutes Resource • Workbook, p. 15

Build Background

Activity

Welcome!

 **Time** 15–20 minutes

Have children draw pictures either of their homes or their schools. Give each child a strip of paper with the name of his/her street or the name of the school's street on it. Have children paste the labels onto the backs of their pictures.

As children share their work, have them tell the name of the street on which their homes or school is located. Children who live on the same street might line up to show their pictures—and neighborhoods.

If time is short, **ask children to tell the name of the street on which they live or on which the school is located. Write the street names on the board.**

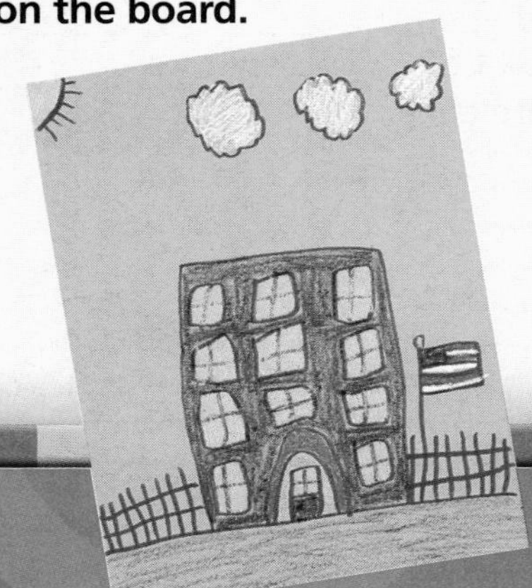

Read Aloud

Hi, Neighbor!

by Peri Jones

I live in a house
On a nice quiet street.
My neighbors say HI!
Whenever we meet.

They come to my home
And I go to theirs.
We sit and we talk—
Have done so for years.

Welcome to My Neighborhood

Objectives

- Identify buildings in relation to the school and neighborhood.
- Recognize that communities include people who have diverse ethnic origins, customs, and traditions and who make contributions to their communities.

Vocabulary

neighborhood a place where people live, work, and play (p. 52)

QUICK Teaching Plan

If time is short, have children look at the pictures and then tell:

- how their own neighborhoods are like Kim's and
- how their own neighborhoods are different from Kim's.

1 Introduce and Motivate

Preview Display the Vocabulary Card **neighborhood**. Pronounce the word, and spell it aloud for children. Share its meaning as "a place where people live, work, and play." Have children locate the term as they preview the lesson.

Warm Up To activate prior knowledge, ask children to tell briefly about some of their own neighbors. If necessary, point out that neighbors are the people who live nearby. Then have children tell how neighbors help each other.

Lesson

Welcome to My Neighborhood

My home has an address. An address can help you find a home or another building. An address has a number and a street name. My address is 9 Maple Street. 1

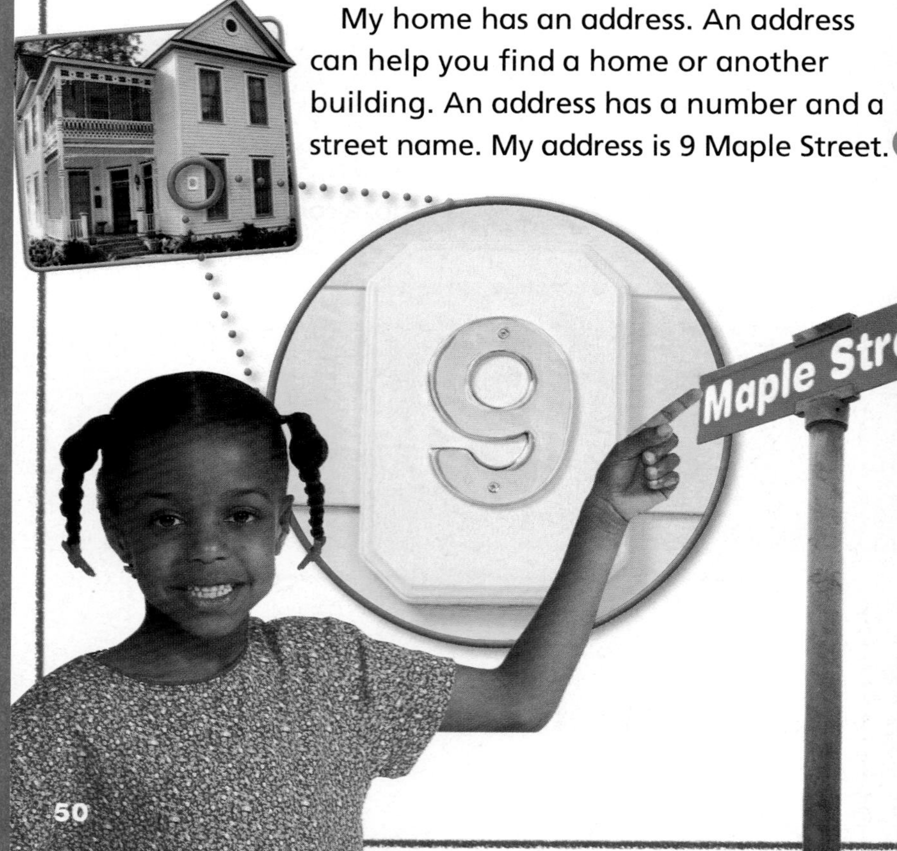

50

Practice and Extend

READING SKILL Alike and Different

Compare and Contrast Remind children that they can use the word *alike* to tell how things are the same and *different* to tell how things are not the same.

- After children finish p. 53, make a chart like the one shown below.
- Have children look at the two neighborhoods shown on p. 52. Guide them in finding ways in which the neighborhoods are alike and different.

Alike	Different

Look on the map. Find my home. Now find my school. What is the address of my school?

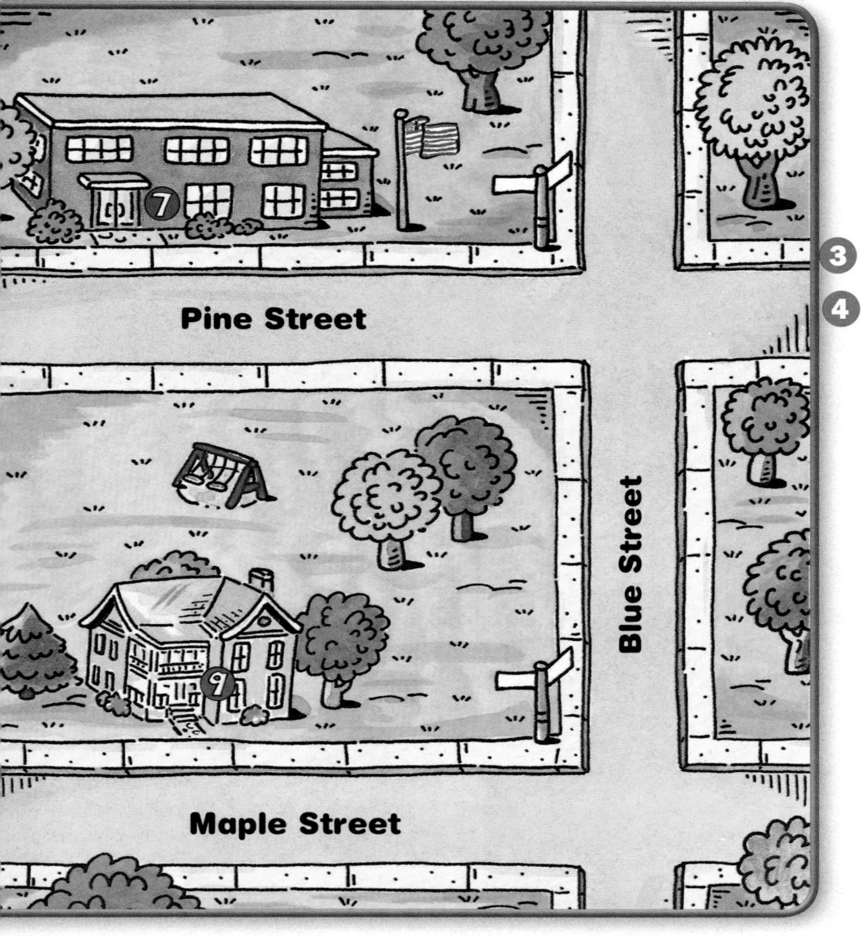

51

CURRICULUM CONNECTION
Art

Design a Street Sign

- Point out the street sign Kim is pointing to on p. 50.
- Ask children to make a street sign that tells the address of Kim's school.
- Provide strips cut from index cards. Have children write the street name on their strip.
- Give children pencils or dowels and tape. Show them how to tape their sign strip onto the pencil.

WEB SITE
Technology

You can look up vocabulary words online. Click on *Social Studies Library* and select the dictionary at **www.sfsocialstudies.com.**

2 Teach and Discuss

Page 50

Identify Kim in the photograph. Ask what Kim is doing.

1 **What is the name of Kim's street? What is the number of her house on Maple Street?** Maple Street; nine **Recall and Retell**

2 **Why do you think most addresses have a street name and a number?** Possible answer: So people can find the specific house they are looking for **Draw Conclusions**

Page 51

Point out the map of Kim's neighborhood. Help children find Kim's home and school.

Themes of Geography: Location

3 **Tell how Kim uses street names to find her home on the map.** She looks for Maple Street, which is the name of her street. **Interpret Maps**

4 **Find Kim's house on the map. Is the school near her house? Explain.** Yes, the school is on the next block. **Interpret Maps**

Lesson 1 continued

Page 52

Have children compare and contrast the two photographs on p. 52.

Test Talk

Locate Key Words in the Question

5 How is a big neighborhood different from a small neighborhood? Call attention to the key words *different from* in the question. Remind children that they need to tell how the two neighborhoods are *not* the same. Elicit that a big neighborhood has more buildings, more traffic, more people, and more noise.
Compare and Contrast

6 How are people in these neighborhoods alike? Possible answer: They are doing things in their communities; they are helping to make their communities nice places in which to live.
Compare and Contrast

7 How can people in a neighborhood help each other? Possible answer: Police officers help keep people safe. Shop owners sell the things people need. **Make Inferences**

My home and school are part of my neighborhood. A **neighborhood** is a place where people live, work, and play.

Neighborhoods can be big or small. They can be noisy or quiet. They can have many buildings or just a few buildings.

Tell how these neighborhoods are alike and different.

5 6 7

52

Practice and Extend

EXTEND LANGUAGE
ESL Support

Telling About Neighborhoods Use the neighborhood pictures in Lesson 2 to help children learn new words about things found in neighborhoods.

Beginning Point to such things as stores, schools and cars. Name items in the pictures as you point to them. Have children repeat the names.

Intermediate Help children name the various items in the neighborhood pictures. Ask if they have those same things in their neighborhoods. Encourage them to answer in sentences: *I have ___ in my neighborhood.*

Advanced After talking about the pictures, ask children to draw pictures of their own neighborhoods. Have them take turns telling each other about their neighborhoods.

For additional ESL support, use Every Student Learns Guide, pp. 18–21.

Meet some people who work in my neighborhood.

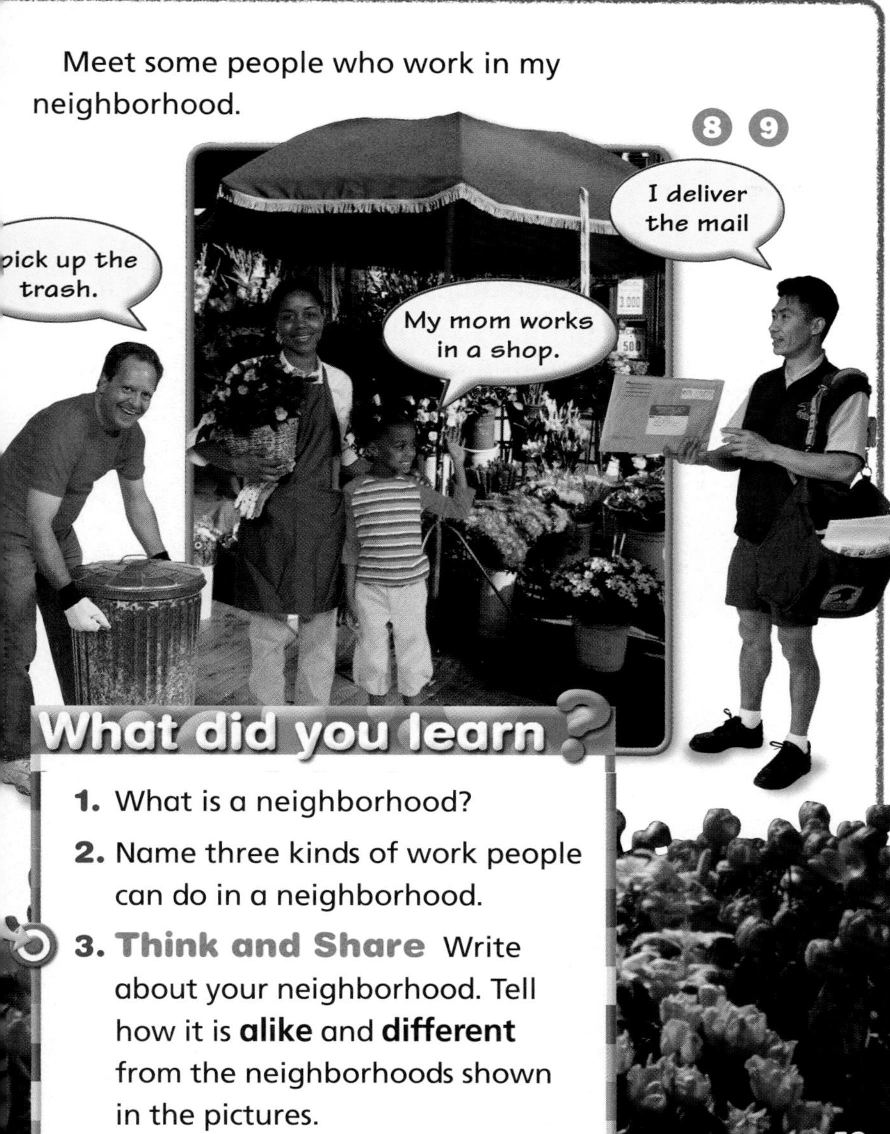

8 9
pick up the trash.
I deliver the mail
My mom works in a shop.

What did you learn?

1. What is a neighborhood?
2. Name three kinds of work people can do in a neighborhood.
3. **Think and Share** Write about your neighborhood. Tell how it is **alike** and **different** from the neighborhoods shown in the pictures.

53

FYI

SOCIAL STUDIES Background

About Addresses

- Write a mailing address on the board, including name, street address, city or town, state, and Zip Code. Point to each element as you name it.
- Mention that Zip Codes were added to help the post office sort letters. The numbers indicate the part of the country, the part of the state, and the part of the city or town.

Workbook, p. 14

Welcome to My Neighborhood

Cut out the boxes at the bottom.
Paste three of them where they belong.

I take away your trash.
I keep your neighborhood safe.
I bring your mail.

I help put out fires.
I keep your neighborhood safe.
I bring your mail.
I take away your trash.

Also on Teacher Resources CD-ROM.

Page 53

Point out Kim, the trash collector, and the mail carrier.

8 **How does the mail carrier help the people in Kim's neighborhood?** He brings them their mail. Make Inferences

9 **How does a mail carrier know where to take each letter?** He or she looks at the address on the envelope and takes the letter to that address. Make Inferences

3 Close and Assess

Have children describe their own school neighborhood. Tell them to include the school's address and to describe the buildings near the school. Ask where they live in relation to the school.

What did you learn?

1. It's a place where people live, work, and play.
2. Possible answers: Sell things in a store, collect trash, deliver mail

Test Talk

Write Your Answer
Ask children to reread their answers to make sure they are correct.

3. **Think and Share** Answers might include more buildings, more people, the same workers.

Use a Map Key

Objectives

- Create and use simple maps to identify the location of places in the classroom.
- Construct a map using basic map symbols.

Vocabulary

symbol a picture that stands for a real thing (p. 54)

map key a set of pictures and words that tell what the symbols on a map mean (p. 55)

1 Introduce and Motivate

Preview Write the vocabulary words on the board, and share the definitions with children. Then point to the map key on p. 55, and identify it for children. Tell children that a map key is sometimes called a map legend.

Warm Up To activate prior knowledge, remind children that a map is a drawing that shows what a place looks like from above. Then remind them of symbols they use in math, such as the plus sign and the equals sign. Then display two simple drawings: one of a can of soup and the other of a box of cereal. Tell children to imagine they are at a supermarket and these pictures are hung at the beginning of two different aisles. Ask: *Which sign would you look for if you wanted to buy soup? Which would you look for if you wanted to buy cereal?* Explain that the pictures are symbols because they stand for something else that is real.

Use a Map Key

Some maps use pictures to stand for real things. A picture that stands for a real thing is called a **symbol.** On this map, the stands for a tree.

54

Practice and Extend

Creating Symbols

- Have children take turns pointing to different areas of the classroom, such as learning centers, and describing each area.
- Point out any signs you have put up to name special areas. Help children read the signs. Then tell children you need their help in adding some picture symbols to show what the different areas are for.
- Assign each child a partner and an area. Ask the pair to design a picture symbol for it. If necessary, brainstorm ideas: a picture of a book for the classroom library, a pencil for the writing center, a paintbrush for the art center.
- Have partners work together to create pictorial symbols. Post these in the appropriate areas.

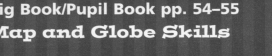

This is a map of the park near Kim's home. The map has a map key. A **map key** tells what the symbols (1) on the map mean.

Try it!

1. Why are symbols on a map important?
2. What is next to the [trash can] in the park?
3. **On Your Own** Draw a map and map key of your classroom. Show how you go from your desk to your teacher's desk.

55

SOCIAL STUDIES STRAND
Geography

- Have each child draw a map of the street on which he or she lives. Give children colored paper to cut out shapes for homes, shops, and other buildings on the street. Then ask children to put their cut-outs on the drawings in the place they think each belongs.
- Have children make a map key for their maps. Remind them to put both pictures and words in their map keys.

Workbook, p. 15

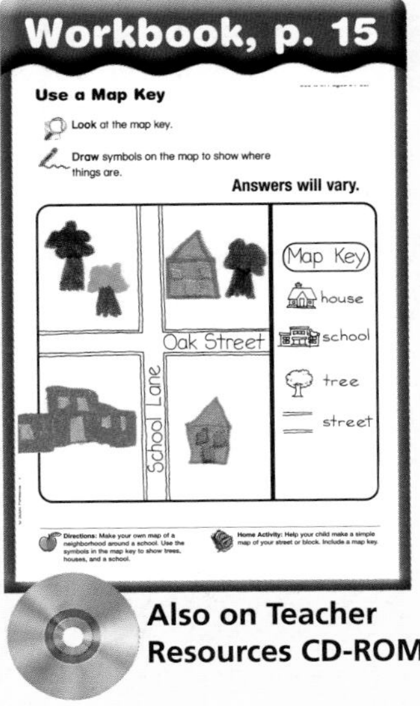

Use a Map Key
Look at the map key.
Draw symbols on the map to show where things are.
Answers will vary.
Map Key
house
school
tree
street
Oak Street
School Lane

Also on Teacher Resources CD-ROM.

2 Teach and Discuss

Pages 54-55

Read pp. 54–55 with children. Then have them point to the map key on p. 55. Tell them that a map key is also known as a map legend. Most maps have map keys, or legends, that include symbols that represent objects.

(1) **What is the purpose of a map key?** It tells what the symbols on a map mean. **Main Idea and Details**

(2) **What play equipment does this park have? How do you know?** It has a swingset. The map key shows the symbol for swingset. That same symbol appears on the map. **Interpret Maps**

3 Close and Assess

Try it!

1. They show where to find things and places.
2. The park bench
3. **On Your Own** Maps will vary but should include a map key and features of the classroom, such as children's desks, teacher's desk, board, and perhaps doors or windows. Maps should show the correct route to the teacher's desk

Use with pages 50–55

Lesson 1 Wrap-Up

MEETING INDIVIDUAL NEEDS

Leveled Practice

Comparing and Contrasting Neighborhoods

Have each child draw pictures of two familiar neighborhoods. Suggest that children choose from among these neighborhoods: their own, a friend's, the school, Kim's.

Easy Direct children to put their two pictures side by side for study. Each child can then tell one way in which the two neighborhoods are alike and one way in which they are different. **Reteach**

On-Level Have children add one street name and an address for one building in each of their pictures. Then have children tell classmates how the neighborhoods they have drawn are alike and different. **Extend**

Challenge Encourage children to write captions for their pictures. Each caption should define the neighborhood and tell some of its features. Children can then use their captions to tell how the neighborhoods are alike and different. **Enrich**

Hands-on Activities

CURRICULUM CONNECTION

Writing

Add to "My Word Book"

Objective Define and illustrate the words *neighborhood, symbol,* and *map key*.

Resources Vocabulary Cards **neighborhood, symbol, map key**

Materials crayons, pencils

Learning Style Visual

Individual

Time 20–25 minutes

1. Display the Vocabulary Card for *neighborhood*. Direct children to find the "N" page in their Word Books and have them write *neighborhood* in a word space.

2. Have children draw pictures to illustrate the word. Also encourage them to write a sentence using the word.

3. Follow a similar procedure for *symbol* and *map key*. Children may want to draw simple map keys to illustrate the latter.

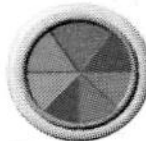

CURRICULUM CONNECTION

Drama

Plan a Street

Objective Create a make-believe neighborhood.

Materials classroom desks, paper, crayons or markers, tape, any classroom costume or role-play objects

Learning Style Kinesthetic/Verbal

Group

Time 15–30 minutes

1. Help children organize their desks into two rows with a path between.

2. Direct each child to develop one desk into a home. Have children use props or make signs to individualize their desk-homes. They might show its color or building material, or decorate its "front yard" with flowers, or use classroom props to show typical activities.

3. Invite children to take you on a tour of their "neighborhood."

SOCIAL STUDIES STRAND

Geography

Make a Map

Objective Make a map of a familiar area, using map symbols.

Materials large sheets of construction paper, pencils, crayons

Learning Style Visual/Kinesthetic

Group

Time 15–30 minutes

1. Visit the playground with children. Have them dictate a list of its features for you to record. Also have them make rough sketches of a map of the area.

2. Back in the classroom, guide children in making a map key that includes the important features of the playground. Display the key.

3. Have children make maps of the playground. Have them copy the key onto construction paper. Then have them draw a map, referring to their sketches and using items from the key to locate features.

Lesson 2 Overview

Different Kinds of Communities

pages 56–57

Children will learn the meaning of the word *community* and explore ways in which a community is different from a neighborhood.

Time 20 minutes

Resources

- Workbook, p. 16
- Vocabulary Card **community**
- Every Student Learns Guide, pp. 22–25

How a Community Changed

pages 58–59

Children will use pictures to learn how communities can change over time.

Time 15–20 minutes

Use Four Directions

pages 60–61

Children will learn the meanings of the four cardinal directions and practice using them to locate places on a map.

Time 15–20 minutes

Resource

- Workbook, p. 17

Build Background

Activity

Picture Places

Time 20–25 minutes

Provide children with magazines. Have them cut out pictures that show where people live or work. Encourage them to find a variety of such places—large and small, busy and quiet, near and far, from long ago or from today.

Ask children to sort pictures into "places we work" or "places we live." Have children mount the pictures on construction paper and save them for later use. (As children learn more about communities, they can put the pictures into groups and bind the pages to make books.)

If time is short, show children pictures of different communities and ask them to describe these places.

Read Aloud

Points of View

by Mara McDuff

I love the city!
It's big and it's bold.
But country is better—
Or so I am told.

I love the country.
It's quiet, it's green.
Best place in the world
That I've ever seen!

I love my town.
It's neat, it's clean.
Not city or country
But right in between.

Different Kinds of Communities

Objective

- Explain similarities and differences between life in city, town, and farm communities.

Vocabulary

community a group of people and the place where they live (p. 56)

QUICK Teaching Plan

If time is short, brainstorm with children ways in which communities can be alike yet different.

- Use the photographs on pp. 56–57 to help children identify features of a city, a town, and a farm community.

1 Introduce and Motivate

Preview Display the Vocabulary Card **community**, read the word, and ask children what they think it means. Then share the meaning of the word, pointing out that many neighborhoods together make up a community.

Warm Up To activate prior knowledge, ask children to name schoolmates NOT in your class. Elicit times and places that children see these schoolmates, such as on the bus or playground. Explain that your class is like a neighborhood—you see the people in it a lot—but that the whole school is like a community—you might see the people in it only sometimes.

2 Teach and Discuss

Page 56

Discuss with children the city community pictured on p. 56. Point out the things made by people: buildings, roads, and so on. Tell children that we call these things *human features*.

Lesson

Different Kinds of Communities

My neighborhood is part of a community. A **community** is a group of people and the place where they live. A community is bigger than a neighborhood. Many 1 different neighborhoods can be part of a community.

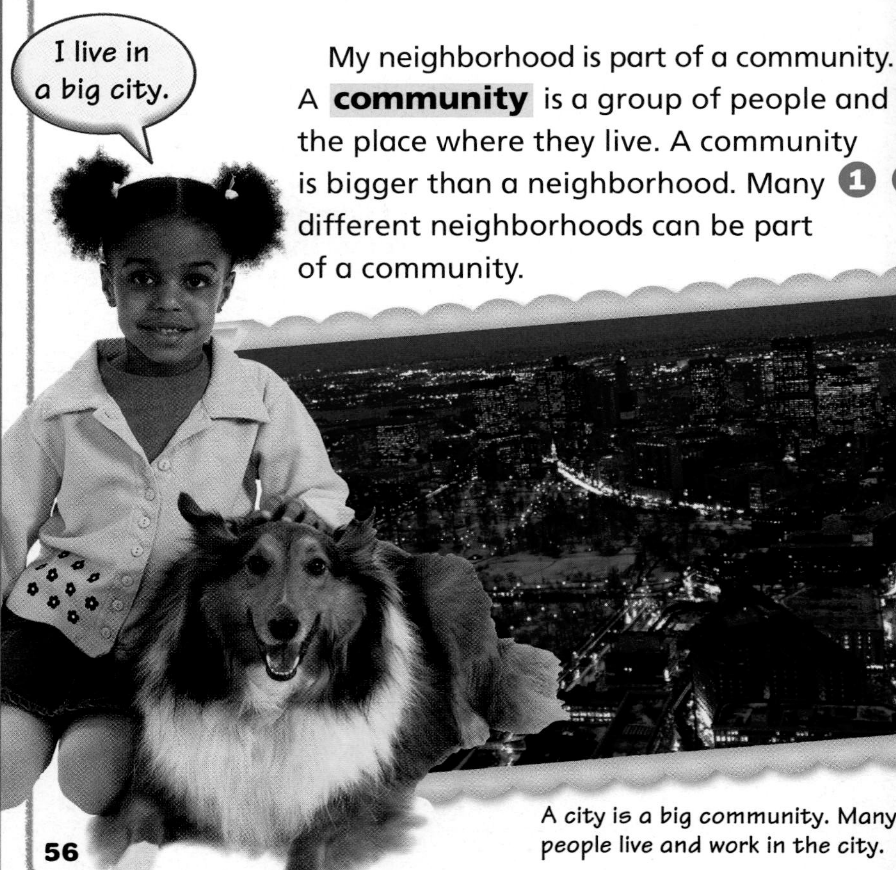

A city is a big community. Many people live and work in the city.

Practice and Extend

READING SKILL Alike and Different

Target Skill

Make Word Webs

- On the board, begin a word web:

- Have children identify details in the photo on p. 56. Ask them to suggest words to add under *city*.
- Follow a similar procedure for *town* and *farm*. Then have children use the completed web to compare and contrast the three communities.

WEB SITE Technology

You can look up vocabulary words online. Click on *Social Studies Library* and select the dictionary at **www.sfsocialstudies.com.**

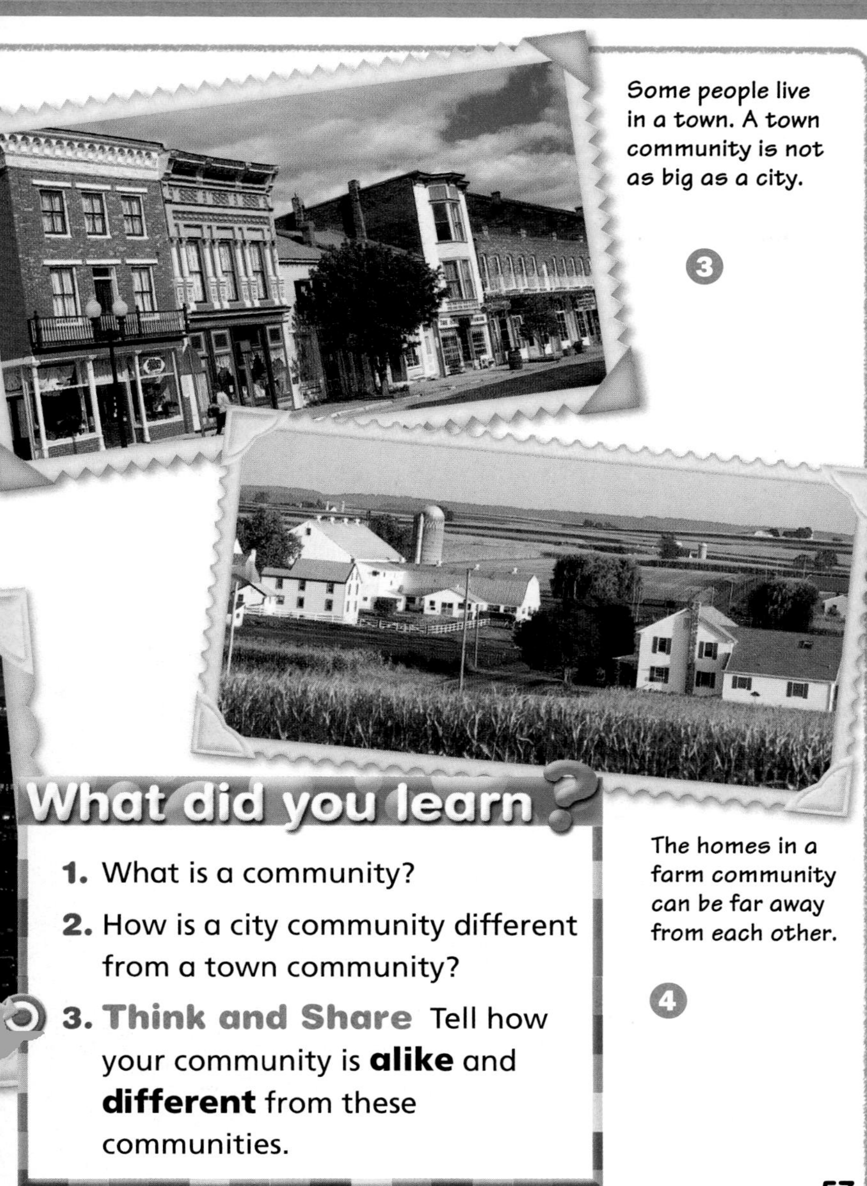

Some people live in a town. A town community is not as big as a city.

3

The homes in a farm community can be far away from each other.

4

What did you learn?

1. What is a community?
2. How is a city community different from a town community?
3. **Think and Share** Tell how your community is **alike** and **different** from these communities.

57

CURRICULUM CONNECTION
Literature

Read *My New York*

- Use *My New York,* by Kathy Jakobsen (Little Brown, 1993; ISBN 0-316-45653-5), to explore different neighborhoods found in a big city.
- Contrast the last scene, which shows a farm community, with the city community.
- Note that the World Trade Center appears on the fly-leaf map and in two pictures. You may want to talk about the tragic events of September 11, 2001, with children. See also pages TR1–TR2.

Workbook, p. 16

Different Kinds of Communities
Write city, town, or farm.
Color the picture that shows a community like yours.
Answers will vary.
farm
city
town

Also on Teacher Resources CD-ROM.

1 **How is a community different from a neighborhood?** It is bigger. It has several neighborhoods. Compare and Contrast

2 **Look at the photo on p. 56. How would you describe a city community?** Possible answer: It's big and busy; there are many people and tall buildings. Analyze Pictures

Page 57

3 **How is a town like a city?** Both communities have people, homes, shops and other buildings. Compare and Contrast

4 **How is a town different from a farm community?** The homes and buildings are closer together in a town. Compare and Contrast

SOCIAL STUDIES STRAND
Technology

Today, technology helps people from different communities stay in touch. For example, people can communicate by telephone or by e-mail. They can learn about people in other places through radio, television, and the Internet. Talk about how these advances in technology have changed the way people communicate and do business.

3 Close and Assess

Begin a three-column chart of kinds of communities: city, town, farm. Ask children to suggest words for you to write in each column.

✓ What did you learn?

1. A community is a group of people and the place where they live. It contains several neighborhoods.
2. A city community is bigger. It has more people and more buildings.
3. **Think and Share** Children should identify at least one similarity and one difference.

How a Community Changed

Objective

- Distinguish among past, present, and future and identify changes in the community.

1 Introduce and Motivate

Preview Tell children that most things—including communities— don't stay the same forever; they *change*. *Change* means to make or become different. Ask children how they have changed since they were babies.

Warm Up To activate prior knowledge, write *past, present,* and *future* as column headings. Display pictures of a log cabin, a modern apartment house, and a space station. Use the words *past, present,* and *future* as you talk about the pictures with children.

2 Teach and Discuss

Page 58

Review ways to get clues from pictures, and then ask children to study the photograph on p. 58. Be sure they understand that it shows the past.

1 What did Kim's community look like in the past? Possible answers: Buildings were not very tall; people rode horses or used horse-drawn carts.
Analyze Pictures

SOCIAL STUDIES STRAND
History

Tell children that all communities change over time. Show children past and present pictures of your own community. (Copies can often be obtained from a local historical society or library.) After talking about the pictures and the changes they show, help children put the pictures in an order that shows changes over time.

How a Community Changed

This picture shows what Kim's community looked like in the past. Her community has changed since then.

58

Practice and Extend

ESL SUPPORT
Extend Language

Work with New Words Review the meaning of *past, present, and future*. Have children write each word on a card and then a word in their home language to remind them of the English meaning. Display pictures showing past, present, and future communities.

Beginning Have children match a card to each picture. Say something about each picture, using phrases such as *in the past, long ago; today, now;* and *in the future.*

Intermediate Follow the procedure for Beginning, but have children use the terms *past, present,* and *future* to tell something about each picture.

Advanced Have children sort the pictures according to whether they show a community from the past, the present, or the future. Have children label the group of pictures and then share their ideas about them.

This is Kim's community today. More people live and work in her community now. The community has more homes and stores. Look how it has changed. 

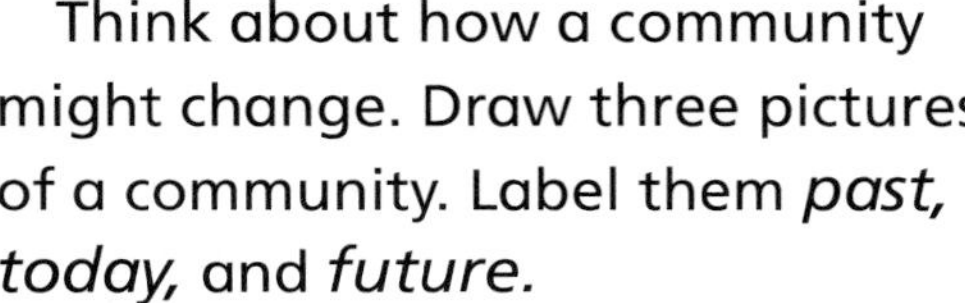

Hands-on History

Think about how a community might change. Draw three pictures of a community. Label them *past, today,* and *future.*

59

CURRICULUM CONNECTION

Literature

Smoky Night

- To help children deal with disasters that may change a community, read aloud the 1995 Caldecott Medal winner *Smoky Night* by Eve Bunting (Harcourt, ISBN 0-15-269954-6, 1994). In the story, Daniel and his mother witness a riot, after which their apartment building catches fire.
- After reading, discuss what Daniel learned about the importance of getting along with others regardless of race or background. Ask children to comment on Daniel's suggestion that the cats belonging to him and to Mrs. Kim were enemies only because they didn't know each other well enough. Invite predictions about how the story characters will treat each other in the future.
- For activities to help children deal with fear and loss, see pp. TR1–TR2.

Page 59

Have volunteers describe the people and buildings in the photograph of modern-day Houston.

2 **How has Kim's community changed since the past? Look at the pictures for clues.** Possible answers: More people live and work there. There are many tall buildings now. **Compare and Contrast**

3 **Why do you think there are more shops in Kim's community now than long ago?** Possible answer: More people live there now and need to buy things. **Make Inferences**

4 **What is one way that change might hurt a community?** Answers might relate to crowding or pollution. **Predict**

Themes of Geography: Places and People Change Each Other

5 **What has changed in your community?** Possible answer: More people have moved in, and more houses have been built; new stores have opened; there is more traffic and less open space. **Apply Information**

3 Close and Assess

Hands-on History

Review the meaning of the words *past, present,* and *future*. After children draw their pictures, have them cut the pictures apart. They can then exchange sets of pictures with partners. Tell partners to put the pictures in an order that shows first (yesterday or past), next (today or present), and last (tomorrow or future).

Use Four Directions

Objective

- Locate places using the four cardinal directions.

Vocabulary

directions things on a map that tell which way to go (p. 60)

1 Introduce and Motivate

Preview Write the vocabulary word on the board, and read the word for children. Explain that on a map, directions tell which way to go: north, south, east, or west. Point out where north is in your classroom. Post a sign saying *north* on this wall (or in this area). Do the same for south, east, and west.

Warm Up To activate prior knowledge, have children identify the *north, south, east,* and *west* signs in your classroom. Ask a volunteer to walk toward the north sign. Explain that he or she is moving north. Repeat with other volunteers and directions. Then add the abbreviations *N, S, E,* and *W* to the signs. Tell children that we sometimes use just the letters to stand for the directions.

2 Teach and Discuss

Page 60

Have children look at the map and find the labels *North, South, East,* and *West.*

1 **Which direction is at the top of the map?** North **Where is south?** At the bottom; opposite north Interpret Maps

2 **Looking at the map, which direction is opposite east?** West Interpret Maps

3 **Is the post office east or west of Pine Street?** West Interpret Maps

Map and Globe Skills

Use Four Directions

Kim uses the directions on a map to find places in her community. **Directions** tell her which way to go. North, south, east, and west are the four main directions.

1 2 3 4

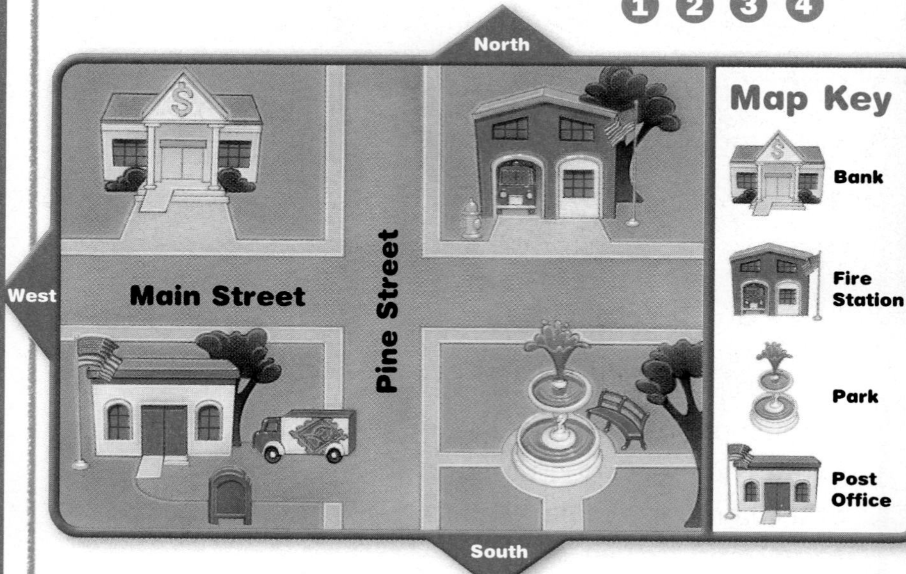

60

Practice and Extend

CURRICULUM CONNECTION
Science

Draw to Show Weather Changes

- Point out the United States on a map. Be sure the map has directional arrows. Explain that in the United States, the weather usually gets colder the farther north you travel.
- Point to Houston on the map. Mention that in January, the temperature here is usually around 50°F, so people need to wear sweaters or light jackets. Point to Chicago. Explain that this city is farther north. Since the January temperature is usually around 20°F, people need to wear much warmer clothing.
- Tell children to imagine that the north end of your classroom is colder than the south end. Have them draw pictures to show how people might dress in the north end or the south end of your room. Post the pictures in the appropriate parts of the room.

Put your finger on Pine Street. Move your finger toward the arrow that points south. You are moving south. Now move your finger toward the arrow that points north. Which direction are you moving? When you move north, east is on your right. What direction is on your left?

Try it!

1. Is the park north or south of Main Street?
2. Find the fire station. What direction would you go to get to the bank?
3. **On Your Own** Stand by your desk. Face north. Tell where things are in your classroom and school. Use the words *north, south, east,* and *west.*

BUILD BACKGROUND
ESL Support

Locating Places Hide several objects. Tell children that you will give directions for finding the objects.

Beginning Give children explicit clues, such as: *It is under the reading table*. Have children try to find the objects.

Intermediate Describe where you have hidden one object. Have children take turns trying to identify the place.

Advanced Use directional words to provide clues, for example: *It is two steps north of my desk.*

Workbook, p. 17

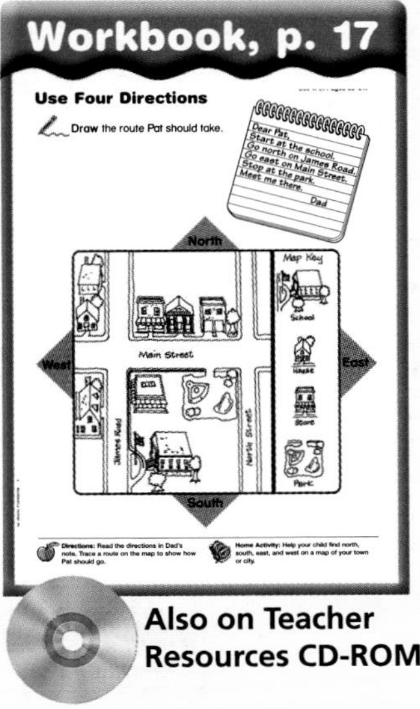

Also on Teacher Resources CD-ROM.

SOCIAL STUDIES STRAND
Geography

Show children a globe. Explain that a globe stands for the Earth. Point out that on a globe, north is at the top and south is at the bottom. Point out the poles, and explain that people reach the poles when they travel as far they can to the north or to the south. Point out the equator. Tell children the equator is an imaginary circle around the middle of the Earth, halfway between the North Pole and South Pole. Have children take turns putting their fingers on the equator and then moving north or south as you give directions.

Page 61

4 In which directions does Main Street go?
East and west **Interpret Maps**

Ongoing Assessment

If... children cannot correctly identify directions on the map, **then...** reconstruct the map in the classroom by labeling desks as the buildings. Orient the three-dimensional model of the map to your posted direction markings. Then have children walk the routes discussed in the lesson questions.

3 Close and Assess

Try it!

1. South
2. West
3. **On Your Own** Children should use the words *north, south, east,* and *west* as they describe where things are in the classroom. As you discuss children's answers with them, be sure to use cardinal directions when referring to places outside the classroom.

Use with pages 56–61

Lesson 2 Wrap-Up

MEETING INDIVIDUAL NEEDS Leveled Practice

Compare and Contrast Community Pictures

Provide children with a selection of picture books that shows different communities. Have them browse through the books.

Easy Present two pictures to children and ask questions such as: *Which of these communities is bigger? Which is a farm community? Which community is more like your community?* **Reteach**

On-Level Remind children of what they learned about their own community during the lesson. Then, as you show them pictures from the books, ask them to tell how each community is similar to and different from their own community. **Extend**

Challenge Have children find pictures in the books that show communities from the past. Challenge them to put a few books in order, according to whether their pictures show past, present, or future. **Enrich**

Hands-on Activities

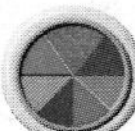

CURRICULUM CONNECTION

Literature

City, Country

Objective Compare and contrast two communities.

Materials *City Mouse—Country Mouse* and *Two More Mouse Tales from Aesop* by John C. Wallner (illustrator) crayons, drawing paper

Learning Style Auditory/Kinesthetic

Partners

Time 20–25 minutes

1. Share the illustrations as you read. Talk about how the artist depicts the two communities.

2. Have partners draw the story settings. One child can draw the city scenes; the other, the country.

3. Have partners present their work and tell how the two communities are alike and different.

4. Remind children to add the words *community* and *directions* to their Word Books.

CURRICULUM CONNECTION

Math

Simon Says

Objective Use cardinal directions to locate places in the classroom.

Learning Style Auditory/Kinesthetic

Partners

Time 10–15 minutes

1. Review the cardinal directions posted in the classroom. Then position pairs of children randomly in the room. Have partners choose who will play the part of Simon first.

2. Explain that Simon's role is to give his/her partner a series of directions to get to another part of the classroom. Tell children that they must include a number (for steps) and a direction word. Remind them how Simon speaks: "Simon says: Go 3 steps north."

3. Have partners change roles.

CURRICULUM CONNECTION

Science

Where's North?

Objective Observe how a compass helps one find cardinal directions.

Materials a compass

Learning Style Visual

Group

Time 20–25 minutes

1. Display a compass. Allow children to experiment with it. Have them note that the needle points north.

2. Take children outdoors. Have them use the compass to find north. Then help them locate south, east, and west.

3. Change your position several times, and have children take turns using the compass to find north. Ask them to explain how to find south—with or without the compass.

Lesson 3 Overview

Special Things We Do **pages 62–65**	Children will learn about the special customs that people from different cultures share.	Time 20–30 minutes Resources • Workbook, p. 18 • Every Student Learns Guide, pp. 26–29
Chinese New Year **pages 66–67**	Children will learn how to use visual sources, such as pictures, to gather information about the custom of Chinese New Year.	Time 15–20 minutes
Learning About Each Other **pages 68–69**	Children will learn about a group of young people who teach their customs to others.	Time 15–20 minutes

Build Background

Activity

Celebrate a Custom

Time 20–25 minutes

Beforehand, cut a large star from cardboard and cover it with gold foil paper.

Tell children that you have a custom you'd like to share with them. Explain that every time there is perfect attendance in your class, you like to celebrate by hanging the star on your door. Show children the star. Brainstorm ideas for another way to celebrate perfect attendance.

List children's ideas on the board, and have children vote to choose just one.

The next time you do have perfect attendance, remind children of the custom—and proceed to celebrate.

If time is short, have children tell about ways they like to celebrate special days or events.

Read Aloud

Flag Song

Our flag shines bright and true,
Waving red, white, and blue,
Looking so grand.

Protecting all who come,
Welcoming everyone,
To our homeland.

Lesson 3

Special Things We Do

Objectives

- Describe various customs and traditions and explain their importance.
- Obtain information about a topic using a variety of oral sources, such as conversations.
- Describe selected customs.

QUICK Teaching Plan

If time is short, guide children in making a list of customs they already know.

- Then refer children to the pictures in the lesson for ideas about some common customs associated with special days.

1 Introduce and Motivate

Preview Tell children that a custom is an old or popular way of doing things. Give an example, such as having a cake on one's birthday. Explain that customs are part of tradition. Tradition is the combination of beliefs and customs we get from our family, religion, or culture. Tell children that some traditions can help make families closer. Some traditions help us remember our heritage. Traditions and celebrations are important because they help us celebrate who we are.

Warm Up To activate prior knowledge, ask what children do with their families on holidays or on special days, such as birthdays. Invite children to share information about favorite foods, decorations, or activiities. Ask them why they think everyone enjoys special occasions. Encourage children to ask questions about any customs mentioned that are unfamiliar to them.

Lesson 3

Special Things We Do

People in my community share different customs. A custom is the way people usually do something. My scrapbook has pictures of special customs we have.

We have a picnic on Independence Day. It is our country's birthday.

1 2 3

We give a basket of fruit to new neighbors. Welcome to our neighborhood!

62

Practice and Extend

READING SKILL Alike and Different

Target Skill

Common Customs

- Help children compare and contrast the customs pictured on pp. 62–63. Ask which pictures show something Kim does only once a year. Ask which picture shows something Kim and her family may do whenever a new family moves into the neighborhood.
- Ask children if they have any of these same customs. Chart their responses, as follows:

	Independence Day	Mother's Day	To welcome neighbors
Kim			
Us			

- Follow a similar procedure to compare and contrast the customs pictured on pp. 64–65.

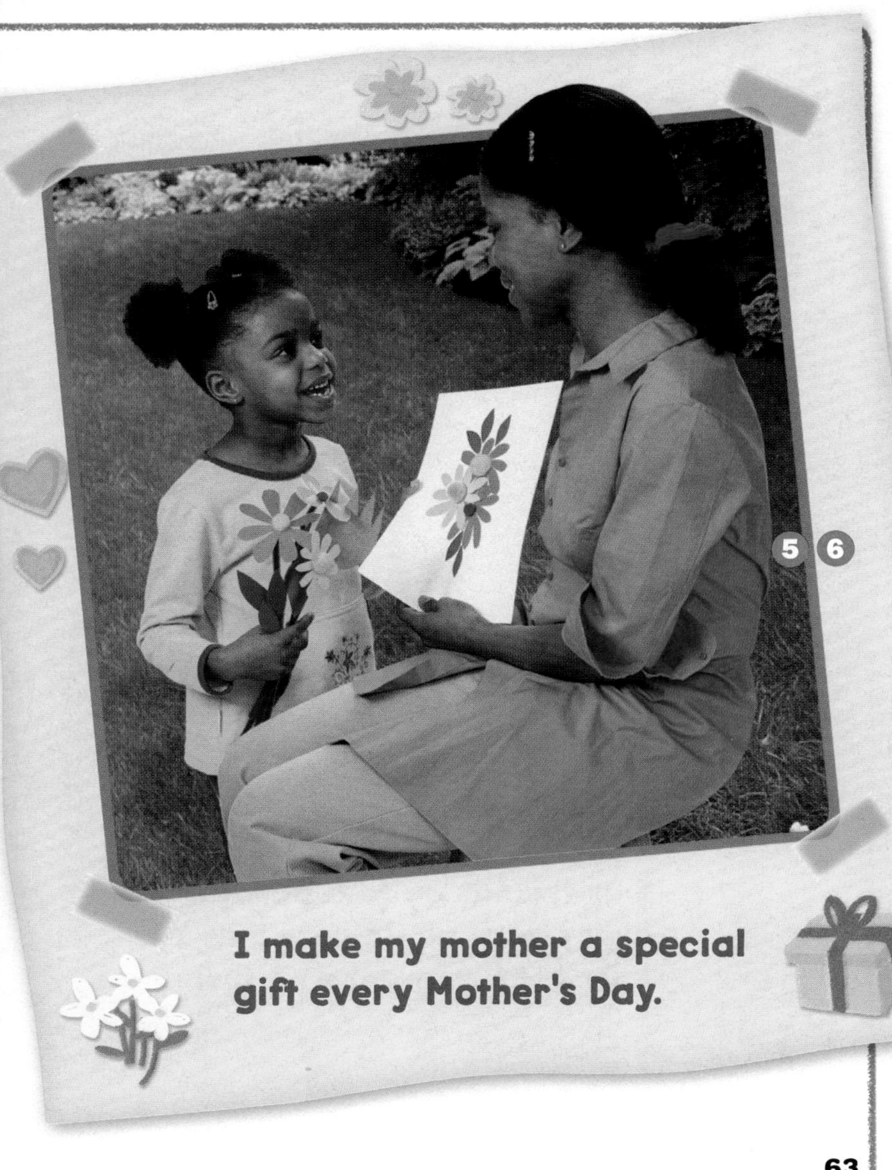

I make my mother a special gift every Mother's Day.

63

SOCIAL STUDIES
Background

About Mother's Day

- In 1872, Julia Ward Howe (who wrote the words to *Battle Hymn of the Republic*) suggested the idea of Mother's Day, which she saw as a day dedicated to peace.
- In 1907, Ana Jarvis began a campaign to establish a national Mother's Day. By 1911, Mother's Day was celebrated in almost every state.
- In 1914, President Woodrow Wilson made Mother's Day a national holiday.
- Mother's Day in the United States falls on the second Sunday in May.
- Wearing a carnation is a tradition associated with Mother's Day.

2 Teach and Discuss

Page 62

After reading p. 62, point out that many of the pictures in this lesson show pages from Kim's scrapbook.

1 **Why is Kim wearing red, white, and blue to celebrate Independence Day?** Possible answer: She is wearing the colors of our country's flag; those colors are symbols of our country. **Make Inferences**

2 **What does Kim do on Independence Day?** Go on a picnic **Main Idea and Details**

3 **How do you celebrate Independence Day?** Possible answers: Go to a parade; have a picnic; watch fireworks **Apply Information**

4 **What does Kim's family do when new neighbors move in? Why?** Give them a basket of fruit to welcome them **Cause and Effect**

Page 63

5 **How does Kim celebrate Mother's Day?** She gives her mother a card and some flowers. **Analyze Pictures**

6 **In some countries, people celebrate Children's Day. Would you like such a day? What would you do?** Most children will probably agree that Children's Day is a great idea; accept all reasonable responses to the second part of the question. **Express Ideas**

continued

Page 64

Discuss what Kim's scrapbook picture on p. 64 shows. Emphasize that people can share in the customs of their friends.

7 **How do Kim's friends celebrate Chinese New Year?** They go to a parade. **Recall and Retell**

8 **How else do people celebrate the beginning of a new year?** Possible answers: They go to First Night celebrations; they watch parades and football on TV on New Year's Day. **Apply Information**

SOCIAL STUDIES STRAND
Culture

Point out that families in a community can have different beliefs, traditions, and customs that come from their religious beliefs, their ethnicity, or their cultures. Have volunteers share examples of such customs, beliefs, or traditions (such as Kwanzaa, Hanukkah, Lent, and Christmas) and explain their importance. Discuss ways in which customs may be alike—even if they come from different cultures.

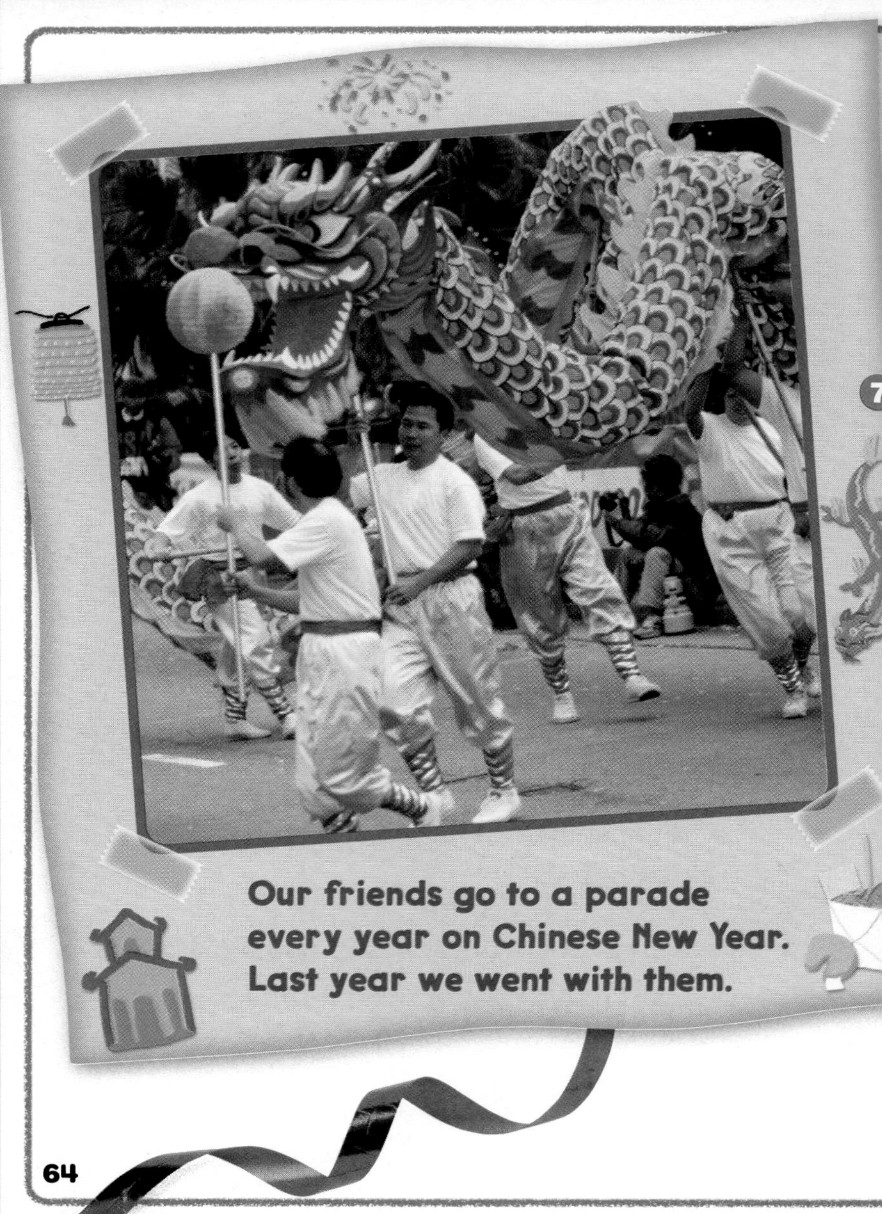

Our friends go to a parade
every year on Chinese New Year.
Last year we went with them.
64

Practice and Extend

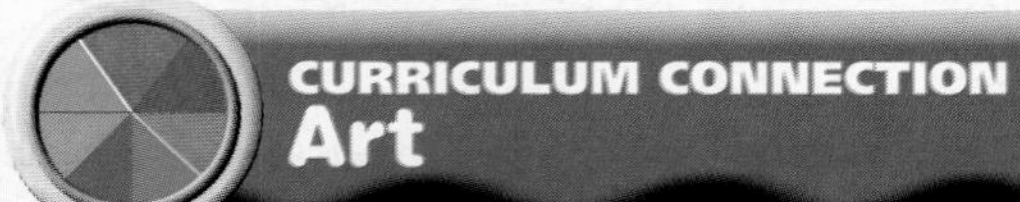

CURRICULUM CONNECTION
Art

Make a "Customs" Calendar

- Give each child a blank calendar for the current month. Remind them of what they learned about calendars in Unit 1. Have them number the days of the month.
- Brainstorm a list of special days for the month. Include events celebrated by the class, by children's families, and by the community—as well as state and national holidays. Have children share their knowledge of the holidays or customs identified.
- Read about a few unfamiliar holidays for the currrent month from a children's encyclopedia.
- Distribute self-stick notes. Have children draw pictures to show the holidays you've learned about. Stick them onto the calendar grid.

BUILD BACKGROUND
ESL Support

Using Pictures Provide several pictures that show typical American holidays and the customs associated with them.

Beginning Ask children to name holidays in their home language. When possible, link these holidays to American holidays by pointing to any appropriate pictures.

Intermediate Have children look at the pictures and point out customs with which they are familiar. Encourage them to ask questions about customs they don't recognize. Provide answers, or have others in the class do so.

Advanced Follow a procedure similar to that suggested for Intermediate. Then give children a calendar showing pictorial representations of common holidays. Talk about when each holiday occurs—and about any that may be coming up.

For additional ESL Support, use Every Student Learns Guide, pp. 26–29.

My mom and I read a book each night before bedtime. This is our special time together!
9

What did you learn?

1. What special times does your family share?
2. Why do we celebrate Independence Day?
3. **Think and Share** Draw a picture of one way to celebrate a special day. Tell what is happening in your picture.

65

Also on Teacher Resources CD-ROM.

Page 65

Explain that customs can be any special activities that people do again and again.

9 **Is the time Kim spends with her mom each night a custom? Tell why.** Possible answer: Yes, it is a custom because they spend this time together every night, doing the same thing.
Main Idea and Details

3 Close and Assess

Have children work with partners to brainstorm a special custom the class could begin. Tell each pair to agree on one suggestion. Then have each child draw a picture and write a sentence about the idea.

✓ What did you learn?

1. Answers will vary but may include birthday celebrations, religious or cultural traditions, and/or any activities family members do together on a regular basis.
2. It is the birthday of the United States.
3. **Think and Share** Children should identify the special days celebrated in their pictures; they should also tell what they do on those days, and why the days are important to them.

Chinese New Year

Objectives

- Describe community celebrations.
- Describe various customs of families.
- Obtain information about a topic using a variety of visual sources, such as pictures.

1 Introduce and Motivate

Preview Discuss with children the fact that many communities in their state include people of different ethnic origins. Many of these people come from different places around the world. Remind children of the picture of Chinese New Year in Kim's scrapbook (p. 64). Then read the title of this lesson, and have children look at the pictures on pp. 66-67. Ask if they would like to take part in a Chinese New Year celebration.

Warm Up To activate prior knowledge, ask children to tell about any New Year celebrations they have taken part in.

Read the introduction with children. Ask if they agree with Man Po that Chinese New Year is a colorful celebration. Ask what they think makes it so colorful.

2 Teach and Discuss

Have children point to the photos as you read the captions. Allow time for them to respond to the pictures.

1 Find the message that Man Po has written. How is Chinese writing different from writing in English? Chinese writing uses characters that look like little pictures; English writing uses letters of the alphabet. **Compare and Contrast**

2 What will Man Po find in the envelope to help her get rich? She'll find money in it. **Draw Conclusions**

CELEBRATIONS

Chinese New Year

Man Po is nine years old and lives in China. She likes Chinese New Year. It is one of the world's most colorful celebrations.

Thousands of people watch the floats in the New Year parade.

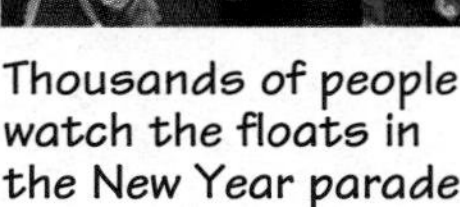

Tangerines with leaves are the lucky fruits of the New Year.

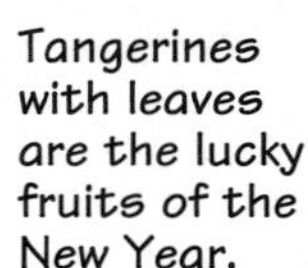

The Chinese believe that peach blossoms are lucky.

This float is shaped like an ox.

A kumquat tree is thought to bring luck for the new year.

66

Practice and Extend

FYI SOCIAL STUDIES Background

About Chinese New Year

- The Chinese calendar year begins sometime between the end of January and the middle of February.
- Each year of the calendar gets an animal name, chosen from a series of 12 animals. For example, the year 2002: the year of the horse; the year 2003: the year of the sheep.
- Chinese New Year celebrations last for about three days. To get ready for the new year, families give their homes a thorough cleaning. They may paint their doors and windows a bright red.

“My outfit is made of silk. It is very beautiful.”
1
恭喜發財
“I have written words in Chinese that wish a person riches.”
2 On New Years morning, Chinese children get money in red envelopes.
4 One of Man Po’s favorite foods is Law Pak Ko, a cake with shrimps.
Law Pak Ko
3 Red is the main color for clothes and decorations at New Year. It is a color of happiness.
67

SOCIAL STUDIES STRAND Culture

Chinese New Year Celebration

- Explain that Chinese New Year marks the beginning of a new year and is also a religious holiday
- Suggest that the class plan its own Chinese New Year celebration.
- Provide additional details about the holiday, such as its being about cleaning your house for good luck in the new year.
- Plan how to decorate the classroom. Have children make masks from paper bags.
- Invite children to put on their masks and have a parade.

Test Talk

Use Information from the Text

3 Why does Man Po wear red on Chinese New Year? Red is a color of happiness; it’s a color that many Chinese people wear on this day. Ask children to listen as you reread the question. Ask if they have given the right information from the text.
Make Inferences

4 What is one food that people enjoy on Chinese New year? A cake with shrimps
Analyze Pictures

3 Close and Assess

- Ask children what part of the Chinese New Year celebration they would enjoy most. Encourage them to give reasons for their choices.
- Tell children that Man Po has written *Kung Hei Fat Choy* in Chinese. Have them practice saying it with you in Chinese. (/kŭng hā făt choi/) Ask what else people say to wish others a happy new year.

CITIZEN HEROES

Learning About Each Other

Objective

- Identify characteristics of good citizenship, such as a belief in equality.

1 Introduce and Motivate

Preview Using a globe, point out the Pacific Ocean. Then locate China for children, as well as a few other Asian Pacific countries. Then have children look at the photos on pp. 68–69. Explain that the people in the pictures are Asian Pacific Americans.

Warm Up To activate prior knowledge, remind children of Kim's visit to the Chinese New Year parade. Ask why people who have come to the United States from other countries would want to keep their old customs. Why would they want to share them with others?

Introduce Vira, who founded CAPAY. Explain that CAPAY stands for Coalition for Asian Pacific American Youth—and that this is a group to which many Asian Pacific Americans belong.

2 Teach and Discuss

1 Why did Vira start CAPAY? She wanted to teach people in her community about being Asian Pacific; she wanted people to treat Asian Pacific Americans fairly. **Recall and Retell**

2 What do you think "to be treated fairly" means? Possible answer: The rules are the same for everyone; what goes for one, goes for everyone. **Generalize**

3 Do you agree with Vira that all people should be treated fairly? Why? Most children will agree; at this age, most have strong feelings about fairness. **Point of View**

CITIZEN HEROES

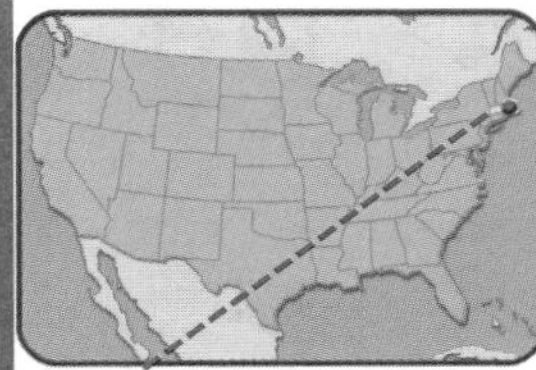

CAPAY was started in Boston, Massachusetts.

Vira helped start CAPAY.

Learning About Each Other

Some people want to teach others about different customs and ways of life. Vira is an Asian Pacific American. She wanted people in her community to understand more about being Asian Pacific American.

Vira and her friends started a group called CAPAY. Members of CAPAY want Asian Pacific people to be treated fairly. They work together to make their community a better place to live.

68

Practice and Extend

SOCIAL STUDIES **Background**

About CAPAY

- The term *Asian Pacific American* refers to an American who has come from any country or territory in Asia or the Pacific Islands.
- The coalition was founded in the early 1990s by a group of Asian Pacific Americans, including Vira Douangmany, a Laotian American student.
- According to its mission statement, CAPAY's goals are to abolish stereotypes, to educate people about Asian Pacific Americans, to celebrate their heritage, and to improve race relations.

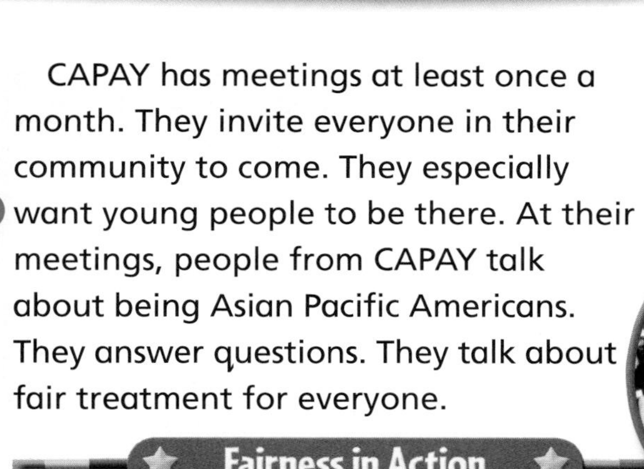

BUILDING CITIZENSHIP
Caring
Respect
Responsibility
Fairness
Honesty
Courage

CAPAY has meetings at least once a month. They invite everyone in their community to come. They especially
5 want young people to be there. At their meetings, people from CAPAY talk about being Asian Pacific Americans. They answer questions. They talk about fair treatment for everyone.

Fairness in Action

What can you and your classmates do to be sure everyone is treated fairly?

69

Problem Solving

Use a Problem-Solving Process

- Present this problem-solving scenario: *A boy from another country has just joined our class. Some children in the class are being mean to the boy. They are not treating him fairly.*
- For each step in the process, have children discuss what to do to solve the problem.

1. Identify a problem.
2. Gather information.
3. List and consider options.
4. Consider advantages and disadvantages.
5. Choose and implement a solution.
6. Evaluate the effectiveness of a solution.

After children have worked through the process, ask them to compare their solutions to the one that Vira and her friends decided upon.

4 Do you think having a meeting and talking about problems is a good thing to do? Why or why not? Possible answer: Yes. Talking things through is often the first step in finding a solution to a problem. **Evaluate**

5 Vira wants people to know about her Asian Pacific way of life. What would you like to tell people about your way of life? Answers will vary but should reflect children's understanding of *ways of life*. **Apply Information**

SOCIAL STUDIES STRAND
Citizenship

Point out that Vira shows she is a good citizen by working to get fair treatment for Americans from all different countries. She also helps her community by teaching young people about another culture. This encourages young people to have respect for all people. Ask children to tell about ways in which they can show respect for other people.

3 Close and Assess

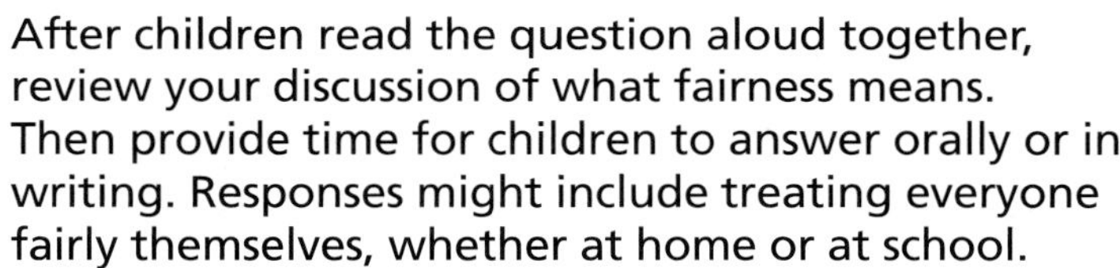

Fairness in Action

After children read the question aloud together, review your discussion of what fairness means. Then provide time for children to answer orally or in writing. Responses might include treating everyone fairly themselves, whether at home or at school.

Use with pages 62–69

Lesson 3 Wrap-Up

MEETING INDIVIDUAL NEEDS Leveled Practice

Make a Scrapbook

Guide children in making a scrapbook of familiar customs. To prepare, have children bring in photos from home or draw their own pictures.

Easy Ask each child to choose a picture and then tell about the custom it shows. After children talk about the pictures, have them dictate a title for each one. **Reteach**

On-Level Have children work in pairs to develop captions for their pictures. Partners should discuss what the picture shows and then write or dictate a sentence describing it. Ask how the customs shown in various pictures are alike and different. **Extend**

Challenge Have children help you organize the scrapbook. Lead them in choosing appropriate categories—for example, birthdays—for the pictures. Then ask them to write or dictate a short description of the category. **Enrich**

Hands-on Activities

CURRICULUM CONNECTION **Writing**

Customs

Objective Describe various *customs*.

Materials poster paper, pencils, colored markers, plastic clothespins, yarn or twine

Learning Style Verbal/Visual

Group 

Time 10–15 minutes

1. Have children work in groups to choose a custom from among those they learned about in the lesson.

2. Have groups make posters to tell others about their chosen customs. As children are working, help them write short captions that tell what each custom is and why it is important.

3. Using plastic clothespins, hang children's posters so that they stretch out across the room.

CURRICULUM CONNECTION **Music/Drama**

Sing Out!

Objective Learn and perform songs from different countries and cultures.

Materials Book of songs from around the world, such as *Wee Sing Around the World* by Pamela Conn Beall and Susan Hagen Nipp (Penguin Putnam 1994, ISBN 0-8431-3740-1); world map

Learning Style Auditory

Group 

Time 25–30 minutes

1. Tell children that the songs people sing can be customs too. Explain they will now learn some songs sung by children from around the world.

2. Sing (or play) one of the songs for children. Name the country the song comes from. Then, using a world map, locate the country for children.

3. Follow a similar procedure with several other songs. Invite children to choose a few songs they wish to learn. The whole class might learn all the songs. Or, small groups of children can learn different songs.

4. Provide children with outline maps that show where the songs they have learned come from. Children can color the maps and display them as they sing.

5. Invite parents and/or another class to come to your "sing out." Introduce each song before children sing it—or have a child act as narrator.

Lesson 4 Overview

Community Laws and Leaders

pages 70–71

Children will learn the meaning of the words *law* and *leader* and about the responsibilities of community leaders. They will also learn about the importance of community laws.

Time 20 minutes

Resources

- Workbook, p. 19
- Vocabulary Cards **law** **leader**
- Transparency 15
- Every Student Learns Guide, pp. 30–33

Meet Jane Addams

pages 72–73

Children will identify the contributions of Jane Addams, a historical figure who influenced the nation and demonstrated good citizenship.

Time 15–20 minutes

Build Background

Activity

Choose a Rule

Time 15–20 minutes

Ask each child to draw a picture or pantomime to tell about a rule from home or school. Direct children to choose rules that they have to follow often. As children share their rules, ask them who they think made each rule—and why it might be important to follow it.

If time is short, ask children to name some school rules and to tell why each rule is important.

Read Aloud

Signs

by D. G. Chester

Look around and you will see
Signs that help you and me.

At the corner there's a sign
For cars to stop at the line.

There's a light to help you know
When to wait and when to go.

Heed the signs. Do what they say.
It's the law! You must obey.

Community Laws and Leaders

Objectives

- Explain the need for laws in the community.
- Identify the responsibilities of authority figures in the community.
- Describe the role of public officials including mayor.

Vocabulary

law a rule that people must obey (p. 70)

leader someone who helps people decide what to do (p. 71)

QUICK Teaching Plan

If time is short, identify Officer Taylor and Mayor Garza and read the sentences in their speech balloons.

- Have children tell one thing each person pictured does to help the community.

1 Introduce and Motivate

Preview Display the Vocabulary Cards **law** and **leader**. Ask children what they think each word means. Share the meaning for each word and use it in a sentence: *People must obey each law of our state. The President of the United States is the leader of our country.*

Warm Up To activate prior knowledge, ask children if they can name people at school who make rules or who are leaders. Mention that you made rules for the classroom, but that the principal makes rules for the school, since he/she is the leader of the school. Then say that when leaders of a community or nation make rules, they are called laws.

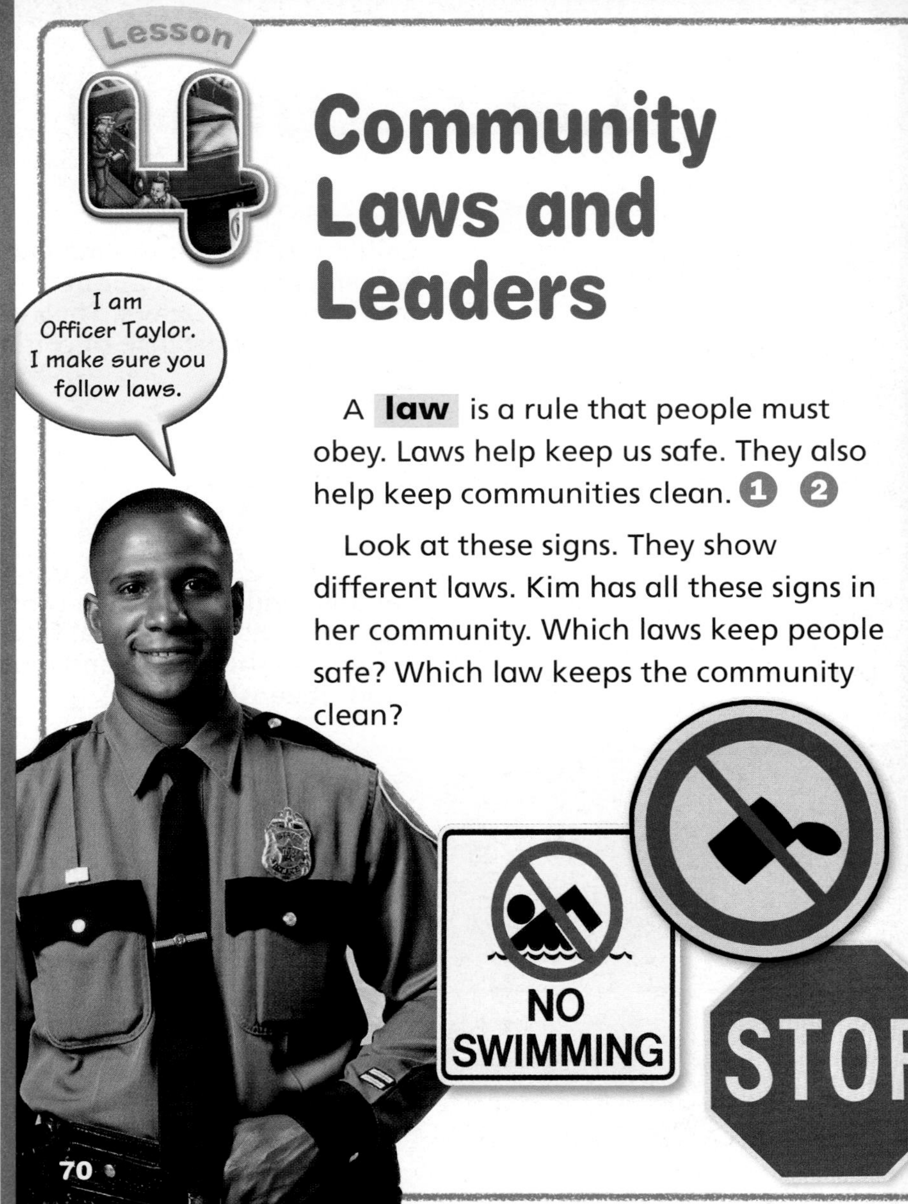

Lesson 4
Community Laws and Leaders
I am Officer Taylor. I make sure you follow laws.
A **law** is a rule that people must obey. Laws help keep us safe. They also help keep communities clean. 1 2
Look at these signs. They show different laws. Kim has all these signs in her community. Which laws keep people safe? Which law keeps the community clean?
NO SWIMMING
STOP
70

Practice and Extend

READING SKILL Cause and Effect

Telling Why

- Discuss the laws suggested by the signs on p. 70. Have children tell why these laws are important. Ask what might happen if people didn't obey them.
- Display Transparency 15. Tell children to first draw a picture that shows someone breaking one of the laws from p. 70. Then have them draw a picture to show the result.

WEB SITE Technology

You can look up vocabulary words online. Click on *Social Studies Library* and select the dictionary at **www.sfsocialstudies.com.**

A mayor is a leader of a community. A **leader** helps people decide what to do. ③

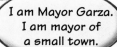

Mayor Garza works with other community leaders. They make decisions about their community. They make their community a great place to live!

I am Mayor Garza.
I am mayor of
a small town.

What did you learn?

1. Why do we need rules and laws?
2. What do leaders do? Who are the leaders in your school and community?
3. **Think and Share** Think of two laws. Draw signs for them. Share your signs.

71

Decision Making

Use a Decision-Making Process

- Say: *Suppose you are the class leader. You want to make it easier for children to see the teacher. You want to change how the desks are arranged in the classroom. What is the best way to put the desks?*
- Children should use the decision-making process to decide what arrangement best achieves their goal.
- For each step in the process, have children discuss what to consider as they make their decision. You can refer to the steps listed here. To guide children, read aloud the steps as they are listed on p. H5.

1. Identify a situation that requires a decision.
2. Gather information.
3. Identify options.
4. Predict consequences.
5. Take action to implement a decision.
6. Evaluate the decision.

Workbook, p. 19

Community Laws and Leaders

Circle the picture that goes with the sentence.

It is safe to cross.

Keep our park clean.

Walk your dog on a leash.

Also on Teacher Resources CD-ROM.

2 Teach and Discuss

Page 70

After reading p. 70, direct children's attention to the signs.

① **What is the job of a police officer like Officer Taylor?** A police officer's job is to make sure people obey laws. **Generalize**

② **What are some laws that Officer Taylor wants you to follow?** Stop at stop signs, don't litter, no swimming **Analyze Pictures**

Page 71

③ **Why do communities need leaders?** Possible answers: To make the community a good place to live, to make decisions about how the community should be run **Generalize**

3 Close and Assess

✓ What did you learn?

Name the mayor and/or other leaders in your community. Ask children what they think these leaders do.

1. To keep our communities safe and clean and to help people get along with each other
2. Leaders make decisions for the community. The school principal is a school leader and a mayor is a community leader.
3. **Think and Share** Possible answers: Octagon with the word "stop" in it, circle with a bar through a person walking

Jane Addams

Objective

- Identify contributions of historical figures.
- Identify historic figures who have exemplified good citizenship.

1 Introduce and Motivate

Preview Point out the term *social worker* in the lesson subtitle. Tell children that a social worker helps people in many different ways. Point out that in this lesson, children will learn about one social worker and the ways she helped people in her community.

Warm Up To activate prior knowledge, invite children to suggest some ways that people at school help them. Prompt children by naming staff members, such as school nurse, school social worker or psychologist, playground supervisors, office staff, cafeteria staff. List these on the board.

Have children look at the pictures on pp. 72–73. Identify the woman as Jane Addams, and ask children what they think she is doing.

2 Teach and Discuss

Read the biography together. Tell children that Jane Addams was a leader of the settlement house movement. Explain that settlement houses are centers to which people who need help can go.

1 Why did Jane Addams start Hull House? So people in the community would have a place to go for help **Main Idea and Details**

2 What is one way you could help people in your community? Possible answers: Give food to hungry people, give clothes to people who need them, keep lonely older people company **Solve Problems**

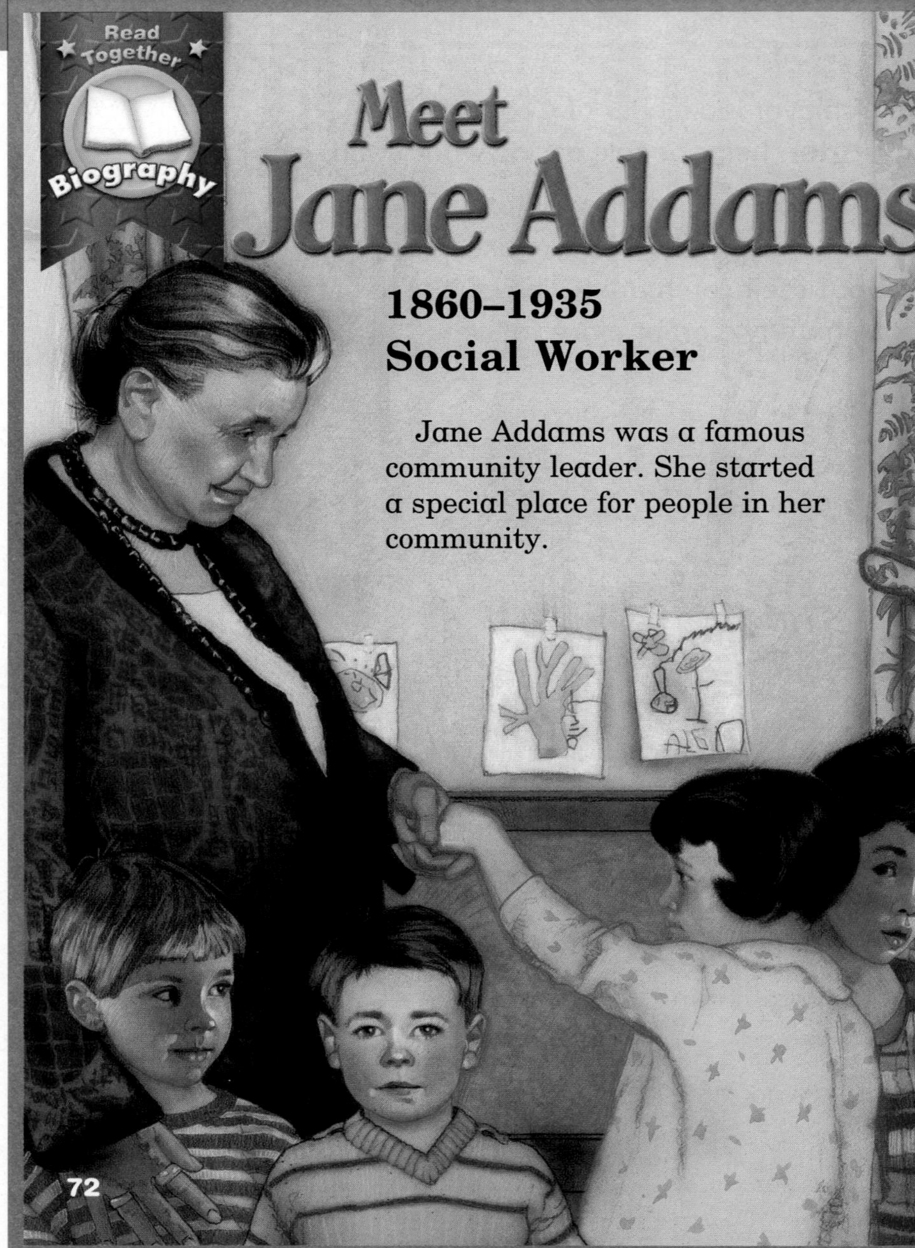

Read Together
Biography
Meet
Jane Addams
1860–1935
Social Worker
Jane Addams was a famous community leader. She started a special place for people in her community.
72

Practice and Extend

SOCIAL STUDIES Background

About Jane Addams and Hull House

- Jane Addams fought for the rights of poor women and children. She set up a nursery at Hull House, so women had access to child care.
- Addams believed in justice and equality. She helped create playgrounds that *all* children could use.
- Alfred Nobel wanted to honor people who worked for the good of humanity. Jane Addams won the Nobel Peace Prize as a result of her work for the common good of her community.

WEB SITE Technology

You may help children find out more about Jane Addams by clicking on *Meet the People* at **www.sfsocialstudies.com.**

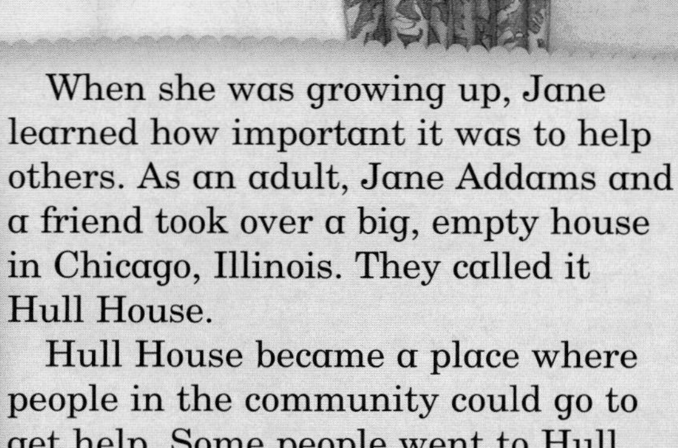

When she was growing up, Jane learned how important it was to help others. As an adult, Jane Addams and a friend took over a big, empty house in Chicago, Illinois. They called it Hull House.

Hull House became a place where people in the community could go to get help. Some people went to Hull House because they were sick. Others went because they had questions about the law. Some people needed care for their children. People also went there to take classes. Hull House had a community kitchen, playground, and nursery. ❶

In 1931, Jane Addams was the first American woman to win an important prize called the Nobel Peace Prize. ❷ ❸

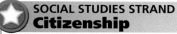

Jane Addams was born in Cedarville, Illinois.

Hull House Museum

Think and Share

How did Jane Addams help people in the community ?

For more information, go online to *Meet the People* at **www.sfsocialstudies.com.**

MEETING INDIVIDUAL NEEDS

Leveled Practice

Make a Collage

Help children make a list of things Jane Addams did to help others. Tell children that they will use this list as they make a collage celebrating her work.

Easy Have children draw pictures to illustrate the items on the list. **Reteach**

On-Level Have children refer to the list to write sentences about the work of Jane Addams. Provide index cards and have children write one sentence on each card. **Extend**

Challenge Help children brainstorm a list of words and phrases that describe a good citizen. Have children write the words and phrases on colored index cards. **Enrich**

Have groups of children arrange the pictures and cards on poster board and paste them in position. Display the collages.

❸ **Why was winning the Nobel Peace Prize such an honor for Jane Adams?** She was the first American woman to win the prize.
Make Inferences

SOCIAL STUDIES STRAND

Citizenship

Explain that Jane Addams showed she was a good citizen by helping poor immigrants help themselves. By providing child care and schooling, Jane Addams gave these people the tools they needed to make their own lives better. By teaching them English and an understanding of American laws, she helped them speak for themselves and try to get fair treatment. Ask children if they think Jane Addams deserved the prize she won, and if so, why.

3 Close and Assess

Think and Share

Have children review the lesson pictures and text before they answer. Answers should suggest that Jane Addams provided a place where people could go to learn or to get help—because they were sick, because they had questions about the law, because they needed care for their children.

Use with pages 70–73

Lesson 4 Wrap-Up

MEETING INDIVIDUAL NEEDS Leveled Practice

Make a Web

Lead children in making a concept web about community leadership. Place the words *community leader* in the center cell.

Easy Have children draw pictures showing things that community leaders do. Ask them to put their pictures on the outer cells of the web. Tell children they may include pictures of Jane Addams or other community leaders they know about. **Reteach**

On-Level Have children brainstorm additional ways leaders help a community. Add more cells to the web. Then have children add their pictures. Ask how the leader is helping his/her community. **Extend**

Challenge Review earlier lessons about the qualities of a good citizen. Then have children choose one picture from the expanded web. Ask them to tell how the community leader pictured is a good citizen. **Enrich**

Hands-on Activities

CURRICULUM CONNECTION
Writing

Class Letter

Objectives Use lesson vocabulary; explain the need for leadership and laws.

Resources Vocabulary Cards **law, leader**

Materials lined paper, pencils

Learning Style Verbal

Group

Time 10–15 minutes

1. Show children the Vocabulary Cards *law* and *leader*. Review the meaning of these words.

2. Invite children to write a class letter to a school or community leader.

3. Discuss laws identified in Lesson 4 or others children know. Have them choose a few laws they feel are important and dictate sentences telling why the laws are good for the community.

4. Remind children to add *law* and *leader* to their Word Books.

SOCIAL STUDIES STRAND
Citizenship

Help Hints

Objective Interview to learn about the roles of public officials.

Learning Style Verbal

Group

Time 20–30 minutes

1. Invite the mayor or other leader in your community to visit the classroom. Prepare the guest by providing a list of probable questions.

1) What is your job?
2) How did you get elected?
3) What is a problem in our community?

2. Tell children about the visit, and ask them to help you make a list of questions to ask the leader.

3. After the guest tells about his or her role in the community, have children take turns asking their questions.

SOCIAL STUDIES STRAND
Government

Mayor for a Day

Objectives Act out the roles of public officials, including a mayor; demonstrate the importance of voting to make choices about leaders.

Learning Style Kinesthetic/Verbal

Group

Time 15 minutes

1. Provide a "mayor" costume, such as a special hat or coat.

2. Ask a child with good leadership qualities to start out as classroom mayor (or have children vote to select a mayor). Tell children that this job will rotate.

3. Have other children play the role of classroom council leaders. Together, the mayor and the leaders can think of problems in the classroom—and can then suggest ways to solve these problems.

Lesson 5 Overview

Where in the World Do I Live? **pages 74– 77**	Children will learn the meaning of the words *state, continent,* and *ocean* and how a community fits into a state, a country, and a continent. They will also learn how to find continents on a world map.	 Time 20–30 minutes Resources • Workbook, p. 20 • Vocabulary Cards **state** **continent** **ocean** • Transparency 13 • Every Student Learns Guide, pp. 34–37
Meet Sam Houston **pages 78–79**	Children will identify the contributions of Sam Houston, a historical figure who influenced the nation.	 Time 15–20 minutes

Build Background

Activity

Map It!

 **Time** 20–30 minutes

Display several maps in the classroom. Include maps of the United States, North America, and the world.

Direct children to the appropriate map, and show them how to trace their state, the United States of America, and the continent of North America. Have them cut out the shapes they traced. Then ask children if they can tell in which cutouts their community belongs.

If time is short, ask children if they know what state or country their community is in.

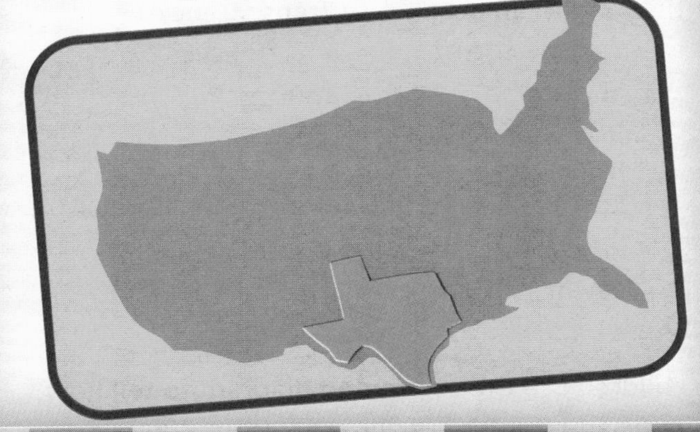

Read Aloud

Our Round Earth

by Mae Carroll

Our Earth is round
Like a ball.
Our Earth is big
But I am small.

Our Earth has land,
Called continents,
And water too,
Called oceans,
hence—

If you could fly
To the moon
You'd see a ball
With lots of blue.

Where in the World Do I Live?

Objective

- Locate places of significance on maps.

Vocabulary

state a part of a country (p. 75)

continent a very large piece of land (p. 76)

ocean a very large body of salt water (p. 76)

QUICK Teaching Plan

If time is short, help children use the map on p. 75 to locate their state.

- Have them use the map on pp. 76–77 to identify large bodies of land and water.
- Read the captions for the world map. Point out the United States and North America.

1 Introduce and Motivate

Preview Display the Vocabulary Card **state**, **continent**,and **ocean**. Ask children what they think each word means. Share the meaning of each word. Ask children to name their state and country. Then have children look at the map on p. 75 as you point out the two oceans that border the contiguous United States.

Warm Up To activate prior knowledge, ask if children have traveled to other states. List the states children name on the board; then point them out on a map of the United States. (If children name countries or cities, list these on a separate section of the board.)

Where in the World Do I Live?

Here is my community. My community is a city called Houston. It was named after a famous leader called Sam Houston. 1

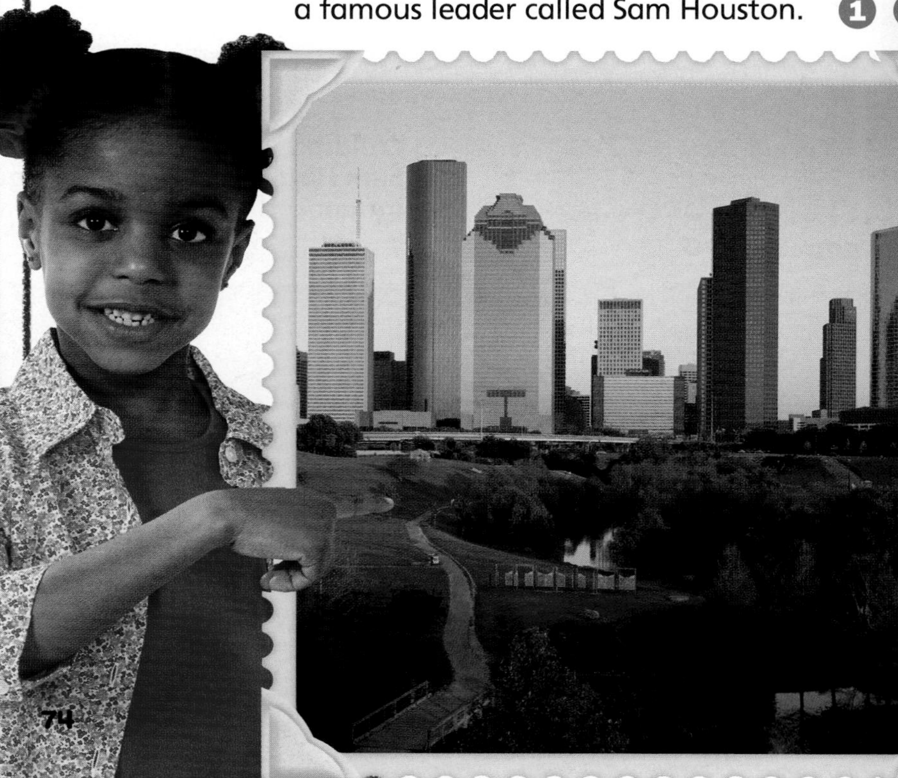

Practice and Extend

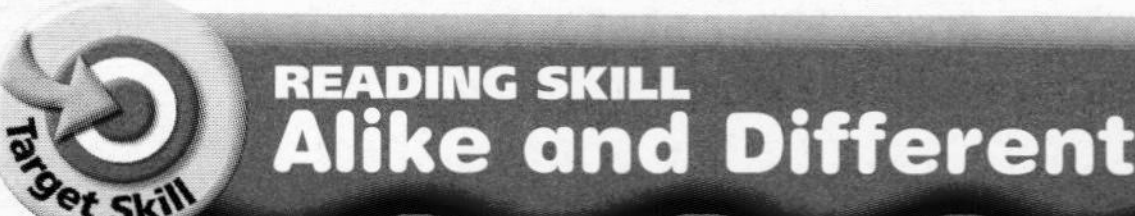

Venn Diagram Remind children that thinking about how things are alike and different can help us understand those things better. After they finish reading p. 76, help them complete a Venn diagram to compare and contrast a continent with an ocean. Use Transparency 13.

continent	both	ocean
• piece of land • one of seven	• part of the earth • large in size	• body of salt water • one of four

Have children use the completed diagram to tell how continents and oceans are alike and different.

I live in the state of Texas. A **state** is part of a country. The United States of ③ America is my country. We have fifty states in the United States. What is the name of your state? Find it on the map.

④

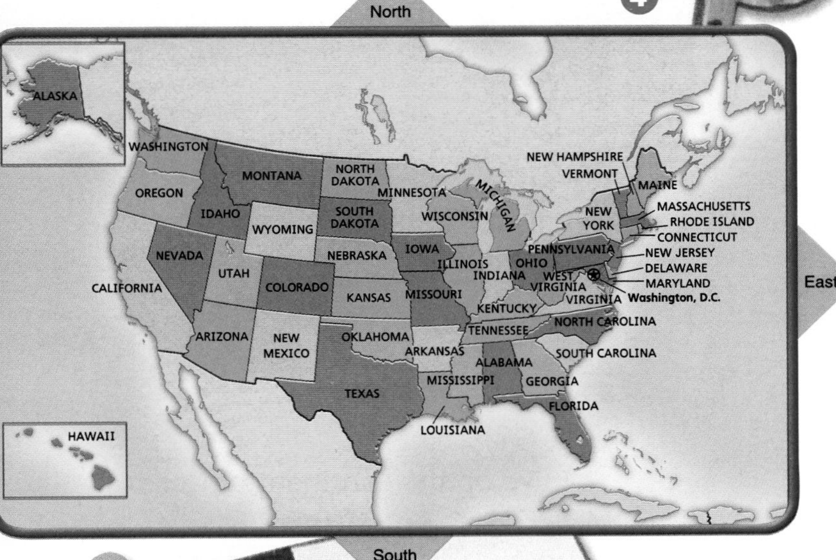

75

2 Teach and Discuss

Page 74

Explain that in this lesson, Kim tells us about her community—and where in the world it is. Point out that children can use the information Kim shares to learn more about their own community.

① **What does the picture Kim is pointing to show?** The city of Houston **Make Inferences**

② **How is Kim's community like your community? How is it different?** Possible answers: Kim lives in a city, but I live in a town. Her city is bigger, and buildings are taller and closer together than those in my town.
Compare and Contrast

Page 75

Point out that the map shows the whole United States. Locate the United States on a globe before reading the page. Point out Alaska and Hawaii, explaining that these two states do not touch the other states.

③ **What is the name of Kim's state?** Texas
Recall and Retell

④ **What other states touch your state?** Answers will vary, depending on where children live.
Interpret Maps

Themes of Geography: Location

Have children locate the cardinal directions on the map. Ask which direction—north, south, east, or west—best describes the location of their state in the United States. Explain that we sometimes call a state such as Florida a southern state.

CURRICULUM CONNECTION Art

Make a State Puzzle

- Provide each child with an outline map of your state. Have children note the shape of their state.
- Have children paste the outline onto oaktag and then color and cut it out.
- Next, have children cut their state into four or five "puzzle" pieces.
- Have partners trade puzzle pieces and try to put them back together to make the shape of your state.

WEB SITE Technology

You can look up the vocabulary words online. Click on *Social Studies Library* and select the dictionary at **www.sfsocialstudies.com.**

continued

Page 76

Explain that the map on pp. 76–77 shows the whole world. Help children locate the United States on this map. Point out a few physical features, such as the Florida peninsula, that might help children find the United States on any world map.

5 **What continent is the United States a part of? How do you know?** The caption by the map says that it is part of North America. **Interpret Maps**

SOCIAL STUDIES STRAND
Geography

Mention that the United States is just one country on the continent of North America. Point out the location of Mexico, and explain that it is also in North America. Follow a similar procedure for Canada.

6 **How can you tell land from water on a map?** Water is blue in color. **Interpret Maps**

7 **What are the names of the world's four oceans?** Atlantic, Pacific, Arctic, Indian **Interpret Maps**

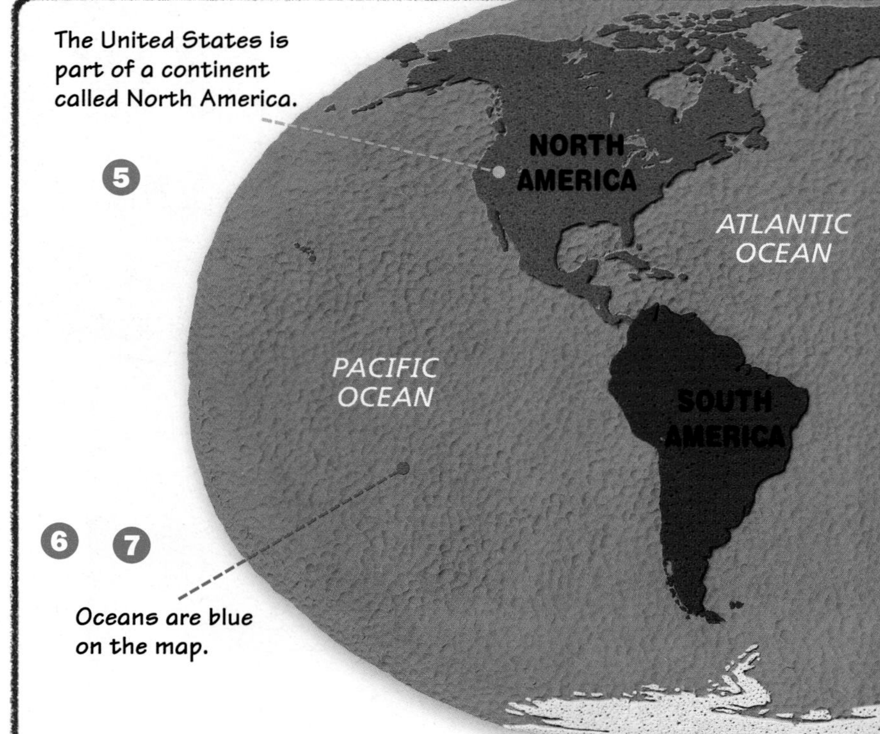
The United States is part of a continent called North America.
5
NORTH AMERICA
ATLANTIC OCEAN
PACIFIC OCEAN
SOUTH AMERICA
6
7
Oceans are blue on the map.

I live on the continent of North America. A **continent** is a very large piece of land. The world has seven continents. Find them on the map.

The world has four oceans too. An **ocean** is a very large body of water. Ocean water is very salty.

76

Practice and Extend

ESL

EXTEND LANGUAGE
ESL Support

A Spinning Game Invite children to practice using words that relate to maps by playing a game.

Beginning Place your finger lightly on the globe, and then spin it around. When the globe stops spinning, ask children if you are on land or on water.

Intermediate Follow a similar procedure as for Beginning. Have children tell whether you have touched an ocean or a continent. Name the ocean or continent.

Advanced Follow a similar procedure as for Beginning, but have children try to name the continent or the ocean on which your finger lands. Allow them to use their home language first, if need be. Then provide the English name, and have children repeat it.

For additional ESL Support, use Every Student Learns Guide, pp. 34–37.

FAST FACTS

You may want to share these facts about the continents with children.

- Asia is the largest continent. Australia is the smallest.
- Antarctica is the coldest continent. It is covered with ice, much of which extends out into the waters around Antarctica.
- The Sahara Desert in Africa is almost as big as the United States.
- Australia is the only continent that is also a country. The country is also called Australia.
- Europe is part of the same piece of land as the continent of Asia. Some people call the two continents by one name: *Eurasia*.

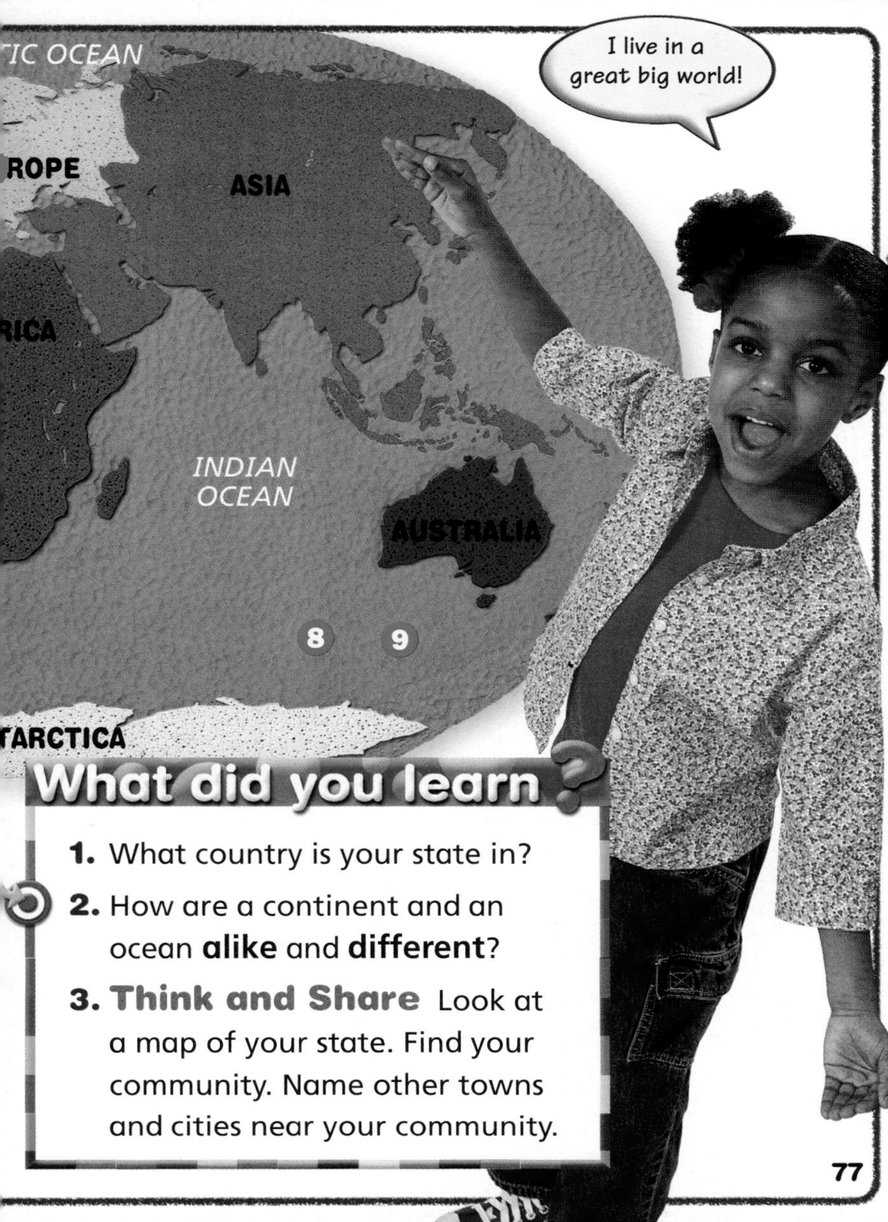

I live in a great big world!

What did you learn?

1. What country is your state in?
2. How are a continent and an ocean **alike** and **different**?
3. **Think and Share** Look at a map of your state. Find your community. Name other towns and cities near your community.

77

WEB SITE
Technology

You may help children find out more about your state by going online. Click on *Atlas* at **www.sfsocialstudies.com.**

Workbook, p. 20

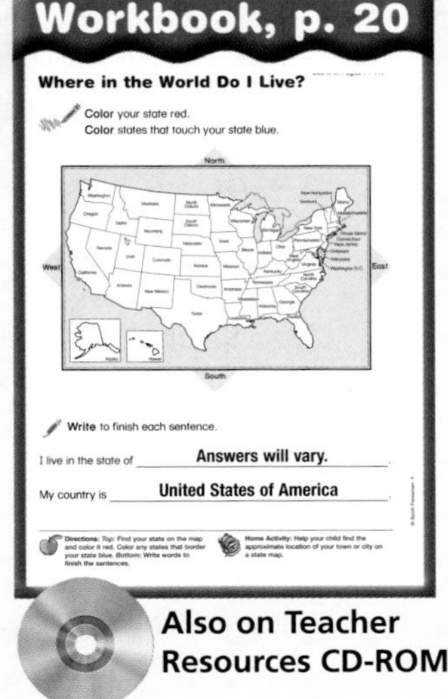

Where in the World Do I Live?
Color your state red.
Color states that touch your state blue.
Write to finish each sentence.
I live in the state of Answers will vary.
My country is United States of America

Also on Teacher Resources CD-ROM.

Page 77

Help children find the approximate locations of their home states on the world map.

8 Do you live near an ocean? If so, which one? Answers will vary, depending on where children live. **Interpret Maps**

9 What are the names of the seven continents? North America, South America, Europe, Asia, Africa, Australia, Antarctica.

SOCIAL STUDIES STRAND
Economics

Point out the continent of Europe on the map. Tell children that the United States trades goods with many other countries—including countries in Europe. Ask them to trace a route on the map from the United States to Europe. Ask what ocean the goods need to cross to get to Europe. Follow a similar procedure for Asia.

3 Close and Assess

Trace and cut out two states, including your own. Ask children to point out which outline is your state. Repeat this activity with two country outlines, including the United States.

What did you learn?

1. The United States of America
2. Both a continent and ocean are very big. A continent is a piece of land. An ocean is a body of salt water.
3. **Think and Share** Children should be able to locate their community and name at least two nearby communities.

Sam Houston

Objective

- Identify contributions of historical figures.

1 Introduce and Motivate

Preview Review with children the qualities that make someone a leader. Then ask if they know what a lawyer is. Write the word on the board, underlining the first part of the word—*law*. Explain that a lawyer is someone who has studied law and whose job is to advise people about matters of law.

Warm Up To activate prior knowledge, ask if children recall the name of the city in which Kim lives. If necessary, show them the picture of Houston on p. 74. Explain that Kim's community was named for Sam Houston.

Have children preview the pictures on pp. 78–79. Identify Sam Houston, and ask children what they think he is doing. Point out the early Texas flag on p. 79, and ask if children have ever seen one like it. Show children a picture of the current Texas flag, and have them note the similarities.

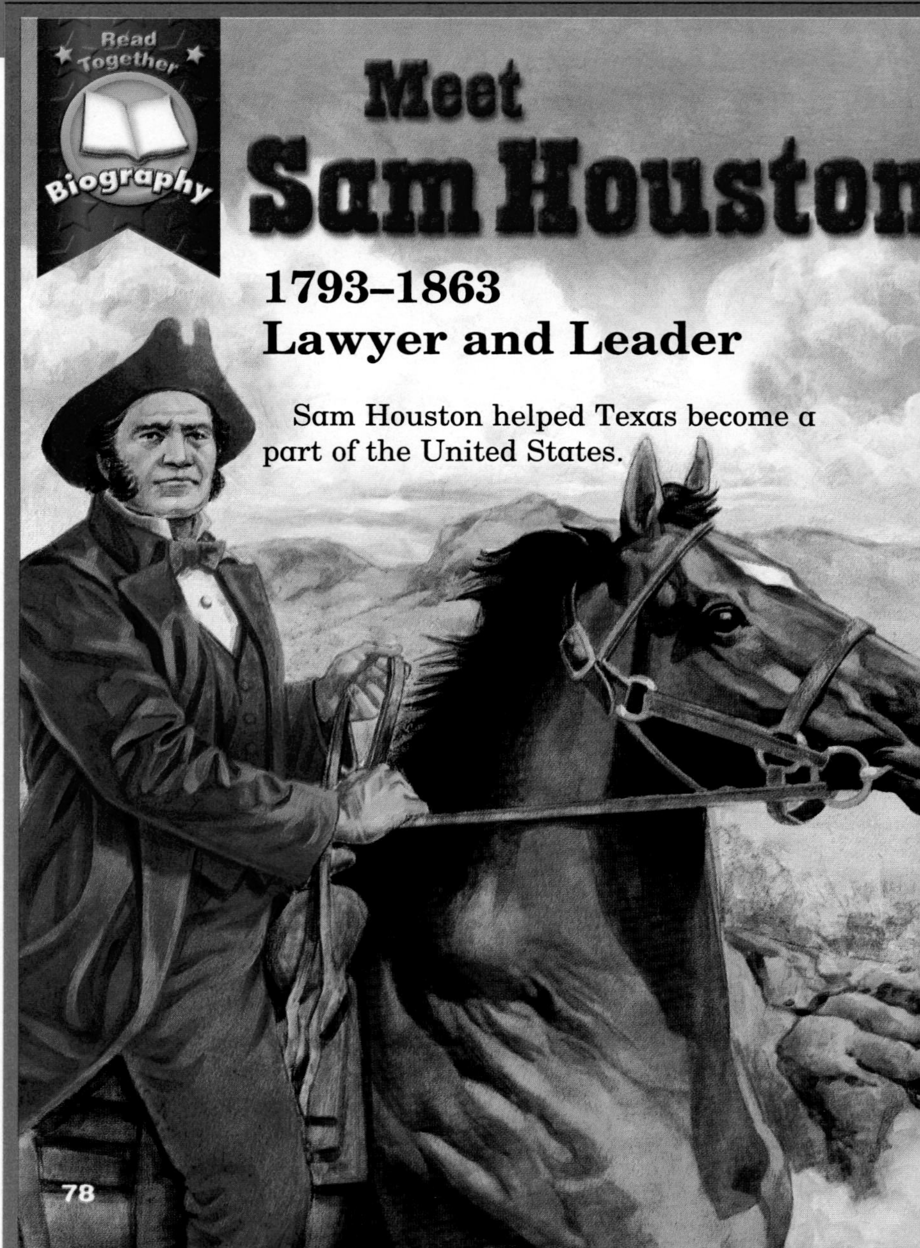

Read Together
Biography
Meet
Sam Houston
1793–1863
Lawyer and Leader
Sam Houston helped Texas become a part of the United States.
78

Practice and Extend

SOCIAL STUDIES Background

About Sam Houston

- Sam Houston was the first official president of the Lone Star Republic.
- After Texas became a state, Sam Houston served as its governor and as its U.S. senator.
- Fort Sam Houston (which is in San Antonio, Texas) is named for Sam Houston.
- For a while, Sam Houston lived in the state of Tennessee. He was its governor too.

WEB SITE Technology

You may help children learn more about Sam Houston by clicking on *Meet the People* at **www.sfsocialstudies.com.**

Young Sam lived on farms in Virginia and Tennessee. When he was a teenager, he left home to live with Native Americans called the Cherokee. He learned the Cherokee language and customs. 1

When Sam Houston grew older, he became a lawyer. He was also one of the leaders of Texas before it became a state. During that time, Texas was part of Mexico. The people of Texas wanted to control their land by themselves. Texas went to war with Mexico. Sam Houston led his army against Mexico and won. Texas became independent. 2

In later years, Sam Houston helped Texas become a state in the United States of America. 3

Sam Houston was born near Lexington, Virginia.

The Texas flag

Think and Share

What are two ways Sam Houston helped Texas?

For more information, go online to *Meet the People* at **www.sfsocialstudies.com.**

2 Teach and Discuss

Tell children that Texas was once part of Mexico. It became a state in the United States in 1845. Then read the biography together.

1 **How did Sam Houston get to know the Cherokee?** He lived with them and learned their language and customs. **Make Inferences**

SOCIAL STUDIES STRAND
History

The Cherokee, or Keetoowha, are a group of native Americans. One of their leaders was a man named Sequoyah, who invented a system of writing the Cherokee language.

2 **How did Sam Houston help Texas become independent from Mexico?** He led an army against Mexico and won. **Recall and Retell**

3 **Why do you think Kim's community is named after Sam Houston?** Possible answer: The people of Texas remember Sam Houston as a good leader who helped them gain statehood. **Make Inferences**

3 Close and Assess

Think and Share

Possible answers: He helped Texas become independent from Mexico. He helped Texas become a state in the United States.

SOCIAL STUDIES STRAND
Geography

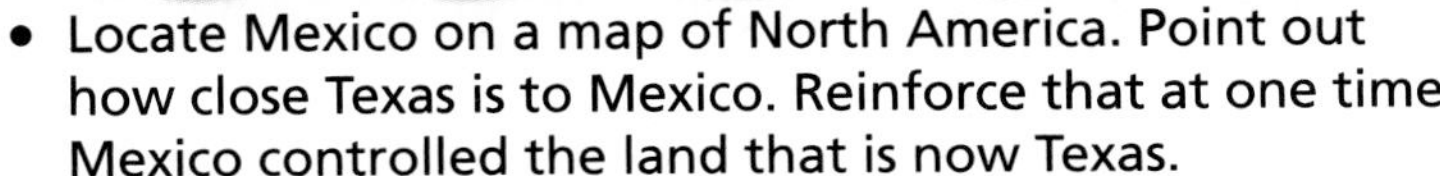

- Locate Mexico on a map of North America. Point out how close Texas is to Mexico. Reinforce that at one time Mexico controlled the land that is now Texas.
- Then locate San Jacinto on the map. Explain that this is where Sam Houston fought a famous battle against the Mexican army. He captured a Mexican leader, General Santa Anna. After this battle, Texas became independent.
- Ask children to share any knowledge they have of the battle for Texas independence.

Use with pages 74–79

Lesson 5 Wrap-Up

MEETING INDIVIDUAL NEEDS

Leveled Practice

State Shapes

Guide children in getting to know the shape of their state. Using a wall map, trace the shape of three states, including your own state, and duplicate for children.

Easy Have children find your state on a wall map. Then display three of the state shapes, and have children point out which of the three is their state. Ask what clues children used to decide which state was theirs. **Reteach**

On-Level Distribute all three state shapes to children. Have them identify their own state, cut it out, and label it. Then have them refer to a wall map of the United States to identify the other two states. **Extend**

Challenge Give children all three state shapes, and have them cut them out and label them. Then guide children in writing clues to your own state. Help children write their clues on index cards. Others in the class can then try to match the cards with their states. **Enrich**

Hands-on Activities

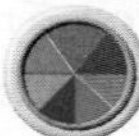

CURRICULUM CONNECTION

Reading

Name Game

Objective Use lesson vocabulary.

Resources Vocabulary Cards **state, continent, ocean**

Materials index cards, pencil, scissors, glue

Learning Style Verbal/Kinesthetic

Partners

Time 20–25 minutes

1. Prepare simple word clues for each vocabulary word: *state, continent, ocean*. For *continent*, you might say: *There are seven of me*. Write the clues on index cards.

2. Give pairs of children a few index cards. Have them discuss the clues and try to guess the words.

3. Once children guess the words, have them cut out magazine pictures or draw their own pictures to illustrate each index card.

4. Remind children to add the lesson vocabulary to their Word Book.

There are seven of me.

CURRICULUM CONNECTION

Literature

Routes

Objective Locate places and trace a route on a map or globe.

Materials *How to Make an Apple Pie and See the World,* by Marjorie Priceman (Alfred A. Knopf, ISBN 0-673-61098-5, 1994), world map

Learning Style Verbal/Visual

Group

Time 20–25 minutes

1. Display the map at the beginning of the book. Have children compare it with the map on pp. 76–77.

2. Read the story aloud, sharing the pictures. As the storyteller arrives in each new place, locate it on a wall map. Have children point to the corresponding location on the map on pp. 76–77.

3. Finally, help children trace the storyteller's route.

4. Children may enjoy making up their own travel stories for the missing ice cream.

SOCIAL STUDIES STRAND

History

What's in a Name?

Objective Use oral sources to learn how a community got its name.

Learning Style Verbal/Kinesthetic

Individual

Time 20–25 minutes

1. Help children brainstorm possible explanations for the name of your community. For example, it might be named for a geographical feature, such as a river or mountain.

2. If your community is named for a person, provide children with information about this person.

3. Have each child draw a community logo. Logos should include the name of the community, decorated with drawings that explain the name of the community or its history.

Ending Unit 2

End with a Poem pages 80–81	Children will listen to and talk about a poem—"One Great Big Community" by Toni Barkley—that tells about a child and where his home fits into the world.	
Unit 2 Review pages 82–85	Children will review unit vocabulary words and the unit skills of identifying alike and different, using a map key, and using four directions. Children will answer questions about what they learned in the unit. Children will learn about several books about communities and geography.	Resources • Workbook, p. 21 ✓• Assessment Book, pp. 5–8
Unit 2 Project page 86	Children will create posters and give news reports about community events. They will also be directed to a Web site where they can learn more about communities.	Resource • Workbook, p. 22

Wrap-up

Activity

Helping My Community

Have children make trading cards to show how people help care for their own neighborhoods and communities.

- On the cards, children can write descriptions or draw pictures to show ways in which people help other people in their own communities. Brainstorm ideas with them, such as: by being leaders, by helping to keep places clean, and by caring for sick people.
- On each card, have children add a small picture of a child if the activity is one in which children can participate.

Performance Assessment

You can use the activity on this page as a performance assessment.

✓ **Assessment Scoring Guide**

Make Trading Cards About Helping Communities	
4	Describes helping options very clearly and completely, with many details.
3	Describes helping options clearly and completely, with some details.
2	Describes helping options with a few gaps in information and few details.
1	Describes helping options with little or inaccurate information and few or vague details.

One Great Big Community

Objectives

- Obtain information about a topic using a variety of visual sources, such as pictures and literature.
- Identify main ideas from oral, visual, and print sources.

1 Introduce and Motivate

Preview Point to and read the title; then identify the author of the poem. Ask children what they think the poem is about. Suggest that they think about the title and look at the picture before they answer.

Warm Up Remind children of the song with which they began this unit. You may want to turn to p. 44 and sing the song with children once again.

2 Teach and Discuss

Explain that a poem is a kind of writing that often has rhyming words. Read the poem aloud, and then have children read it with you.

1 **What are some ways to describe the boy's house?** Answers might include very tall and just the right size. **Recall and Retell**

2 **What things do you see in the boy's neighborhood?** Different houses, trees, hills **Analyze Pictures**

3 **How is the boy's neighborhood different from his community?** His neighborhood is smaller than his community. **Compare and Contrast**

UNIT 2
End with a Poem
One Great Big Community
by Toni Barkley
Here is my home.
It's very tall.
It's just the right size
To fit us all.
Here is my neighborhood
All around me.
It's part of a bigger
Community.
1 2 3
80

Practice and Extend

SOCIAL STUDIES STRAND
Economics

Community Connections

- Talk with children about the many communities to which the boy in the poem—and they—belong. Help children list these: home, neighborhood, community, state, country, world.
- Point out that all these communities can connect to one another in many ways. One way is that people travel across town, to other states, and even around the world for fun and for work. They take things with them. They also bring things back to their homes with them.
- Explain to children that the things they wear, eat, and use often come from the different communities they listed above. Tell children that in Unit 3 they will learn more about the ways people depend on many communities to get what they need and want.

Here is my state.
It's one of fifty.
It's part of my country.
It's very nifty!

Here is my world.
It's special, you see.
It's the perfect home
For you and me!
4
81

Page 81

Explain to children that the word *nifty* means "attractive or stylish." Point out the state silhouette and help children identify the state shown.

4 Name two very big communities in which the boy lives. Possible answers: His state, his country, the world **Main Idea and Details**

3 Close and Assess

- Organize children in six groups: home, neighborhood, community, state, country, world. Divide up a set of nesting boxes or cups, giving each group an ascending size box or cup.
- Have groups read the lines of the poem related to their assigned community. As they read, help children assemble the stack of boxes or cups. Demonstrate how each fits into the next biggest size box or cup.
- Reread the poem again as a group. Ask children what they think the title means now. Explain that the boy sees the world as a huge community in which there are other communities of smaller and smaller size, all the way down to his own home.

Books About Community

Children might enjoy reading these books.

Officer Buckle and Gloria, by Peggy Rathmann (Putnam, ISBN 0-399-22616-8, 1995) A police officer and a very special dog team up to present school safety programs. **Easy** ***Caldecott Medal 1996***

Me on the Map, by Joan Sweeney and Annette Cable (illustrator), (Dragonfly, ISBN: 0-517-88557-3, 1998) In a game children love to play, a girl describes herself and her surroundings in ever-widening circles. **On-Level**

Miss Rumphius, by Barbara Cooney (Viking, ISBN 0-140-50539-3, 1985) A gentle story about a world traveler who made her own part of the world more beautiful for later generations. **Challenge** ***Notable Social Studies Book.***

Review

Resources

- Assessment Book, pp. 5–8
- Workbook, p. 21: Vocabulary Review

Vocabulary Review

1. neighborhood
2. leader
3. state
4. continent
5. ocean

Answers to Test Prep

1. law
2. community

UNIT 2

Review

Vocabulary Review

neighborhood
continent
ocean
leader
state

Tell which word completes each sentence.

1. People live, work, and play in a _____.
2. A mayor is a community _____.
3. Texas is a _____.
4. A very large piece of land is a _____.
5. A very large body of salt water is called an _____.

★ ★ ★ ★ ★ ★ ★ ★

Which word completes the sentence?

1. A rule you must obey is a _____.
   a. law **b.** state
   c. leader **d.** community

2. A city is a big _____.
   a. neighborhood **b.** continent
   c. ocean **d.** community

82

Practice and Extend

Assessment Options

✓ Unit 2 Assessment

- Unit 2 Content Test: Use Assessment Book, pp. 5–6
- Unit 2 Skills Test: Use Assessment Book, pp. 7–8

Standardized Test Prep

- Unit 2 tests contain standardized test formats.

✓ Unit 2 Performance Assessment

- See p. 86 for information about using the Unit 2 Project as a means of performance assessment.
- A scoring guide for the Unit 2 Project is provided in the teacher's notes on p. 86.

Test Talk

- Test Talk Practice Book

Skills Review

Alike and Different

Tell or write about how laws can be **alike** and **different.**

Use a Map Key

1. What does [library symbol] stand for?
2. How many symbols are on the map key?
3. Draw a symbol for something on the map that is not in the map key.

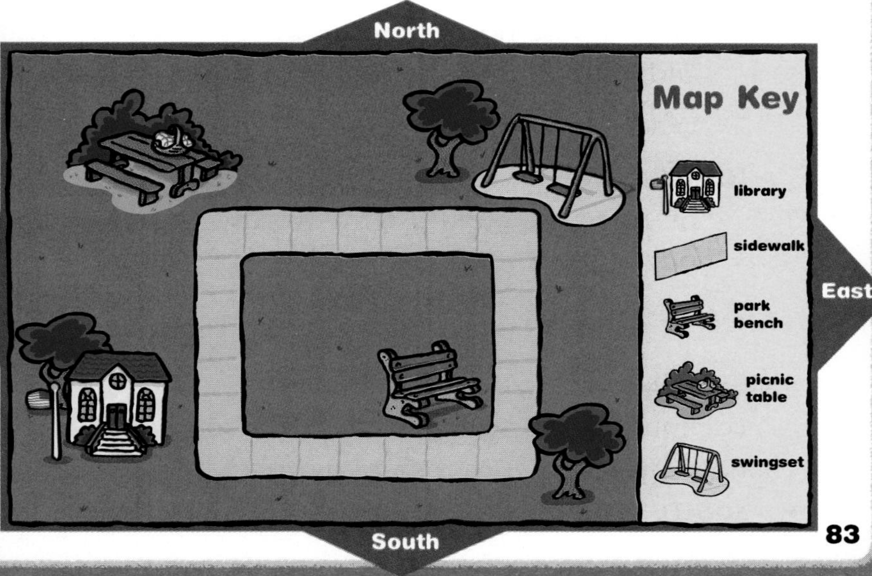

Practice and Extend

For more information, you can select the dictionary or encyclopedia from *Social Studies Library* at **www.sfsocialstudies.com.**

Workbook, p. 21

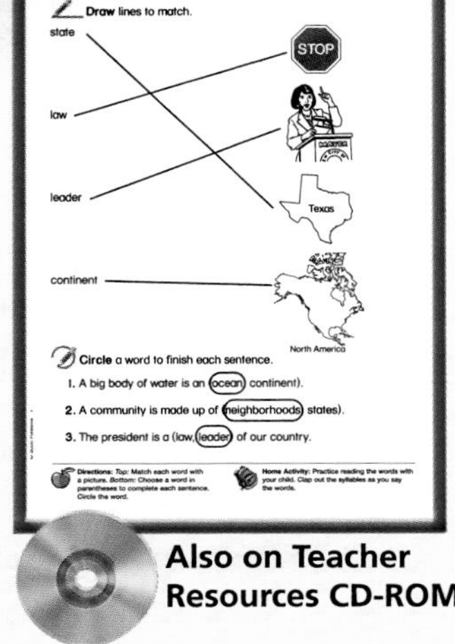
Draw lines to match.
state
law
leader
continent
STOP
Texas
North America
Circle a word to finish each sentence.
1. A big body of water is an (ocean continent).
2. A community is made up of (neighborhoods states).
3. The president is a (law leader) of our country.

Also on Teacher Resources CD-ROM.

Skills Review

Alike and Different

- Possible answer: Some laws help keep us safe. Other laws help keep our community clean. All laws must be obeyed by people who live in a community.

Use the following scoring guide.

✓ Assessment Scoring Guide

Compare and Contrast Laws	
4	Explains that laws are alike in that all laws must be obeyed. Explains that laws are different in that some laws keep people safe while others help keep the community clean; gives an example of each kind of law.
3	Explains that laws are alike in that laws must be obeyed. Explain how laws are different but gives an example of only one kind of law, not both.
2	Explains that laws are alike in that all laws must be obeyed. Explains how laws are different but does not give an example of either kind of law.
1	Explains that all laws must be obeyed but is unable to tell how laws are different.

Use a Map Key

1. Library
2. 5
3. Children should draw a symbol for a tree.

Review

continued

Skills Review

Use Four Directions

1. North
2. The park
3. I would go west on Old Street and south on New Street.

Skills on Your Own

- Children's maps should include cardinal directions and a map key, as well as symbols showing their homes and school. They should use cardinal direction words to tell how to get from their home to school.

Use the following scoring guide.

✓ Assessment Scoring Guide

	Make a Map
4	Map includes home and school, as well as cardinal directions and a map key. Child is able to tell how to get from home to school, using direction words *north, south, east, west.*
3	Map includes home and school, as well as cardinal directions and a map key. Child is able to tell how to get from home to school but does not use direction words *north, south, east, west.*
2	Map includes home and school but is lacking either cardinal directions or a map key. Child is unable to tell how to get from home to school.
1	Map includes only one of the four required features.

Review

Skills Review

Use Four Directions

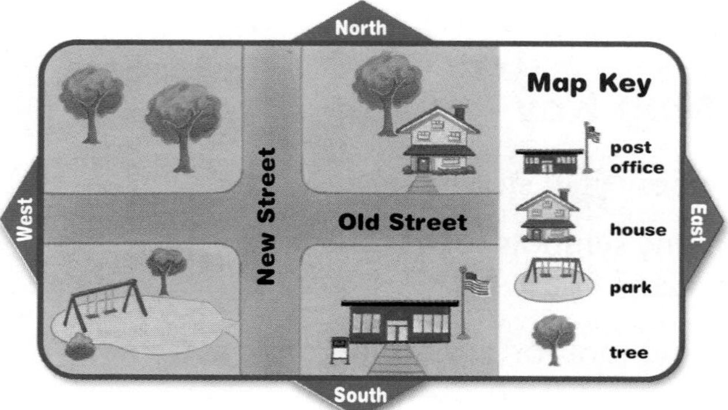

1. Is the house north or south of Old Street?
2. What place is west of New Street?
3. Tell how you would go from the house to the park. Use the words *north, south, east,* or *west.*

Skills On Your Own

Draw a map and map key of your community. Tell how you would go from home to school. Use the words *north, south, east,* and *west.*

84

Practice and Extend

Revisit the Unit Question

✓ Unit 2 Portfolio Assessment

- Have children look back at the list that they suggested on p. 43.
- Ask if children would like to add to that list now.
- Encourage children to tell what has prompted them to make the additions. Did the lessons in the unit give them more ideas?
- Help children prioritize the list to show what they like best, next best, and so on.

What did you learn?

1. Why is it important to know your home address?
2. How can you live in a community and state at the same time?
3. Name two ways a community might change over time.
4. **Write and Share** Write about a mayor and a principal. Tell how these leaders are **alike** and **different.**

Find key words in the text.

ead About Communities

ok for books like these in the library.

85

What did you learn?

1. Answers will vary but may include so you can tell people where you live.
2. A community is part of a state. A state is made up of many communities.
3. Possible answers: A community might get bigger in size and have more people or it might get smaller and have fewer people.
4. **Write and Share** Children may suggest that a principal is a school leader and a mayor is a community leader.

Locate Key Words in the Text
Use Question 2 of What did you learn? to model the Test Talk strategy.

Decide where you will look for the answer.
Have children make notes about details from the text that answer the question.

Use information from the text.
Have children check their notes and then ask themselves, "Do I have the right information?"

For additional practice, use the Test Talk Practice Book.

Read About Community

Invite children to read one or more of these books:

Where I Live, by Christopher Wormell (Dial, ISBN 0-8037-2056-4,1996) This book introduces fourteen animals in their natural habitats.

As the Roadrunner Runs: A First Book of Maps, by Gail Hartman (Bradbury, ISBN 0-02-743092-8, 1994) A lizard, a jackrabbit, a roadrunner, a deer, and a mule roam the Southwest.

A Home Album, by Peter and Connie Roop (Heineman, ISBN 1-57572-602-5, 1998) This book traces patterns of continuity and change in homes people live in.

Unit 2 Project

News for All

Objective

- Identify, describe, and communicate information about an event in the community.

Resource

- Workbook, p. 22

Materials

poster board, crayons or markers, construction paper, fabric cords, balls

Follow This Procedure

- Discuss how reporters relate news about local and world events, weather, and other topics.
- Explain that reporters ask questions, especially *who*, *what*, *where*, *when*, and *why*. Write these words on the board.
- Explain to children that they will work in small groups to act as news reporters covering an event in the community. Assign children to work in groups of five to report *who*, *what*, *where*, *when*, and *why*.
- Have children create a poster about the event and then give a news report about it.
- Some children may want to make a model of a microphone for the news reports.

✓ Assessment Scoring Guide

	News for All
4	Describes, identifies, and communicates a good understanding of how to present information about an event with specific details.
3	Describes and communicates a fair understanding of how to present information about an event but does not identify specific details of that event.
2	Has difficulty describing, identifying, and communicating a good understanding of how to present information about an event with specific details.
1	Is unable to describe, identify, and communicate an understanding about an event and/or provides few if any specific details.

Discovery CHANNEL SCHOOL

UNIT 2 Project

News for All

TV news reporters tell us what goes on in the world. You can report what goes on in your community.

1 **Choose** an event that happened or might happen in your community.

2 **Make** a poster about the event. At the bottom of your poster, write words that describe what is happening.

3 **Give** a news report about the event. Tell what happened and who was there. Tell when and where the event happened. Tell why it is news.

Internet Activity

Go to www.sfsocialstudies.com/activities to learn more about events that might happen in a community.

86

Practice and Extend

Hands-on Unit Project

✓ Performance Assessment

- The Unit Project can also be used as a performance assessment activity.
- Use the scoring guide to assess each group's work.

WEB SITE Technology

Children can launch the activity by clicking on *Grade 1, Unit 2* at **www.sfsocialstudies.com/activities.**

Workbook, p. 22

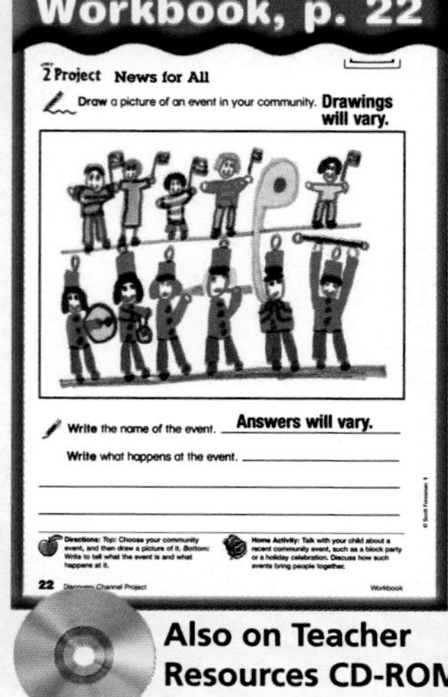
2 Project News for All
Draw a picture of an event in your community. Drawings will vary.
Write the name of the event. Answers will vary.
Write what happens at the event.

Also on Teacher Resources CD-ROM.

★ Unit 3 ★

Work! Work! Work!

Work! Work! Work!

UNIT 3

UNIT 3

Unit 3 Planning Guide

Work! Work! Work!

Begin with a Song pp.88–89 **Vocabulary Preview** pp. 90–91

Target Skill **Reading Social Studies, Sequence** pp. 92–93

Lesson Titles	Pacing	Main Ideas
Lesson 1 **Ben's Jobs** pp. 94–97 **Chart and Graph Skills: Use a Chart** pp. 98–99	2 days	• Children do jobs at home and at school. • A chart is a way to show things using words and pictures.
Lesson 2 **Needs and Wants** pp. 100–101 **Then and Now: Changing Toys** pp. 102–103	2 days	• Families have needs and wants. • Some types of toys have changed over time.
Lesson 3 **Spending and Saving** pp. 104–105 **Here and There: Money Around the World** pp. 106–107	2 days	• People who earn money must make choices about spending and saving. • People all over the world spend and save money.
Lesson 4 **Welcome to Job Day!** pp. 108–111 **Citizen Heroes:** Caring **Kid's Kitchen** pp. 112–113 **Biography: Clara Barton** pp. 114–115	3 days	• Workers provide goods and services. • Some volunteers show they care by helping people in their communities. • Clara Barton started the American Red Cross, a volunteer group that helps many people.
Lesson 5 **Interview with a Farmer** pp. 116–119 **Map and Globe Skills: Follow a Route** pp. 120–121 **Biography: George Washington Carver** pp. 122–123	3 days	• A farmer provides goods by growing the food we buy at the store. • We can use a map to find out how to get from one place to another. • George Washington Carver taught farmers how to grow peanuts and found ways to make many other products from peanuts.
Lesson 6 **From Place to Place** pp. 124–125 DK **Transportation** pp. 126–127	2 days	• Transportation moves people and goods from place to place. • Different kinds of trucks help people do different jobs.

✓ **End with a Poem** pp. 128–129 ✓ **Unit 3 Review** pp. 130–133 ✓ **Unit 3 Project** p. 134

✓ = Assessment Options

Vocabulary	Resources	Meeting Individual Needs
job	• Workbook, pp. 25–26 • Transparency 9 • Vocabulary Card: job • Every Student Learns Guide, pp. 38–41	• ESL Support, TE p. 96 • Leveled Practice, TE p. 99a
needs **wants**	• Workbook, p. 27 • Vocabulary Cards: needs, wants • Every Student Learns Guide, pp. 42–45	• ESL Support, TE p. 101 • Leveled Practice, TE p. 103a
	• Workbook, p. 28 • Every Student Learns Guide, pp. 46–49	• ESL Support, TE p. 105 • Leveled Practice, TE p. 107a
tools **goods** **service** **volunteer**	• Workbook, p. 29 • Vocabulary Cards: tools, goods, service, volunteer • Every Student Learns Guide, pp. 50–53	• ESL Support, TE p. 110 • Leveled Practice, TE p. 115a
	• Workbook, pp. 30–31 • Transparency 9 • Every Student Learns Guide, pp. 54–57	• ESL Support, TE p. 118 • Leveled Practice, TE p. 123a
transportation	• Workbook, p. 32 • Vocabulary Card: transportation • Every Student Learns Guide, pp. 58–61	• ESL Support, TE p. 126 • Leveled Practice, TE p. 127a

Providing More Depth

Multimedia Library

- ***Money* by Joe Cribb**
- ***Jobs People Do— A Day in the Life of a Builder* by Linda Hayward**
- **Songs and Music**
- **Video Field Trips**
- **Software**

Additional Resources

- Family Activities
- Vocabulary Cards
- Daily Activity Bank
- Social Studies Plus!
- Big Book Atlas
- Outline Maps
- Desk Maps

ADDITIONAL Technology

- AudioText
- TestWorks
- Teacher Resources CD-ROM
- Map Resources CD-ROM
- **www.sfsocialstudies.com**

To establish guidelines for children's safe and responsible use of the Internet, use the **Scott Foresman Internet Guide.**

Additional Internet Links

To find out more about:

- being a smart consumer, visit **www.zillions.org.**
- trains, past and present, visit the California State Railroad Museum at **www.csrmf.org.**

Key Internet Search Terms

- money
- Clara Barton
- George Washington Carver
- peanuts

Unit 3 Objectives

Beginning of Unit 3

- **List the different jobs that many people do.** (pp. 88–89)
- **Determine the meanings of words.** (pp. 90–91)
- **Recognize words that help tell order.** (pp. 92–93)
- **Analyze pictures and text to identify sequence.** (pp. 92–93)
- **Sequence information.** (pp. 92–93)

Lesson 1
Ben's Jobs
pp. 94–97

- **Describe the requirements of various jobs and the characteristics of a job well-performed.**
- **Express ideas orally based on knowledge and experiences.**
- **Sequence information.**
- **Obtain information about a topic using visual sources, such as graphics and pictures.** (pp. 98–99)
- **Recognize a chart, its parts, and its function.** (pp. 98–99)
- **Read and understand a chart.** (pp. 98–99)

Lesson 2
Needs and Wants
pp. 100–101

- **Describe ways that families meet basic human needs.**
- **Distinguish between wants and needs.**
- **Explain how people fulfill needs and wants.**
- **Distinguish among past, present, and future.** (pp. 102–103)
- **Compare and contrast toys from the past and today.** (pp. 102–103)

Lesson 3
Spending and Saving
pp. 104–105

- **Identify examples of people wanting more than they can have.**
- **Explain why wanting more than they can have requires that people make choices.**
- **Identify examples of choices families make when buying goods and services.**
- **Obtain information about a topic using visual sources, such as pictures and maps.** (pp. 106–107)

Lesson 4
Welcome to Job Day!
pp. 108–111

- **Identify examples of goods and services in the home, school, and community.**
- **Describe the requirements of various jobs and the characteristics of a job well-performed.**
- **Describe how specialized jobs contribute to the production of goods and services.**
- **Describe characteristics of good citizenship, as exemplified by ordinary people.** (pp. 112–113)
- **Identify characteristics of good citizenship, such as responsibility for the common good.** (pp. 112–113)
- **Explain that people can both give and receive care.** (pp. 112–113)
- **Identify contributions of historical figures who have influenced the nation.** (pp. 114–115)
- **Identify historic figures, such as Clara Barton who have exemplified good citizenship.** (pp. 114–115)

Lesson 5
Interview with a Farmer
pp. 116–119

- **Describe how specialized jobs contribute to the production of goods and services.**
- **Obtain information about a topic using a variety of oral sources, such as interviews.**
- **Identify the role of markets in the exchange of goods and services.**
- **Sequence information.**
- **Use a simple map to identify the location of places.** (pp. 120–121)
- **Locate places of significance on maps.** (pp. 120–121)
- **Identify a historic figure who has exhibited a love of individualism and inventiveness.** (pp. 122–123)
- **Identify contributions of historical figures who have influenced the nation.** (pp. 122–123)

Lesson 6
From Place to Place
pp. 124–125

- **Identify the role of transportation in the exchange of goods.**
- **Describe how technology has changed transportation.**
- **Obtain information about a topic using a variety of visual sources, such as pictures and graphics.** (pp. 126–127)
- **Identify ways people exchange goods and services.** (pp. 126–127)

End of Unit 3

- **Obtain information about a topic using a variety of visual sources, such as pictures and literature.** (p. 128–129)
- **Describe the requirements of a job.** (p. 134)

Assessment Options

✓ Formal Assessment

- **What did you learn?** PE/TE pp. 97, 101, 105, 111, 119, 125
- **Unit Review,** PE/TE pp. 130–133
- **Unit 3 Test,** Assessment Book pp. 9–12
- **TestWorks,** test-generator software

✓ Informal Assessment

- **Teacher's Edition Questions,** throughout Lessons and Features
- **Close and Assess,** TE pp. 93, 97, 99, 101, 103, 105, 107, 111, 113, 115, 119, 121, 123, 125, 127
- **Try it!** PE/TE pp. 93, 99, 121
- **Think and Share,** PE/TE pp. 97, 101, 105, 111, 115, 119, 123, 125
- **Caring in Action,** PE/TE p. 113
- **Hands-on History,** PE/TE p. 103

Ongoing Assessment

Ongoing Assessment is found throughout the Teacher's Edition lessons using an **If...then** model.

If = students' observable behavior, **then =** reteaching and enrichment suggestions

✓ Portfolio Assessment

- **Portfolio Assessment,** TE pp. 87, 132
- **Leveled Practice,** TE pp. 90, 99a, 103a, 107a, 115a, 123a, 127a
- **Workbook Pages,** pp. 23–34
- **Unit Review: Skills on Your Own,** PE/TE p. 132
- **Curriculum Connection: Writing,** TE pp. 99a, 103, 103a, 115, 115a, 127a

✓ Performance Assessment

- **Hands-on Unit Project** (Unit 3 Performance Assessment), PE/TE pp. 87, 130, 134
- **Internet Activity,** PE p. 134
- **Scoring Guides,** TE pp. 131, 132, 134

Test Talk

Test-Taking Strategies

Understand the Question

- **Locate Key Words in the Question,** TE p. 95
- **Locate Key Words in the Text,** TE p. 102

Understand the Answer

- **Choose the Right Answer,** TE p. 130
- **Use Information from the Text,** TE p. 107
- **Use Information from Graphics,** TE p. 91
- **Write Your Answer,** TE p. 93

For additional practice, use the Test Talk Practice Book.

Featured Strategy

Choose the Right Answer

Children will:

– Narrow the answer choices and rule out choices they know are wrong.

– Choose the best answer.

PE/TE p. 130

Curriculum Connections

Integrating Your Day

The lessons, skills, and features of Unit 3 provide many opportunities to make connections between social studies and other areas of the elementary curriculum.

Reading

Make a Picture Glossary, TE p. 91

Reading Skill—Put Things in Order (Sequence), PE/TE pp. 92–93, 94, 116–119

Sequence Stories, TE p. 93

Add to My Word Book, TE p. 99a

Reading Skill—Compare and Contrast, TE p. 100

Reading Skill—Categorize, TE p. 104

Reading Skill—Main Idea and Details, TE p. 108

I Spy a Job, TE p. 115a

What a Plot! TE p. 123a

Reading Skill—Analyze Pictures, TE p. 124

Rhyming Words, TE p. 128

Math

Measure to Make Lemonade, TE p. 93

Ordinal Numbers, TE p. 98

A Wish List, TE p. 103a

Count Pennies, TE p. 107

From Most to Least, TE p. 107a

Writing

Job Coupons, TE p. 99a

Naming Toys, TE p. 103

Give Thanks, TE p. 103a

Book of Homes, TE p. 103a

Helping Someone, TE p. 115

Who's Working? TE p. 115a

Poem, TE p. 127a

Social Studies

Literature

Read a Story, TE p. 111

All Aboard, TE p. 127a

Books About Work, TE p. 129

Read About Work, PE/TE p. 133, TE p. 133

Science

What a Plant Needs, TE p. 117

How Wheels Work, TE p. 127

Music/Drama

Write Other Song Versions, p. 89

Sing a Song, TE p. 96

Who Am I? TE p. 99a

Perform a Skit, TE p. 113

What's My Line? TE p. 115a

Dramatize an Interview, TE p. 118

Art

Hands on the Job, TE p. 94a

What Will You Pack? TE p. 100a

How Will You Go? TE p. 124a

Look for this symbol throughout the Teacher's Edition to find **Curriculum Connections.**

Professional Development

Teaching Curriculum Goals and Standards

by Dr. M. Gail Hickey
Indiana University/Purdue University

Effective social studies learning experiences must be defensible in light of national and state level curriculum standards. The National Council for Social Studies (NCSS) identified ten thematic strands in social studies. Below are several ways to incorporate two such strands as you teach *Scott Foresman Social Studies*.

Strand: Production, Distribution, and Consumption

- Students dealing with economic concepts and issues need to understand and answer questions such as: What goods are to be made? What services are to be done? How do goods and services reach the people who need them?
- *Have children study the pictures and captions found on pp. 108–109 in Lesson 4 and pp. 118–119 in Lesson 5. Make sure that children understand the similarities and differences between goods and services. Have children describe how the people shown make or produce goods or provide services to others.*

Strand: Global Connections

- Connections across the globe are becoming increasingly important. The theme of global connections typically appears in units dealing with geography, culture, and economics.
- *The Here and There feature "Money Around the World" (pp. 106–107) shows a world map and pictures of coins to create students' awareness that people all over the world spend and save money.*

ESL Support

by Jim Cummins, Ph.D.
University of Toronto

The social studies concepts students are learning are also linguistic concepts.The language of a Social Studies text will likely be challenging for ESL students to learn.

Access Content

One way to make the input comprehensible for ESL students is to modify how we present the content. We do this through extensive use of visuals such as graphic organizers, photographs, drawings, and so on. Other ways to help ESL students understand meaning are through paraphrasing the language and by use of examples and demonstrations that connect with students' prior knowledge.

The following examples in the Teacher's Edition will help you to enable ESL students to access the content:

- *"**Analyze Pictures**" on p. 96 helps English Language Learners learn and use job words. This will aid in their understanding of various jobs and their requirements.*
- *"**Using Graphic Organizers**" on p. 118 has children use graphic organizers to put things in order to show steps in a process. This activity will reinforce the use of the words* first, next, *and* last, *as well as help children understand the processes of growing peanuts and sending them to market.*

Read Aloud

Allowance

by Aiko Saubi

My mom gives me allowance
For doing all my chores.
I can spend my money
When she takes me to the store.

But I don't spend all my money
I put half of it away,
Mom calls it my savings
For a very special day.

Build Background

- Ask children to tell about any jobs they have had in which they earned money.
- Ask children how they might save money they have earned.

Read Alouds and Primary Sources

Read Alouds and Primary Sources contains additional selections to be used with Unit 3.

Bibliography

My Town, by Rebecca Treays (EDC, ISBN 0746030797, 1998) **Easy** Notable Social Studies Book, 1999

Sam and the Lucky Money, by Karen Chinn (Lee and Low, ISBN 1-880-00013-X, 1995) **Easy**

3 Pigs Garage, by Peter Lippman (Workman Publishing International Ltd., ISBN 0-7611-1361-4, 1998) **Easy**

Trucks That Build, by Lars Klove (Simon & Schuster, ISBN 0-68-98176-22, 1999) **Easy**

Buzby, by Julia Hoban and John Himmelman (illustrator), (Harper Audio, ISBN 0-694-70044-4, 1996) **On-Level**

Jamal's Busy Day, by Wade Hudson and George Ford (illustrator), (Just Us Books, ISBN 0-940975-21-1, 1991) **On-Level**

AWARD ***Night Worker, The*** by Katie Banks and Georg Hallensleben (illustrator), (Farrar Straus & Giroux, ISBN 0-374-35520-7, 2000) **On-Level** ***2001 Charlotte Zolotow Award, An ALA Notable Children's Book***

Tight Times, by Barbara Shook Hazen and Trina Shart Hyman (illustrator), (Viking, ISBN 0-140-504427-7, 1983) **On-Level**

Animal Rescue: The Best Job There Is, by Susan E. Goodman (Simon & Schuster, ISBN 0-689-81794-0, 2000) **Challenge**

AWARD ***Boy Who Loved to Draw, Benjamin West, The*** by Barbara Brenner (Houghton Mifflin, ISBN 0-395-85050-0, 1999) **Challenge** ***Notable Social Studies Trade Book, 2000***

Magic School Bus Gets Programmed, by Joanna Cole (Scholastic Books, ISBN 0-590-187-37, 1999) **Challenge**

Steven Caney's Kids' America, by Steven Caney (Workman, ISBN 0-911-10480-1, 1978) **Teacher Reference**

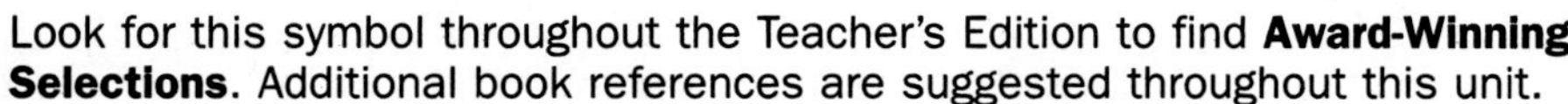

AWARD Look for this symbol throughout the Teacher's Edition to find **Award-Winning Selections**. Additional book references are suggested throughout this unit.

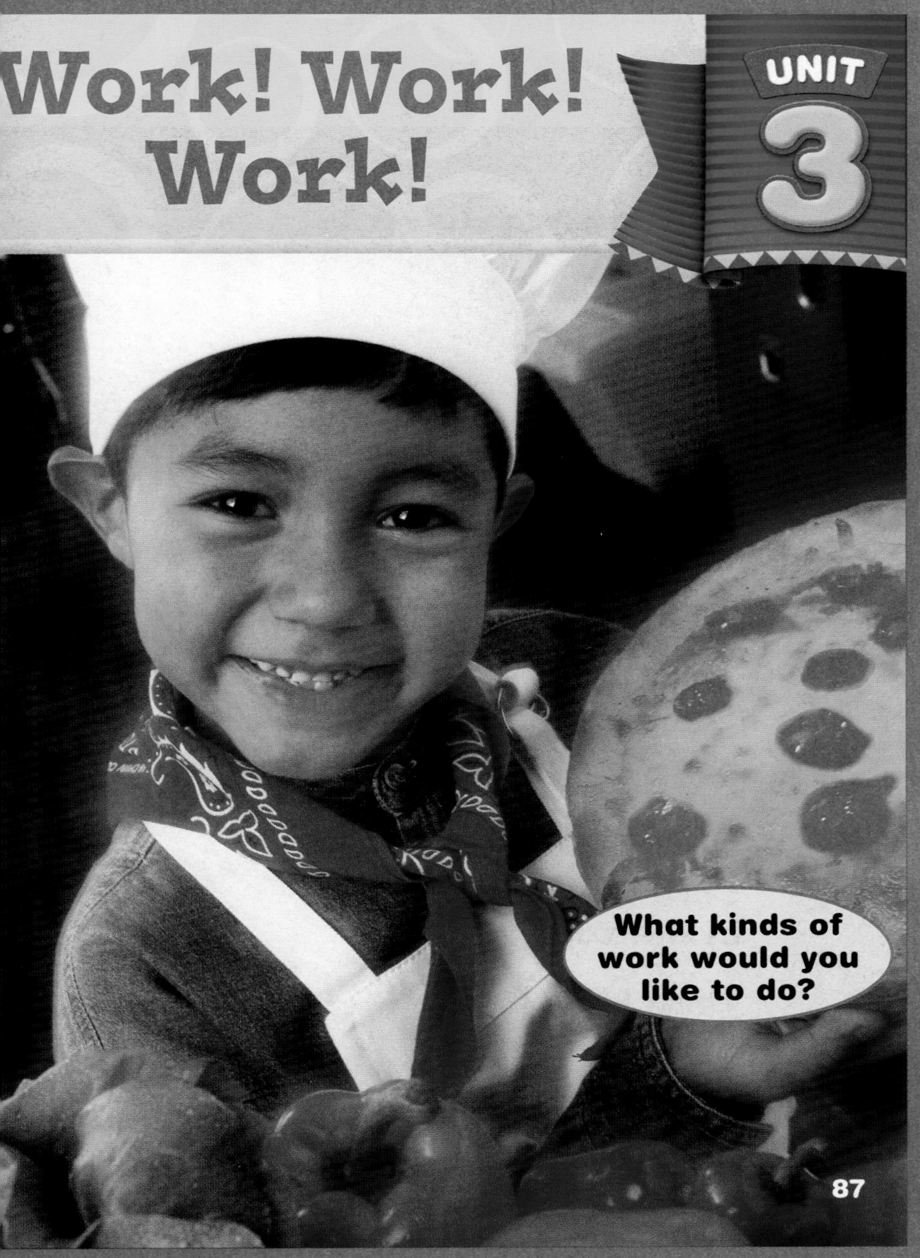

Work! Work! Work!
UNIT 3
What kinds of work would you like to do?
87

Practice and Extend

✓ **Unit 3 Performance Assessment**

The Unit 3 Project, *Jobs in Your Community*, on p. 134, is an ongoing performance assessment project to enrich children's learning throughout the unit.

- This project, which has children making a puppet and giving an interview, may be started now or at any time during this unit of study.
- A performance assessment scoring guide is located on p. 134.

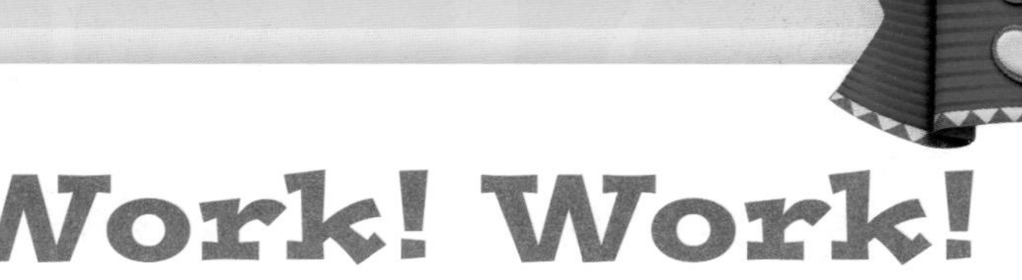

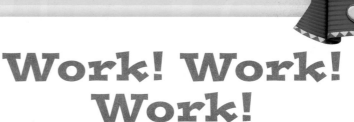

Work! Work! Work!

Unit Overview

This unit introduces children to the concepts of jobs at home and at school and explores basic economic concepts relating to how people work to fulfill their economic needs and wants.

Introduce Ben

Read the unit title and then introduce the featured child for this unit as a first-grader named Ben. Talk about what kind of work Ben might like to do.

Unit Question

- Ask children the question on this page.
- Initiate a discussion of the kinds of work children would like to do when they are grown up.
- To activate prior knowledge, list on the board the jobs children name.

✓ **Portfolio Assessment** Keep a copy of this list for the Portfolio Assessment at the end of the unit on p. 132.

Lots of Jobs

Objective

- List the different jobs that many people do.

Resources

- *Songs and Music* CD "Lots of Jobs"
- Poster 5
- Social Studies Plus!

Introduce the Song

Preview Tell children that they will be singing a song about jobs. Focus attention on the picture of Ben and review what job Ben would like to do. (Be a cook; own a pizza shop)

Warm Up To activate prior knowledge, invite children to name a place of work for each worker on the list generated on p. 87. Remind children that people can work at home or at places outside the home, such as an office, a factory, a store, or a restaurant. Ask volunteers to identify and describe what the workers at each of these places do to earn a living.

Sing the Song

- Have children sing the song "Lots of Jobs."
- Have children act out the jobs named in the song.
- You may want to have children act out other jobs from the list.

UNIT 3
Begin with a Song
Lots of Jobs
by Latrice Butler
Sung to the tune of "Skip to My Lou"
Baker, teacher,
doctor, too.
Lots of jobs
I'd like to do.
Care for animals
in the zoo.
What kinds of work
would you do?
88

Practice and Extend

Possible Misconceptions

To avoid stereotypes in occupational roles, you might encourage children to use names like homemaker for housewife, firefighter for fireman, police officer for policeman, salesperson for salesman, and so on.

Play the CD, *Songs and Music*, to listen to "Lots of Jobs."

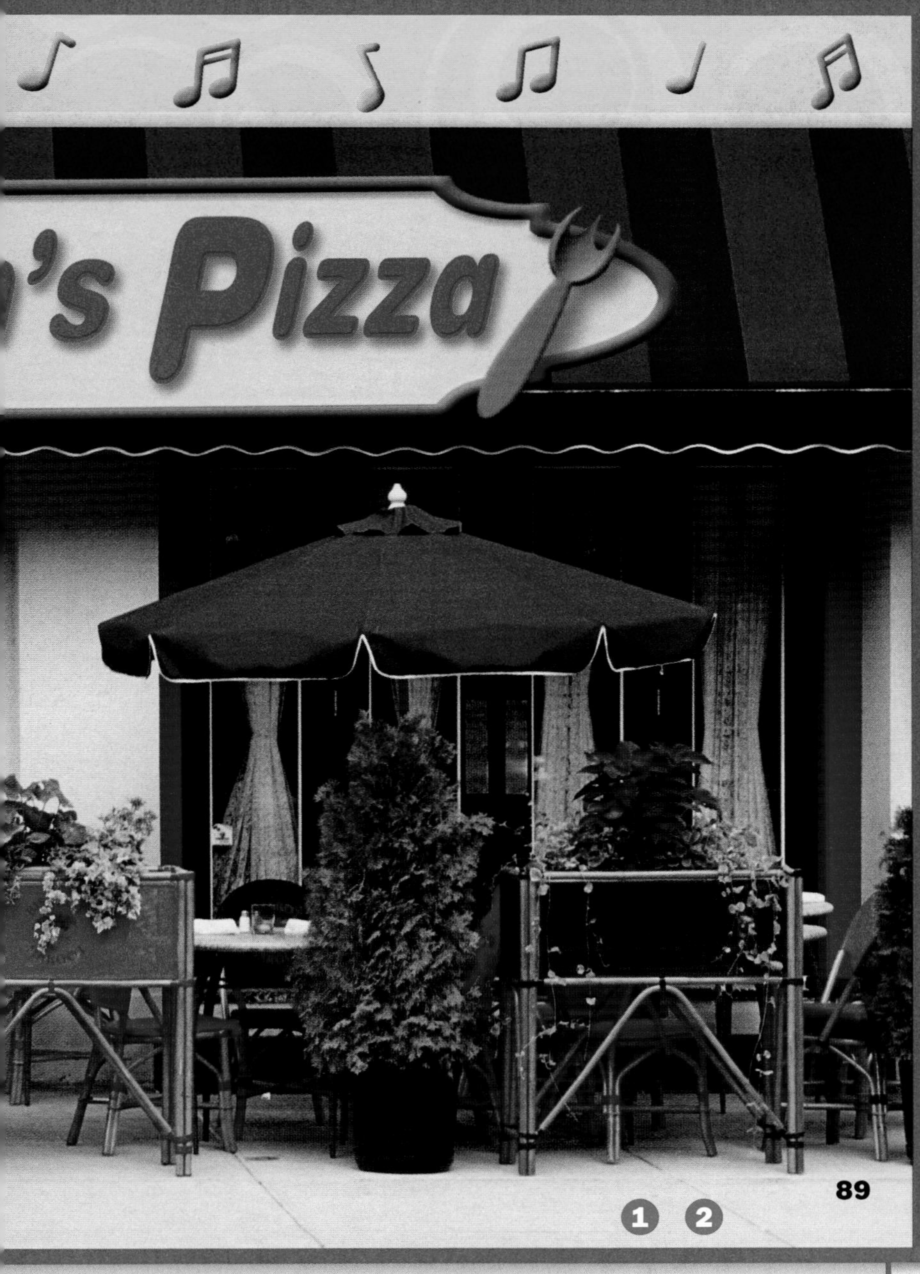

Write Other Song Versions

- Write the song "Lots of Jobs" on the board, as follows.

Lots of Jobs

__________, ____________, __________, too.
Lots of jobs I'd like to do.
____________________________.
What kinds of work would you do?

- Work with children to create their own personal version of the song "Lots of Jobs" by rewriting the first and third sentences.
- Point out that the last word in the third line should rhyme with *too* and *do*.
- Sing the new versions of the song. Children may illustrate the jobs shown in the new verses of the song.

Talk About the Picture

Direct children's attention to the photograph on these two pages. Talk with children about how this photograph differs from the one on p. 87.

1 **What does this photograph show that we did not see when we met Ben on the last page?** Answers may include a restaurant with an outside dining area and Ben in restaurant whites instead of an apron. **Compare and Contrast**

2 **What clues tell you that the photograph shows a restaurant?** Answers may include the name "Ben's Pizza," the utensils shown in the restaurant's sign, or the outside dining area. **Interpret Pictures**

Objective

- Determine the meanings of words.

Resources

- Workbook, p. 23
- Vocabulary Cards
- Poster 6

Introduce the Vocabulary

Read aloud and point to each vocabulary word and the photograph illustrating it. Have volunteers give the meanings of the words. Then have children find several examples of vocabulary words in the illustration. Write these examples on the board:

Vocabulary Word	Illustrated Examples
job	boy carrying trash, adults working
needs	home, groceries
wants	bike, toy
tools	wrench, jackhammer, rake
goods	fruits, vegetables, cars
service	paper delivery, road workers
volunteer	crossing guard, candy striper
transportation	bus, trucks, cars

SOCIAL STUDIES STRAND
Economics

Listed below are some basic principles of economics for young children. Direct your discussion of the illustration toward the development of these concepts.

- needs and wants
- goods and services
- types of jobs
- choices people make
- ways people exchange goods and services
- ways people use money
- role of stores in the exchange of goods and services
- people producing and consuming goods and services

Vocabulary Preview

job

needs

wants

tools

Practice and Extend

MEETING INDIVIDUAL NEEDS
Leveled Practice

Take a Tour

Invite children to take a tour through the community in the illustration.

Easy Explain that you will be their tour guide. Begin at one end of a specific street and describe in detail all the buildings, people, signs, vehicles and other things along the way. Have children repeat the vocabulary words as you guide them from one end of the street to the other. **Reteach**

On-Level Have children take turns leading a tour through the community, using vocabulary words to describe what they see. **Extend**

Challenge Invite children to describe something in the community using some of the vocabulary words. Have others guess what is being described. **Enrich**

Talk About the Illustration

Allow children time to study the illustration. The picture shows a community with many kinds of workers and stores. Encourage children to talk about what various workers in the illustration are doing.

Use Information from Graphics

1 **How are people using tools?** Possible answers: digging up the street, cooking, painting. Tell students to use details from the picture to support their answers. **Apply Information**

2 **How are volunteers helping people?** As volunteer hospital workers, firefighters, and crossing guards **Apply Information**

Look Ahead

Tell children that they will learn more about each of these words as they study Unit 3.

You may want to revisit the picture with children to review the concepts and vocabulary in the unit.

3 **How are the types of transportation shown in the picture alike and different?** Possible answers: All shown have wheels; some carry many people, and some carry few. **Compare and Contrast**

4 **What do you think would happen if these people didn't do their jobs?** Possible answers: Someone might get hurt; you could not buy what you need and want. **Predict**

CURRICULUM CONNECTION
Reading

Make a Picture Glossary

Children can add the vocabulary for Unit 3 to "My Word Book." Words may be entered at the beginning of the unit or added as they are introduced.

WEB SITE
Technology

You can look up vocabulary words online. Click on *Social Studies Library* and select the dictionary at **www.sfsocialstudies.com.**

Workbook, p. 23

Draw a picture for each word. Drawings will vary.

job	tools
goods	wants
service	needs
volunteer	transportation

Also on Teacher Resources CD-ROM.

Ben at Work

Put Things in Order (Sequence)

Target Skill

Objectives

- Recognize words that help tell order.
- Analyze pictures and text to identify sequence.
- Sequence information.

Resource

- Workbook, p. 24

About the Unit Target Skill

- The target reading skill for this unit is Put Things in Order.
- Children are introduced to the unit target skill here and are given an opportunity to practice it.
- Further opportunities to put things in order are found throughout Unit 3.

1 Introduce and Motivate

Preview To determine if children understand the concept of putting things in order, or sequencing, ask children to tell when they do things in a certain order. Possible answers may include their routines for getting ready for school or going home from school. Write the word *order* on the board and explain that the word means "to tell when things happen."

Warm Up To activate prior knowledge, direct children's attention to today's class schedule. Ask a volunteer to name three activities the class will do before lunch. Record their responses in complete sentences as they are given. Have children arrange the activities in order to tell about the morning at school.

UNIT 3
Reading Social Studies

Ben at Work

Put Things in Order

Target Skill

Hi! I'm Ben. Someday I want to own a pizza shop.

Saturday I had a lemonade stand. These pictures show the order in which things happened. Use your own words to tell what I did.

First

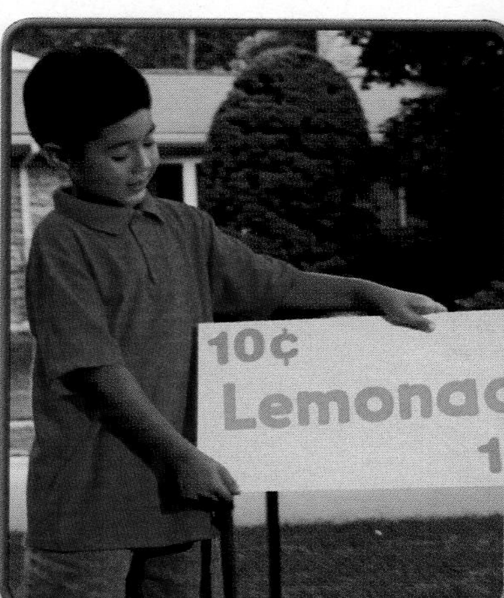

Next

Practice and Extend

ESL

ACCESS CONTENT

ESL Support

Work with New Words Discuss the meaning of the words *first, next,* and *last*. Have children write each word on a card and then write a word in their home language below it to remind them of the English meaning.

Beginning Display pictures that show time order and have children display the appropriate card for each event or step pictured. Some children may benefit from numbering the cards *1–3*.

Intermediate As children become more proficient using the terms, mix the events or steps and repeat.

Advanced Have children work in pairs. Ask one child to give oral examples of time order and the other to hold up the appropriate card. Then have them reverse roles.

Did you use words like **first, next,** and **last?** Those words tell the order in which things happened.

First, I made the lemonade.

Next, I set up my stand.

Last, I sold a cup to my friend.

Look for **first, next,** and **last** as you learn more about people at work.

10¢
Lemonade
10¢

Last

Try it!

Tell or write about how Ben could make a pizza. Use the words **first, next,** and **last.** Draw pictures to show the order in which things happen.

93

CURRICULUM CONNECTION Math

Measure to Make Lemonade

Help children to measure the ingredients and then make lemonade. Direct children to stir the following ingredients together until dissolved: 5 cups cold water, 2/3 cup granulated sugar, 1 cup lemon juice. Then help children pour the lemonade over ice.

Workbook, p. 24

Put Things in Order
Write 1, 2, and 3 to show the order.
3
1
2
Write first, next, and last to show the order.
first
last
next

Also on Teacher Resources CD-ROM.

2 Teach and Discuss

Read p. 92 and have children examine the three pictures on pp. 92–93. Invite three volunteers to tell what Ben is doing in each picture.

Read p. 93 and focus on the terms *first, next, last*. Point out that these words help connect parts of the story. Reread the story while children focus on the pictures. Point out that there may be more than one way to order some of the steps (for example, Ben could set up the lemonade stand first and make the lemonade next).

Ongoing Assessment

If... children do not understand that the words *first, next,* and *last* tell order,

then... list *first, next, last* on the board and write *1* next to *first*, *2* next to *next*, and *3* next to *last*.

Tell children that putting things in order when we read helps us understand when things happened.

3 Close and Assess

Try it!

Test Talk

Write Your Answer

Review with children the steps in making a pizza. Be sure they are familiar with pizza and know its ingredients. Children's stories and drawings should correctly show the order for making a pizza and correctly use the words *first, next,* and *last*. Have partners read each other's written answers and look at each other's pictures. Partners can check that the steps are in order. Then they can talk about what would happen if the order of the steps was changed.

Workbook Support

Use the following Workbook pages to support content and skills development as you teach Unit 3. You can also view and print Workbook pages from the Teacher Resources CD-ROM.

Workbook, p. 23

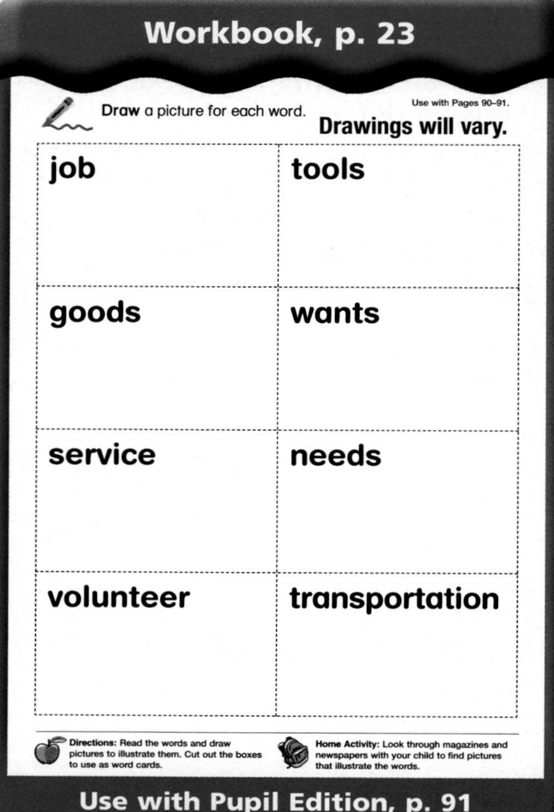

Use with Pages 90–91.

Draw a picture for each word. **Drawings will vary.**

job	tools
goods	wants
service	needs
volunteer	transportation

Directions: Read the words and draw pictures to illustrate them. Cut out the boxes to use as word cards.

Home Activity: Look through magazines and newspapers with your child to find pictures that illustrate the words.

Use with Pupil Edition, p. 91

Workbook, p. 24

Use with Pages 92–93.

Put Things in Order

Write *1*, *2*, and *3* to show the order.

3 **1** **2**

Write *first*, *next*, and *last* to show the order.

first **last** **next**

Directions: *Top:* Show the order in which things happen by writing *1*, *2*, and *3*. *Bottom:* Write *first*, *next*, and *last* to show the order.

Home Activity: Share a comic strip with your child. Then cut apart the boxes, mix them up, and help your child put them back in order.

Use with Pupil Edition, p. 93

Workbook, p. 25

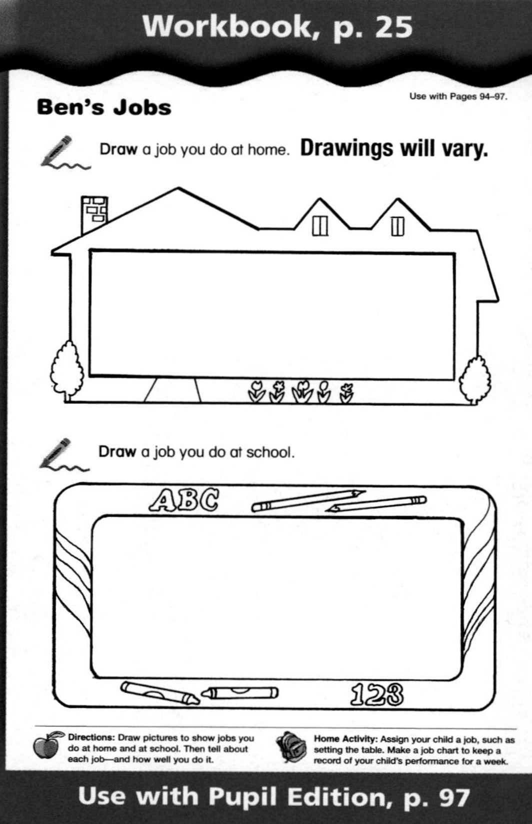

Use with Pages 94–97.

Ben's Jobs

Draw a job you do at home. **Drawings will vary.**

Draw a job you do at school.

Directions: Draw pictures to show jobs you do at home and at school. Then tell about each job—and how well you do it.

Home Activity: Assign your child a job, such as setting the table. Make a job chart to keep a record of your child's performance for a week.

Use with Pupil Edition, p. 97

Workbook, p. 26

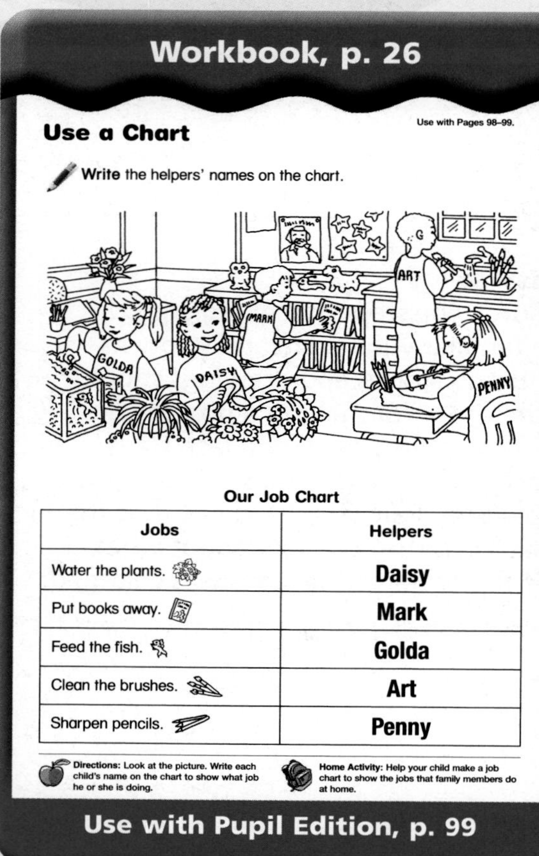

Use with Pages 98–99.

Use a Chart

Write the helpers' names on the chart.

Our Job Chart

Jobs	Helpers
Water the plants.	**Daisy**
Put books away.	**Mark**
Feed the fish.	**Golda**
Clean the brushes.	**Art**
Sharpen pencils.	**Penny**

Directions: Look at the picture. Write each child's name on the chart to show what job he or she is doing.

Home Activity: Help your child make a job chart to show the jobs that family members do at home.

Use with Pupil Edition, p. 99

Workbook, p. 27

Use with Pages 100–101.

Needs and Wants

Circle things you need to stay alive.

Draw something you want. **Drawings will vary.**

Directions: *Top:* Circle the pictures of things you *need* in order to live. *Bottom:* Draw a picture of something you *want* rather

Home Activity: During a shopping trip, help your child distinguish between needs and wants.

Use with Pupil Edition, p. 101

Workbook, p. 28

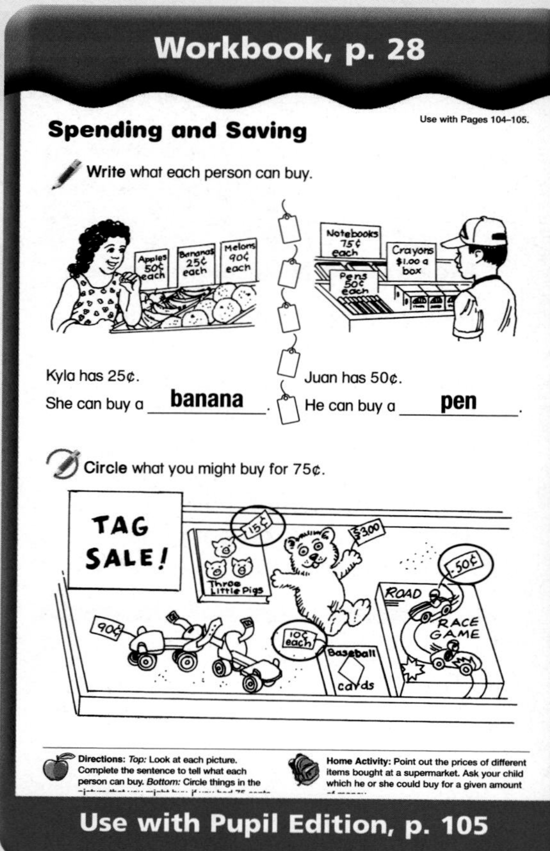

Use with Pages 104–105.

Spending and Saving

Write what each person can buy.

Kyla has 25¢. She can buy a **banana**.

Juan has 50¢. He can buy a **pen**.

Circle what you might buy for 75¢.

Directions: *Top:* Look at each picture. Complete the sentence to tell what each person can buy. *Bottom:* Circle things in the

Home Activity: Point out the prices of different items bought at a supermarket. Ask your child which he or she could buy for a given amount

Use with Pupil Edition, p. 105

Workbook Support

Workbook, p. 29

Welcome to Job Day!

Use with Pages 108–111.

Circle people who have service jobs.

Draw a job you might like to have. **Drawings will vary.**

Directions: *Top:* Circle pictures of workers who provide services. *Bottom:* Draw a job you might like to do.

Home Activity: Point out to your child examples of people who provide services in your community.

Use with Pupil Edition, p. 111

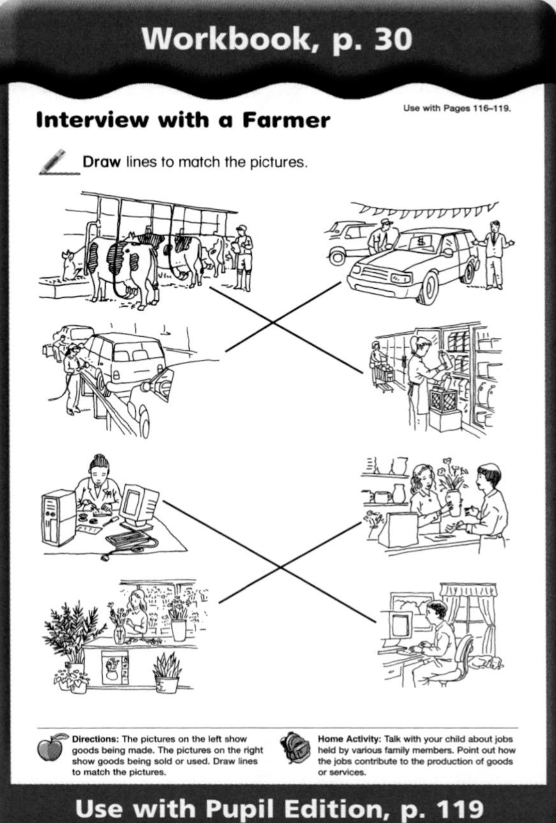

Workbook, p. 30

Interview with a Farmer

Use with Pages 116–119.

Draw lines to match the pictures.

Directions: The pictures on the left show goods being made. The pictures on the right show goods being sold or used. Draw lines to match the pictures.

Home Activity: Talk with your child about jobs held by various family members. Point out how the jobs contribute to the production of goods or services.

Use with Pupil Edition, p. 119

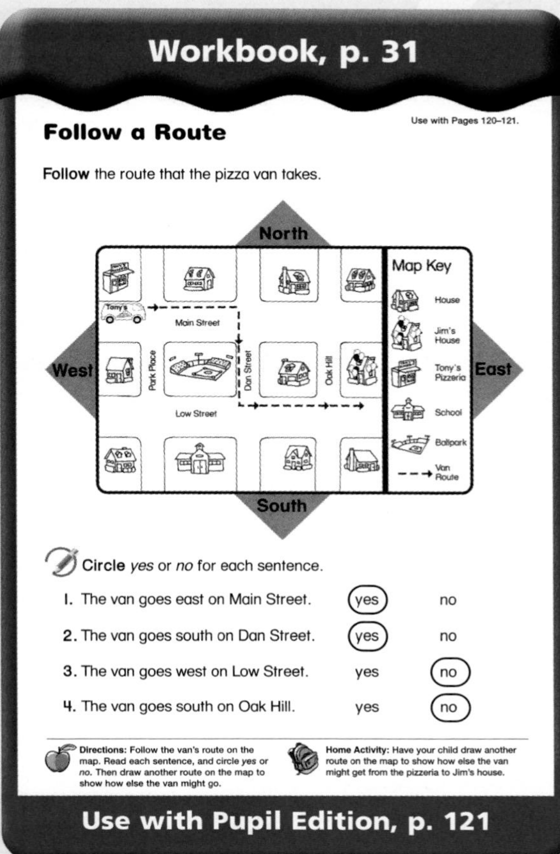

Workbook, p. 31

Follow a Route

Use with Pages 120–121.

Follow the route that the pizza van takes.

Circle *yes* or *no* for each sentence.

1. The van goes east on Main Street. (yes) no
2. The van goes south on Dan Street. (yes) no
3. The van goes west on Low Street. yes (no)
4. The van goes south on Oak Hill. yes (no)

Directions: Follow the van's route on the map. Read each sentence, and circle *yes* or *no*. Then draw another route on the map to show how else the van might go.

Home Activity: Have your child draw another route on the map to show how else the van might get from the pizzeria to Jim's house.

Use with Pupil Edition, p. 121

Workbook, p. 32

From Place to Place

Use with Pages 124–125.

Make a chart to show then and now.
Cut out the pictures.
Paste them on the chart.

Now	Then	Now
Then	Now	Then
Now	Now	Then
Now	Then	Then

Directions: Make a two-column Transportation chart with the headings *Then* and *Now*. Cut out the pictures and paste them under the correct heading.

Home Activity: Talk with your child about how means of transportation have changed since you were a child.

Use with Pupil Edition, p. 125

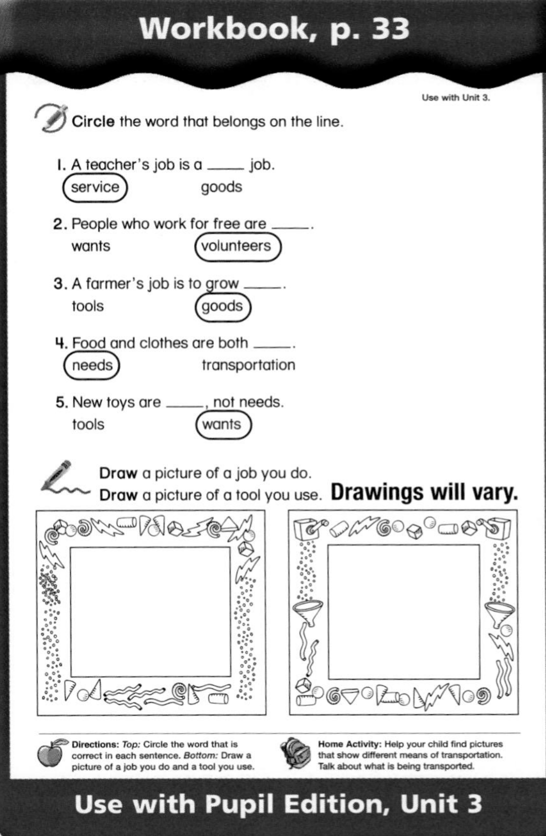

Workbook, p. 33

Use with Unit 3.

Circle the word that belongs on the line.

1. A teacher's job is a ____ job.
   (service) goods
2. People who work for free are ____.
   wants (volunteers)
3. A farmer's job is to grow ____.
   tools (goods)
4. Food and clothes are both ____.
   (needs) transportation
5. New toys are ____, not needs.
   tools (wants)

Draw a picture of a job you do.
Draw a picture of a tool you use. **Drawings will vary.**

Directions: *Top:* Circle the word that is correct in each sentence. *Bottom:* Draw a picture of a job you do and a tool you use.

Home Activity: Help your child find pictures that show different means of transportation. Talk about what is being transported.

Use with Pupil Edition, Unit 3

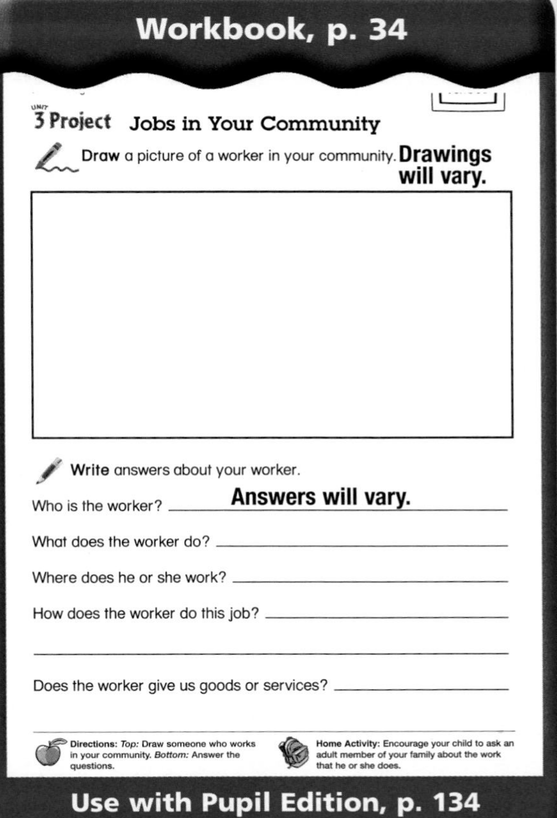

Workbook, p. 34

Unit 3 Project **Jobs in Your Community**

Draw a picture of a worker in your community. **Drawings will vary.**

Write answers about your worker.

Who is the worker? **Answers will vary.**

What does the worker do? ____

Where does he or she work? ____

How does the worker do this job? ____

Does the worker give us goods or services? ____

Directions: *Top:* Draw someone who works in your community. *Bottom:* Answer the questions.

Home Activity: Encourage your child to ask an adult member of your family about the work that he or she does.

Use with Pupil Edition, p. 134

Assessment Support

Use the following Assessment Book pages and TestWorks to assess content and skills in Unit 3. You can also view and print Assessment Book pages from the Teacher Resources CD-ROM.

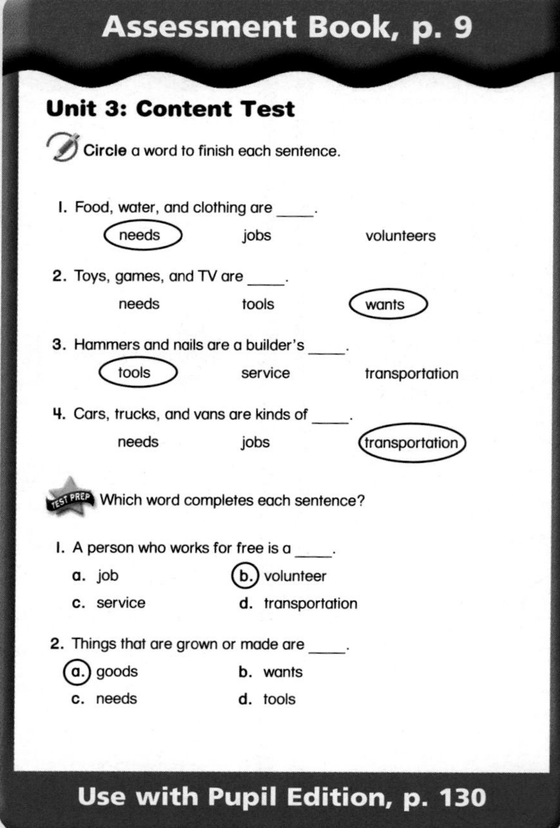

Assessment Book, p. 9

Unit 3: Content Test

Circle a word to finish each sentence.

1. Food, water, and clothing are ____.
   (needs) jobs volunteers
2. Toys, games, and TV are ____.
   needs tools (wants)
3. Hammers and nails are a builder's ____.
   (tools) service transportation
4. Cars, trucks, and vans are kinds of ____.
   needs jobs (transportation)

Which word completes each sentence?

1. A person who works for free is a ____.
   a. job (b.) volunteer
   c. service d. transportation
2. Things that are grown or made are ____.
   (a.) goods b. wants
   c. needs d. tools

Use with Pupil Edition, p. 130

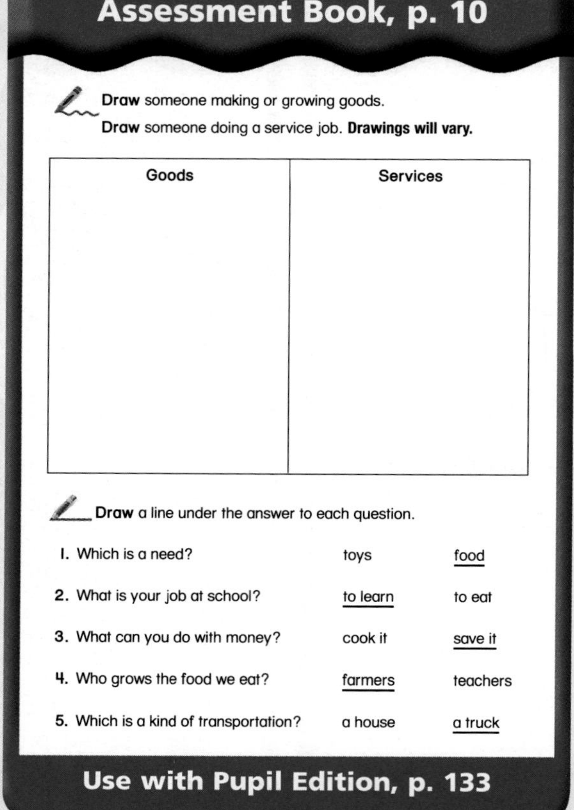

Assessment Book, p. 10

Draw someone making or growing goods.
Draw someone doing a service job. **Drawings will vary.**

Goods	Services

Draw a line under the answer to each question.

1. Which is a need? toys <u>food</u>
2. What is your job at school? <u>to learn</u> to eat
3. What can you do with money? cook it <u>save it</u>
4. Who grows the food we eat? <u>farmers</u> teachers
5. Which is a kind of transportation? a house <u>a truck</u>

Use with Pupil Edition, p. 133

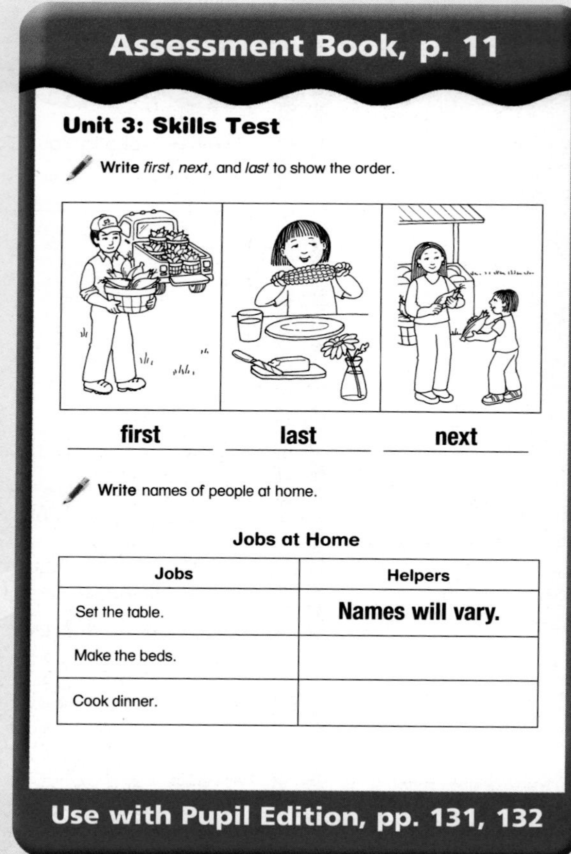

Assessment Book, p. 11

Unit 3: Skills Test

Write *first*, *next*, and *last* to show the order.

first **last** **next**

Write names of people at home.

Jobs at Home

Jobs	Helpers
Set the table.	**Names will vary.**
Make the beds.	
Cook dinner.	

Use with Pupil Edition, pp. 131, 132

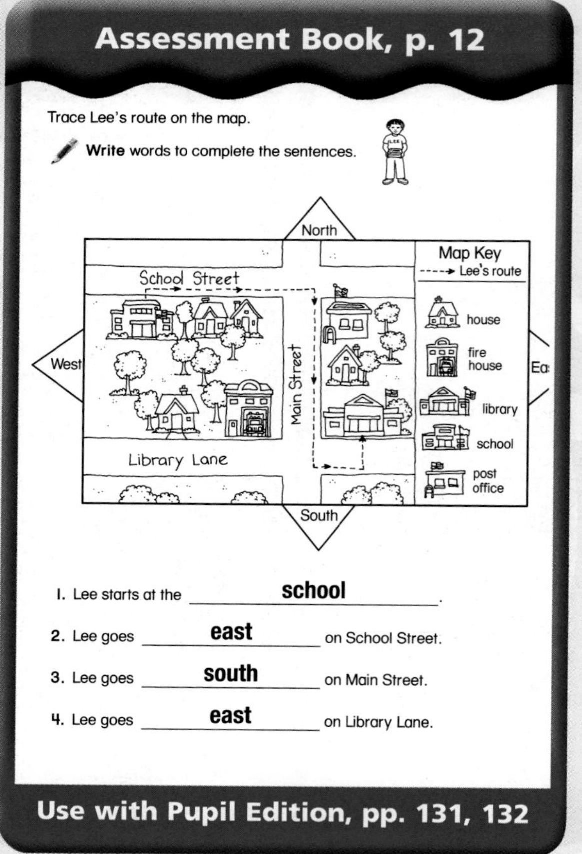

Assessment Book, p. 12

Trace Lee's route on the map.

Write words to complete the sentences.

1. Lee starts at the **school**.
2. Lee goes **east** on School Street.
3. Lee goes **south** on Main Street.
4. Lee goes **east** on Library Lane.

Use with Pupil Edition, pp. 131, 132

Lesson 1 Overview

Ben's Jobs pages 94–97	Children will learn the meaning of the word *job* and explore the kinds of jobs that children perform at home and at school.	Time 20–30 minutes Resources • Workbook, p. 25 • Vocabulary Card job • Transparency 9 • Every Student Learns Guide, pp. 38–41
Use a Chart pages 98–99	Children will learn how to use charts, such as jobs charts.	Time 15–20 minutes Resource • Workbook, p. 26

Build Background

Activity

Hands on the Job

Time 15–20 minutes

Create a "Hands on the Job" chart similar to the one shown. Have children trace their hands on two different colors of paper. Children then write or draw one thing they do to help at home on one hand and a way they help at school on the other hand.

If time is short, have children suggest ways they help at home and at school. You can then write their ideas inside the large hand outlines.

Read Aloud

Little Helper

by Andy Parker

I run for Daddy's slippers.
I wheel the baby out.
I find my Grandma's glasses.
You never see me pout.
I help when Mommy's busy.
I am always kind and glad.
I am the kindest
little helper
A family
ever had.

Ben's Jobs

Objectives

- Describe the requirements of various jobs and the characteristics of a job well-performed.
- Express ideas orally based on knowledge and experiences.
- Sequence information.

Vocabulary

job the work people do (p. 94)

QUICK Teaching Plan

If time is short, have children look at the pictures and brainstorm a list of jobs at home.

- Have them brainstorm a list of jobs at school.

1 Introduce and Motivate

Preview Display the Vocabulary Card **job** and ask children what a job is. Then share its meaning as "the work people do." Have children locate the term as they preview the lesson.

Warm Up To activate prior knowledge, ask children to give examples of work they do at home. Then ask children to suppose they are visiting Ben's family. Have them name jobs they might see people in the family doing. Invite volunteers to take turns selecting one of the jobs and acting it out for the class.

Ben's Jobs

I do lots of jobs to help at home. A **job** is the work people do. **First,** I put away my toys all by myself.

1 2

Next, I feed our dog. My whole family takes turns caring for Rusty.

94

Practice and Extend

READING SKILL Put Things in Order

Target Skill

Sequence Tell children that this lesson includes words to help them tell order.

- After they read pp. 94–97, give children a copy of Transparency 9.
- Have them complete it to show what Ben did first, next, and last at home.

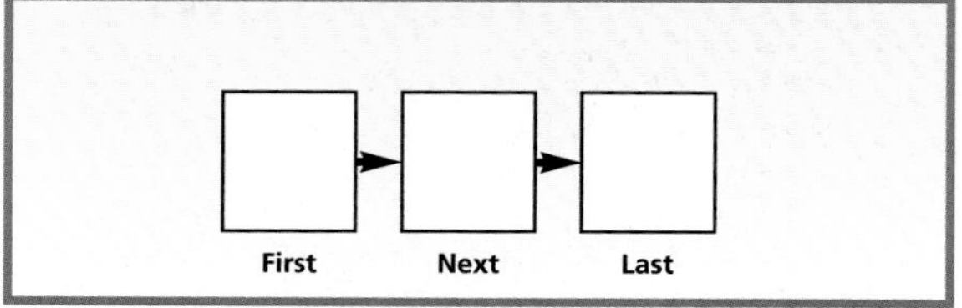

Last, my family and I work together to make dinner. I like to help cook. When the work is done, we all eat. I like that part the best! ❸ ❹ ❺

95

SOCIAL STUDIES
Background

Possible Misconceptions

- Children may think that work performed at home has less value than work performed outside of the home.
- Work performed at home can include such activities as child care and housework, as well as work done for an outside employer.
- Discuss how work done at home is important.

WEB SITE
Technology

You can look up vocabulary words online. Click on *Social Studies Library* and select the dictionary at **www.sfsocialstudies.com.**

2 Teach and Discuss

Page 94

Identify Ben in the photographs. Invite volunteers to name the jobs Ben is doing. Point out that Ben is doing each job by himself.

❶ **What jobs can you do by yourself?** Answers will vary but should reflect jobs children can perform individually. **Apply Information**

Test Talk

Locate Key Words in the Question

❷ **Compare two jobs that you can do.** Tell children that the word *compare* means to tell how two or more things are alike. Encourage children to tell about two jobs—and to tell what is the same about those jobs. **Compare and Contrast**

Page 95

Point out the members of Ben's family. Discuss the jobs involved in making dinner.

❸ **Tell how Ben knows when he has done a job well.** Possible answers: The toys are all put away; the dog is no longer hungry; the dinner is delicious. **Make Inferences**

❹ **Why might family members work together to do some jobs?** Possible answers: to get jobs done more quickly, to make things fair for everyone, to spend time together, or to make more time for fun **Make Inferences**

❺ **What other jobs might Ben's family do together?** Answers will vary but should reflect jobs performed by two or more people. **Make Inferences**

continued

Page 96

Have children name the school jobs shown in the drawing.

6 **What is your big job in school?** To learn **Apply Information**

7 **How might you be rewarded for a job well done at school?** Answers may include feeling proud, getting a sticker on a paper, getting a tally on a chart, or getting praise. **Apply Information**

SOCIAL STUDIES STRAND
Economics

Point out that going to school is similar to grown-ups going to work or working at home. Invite volunteers to discuss jobs done by adults.

8 **Your job is to go to school and learn. Why is this such an important job?** Possible answers: to prepare for work as an adult, to understand things about the world, to learn how things work, to learn how to cooperate with others **Make Inferences**

6 7 8 I have jobs at school. My big job is to learn. That is your job at school too.

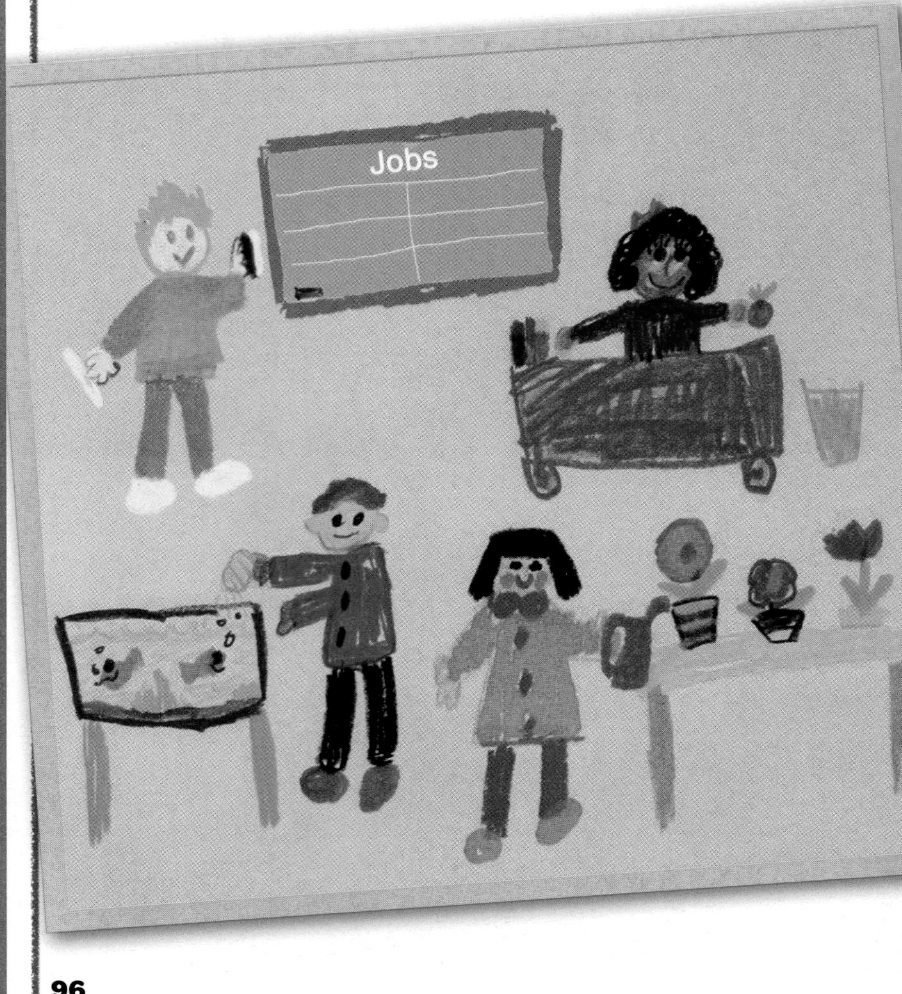

96

Practice and Extend

ACCESS CONTENT
ESL Support

Analyze Pictures The pictures in Lesson 1 show jobs children can do at home and at school.

Beginning Model pointing to each picture while telling about each job. Have children point to the pictures and repeat the job words.

Intermediate Demonstrate the jobs pictured and invite children to identify them. Invite children to take turns performing jobs for others to identify.

Advanced Invite children to draw a picture on an index card about jobs they do at home. Mix the cards. Have children take turns picking a card and dictating a sentence describing how to do the job.

For additional ESL support, use Every Student Learns Guide, pp. 38–41.

CURRICULUM CONNECTION
Music

Sing a Song

Using lesson vocabulary words in songs not only reinforces the word and its meaning, but also helps reach children with other learning styles and talents. Have children take turns acting out a school job for others to guess. Children might pretend to pass out papers, hold the flag, or do other school tasks. Other related song adaptations could be "This Is a Job I Do at Home "or "This Is a Job I'd Like to Do."

Sing to the tune of
This Is the Way We Go to School

This Is a Job I Do at School

This is a job I do at school,
Do at school,
Do at school.
This is a job I do at school.
Guess what it could be.

Today I have a special job. I get to feed our hamster. What are your special jobs at school?

  11

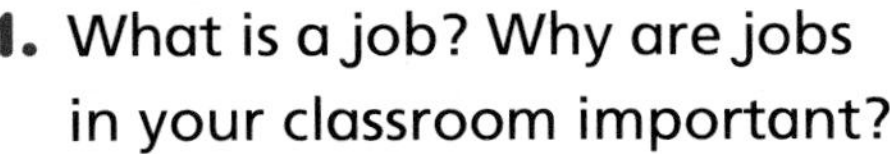

What did you learn?

1. What is a job? Why are jobs in your classroom important?
2. How are jobs at home and at school the same? How are they different?
3. **Think and Share** Tell or write about a job you do well. Use the words **first, next,** and **last** in your story.

97

Workbook, p. 25

Ben's Jobs

Draw a job you do at home. Drawings will vary.

Draw a job you do at school.

Also on Teacher Resources CD-ROM.

Page 97

Discuss the special school job in the photograph.

9 **What things does Ben need to know to do his special job?** Possible answers: He needs to know how often to feed the hamster and where the hamster food is kept. **Make Inferences**

Ongoing Assessment

If... children do not understand why Ben's job is special,	**then...** explain that a special job is a job you don't get to do every day.

10 **What special jobs might you do in art class?** Answers will vary but may include handing out or putting away art supplies. **Apply Information**

11 **Tell how you might know when someone else has done a job well.** Possible answer: It is done completely, neatly, and on time. **Make Inferences**

3 Close and Assess

Have children brainstorm a list of all the special jobs they do. Encourage children to name jobs both inside and outside school. Then have children talk to a partner about what is required for them to do in their favorite special job and how they know when they did the job well.

What did you learn?

1. A job is the work someone does. Classroom jobs are important because they help make things run smoothly—so everyone can learn.
2. Answers will vary but should reflect jobs of children and the similarities and differences between those done at home and at school.
3. **Think and Share** Answers should explain the steps in the job.

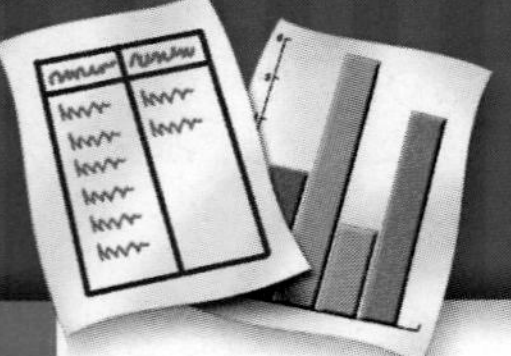

Use a Chart

Objectives

- Obtain information about a topic using visual sources, such as graphics and pictures.
- Recognize a chart, its parts, and its function.
- Read and understand a chart.

Skill Vocabulary

chart a way to show things using words and pictures (p. 98)

1 Introduce and Motivate

Preview Ask children to say what they think a chart is. Tell children that a chart is a special way to show information. Mention that a chart often uses both words and pictures.

Warm Up To activate prior knowledge, have children identify any charts displayed in your classroom, such as the class schedule, a calendar, and so on. Explain that learning how to read a chart will help them understand a different way to get organized information.

2 Teach and Discuss

Read the introduction. Prior to reading the chart and discussing its parts, ask children to identify their left and right hands.

1 **What does the right side of the chart show?** Helpers **Interpret Charts**

2 **How many helpers are there on the chart?** Three **Interpret Charts**

3 **What job will Sam do? How do you know?** He will clean the board; his name is next to that job. **Interpret Charts**

Chart and Graph Skills

Use a Chart

A **chart** is a way to show things using words and pictures. This chart shows some special jobs children do in school.

1 2 3

Jobs at School	
Jobs	**Helpers**
Feed hamster.	**Ben**
Water plants.	**Mary**
Clean board.	**Sam**

- The title tells what the chart is about. What is this chart about?
- The left side of the chart lists the jobs.
- Look at the name next to the first job. Which helper feeds the hamster?

98

Practice and Extend

CURRICULUM CONNECTION
Math

Ordinal Numbers

- The lesson requires children to find the first job on the "Jobs at School" chart. Children less familiar with ordinal numbers will benefit from a quick review.
- To make discussion of charts easier, prepare and label rows of classroom charts with the number and the ordinal word cards.

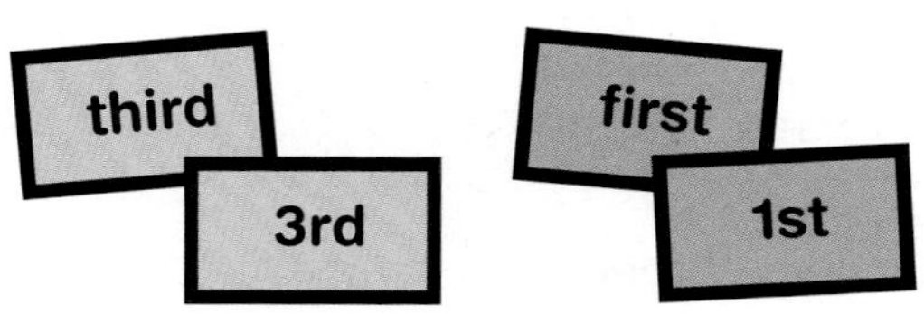

Ben and his sister Rita have jobs at home. This chart shows the jobs they do. Use the chart to answer the questions.

Jobs at Home	
Jobs	**Helper**
Set table.	Ben
Clear table.	Rita
Walk dog.	Ben
Feed dog.	Rita

4

1. Who clears the table?
2. Who walks the dog?
3. **On Your Own** Make a chart to show the jobs your family does at home.

99

Workbook, p. 26

Use a Chart

Write the helpers' names on the chart.

Our Job Chart

Jobs	Helpers
Water the plants.	Daisy
Put books away.	Mark
Feed the fish.	Golda
Clean the brushes.	Art
Sharpen pencils.	Penny

Also on Teacher Resources CD-ROM.

4 **Look at the chart on p. 99. Why do you think Ben and Rita made this chart?** So that each would know what job to do **Make Inferences**

3 Close and Assess

To increase awareness of charts, have children go on a "chart hunt." As you go through the day, have children try to find charts in the classroom, halls, and in books. Keep a tally of how many charts are found. Have each child tell a partner what one of the charts shows.

Try it!

1. Rita clears the table.
2. Ben walks the dog.
3. **On Your Own** Charts will vary but should reflect jobs of family members.

Use with pages 94–99

Lesson 1 Wrap-Up

MEETING INDIVIDUAL NEEDS

Leveled Practice

Find Pictures of Jobs

Ask children to draw or cut out magazine pictures that show people doing work.

Easy Use the pictures to make a classroom poster. Have each child tell about one of the jobs on the poster. **Reteach**

On-Level Use the pictures to make a classroom poster. Draw a word web on the board. Ask children to choose a picture from the poster for the topic of the web. Have children fill in the web with words that relate to the job. **Extend**

Challenge Use the pictures to make a classroom poster. Have children write and illustrate a story about one of the jobs pictured on the poster. Volunteers may share their stories with the class. **Enrich**

Hands-on Activities

CURRICULUM CONNECTION

Reading

Add to "My Word Book"

Objective Define and illustrate the word *job*.

Resources Vocabulary Card **job**

Materials crayons, pencils

Learning Style Visual

Individual 

Time 10–15 minutes

1. Display the Vocabulary Card. Direct children to find the "J" page in their word book and have them write the word *job* in a word space.

2. Have children draw a picture to illustrate the word and write a sentence below or next to the picture using the word.

CURRICULUM CONNECTION

Drama

Who Am I?

Objective Recognize jobs done at home.

Materials chart paper, marker

Learning Style Visual/Verbal/ Kinesthetic

Group 

Time 15–30 minutes

1. Help children make a class list of jobs people do at home.

2. Invite volunteers to select a job and act it out for the class.

3. The other children can use the list to figure out which job is being done.

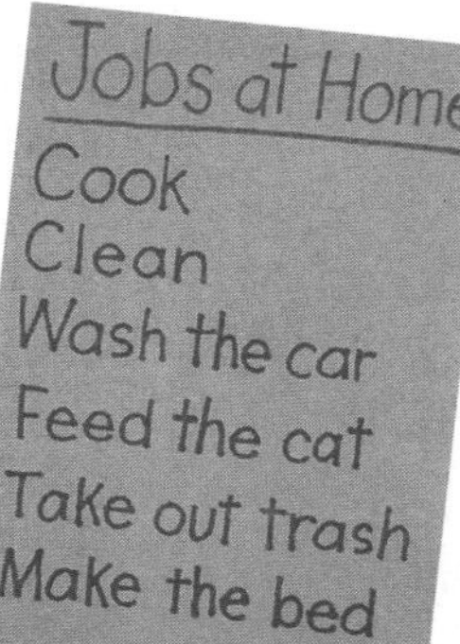

Jobs at Home
Cook
Clean
Wash the car
Feed the cat
Take out trash
Make the bed

CURRICULUM CONNECTION

Writing

Job Coupons

Objective Demonstrate how doing a job helps others.

Materials paper, crayons

Learning Style Visual

Group

Time 10–15 minutes

1. Children will make a job coupon to see how their work benefits others. Provide children with half-sheets of drawing paper. Draw a sample coupon on the board for children to copy.

Job Coupon
To:
Take a break!
I'll
today.
From:
Job Coupon
To: Mom
Take a break!
I'll
today.
From: Chad

2. Tell children to write or draw a job on the line that they do not do at home but could do. The job should give another family member or caregiver a break.

Lesson 2 Overview

Needs and Wants **pages 100–101**	Children will learn meanings of the words *needs* and *wants*. They will identify basic human needs and contrast needs with wants.	 Time 20 minutes Resources • Workbook, p. 27 • Vocabulary Cards **needs** **wants** • Every Student Learns Guide, pp. 42–45
Changing Toys **pages 102–103**	Children will learn how to use visual sources, such as charts, to compare and contrast.	Time 15–20 minutes

Build Background

Activity

What Will You Pack?

 **Time** 15–20 minutes

Ask children to suppose that they're going on a trip together. Have each child draw a picture of one thing to take. Then "pack" the pictures in a class shoe box.

Suggest a situation that reflects a need, such as: "I'm so thirsty! Did anyone pack a drink?" Select a volunteer to check the box to see if it contains a drink. Next, suggest a situation that reflects a want, such as: "I want to write in my journal. Did anyone pack a pencil?"

If time is short, have children suggest things they would pack for a trip. Ask the questions suggested above.

Read Aloud

What Do I Need?

by Michael Brown

What do I need? Only these three:

Food to eat that's good for me.

Clothes to keep my body warm.

A home to keep me safe from harm.

That's all? you ask. Nothing more?

Just your love—and that makes four.

Needs and Wants

Objectives

- Describe ways that families meet basic human needs.
- Distinguish between wants and needs.
- Explain how people fulfill needs and wants.

Vocabulary

needs things we must have to live (p. 100)

wants things we would like to have (p. 101)

QUICK Teaching Plan

If time is short, guide children in making a two-column list of needs and wants.

1 Introduce and Motivate

Preview Display the Vocabulary Cards **needs** and **wants**. Ask children what they think each word means. Then share the meaning of each word.

Warm Up To activate prior knowledge, ask children which they need: food or toys. Ask children to guess the things inside Ben's box. Ask them to group, or categorize, what they think is in Ben's box as a need or a want.

2 Teach and Discuss

Page 100

Point out that Ben is continuing to tell his story.

1 **What are some similarities in the ways families might meet their needs?** Possible answers: Many parents cook, provide a home, work to earn money to buy things that meet needs, and so on. **Draw Conclusions**

Needs and Wants

My family gives me many things I need. **Needs** are the things we must have to live. The pictures show some needs people have. 1 2

We need clothes to keep us warm.

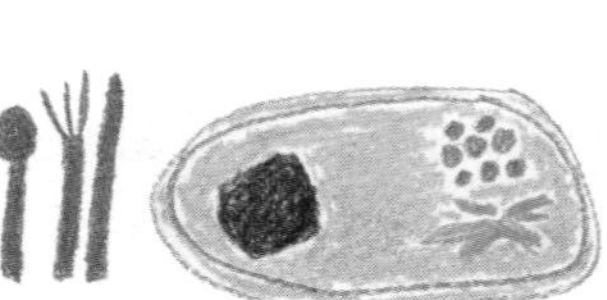

We need food and water to help us stay well and grow.

We need a place to live.

100

Practice and Extend

READING SKILL
Compare and Contrast

Tell children that this lesson talks about two kinds of things that are important to people. Ask children to read pp. 100–101. Then have them fold a piece of paper in half. Ask them to write the word *Needs* at the top of one half and the word *Wants* at the top of the other half. Tell them to draw or write about things people need to live and things people want under the correct headings.

WEB SITE
Technology

You can look up vocabulary words online. Click on *Social Studies Library* and select the dictionary at **www.sfsocialstudies.com.**

Wants are things we would like to have. Not everyone wants the same things. Rita wants music lessons. I want a robot car. If you were opening this gift, what would you want to find inside?

3 4

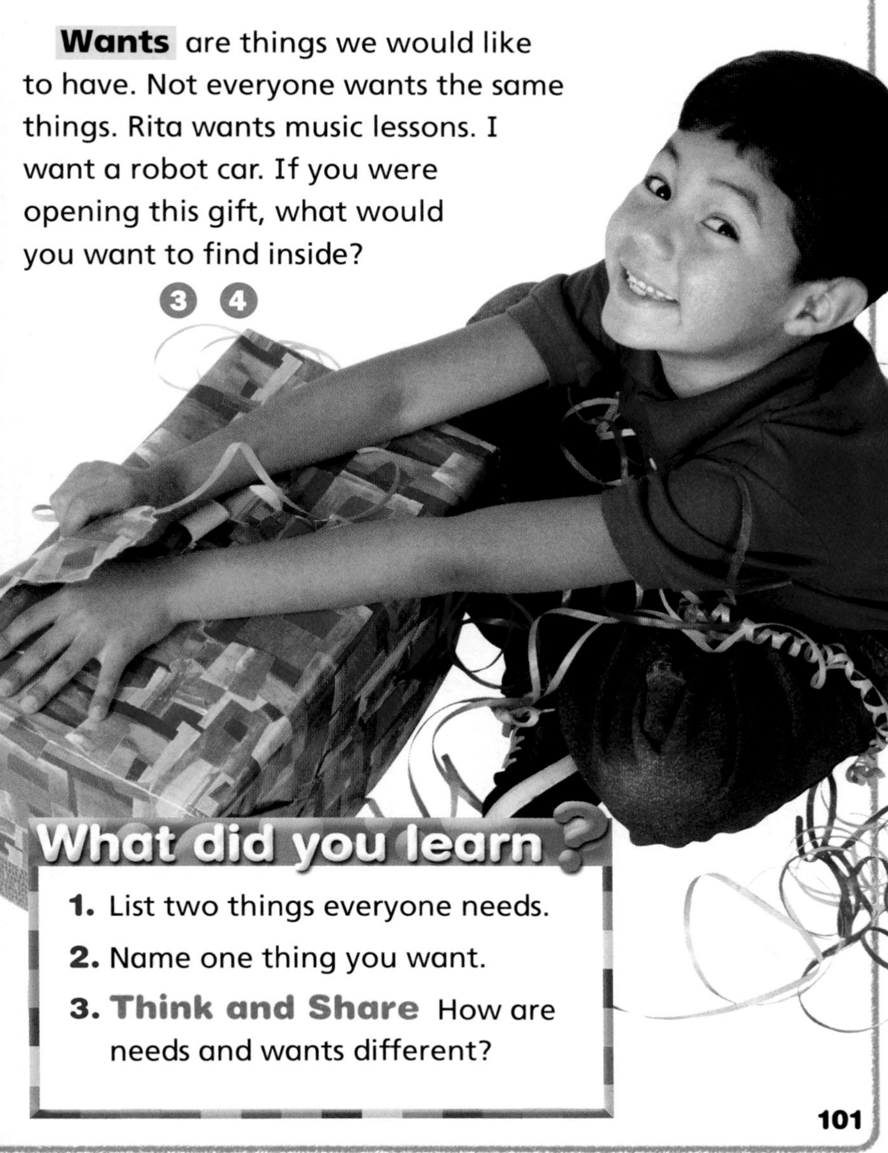

What did you learn?

1. List two things everyone needs.
2. Name one thing you want.
3. **Think and Share** How are needs and wants different?

101

2 What are some differences in the ways families might meet their needs? Possible answers: cooking different foods; living in different kinds of homes; growing foods that others might buy
Make Inferences

Page 101

3 What do you think Ben's gift is? It may be the robot car Ben wants. **Draw Conclusions**

4 What are some ways people get the things they need and want? Answers might indicate that parents or guardians usually provide for the needs and many of the wants children have or that people work to earn money to buy goods and services. **Make Inferences**

3 Close and Assess

Begin a two-column chart of needs and wants. Ask children to suggest items to place in each column. Then have each child tell a partner about one need and one want.

✓ **What did you learn?**

1. Answers should include two of the following: clothes, food, water, a place to live.
2. Children may suggest such things as toys, participation in activities, books, games, and pets.
3. **Think and Share** Needs are the same for everyone. Needs are things you must have in order to stay alive. Wants are not the same for everyone. Wants are things a person would like to have but can live without.

FYI SOCIAL STUDIES Background

Possible Misconceptions

- Children often say that they "have to have" something when they are talking about a "want," such as a particular toy.
- Many things that children would like to have are "wants" rather than "needs." People must have their needs met in order to live, but people can live without their wants.

Workbook, p. 27

Needs and Wants

Circle things you need to stay alive.

Draw something you want. Drawings will vary.

Also on Teacher Resources CD-ROM.

ESL ACCESS CONTENT ESL Support

For additional ESL support, use Every Student Learns Guide, pp. 42–45.

Changing Toys

Objectives

- Distinguish among past, present, and future.
- Compare and contrast toys from the past and today.

1 Introduce and Motivate

Preview Ask children for different meanings of the word *change*. Explain that on pp. 102–103, *change* means that things do not stay the same. Have volunteers name some toys they play with and discuss whether they think toys have always been the same.

Warm Up To activate prior knowledge, review the difference between wants and needs with children, making sure they recognize toys as "wants." Also, have children brainstorm words people use when they talk about the past (*yesterday, last week,* etc.) and the present (*now, today,* etc.).

2 Teach and Discuss

Review the parts of a chart by having volunteers identify the two columns and their headings.

Locate Key Words in the Text

1 What does the chart show? Have children point to the words at the top of the chart on p. 102. Explain that the words *Then* and *Now* are key words that will help them answer the question. Elicit that the chart shows toys *Then* and *Now*.
Main Idea and Details

Changing Toys

Ben wants a robot car. Children have always played with toys. These are toys that children have wanted then and now.

1 2 3

4

102

Practice and Extend

SOCIAL STUDIES
Background

About Toys in History

- Until the middle 1880s, most toys were made by families at home. Native American and colonial toys were usually made from local resources.
- Large-scale manufacturing of toys dates from after the Civil War. Toys made in Europe dominated the American market until World War I.
- One of the most popular toys of all time is the teddy bear, which was named for Theodore (Teddy) Roosevelt. The first one was made in 1903.
- Today the federal government regulates the safety of toys.

Where on the chart would you put these toys?
5 6
United States

Think about a new toy children might want in the future. Draw a picture of it.

103

CURRICULUM CONNECTION
Writing

Naming Toys

- List the names of the class's favorite toys on the board.
- Ask each child to choose one toy and to rename it based on what it does or how it works.
- Have children write one or two sentences explaining why they chose the new name.

2 Which word on the chart tells that you are looking at toys from long ago? Possible answer: The word *Then* **Analyze Information**

3 What word on the chart means the same as *today*? *Now* **Analyze Pictures**

4 In what ways are the bicycles from THEN and NOW alike? Possible answers: Both have pedals, two wheels, a seat, and handlebars. **Compare and Contrast**

Page 103

Have volunteers identify the toys on this page and explain how they are alike and different. Then have children tell where on the chart each belongs.

5 Why do toys and other things change? Answers should reflect understanding of changing wants and technologies. **Draw Conclusions**

6 How do people learn about changes in toys? Possible answers: Television and print advertisements, word of mouth, and so on **Make Inferences**

3 Close and Assess

Have the class brainstorm possible future toys before they make their drawings. Make a bulletin board labeled "Toys of the Future" with their drawings.

Use with pages 100–103

Lesson 2 Wrap-Up

MEETING INDIVIDUAL NEEDS
Leveled Practice

Find Pictures of Needs and Wants

Have children cut out magazine pictures that show things they need and want.

Easy Have children sort the magazine pictures into two groups: one for needs and another for wants. This can be done by having children put the pictures into boxes—one labeled *needs*, and the other labeled *wants*. **Reteach**

On-Level Ask each child to choose a picture, identify the item as a need or a want, and then explain how it is—or is not—necessary for survival. **Extend**

Challenge Have each child select one picture that shows a need and one picture that shows a want. Write a story about a character who has the selected need and want. Children's stories should say how their characters get what they need and want. **Enrich**

Hands-on Activities

CURRICULUM CONNECTION
Writing

Give Thanks

Objective Demonstrate an understanding of the words *needs* and *wants*.

Resources Vocabulary Cards: **needs, wants**

Materials crayons or markers, construction paper

Learning Style Visual/Verbal

Individual

Time 20–25 minutes

Dear Mom,
Thanks for giving me a great home!
I need that!
Love,
Joey

1. Write the following sentence frames on the board:

Thanks for giving me ___.
I needed that!

Thanks for giving me___.
I wanted one!

2. Have children complete the sentence frames to make thank-you cards for people who gave them things.
3. Remind children to add their new words to the Word Book.

CURRICULUM CONNECTION
Writing

Book of Homes

Objective Describe different kinds of homes.

Materials old magazines, safety scissors, construction paper, glue

Learning Style Visual/Verbal/Kinesthetic

Individual

Time 20–30 minutes

1. Ask children to find and cut out pictures that show different kinds of homes people live in.
2. Have children glue their pictures onto construction paper.
3. Ask children to write or dictate sentences that describe the homes.
4. Bind the pages together to make a book.

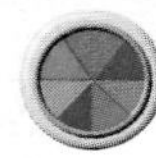

CURRICULUM CONNECTION
Math

A Wish List

Objective Compare and contrast things people want.

Materials chart paper, marker

Learning Style Visual/Verbal

Group

Time 15–20 minutes

1. Have each child make a list to show three things he or she would like to have. (You may want to help children think of non-material wants, such as more play time.)
2. As a group, compare and contrast the items on the lists.
3. If time permits, make a graph to show the results. Have children use the graph to rank items as chosen most often, chosen least often, and so on.

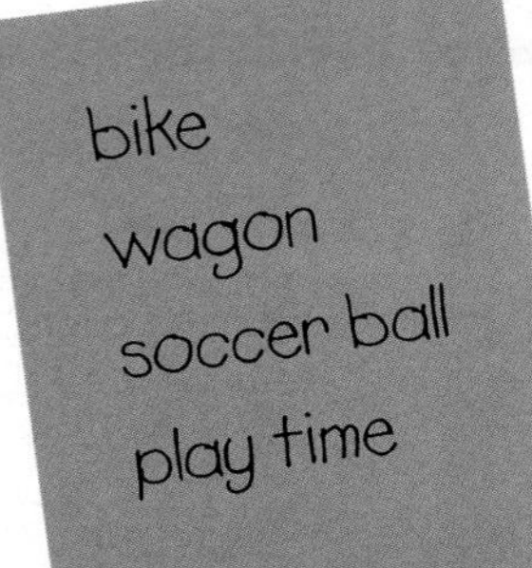

Lesson 3 Overview

Spending and Saving pages 104–105	Children will learn how money is used to buy things people need or want. They will also learn the importance of saving money for future use. 	Time 20 minutes Resources • Workbook, p. 28 • Every Student Learns Guide, pp. 46–49
Money Around the World pages 106–107	Children will use a map to learn about coins from around the world.	Time 15–20 minutes

Build Background

Activity

What Will You Buy?

 **Time** 15–20 minutes

Tell children that before there was money, people used to trade things. They would trade something they already had for something they didn't have.

Set up a "trading post" or "swap shop" where children can pretend to exchange something they have for something they want or need. Be sure children's names are on the items so they can be returned to their owners at the end of the activity.

If time is short, have children dictate a short list of things they might like to buy for the classroom. Then, for each item, ask what other item they would trade in exchange for the desired item.

Trading Post

Read Aloud

The Rainy Day

by Andrea Johnston

A nickel from Mom,
A quarter from Dad.
Two dimes from Gramps,
That's all that he had.

I've got fifty cents.
I've counted it twice.
I can go shopping
For something nice.

Or I could save up
For a rainy day.
But look! It's raining!
Hip-hip-hooray!

Spending and Saving

Objectives

- Identify examples of people wanting more than they can have.
- Explain why wanting more than they can have requires that people make choices.
- Identify examples of choices families make when buying goods and services.

QUICK Teaching Plan

If time is short, ask which of the pictures on p. 104 show things that cost 70 cents or less.

1 Introduce and Motivate

Preview Have children point to each item shown in the pictures and name the price.

Warm Up To activate prior knowledge, have children pass real coins around and tell what they would do with the money, if it was theirs to spend.

2 Teach and Discuss

Page 104

Remind children that on pp. 92–93, they read about Ben's lemonade stand.

1 Which things shown on p. 104 can Ben buy with 70 cents or less? Pen, apple
Draw Conclusions

2 What is an example of a person wanting more than he or she can have? Possible answers: A person wanted a book but did not have enough money; a family wanted to go to the movies and dinner but had only enough money to do one thing. Make Inferences

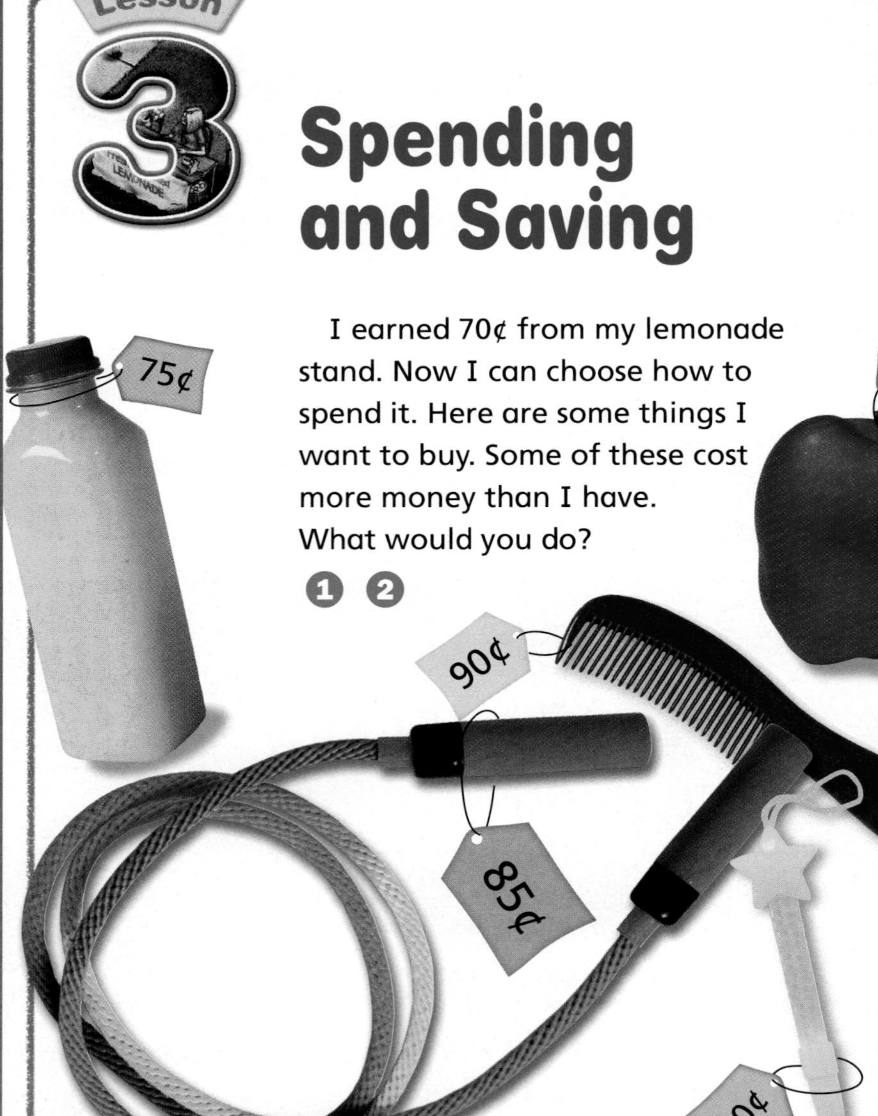

Lesson
Spending and Saving
I earned 70¢ from my lemonade stand. Now I can choose how to spend it. Here are some things I want to buy. Some of these cost more money than I have. What would you do?
1 2
75¢
90¢
85¢
50¢
104

Practice and Extend

READING SKILL Categorize

Sorting Things

- Ask children to describe the objects pictured on p. 104. Encourage children to tell about price, shape, texture, and how each item is used. Have children point to the juice. Ask if there is another food item. (apple)
- Ask children to sort the items by price. Which things have a price of 50¢ or less? (pen, apple) Which things have a price of more than 50¢? (jump rope, juice, comb)
- Have children think of other ways to sort the objects, such as by color. Then have them name their groups.

I can spend my money now or save it for later. To save money means to put it away to use at another time. After my next lemonade stand, I'll have even more money! 3 4

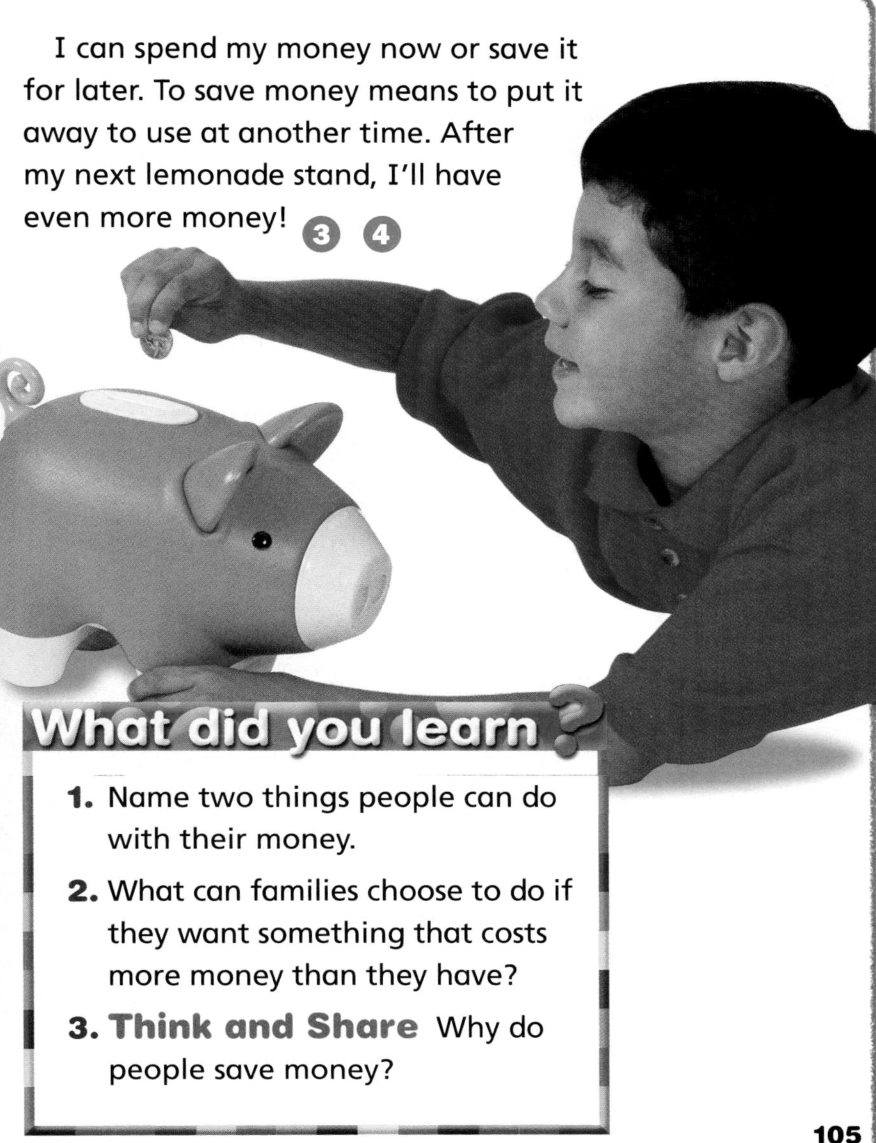

What did you learn?

1. Name two things people can do with their money.
2. What can families choose to do if they want something that costs more money than they have?
3. **Think and Share** Why do people save money?

105

BUILD BACKGROUND ESL Support

Using Coins Display samples of U.S. coins, such as pennies, nickels, dimes, and quarters.

Beginning Help children point to the coins as you name them. Say: *This is a penny*, and so on.

Intermediate Have children name the coins and state how much each coin is worth.

Advanced Have children dramatize using coins to buy something. Children can talk about their exchanges.

For additional ESL Support, use Every Student Learns Guide, pp. 46–49.

Workbook, p. 28

Also on Teacher Resources CD-ROM.

Page 105

Point out to children that most people cannot have everything they want. Lead a discussion about the need for people to make choices.

3 **What are some examples of choices families make when buying things?** Possible answers: Choosing different kinds and price ranges of foods and other products **Analyze Information**

Ongoing Assessment

If... children have difficulty thinking of examples of choices,	**then...** have them dramatize going to a market. Display items that could be purchased.

Decision making

4 **What would you do if you were Ben and you wanted to buy the comb?** Possible answers: Save the 70 cents and wait until I earn 20 cents more; buy something that costs less now and wait until I have 90 cents before I buy the comb. **Make Decisions**

3 Close and Assess

Have children tell what they would buy or how they would save if they were in Ben's place.

What did you learn?

1. People can save or spend their money.
2. Families can choose to save their money until they have enough to buy the item, or they can choose to buy something else that costs less.
3. **Think and Share** People save money so they can buy things they need or want at a later time.

Money Around the World

Objective

- Obtain information about a topic using visual sources, such as pictures and maps.

1 Introduce and Motivate

Preview Ask if children have ever seen coins or paper money from another country. If you have any foreign coins, share them with children.

Warm Up To activate prior knowledge, hold up a penny and ask what it is worth. (one cent) Pass a few pennies around so children can examine them. Challenge children to find the words *United States of America* on the pennies. Then have children name other coins used in the United States. Point out that we use both coins and paper bills as money.

2 Teach and Discuss

Pages 106–107

Help children identify the continents shown on the world map. Then name the coins pictured on pp. 106–107: dollar, boliviano, zloty, yen, dollar, pound. As you name each one, have children use their fingers to follow the dashed leader line to the country from which the coin comes.

1 **What do these pages show?** Different kinds of money used around the world
Main Idea and Details

2 **In what country do people use bolivianos as money?** Bolivia **Analyze Pictures**

3 **Where is Bolivia? How do you know?** It's in South America; the dashed line goes from the words *Bolivia/Boliviano* to *South America*.
Analyze Pictures

Money Around the World

People all over the world spend and save money.

1 2 3

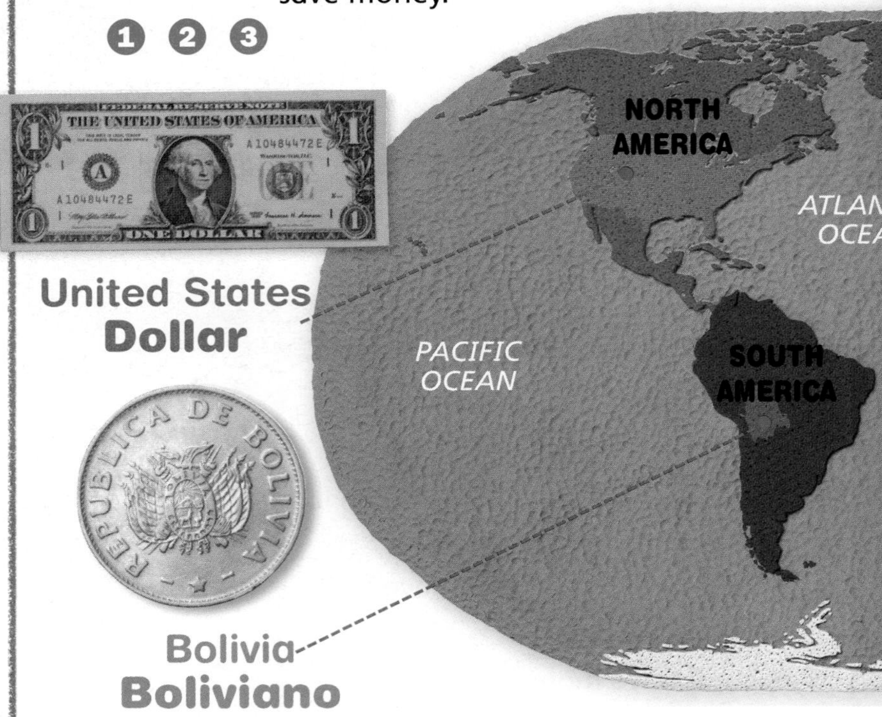

United States Dollar

Bolivia Boliviano

106

Practice and Extend

SOCIAL STUDIES Background

About Money

- Before there was a system of money, people used the barter system to trade by exchanging one kind of goods for other goods. In some places, people still barter.
- In the past, people used beads, salt, shells, and stones as money. They also used metals such as copper, gold, and silver.
- Paper money was first used in China.

WEB SITE Technology

You may help children find out more about places on these pages by clicking on *Atlas* at **www.sfsocialstudies.com.**

4 If you were traveling in Japan, what money might you use? Yen **Analyze Pictures**

SOCIAL STUDIES STRAND
Culture

In the past, many cultures in Africa and the Pacific used shells as money. Some Native American cultures used pieces of shell rubbed smooth and strung together like beads. Other cultures have used nails and sheep as money. Show children objects or pictures of objects that have been used as money in other cultures. Children can dramatize paying for a book with one of the objects presented.

Use Information from the Text

5 Which two countries use dollars? Have students jot their answers on a slip of paper. Reread the question and have children check to be sure they have written the words *United States* and *Australia*. **Compare and Contrast**

3 Close and Assess

SOCIAL STUDIES STRAND
Geography

Have children plan a trip around the world. Have them tell where they would go and what kind of money they would need. Remind them to refer to the coins and bills and the places pictured on the map on pp. 106–107.

CURRICULUM CONNECTION
Math

Count Pennies

- Provide small groups of children with 7 to 15 pennies to count.
- Have one child from each group say how many pennies were counted, and write the answer on the board.
- Tell children that in some countries, people use coins similar to our penny.
- Ask each group to imagine the pennies they counted are coins from another country, such as Guatemala, where centavos are used. Have children use that country's coin name, for example, 10 centavos.

Lesson 3 Wrap-Up

MEETING INDIVIDUAL NEEDS
Leveled Practice

Using Pictures to Shop for Food
Have children cut out newspaper pictures and prices of grocery items.

Easy Have children sort through the grocery pictures. Have children choose the items they would need to buy. **Reteach**

On-Level Make a classroom poster with the food pictures and use these prices: 55¢, 50¢, 40¢, 33¢, and 20¢. Designate children to be "shoppers." They choose cards that tell how much money they can spend. Each shopper then decides which items he or she can afford to buy. **Extend**

Challenge Have children work with partners. One partner chooses two items from the poster. He or she "purchases" one of the items, then tells the partner which coins were used to make the purchase. The partner must guess which item was chosen, based on the coin combination. **Enrich**

Hands-on Activities

SOCIAL STUDIES STRAND
Economics

Choosing One of Three

Objective Give reasons for making choices.

Materials mail-order catalogs, scissors

Learning Style Visual/Verbal/ Kinesthetic

Group

Time 15–20 minutes

1. Have each child cut out three items that he or she would like to have (want).

2. Tell children that they must now eliminate two of the three items they have chosen.

3. Have each child display his/her final choice and give a reason for its selection.

SOCIAL STUDIES STRAND
Economics

Piggy-Bank Fun

Objective Make a plan for saving money.

Materials disposable cups (with lids), tape, colored markers and other arts/crafts materials

Learning Style Kinesthetic

Individual

Time 25–30 minutes

1. Give each child a cup and a lid, into which you've cut a slot.

2. Have children tape down the lids and then decorate the cups. They might create animal shapes, using construction paper, pipe cleaners, and so on.

3. Ask each child to formulate a plan for saving, such as putting away a penny each week.

4. Have children take their banks home so they can put their plans into practice.

CURRICULUM CONNECTION
Math

From Most to Least

Objective Collect data to solve a problem.

Materials mail-order catalogs, scissors, glue, play money

Learning Style Verbal/Visual

Partner

Time 15–20 minutes

1. Have partners choose and cut out several pictures of things they might wish for. Tell children to be sure to include the price of each.

2. Have children arrange and glue down the items in order, from most to least expensive.

3. Give pairs play money (including paper bills). Have children buy items from each other with play money.

Lesson 4 Overview

Welcome to Job Day! **pages 108–111**	Children will learn about a variety of jobs in which people provide goods and services. They will explore volunteerism and the importance of all jobs. 	Time 20 minutes Resources • Workbook, p. 29 • Vocabulary Cards **tools** **goods** **service** **volunteer** • Every Student Learns Guide, pp. 50–53
Kid's Kitchen **pages 112–113**	Children will learn about volunteer work performed by children.	Time 15–20 minutes
Meet Clara Barton **pages 114–115**	Children will identify the contributions of Clara Barton, a person who exemplified good citizenship. They will use a map to locate Barton's birthplace.	Time 15–20 minutes

Build Background

Activity

Guess My Job

 **Time** 10–15 minutes

Ask a volunteer to think of a job he or she might like to have as an adult. Have other children ask questions that will help them guess what the job is.

If time is short, show several pictures of people at work. Have children tell what kind of job is shown in each picture.

Read Aloud

When I Grow Up

by Jennifer Cline

When I grow up, I'd like to be
A sailor who goes out to sea.
Or maybe I won't choose to roam.
I'll raise a family, stay at home.

When I grow up, I could teach,
Or be a lifeguard at the beach.
Or drive a truck or moving van,
Or play my trumpet in a band.

When I grow up, I'd be thrilled
Houses, bridges, and towns to build!
There are so many jobs to do.
What's the very best job for you?

Welcome to Job Day!

Objectives

- Identify examples of goods and services in the home, school, and community.
- Describe the requirements of various jobs and the characteristics of a job well-performed.
- Describe how specialized jobs contribute to the production of goods and services.

Vocabulary

tools things people use to help them do work (p. 108)

goods things that are grown or made (p. 108)

service a job people do to help others (p. 109)

volunteer a person who works for free (p. 110)

QUICK Teaching Plan

If time is short, have children look at the pictures and brainstorm a list of jobs.

- Ask children what goods or services the jobs might provide.

1 Introduce and Motivate

Preview Display the Vocabulary Card **tools**, **goods**, **service**, and **volunteer**. Ask children what they think each word means. Share the meaning of each word and use it in a sentence for children. Point out that goods satisfy people's needs and wants.

Warm Up To activate prior knowledge, ask children to name some jobs they might like to do when they grow up. Then ask children to suppose that they have accompanied one of the workers pictured in the lesson to his or her job. Ask volunteers to tell about their day at work.

Welcome to Job Day!

Workers have come to our class to tell us about the work they do. Some workers use tools. **Tools** are things that are used to help people do work. Some workers earn money by growing or making goods. Things that are grown or made are **goods.**

❶ ❷

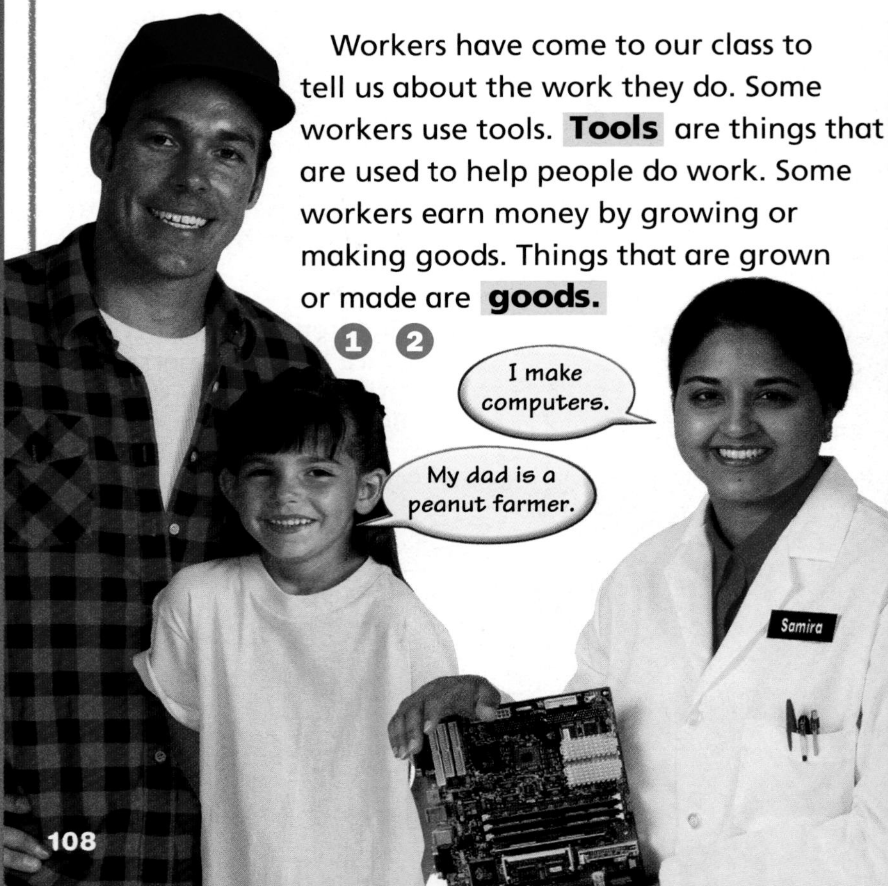

I make computers.
My dad is a peanut farmer.
Samira

108

Practice and Extend

READING SKILL
Main Idea and Details

All About Job Day

- Have children read Lesson 4. Then have them draw pictures or write sentences that tell what Job Day is all about.
- Invite volunteers to share their drawings and sentences with the class.

Some workers earn money by having service jobs. A **service** is a job people do to help others. It helps people meet their wants and needs. Do you know someone who has a service job? What does the person do? ❸ ❹ ❺

I help children learn. I am a teacher.
My dad is a plumber. He fixes broken pipes.

109

SOCIAL STUDIES
Background

About Different Kinds of Jobs

- According to the U.S. Census Bureau, the majority of jobs in the United States are in manufacturing and retail. Other major job categories are health services, educational services, and financial services.
- One hundred years ago, most U.S. workers were farmers. Today, farming is near the bottom of the list, followed only by public utilities, entertainment, miscellaneous personal services, and mining.

WEB SITE
Technology

You can look up vocabulary words by going online. Click on *Social Studies Library* and select the dictionary at **www.sfsocialstudies.com.**

2 Teach and Discuss

Page 108

Have children identify the workers pictured on pp. 108–109. Read aloud the words in the speech balloons.

❶ **What goods do the workers on this page provide?** The peanut farmer grows peanuts. The woman in the white coat makes computers. **Interpret Pictures**

❷ **What are some examples of goods you use in your home? your school? your community?** Answers will vary but may include for home: appliances, clothes; for school: books, pens, computer; for community: playground equipment, water fountain. **Apply Information**

Page 109

❸ **How might the plumber and the teacher know they have done a good job?** The pipes would no longer be broken and leak. Children in the teacher's class would learn many things. **Draw Conclusions**

❹ **What are other examples of services you might use in your home? your school? your community?** Answers will vary but may include for home: painter, carpenter; for school: principal, cafeteria worker, teacher aide; for community: doctor, check-out clerk, or any other service job. **Apply Information**

❺ **Was the lemonade Ben sold at his lemonade stand a good or a service? How do you know?** A good, because he made it **Apply Information**

continued

Page 110

Discuss what the adults shown on the page do to help other people. Point out that some volunteers have paid jobs in addition to the work they do for free. They do volunteer work in their spare time.

6 How do these workers help others meet their needs? They volunteer in a place that provides food, clothing, and shelter.
Interpret Pictures

7 Are there any volunteers in your school? What do they do? Answers will vary but may include parents, older siblings, guardians and community members who help in the classroom, on the playground, on class trips, and so on.
Apply Information

Page 111

Help children identify the workers doing specialized jobs pictured on p. 111.

8 Which job pictured provides goods? Which jobs provide services? The baker provides goods; the musician and doctor provide services.
Use Picture Clues

✓ Ongoing Assessment

If... children do not know if what a particular worker provides is a good or a service,

then... remind them that goods are what workers make or grow and services are what workers do to help others.

Some people do not earn money for their work. They are volunteers. A **volunteer** works for free. Volunteers help others. 6

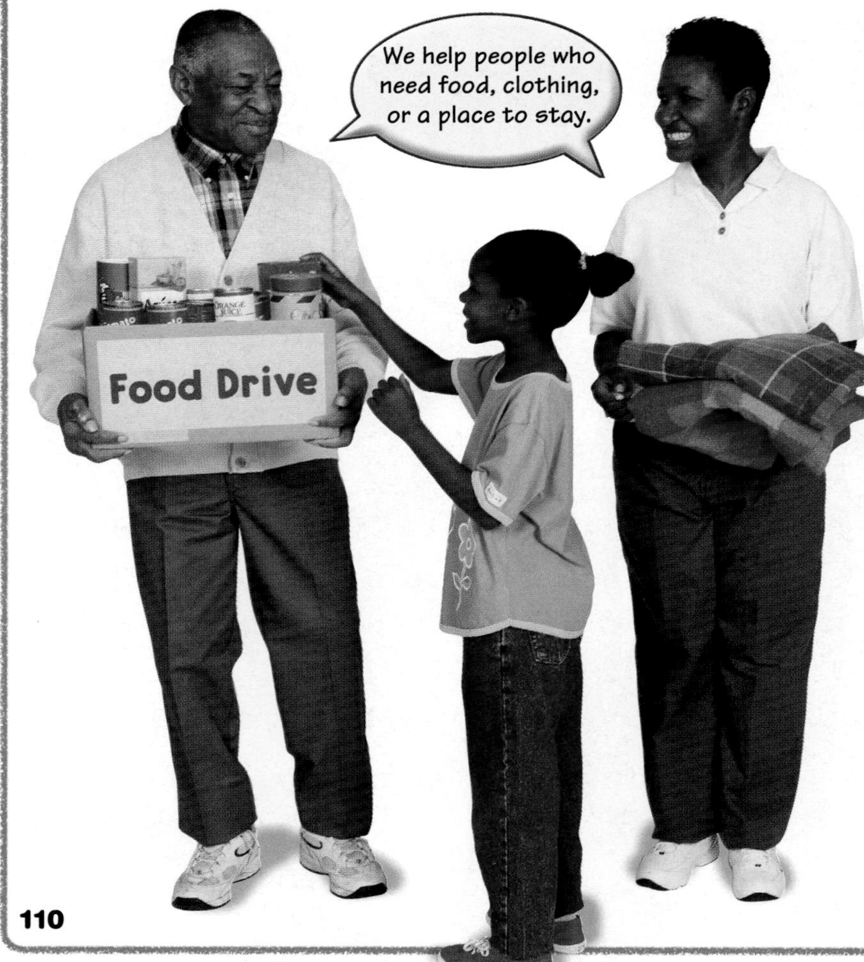

We help people who need food, clothing, or a place to stay.
Food Drive

110

Practice and Extend

ESL Support

Using Pictures Show children pictures of modern-day soup kitchens or other places people can go for help in the community.

Beginning Ask children to point to the pictures as they repeat the names of jobs of the workers pictured on pp. 108–111. Then show other job pictures and help children brainstorm a list of other jobs.
Intermediate Have children follow along as you read the sentences in speech balloons on pp. 108–110. Then have children name the workers pictured on p. 111 and dictate sentences the workers might say.
Advanced After children identify the workers pictured in the book, they can find pictures of other workers and use them to talk about the jobs these people do and the goods or services they provide.

For additional ESL support, use Every Student Learns Guide, pp. 50–53.

There are many kinds of jobs. Which would you choose? Would you make or grow something? Would you work helping others? All kinds of work are important! How do all these workers help us? 

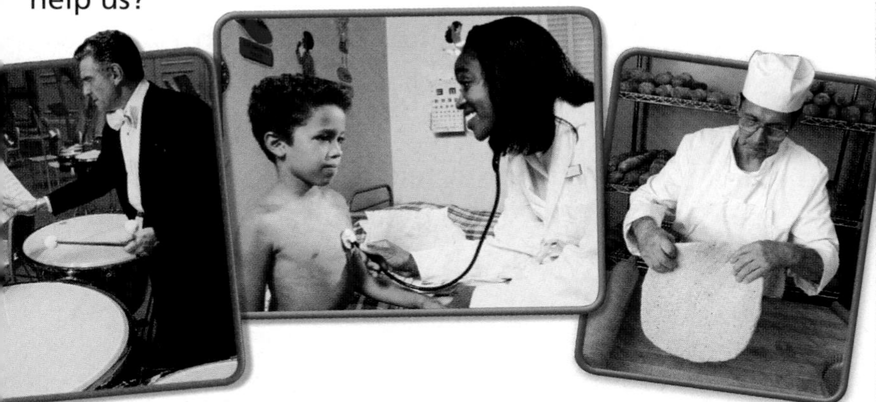

What did you learn?

1. What are some services that help us?
2. How do volunteers help people?
3. **Think and Share** Name three goods you use every day. How do you use them?

111

CURRICULUM CONNECTION Literature

Read a Story

- Read aloud *The Dream Jar* by Bonnie Pryor (Morrow, 1996). In this story, which is set in New York City in the early 1900s, each family member works hard to contribute to the family's dream of owning a store.
- After reading, talk about the job each family member did—and how well he or she did it.
- Guide children in comparing and contrasting the jobs people did long ago with those that people do today.

Workbook, p. 29

Welcome to Job Day!
Circle people who have service jobs.
Draw a job you might like to have. Drawings will vary.

Also on Teacher Resources CD-ROM.

3 Close and Assess

Have children draw and write to show the kinds of jobs they would like to have as adults. Then have them tell partners about those jobs. Partners can make a list of the jobs. Ask children to tell whether the jobs involve providing goods or services. Help children see how some jobs, which may be specialized, contribute to the production of goods or services.

✓ What did you learn?

1. Answers will vary but may include dentist, police officer, plumber.
2. Volunteers help people by doing things for them for free.
3. **Think and Share** Answers will vary but may include such things as books, pencils, hairbrushes, dishes, foods, and so on. Children should tell how each item is used.

CITIZEN HEROES

Kid's Kitchen

Objectives

- Understand characteristics of good citizenship as exemplified by ordinary people.
- Identify characteristics of good citizenship, such as responsibility for the common good.
- Understand that people can both give and receive care.

1 Introduce and Motivate

Preview Encourage children to recall the definition of *volunteer* that they read in the previous lesson. Have them suggest some things they think volunteers could do.

Warm Up To activate prior knowledge, ask children what the word *caring* means to them. Help children to understand that caring may include concern, or interest in others, liking or loving another, or providing for or helping another.

Introduce the featured child, Sagen. Tell children that they will learn reasons why Sagen is a citizen hero.

2 Teach and Discuss

Read p. 112, including the caption for the map. You may wish to add to children's geography awareness by having them locate Georgia on your classroom map.

1 **Who does Kid's Kitchen help?** Families in need of food **Analyze Information**

CITIZEN HEROES

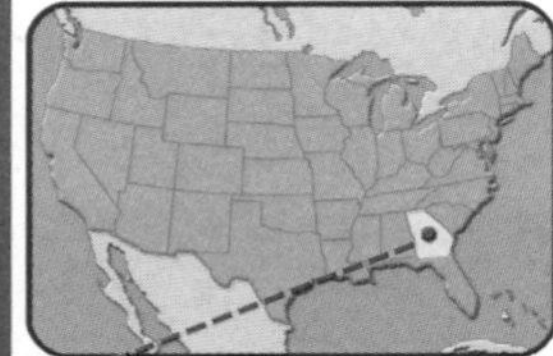

Kid's Kitchen is in Warner Robins, Georgia.

Kid's Kitchen

When Sagen was in second grade, she saw something interesting on TV. It was about helping her community. She decided to be a volunteer.

1 Sagen started a group called Kid's Kitchen. The group gives lunch to families in need. It is open one day a week.

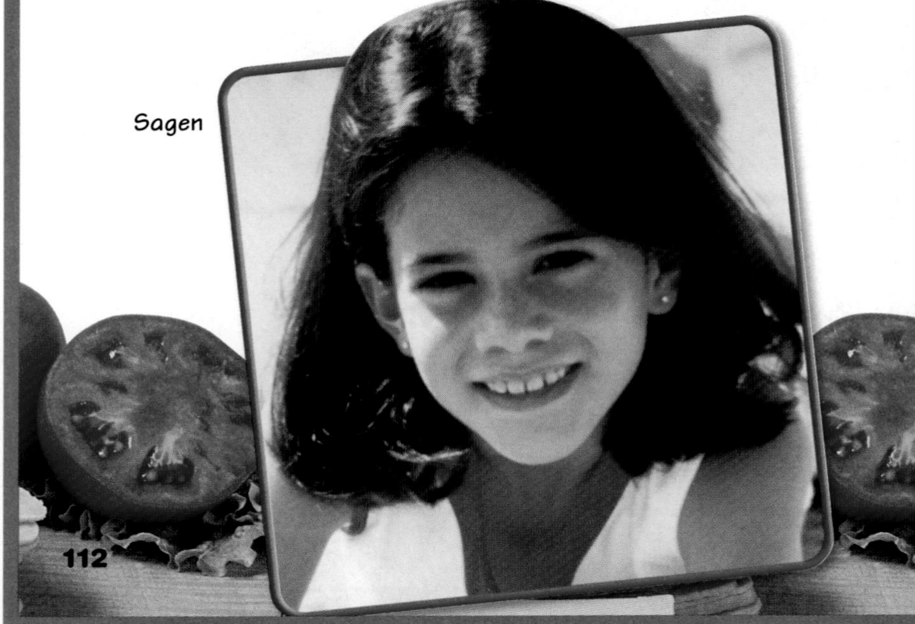

Sagen

112

Practice and Extend

SOCIAL STUDIES
Background

About Kid's Kitchen

- With help from the director of a local soup kitchen, Sagen planned menus and solicited money and donations of food for Kid's Kitchen.
- Kid's Kitchen is open every Wednesday during the summer. It is run completely by 8- to 12-year-olds.
- Sagen received the Spirit of Community Award for 2000. She also was commended by the Georgia Senate for her work as a Georgia Youth Volunteer.

Many children volunteer. They make hundreds of sandwiches each week. Some people take home leftovers for dinner. 2 3

"When I tell someone about Kid's Kitchen, I hope it will inspire them to do something in their town," says Sagen. 4

Caring in Action

What can you do to show you care for someone?

113

2 **Why might a volunteer be considered a good citizen?** Possible answer: He or she helps people for free. **Draw Conclusions**

Problem Solving

3 **What should the children working at Kid's Kitchen do if they need to make more sandwiches in a week than they usually do?** Possible answers: Find more volunteers to work; get more ingredients for sandwiches **Solve Problems**

4 **What has Sagen done that is a good example of caring?** Answers may include that she started Kid's Kitchen and that the group helps people by making lunch for them. **Main Idea and Details**

SOCIAL STUDIES STRAND Citizenship

Point out that Sagen showed that she is a caring citizen by starting a group that gives food to families in need. Ask children to say names of people they know who are caring citizens and how those citizens show they care about others. Answers may include a parent or a school worker.

3 Close and Assess

Caring in Action

Read the question and have children discuss possible answers. Responses may include giving a family member a hug or kiss, helping another person in some way, making a card for someone, saying a kind word to another, and so on.

CURRICULUM CONNECTION Drama

Perform a Skit

- Work with pairs or small groups of children to create and perform short skits showing examples of caring.
- Suggest that some children pantomime their actions while others share their examples orally.
- For both kinds of skits, have children pay close attention to facial expressions and body language.

Clara Barton

Objectives

- Identify contributions of historical figures who have influenced the nation.
- Identify historic figures such as Clara Barton who have exemplified good citizenship.

1 Introduce and Motivate

Preview Begin a word web with *volunteer* in the center circle. Remind children that a volunteer helps other people but does not get paid.

Warm Up To activate prior knowledge, ask children to suggest some things they can do to help other people. Record their suggestions on the word web.

Have children look at the pictures on pp. 114–115. Identify the woman as Clara Barton, and ask children what they think she is doing. Point out the red cross on page 115. Ask children if they have ever seen this symbol before, and if so, where.

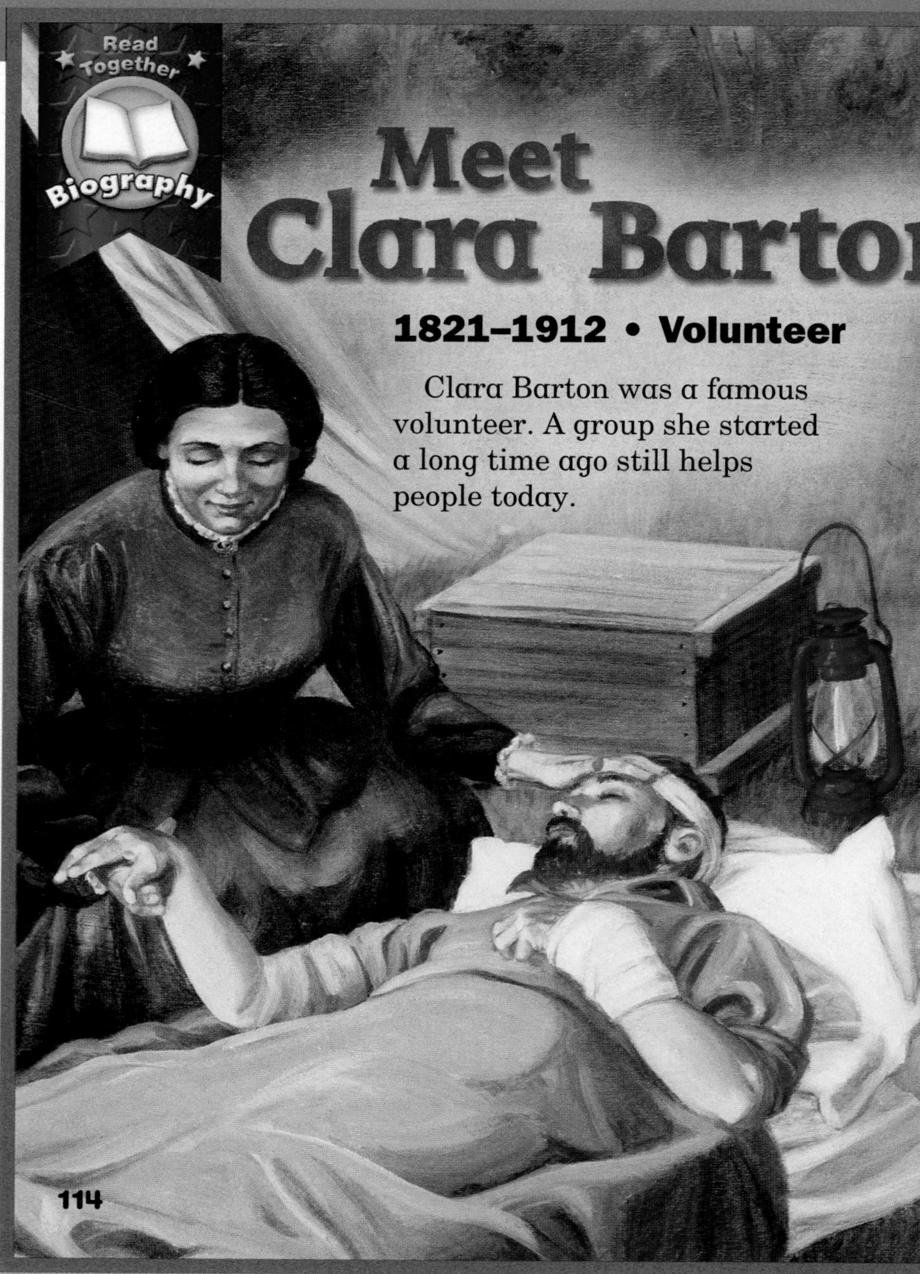

Read Together
Biography
Meet Clara Barton
1821–1912 • Volunteer
Clara Barton was a famous volunteer. A group she started a long time ago still helps people today.
114

Practice and Extend

SOCIAL STUDIES Background

About Clara Barton

- Although most famous for founding the American Red Cross, Clara Barton was also a teacher, a patent office clerk, a nurse, a writer, and a lecturer.
- During the Civil War, Barton became known as the "Angel of the Battlefield." Although not a trained nurse, she carried supplies to and nursed the wounded. After the war, she helped search for missing soldiers.
- In 1869, Barton went to Switzerland, where she learned of the International Committee of the Red Cross. After returning to the United States, she tried to interest others in the work of the Red Cross. Her work led to the establishment of the American branch in 1881.

WEB SITE Technology

You may help children find out more about Clara Barton by clicking on *Meet the People* at **www.sfsocialstudies.com.**

Clara Barton worked hard to help people. When she was just a girl, she helped take care of her brother. He was sick for about two years! 1

During the Civil War, Clara Barton was a volunteer. She helped soldiers who were hurt. She handed out bandages and medicine. Her work saved many lives. 2

After the war, Clara Barton wanted to keep on helping people. She started the American Red Cross. Today the Red Cross 3 4 gives food, clothing, and shelter to people who need help all over the world.

Clara Barton was born in Oxford, Massachusetts.

Clara Barton made a red cross from a ribbon she wore.

Think and Share

Tell two ways Clara Barton helped people.

For more information, go online to *Meet the People* at **www.sfsocialstudies.com.**

CURRICULUM CONNECTION Writing

Helping Someone

Ask children to listen to this story:

In 1884, there was a terrible flood. The waters of the Mississippi and Ohio Rivers poured out over the land. Many people lost their homes. Clara Barton wanted to help these people, and so did six children from Pennsylvania.

The children decided to put on a play. They charged admission—and earned $50.00! They sent this money to Clara Barton to help a homeless family. Here's what the children wrote in a letter to Clara Barton: "Sometime again when you want money for your good work, call on—the Little Six."

Ask children to draw a picture of something they could do to help someone. Then have children dictate or write a sentence telling about their picture.

2 Teach and Discuss

Read the biography together. Tell children that the Civil War was fought in the United States and that the two sides were the North and the South.

1 **How did Clara Barton learn to help people?** When she was a girl, she took care of her sick brother for about two years. **Cause and Effect**

2 **Clara Barton helped soldiers who were on different sides during the Civil War. What kind of a citizen do you think she was?** She was kind and caring. The side of the war the soldiers were on didn't matter to her. **Draw Conclusions**

3 **What made Clara Barton a famous volunteer?** She started the group called the American Red Cross. The American Red Cross still helps people today. **Main Idea and Details**

4 **When might people need the help of the Red Cross?** When bad weather or war causes people to need food, clothing, or shelter **Make Inferences**

3 Close and Assess

Think and Share

She cared for her sick brother; she brought bandages and medicine to wounded Civil War soldiers; she helped save lives; she started the American Red Cross.

Use with pages 108–115

Lesson 4 Wrap-Up

MEETING INDIVIDUAL NEEDS Leveled Practice

Make a Chart

Guide children in making a jobs chart with the column headings *Goods* and *Services*.

Easy Have children look in magazines for pictures showing different jobs. Ask them to place the pictures into the goods column or the services column. **Reteach**

On-Level Have children brainstorm other workers who grow/make goods or provide services. Add these workers to the appropriate column in the chart. Ask volunteers to tell the duties of each job and how the worker would know if they did their job well. **Extend**

Challenge Have partners choose one worker from each column of the chart. Ask them to write or dictate brief descriptions of the workers' jobs. Encourage them to tell about job requirements including the amount of schooling and on-the-job training. **Enrich**

Hands-on Activities

CURRICULUM CONNECTION **Reading**

I Spy a Job

Objective Demonstrate an understanding of lesson vocabulary.

Materials Pupil Book, pp. 90–91

Learning Style Visual/Verbal

Partners

Time 15–20 minutes

1. Have one partner give clues about a worker on pp. 90–91. If the worker is, for example, the paperboy, clues might be: *I spy someone with a service job. This person helps by delivering something.*

2. Children take turns spying workers. Encourage children to use lesson vocabulary.

3. Remind children to add the lesson vocabulary in their Word Book.

CURRICULUM CONNECTION **Writing**

Who's Working?

Objective Describe jobs and their requirements.

Materials paper, scissors, arts/crafts materials

Learning Style Visual/Verbal/Kinesthetic

Partners

Time 20–30 minutes

1. Cut out paper-doll outlines of people. You might want to have children work with partners and trace around each other's bodies. Children can dress and/or decorate the paper dolls to correspond to the jobs people do. Encourage them to include any tools that the workers may use.

2. Have children dictate sentences telling what each worker does and what skills they think the worker might need. Children can write these sentences on their paper dolls.

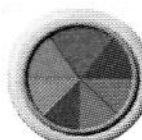

CURRICULUM CONNECTION **Drama**

What's My Line?

Objective Identify certain jobs.

Materials old magazines, scissors, glue, index cards

Learning Style Visual/Kinesthetic

Group

Time 20–25 minutes

1. Ask children to find and cut out as many pictures of workers as they can find. Children should glue each picture onto an index card.

2. Ask the children to pantomime what the workers do. Others in the class try to guess the job.

Lesson 5 Overview

Lesson	Description	Time and Resources
Interview with a Farmer **pages 116–119**	Through an interview, children will learn about the work of a farmer. They will also discover how farm produce gets to the market. 	Time 20–30 minutes Resources • Workbook, p. 30 • Transparency 9 • Every Student Learns Guide, pp. 54–57
Follow a Route **pages 120–121**	Children will learn how to follow a route on a map.	 Time 20–35 minutes Resource • Workbook, p. 31
Meet George Washington Carver **pages 122–123**	Children will identify the contributions of George Washington Carver, a historical figure who has influenced the nation.	 Time 15 minutes

Build Background

Activity

What Foods Do You Like?

 **Time** 15–20 minutes

Ask each child to find and cut out a picture of a favorite food. As children display their foods, ask where they think the food came from—and how it got to them.

If time is short, ask children to name a food. Ask children where they think the food came from—and how it got to them.

Read Aloud

Oats, Peas, Beans, and Barley Grow

Oats, peas, beans, and barley grow;
Oats, peas, beans, and barley grow.
Can you or I or anyone know
How oats, peas, beans, and
barley grow?

Thus the farmer sows his seed,
Stands erect, and takes his ease.
He stamps his foot and claps his
hands
And turns around to view his lands.

Lesson 5 Interview with a Farmer

Objectives

- Describe how specialized jobs contribute to the production of goods and services.
- Obtain information about a topic using a variety of oral sources, such as interviews.
- Identify the role of markets in the exchange of goods and services.
- Sequence information.

QUICK Teaching Plan

If time is short, have children use the photos on pp. 117–118 to summarize the steps in growing and marketing peanuts.

- Have children make a graphic organizer summarizing the three steps shown for growing peanuts. Then have them do the same for marketing peanuts.

1 Introduce and Motivate

Preview Ask children to tell what they think a farmer does. Remind children that a farmer earns money from his or her job. A farmer can use the money to buy goods and services. Then ask children to suppose they were talking with a farmer. What questions would they ask to learn more about a farmer's job?

Warm Up To activate prior knowledge, ask children to think about the steps in their school day. Brainstorm three school activities. Then discuss with children how to put the activities in the order that they do them.

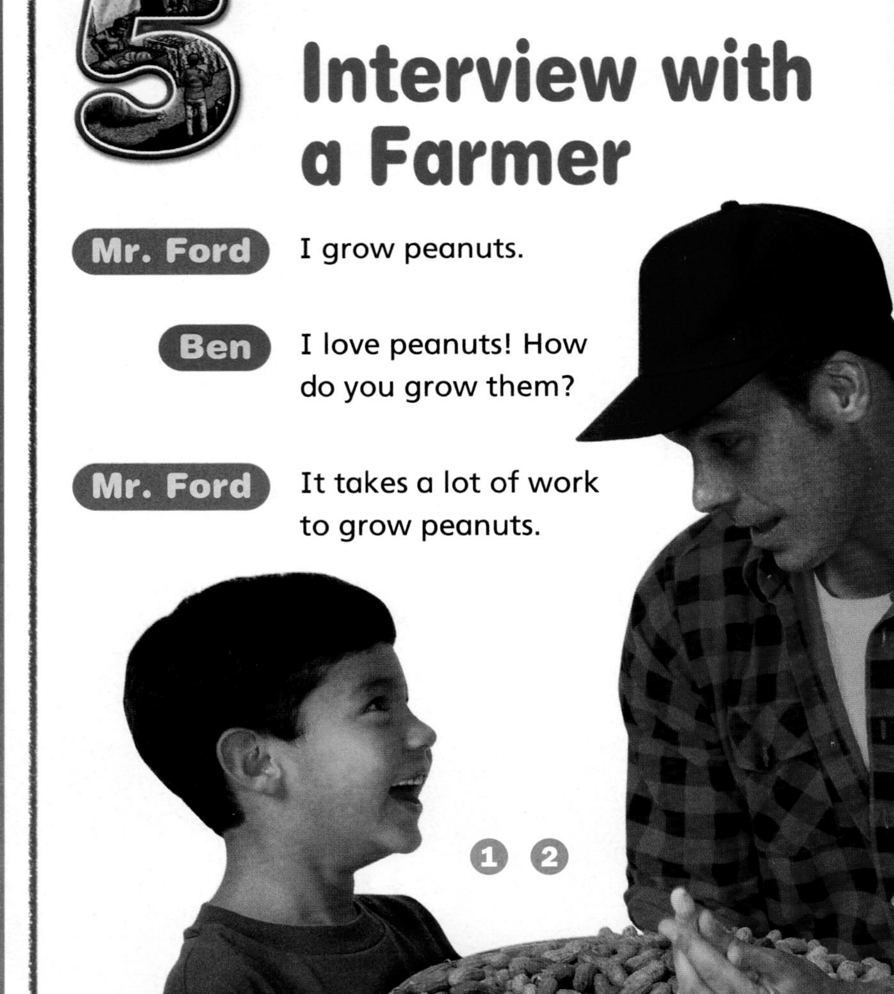

Lesson 5
Interview with a Farmer
Mr. Ford I grow peanuts.
Ben I love peanuts! How do you grow them?
Mr. Ford It takes a lot of work to grow peanuts.
1 2
116

Practice and Extend

READING SKILL Put Things in Order

Target Skill

Sequence In this lesson, children will use words to understand the order in which things happen.

- After children read pp. 116–117, display Transparency 9. Help them complete it to show what Mr. Ford does first, next, and last.
- You may want to use the transparency again after reading p. 118.

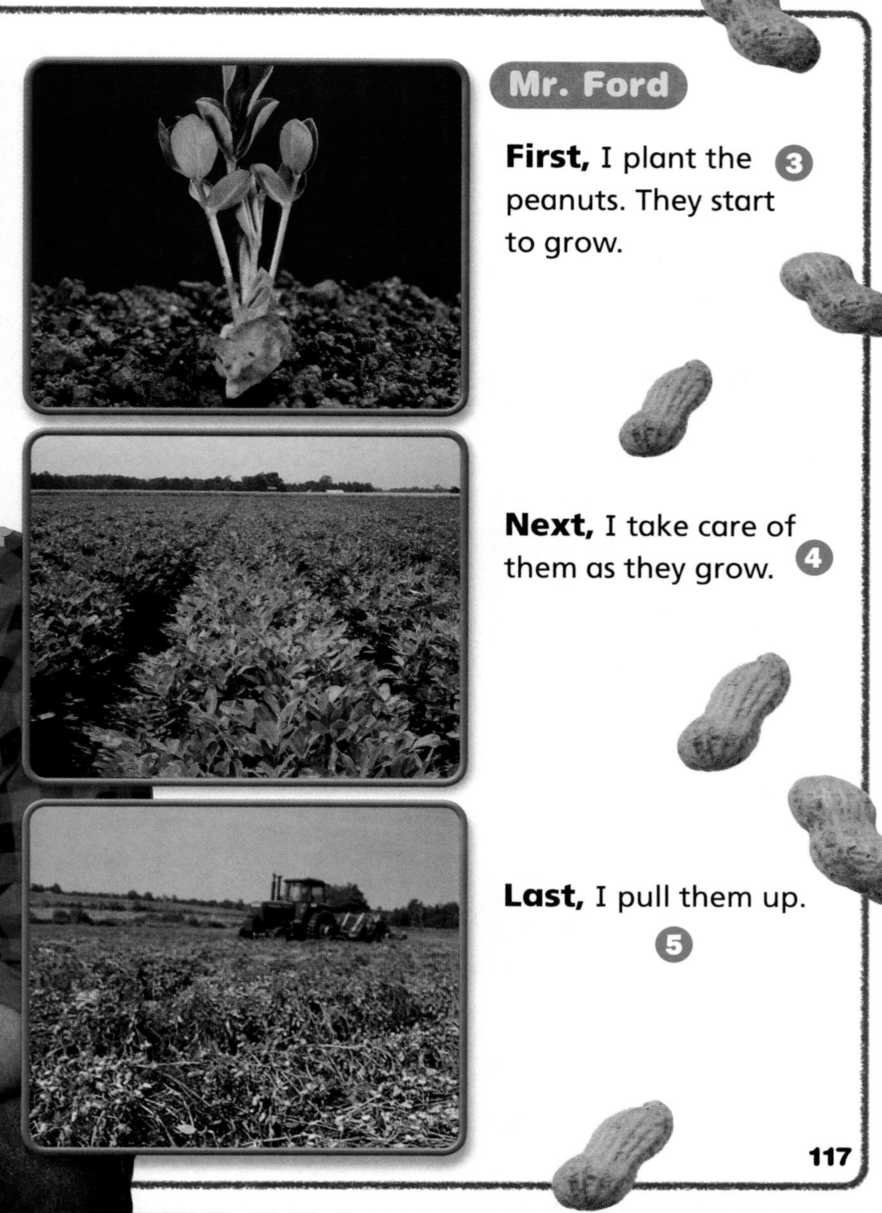

Mr. Ford

First, I plant the peanuts. They start to grow. 3

Next, I take care of them as they grow. 4

Last, I pull them up. 5

117

2 Teach and Discuss

Page 116

Remind children that Mr. Ford is a farmer they saw in Lesson 4. Point out that Lesson 5 is an interview, or a meeting of people to talk something over or ask questions. Ben is interviewing Mr. Ford about his job.

1 **Look at the shell that Mr. Ford is holding. What is inside the shell?** The peanuts
Make Inferences

2 **A farmer needs to know many special things to do his or her job. What are some things farmers do to produce peanuts?** A farmer plants the peanuts, cares for them, then digs them up. **Make Inferences**

Page 117

3 **What is the first thing Mr. Ford does?** He plants the peanuts. **Sequence**

4 **What does he do next?** He takes care of them as they grow. **Sequence**

5 **What does Mr. Ford do last?** He pulls them up with his tractor. **Sequence**

CURRICULUM CONNECTION
Science

What a Plant Needs

- Help children identify the things a plant needs in order to grow. (soil, water, sunlight)
- Have children investigate by placing one seedling in a sunny window and watering it regularly. Place another in a dark corner and withhold water. After a few days, compare the plants. Compare again after a week.
- Alternatively, have children make three drawings to show stages in a plant's growth from seedling to mature plant. Have children label their pictures with terms such as *roots, stem, leaves*.

continued

Page 118

6 Are the peanuts roasted before or after they are taken to the factory? After
Sequence

Ongoing Assessment

If... children do not understand that the peanuts are roasted after they are taken to the factory,	**then...** have children copy the sentences beginning with *First* and *Next* and number them *1* and *2*. Then have them reread the sentences.

7 What is the last thing that workers do with the peanuts? They put them into bags and send them to stores. Sequence

8 What do you think workers in stores do after they receive the peanuts? Possible answers: They put the peanuts in bins where shoppers can see them; they put up a sign showing the price of the peanuts; they sell the peanuts to people who want to eat peanuts. Make Inferences

Ben How do peanuts get from the farm to me?

Mr. Ford

First, a truck takes the peanuts to the factory.

Next, they are dried, cleaned, and roasted. 6

Last, they are put into bags and sent to the stores. 7 8

118

Practice and Extend

ACCESS CONTENT ESL Support

Using Graphic Organizers Make drawings of the steps of growing peanuts and the steps of peanuts going to market. Cut out the drawings, and then mix them up.

Beginning Have children arrange the drawings of growing peanuts in the proper order to form a graphic organizer. Have children say *first, next,* and *last* as they point to the pictured steps.

Intermediate Have children put all six steps in order. Have children describe what is happening in each step.

Advanced Have children use a sequence graphic organizer to write the six steps. They can also make their own graphic organizer showing the steps in a process familiar to them, such as making a sandwich.

For additional ESL support, use Every Student Learns Guide, pp. 54–57.

CURRICULUM CONNECTION Drama

Dramatize an Interview

- Have children work in small groups to dramatize the interview with Mr. Ford. Two children can read aloud the lines of Ben and Mr. Ford.
- Others can act out through pantomime the steps in growing the peanuts and getting them to market to be sold.
- Encourage the readers to pause after each step so that those doing the pantomime can elaborate on the actions.

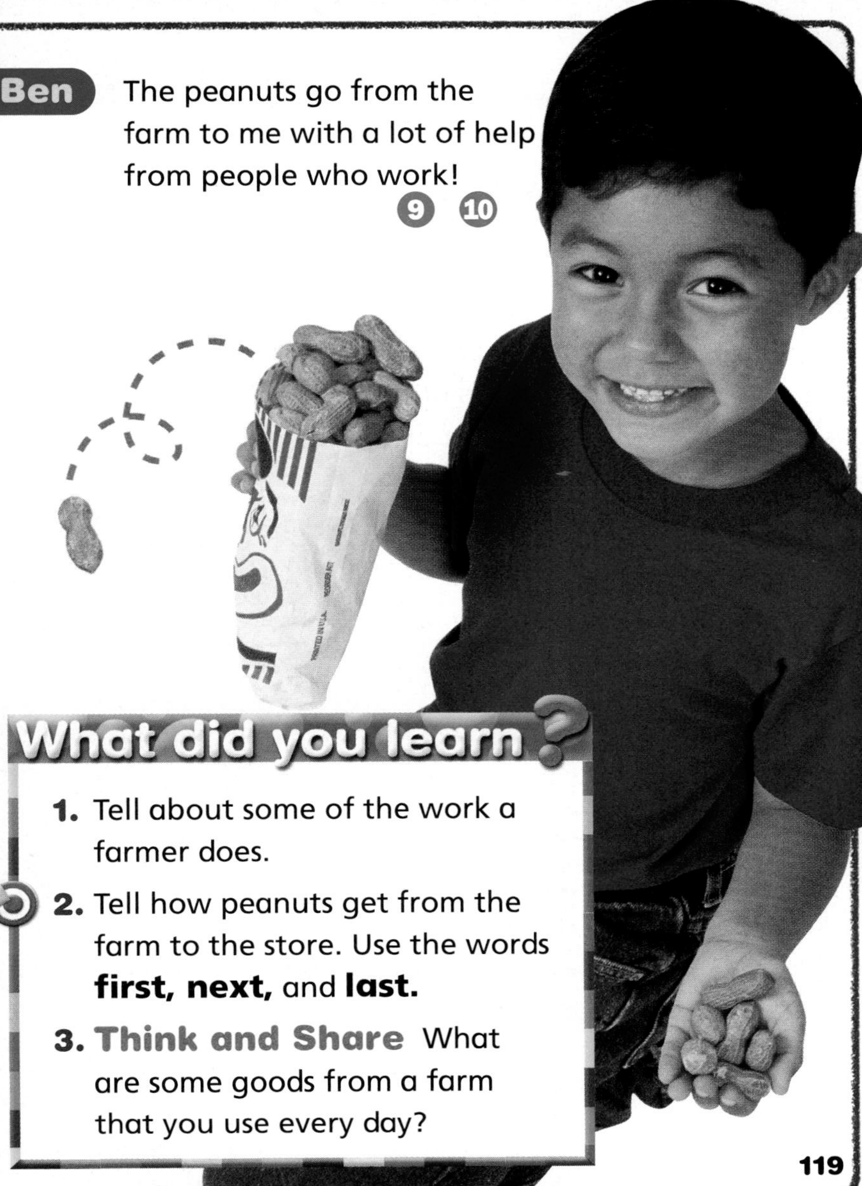

Ben The peanuts go from the farm to me with a lot of help from people who work! 9 10

What did you learn?

1. Tell about some of the work a farmer does.
2. Tell how peanuts get from the farm to the store. Use the words **first, next,** and **last.**
3. **Think and Share** What are some goods from a farm that you use every day?

119

FAST FACTS

- The part of the peanut plant that we eat grows in a pod under the ground.
- The first peanut butter was made by South Americans 3,000 years ago, when they ground peanuts into a paste and mixed it with cocoa.
- The first peanut farmers in the United States grew peanuts only for feeding their turkeys, chickens, and pigs.

Workbook, p. 30

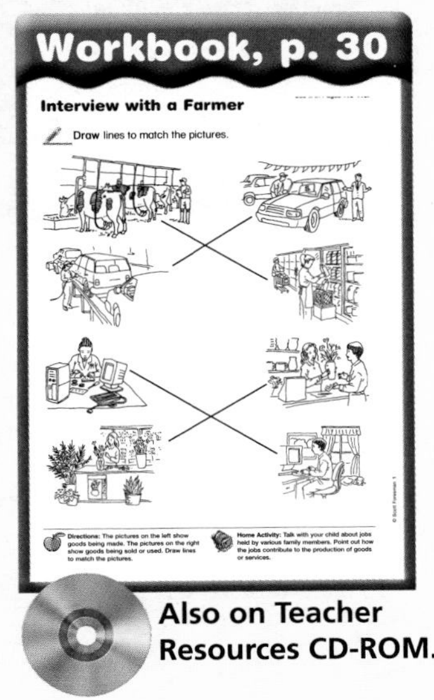

Interview with a Farmer
Draw lines to match the pictures.

Also on Teacher Resources CD-ROM.

Page 119

Before reading p. 119, point out to children that the store pays the factory for the peanuts, and that the factory pays Mr. Ford. Ask children where they think Ben got the bag of peanuts he is holding in the photo on p. 119. Elicit that he probably bought them at a store or a food stand.

9 **The peanuts you see here are still in their shells. How else can you buy peanuts?** Answers will vary, but may include jars or cans of peanuts without shells, as peanut butter, as peanut oil. **Main Idea and Details**

10 **Which do you think is harder: growing peanuts or getting them to market?** Answers may vary but children should note that both processes probably take a lot of work. **Evaluate**

3 Close and Assess

Have children fold a sheet of drawing paper into thirds. On the front side of the paper, have children write a sentence in each section about the three steps in growing peanuts. On the back, have them do the same for the steps in marketing the peanuts.

✓ What did you learn?

1. Answers will vary, but may include planting crops, caring for them, and harvesting them.
2. First, a truck takes them to a factory. Next, the peanuts are cleaned and roasted. Last, they are bagged and sent to stores.
3. **Think and Share** Answers will vary, but may include such things as fruits, vegetables, dairy products, and grains.

Follow a Route

Objectives

- Use a simple map to identify the location of places.
- Locate places of significance on maps.

Skill Vocabulary

route one way to get from one place to another (p. 120)

1 Introduce and Motivate

Preview Write the word *route* on the board, and ask children what they think it means. Then share the definition of the word.

Warm Up To activate prior knowledge, discuss the routes children take to get from one place to another. Begin by describing the route you take to get from one part of the classroom to another. Ask several volunteers to do the same. Then talk about the route you would take to get to the principal's office. Ask children to tell what route they would take to get to another classroom.

Map and Globe Skills

Follow a Route

1 The map shows the route the truck takes from the farm to the factory. A **route** is one way to get from one place to another.

2

3

4

5

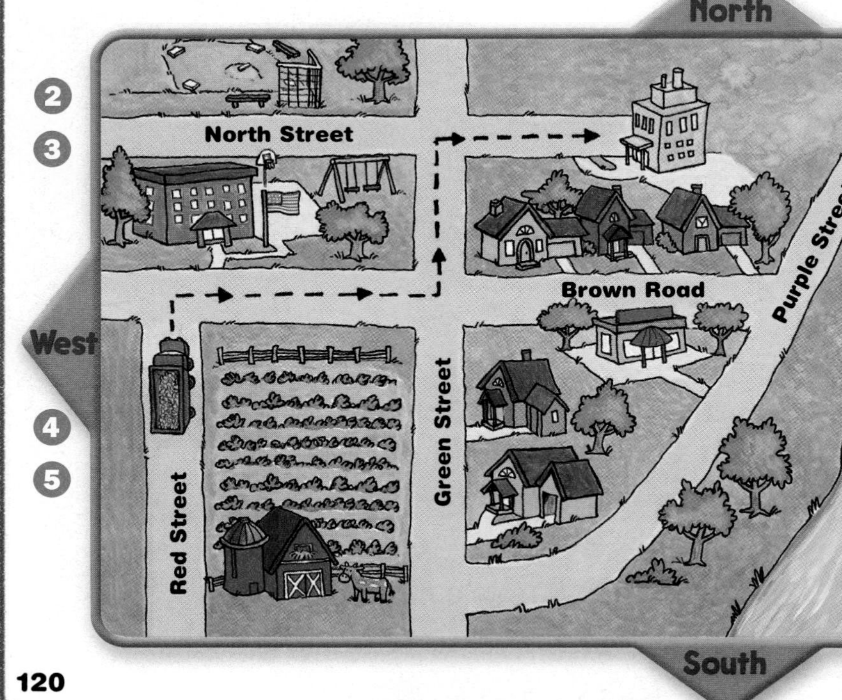

120

Practice and Extend

SOCIAL STUDIES STRAND
Geography

Giving Directions

- Assign each child a partner.
- Have one partner give oral directions for getting from one place on the map to another. The other partner traces the route with his or her finger.
- Partners reverse roles to retrace the route for the return trip.

Look at the map. Tell what building is just north of the truck. What does the arrow show? Where does the route begin? Follow the route with your finger.

1. What does the [store symbol] stand for? How do you know?
2. What direction does the truck go on each street?
3. **On Your Own** Make a map and a map key of your school. Tell what route you would take to get from your classroom to the office.

Map Key

Farm

Store

Factory

School

House

- - -→ **Truck Route**

East

Workbook, p. 31

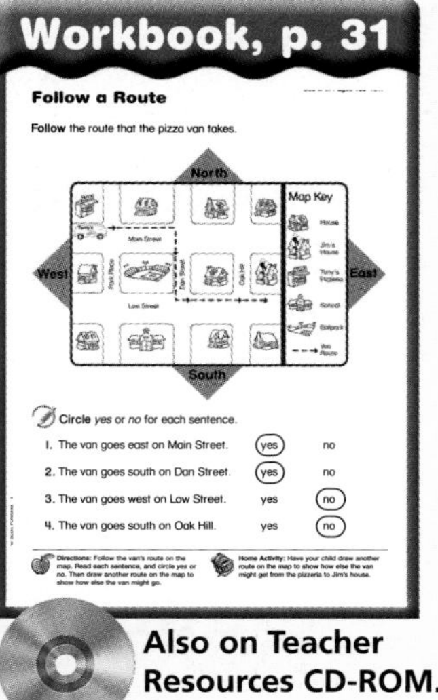

Follow a Route

Follow the route that the pizza van takes.

Circle yes or no for each sentence.

1. The van goes east on Main Street. (yes) no
2. The van goes south on Dan Street. (yes) no
3. The van goes west on Low Street. yes (no)
4. The van goes south on Oak Hill. yes (no)

Also on Teacher Resources CD-ROM.

2 Teach and Discuss

Pages 120–121

Have children use the map key to locate the farm and the factory. Then have them find the truck on the map. Explain that it is the truck with Mr. Ford's peanuts.

1. **What do the lines with arrows show?** The route the truck takes from the farm to the factory **Interpret Maps**

2. **What street does the truck take first?** Red Street **Interpret Maps**

3. **At the end of Red Street, the truck makes a turn. Onto what street does it turn?** Brown Road **Interpret Maps**

4. **Where does the truck go last?** The factory **Interpret Maps**

5. **Is there another route the truck could take? Would that route be shorter or longer?** Accept other possible routes, including entering Green Street from the farm. **Analyze Information**

3 Close and Assess

Try it!

1. It stands for the store. It matches the symbol on the map key.
2. North on Red Street, east on Brown Road, north on Green Street, east on North Street
3. **On Your Own** Children's maps will vary but should include a route from the classroom to the office.

George Washington Carver

Objectives

- Identify a historic figure who has exhibited a love of individualism and inventiveness.
- Identify contributions of historical figures who have influenced the nation.

1 Introduce and Motivate

Preview Hold up a jar of glue, a piece of paper, a rubber ball, and a plastic cup. Have children name the products. Write the names on the lines of a word web. Leave the center circle blank.

Write *peanut* in the center of the word web. Explain that peanuts can be used to make all of the things named on the web.

Tell children that many other products can be made using peanuts as one of the ingredients. Name and add these products to the web: cheese, shaving cream, cooking oil, flour, mayonnaise, bleach, ink, and shoe polish.

Warm Up Point to each word on the web and ask children to tell if they use or eat any of the products.

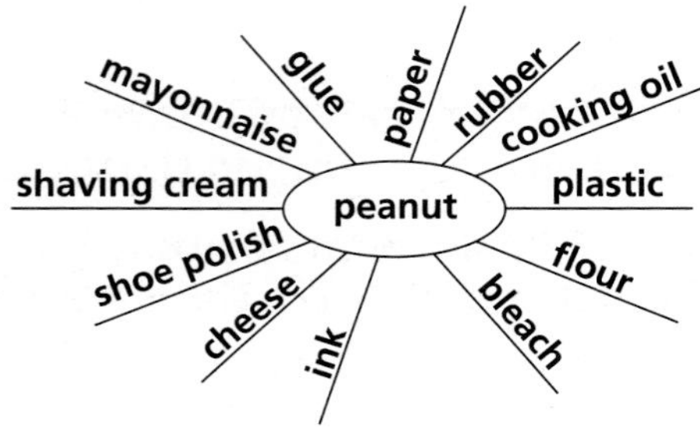

Caution! Because some children may be allergic to peanuts, do not bring peanuts into the classroom. Peanut allergies are very serious and can be life-threatening.

Have children preview the pictures on pp. 122–123. Invite children to describe what they see.

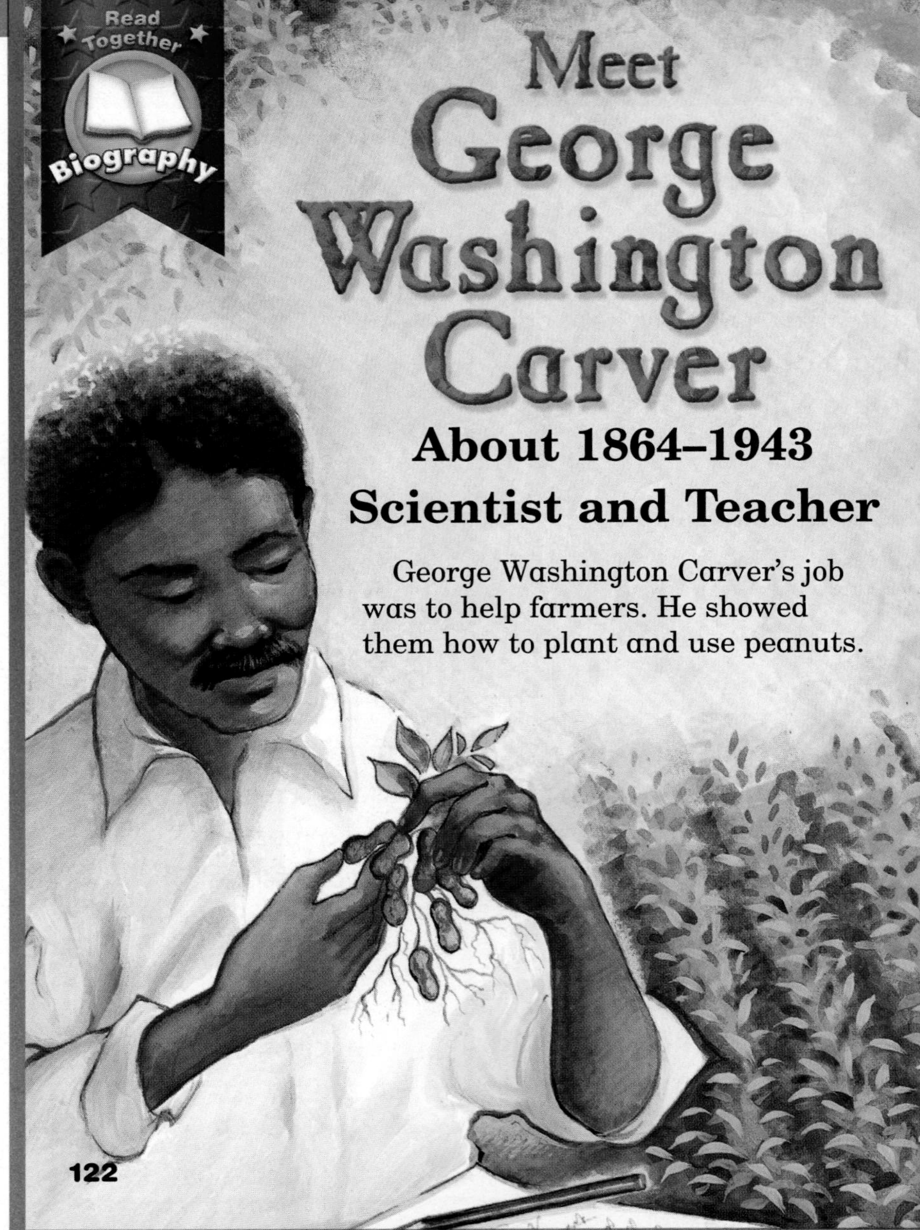

Read Together
Biography
Meet George Washington Carver
About 1864–1943
Scientist and Teacher
George Washington Carver's job was to help farmers. He showed them how to plant and use peanuts.
122

FYI SOCIAL STUDIES Background

About George Washington Carver

- George Washington Carver was born into slavery near Diamond Grove, Missouri. Due to the lack of detailed records, the exact year of his birth is uncertain.
- Carver studied agricultural science at Iowa State Agricultural College, where he received a bachelor's degree in agricultural science in 1894 and a master of science degree in 1896.
- George Washington Carver developed a system of crop rotation and discovered hundreds of products that could be made from peanuts, soybeans, and sweet potatoes. Carver taught at Tuskegee Institute in Alabama for most of his life.
- In his later years, George Washington Carver gave 1864 as the date of his birth.

As a young boy, George liked plants. Later, he went to school to learn about plants and farming. He became a teacher to help farmers. 1

George Washington Carver taught farmers how to grow peanuts. He knew that peanut plants help to 2 make the soil healthy so other crops can grow. He also made many new things from peanuts. You may even use some of the things he learned to make. Did you know that soap, candy, and paint can be made from peanuts? 3

George Washington Carver was born in Diamond Grove, Missouri.

Peanuts with roots and stems

Think and Share

How did George Washington Carver's work help people?

For more information, go online to *Meet the People* at **www.sfsocialstudies.com.**

123

2 Teach and Discuss

Read the biography together. Tell children that when George Washington Carver was a child, his nickname was "the plant doctor."

1 What did George Washington Carver do before he became a teacher? He went to school to learn about plants and farming. **Sequence**

2 How did George Washington Carver help farmers? He helped them grow peanuts. Growing peanuts made their soil healthy. **Cause and Effect**

3 Which goods made from peanuts have you used? Answers may include soap, milk, paint, candy, peanut butter, and so on. **Apply Information**

3 Close and Assess

Think and Share

He taught farmers how to grow peanuts. He also made many new things from peanuts so the farmers had a market for their peanuts.

WEB SITE Technology

You may help children find out more about George Washington Carver by clicking on *Meet the People* at **www.sfsocialstudies.com.**

Use with pages 116–123

Lesson 5 Wrap-Up

MEETING INDIVIDUAL NEEDS
Leveled Practice

Draw Sequential Pictures
Have children draw pictures of the steps in growing peanuts and marketing the peanuts.

Easy Have children pantomime some of the steps in growing peanuts and getting them to market. Classmates can try to guess which of the steps described in their pictures is being acted out. **Reteach**

On-Level Remind children that Mr. Ford thinks growing peanuts is hard work. Ask children to point to their drawing and tell why they think each step pictured might be hard work. **Extend**

Challenge Have children work with partners. Have them dramatize interviewing a farmer about the steps in growing peanuts and marketing them. The "farmer" may use pictures as visual aids. **Enrich**

Hands-on Activities

CURRICULUM CONNECTION
Reading

What a Plot!

Objective Recognize story plot.

Materials *The Little Red Hen (Makes a Pizza),* by Philemon Sturges (Dutton, ISBN 0-525-45953-7, 1999)

Learning Style Visual/Verbal

Group

 **Time** 20 minutes

1. Share the pictures as you read the story to children.

2. Help children identify the story problem. Elicit that when the hen wanted to make a pizza, she got no help from the duck, the dog, or the cat.

3. Ask how the hen solved her problem. Elicit that she did all the work herself.

4. Invite children to tell how the story ends. If they know the original tale, have them contrast the story endings. (In this version, the hen shares the pizza and the animals agree to wash the dishes.)

SOCIAL STUDIES STRAND
Geography

Placemat Maps

Objective Follow a route.

Materials old placemats, markers, blocks, toy cars

Learning Style Kinesthetic

Partners

 **Time** 15–20 minutes

1. Draw simple map outlines on several old placemats. Have children add buildings with blocks or other small objects. Children can "drive" small-sized cars around their maps.

2. Ask children to draw copies of their maps and show the routes they "drove."

SOCIAL STUDIES STRAND
Economics

Interview

Objective Interview a person about skills required for a job.

Learning Style Verbal

Individual

 **Time** 20–25 minutes

1. Have each child interview a family member or a neighbor about his or her job.

2. Encourage children to ask how the person being interviewed prepared for his or her job. Did they need to learn special skills? Where did they learn those skills?

3. Children can give oral reports to share what they learned about the job of the person they interviewed.

Lesson 6 Overview

From Place to Place **pages 124–125**	Children will explore different modes of transportation and how transportation is used to move goods. They will also learn how technology has changed transportation.	Time 20 minutes Resources • Workbook, p. 32 • Vocabulary Card **transportation** • Every Student Learns Guide, pp. 58–61
Big Wheels **pages 126–127**	Children will use pictures to learn how different types of transportation help people do jobs.	Time 15–20 minutes

Build Background

Activity

How Will You Go?

Time 15–20 minutes

Ask children to draw pictures to show how they get to school each day. When children are finished, have them hold up their pictures and identify the modes of transportation used. Make a pictogram to show the results.

If time is short, have children tell how they get to school. Ask if they walk, come by car, ride on the school bus, or get there some other way.

Read Aloud

Getting There

by Janet Carroll

To get to school, I ride the bus.
Gramps comes by car to visit us.

Subways run below the ground
So city folks can get around.

Trucks move on roads; trains, on rails.
Sailors need wind to blow their sails.

Jet planes travel through the air.
They fly so fast—from here to there.

But when I go next door to play,
I use my skates—they're quite OK.

From Place to Place

Objectives

- Identify the role of transportation in the exchange of goods.
- Describe how technology has changed transportation.

Vocabulary

transportation things that move people and goods from place to place (p. 124)

QUICK Teaching Plan

If time is short, brainstorm with children a list of vehicles that move people and goods.

- Use pp. 124–125 to explore with children different means of transportation.

1 Introduce and Motivate

Preview Display the Vocabulary Card **transportation** and ask children what they think it means. Then share its meaning. Have children locate the word as they preview the lesson.

Warm Up To activate prior knowledge, ask children to tell ways in which they get from place to place, other than by walking. Ask children to suppose they want to visit a friend who lives across the country. How can they get there? Then ask children to suppose they want to visit a friend who lives across the ocean. How could they get there?

From Place to Place

Mr. Ford drives a tractor and a truck on his farm. The tractor and truck are his transportation. **Transportation** moves people and goods from place to place.

Sometimes Ben travels by bike or car. What kinds of transportation do you use?

1

124

Practice and Extend

READING SKILL
Analyze Pictures

Look Again!

- Ask children to describe the photographs around the edge of these pages.
- Have children point to each kind of transportation in the drawing that matches a photograph.
- Ask how photographs and drawings are the same. (They can picture the same objects.) Ask how they are different. (Photographs show real objects; drawings can show real or imagined objects.)

WEB SITE
Technology

You can look up vocabulary words online. Click on *Social Studies Library* and select the dictionary at **www.sfsocialstudies.com.**

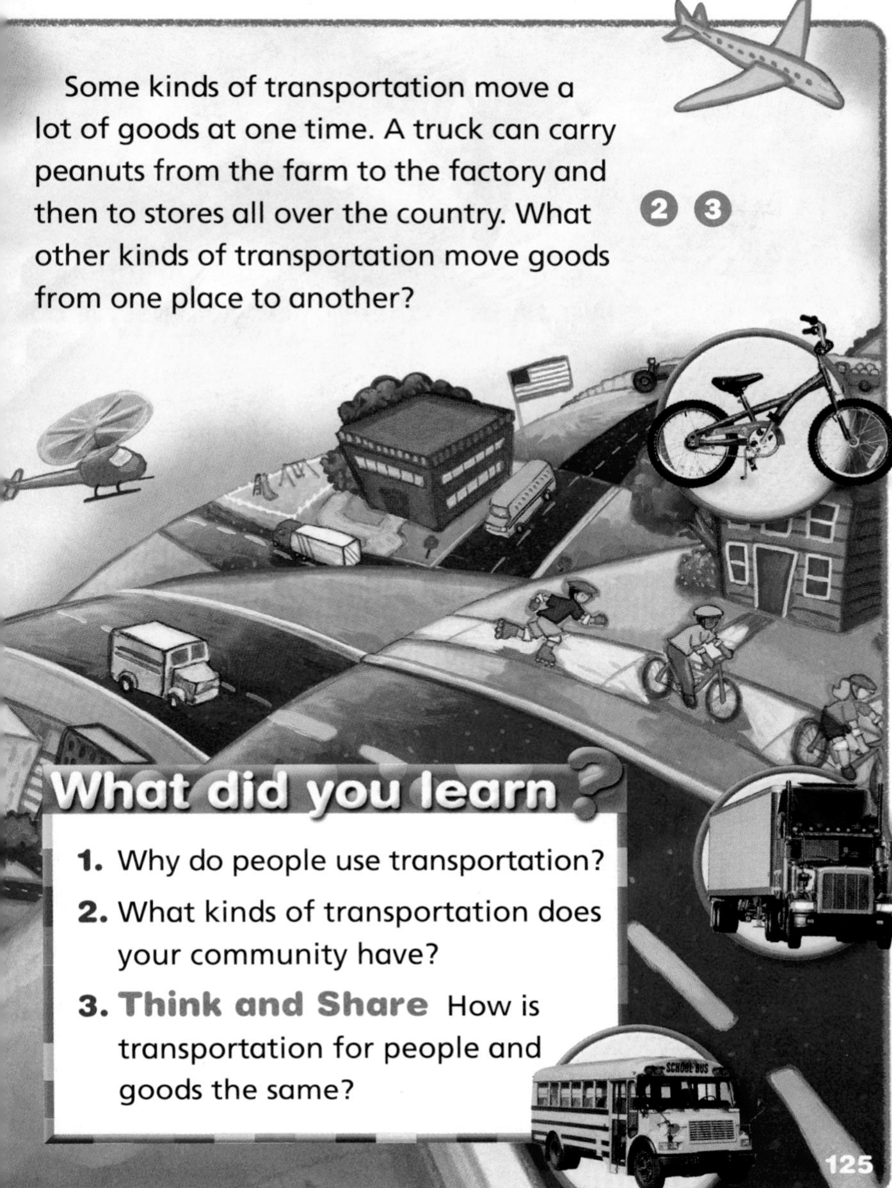

Some kinds of transportation move a lot of goods at one time. A truck can carry peanuts from the farm to the factory and then to stores all over the country. What other kinds of transportation move goods from one place to another? ❷ ❸

What did you learn?

1. Why do people use transportation?
2. What kinds of transportation does your community have?
3. **Think and Share** How is transportation for people and goods the same?

125

2 Teach and Discuss

Pages 124–125

Challenge children to see how many kinds of transportation they can name on pp. 124–125.

❶ **What are some ways people can move from place to place in a big city?** Possible answers: taxis, buses, and trains **Analyze Pictures**

❷ **Which pictures show ways to move goods?** The trucks, the boat, perhaps the jet **Analyze Pictures**

SOCIAL STUDIES STRAND History

Transportation has changed as technology has improved. Remind children that before there were cars, people walked from place to place and rode in horse-drawn vehicles. Ask children to recall old pictures they have seen of bikes, cars, trucks, or planes, or anything their grandparents have told them about how transportation used to be. Discuss how various means of transportation have changed.

❸ **Why is it important to move peanuts from farms to stores?** So they can be sold **Draw Conclusions**

3 Close and Assess

✓ What did you learn?

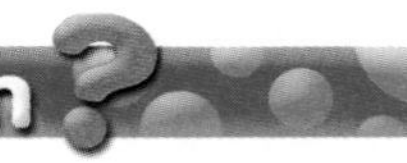

1. To move people and goods from place to place.
2. Answers will vary but should reflect how location and surroundings affect transportation.
3. **Think and Share** Both people and goods are moved from place to place.

SOCIAL STUDIES Background

Possible Misconceptions

- Children may not realize that wheels, sails, steam engines, internal-combustion engines, electric motors, and rockets have revolutionized transportation.
- There were few suburbs around cities until streetcars and trains became popular. Before commercial air travel, long journeys often took weeks or months.

Workbook, p. 32

From Place to Place

Make a chart to show then and now.
Cut out the pictures.
Paste them on the chart.

Now	Then	Now
Then	Now	Then
Now	Now	Then
Now	Then	Then

Also on Teacher Resources CD-ROM.

Big Wheels

Objectives

- Obtain information about a topic using a variety of visual sources, such as pictures and graphics.
- Identify ways people exchange goods and services.

1 Introduce and Motivate

Preview Ask children what they think the phrase *Big Wheels* means. Tell them that in this lesson, *Big Wheels* is another way of saying *trucks*. Have children locate the title *Big Wheels* as they preview the lesson.

Warm Up To activate prior knowledge, ask children what kinds of transportation they talked about in Lesson 6. Ask which kinds had wheels. (cars, buses, trucks, and so on) Tell children that they will now take a closer look at some trucks with big wheels.

Read the introduction with children. Ask them to try to guess what kinds of jobs these trucks do.

2 Teach and Discuss

Point out the two pictures of a concrete truck. Using the larger picture, have children identify the mixing drum and the hood.

❶ **Look at the smaller picture. What is coming out of the back of the truck?** Accept reasonable answers, including concrete or cement.
Analyze Pictures

❷ **Why do people need concrete?** To make sidewalks, streets, foundations for houses, and so on
Make Inferences

❸ **What do you think happens in the mixing drum?** As the drum turns, the contents move around and around. This keeps the concrete well mixed; it also prevents it from hardening too soon.
Make Inferences

Big Wheels

Look at some types of transportation. What jobs do these trucks help people do?

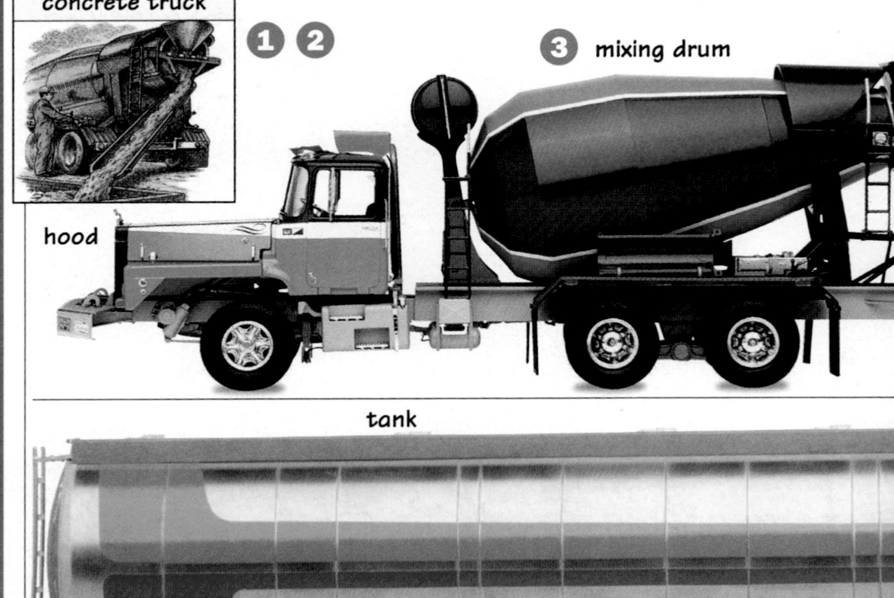

Practice and Extend

SOCIAL STUDIES Background

About Trucks

- Concrete is a mixture of cement, sand, gravel, and water.
- The larger the truck and the heavier its load, the more tires it requires. The additional tires help distribute the weight of the load more evenly. The tires also help protect the road surface.
- Sitting up high in the cab helps the truck driver to see long distances. However, if the hood of the truck sticks out, the driver can't see what is directly in front.

ACCESS CONTENT ESL Support

For additional ESL support, use Every Student Learns Guide, pp. 58–61.

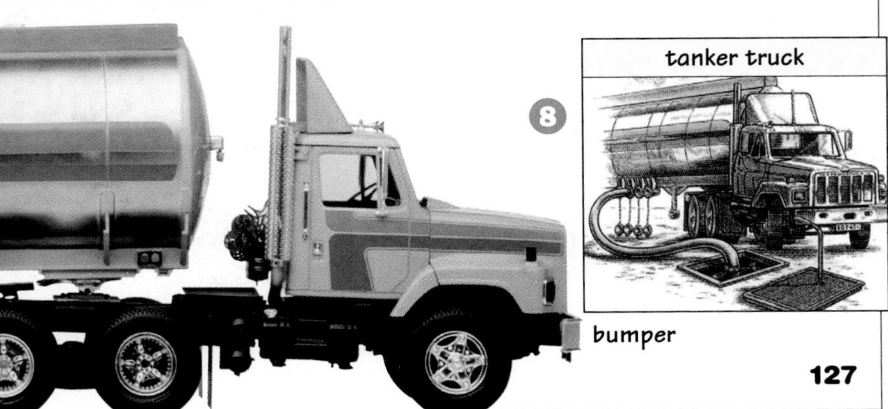

Next, have children focus on the two pictures of a delivery truck on p. 127. Remind children that trucks are a type of transportation that can move a lot of goods at one time.

4 **What does a delivery truck do?** It takes goods to stores and to people who need the goods. **Make Inferences**

5 **What is the part where the driver sits called?** The cab **Main Idea and Details**

Next, children should look at the pictures of a tow truck. Have children point to the crane arm and the hook in the larger picture.

6 **What is a tow truck used for?** To pull cars or trucks from one place to another **Make Inferences**

7 **Does a tow truck give people a good or a service?** A service **Analyze Information**

Finally, focus on the two pictures of the tanker truck. Explain that a tanker truck delivers fuel, and that the gas used to run cars is a fuel.

8 **How do you think fuel gets from the tank into the containers underground?** It goes through the big hose attached to the tank. **Analyze Pictures**

3 Close and Assess

- Ask children to point out where the driver sits in each truck. Have them compare the fronts of the trucks by naming the truck with a flat front (delivery truck), and the trucks with fronts that stick out (concrete mixer, tow truck, tanker truck).
- Have children look at the wheels on the trucks. Talk about why the tanker truck has more wheels than the other trucks.
- Ask children to tell how different kinds of trucks provide goods and services.

CURRICULUM CONNECTION Science

How Wheels Work

Mention that wheels on a truck are attached to an axle. Explain that a wheel and axle is a simple machine. A wheel and axle is made of a rod, or axle, attached to the center of a wheel. The wheel turns around the axle. A wheel and axle moves or turns an object. Have children work in small groups to observe the workings of these wheel-and-axle tools.

- doorknob
- screwdriver
- egg-beater
- pencil sharpener
- pepper mill

Use with pages 124–127

Lesson 6 Wrap-Up

MEETING INDIVIDUAL NEEDS
Leveled Practice

Find Transportation Pictures
Ask children to cut out magazine or newspaper pictures that show different means of transportation.

Easy Divide a bulletin board into three sections: **Air, Land, Water**. Have children categorize and display the pictures in the appropriate sections. **Reteach**

On-Level Have each child choose a picture and paste it on a sheet of paper. Then have each student dictate or write sentences telling how that means of transportation moves people and/or goods. **Extend**

Challenge Have children find information on and then draw examples of vehicles used long ago. Children can use the pictures to make "Now and Then" posters to compare and contrast various means of transportation from the past and present. **Enrich**

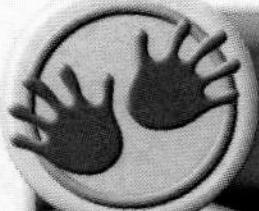

Hands-on Activities

CURRICULUM CONNECTION
Writing

A Poem

Objective Write a poem using lesson vocabulary.

Materials chart paper, markers

Learning Style Visual/Verbal

Group

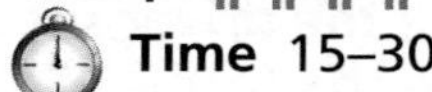

Time 15–30 minutes

1. Create a word web around the word *transportation* and the phrases *on land, on water,* and *in the air*.

2. Ask children to pick a favorite mode of transportation. Write the word vertically, one letter under the other, on chart paper. Help children create a poem for the mode of transportation by suggesting a word or phrase for each letter.

3. Remind children to add their word *transportation* to the Word Book.

CURRICULUM CONNECTION
Literature

All Aboard

Objectives Describe how trains move people; compare/contrast trains then and now.

Materials *Window Music,* by Anastasia Sven (Viking, ISBN 0-670-87287-3, 1998)

Learning Style Auditory/Visual

Group

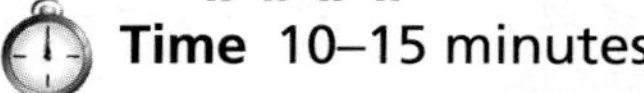

Time 10–15 minutes

1. Read the book aloud, displaying the pictures. Have children note how the scenery changes as the train moves.

2. Ask children to find pictures of modern trains. Compare them with the train shown in the book. Talk about how technology has changed the way trains look and run.

3. Reread the story, inviting children to join in.

SOCIAL STUDIES STRAND
Economics

Trucks That Work

Objective Demonstrate how trucks help people.

Materials toy and/or model trucks

Learning Style Visual/Verbal/Kinesthetic

Group

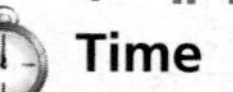

Time 10–15 minutes

1. Ask children who have toy or model trucks at home to bring them to school.

2. Have the owners demonstrate how the trucks work. Encourage them to tell what the trucks help people do.

3. Ask children to look for real trucks that do some of these same things in their own communities.

Ending Unit 3

End with a Poem pages 128–129	Children will listen to and talk about a poem, "Work Day" by Kate Greenwood, that tells about a child who goes to work with her mother.	
Unit 3 Review pages 130–133	Children will review unit vocabulary words and the unit skills of put things in order, follow a route, and use a chart. They will answer questions about what they learned in the unit. Children will also learn about several books relating to jobs and work. 	Resources • Workbook, p. 33 ✓• Assessment Book pp. 9–12
Unit 3 Project page 134	Children will learn how to make a community worker puppet. They will also be directed to a Web site where they can learn more about people at work.	Resource • Workbook, p. 34

Wrap-up

Activity

My Book About Work

Have each child make a small book by folding two sheets of plain paper in half. The front page should carry the title, *My Book About Work.*

- On the inside pages, ask children to write descriptions or draw pictures showing work they do now including schoolwork, chores at home, and so on.
- The last page should be devoted to the kind of work they would like to do as adults. Encourage children to include volunteer work.

Performance Assessment
You can use the activity on this page as a performance assessment.

✓ Assessment Scoring Guide

Make Books About Work	
4	Describes work and work goals in depth very clearly and completely.
3	Describes work and work goals clearly and completely, including some details.
2	Describes work and work goals with a few gaps in information and few details.
1	Describes work and work goals with little information or details.

Work Day

Objective

- Obtain information about a topic using a variety of visual sources, such as pictures and literature.

1 Introduce and Motivate

Preview Point to and read the title, then identify the author of the poem. From the title and art, ask children what the poem could be about. Write their responses on the board and review them after the reading.

Explain that a poem is a kind of writing that often has rhyming words.

Warm Up To activate knowledge, ask children if they have ever visited a place of work of someone they know. Encourage them to tell what they saw and did there.

2 Teach and Discuss

Invite children to listen as you read the poem. Encourage them to picture in their minds the actions of the poem.

1 In what kind of place do you think the mother works? Possible answer: An office
Make Inferences

2 What do you think the child might have done at work? Possible answers: Played with her doll or other toys she brought from home; played with office supplies, such as paper and pencils
Make Inferences

Have children listen for rhyming words at the ends of the phrases as you read the poem aloud again.

UNIT 3

End with a Poem

Work Day

by Kate Greenwood

My mom and I
went to work today.

Well, she went to work
and I went to play.

She met with people
and talked on the phone.

I wonder what I'll do 1 2
when I'm all grown.

128

Practice and Extend

Rhyming Words

Direct small groups of children to locate and write pairs of rhyming words from the poem—*today* and *play, phone* and *grown.* Encourage them to add other rhyming words to each pair. Upon completion, each group can share their groups of words.

3 Close and Assess

- Divide children into two groups.
- Have children do a choral reading of the selection, with each group reading alternate stanzas.
- After children have read the poem aloud, invite them to share what they like most about the poem.

CURRICULUM CONNECTION
Reading

Books About Work

Children might enjoy reading these books related to work.

Career Day, by Anne F. Rockwell (HarperCollins Children's Book Group, ISBN 0-06-027565-0, 2000). In this picture book, children in a class introduce parents and grandparents who demonstrate their occupation. **Easy**

Work Song, by Gary Paulsen (Harcourt Brace, ISBN 0-015-200980-9, 1997) The rhyming text and visuals in this book celebrate the world of work. **On-Level**

AWARD ***Mama & Papa Have a Store,*** by Amelia Lau Carling (Dial Books for Young Readers, ISBN 0-8037-2044-0, 1998) A young Chinese girl describes a typical day in her parents' general store in Guatemala City. **Challenge** ***Pura Belpré Honor, 2000***

Review

Resources

- Assessment Book, pp. 9–12
- Workbook, p. 33: Vocabulary Review

Vocabulary Review

1. needs
2. job
3. service
4. volunteer
5. transporation
6. goods

Answers to Test Prep

1. wants
2. tools

Test Talk

Use Question 1 to model the Test Talk strategy.

Narrow the answer choices.
Tell children to read each answer choice carefully. Children should rule out any choice that they know is wrong.

Choose the best answer.
After children make their answer choice, tell them to check their answer by comparing it to the text.

For additional practice, use the Test Talk Practice Book.

UNIT 3

Review

Vocabulary Review

transportation
job
service
goods
volunteer
needs

Tell which word completes each sentence.

1. Food and clothing and a place to live are _____.
2. Work that people do is a _____.
3. A job workers do to help others is a _____
4. A person who works for free is a _____.
5. A plane is one type of _____.
6. Things that are grown or made are _____

★ ★ ★ ★ ★ ★ ★ ★

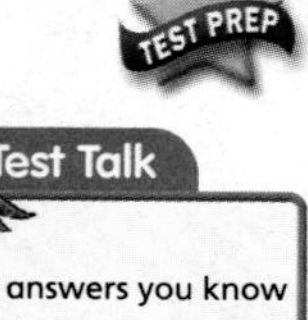

Test Talk

Rule out answers you know are wrong.

TEST PREP Which word completes each sentence?

1. Things we would like to have are _____.

   a. goods b. transportation
   c. tools d. wants

2. Pliers and a hammer used by a carpenter are called _____.

   a. service b. transportation
   c. tools d. wants

130

Practice and Extend

Assessment Options

✓ Unit 3 Assessment

- Unit 3 Content Test: Use Assessment Book, pp. 9–10
- Unit 3 Skills Test: Use Assessment Book, pp. 11–12

Standardized Test Prep

- Unit 3 tests contain standardized test formats.

✓ Unit 3 Performance Assessment

- See p. 134 for information about using the Unit 3 Project as a means of performance assessment.
- A scoring guide for the Unit 3 Project is provided in the teacher's notes on p. 134.

Test Talk

- Test Talk Practice Book

Skills Review

Put Things in Order

Write about a job you want to do some day. Tell what you would do **first, next,** and **last.**

Follow a Route

1. What buildings are east of the store?
2. Follow the route with your finger. Where does Pat's route begin?
3. Tell what direction Pat goes on each street.

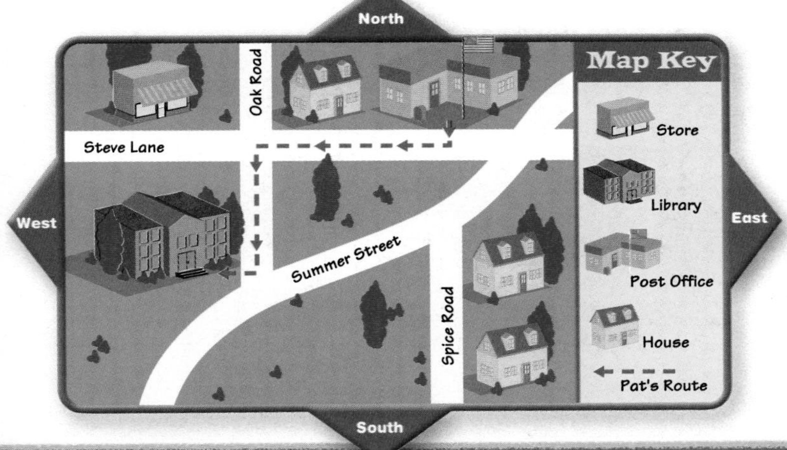

131

Practice and Extend

For more information, you can select the dictionary or encyclopedia from *Social Studies Library* at **www.sfsocialstudies.com.**

Workbook, p. 33

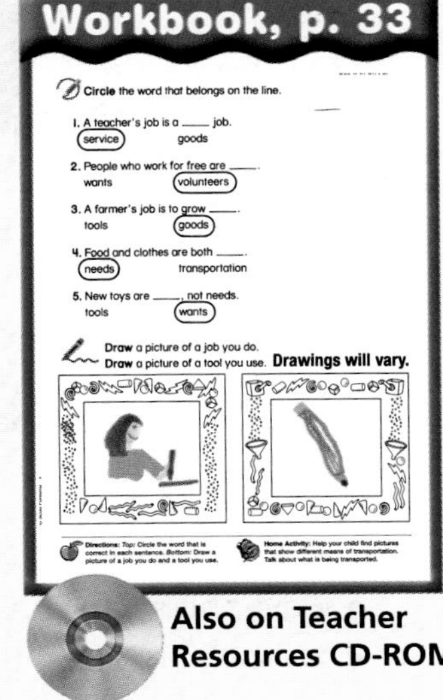

Circle the word that belongs on the line.

1. A teacher's job is a ___ job. (service) goods
2. People who work for free are ___. wants (volunteers)
3. A farmer's job is to grow ___. tools (goods)
4. Food and clothes are both ___. (needs) transportation
5. New toys are ___, not needs. tools (wants)

Draw a picture of a job you do.
Draw a picture of a tool you use. **Drawings will vary.**

Also on Teacher Resources CD-ROM.

Skills Review

Put Things in Order

- Children's answers should show an understanding of the concept of jobs. Children's answers should include correct use of the words *first, next,* and *last.*

Use the following scoring guide.

✓ Assessment Scoring Guide

	Write About Sequence Related to a Job
4	Describes a job with many precise details, using the words *first, next,* and *last* correctly.
3	Describes a job with adequately clear details, using the words *first, next,* and *last* correctly.
2	Describes a job with few clear details, using two of the words *first, next,* and *last* correctly.
1	Describes a job with few or no details, using one or none of the words *first, next,* and *last* correctly.

Follow a Route

1. A house and the post office
2. At the post office
3. West on Steve Lane, south on Oak Road

Review

Skills Review

Use a Chart

1. Four

2. Lisa

3. Sara

Skills On Your Own

- Children's charts should be in the correct format and accurately reflect class jobs.

Use the following scoring guide.

✓ Assessment Scoring Guide

Make a Chart	
4	Shows precise class jobs information in an easy-to-read, correct chart format.
3	Shows accurate class jobs information in a correct chart format.
2	Shows class jobs information with a few errors in a format that is similar to a chart.
1	Shows class jobs information with many errors in a format that is not a chart.

Review

Skills Review

Use a Chart

Use the chart to answer the questions.

1. How many tools does the chart show?

2. Who used a ruler?

3. Who used a pencil?

Tools We Used Today	
Tools	**People**
Pencil	Sara
Computer	Tony
Brush	Ryan
Ruler	Lisa

Skills On Your Own

Make a chart of some jobs in your class. Write a title for your chart. Write the jobs on the left. Write the names of the helpers next to the jobs they do.

Jobs in Our Class	
Hand out tools.	Anna
Be line leader.	Maria
Clean board.	Henry
Hand out milk.	Mark

132

Practice and Extend

Revisit the Unit Question

✓ Unit 3 Portfolio Assessment

- Have children look back at the list of jobs they made on p. 87.
- Have children list details about the job they would like to have.
- Ask children to underline the details they learned about jobs from studying this unit.
- Ask children to draw a picture of a job they would like to do when they are grown.
- Have children write two sentences about the job.
- Have children add their lists, drawings, and sentences to their Social Studies Portfolio.

What did you learn?

1. Why do people work?
2. How are goods different from services?
3. Name some jobs. Tell what good or service each job provides.
4. **Write and Share**
Write what you could do if you wanted to buy a toy that costs more money than you have.

Read About Work

Look for books like these in the library.

133

What did you learn?

1. People work to earn money, to help people, and because they like what they do.
2. Goods are things people grow or make; services are jobs people do to help others.
3. Possible answers include: Doctors help keep people well and salespeople sell different goods.
4. **Write and Share** Children's answers should reflect understanding of the concept that wanting more than one can have requires that people make choices.

Read About Work

You might want to have these or other books about work available in the classroom. Invite children to read one or more of the books and write a short book report or tell why they liked the book.

Cowboy Bunnies, by Christine Loomis (Putnam, ISBN 0-399-22625-7, 1997) The bunnies in this book are indeed cowboys who "Start at sunup/Work all day/Roping cows/Tossing hay." **Easy**

Dancin' in the Kitchen, by Wendy Gelsanliter and Frank Christian (Putnam, ISBN 0-399-23035-1, 1998) Three generations of a family help to prepare a meal—while dancing to the music on the radio. **On-Level**

A Weed Is a Flower: The Life of George Washington Carver, by Aliki (Aladdin, ISBN 0-671-66490-5, 1988) This inspiring biography includes dramatic action—and makes for good class read-aloud. **Challenge**

Unit 3 Project

Jobs in Your Community

Objective

- Understand jobs done by different workers in the community.

Resource

- Workbook, p. 34

Materials

paper bags, scissors, construction paper, crayons, glue, paper, pencil

Follow This Procedure

- Review different kinds of workers in the community. Discuss any special clothes they wear, tools they use, and how they provide goods or services.
- Tell children they will be making a worker puppet and then interviewing each other's puppets.
- Reproduce or have children trace patterns of arms, hats, and special tools, clothing, or accessories on construction paper.
- Have children color, cut, and glue the pieces onto the bag.
- Explain to children that they're going to act as the worker and give an interview about the worker's job.

✓ **Assessment Scoring Guide**

	Jobs in Your Community
4	Describes a worker's job and ways of exchanging goods or services and answers questions very clearly and completely.
3	Describes a worker's job and ways of exchanging goods or services and answers questions clearly and completely.
2	Describes a worker's job and ways of exchanging goods or services and answers questions with gaps in information.
1	Describes a worker's job and ways of exchanging goods or services and answers questions with confusing information and few details.

Unit 3 Project

Jobs in Your Community

Make a community worker puppet. Give an interview about your community worker's job.

1. **Choose** a kind of worker in your community.
2. **Make** a puppet of your worker. Show any special clothes or tools.
3. **Tell** how your worker gives us goods or services.
4. **Answer** questions from your classmates about your worker's job.

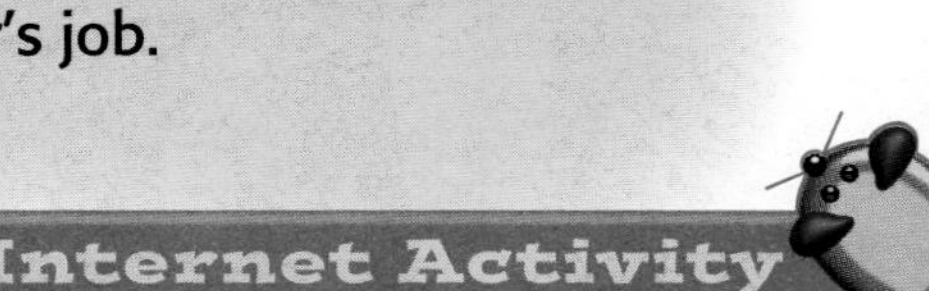

Internet Activity

Go to www.sfsocialstudies.com/activities to learn more about people at work.

134

Practice and Extend

Hands-on Unit Project

✓ **Performance Assessment**

- The Unit Project can also be used as a performance assessment activity.
- Use the scoring guide to assess each group's work.

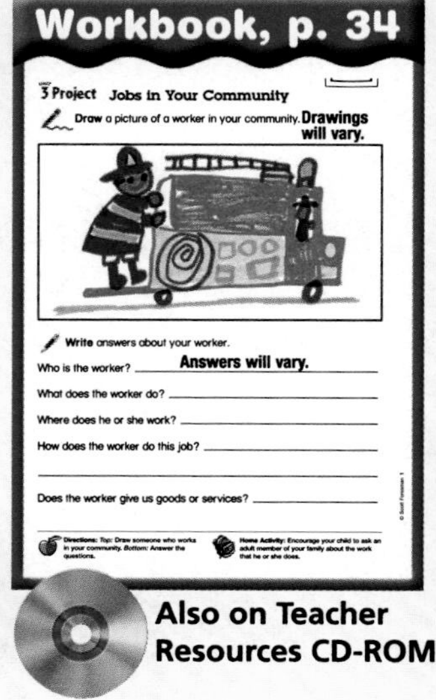

Workbook, p. 34

3 Project Jobs in Your Community

Draw a picture of a worker in your community. **Drawings will vary.**

Write answers about your worker.

Who is the worker? **Answers will vary.**

What does the worker do?

Where does he or she work?

How does the worker do this job?

Does the worker give us goods or services?

Also on Teacher Resources CD-ROM.

WEB SITE Technology

Children can launch the activity by clicking on *Grade 1, Unit 3* at **www.sfsocialstudies.com/activities.**

★ Unit 4 ★

Our Earth, Our Resources

Our Earth,
Our Resources
UNIT
4

UNIT 4

Unit 4 Planning Guide

Our Earth, Our Resources

Begin with a Song pp. 136–137 **Vocabulary Preview** pp. 138–139

Target Skill **Reading Social Studies, Find the Main Idea** pp. 140–141

Lesson Titles	Pacing	Main Ideas
Lesson 1 **Different Kinds of Weather** pp. 142–145 **Chart and Graph Skills: Read a Time Line** pp. 146–147 **Smithsonian Institution: Weather and Fun** pp. 148–149	2 days	• Weather can vary from day to day and from place to place; weather affects what we wear and what we do. • A time line is a graphic organizer used to show the order in which things happen. • Climate and weather can affect what people do for recreation.
Lesson 2 **Looking at Our Land and Water** pp. 150–153 **Map and Globe Skills: Locate Land and Water** pp. 154–155	2 days	• Earth has different kinds of land (such as mountains, hills, and plains) and water (such as oceans, lakes, and rivers). • A globe is a round model of Earth; like a map, it shows landforms and bodies of water.
Lesson 3 **Our Earth's Resources** pp. 156–159 **Citizen Heroes: Responsibility Tree Musketeers** pp. 160–161 **Read Together Biography: Elvia Niebla** pp. 162–163	3 days	• Among Earth's natural resources are land, water, air, trees, oil, and gas. It is important to conserve our natural resources. • Tree Musketeers helps take care of Earth. • Elvia Neibla, a Mexican American, is a scientist who studies forests and works for their conservation.
Lesson 4 **Interview About Farm History** pp. 164–167 **Biography: Sacagawea** pp. 168–169	2 days	• A visit to "Living History Farms" is one way to learn about the history of an area—and how farming has changed over the years. • Sacagawea was a Shoshone who guided explorers Lewis and Clark during their search for a water route to the Pacific Ocean.
Lesson 5 **Caring for Our Resources** pp. 170–173 **Here and There: Endangered Animals** pp. 174–175	2 days	• To conserve our natural resources, people can observe the 3 *R*s: reduce, reuse, and recycle. • When people care for Earth, they also help endangered animals, such as giant pandas and tigers.

✓ **End with a Legend** pp. 176–177 ✓ **Unit 4 Review** pp. 178–181 ✓ **Unit 4 Project** p. 182

✓ = **Assessment Options**

Vocabulary	Resources	Meeting Individual Needs
weather	• Workbook, pp. 37–39 • Vocabulary Card: weather • Every Student Learns Guide, pp. 62–65	• ESL Support, TE p. 144 • Leveled Practice, TE p. 149a
mountain **plain** **lake** **river**	• Workbook, pp. 40–41 • Vocabulary Cards: mountain, plain, lake, river • Every Student Learns Guide, pp. 66–69	• ESL Support, TE pp. 151, 154 • Leveled Practice, TE p. 155a
natural resource	• Workbook, p. 42 • Vocabulary Card: natural resource • Every Student Learns Guide, pp. 70–73	• ESL Support, TE pp. 157, 162 • Leveled Practice, TE p. 19a
history	• Workbook p. 43 • Vocabulary Card: history • Every Student Learns Guide, pp. 74–77	• ESL Support, TE p. 166 • Leveled Practice, TE p. 169a
	• Workbook p. 44 • Every Student Learns Guide, pp. 78–81	• ESL Support, TE p. 171 • Leveled Practice, TE p. 175a

Providing More Depth

Multimedia Library

- ***Weather* by Brian Cosgrove**
- ***The Secret Life of Trees* by Chiara Chevallier**
- **Songs and Music**
- **Video Field Trips**
- **Software**

Additional Resources

- Family Activities
- Vocabulary Cards
- Daily Activity Bank
- Social Studies Plus!
- Outline Maps
- Big Book Atlas
- Desk Maps

ADDITIONAL Technology

- AudioText
- TestWorks
- Teacher Resources CD-ROM
- Map Resources CD-ROM
- **www.sfsocialstudies.com**

To establish guidelines for children's safe and responsible use of the Internet, use the **Scott Foresman Internet Guide.**

Additional Internet Links
To find out more about:

- Tree Musketeers, visit **Info@TreeMusketeers.org**
- Living History Farms, visit **http://www.ioweb.com**

Key Internet Search Terms

- weather
- recycle
- endangered

Unit 4 Objectives

Beginning of Unit 4

- **Obtain information about a topic using a variety of oral sources such as music.** (pp. 136–137)
- **Determine the meanings of words.** (pp. 138–139)
- **Identify main ideas from print sources.** (pp. 140–141)

Lesson 1
What Is the Weather Today?
pp. 142–145

- **Identify and describe the physical characteristics of places such as weather and climate.**
- **Describe how climate affects the way people live, including their clothing and recreation.**
- **Use vocabulary related to chronology, including *yesterday, today,* and *tomorrow*.**
- **Distinguish among past, present, and future.** (pp. 146–147)
- **Create a time line.** (pp. 146–147)
- **Create visual and written material including time lines.** (pp. 146–147)
- **Interpret information presented in picture time lines to show sequence of events.** (pp. 146–147)
- **Describe how weather affects people's choice of recreational activities.** (pp. 148–149)

Lesson 2
Looking at Our Land and Water
pp. 150–151

- **Identify and describe the physical characteristics of places such as landforms and bodies of water.**
- **Describe how location and physical surroundings affect the way people live, including their recreation.**
- **Identify a globe as a model of the Earth.** (pp. 154–155)
- **Distinguish between land and water on globes and maps.** (pp. 154–155)
- **Relate locations on globes to locations on the Earth.** (pp. 154–155)

Lesson 3
Our Earth's Resources
pp. 156–159

- **Identify and describe the physical characteristics of places such as their natural resources.**
- **Identify examples of and uses for natural resources in the community, state, and nation.**
- **Identify characteristics of good citizenship such as responsibility for the common good.** (pp. 160–161)
- **Identify ordinary people who exemplify good citizenship.** (pp. 160–161)
- **Identify characteristics of good citizenship such as responsibility for the common good.** (pp. 162–163)

Lesson 4
Interview About Farm History
pp. 164–167

- **Distinguish among past, present, and future.**
- **Identify examples of and uses for natural resources.**
- **Identify contributions of historical figures who have influenced the nation.** (pp. 168–169)

Lesson 5
Caring for Our Resources
pp. 170–173

- **Identify ways that natural resources can be used and reused.**
- **Obtain information about a topic using maps and pictures.** (pp. 174–175)
- **Identify ways that protecting natural resources helps animals.** (pp. 174–175)
- **Respond to important problems with the Earth's natural resources.** (pp. 174–175)

End of Unit 4
pp. 176–177

- **Retell stories from selected folktales and legends.**

Assessment Options

✓ Formal Assessment

- **What did you learn?** PE/TE pp. 145, 153, 159, 167, 173, 181
- **Unit Review,** PE/TE pp. 178–181
- **Unit 4 Test,** Assessment Book pp. 13–16
- **TestWorks,** (test generator software)

✓ Informal Assessment

- **Teacher's Edition Questions,** throughout Lessons and Features
- **Close and Assess,** TE pp. 9, 11, 13, 17, 19, 21, 25, 27, 31, 33, 35, 37
- **Try it!** PE/TE pp. 141, 147, 155
- **Think and Share,** PE/TE pp. 145, 153, 159, 163, 167, 173
- **Responsibility in Action,** PE/TE p. 161

Ongoing Assessment

Ongoing Assessment is found throughout the Teacher's Edition lessons using an **If...then** model.

If = students' observable behavior,	**then** = reteaching and enrichment suggestions

✓ Portfolio Assessment

- **Portfolio Assessment,** TE pp. 180
- **Leveled Practice,** TE pp. 138, 149a, 155a, 163a, 169a, 175a
- **Workbook,** pp. 35–46
- **Unit Review: Skills on Your Own,** PE/TE p. 180
- **Curriculum Connection: Writing,** TE pp. 136, 149a, 155a, 163a, 169a, 175a

✓ Performance Assessment

- **Hands-on Unit Project** (Unit 4 Performance Assessment), PE/TE pp. 135, 182
- **Internet Activity,** PE p. 182
- **Hands-on Unit Project,** PE/TE p. 182
- **Scoring Guides,** TE pp. 176a, 179, 180, 182

Test Talk

Test-Taking Strategies

Understand the Question

- **Locate Key Words in the Question,** TE p. 152
- **Locate Key Words in the Text,** TE p. 172

Understand the Answer

- **Choose the Right Answer,** Test Talk Practice Book
- **Use Information from the Text,** TE p. 144
- **Use Information from Graphics,** TE p. 166
- **Write Your Answer,** TE p. 161

For additional practice, use the Test Talk Practice Book.

Featured Strategy

Use Information from the Text

Children will:

– Decide where they will look for the answer and make notes about details from the text.

– Use information from the text, then look back at the question and the text to make sure they have the right answer.

PE/TE p. 179, **TE** p. 144

Curriculum Connections

Integrating Your Day

The lessons, skills, and features of Unit 4 provide many opportunities to make connections between social studies and other areas of the elementary curriculum.

Reading

Reading Skill—Find the Main Idea, PE/TE pp. 140–141, TE p. 142

Reading Skill—Time Lines, TE p. 147

Reading Skill—Alike and Different, TE p. 150

Reading Skill—Find the Main Idea, TE pp. 156, 170

Reading Skill—Sequence, TE p. 164

Books About Things That Grow, TE p. 176

Writing

Office Recycling Can, TE p. 136

Weather Word Puzzle, TE p. 149a

Where Am I? TE p. 155a

Poster, TE p. 163a

Farm Contest, TE p. 169a

Save Animals, TE p. 175a

Math

Water, Water, Everywhere, TE p. 163a

Social Studies

Literature

A Prairie Boy's Winter, TE p. 148

Blue Whales, TE p. 175a

Books About Caring for Earth and About People Around the World, TE p. 181

Science

Planting Trees, TE p. 141

Weather Prediction Chart, TE p. 143

Make a Weather Time Line, TE p. 146

Between a Rock and a Soft Place, TE p. 163

Trees, Above and Below, TE p. 163a

Research an Endangered Animal, TE p. 175

Music/Drama

Living Times Lines, TE p. 149a

Take a Tour, TE p. 169

Jill and Johnny Appleseed's Dance, TE p. 177

Art

Make a Globe, TE p. 155

Build It! TE p. 155a

Look for this symbol throughout the Teacher's Edition to find **Curriculum Connections.**

Professional Development

The Place of Literature in a Social Studies Program

by Valerie Pang

Children's literature is one of the most important tools we, as teachers, can use in social studies education. Literature brings the hope and joy of life into the classroom. It celebrates the human spirit. Literature also describes the human condition. Well-written books can demonstrate how people from diverse communities work together to create a more compassionate and just society. Literature can also show the struggle of many individuals who have fought against oppressive practices and triumphed. It also provides children with the opportunity to look at life from many different people's perspectives.

This unit provides several opportunities to incorporate children's literature into Scott Foresman Social Studies.

- ***For Lesson 1,*** *read the hilarious spoof* Cloudy With a Chance of Meatballs *by Judi Barrett.*
- ***For Lesson 2,*** *read* Three Days on a River in a Red Canoe *by Vera B. Williams.*
- ***For Lesson 3,*** *read the Caldecott winner* The Gardener *by Sarah Stewart, illustrated by David Small.*
- ***For Lesson 4,*** *read* Aliki's Corn Is Maize: The Gift of the Indians*, as well as the biography of Sacagawea recommended on TE p. 169a.*
- ***For Lesson 5,*** *read the nonfiction book* Recycle! *by Gail Gibbons.*

ESL Support

by Jim Cummins, Ph. D.
University of Toronto

Inviting students to contribute what they already know to the class discussion communicates to students that the cultural and linguistic knowledge they are bringing into the classroom is important. It also enables teachers to get to know their students much better than if students are confined to more passive roles in the classroom.

Strategies for Activating Prior Knowledge and Building Background Knowledge

Teachers can use a variety of strategies to activate students' prior knowledge. Some of the most useful strategies are:.

- ***Brainstorming/discussion*** *as a whole class, in small groups, or in pairs*
- ***Visuals in texts*** *such as posters, photographs, etc., can be used to stimulate discussion about aspects of their meaning*
- ***Direct experiences*** *such as taking a walk around the neighborhood of the school or going on a field trip followed by a group language experience narrative.*

The following examples in the Teacher's Edition will help you to activate ESL students' prior knowledge and to build background for the content of the lesson.

- ***Relate to Personal Experience*** *on p. 140 encourages children to identify things they have seen that are named in the unit song.*
- ***Using Pictures*** *on p. 151 helps English language learners compare and contrast the physical characteristics of the plains to where they live.*
- ***The Grand Tour of the Classroom*** *on p. 158 asks children to identify things in their classroom made from natural resources, such as a pencil, jump rope, or paper bag.*

Read Aloud

Water

By Hilda Conkling

The world turns softly
Not to spill its lakes and rivers.
The water is held in its arms
And the sky is held in the water.
What is water,
That pours silver,
And can hold the sky?

Build Background

- Ask children to show on a globe how the world "turns softly."
- Ask children to tell about reflections they have seen in water.

Read Alouds and Primary Sources

Read Alouds and Primary Sources contain additional selections to be used with Unit 4.

Bibliography

I Celebrate Nature, by Diane Iverson (Dawn Pubns, ISBN 1-883-22000-9, 1995) **Easy** ***Notable Social Studies Book***

I Took a Walk, by Henry Cole (Greenwillow, ISBN 0-688-15115-9, 1998) **Easy**

Morning, Noon, and Night, by Jean Craighead George and Wendell Minor (Illustrator) (Harpercollins, ISBN 0-060-23628-0, 1999) **Easy**

Backyard, by Donald M. Silver and Patricia J. Wynne (Illustrator) (McGraw-Hill, ISBN 0-070-57930-X, 1997) Encourages children to explore their own backyards for interesting sights, sounds, and smells from the ground up. **On-Level**

Birdsong, by Audrey Wood and Robert Florczak (Illustrator) (Voyager, ISBN 0-152-02419-0, 2001) Children interact with birds in the wild, listening to their songs and viewing their habitats, through the course of a day. **On-Level** ***Notable Social Studies Book***

Where Once There Was a Wood, by Denise Fleming (Henry Holt, ISBN 0-805-06482-6, 2000) Celebrates in simple words and pictures the natural world that existed before a housing development appeared. **On-Level** ***Notable Social Studies Book***

Turtle Bay, by Saviour Pirotta and Nilesh Mistry (Illustrator) (Farrar Straus & Giroux, ISBN 0-374-37888-6,1997) Through his friendship with an old man, a boy learns about caring for Japanese sea turtles. **Challenge** ***Notable Social Studies Book***

Where Does the Garbage Go? by Paul Showers, Randy and Paul Chewning (Illustrators) (Harpercollins, ISBN 0-064-45114-3, 1994) **Challenge**

Mapmaking with Children: Sense of Place Education for the Elementary Years, by David Sobel (Heinemann, ISBN 0-325-00042-5, 1998) **Teacher Reference**

Look for this symbol throughout the Teacher's Edition to find **Award-Winning Selections**. Additional book references are suggested throughout this unit.

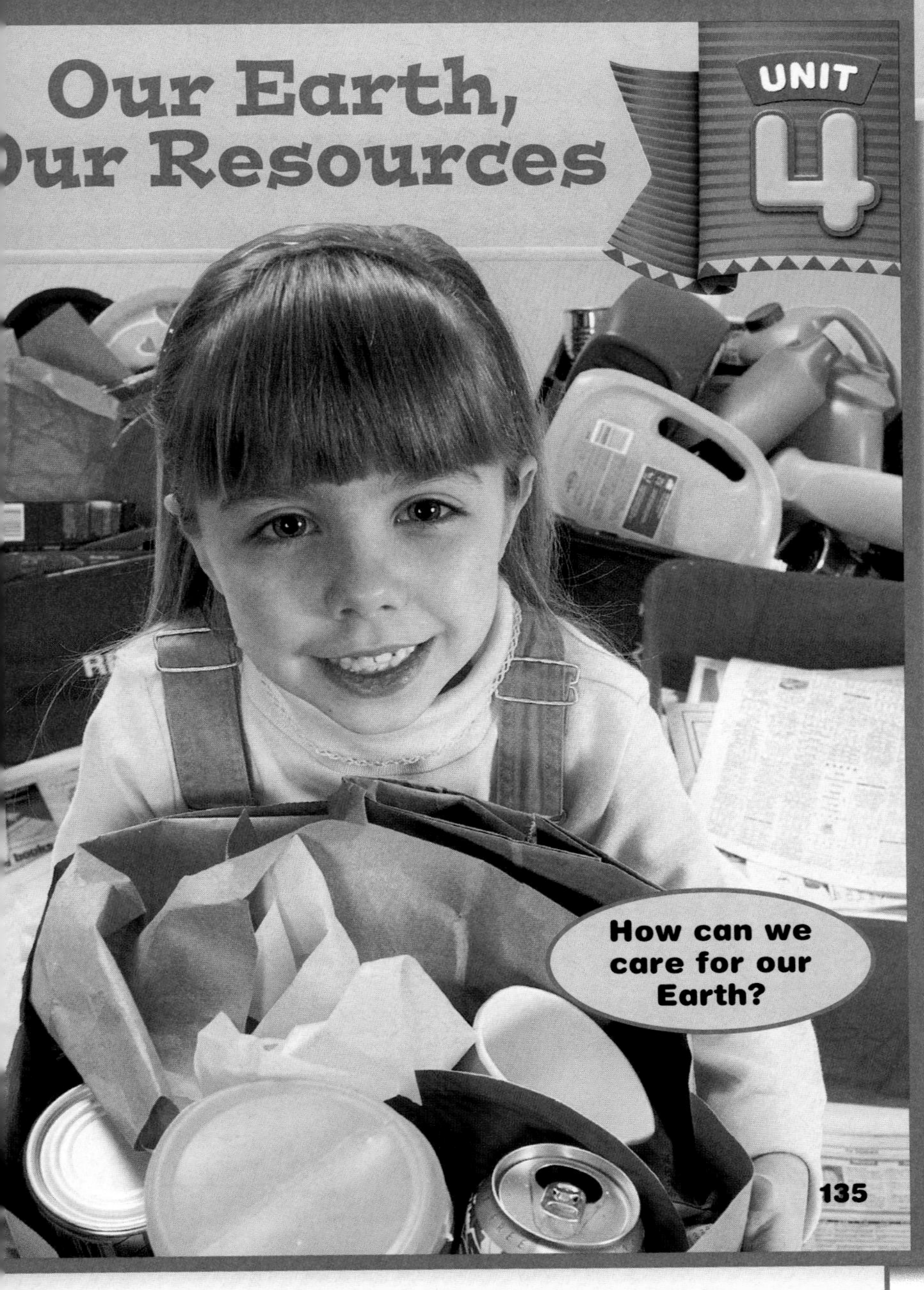
Our Earth, Our Resources
UNIT 4
How can we care for our Earth?
135

Our Earth, Our Resources

Unit Overview

This unit introduces children to our Earth and its resources, and identifies and describes physical characteristics of places such as landforms, bodies of water, and weather.

Introduce Debby

Read the unit title and then introduce the featured child for this unit as a first-grader named Debby. Talk about how Debby might take care of Earth.

Unit Question

- Ask children the question on this page "How can we care for our Earth?"
- Initiate a discussion of ways people can care for Earth.
- To activate prior knowledge, make a list on the board of ways children name to care for Earth.

✓ **Portfolio Assessment** Keep a copy of this list for the Portfolio Assessment at the end of the unit on p. 180.

Practice and Extend

Hands-on Unit Project

✓ **Unit 4 Performance Assessment**

The Unit 4 Project, *Create a Weather Television Program of Your Own*, found on p. 182, is an ongoing performance assessment project to enrich children's learning throughout the unit.

- This project, which has children giving a television weather report, may be started now or at any time during this unit of study.
- A performance assessment scoring guide is located on p. 182.

Show You Care

Objective

- Obtain information about a topic using a variety of oral sources such as music.

Resources

- *Songs and Music* CD "Show You Care"
- Poster 7
- Social Studies Plus!

Introduce the Song

Preview Tell children that they will be singing a song about caring for our Earth. Point out that the song suggests ways for people to show they care in their daily life.

Warm Up To activate prior knowledge, discuss with children ways to care for our Earth at home, school, and recreational locations, such as a park or beach.

Sing the Song

- Have children sing the song "Show You Care."
- Have children mime the ways to care described in the song.
- Have children mime other ways to care for our Earth.

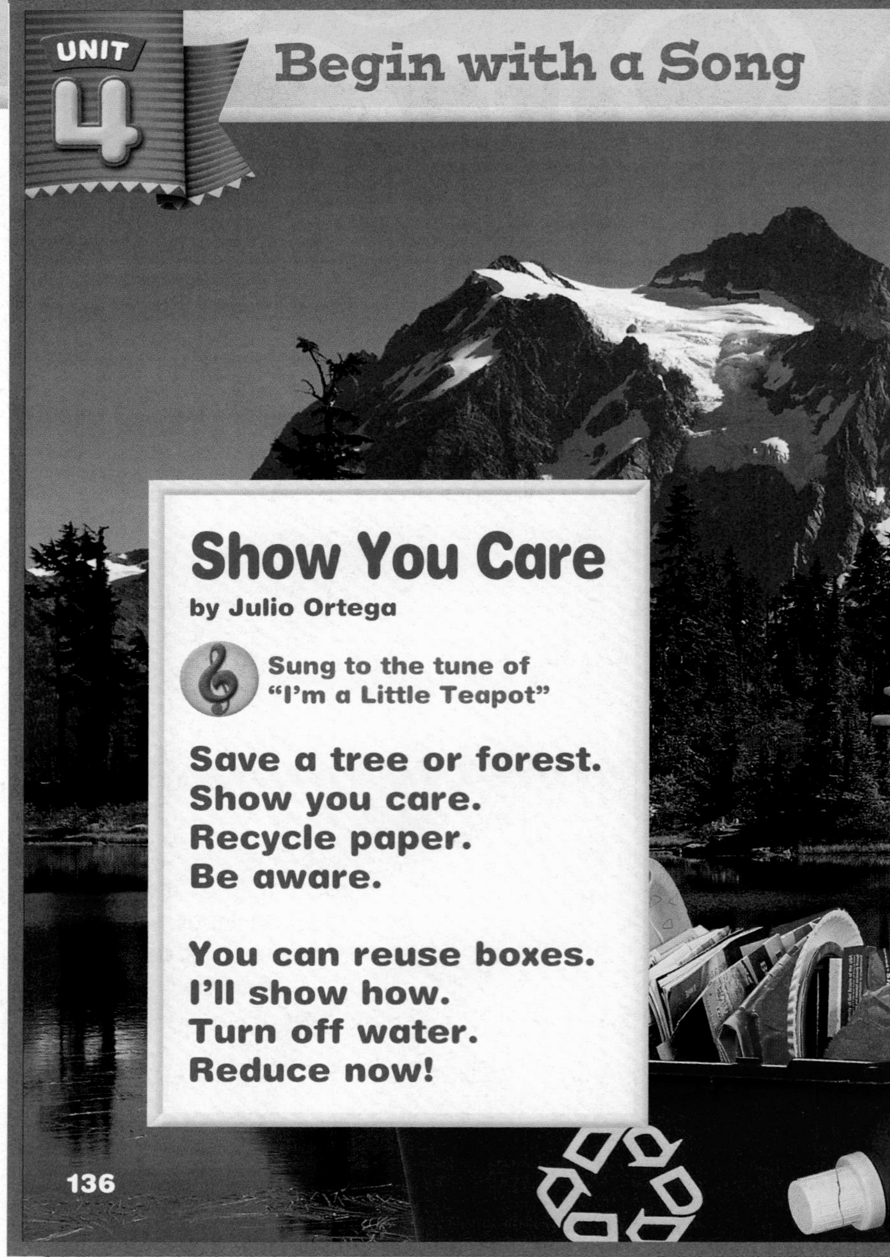

UNIT 4 Begin with a Song

Show You Care
by Julio Ortega

Sung to the tune of "I'm a Little Teapot"

Save a tree or forest.
Show you care.
Recycle paper.
Be aware.

You can reuse boxes.
I'll show how.
Turn off water.
Reduce now!

136

Practice and Extend

CURRICULUM CONNECTION
Writing

Office Recycling Can

Explain to children that many offices have recycling cans for white paper only.

- Have children write *Recycle These* and *Not These* across the top of a sheet of paper.
- As you read the following to children, tell them to write down the papers under the appropriate headings: white photocopy paper, food wrappers, white paper for letters, newspapers, magazines.

AUDIO CD
Technology

Play the CD, *Songs and Music*, to listen to "Show You Care."

Talk About the Picture

Focus attention on the picture of Debby. Ask children to tell what is in the foreground (recycling bins) and the background (sky, mountains, trees, lake).

1 **What things are in the recycling bins?** Possible answers include plastic bottles, aluminum cans, paper plates, magazines, and cardboard boxes. Interpret Pictures

2 **Describe the landform and body of water.** Answers will vary but may include a snow-capped mountain and a wide lake with still water. Interpret Pictures

SOCIAL STUDIES Background

Possible Misconceptions

Children may not understand the connection between recycling paper and saving the trees shown in the picture. Explain that trees and forests are valuable not only for their beauty and recreational use but also for their wood. Tell children that recycling paper helps protect these trees from people who might want to cut them down for wood.

Vocabulary Preview

Objectives

- Determine the meanings of words.
- Use pictures to obtain information.

Resources

- Workbook, p. 35
- Vocabulary Cards
- Poster 8

Introduce the Vocabulary

Read aloud and point to each vocabulary word and the photograph illustrating it. Have volunteers give the meanings of the words. Then have children find examples of geography vocabulary words in the picture in the following locations: the exhibit of landforms and bodies of water within the national park; the rest of the park; and beyond the park. Then have children find examples of history in the park.

Vocabulary Word	Illustrated Examples
weather	partly cloudy, mildly windy, cool
mountain	exhibit of mountain, base of mountain
plain	exhibit of plain
lake	exhibit of lake
river	exhibit of river, river
natural resource	air, trees, water, land
history	house, bridge, canoe

Social Studies Strand
Geography

Listed below are some basic principles of geography for children. Direct most of your discussion of the picture toward the development of these concepts.

- kinds of weather
- kinds of landforms
- kinds of bodies of water
- kinds of natural resources
- uses of natural resources

Then explain that history is the story of people and places from the past. Direct the rest of your discussion toward the development of this concept.

Vocabulary Preview

weather

mountain

plain

Practice and Extend

MEETING INDIVIDUAL NEEDS
Leveled Practice

Visit a National Park

Invite children to visit the national park in the picture.

Easy Have children lead a tour through the exhibit of landforms and bodies of water, using vocabulary words. **Reteach**

On-Level Have children lead a tour through the park and beyond, describing things that show the weather, such as the cloud shows it's partly cloudy, the kite shows it's mildly windy, the sweaters, long-sleeved shirts, and long pants show it's cool. **Extend**

Challenge Have children lead a tour through the park, describing things that might have been made in the past, such as the house, bridge, canoe, and fence. Ask children to describe how these things might be made in the present. **Enrich**

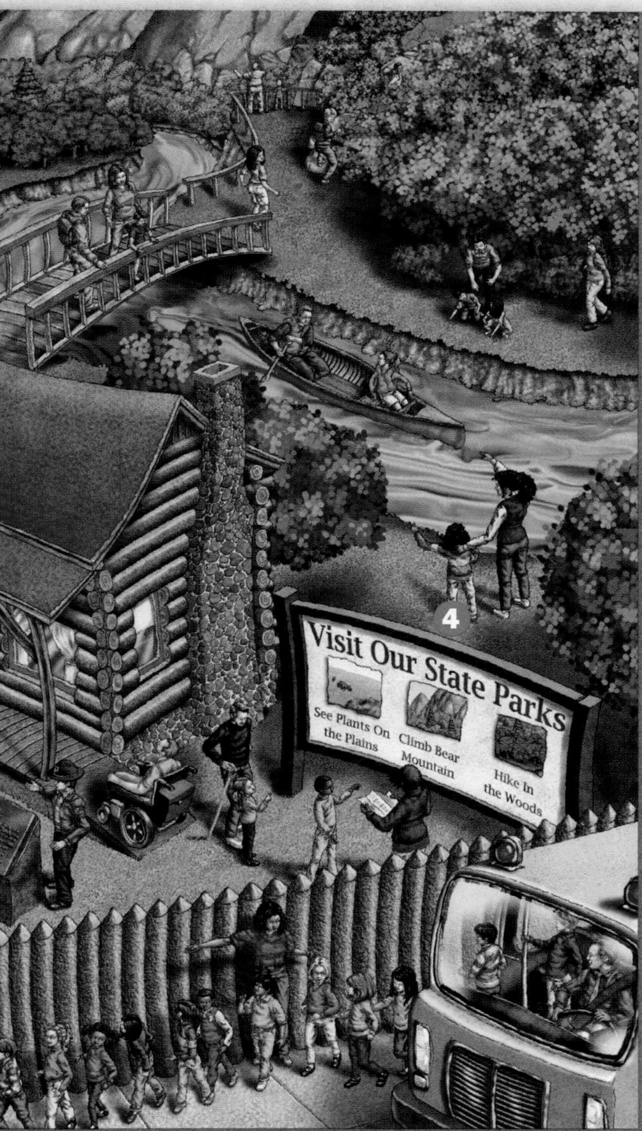

139

Talk About the Picture

Allow children time to study the picture. The picture shows a national park with both physical and human characteristics of the environment. Encourage children to identify and describe both of these characteristics.

1 **Look at the sky. What is the weather?** Cloudy **Analyze Pictures**

2 **What body of water is nearest the "Enter" sign?** River **Analyze Pictures**

3 **What things in the picture were made by people?** Answers will vary but may include the house, the bridge, the boat, and the fences. **Make Inferences**

Look Ahead

Tell children they will learn more about each of the vocabulary words as they study Unit 4.

You may want to revisit the picture with children to review the concepts and vocabulary in the unit.

4 **Look at the sign. What three activities might you do in the national park?** See plants on the plains, climb Bear Mountain, and hike in the woods. **Analyze Information**

WEB SITE Technology

You can look up vocabulary words online. Click on *Social Studies Library* and select the dictionary at **www.sfsocialstudies.com.**

Workbook, p. 35

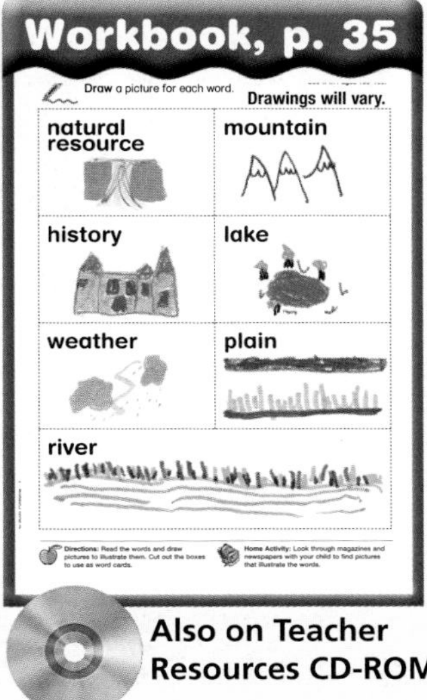

Also on Teacher Resources CD-ROM.

Celebrate the Earth

Find the Main Idea

Objective

Identify main ideas from print sources.

Resource

- Workbook, p. 36

About the Unit Target Skill

- The target reading skill for this unit is Find the Main Idea.
- Children are introduced to the unit target skill here and are given an opportunity to practice it.
- Further opportunities to find the main idea are found throughout Unit 4.

1 Introduce and Motivate

Preview To determine if children understand how to find the main idea, write the following on the board: *Then they visit other flowers. The butterflies stop at a flower to drink the nectar. Nectar is a sweet liquid found in many flowers.* Ask a volunteer to rearrange the sentences and tell the main idea in his or her own words. (Possible answer: Butterflies drink nectar from flowers.) Then write the words *main idea* on the board and explain that the main idea is the most important idea.

Warm Up To activate prior knowledge, direct children's attention to the unit song on p. 136. Ask children what the song is about. Record their responses on the board. Discuss with children which response best describes the main idea. (Show you care about Earth.)

Celebrate the Earth

Find the Main Idea

Hi! My name is Debby. My class wrote a story for the school newspaper. Every story tells about something. What the story tells about is called the **main idea.** Read our story. Find the **main idea.**

Butterfly Garden

Our class will take care of our Earth. We will plant a butterfly garden. We will plant flowers that butterflies like. We hope to have many butterfly visitors soon.

140

Practice and Extend

ACTIVATE PRIOR KNOWLEDGE
ESL Support

Relate to Personal Experience Remind children that the main idea of the song is *Show you care about Earth.* Have children draw pictures of three things they've seen that are named in the song. (Tree, forest, paper, or water)

Beginning Have children tell about their drawings.

Intermediate Have children identify their drawings by writing labels for them.

Advanced Have children write directions under their drawings telling how to show you care.

(Possible directions: "Recycle paper," "Reuse boxes," and "Turn off water.")

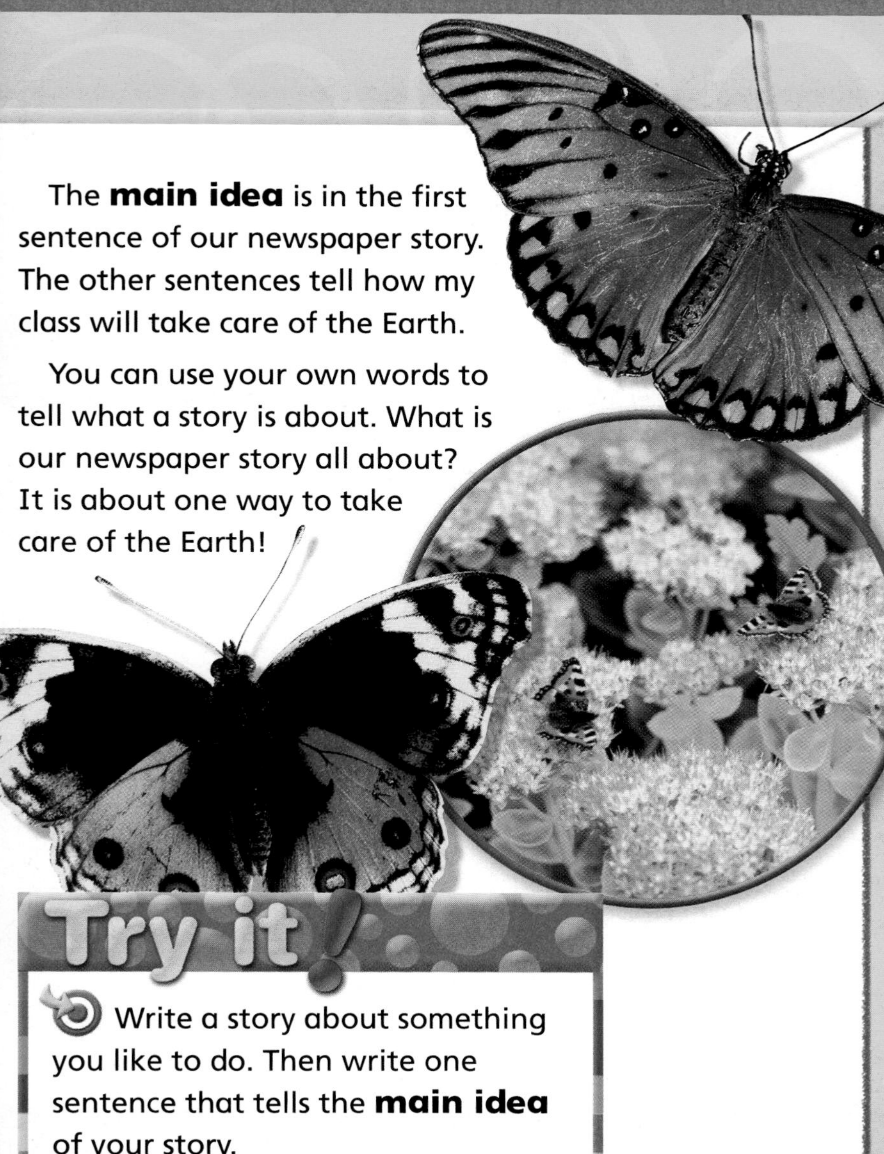

The **main idea** is in the first sentence of our newspaper story. The other sentences tell how my class will take care of the Earth.

You can use your own words to tell what a story is about. What is our newspaper story all about? It is about one way to take care of the Earth!

Write a story about something you like to do. Then write one sentence that tells the **main idea** of your story.

141

2 Teach and Discuss

Page 140

Read p. 140 and ask children to define *main idea*. (What a story tells about)

Page 140

What sentences in the newspaper story support the main idea? We will plant a butterfly garden. We will plant flowers that butterflies like. We hope to have many butterfly visitors soon. **Main Idea and Details**

If... children think that a main idea can only be identified from print sources, **then...** tell them that sometimes a main idea can be identified from oral and visual sources as well.

3 Close and Assess

Try it!

The sentences about the story will vary but should summarize the story.

CURRICULUM CONNECTION Science

Planting Trees

- Tell children that another way people can care for Earth is to plant trees.
- Explain to children that topsoil can be washed away by rain if grass, flowers, and trees do not hold it in place.
- Have children make drawings of grass, flowers, and trees above the ground and their roots under the ground.
- Remind students that grass has the smallest roots and trees have the biggest roots.

Workbook, p. 36

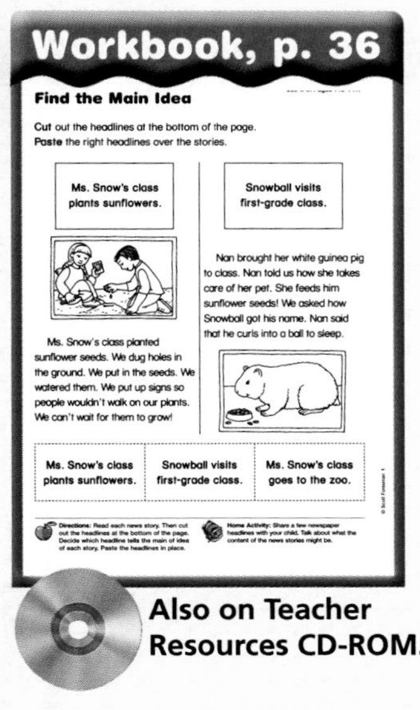

Find the Main Idea

Cut out the headlines at the bottom of the page. Paste the right headlines over the stories.

Ms. Snow's class plants sunflowers.

Snowball visits first-grade class.

Nan brought her white guinea pig to class. Nan told us how she takes care of her pet. She feeds him sunflower seeds! We asked how Snowball got his name. Nan said that he curls into a ball to sleep.

Ms. Snow's class planted sunflower seeds. We dug holes in the ground. We put in the seeds. We watered them. We put up signs so people wouldn't walk on our plants. We can't wait for them to grow!

Ms. Snow's class plants sunflowers.	Snowball visits first-grade class.	Ms. Snow's class goes to the zoo.

Also on Teacher Resources CD-ROM.

Workbook Support

Use the following Workbook pages to support content and skills development as you teach Unit 4. You can also view and print Workbook pages from the Teacher Resources CD-ROM.

Workbook, p. 35

Use with Pages 138–139.

Draw a picture for each word. **Drawings will vary.**

natural resource	mountain
history	lake
weather	plain
river	

Directions: Read the words and draw pictures to illustrate them. Cut out the boxes to use as word cards.

Home Activity: Look through magazines and newspapers with your child to find pictures that illustrate the words.

Use with Pupil Edition, p. 139.

Workbook, p. 36

Find the Main Idea

Use with Pages 140–141.

Cut out the headlines at the bottom of the page.
Paste the right headlines over the stories.

Ms. Snow's class plants sunflowers.

Ms. Snow's class planted sunflower seeds. We dug holes in the ground. We put in the seeds. We watered them. We put up signs so people wouldn't walk on our plants. We can't wait for them to grow!

Snowball visits first-grade class.

Nan brought her white guinea pig to class. Nan told us how she takes care of her pet. She feeds him sunflower seeds! We asked how Snowball got his name. Nan said that he curls into a ball to sleep.

Ms. Snow's class plants sunflowers.	Snowball visits first-grade class.	Ms. Snow's class goes to the zoo.

Directions: Read each news story. Then cut out the headlines at the bottom of the page. Decide which headline tells the main of idea of each story. Paste the headlines in place.

Home Activity: Share a few newspaper headlines with your child. Talk about what the content of the news stories might be.

Use with Pupil Edition, p. 141.

Workbook, p. 37

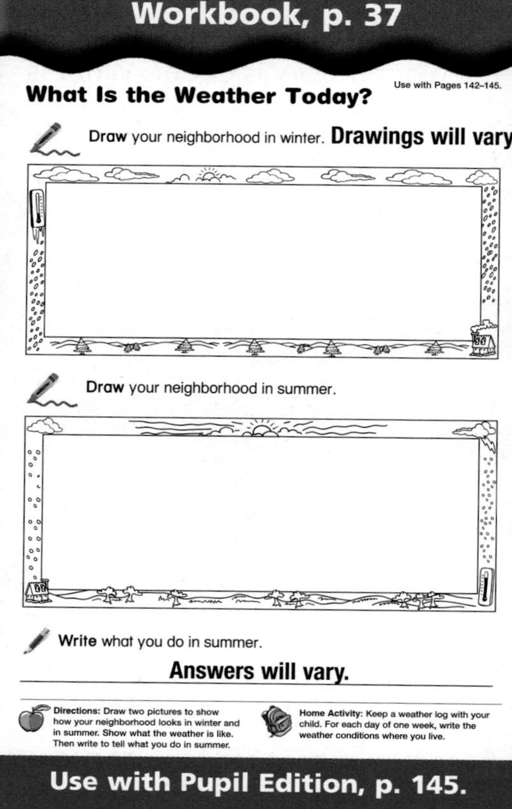

What Is the Weather Today?

Use with Pages 142–145.

Draw your neighborhood in winter. **Drawings will vary.**

Draw your neighborhood in summer.

Write what you do in summer.

Answers will vary.

Directions: Draw two pictures to show how your neighborhood looks in winter and in summer. Show what the weather is like. Then write to tell what you do in summer.

Home Activity: Keep a weather log with your child. For each day of one week, write the weather conditions where you live.

Use with Pupil Edition, p. 145.

Workbook, p. 38

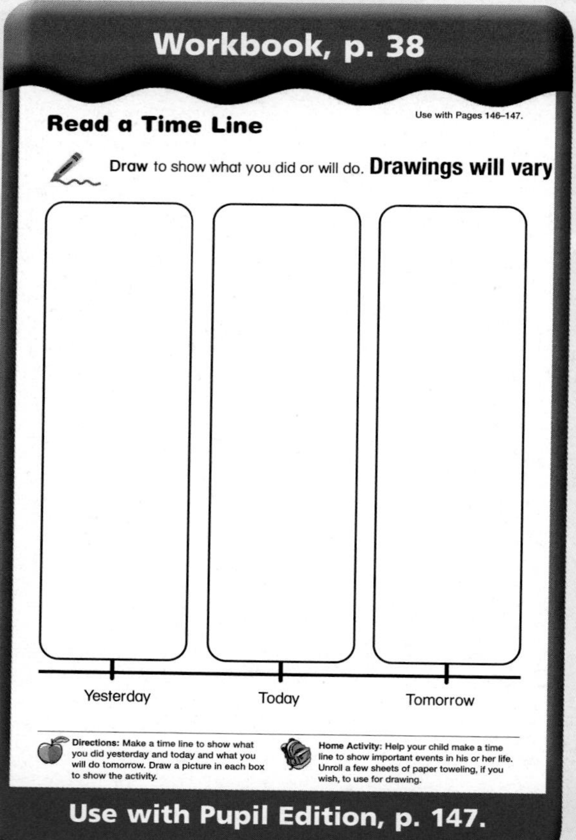

Read a Time Line

Use with Pages 146–147.

Draw to show what you did or will do. **Drawings will vary**

Yesterday — Today — Tomorrow

Directions: Make a time line to show what you did yesterday and today and what you will do tomorrow. Draw a picture in each box to show the activity.

Home Activity: Help your child make a time line to show important events in his or her life. Unroll a few sheets of paper toweling, if you wish, to use for drawing.

Use with Pupil Edition, p. 147.

Workbook, p. 39

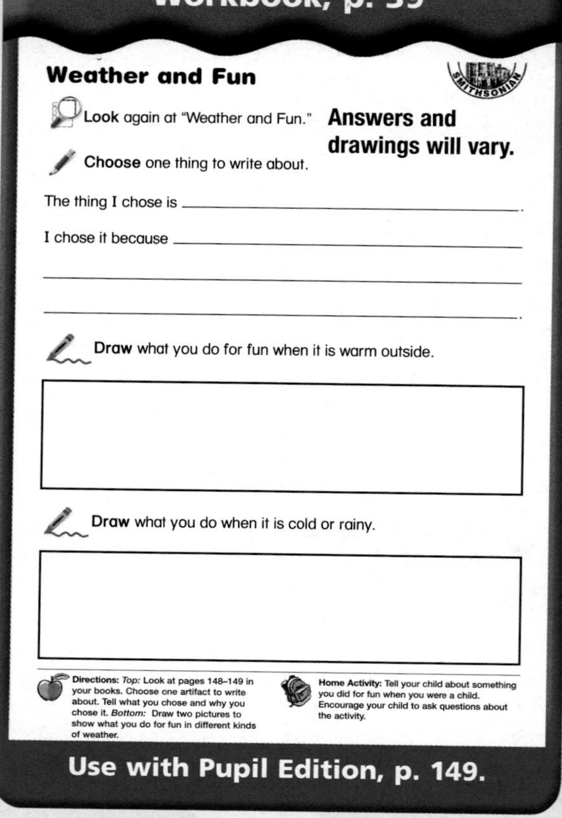

Weather and Fun

Look again at "Weather and Fun." **Answers and drawings will vary.**

Choose one thing to write about.

The thing I chose is ________.

I chose it because ________

Draw what you do for fun when it is warm outside.

Draw what you do when it is cold or rainy.

Directions: *Top:* Look at pages 148–149 in your books. Choose one artifact to write about. Tell what you chose and why you chose it. *Bottom:* Draw two pictures to show what you do for fun in different kinds of weather.

Home Activity: Tell your child about something you did for fun when you were a child. Encourage your child to ask questions about the activity.

Use with Pupil Edition, p. 149.

Workbook, p. 40

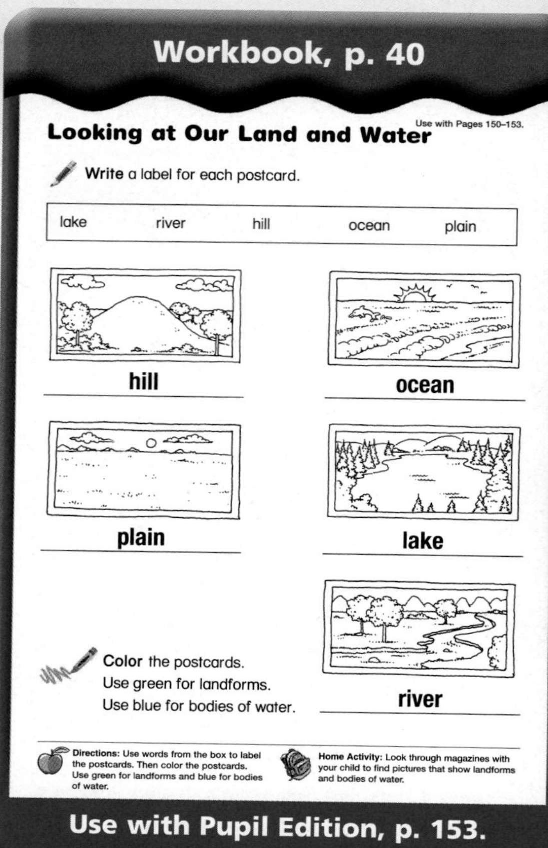

Looking at Our Land and Water

Use with Pages 150–153.

Write a label for each postcard.

lake	river	hill	ocean	plain

hill — ocean — plain — lake — river

Color the postcards.
Use green for landforms.
Use blue for bodies of water.

Directions: Use words from the box to label the postcards. Then color the postcards. Use green for landforms and blue for bodies of water.

Home Activity: Look through magazines with your child to find pictures that show landforms and bodies of water.

Use with Pupil Edition, p. 153.

Workbook Support

Workbook, p. 41

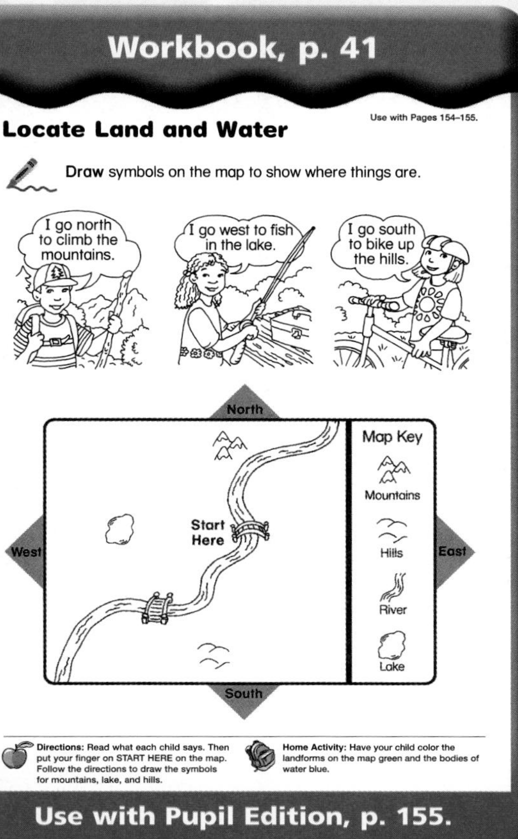

Locate Land and Water Use with Pages 154–155.

Draw symbols on the map to show where things are.

Directions: Read what each child says. Then put your finger on START HERE on the map. Follow the directions to draw the symbols for mountains, lake, and hills.

Home Activity: Have your child color the landforms on the map green and the bodies of water blue.

Use with Pupil Edition, p. 155.

Workbook, p. 42

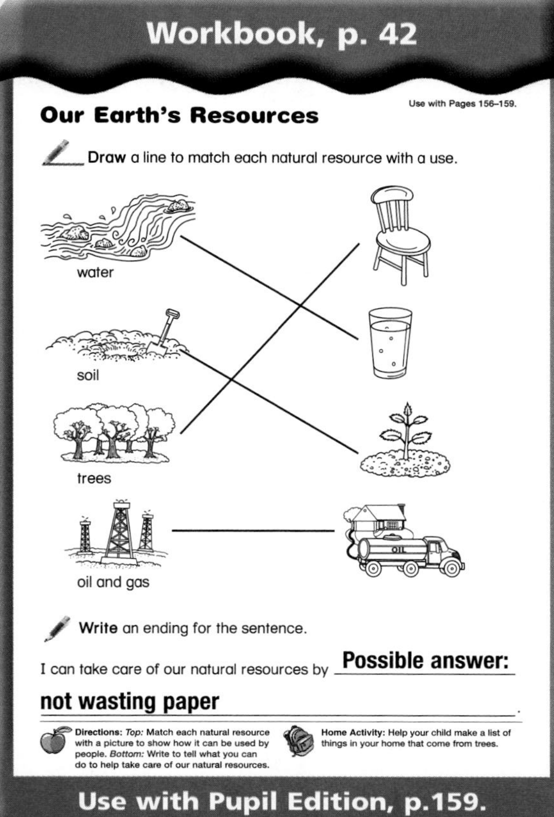

Our Earth's Resources Use with Pages 156–159.

Draw a line to match each natural resource with a use.

Write an ending for the sentence.

I can take care of our natural resources by **Possible answer: not wasting paper**.

Directions: *Top:* Match each natural resource with a picture to show how it can be used by people. *Bottom:* Write to tell what you can do to help take care of our natural resources.

Home Activity: Help your child make a list of things in your home that come from trees.

Use with Pupil Edition, p.159.

Workbook, p. 43

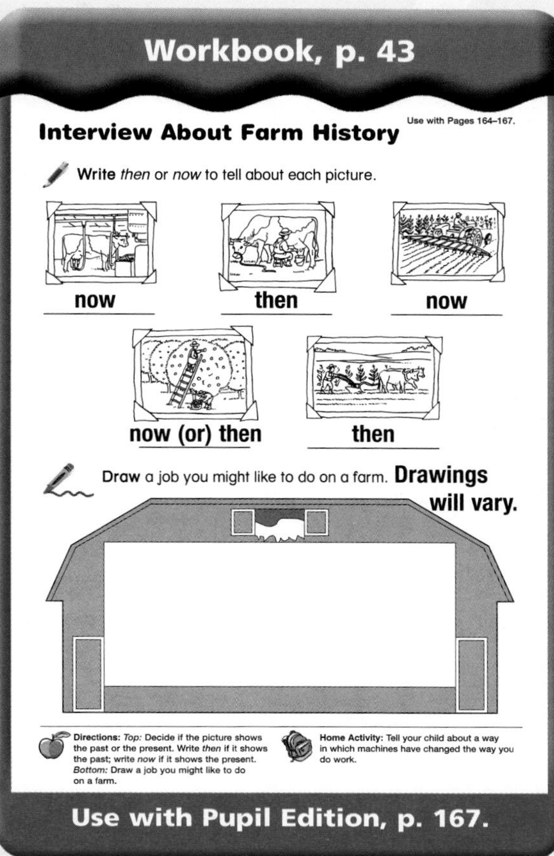

Interview About Farm History Use with Pages 164–167.

Write *then* or *now* to tell about each picture.

now **then** **now**

now (or) then **then**

Draw a job you might like to do on a farm. **Drawings will vary.**

Directions: *Top:* Decide if the picture shows the past or the present. Write *then* if it shows the past; write *now* if it shows the present. *Bottom:* Draw a job you might like to do on a farm.

Home Activity: Tell your child about a way in which machines have changed the way you do work.

Use with Pupil Edition, p. 167.

Workbook, p. 44

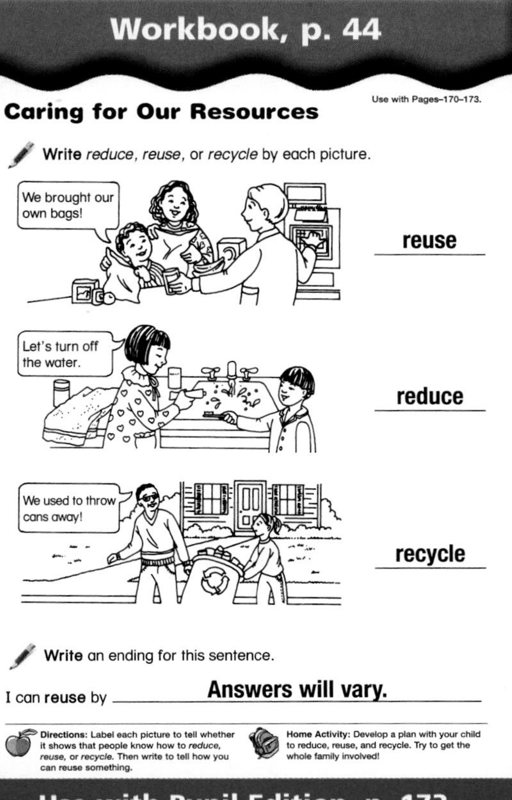

Caring for Our Resources Use with Pages 170–173.

Write *reduce*, *reuse*, or *recycle* by each picture.

reuse

reduce

recycle

Write an ending for this sentence.

I can **reuse** by **Answers will vary.**

Directions: Label each picture to tell whether it shows that people know how to *reduce*, *reuse*, or *recycle*. Then write to tell how you can reuse something.

Home Activity: Develop a plan with your child to reduce, reuse, and recycle. Try to get the whole family involved!

Use with Pupil Edition, p. 173.

Workbook, p. 45

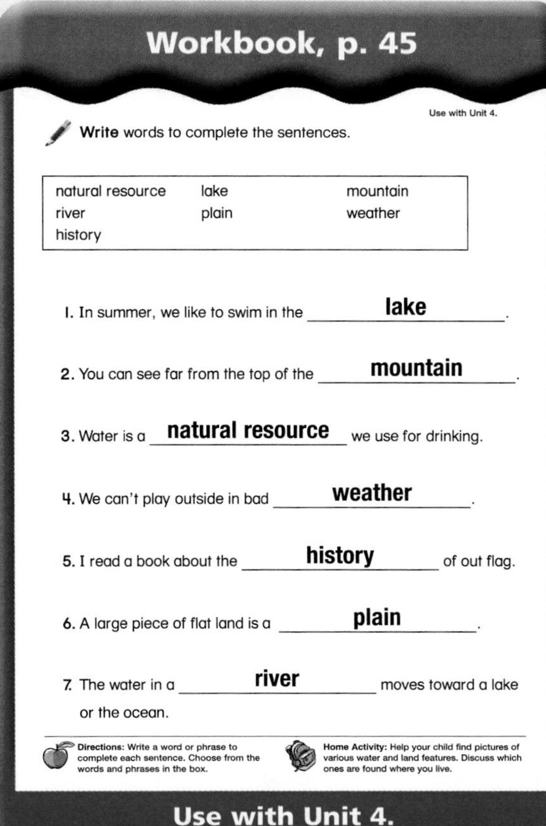

Use with Unit 4.

Write words to complete the sentences.

natural resource	lake	mountain
river	plain	weather
history		

1. In summer, we like to swim in the **lake**.
2. You can see far from the top of the **mountain**.
3. Water is a **natural resource** we use for drinking.
4. We can't play outside in bad **weather**.
5. I read a book about the **history** of out flag.
6. A large piece of flat land is a **plain**.
7. The water in a **river** moves toward a lake or the ocean.

Directions: Write a word or phrase to complete each sentence. Choose from the words and phrases in the box.

Home Activity: Help your child find pictures of various water and land features. Discuss which ones are found where you live.

Use with Unit 4.

Workbook, p. 46

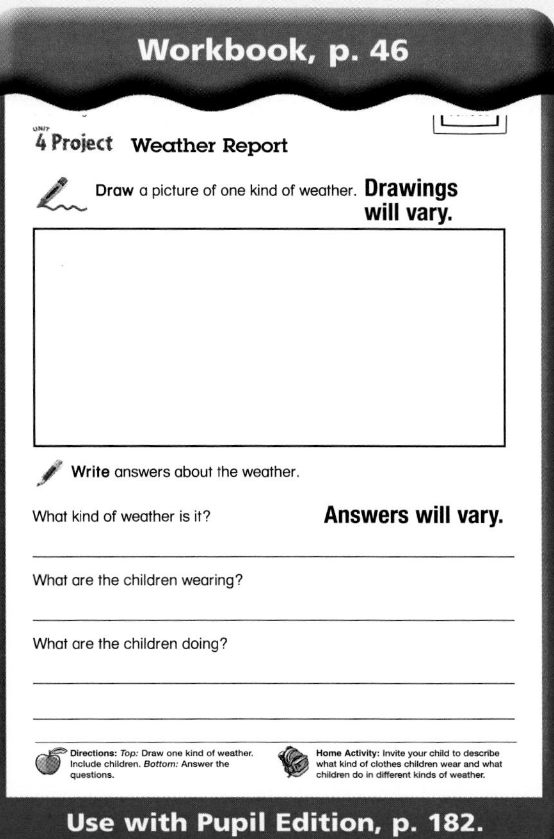

Unit 4 Project **Weather Report**

Draw a picture of one kind of weather. **Drawings will vary.**

Write answers about the weather.

What kind of weather is it? **Answers will vary.**

What are the children wearing?

What are the children doing?

Directions: *Top:* Draw one kind of weather. Include children. *Bottom:* Answer the questions.

Home Activity: Invite your child to describe what kind of clothes children wear and what children do in different kinds of weather.

Use with Pupil Edition, p. 182.

Assessment Support

Use the following Assessment Book pages and TestWorks to assess content and skills in Unit 4. You can also view and print Assessment Book pages from the Teacher Resources CD-ROM.

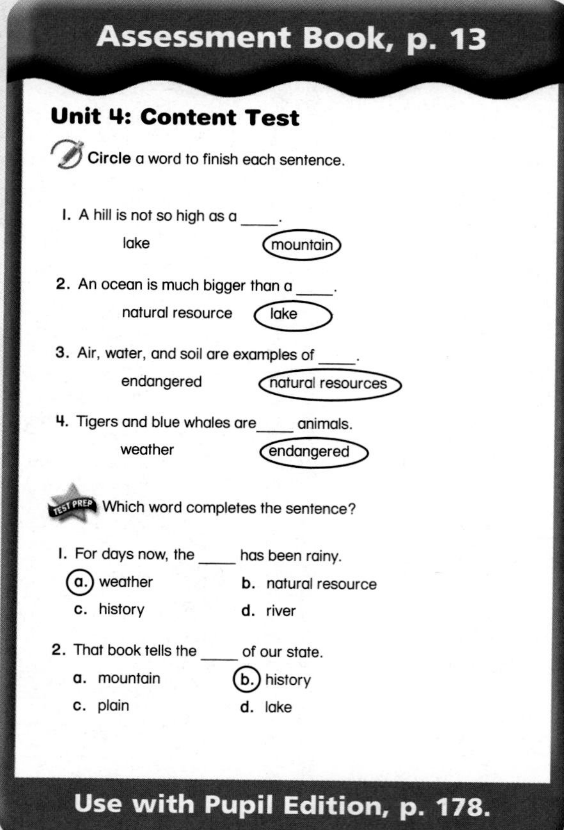

Assessment Book, p. 13

Unit 4: Content Test

Circle a word to finish each sentence.

1. A hill is not so high as a ____.
   lake — (mountain)
2. An ocean is much bigger than a ____.
   natural resource — (lake)
3. Air, water, and soil are examples of ____.
   endangered — (natural resources)
4. Tigers and blue whales are ____ animals.
   weather — (endangered)

TEST PREP Which word completes the sentence?

1. For days now, the ____ has been rainy.
   (a.) weather b. natural resource
   c. history d. river
2. That book tells the ____ of our state.
   a. mountain (b.) history
   c. plain d. lake

Use with Pupil Edition, p. 178.

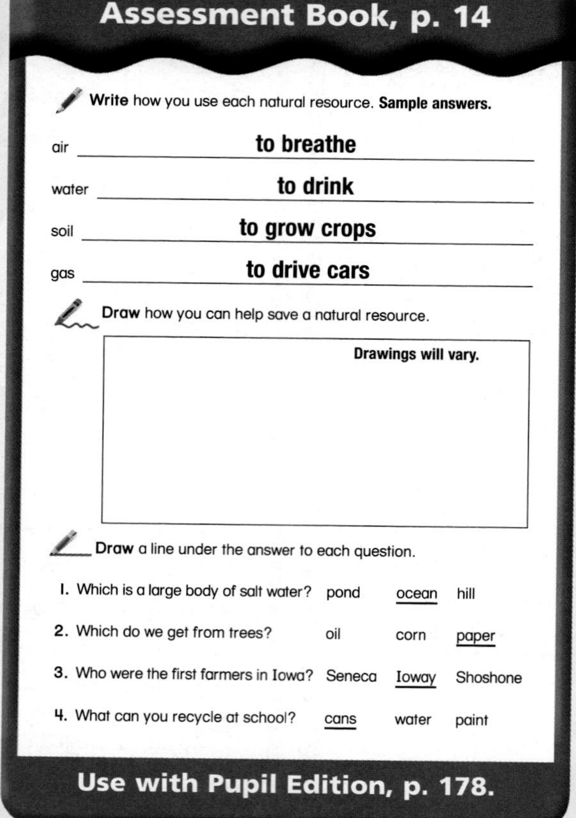

Assessment Book, p. 14

Write how you use each natural resource. **Sample answers.**

air **to breathe**

water **to drink**

soil **to grow crops**

gas **to drive cars**

Draw how you can help save a natural resource.

Drawings will vary.

Draw a line under the answer to each question.

1. Which is a large body of salt water? pond <u>ocean</u> hill
2. Which do we get from trees? oil corn <u>paper</u>
3. Who were the first farmers in Iowa? Seneca <u>Ioway</u> Shoshone
4. What can you recycle at school? <u>cans</u> water paint

Use with Pupil Edition, p. 178.

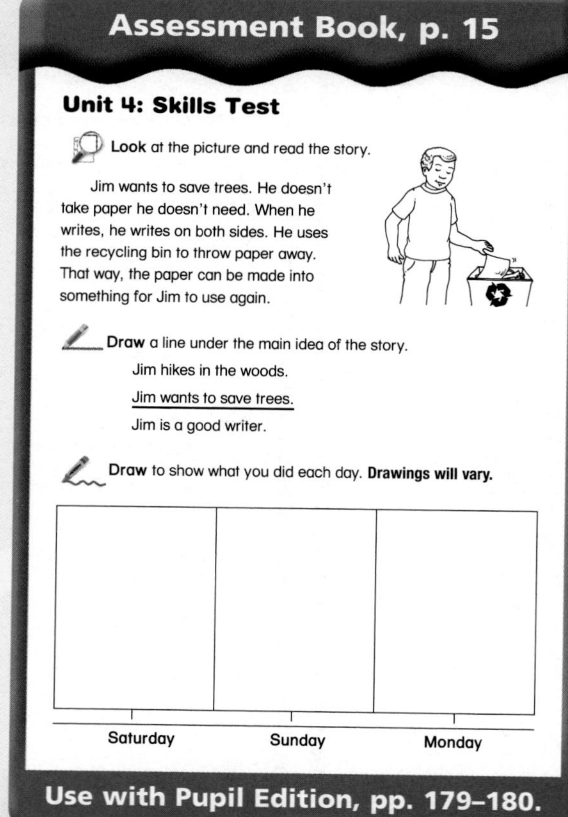

Assessment Book, p. 15

Unit 4: Skills Test

Look at the picture and read the story.

Jim wants to save trees. He doesn't take paper he doesn't need. When he writes, he writes on both sides. He uses the recycling bin to throw paper away. That way, the paper can be made into something for Jim to use again.

Draw a line under the main idea of the story.

Jim hikes in the woods.

<u>Jim wants to save trees.</u>

Jim is a good writer.

Draw to show what you did each day. **Drawings will vary.**

Saturday	Sunday	Monday

Use with Pupil Edition, pp. 179–180.

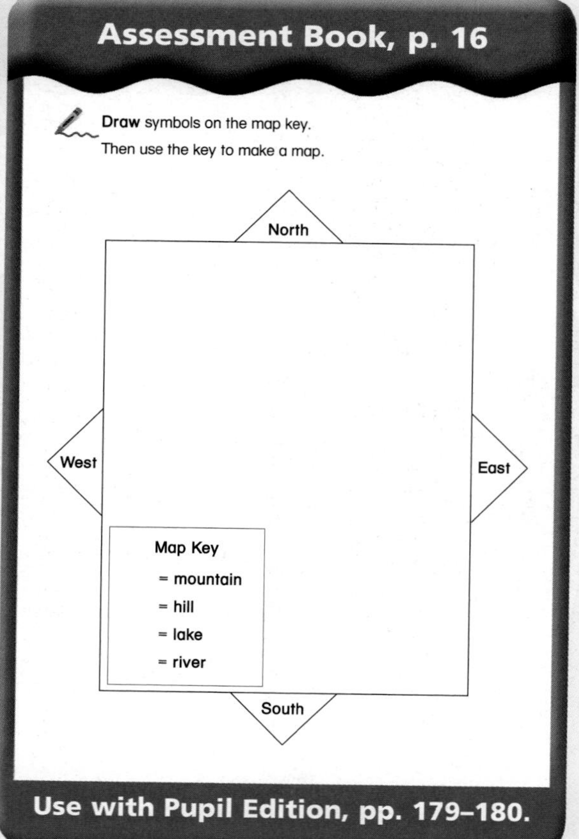

Assessment Book, p. 16

Draw symbols on the map key.
Then use the key to make a map.

Use with Pupil Edition, pp. 179–180.

Lesson 1 Overview

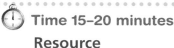

Different Kinds of Weather **pages 142–145**	Children will learn how weather affects their lives, and explore how weather is different in different locations.	 Time 20–30 minutes Resources • Workbook, p. 37 • Vocabulary Card weather • Every Student Learns Guide, pp. 62–65
Read a Time Line **pages 146–147**	Children will learn how to read a time line.	 Time 15–20 minutes Resource • Workbook, p. 38
Smithsonian Institution: Weather and Fun **pages 148–149**	Children will learn how weather affects people's choice of recreational activities.	Time 15–20 minutes Resource • Workbook, p. 39

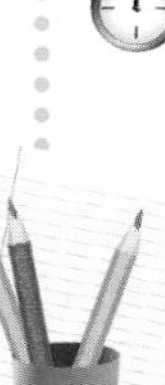

Build Background

Activity

What's the Weather?

 **Time** 15–20 minutes

Make a "What's the Weather?" poster similar to the one shown. Ask children what kind of day today is—is it sunny, cloudy, or windy? Is it cold, warm, or hot? Have children draw pictures of things affected by the weather. Children can add their pictures to the poster.

If time is short, ask children questions about today's weather. Sketch details on the poster reflecting children's answers.

Read Aloud

Fun in the Sun

By Linda Popov

Today the sun will shine,
And fun outdoors will rule!
I love to play in the sun.
But I'm no fool.
When the air is too hot
I swim in a pool
And eat in the shade
Where it's cool.

Different Kinds of Weather

Objectives

- Identify and describe the physical characteristics of places, such as weather and climate.
- Describe how climate affects the way people live, including their clothing and recreation.
- Use vocabulary related to chronology, including *yesterday, today,* and *tomorrow*.

Vocabulary

weather the way it is outside at a certain place and time (p. 142)

QUICK Teaching Plan

If time is short, have children look at the pictures and describe the weather.

- Have children describe the weather outside.
- Have children describe activities they could do outside in this weather.

1 Introduce and Motivate

Preview Display the Vocabulary Card **weather** and say the word. Tell children that weather can be described using words such as *wet* or *dry*, *hot* or *cold*, *clear* or *cloudy*, *calm* or *windy*. Explain that weather can change from day to day. *Climate*, in contrast, is the kind of weather a place has. For example, the climate in southern Texas is usually very warm in summer, and less warm in winter.

Warm Up To activate prior knowledge, have children measure and record the outside temperature with a thermometer. Repeat this activity later in the day. Ask children how the temperature changed.

Lesson

Different Kinds of Weather

Today is hot.

Tomorrow my class is going to plant a butterfly garden. I can hardly wait! I hope the weather is nice. The **weather** is how it is outside at a certain place and time. I am going to check the weather report to see what tomorrow will be like. 2

1

Yesterday was warm and partly cloudy.

142

Practice and Extend

READING SKILL Find the Main Idea

Target Skill

Tell children that this activity provides a main idea and asks them to give information that tells about this main idea.

- Ask children to write "I Wear Warm Things in Very Cold Weather" in the center oval of a spider map. Explain that this is the main idea.
- Then explain that what they wear in cold weather provides more information about the main idea.
- Ask children to draw what they wear in cold weather in the ovals at the end of the spider legs.

If tomorrow is rainy, we can draw.
If tomorrow is sunny, we can plant.
3 4
143

CURRICULUM CONNECTION
Science

Weather Prediction Chart

- Have children predict tomorrow morning's weather.
- First draw a 3-column chart on the board with *Today's Weather*, *Weather Prediction,* and *Actual Weather* as the heads. Then have children fold a piece of paper and copy the chart.
- Ask them to fill in the first two columns today, and the third column tomorrow, using such words as *hot, warm, cool,* or *cold; sunny* or *cloudy; clear* or *rainy.*

WEB SITE
Technology

You can look up vocabulary words online. Click on *Social Studies Library* and select the dictionary at **www.sfsocialstudies.com.**

2 Teach and Discuss

Page 142

Tell children that the first picture shows Debby yesterday. Read the caption. Tell them that the second picture shows her today. Read the speech bubble. Explain that weather words such as *warm, cloudy, hot, rainy,* and *sunny* can be used to describe the physical characteristics of places.

1 **How do you know yesterday's weather was partly cloudy?** The sky seen outside the window has clouds. **Analyze Pictures**

2 **What might you wear on a hot day?** Answers will vary but should include clothing appropriate for hot weather.
Analyze Pictures/Draw Conclusions

Page 143

3 **What are Debby and her father doing in the picture?** They are trying to find out tomorrow's weather. **Analyze Pictures**

4 **What will Debby's class do tomorrow in the sunny weather?** The class will help plant a butterfly garden. **Apply Information**

SOCIAL STUDIES STRAND
Science/Technology

Point out that Debby and her father are learning about tomorrow's weather by reading the newspaper. Ask children what other visual sources they can use to obtain information about a topic such as tomorrow's weather. (Possible answers: Internet, radio, and television)
Make Inferences/Apply Information

continued

Page 144

5 Why does Debby wonder about the weather in Michigan? Her pen-pal class is there. **Make Inferences**

Explain to children that an e-mail can be sent from one computer to another computer far away. Point out that the picture of children planting flowers is part of the e-mail.

Test Talk

Use Information from the Text

6 According to the e-mail, what will the weather be tomorrow in California? Hot and sunny Have children reread the text to make sure they have the right answer. **Apply Information**

6 Where does Debby's pen-pal class live? How do you know? The pen-pal class lives in Michigan. They signed their e-mail "Your pals in Michigan," and there is a map pointing out Detroit, Michigan. **Main Idea and Details**

Page 145

Discuss the e-mail, text, and illustrations on p. 145. Point out that this e-mail letter answers the e-mail on p. 144.

GEOGRAPHY THEMES
Place

7 What ways can you play in a place where it snows? Answers will vary, but may include build a snowman, sled, and ski. **Make Inferences**

8 Decision Making If it was cold outside, would you stay inside or go out to play? Answers will vary, but should include such considerations as clothing, temperature, and availability of playmates.

I live in California. My class has a pen-pal class in Michigan. Our teacher helps us e-mail them. I wonder if the weather will be warm in Michigan tomorro

e-mail

Hi everyone,
Tomorrow we will plant lots of brightly colored flowers. It will be hot and sunny. Some of us will ride our bikes to school. What is the weather like where you live?

Your pen pals in California 

San Diego, California

144

Practice and Extend

EXTEND LANGUAGE
ESL Support

Matching Words with Pictures Have children draw pictures of a favorite warm-weather activity. These may include riding a bicycle, flying a kite, having a picnic, or swimming in the ocean.

Beginning Have children use home-language words to describe the activity. For each home-language word they use, provide the English translation.

Intermediate Have children complete the following sentence: "In my picture I am ________."

Advanced Have children write a one-sentence description of the activity.

For additional support, use Every Student Learns Guide, pp. 62–65.

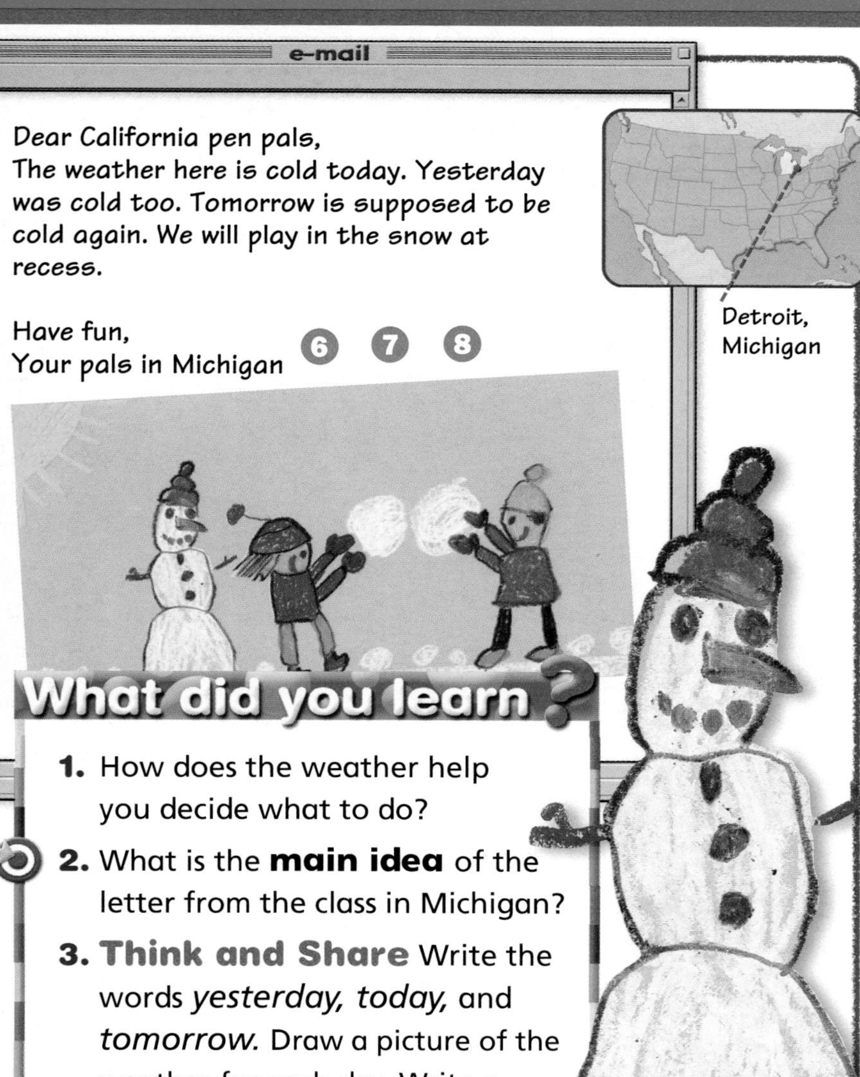
e-mail

Dear California pen pals,
The weather here is cold today. Yesterday was cold too. Tomorrow is supposed to be cold again. We will play in the snow at recess.

Have fun,
Your pals in Michigan 6 7 8

What did you learn?

1. How does the weather help you decide what to do?
2. What is the **main idea** of the letter from the class in Michigan?
3. **Think and Share** Write the words *yesterday, today,* and *tomorrow.* Draw a picture of the weather for each day. Write a sentence about each picture.

145

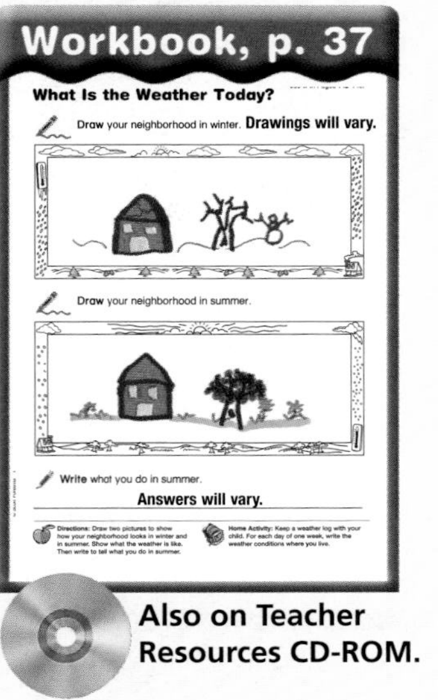
Workbook, p. 37

What Is the Weather Today?

Draw your neighborhood in winter. Drawings will vary.

Draw your neighborhood in summer.

Write what you do in summer.

Answers will vary.

Also on Teacher Resources CD-ROM.

SOCIAL STUDIES STRAND
Geography

Remind children that climate is the kind of weather a place has. Ask them what the climate is during the summer and winter where they live. Suggest that they use such words as *usually, often*, and *mostly* as well as *hot* and *cold, moist* and *dry*, and *clear* and *cloudy*. Have children use the Internet to research the summer and winter climates in northern Michigan and southern California. Then ask children how the summer and winter climates in these places affect people's decisions about clothing and activities.

3 Close and Assess

Have children listen to a weather report on the radio. Remind them that knowing what the weather will be can help them make decisions about what to do and what to wear.

✓ What did you learn?

1. Answers will vary. Possible answers: Knowing what the weather will be can help people decide what to wear, what to do, and where to go.
2. The weather is cold in Michigan.
3. **Think and Share** The drawings under *yesterday* and *today* should accurately show the weather for those days. Answers for the sentence will vary but should describe the weather.

Read a Time Line

Objectives

- Distinguish among past, present, and future.
- Create a time line.
- Create visual and written material including time lines.
- Interpret information presented in picture time lines to show sequence of events.

Vocabulary

time line A line that shows the order in which things happened (p. 146)

1 Introduce and Motivate

Preview Tell children what a **time line** is and point to the time line on pp. 146–147 as an example. Explain that this time line shows how the weather changes over five days.

Warm Up To activate prior knowledge, have children discuss steps they take to prepare for going to school. Tell them that creating a time line for these events can help them more easily explain to people how they prepare for school.

Chart and Graph Skills

Read a Time Line

Debby and her class wanted to show how the weather might change during one school week. They made a time line. A **time line** shows the order in which things happen. Look at the time line. Tell how the weather changed from day to day.

146

Practice and Extend

Make a Weather Time Line

- Help children record how windy it is on a time line using the words *high, medium*, and *low*. Have children hold a ruler with an attached piece of fabric outside the window. Explain that the windier the day, the more the fabric will move.
- Have children use this method to record how windy it is on a time line for five days.

You can look up the vocabulary term by going online. Click on *Social Studies Library* and select the dictionary at **www.sfsocialstudies.com.**

Try it!

1. What day was it windy?
2. What was the weather like on Thursday?
3. **On Your Own** Make a time line about you. Draw yourself in the past, present, and in the future.

147

READING SKILL
Time Lines

- Have children create a time line with pictures that show what they did yesterday and today and what they will do tomorrow.
- Have children exchange time lines with a partner.
- Direct children to describe what their partner did yesterday and today and will do tomorrow. Tell them to use the words *yesterday, today,* and *tomorrow* in their descriptions. Explain that yesterday is about the past, today is about the present, and tomorrow is about the future.

Workbook, p. 38

Also on Teacher Resources CD-ROM.

2 Teach and Discuss

Page 146

① **What is the first day on the time line?** Monday Interpret Time Lines

② **What was the weather like on Tuesday? How can you tell?** It was cloudy. The sky has clouds. Interpret Time Lines/Make Inferences/Analyze Pictures

Page 147

③ **Suppose it is Friday. Tell what the weather is *today*. Then tell what the weather was *yesterday*.** Today it is sunny. Yesterday it was rainy. Interpret Time Lines

④ **How was the weather on Monday and Friday alike?** Both days were sunny. Compare and Contrast/Interpret Time Lines

3 Close and Assess

Try it!

1. It was windy on Wednesday.
2. It was rainy.
3. **On Your Own** Time lines will vary but should include three pictures, labels of children's ages, and depictions of themselves that reflect the past, present, and future.

Weather and Fun

Objective

- Obtain information about a topic using a variety of visual sources such as pictures of artifacts.

Resource

- Workbook, p. 39

1 Introduce and Motivate

Preview Ask children to tell about some of the things they do for fun. Make a list of the activities children name. Ask if they think their parents or grandparents did these same things when they were young.

Warm Up To activate prior knowledge, remind children that in Lesson 1, they talked about different kinds of weather. Ask if the weather changes a lot from season to season in the area where you live. If so, talk about different things people do for fun during the different seasons. If the weather does not change dramatically, ask if children would like to live in a place where it does change. What might they do that they don't do now?

Read the introduction with children. Then read aloud the question that Debby asks. Point out that the pictures on pp. 148–149 show things people did for fun long ago—in different kinds of weather.

2 Teach and Discuss

Direct attention to the painting and identify it as "Skating in Central Park" by Agnes Tait. Explain that Central Park is a large park in New York City, and that the painting, created in 1934, shows how the park looked long ago. Ask what season—and what kind of weather—the painting shows.

LOOK INSIDE THE SMITHSONIAN
Weather and Fun
Look at the pictures from long ago. They show some things people did in different kinds of weather. What do you do for fun when it is warm and sunny outside? What do you do when it is cold or rainy?
1 Listen to the Radio
These radios are very old. It does not matter what the weather is like if you want to listen to the radio.
2 Ice Skate
The weather outside must be cold to ice skate. These skates were used long ago.
What do you do in different kinds of weather?
148

Practice and Extend

A Prairie Boy's Winter

- Use *A Prairie Boy's Winter* by William Kurelek (Houghton Mifflin, ISBN 0-395-36609-7, reprint edition 1984) to extend the concept of weather and fun. In this classic picture book, Kurelek paints memories of his boyhood on a 1930 prairie farm in winter.
- Display a few of the illustrations, such as "Fox and Geese," "Rink Making," "Skiing Behind the Hayrack," and "Skating on the Bog Ditch." Ask children to use details from the pictures to tell how these children had fun in winter. Read aloud the text that accompanies each illustration.
- Help children compare and contrast "Skating on the Bog Ditch" and "Skating in Central Park." Both paintings show the same long-ago winter activity but in very different settings: a prairie farm and a big city.

Read
You can read in any kind of weather!
Ride a Bike
This bike is over a hundred years old. It is fun to ride a bike in good weather.
3
Artifacts are from the Smithsonian Institution.
149

Look at each of the artifacts on pp. 148–149 with children. You may want to start with the ice skates, and then continue clockwise around the page. Read aloud the captions as children point to the artifacts described.

1 **Long ago, what were some things people did for fun in any kind of weather?** People of long ago listened to the radio and read books in any kind of weather. **Analyze Pictures**

2 **Long ago, what did some New Yorkers do for fun outside when the weather was cold?** They went ice skating on a pond in Central Park. **Analyze Pictures**

3 **What nice-weather activity did people long ago do that you do today? How do you know?** People of long ago rode bikes. People still ride bikes today, although the bikes look a bit different. **Compare and Contrast**

3 Close and Assess

- Have children use the pictures on pp. 148–149, together with their own experiences, to tell how such things as ice skates, radios, books, and bikes have changed over the years.
- Invite children to make predictions about how things such as these may change in the future.
- Help children create a bulletin board showing things people do today to have fun in different kinds of weather. Encourage children to write or dictate captions for their pictures.
- Use the list developed during the preview to help children categorize the activities. You might make a T-chart such as the one below.

Fun in Good Weather	Fun in Bad Weather
ride bikes play baseball fly kites	read books listen to the radio watch TV

WEB SITE Technology

You can visit the Smithsonian Institution online. Click on Smithsonian at **www.sfsocialstudies.com** or go to **www.si.edu.**

Workbook, p. 39

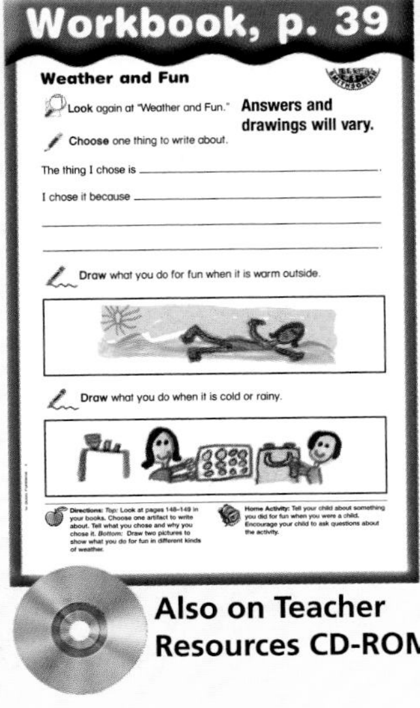

Weather and Fun

Look again at "Weather and Fun." **Answers and drawings will vary.**

Choose one thing to write about.

The thing I chose is ________.

I chose it because ________

Draw what you do for fun when it is warm outside.

Draw what you do when it is cold or rainy.

Directions: *Top:* Look at pages 148–149 in your books. Choose one artifact to write about. Tell what you chose and why you chose it. *Bottom:* Draw two pictures to show what you do for fun in different kinds of weather.

Home Activity: Tell your child about something you did for fun when you were a child. Encourage your child to ask questions about the activity.

Also on Teacher Resources CD-ROM.

Use with pages 142–149

Lesson 1 Wrap-Up

MEETING INDIVIDUAL NEEDS

Leveled Practice

Find Weather Pictures

Provide children with magazines and ask them to cut out pictures showing people in different kinds of weather.

Easy Ask children to sort the pictures into categories such as "sunny," "rainy," "cold," or "hot." Prompt them with pictures from each stack to describe what people are doing. **Reteach**

On-Level Have children choose a picture and tell a story about the people in it. Stories should describe the weather and how it has affected what people are wearing and doing. **Extend**

Challenge Direct children to choose pictures that reflect the local weather yesterday and today. Have them label the pictures in correct time order. Invite children to tell the class about the pictures, using the words *yesterday* and *today*. **Enrich**

Hands-on Activities

CURRICULUM CONNECTION

Writing

Weather Word Puzzles

Objective Demonstrate an understanding of new vocabulary; use weather words to fit shapes.

Resources Vocabulary Card: **weather**

Materials crayons

Learning Style Verbal-Linguistic

Individual

Time 10–15 minutes

1. Hand out weather word puzzles, using the words *cloud, rainy,* and *wind*.
2. Have children write the weather word from the box in the shape that fits.
3. Remind children to add the vocabulary word *weather* to their "My Word Book."

SOCIAL STUDIES STRAND

Geography

Storm Warning

Objective Create a class weather report.

Materials poster board, crayons

Learning Style Verbal-Linguistic

Group

Time 15–20 minutes

1. Help children pretend to predict tomorrow's weather—a big storm—by dramatizing a television weather report.
2. Help children create a large weather map of the local region. Then have children stand next to the map and describe the approaching storm. Have them include suggestions for what people should wear.
3. Invite children to take turns delivering the weather report "in the studio" and "on location."

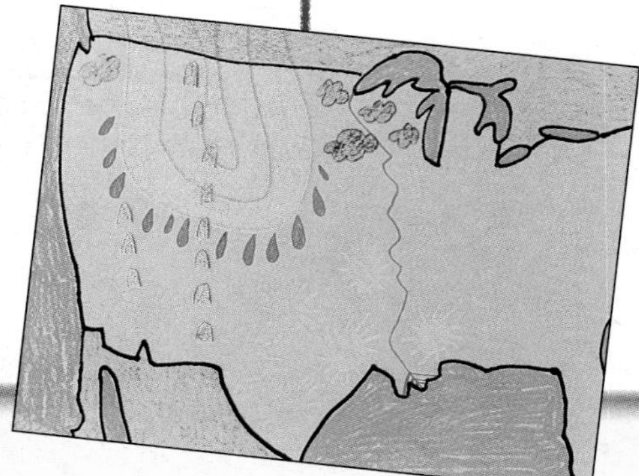

CURRICULUM CONNECTION

Drama

Living Time Lines

Objective Create and dramatize a time line.

Materials paper, pencils, crayons

Learning Style Bodily-Kinesthetic

Partners

Time 15–30 minutes

1. Have children draw a time line using the words"past," "present," and "future." Ask them to draw pictures of themselves traveling to school (past), learning at school (present), and leaving school (future).
2. Invite partners or small groups to dramatize their time lines.

Lesson 2 Overview

Looking at Our Land and Water **pages 150–153**	Children will learn about different landforms including mountains, hills, and plains. They will explore bodies of water, such as oceans, lakes, and rivers.	Time 20–30 minutes Resources • Workbook p. 40 • Vocabulary Cards mountain plain lake river • Every Student Learns Guide, pp. 66–69
Locate Land and Water **pages 154–155**	Children will learn how to recognize land and water on a globe and a map.	Time 15–20 minutes Resource • Workbook, p. 41

Build Background

Activity

Matching Pictures

Have children cut out a magazine photograph of a mountain, plain, hill, lake, river, or ocean. Then have children paste the photograph on paper.

Have children identify the land and water features in their photograph. Write the landform or body of water on an index card.

Invite children to select a card at random and show it to the class. Ask children to tell which photograph the card describes.

If time is short, show children some pictures of different landforms and bodies of water and ask them to describe each one.

Read Aloud

Favorite Places
by Seth Coleman

In winter the mountain
Is covered with snow.
If you like to ski,
That's where to go.

In winter the lake
Is a sheet of ice.
If you like to skate,
The lake is quite nice.

But me—I like summer,
It's sunny; it's hot.
I go to the ocean;
That's *my* favorite spot!

Looking at Our Land and Water

Objectives

- Identify and describe the physical characteristics of places such as landforms and bodies of water.
- Describe how location and physical surroundings affect the way people live, including their recreation.

Vocabulary

mountain the highest kind of land (p. 150)

plain a large piece of land that is mostly flat (p. 151)

lake a body of water with land totally or almost totally around it (p. 152)

river a long body of water that usually moves toward a lake or an ocean (p. 153)

QUICK Teaching Plan

If time is short, guide children in drawing different landforms and bodies of water.

- Use the pictures on pp. 150–153 to prompt children's drawings.

1 Introduce and Motivate

Preview Have children preview the illustrations on pp. 150–153. Then display the Vocabulary Cards **mountain**, **plain**, **lake**, and **river**. Ask children to tell what each word means. Tell children they will learn about some other kinds of land and water in this lesson.

Warm Up To activate prior knowledge, ask children which is bigger, an ocean or a lake and a mountain or a hill. Invite them to name activities they could do at these places.

Looking at Our Land and Water

Places on the Earth can have different kinds of weather. They can have different kinds of land and water too. We can do many things on land and in the water. My class is saving pictures of different kinds of land and water. 1

2 A **mountain** is the highest kind of land. It can snow and get very cold at the top of a mountain.

150

Practice and Extend

READING SKILL
Alike and Different

- Have children point to and describe the different landforms and bodies of water in the photographs on pp. 150–153.
- Name pairs of landforms or bodies of water. Have children use comparison words *bigger, smaller, taller,* and *flatter* to compare the relationship between the two.

WEB SITE
Technology

You can look up vocabulary words online. Click on *Social Studies Library* and select the dictionary at **www.sfsocialstudies.com.**

A hill is land that is higher than the land around it. A hill is not as high as a mountain. Hills have rounded tops.

A **plain** is a large piece of land. A plain is mostly flat. Plains are good for growing different kinds of food.

151

ACITIVATE PRIOR KNOWLEDGE
ESL Support

Using Pictures Tell children that the plains in the picture may be alike or different from the place where they live.

Beginning Ask children how the plains are alike or different from where they live.

Intermediate Ask children to make a comparison chart listing ways the plains are alike or different from where they live. Prompt them by asking such questions as, *Are there few or many buildings on the plains and where you live? Can you see near or far on the plains and where you live? Is it flat or hilly on the plains and where you live?*

Advanced Ask children to write a sentence comparing the plains to where they live.

For additional ESL support, use Every Student Learns Guide, pp. 66–69.

2 Teach and Discuss

Page 150

Have children read the paragraph. Then have a volunteer read the caption aloud as you point to the mountains and snow in the picture.

① **What is the main idea of the paragraph?** Places on Earth can have different kinds of land and water. **Main Idea and Details**

Ongoing Assessment

If... children think that the main idea is always the first sentence of a paragraph,	**then...** remind them that sometimes the main idea may be elsewhere in the paragraph.

② **What kind of weather might you find on a mountain?** It can be cold and snowy. **Recall and Retell**

Page 151

Have children describe the landforms in the two pictures.

SOCIAL STUDIES STRAND
Economics

Point out to students that the work people do may depend on where they live. Tell them plains are good for farming because it is easy to plant and grow things there. Farmers can more easily use tractors and other machines on flat land than on hills. Ask children what kind of job people might do in the mountains. (Possible answers: ski instructor or guide)

continued

Page 152

3 A beach is often next to an ocean. What can you do at the beach? Possible answers: Dig a hole in the sand, look for shells, play catch. **Compare and Contrast**

Test Talk

Locate Key Words in the Question

4 How are a lake and an ocean alike? How are they different? Answers may include: Alike: Oceans and lakes are both made up of water and are good for swimming and fishing. Different: Oceans are much bigger than lakes. Oceans have salt water. Most lakes have fresh water. Tell children that a key word such as *alike* tells them to look for similarities and a key word such as *different* tells them to look for contrast. **Compare and Contrast**

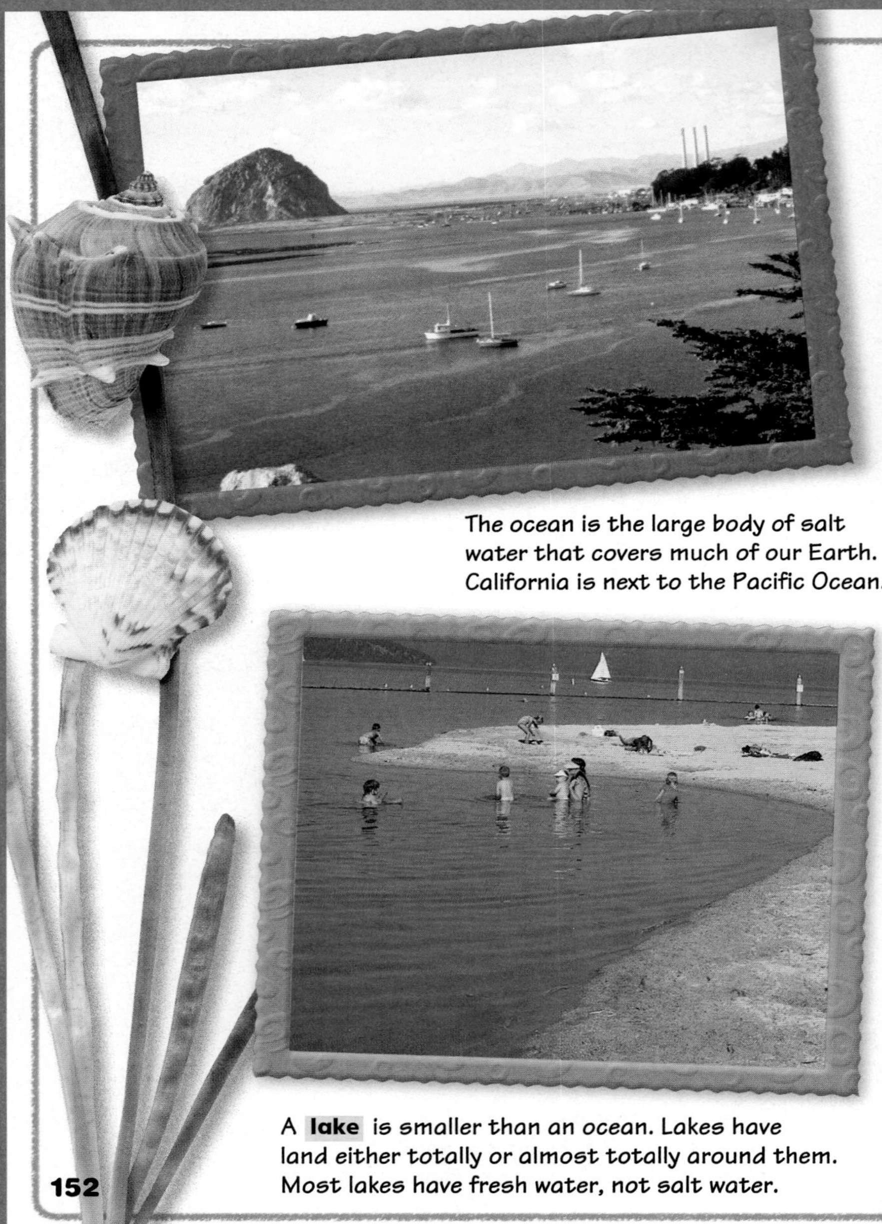

The ocean is the large body of salt water that covers much of our Earth. California is next to the Pacific Ocean.

A **lake** *is smaller than an ocean. Lakes have land either totally or almost totally around them. Most lakes have fresh water, not salt water.*

152

Practice and Extend

SOCIAL STUDIES
Background

About Oceans

- Remind children that there are four oceans: the Atlantic, Pacific, Indian, and Arctic. Help children locate these oceans on a map or globe.
- Explain that the four oceans flow into each other.
- Point out that the Pacific Ocean is the largest ocean, and the Arctic Ocean is the smallest.
- Point out that the Pacific Ocean is also the deepest ocean. It is deeper than the tallest mountain is tall.
- Show children gulfs, bays, or seas that form as oceans meet the land. Explain that they are still part of an ocean.

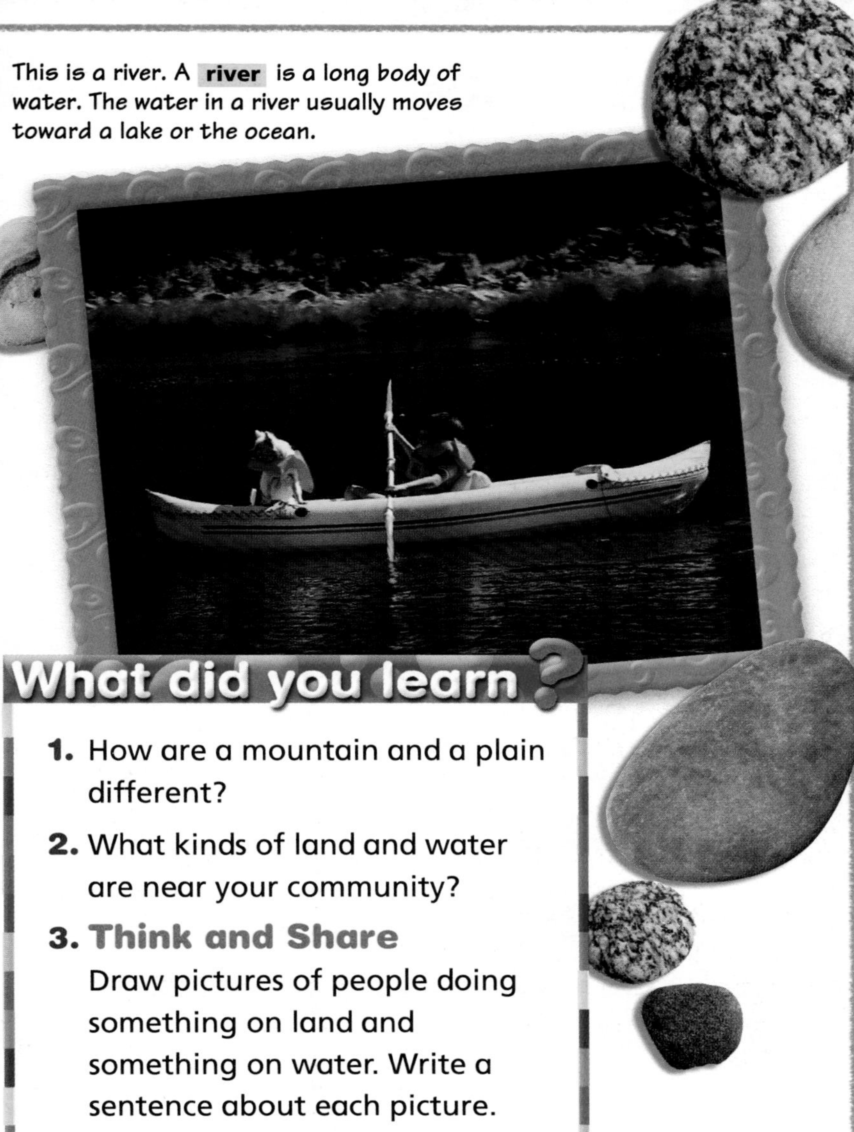

This is a river. A **river** is a long body of water. The water in a river usually moves toward a lake or the ocean.

What did you learn?

1. How are a mountain and a plain different?
2. What kinds of land and water are near your community?
3. **Think and Share** Draw pictures of people doing something on land and something on water. Write a sentence about each picture.

153

Workbook, p. 40

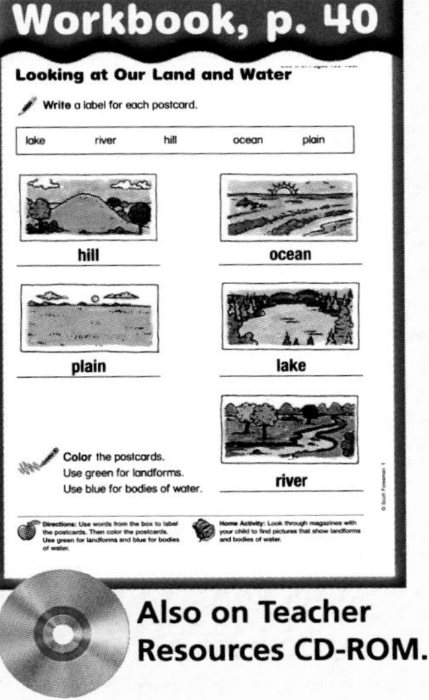

Looking at Our Land and Water

Write a label for each postcard.

lake river hill ocean plain

hill ocean

plain lake

river

Color the postcards. Use green for landforms. Use blue for bodies of water.

Also on Teacher Resources CD-ROM.

Page 153

Discuss the illustration with children.

5 **How is the water in a river different from the water in most lakes?** Answers may include: In a river, the water usually moves toward a lake, ocean, or another river. In most lakes, the water is totally or almost totally surrounded by land. **Compare and Contrast**

6 **What kinds of activities could you do in a river?** Possible answers: Swimming, boating, fishing, and rafting **Apply Information**

3 Close and Assess

Ask children to name some things they could do at each of the places shown in the lesson. Then invite volunteers to tell which place they would most like to visit and why.

✓ What did you learn?

1. A mountain is a very high kind of land. A plain is a flat area of land.
2. Children should correctly identify any nearby mountains, hills, plains, river, lakes, or oceans.
3. **Think and Share** The activities shown in the drawings and described in the sentence should be appropriate to the land and water depicted in the drawings.

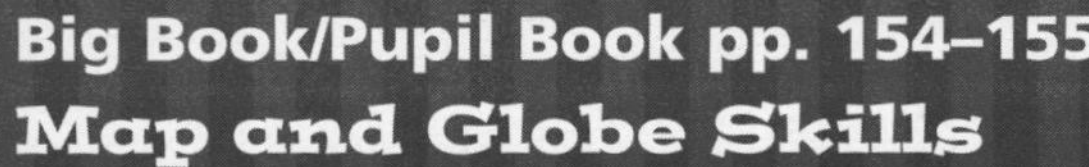

Locate Land and Water

Objectives

- Identify a globe as a model of Earth.
- Distinguish between land and water on globes and maps.
- Relate locations on globes to locations on Earth.

1 Introduce and Motivate

Preview Point out that the word *locate* in the lesson title means *find*. Direct children's attention to the globe and tell them that this is what the Earth looks like from space.

Warm Up To activate prior knowledge, show children a globe. Have them find land and water. Remind them that a continent (such as Europe, North America, Africa, or Asia) is a very large body of land; most continents have countries on them (the continent Australia has only one country, and Antartica has no countries, although it's used by several countries as a scientific research center); and a state (such as California or Florida) is part of a country.

2 Teach and Discuss

Page 154

Read the introduction. Prior to finding locations on the globe, explain to children that a globe is a round model of Earth.

✓ **Ongoing Assessment**

If... children do not understand that a globe is a model of Earth,

then... explain that a model is a small copy of something. Compare other models (such as a dollhouse or a model train) to the things they represent.

Map and Globe Skills

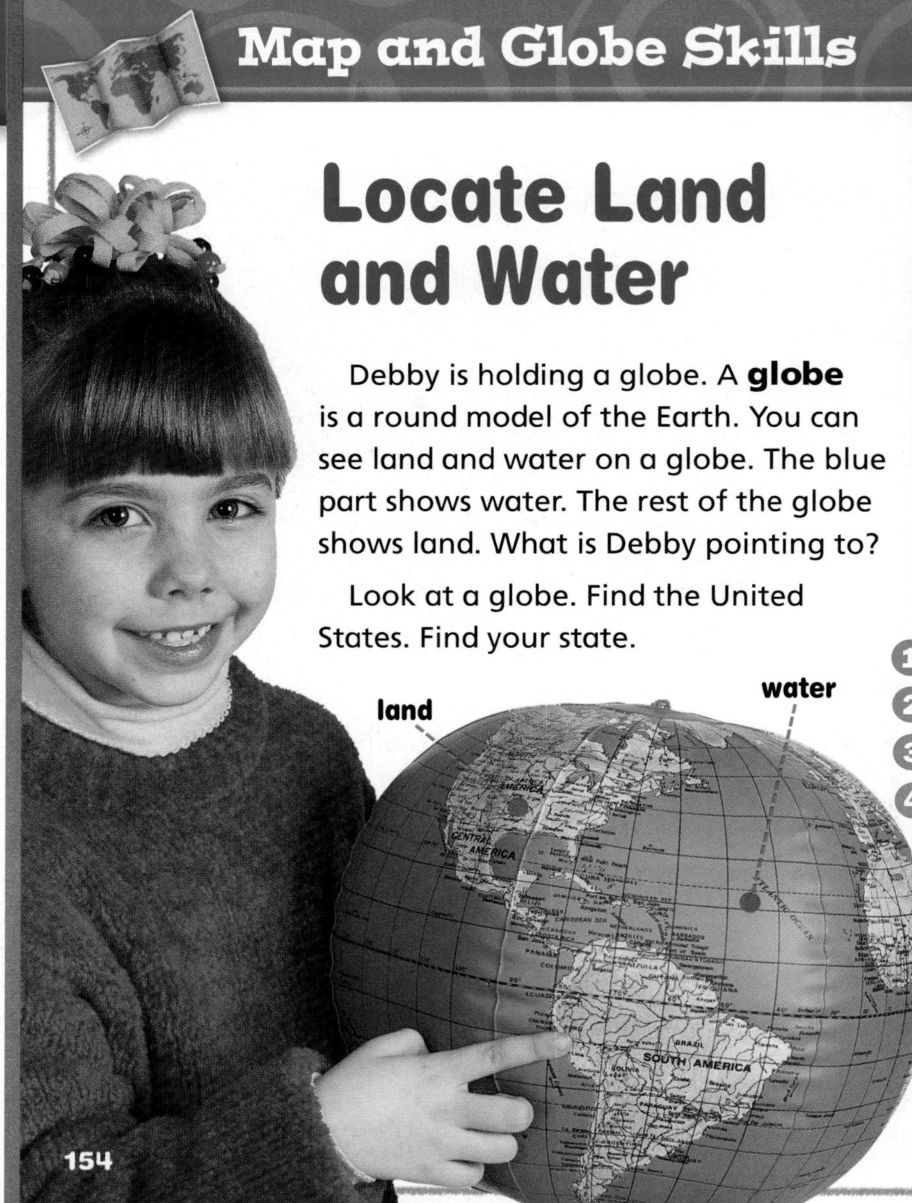

Locate Land and Water

Debby is holding a globe. A **globe** is a round model of the Earth. You can see land and water on a globe. The blue part shows water. The rest of the globe shows land. What is Debby pointing to?

Look at a globe. Find the United States. Find your state.

154

Practice and Extend

ESL — ACCESS CONTENT: ESL Support

Using a Globe Have children plan a trip to Mexico from their home community. Ask what direction they would travel. Model pointing north, south, east, and west on the globe.

Beginning Show children the route from their home community to Mexico, saying the cardinal directions. Have children repeat the directions.

Intermediate Have children trace the route from their home community to Mexico, saying the directions.

Advanced Have children trace a round trip from their home community to Mexico and back, saying the directions.

What kinds of land and water do you see on the map? 5

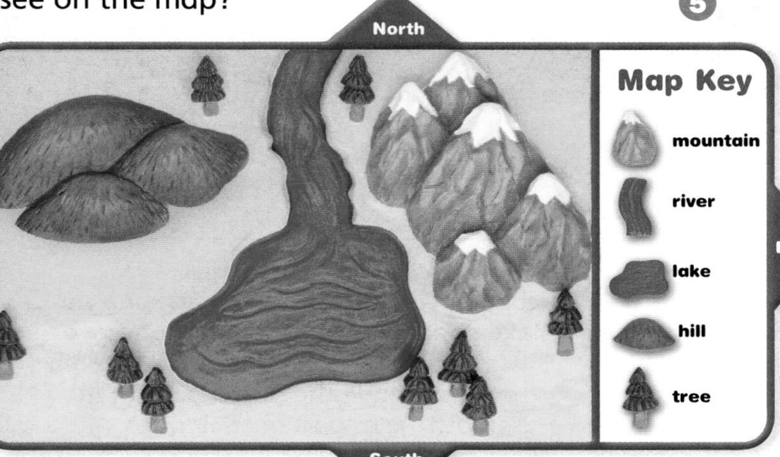

1. What does a globe show? How is it like the Earth?
2. Is the river east or west of the hills?
3. **On Your Own** Look at a map of your state. Name the different kinds of land and water there.

For more information, go online to *Atlas* at **www.sfsocialstudies.com.**

Make a Globe

- Give children a blown-up balloon, tape, and a paper cut-out of North America and South America.
- Then help them tape the continent cut-out to their "globe."

You may help children find out more by clicking on *Atlas* at **www.sfsocialstudies.com.**

Workbook, p. 41

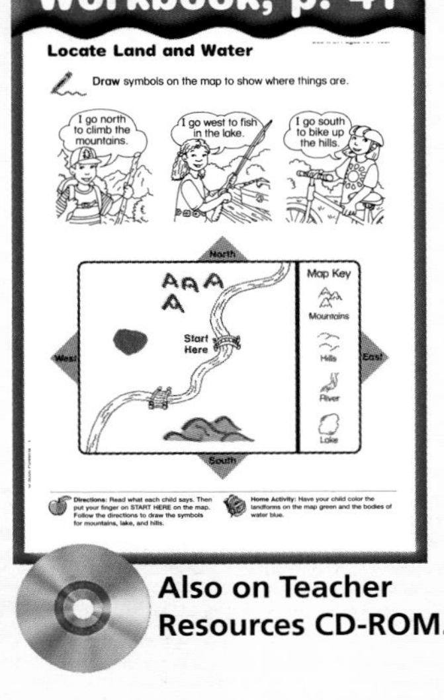

Also on Teacher Resources CD-ROM.

Show children a globe. Briefly discuss the continents. Then help children find the locations in the questions below.

1 **Where is the continent of North America on the globe?** Children should correctly identify North America. **Interpret Globes**

2 **Where is the United States on the globe?** Children should correctly locate the United States. **Interpret Globes**

3 **Where is your state on the globe?** Children should correctly find the approximate location of their state. **Interpret Globes**

4 **Where is your local community on the globe?** Children should correctly find the approximate location of their local community. **Interpret Globe**

Page 155

Discuss each symbol on the map key with children. Then ask them to identify the landforms and bodies of water on the map. Point out the direction tabs.

5 **Look at the map. Are the mountains to the east or west of the river and lake?** East **Interpret Maps**

3 Close and Assess

1. The globe shows the land and water on Earth. Both Earth and a globe are shaped like a ball.
2. The river is east of the hills.
3. **On Your Own** Children should accurately identify land and water in the state.

Use with pages 150–155

Lesson 2 Wrap-Up

MEETING INDIVIDUAL NEEDS Leveled Practice

Draw Pictures of Land and Water

Ask children to draw pictures of a lake including objects in the lake, such as a sailboat, ducks, and a tiny island, and around the lake, such as houses and trees.

Easy Have children identify the objects in and around the lake. **Reteach**

On-Level Have children make their picture into a vacation spot poster. Have them create an inviting title using a made-up name for the lake. **Extend**

Challenge Have children give a TV commercial for the lake, describing the lake as an inviting vacation spot. Have them make up a name for the lake. Tell them to include the objects shown in their picture as part of their pitch. **Enrich**

Hands-on Activities

CURRICULUM CONNECTION

Writing

Where Am I?

Objective Demonstrate the meaning of the words *mountain* and *lake*.

Resources Vocabulary Cards: **mountain, lake**

Materials pencils, paper

Learning Style Verbal

Partners

Time 10–15 minutes

1. Have partners write features of a mountain or lake.

2. Invite partners to prompt each other with "clues" from their list, asking "Where am I?"

3. Partners should provide clues until the location is recognized.

4. Remind partners to add the vocabulary words *mountain, plain, lake,* and *river* to their "My Word Book."

CURRICULUM CONNECTION

Art

Build It!

Objective Make a landform model to identify and describe physical characteristics of places.

Materials modeling clay, water, plastic lunch trays

Learning Style Visual/Kinesthetic

Group

Time 20–25 minutes

1. Have groups use modeling clay on a tray to create a landform model of a river flowing into a lake.

2. Groups may add water to their model.

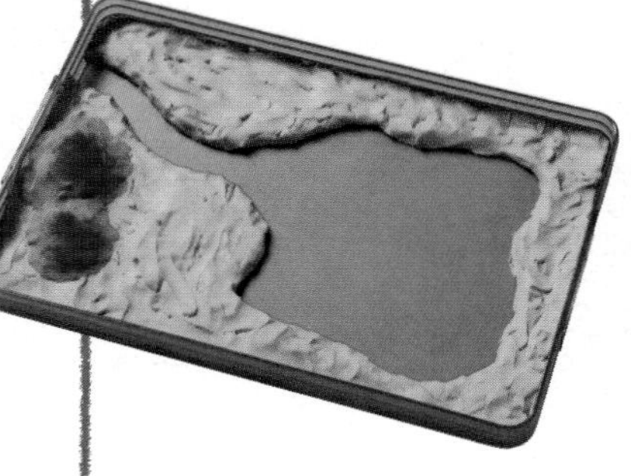

SOCIAL STUDIES STRAND

Geography

Spinning Globes

Objective Use cardinal directions to locate places on a globe.

Materials classroom globe

Partners

Time 10–15 minutes

1. Have a partner slowly spin the globe. Then have the partner stop the spinning by placing a finger on the globe. This spot is the starting place.

2. Then have the other partner trace the most direct route from the starting place to the United States to the home region to the approximate location of the home state, saying the direction of the route (north, south, east, west).

3. Have partners change roles. Repeat the game until all partners have had a turn.

Lesson 3 Overview

Our Earth's Resources pages 156–159	Children will learn the meaning of the term *natural resource* and identify the use of a natural resource and the reason for protecting it.	Time 20–30 minutes Resources • Workbook p. 42 • Vocabulary Card **natural resource** • Every Student Learns Guide, pp. 70–73
Tree Musketeers pages 160–161	Children will learn about volunteers who plant trees.	Time 15–20 minutes
Elvia Niebla pages 162–163	Children will learn about the contributions Elvia Niebla, a scientist, has made to protect forests.	Time 15–20 minutes

Build Background

Activity

Where Does It Come From?

Time 15–20 minutes

Invite children, one by one, to hold up small items that belong to them, such as an apple, pencil, barrette, coin, or mitten. Ask children to tell what they think each item is made of. Prompt them by asking, *Is it made of wood? of plastic?*

If time is short, show children classroom objects. Ask them what each item is made of and whether it comes from something from the Earth or is something created by humans.

Read Aloud

Nature's Gifts

By Mike Paterno

We all need the land,
Even you, dude.
For it's in the soil
We grow our food.

We all need water,
Cool and clean.
We all need fresh air
So we can breathe.

These gifts of Nature,
May come free,
But they need care, dude,
From you and me.

Our Earth's Resources

Objectives

- Identify and describe the physical characteristics of places such as natural resources.
- Identify examples of and uses for natural resources in the community, state, and nation.

Vocabulary

natural resource a useful thing that comes from nature (p. 156)

If time is short, guide children in brainstorming examples of natural resources and ways people use them. Refer children to the web on p. 157 to help them get started.

1 Introduce and Motivate

Preview Display the Vocabulary Card **natural resource** and explain that a natural resource is a useful thing that comes from nature. Ask children for examples.

Warm Up To activate prior knowledge, ask children to recall some of the things they identified as needs and wants in Unit 3. Discuss what these things are made of and where they come from. Point out that many of the things we need and want come directly from nature or are made from things in nature. Examples include air, water, food, and shelter.

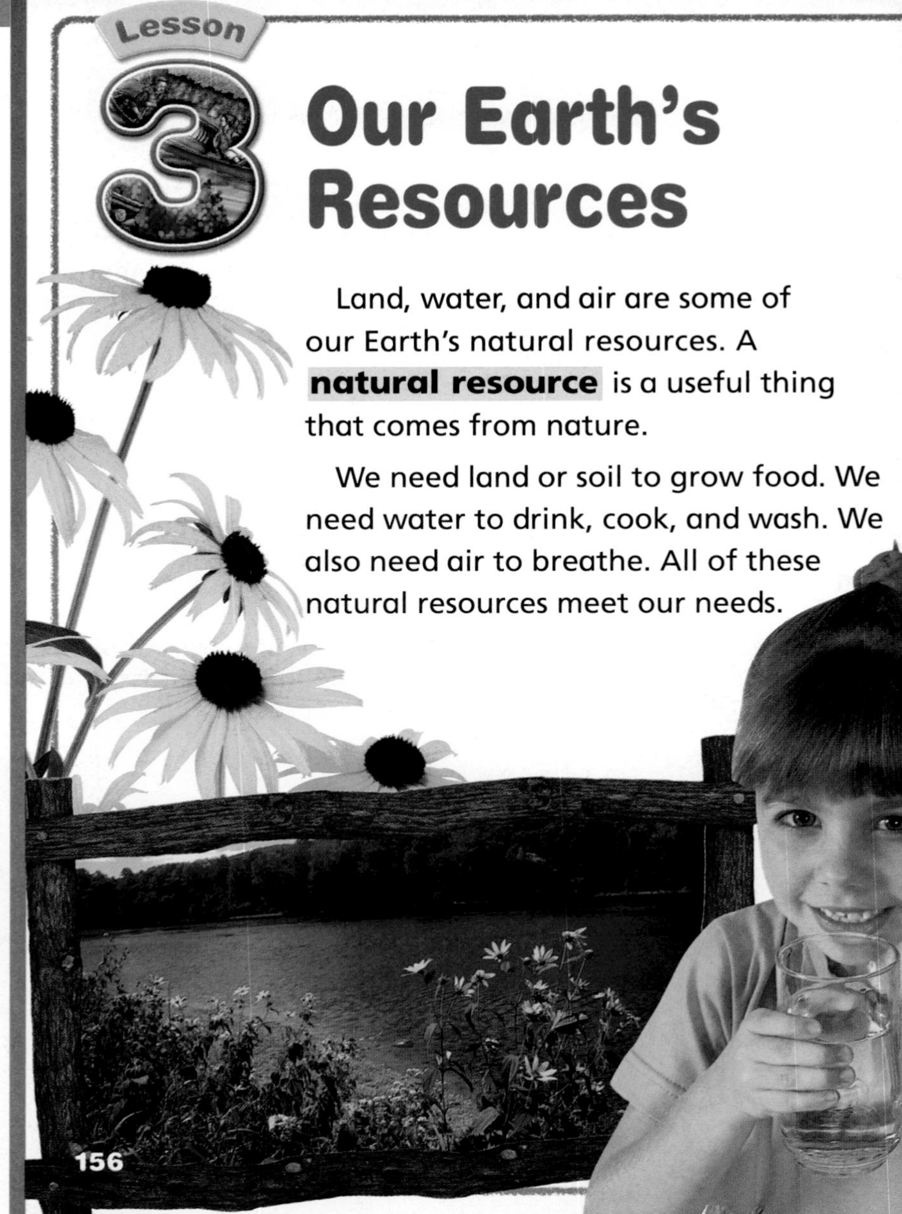

Lesson 3

Our Earth's Resources

Land, water, and air are some of our Earth's natural resources. A **natural resource** is a useful thing that comes from nature.

We need land or soil to grow food. We need water to drink, cook, and wash. We also need air to breathe. All of these natural resources meet our needs.

156

Practice and Extend

READING SKILL
Find the Main Idea

- Tell children that sometimes the main idea of a paragraph is in the last sentence. Read the second paragraph aloud. Note that the final sentence *(All of these natural resources meet our needs.)* is the main idea.
- Point out that the other sentences are details that give examples of ways natural resources meet our needs.
- Have children read the paragraph on p. 157 and find the main idea sentence. *(Trees are another natural resource.)*

WEB SITE
Technology

You can look up vocabulary words online. Click on *Social Studies Library* and select the dictionary at **www.sfsocialstudies.com.**

Trees are another natural resource. Many different things can come from trees. People cut trees into lumber to build homes. They also use the fruits and nuts that grow on trees for food. Look at the pictures. What other things can come from a tree? 2 3

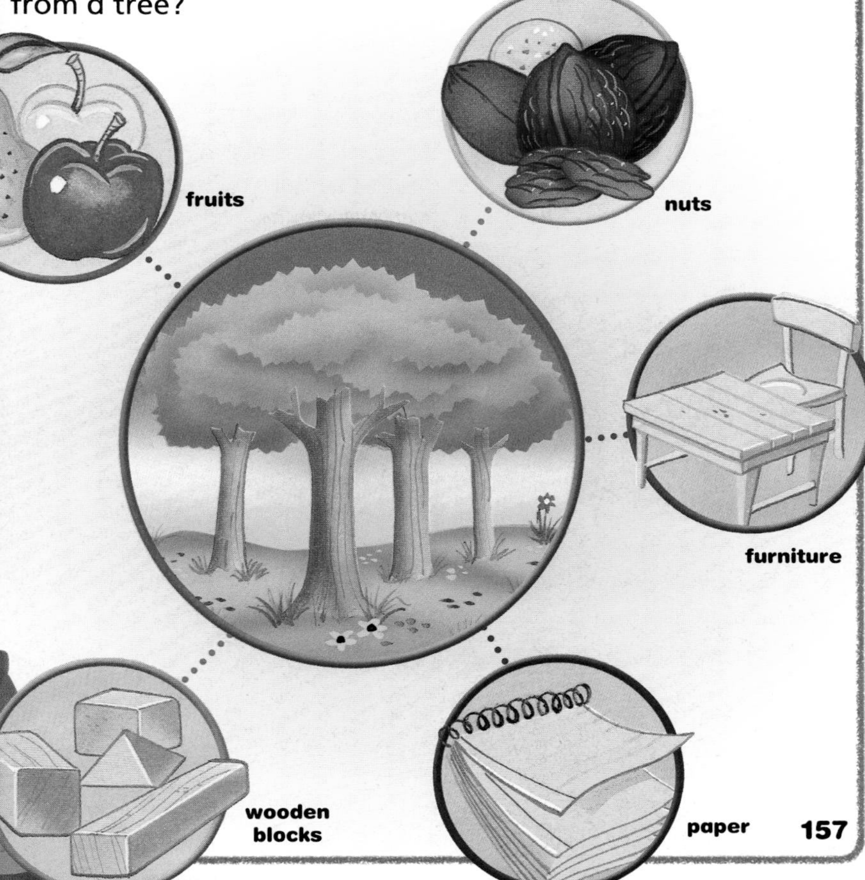

2 Teach and Discuss

Page 156

Have children identify the natural resources in the picture. (water, trees, air, soil)

1 **What can the natural resources be used for?** Possible answers: Water can be used for drinking or swimming. Air is used for breathing. Soil can be used to grow vegetables.

SOCIAL STUDIES STRAND
Economics

Explain to children that many cities in the United States were settled near rivers in order to help the exchange of goods. Many things to be bought and sold were more easily transported by water than land. List several cities along rivers, including ones in your state. Have children locate them on a map. Point out the nearby river.

Page 157

2 **What are some natural resources in your community?** Answers will vary but may include coal, rivers, trees, and lakes. **Apply Information**

3 **How would you make a chair from a tree?** Answers will vary but should include cutting down the tree, making lumber, cutting the lumber into smaller pieces, and fitting the pieces together. **Make Inferences**

BUILD BACKGROUND
ESL Support

Grand Tour of the Classroom Lead children in a tour of the classroom. Have children identify things made from natural resources, such as a pencil, or paper bag. Have children draw pictures of things they found that are made of a natural resource.

Beginning Provide children with the English words for the things, and help them label their pictures.

Intermediate Have children make labels for the things in their home language and in English.

Advanced Have children make labels for the things in their home language and in English. Then have them tell what natural resources the things came from.

For additional ESL support, use Every Student Learns Guide, pp. 70–73.

continued

Page 158

Explain to children that the picture in the circle shows an oil well getting oil from the ground.

4 **What are some ways you use oil or gas at home?** Possible answers: To heat the house and water, to cook, to make the car go. **Apply Information**

Ongoing Assessment

If... children do not understand that gasoline is needed to make a car move, **then...** tell them gasoline in a car is like food in a human: it provides the energy to move.

5 **Remember the kinds of transportation you learned about in Unit 3. What do you think happens to cars, trucks, airplanes, and trains when they don't have gasoline?** They won't go. **Cause and Effect**

SOCIAL STUDIES STRAND
Economics

Tell children that most cars, buses, trucks, trains, and airplanes depend on gasoline to move. Ask children to name transportation-related jobs that indirectly depend on gasoline.

Oil and gas are also natural resources. They come from under the ground. They
4 are used to heat our homes and other buildings. Some oil is made into gasoline for cars, buses, trucks, trains,
5 and airplanes.

Oil wells get oil from the ground.

158

Practice and Extend

FAST FACTS

Lesson 3 discusses national parks. Provide these facts about America's national parks.

- National parks are places where natural resources, sometimes special ones, are protected so people can enjoy them.
- The U.S. National Park System includes 350 park lands of various sizes and kinds.
- Yellowstone National Park, in Wyoming, Montana, and Idaho, created in 1872, was the first national park in the world.
- Through John Muir's efforts, Congress declared Yosemite, in California, a national park in 1890.
- To protect the natural resources in national parks, laws limit the kinds of activities people can do. Usually hunting, mining, or cutting down trees is not allowed. People can fish for their own use.

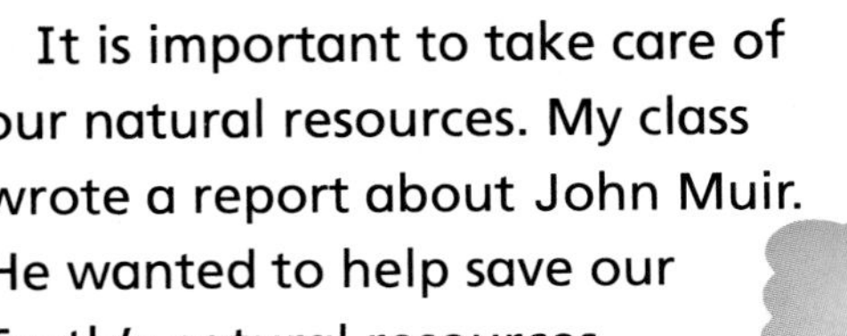

It is important to take care of our natural resources. My class wrote a report about John Muir. He wanted to help save our Earth's natural resources.

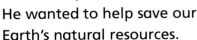

John Muir

John Muir thought natural resources were very important. He loved nature. He wrote about natural resources. He helped start many national parks. 6

What did you learn?

1. Name three ways natural resources meet our needs.
2. What is the **main idea** of the report on John Muir?
3. **Think and Share** Think about a pencil. Draw a picture of it. Name the natural resources that it came from.

159

Page 159

6 Why did John Muir work to create national parks—so that people could make things from natural resources, or so that people could enjoy natural resources? So that people could enjoy natural resources **Make Inferences**

SOCIAL STUDIES STRAND
Citizenship

Point out to students that John Muir was a good citizen because he wanted to establish national parks, not just for himself but for everyone. Ask children how people enjoy national parks. (Possible answer: People hike, camp, fish, and just observe the beauty of mountains, valleys, waterfalls, and trees.)

3 Close and Assess

Have children brainstorm a list of the uses of water. (Answers may include washing, cooking, drinking, swimming, and sailing.)

✓ What did you learn?

1. Answers will vary, but may include air for breathing; soil for growing crops; trees for making lumber.
2. John Muir thought natural resources were very important.
3. **Think and Share** Children should identify trees as one of the natural resources from which pencils are made.

FYI SOCIAL STUDIES
Background

About John Muir

- John Muir's family came to America from Scotland when he was 11. They settled on a farm in Wisconsin. Help children find Wisconsin on a map of the United States.
- Muir's love of nature began when he was a boy.
- In 1892, Muir founded the Sierra Club, a conservation organization. The Sierra Club still works to care for Earth's natural resources.

Workbook, p. 42

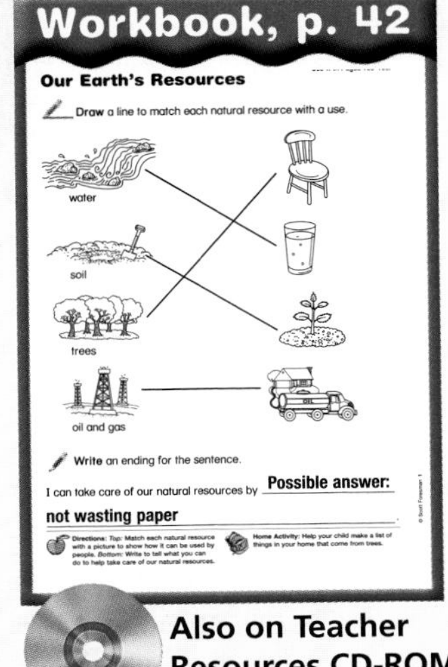

Our Earth's Resources

Draw a line to match each natural resource with a use.

water

soil

trees

oil and gas

Write an ending for the sentence.

I can take care of our natural resources by Possible answer: not wasting paper

Also on Teacher Resources CD-ROM.

CITIZEN HEROES

Tree Musketeers

Objectives

- Identify characteristics of good citizenship, such as responsibility for the common good.
- Identify ordinary people who exemplify good citizenship.

1 Introduce and Motivate

Preview Tell children that the name *Tree Musketeers* is a play on words based on the title of a famous story called *The Three Musketeers*. A long time ago, musketeers were soldiers who protected the king. The Tree Musketeers group protects trees.

Warm Up To activate prior knowledge about good citizenship, discuss with children why they should not pick flowers in the park. Guide them to understand that the flowers are for everyone.

Introduce the featured child, Tara. Tell children that they will learn reasons why Tara and her fellow Tree Musketeers are citizen heroes.

2 Teach and Discuss

Page 160

1 **What step did Tara take to help take care of Earth?** Possible answer: She helped start a group called Tree Musketeers. **Analyze Information**

2 **Why does Tara Church ask volunteers to help plant trees?** Possible answer: The more people who help, the more trees get planted. **Draw Conclusions**

CITIZEN HEROES

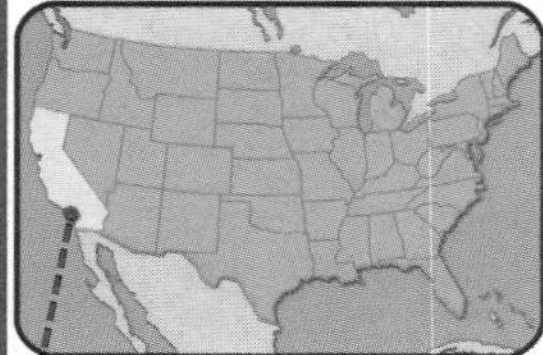

Tree Musketeers is in El Segundo, California.

Tree Musketeers

When Tara was eight years old, she wanted to help take care of the Earth. Tara and a group of children planted a tree in their community.

Tara helped start a group called Tree Musketeers. Tree Musketeers has many volunteers. They take responsibility for helping the Earth. One thing they do is ask people to plant trees. Over one million trees have been planted because of Tara and Tree Musketeers!

Tara

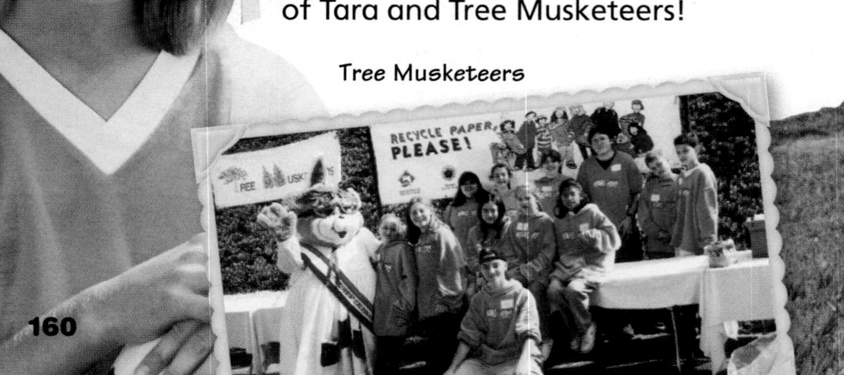

Tree Musketeers

160

Practice and Extend

SOCIAL STUDIES Background

About Tree Musketeers

- Tree Musketeers has a goal called 1-2-3. It wants one million groves of trees planted by two million children during three million hours.
- In addition to its tree-planting work, Tree Musketeers organizes volunteer efforts such as recycling programs and volunteer training.
- Tree Musketeers sends out Youth How-To Kits to teach children about forestry and recycling. You can find information about Tree Musketeers at Info@TreeMusketeers.org.

BUILDING CITIZENSHIP
Caring
Respect
Responsibility
Fairness
Honesty
Courage

Tara and Tree Musketeers have been given many awards for their work. One year, their group was given the President's Volunteer Action Award.

Today, Tara Church is a young adult. She talks to young people about doing volunteer work. Tara Church thinks that volunteering is the best way to make a difference. 3

Responsibility in Action

How can you be more responsible in the way you use natural resources?

4 Tree Musketeers planting

161

Page 161

3 How has Tara shown that she feels a responsibility for all people? Possible answers: She wants to protect the earth for everyone. She wants to plant trees that everyone can enjoy. **Analyze Information**

Test Talk

Write Your Answer

4 What is one of the things that Tree Musketeers volunteers do to help Earth? Write your answer. They ask people to plants trees. Ask children to reread their answer to make sure it is correct. **Analyze Information**

Review the list of citizenship traits in the upper right corner. Tell children that Tara Church has been a good citizen because she took responsibility not only for herself but for others. Ask children for examples of people who take responsibility for others in the home or community.

3 Close and Assess

Responsibility in Action

Read the question and have children discuss answers. Responses might include: Putting trash in receptacles, turning off lights before leaving a room, and recycling.

SOCIAL STUDIES STRAND
Citizenship

What Can You Do?

- Point out that Tara Church is a good citizen not just for planting trees herself, but for encouraging others to plant trees.
- Discuss with children reasons Tara Church might give for volunteering. (Possible answers: It makes you feel good about yourself; it makes the world a better place to live.)
- Invite adults from the community to discuss volunteering appropriate for young children.
- Ask children what kinds of volunteering might interest them, now or in the future.

Elvia Niebla

Objective

- Identify characteristics of good citizenship such as responsibility for the common good.

1 Introduce and Motivate

Preview Direct children's attention to the lesson title. Pronounce the name Elvia Niebla's name (EHL vee uh nee EH bluh) for children and have them repeat it after you. Then tell children that Elvia Niebla is a scientist who studies forests. Ask children what a forest is *(a lot of trees in a large area)*.

Warm Up To activate prior knowledge, ask children if they have ever visited a forest. Ask them to describe what it was like.

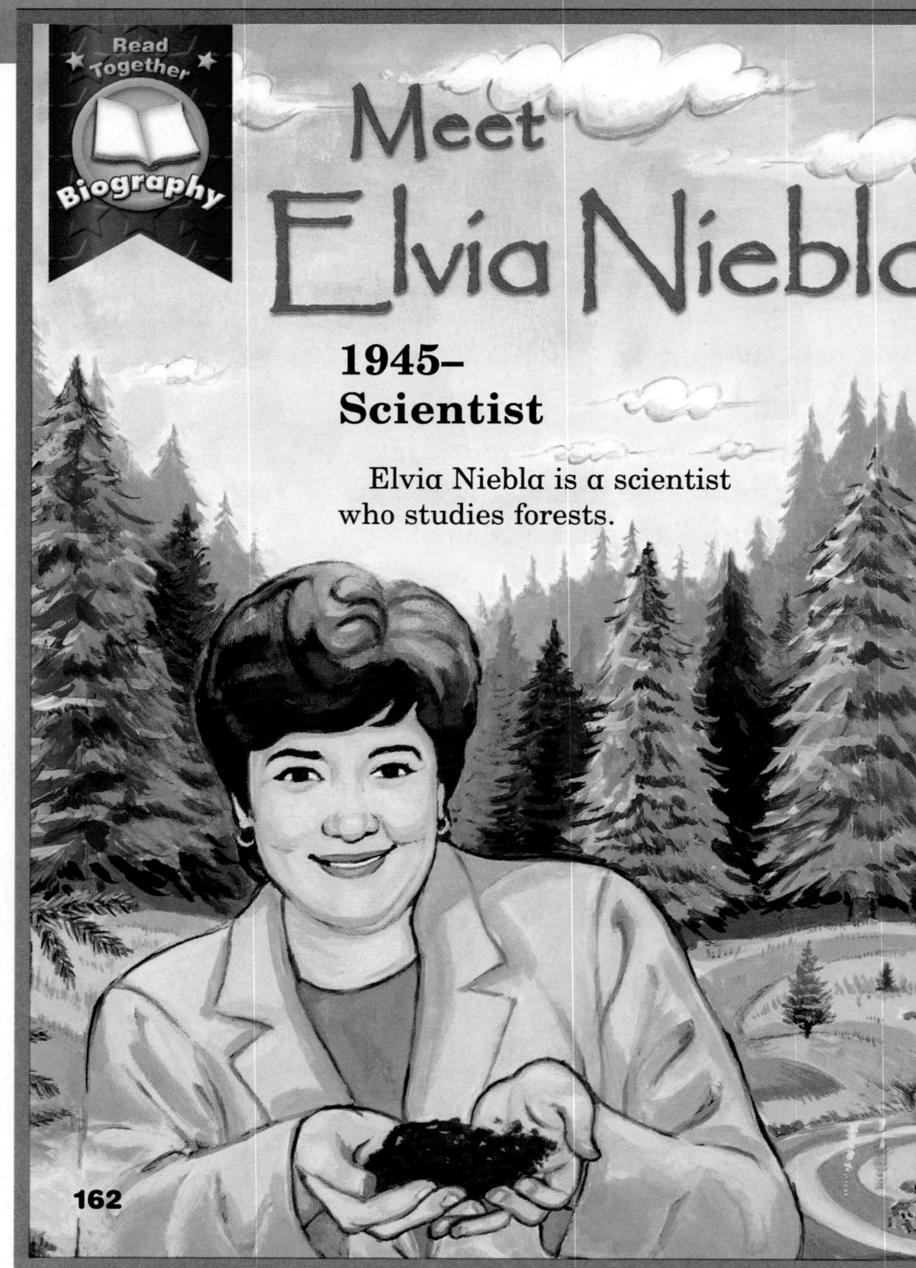
Read Together
Biography
Meet Elvia Niebla
1945–
Scientist
Elvia Niebla is a scientist who studies forests.
162

Practice and Extend

ESL Extend Language: ESL Support

Work with Related Words Have children create a flowchart with the base word *science* at the top. Explain that *science* is the process of gathering knowledge based on observed facts and tested truths; a *scientist* is a person who is specially trained in a field of science; and *scientific* means having to do with science.

Beginning Have children complete the chart with words on pp. 162–163 that are related to the word *science*.

Intermediate Have children complete the flowchart with words on pp. 162–163 that are related to the word *science*. Have them write the sentences containing these words.

Advanced Have children complete the chart with words on pp. 162–163 that are related to the word *science*. Challenge them to write their own sentences using *science, scientist,* and *scientific*.

Elvia was born in Mexico. When she was six years old, her family moved to Arizona. As a child, Elvia liked science. Later, Elvia Niebla went to school to learn more about trees and soil. She learned how some things might
1 harm these natural resources. She also studied ways to protect trees and soil.

Elvia Niebla has helped write rules to protect soil. She leads scientific studies about how different materials and changes in weather can affect the soil. She knows that keeping
2 our air and water clean can also help our forests. Elvia Niebla believes that people need to work together to protect our natural resources.

Elvia Niebla was born in Nogales, Mexico.

Think and Share

How does Elvia Niebla help take care of forests?

For more information, go online to *Meet the People* at **www.sfsocialstudies.com.**

163

2 Teach and Discuss

Pages 162–163

Read the biography together. Point out Elvia Niebla in the pictures on pp. 162–163.

1 **What did Elvia Niebla learn in school about trees and soil?** She learned how some actions might harm trees and soil and ways to protect them. **Analyze Information**

SOCIAL STUDIES STRAND
Government

Point out that Elvia Niebla helped write rules to protect soil and forest plants for the Environmental Protection Agency (EPA), a part of the U.S. government. This rule helps prevent people and corporations from allowing harmful chemicals to enter soil where food is grown.

2 **How do rules keeping the air and water clean help forests?** Possible answer: Dirty air and water are harmful to trees. **Make Inferences/Cause and Effect**

Ongoing Assessment

If... children cannot connect clean air and water to healthy forests,	**then...** explain that trees, like all living things, need clean water and clean air to live.

3 Close and Assess

Think and Share

Children's answers should identify ways that Elvia Niebla's work has helped forests. (Answers may include: She has helped write rules to protect soil. She has helped scientists learn ways that changes in weather and different materials affect the soil.)

CURRICULUM CONNECTION
Science

Between a Rock and a Soft Place

- Ask children if they have ever turned over a rock in the soil. Tell children to describe the living and nonliving things that they might find under a rock. (bugs, pieces of rock, twigs, leaves)
- Have children draw living and nonliving things they might find under a rock.

WEB SITE
Technology

You may help children find our more about Elvia Niebla by clicking on *Meet the People* at **www.sfsocialstudies.com.**

Use with pages 156–163

Lesson 3 Wrap-Up

MEETING INDIVIDUAL NEEDS

Leveled Practice

There's a Tree in the Living Room

Work with children to make a list of things commonly found in the home that come from trees.

Easy Have children draw pictures of things in the home that come from trees. **Reteach**

On-Level Have children make a list of things commonly found in the home that come from trees. **Extend**

Challenge Have children write the names of things surrounding a home that come from trees. Possibilities include a fence, porch, and a dog house. **Enrich**

Hands-on Activities

CURRICULUM CONNECTION

Writing

Poster

Objective Demonstrate an understanding of the term *natural resource.*

Resources Vocabulary Card: **natural resource**

Materials poster paper, markers

Learning Style Verbal/Visual

Individual

Time 10–15 minutes

1. Write the following on the board:

Protect ________. We need this natural resource for ________.

2. Have children copy and complete the sentences. Then have them illustrate their poster.

3. Remind children to add *natural resource* to their Word Book.

CURRICULUM CONNECTION

Science

Trees, Above and Below

Objective To draw a tree.

Learning Style Spatial

Individual

Time 15–20 minutes

1. Have children draw a tree.

2. Have children label the roots, stem, and leaves of the tree.

3. Remind children that even though the roots are under ground, they are an important part of the tree because they take in water.

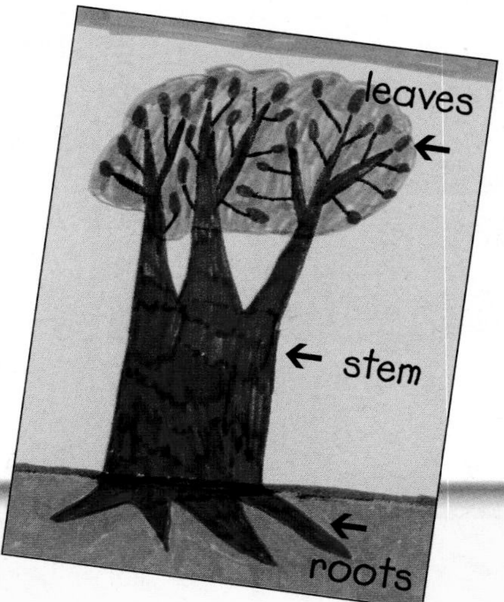

CURRICULUM CONNECTION

Math

Water, Water Everywhere

Objective To identify the uses of water in school.

Learning Style Logical-Mathematical

Partners

Time 15–20 minutes

1. Have partner teams make a list of uses of water in school, such as cleaning the floor, watering plants, filling up the fish tank, and drinking from fountains.

2. With a specific ten-minute time limit, have teams tour the classroom and immediate hallway for uses of water. Tell teams to record and number the examples they found.

3. Chart each teams' results on a simple bar graph.

Lesson 4 Overview

Interview About Farm History pages 164–167	Through an interview, children will learn about farms in history and how farming has changed over time.	 Time 20–30 minutes Resources • Workbook p. 43 • Vocabulary Card **history** • Every Student Learns Guide, pp. 74–77
Sacagawea pages 168–169	Children will identify the contributions of Sacagawea, a Shoshone Indian who helped explorers long ago.	Time 15–20 minutes

Build Background

Activity

Farming Now and Then

 **Time** 15–20 minutes

Show children pictures of oxen performing heavy work on a farm long ago. Explain that a pair of oxen were joined by a yoke—a wooden bar with bows at the ends that fitted around the oxen's necks. Have children draw pictures of oxen helping a farmer.

If time is short, ask children to describe how people grow vegetable gardens.

Read Aloud

Old MacDonald

traditional song

Old MacDonald had a farm,
E-I-E-I-O!
And on that farm he grew some corn, E-I-E-I-O!
With one row here, and one row there,
Here a row, there a row, everywhere a row to hoe.
Old MacDonald had a farm,
E-I-E-I-O!

Interview About Farm History

Objectives

- Distinguish among past, present, and future.
- Identify examples of and uses for natural resources.

Vocabulary

history telling the story of people and places from the past (p. 164)

QUICK Teaching Plan

If time is short, have children use the time line on p. 166 to summarize the ways farming has changed over time.

- Children can write a sentence describing each picture in the time line. The three sentences will form their summaries.

1 Introduce and Motivate

Preview Discuss the lesson title with children and then display the Vocabulary Card **history**. Share the definition above. In order to help children understand the concept of different times in history, explain that the time when their grandparents were children is farther in the past than the time when their parents were children. Explain that the present is now, when they themselves are children. Then explain that in the future they will be grown-ups.

Warm Up To activate prior knowledge, remind children of Unit 3, Lesson 5 "Interview with a Farmer." Review the interview format and the things children learned about farm work. Then ask children to name three things that might be grown on a farm.

Lesson

Interview About Farm History

My family visits friends in Iowa. Our friends live on a farm. One day, we went to a place called "Living History Farms." **History** tells the story of people and places from the past. History also tells about things that happened in the past. 1

164

Practice and Extend

READING SKILL Sequence

- In order to have children understand how events are linked by time, draw on the board a Linear String graphic organizer with three boxes. Label box one "Eat Dinner," box two "Read Book," and box three "Go to Bed."
- Have children describe these events orally.
- Then have children draw pictures of these events in three boxes.

WEB SITE Technology

You can look up vocabulary words online. Click on *Social Studies Library* and select the dictionary at **www.sfsocialstudies.com.**

Mrs. Waters The first farmers in Iowa were Native Americans. Native Americans called the Ioway probably farmed the land we are standing on right now! 4

Debby What did the Ioway grow?

Mrs. Waters They grew many things including corn, beans, pumpkins, and squash.

165

2 Teach and Discuss

Page 164

Tell children that Debby is talking to Mrs. Waters, who works at Living History Farms. This is a place that shows how people farmed in history.

1 **What kind of land do you think is easiest to farm? A mountain, hill, or plain?** Plain **Why?** A plain is mostly flat. **Make Inferences**

2 **What natural resource do you think Debby will find on a farm?** Possible answers: Trees, plants, and soil **Make Inferences**

3 **What does Debby want to know the history of?** She wants to know about the first farmers in Iowa. **Apply Information**

Page 165

Point out the beginning of the interview format. Explain that each lozenge carries the name of the person speaking the words opposite it.

4 **Who were the first farmers in Iowa?** Native Americans called the Ioway **Draw Conclusions**

Ongoing Assessment

If... children are confused about the names of the Native Americans in Iowa,

then... explain that the Ioway are also known as the Iowa. *Iowa* tends to be the legal term, *Ioway* the cultural term. Traditional members of the tribe usually refer to themselves as the Ioway.

SOCIAL STUDIES Background

Water Supply

- Ask children what things plants need to grow. (soil, water, sunlight)
- Remind children of when they planted a seedling and watered it regularly. (Unit 3, Lesson 5, p. 117)
- Explain that some farmers in history depended on a nearby flooding river or rain for water. Other farmers built ditches or canals that directed water from a nearby river or lake to the farmer's field.

continued

Page 166

Have children describe and explain the time line on p. 166. Point out that the word *present* means *now* or *today*.

5 **Why do you think oxen-power replaced man-power on the farm?** Possible answer: Oxen are big and strong. They can pull plows, logs, and other heavy things.
Make Inferences/Analyze Pictures

Use Information from Graphics

6 **Which picture in the time line shows the oldest way to farm and the oldest date?** Children should indicate the drawing of people hoeing in 1700. Tell children to look at the time line again to find the oldest date.
Sequence/Interpret Time Lines

7 **Tell what tool people use to farm in the present.** Tractor **Analyze Pictures**

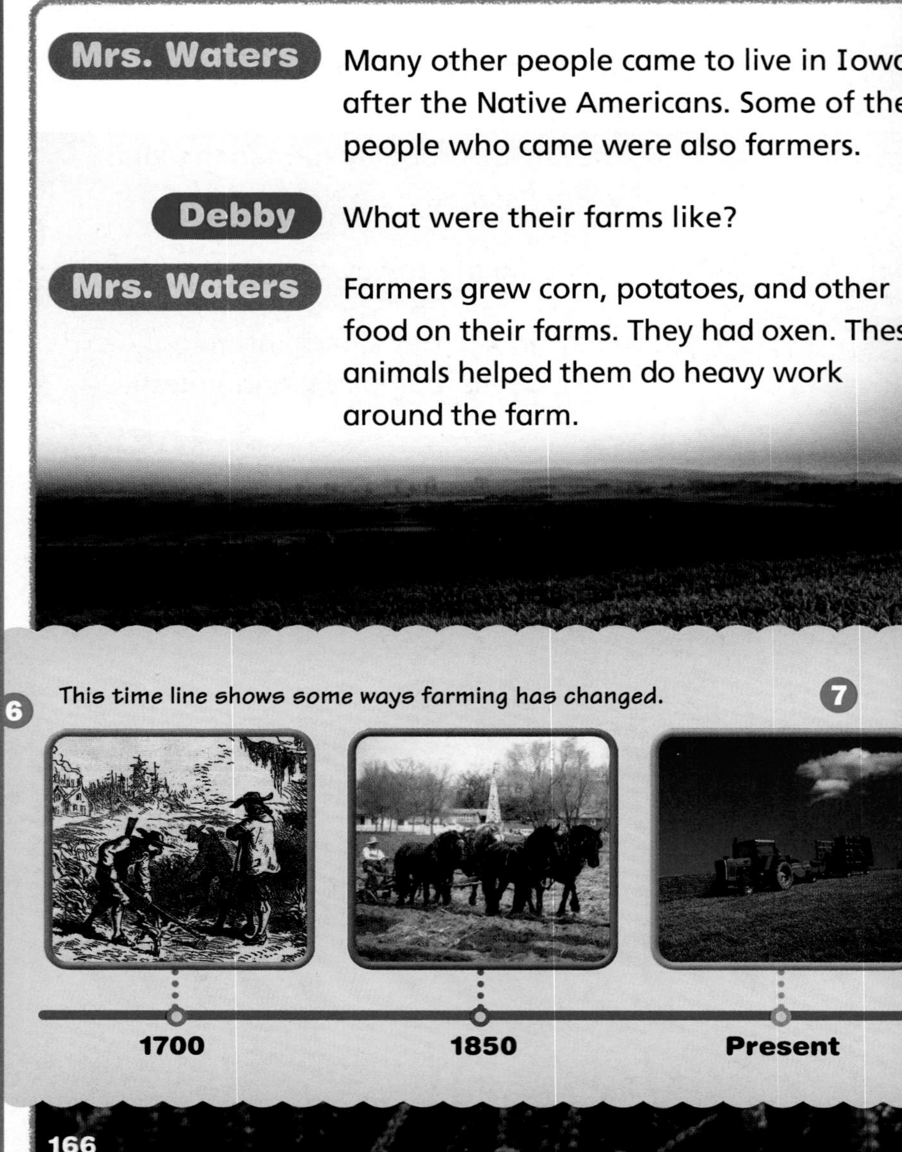

Mrs. Waters
Many other people came to live in Iowa after the Native Americans. Some of the people who came were also farmers.
Debby
What were their farms like?
Mrs. Waters
Farmers grew corn, potatoes, and other food on their farms. They had oxen. These animals helped them do heavy work around the farm.

6 *This time line shows some ways farming has changed.* 7

1700 | 1850 | Present

166

Practice and Extend

ESL SUPPORT
Build Background

Understand Changes Show children a picture of loggers using a chain saw. Discuss how the Ioway used hatchets to cut bark and branches from trees to make their lodges.

Beginning Have children pantomime cutting down a tree with a chain saw. Then have children pantomime Native Americans cutting down a tree with a hatchet.

Intermediate Have children complete the sentence frame: Long ago, people cut down a tree by using a ________. Now, people use a ________.

Advanced Have children complete the sentence frame above. Then ask them to describe the change.

For additional ESL support, use Every Student Learns Guide, pp. 74–77.

SOCIAL STUDIES
Background

First North Americans

Remind children that the groups of people who first lived in North America are called either Native Americans or American Indians. Even among these people, preference for the terms is mixed. Some prefer to be called by their tribal name rather than either general term.

WEB SITE
Technology

You may help children learn more about Living History Farms by going online. Use **http://www.ioweb.com/lhf.**

Mrs. Waters Farming continued to change over time. Some farmers began to use horses ⑧ instead of oxen.

Debby Now farmers use more tools such as tractors to do farm work.

What did you learn?

1. Who were the first farmers in Iowa?
2. How has farming changed over time?
3. **Think and Share** Draw a farm from the past and the present. Tell what a farm might look like in the future.

167

Page 167

⑧ **Why might horses be better helpers on a farm than oxen?** Possible answers: Horses are faster and smarter. **Make Inferences**

3 Close and Assess

Have pairs of children prompt each other with clues about farming in different time periods. Children can respond by identifying the time period as "1700," "1850," or "Present."

✓ What did you learn?

1. Native Americans called the Ioway were the first farmers in Iowa.
2. Today farmers use tools and animals to make their jobs easier.
3. **Think and Share** Children's drawings should show accurate details from historical and modern farms. Their writing should reflect the idea that new tools will probably make farming in the future even easier.

FYI Social Studies Background

Farming

- Explain to children that although farming has changed, in some ways it is still the same. Point out that the same basic natural resources—soil, sun, and water—are used to grow crops on all farms.
- Then point out that most crops on farms are seasonal. Seeds are planted in the spring and the crops are harvested in the fall.

Workbook, p. 43

Interview About Farm History

Write *then* or *now* to tell about each picture.

now — then — now

now (or) then — then

Draw a job you might like to do on a farm. Drawings will vary.

Also on Teacher Resources CD-ROM.

Sacagawea

Objective

- Identify contributions of historical figures who have influenced the nation.

1 Introduce and Motivate

Preview Have children look at the illustration. Tell them that Sacagawea led people across dangerous land and water long ago.

Warm Up To activate prior knowledge, ask children if they remember ever being guided across a dangerous street, rocks, or a stream. Ask children to describe the experience. Discuss with children the responsibilities of a guide.

2 Teach and Discuss

Pages 168–169

Read the biography together. Tell children that Lewis and Clark were two men who were asked by the government to find a way from the middle of the United States to the Pacific Ocean using rivers and lakes, if possible. Show children this region on a map, using St. Louis as the starting point.

1 Why is Sacagawea important to our history? Possible answer: She helped Lewis and Clark on their trip to the Pacific Ocean.
Make Inferences

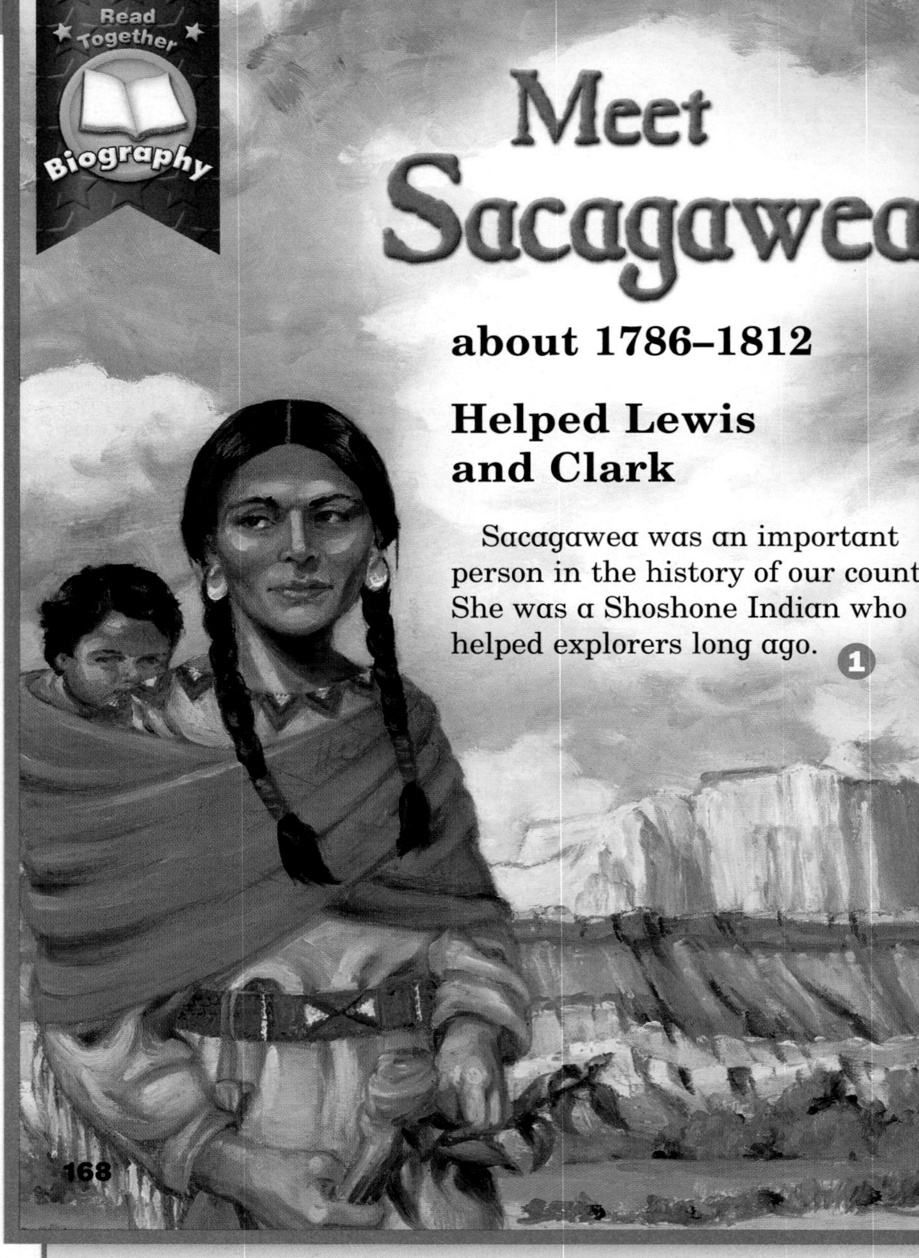

Meet Sacagawea

about 1786–1812

Helped Lewis and Clark

Sacagawea was an important person in the history of our count
She was a Shoshone Indian who helped explorers long ago. 1

168

Practice and Extend

About Sacagawea

- Tell children that Sacagawea (sä cä' gä we ä) was a Native American, a Shoshone. The date of her birth is uncertain. When she was born, her name was Boinaiv, which means "Grass Maiden." When the Hidatsa, who spoke another language, captured her, they changed her name to Sacagawea, which means "Bird Woman."
- Sacagawea's husband was from Canada. When Sacagawea and her husband guided Lewis and Clark, they brought along their newborn baby.
- Sacagawea helped the explorers to make friends with different Native American groups. These groups knew that war parties never traveled with women and children. When they saw Sacagawea and her baby, they knew that Lewis and Clark were friendly.

When Sacagawea was a young child, she was living in a Shoshone village 2 in the Bitterroot Mountains in what is now Idaho. Then the Hidatsas took her to live and work in their village in what is now North Dakota.

Young Sacagawea lived in what is now Idaho.

In 1805 and 1806, a group of men was traveling across the United States. The leaders of the group were Meriwether 3 Lewis and William Clark. They wanted to find a route to the Pacific Ocean.

Sacagawea helped Lewis and Clark on their journey. She showed them how to find food. The American Indians, or Native Americans, that Lewis and Clark met on their journey did not speak English. Sacagawea translated, or changed the words from one language to another. With the help of Sacagawea, Lewis and Clark reached the Pacific Ocean. 4

A picture of Sacagawea is on the one dollar gold coin.

Think and Share

What are two ways Sacagawea helped the explorers?

For more information, go online to *Meet the People* at **www.sfsocialstudies.com.**

169

CURRICULUM CONNECTION Drama

Take a Tour

- Have children take turns role-playing Sacagawea. They can "guide" groups of classmates around parts of the school.
- Encourage children who are role-playing the guide to point out different parts of the school and introduce the other children to people they meet.

WEB SITE Technology

You may help children find out more about Sacagawea by clicking on *Meet the People* at **www.sfsocialstudies.com.**

2 **Where did Sacagawea live with the Shoshone? Point to the state on the classroom map.** Children should identify Idaho. **Make Inferences/Interpret Maps**

C SOCIAL STUDIES STRAND Culture

Explain to children that Sacagawea experienced different cultures during her life. Among them were that of the Shoshone, the Hidatsa, and, after marrying her Canadian husband, Canadians. Ask children what it might be like to experience more than one culture. (Answers will vary but may include: exciting or confusing.)

3 **What direction did Lewis and Clark travel? How do you know?** They traveled west. The Pacific Ocean is west of mainland United States. **Make Inferences**

4 **How did Sacagawea help Lewis and Clark communicate with the American Indians?** She translated. **Apply Information**

3 Close and Assess

Think and Share

Possible answers: She helped them find food, and she translated for them.

Use with pages 164–169

Lesson 4 Wrap-Up

MEETING INDIVIDUAL NEEDS

Leveled Practice

Compare and Contrast Pictures

Have children draw two pictures showing ways that farmers in Iowa used natural resources in the past and use them now. Discuss ways these uses are alike and different.

Easy Direct children's attention to two features common in both drawings, such as soil in which plants grow. Ask them if farmers in both times used this resource. **Reteach**

On-Level Ask children to identify in their drawings ways that farmers in the present work differently from farmers in the past. Have children indicate the tools in their drawings that make farming today different from in the past. **Extend**

Challenge Have partners dramatize a conversation between farmers, one from the past and one from the present, in their drawings. Suggest to children that they talk about farming problems. **Enrich**

Hands-on Activities

CURRICULUM CONNECTION

Writing

Farm Contest

Objective Demonstrate an understanding of the word *history*.

Resources Vocabulary Card: **history**

Materials drawings from "Compare and Contrast Pictures" activity

Learning Style Verbal/Visual

Group 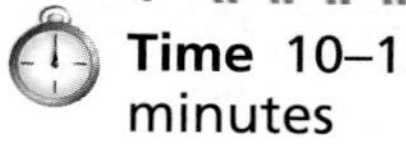

Time 10–15 minutes

1. Place all the drawings from "Compare and Contrast Pictures" (above) in a bag.

2. Show drawings one at a time. Ask children if the drawings show a farm in history or a farm now. Ask how they know.

3. Remind children to add the vocabulary word *history* to their "My Word Book."

SOCIAL STUDIES STRAND

Geography

Find the Way

Objective Follow a route from history.

Materials classroom map of the United States

Learning Style Spatial

Individual

Time 15 minutes

1. Remind children that Lewis and Clark were looking for a way to reach the Pacific Ocean using rivers and lakes.

2. Show children examples of rivers and lakes on your classroom map. Help children find St. Louis. Then have children look at the western United States on the map. Tell them to find rivers and lakes that connect.

3. Ask children whether it is possible to reach the Pacific Ocean from St. Louis without leaving the United States and without traveling over land. (No, it is not.)

SOCIAL STUDIES STRAND

History

Sacagawea

Objective Identify contributions of historical figures who have influenced the nation.

Materials paper, crayons

Learning Style Spatial

Individual

Time 20–30 minutes

1. Read aloud parts of *A Picture Book of Sacagawea* by David A. Adler. Have children identify the settings. Then show the illustrations.

2. Have children respond to the story by drawing pictures of their favorite parts and labeling them.

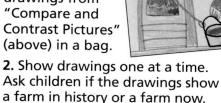

Lesson 5 Overview

Caring for Our Resources

pages 170–173

Children will learn ways to conserve natural resources by reducing, reusing, and recycling.

 Time 20–30 minutes

Resources
- Workbook p. 44
- Every Student Learns Guide, pp. 78–81

Endangered Animals

pages 174–175

Children will learn that helping care for the Earth helps protect endangered animals.

Time 15–20 minutes

Build Background

Activity

Can You Use Less?

 **Time** 15–20 minutes

Have children draw a picture of juice spilled from a glass. Then discuss with them the benefits of cleaning the liquid with a sponge rather than a paper towel. Have children include a sponge in their drawing. Ask them to caption the drawing "Save Paper/Wipe Up with a Sponge."

If time is short, invite children to name some ways that they use paper. Then ask them for ways to use less paper.

Save Paper!
Wipe Up with a Sponge

Read Aloud

Hurt No Living Thing

by Christina Rossetti

Hurt no living thing;
Ladybug, nor butterfly,
Nor moth with dusty wing,
Nor cricket chirping cheerily,
Nor grasshopper so light of leap,
Nor dancing gnat, nor beetle fat,
Nor harmless worms that creep.

Lesson 5 Caring for Our Resources

Objective

- Identify ways that natural resources can be used and reused.

QUICK Teaching Plan

If time is short, brainstorm with children about ways to conserve natural resources.

- Use the pictures and boxed text on pp. 170–173 to prompt children's thinking.

1 Introduce and Motivate

Preview Have children glance at the lesson pages. Explain that the words in the speech bubbles are the advice Debby and her classmates give others about reducing, reusing, and recycling natural resources. Then explain that the words in the boxed text are helpful hints about ways to reduce, reuse, and recycle.

Warm Up To activate prior knowledge, show children the recycling symbol on p. 172 and ask if anyone knows what it means. Ask children how plastic and glass can be recycled in the home. Then ask about recycling newspapers or magazines in the home.

Lesson 5 Caring for Our Resources

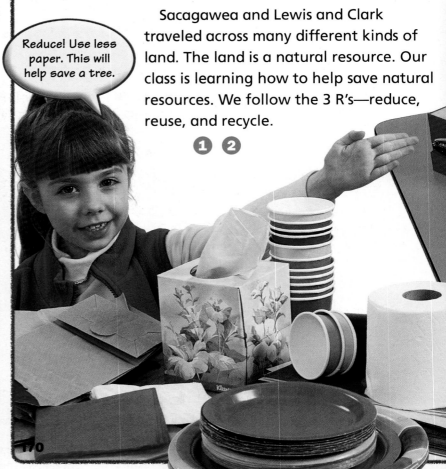

Sacagawea and Lewis and Clark traveled across many different kinds of land. The land is a natural resource. Our class is learning how to help save natural resources. We follow the 3 R's—reduce, reuse, and recycle.

1 2

Reduce! Use less paper. This will help save a tree.

170

Practice and Extend

Target Skill

READING SKILL
Find the Main Idea

- In this lesson children read lists with advice about reducing, reusing, and recycling natural resources.
- Tell children that the title of a list tells them what the list is about. It is the main idea. Each item below the title is a detail or an example.

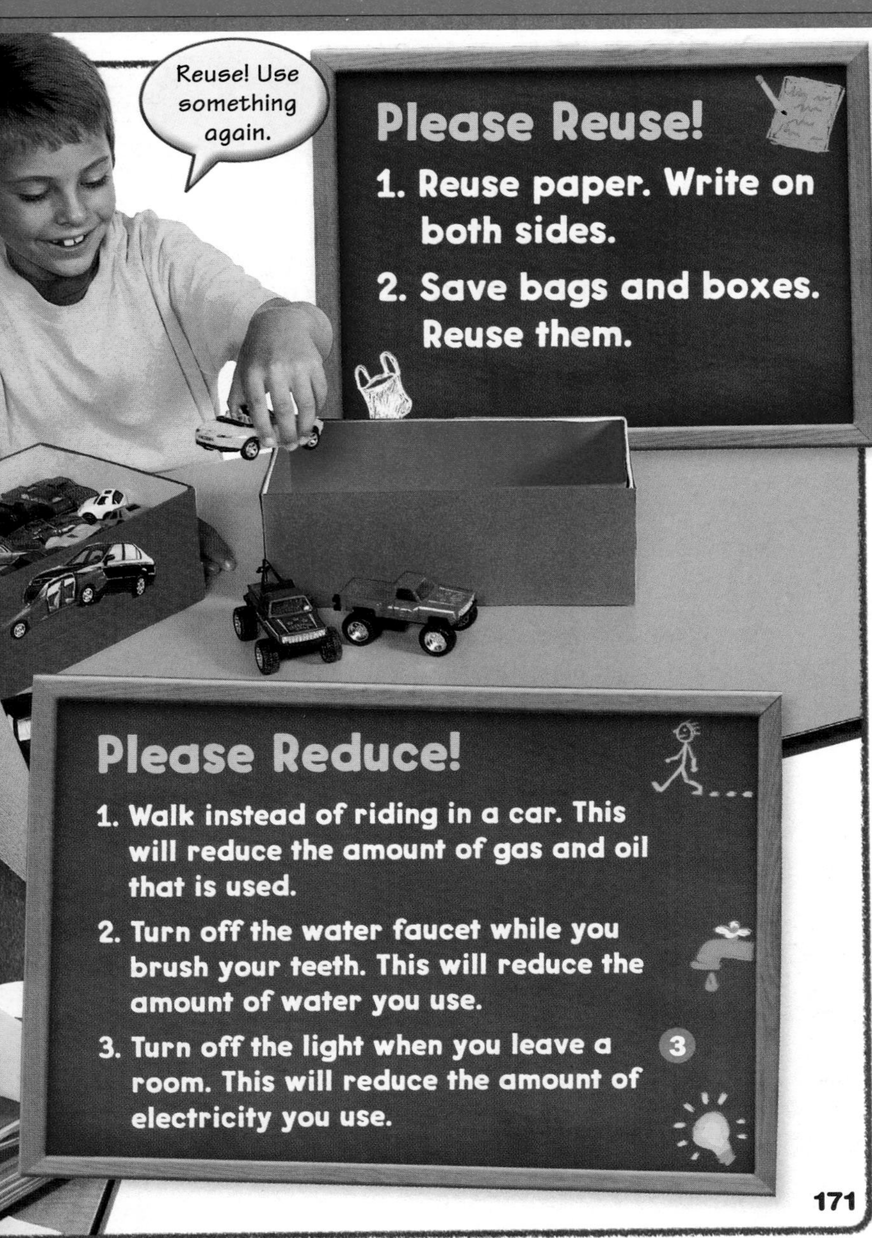

Reuse! Use something again.
Please Reuse!
1. Reuse paper. Write on both sides.
2. Save bags and boxes. Reuse them.
Please Reduce!
1. Walk instead of riding in a car. This will reduce the amount of gas and oil that is used.
2. Turn off the water faucet while you brush your teeth. This will reduce the amount of water you use.
3. Turn off the light when you leave a room. This will reduce the amount of electricity you use.
3
171

ESL SUPPORT Access Content

Make New Words Explain to children that the letters *re* before a word sometimes mean *to repeat an action*. Make word cards containing the prefix *re* and the root words *open, play,* and *use*. Model how to put the cards together to make the words *reopen, replay*, and *reuse*.

Beginning Mix the paper in a bag. Have pairs take turns drawing word cards until they can construct the words *reopen, replay,* and *reuse*.

Intermediate Show children just the slips with *open, play,* and *use*. Have children pantomime these actions. Next, show *re* and have them pantomime repeating the actions.

Advanced Have children use all the cards to display each new word. Ask them to tell what each word means, using the sentence frame: *Re* ______ means to _______ again.

For additional ESL support, use Every Student Learns Guide, pp. 78–81.

2 Teach and Discuss

Page 170

Have children describe the items around Debby. Point out that they are all paper products.

1 **What natural resource is used to make the things around Debby?** Trees
Inferences/Cause and Effect

Ongoing Assessment

If... children cannot identify paper as coming from a natural resource,	**then...** tell them that paper is made, in part, from wood ground into a soft, wet mass.

2 **Why does Debby call *reduce, reuse,* and *recycle* the 3 R's?** All three words start with the letter *R*. Context Clues

Page 171

Review the Reading Skill about understanding lists on TE p. 170 with children.

3 **What is item 3 on the "Please Reduce!" list?** *Turn off the light when you leave a room. This will reduce the amount of electricity you use.*
Analyze Text

SOCIAL STUDIES STRAND
Economics

Point out to children that reducing electricity can save money. Most families pay for the use of electricity each month. The more electricity families use, the more they have to pay. Ask children for ways of reducing the use of electricity. (Answers will vary. Possible answers: Use the air conditioning only for sleeping and shut off the computer when it isn't in use.)

continued

Page 172

Point out that in the picture, Debby's classmates are recycling.

Locate Key Words in the Text

4 **Where are the children putting the things they are recycling?** The children are putting things in recycling bins. Have children locate the key word *recycling* in the text that matches the key word *recycling* in the question. **Analyze Pictures**

5 **What is the boy recycling?** Used bottles and cans **Analyze Pictures**

6 **What are some things you can recycle?** Possible answers: Glass bottles, newspapers, magazines, and metal cans **Apply Information**

If... children cannot name items for recycling,	**then...** display some of the items above.

SOCIAL STUDIES STRAND
Government

Explain to children that many communities have required or voluntary recycling programs. These programs set up a procedure for recycling plastic, glass, paper, and other materials. When trash is collected, the things for recycling are kept separate.

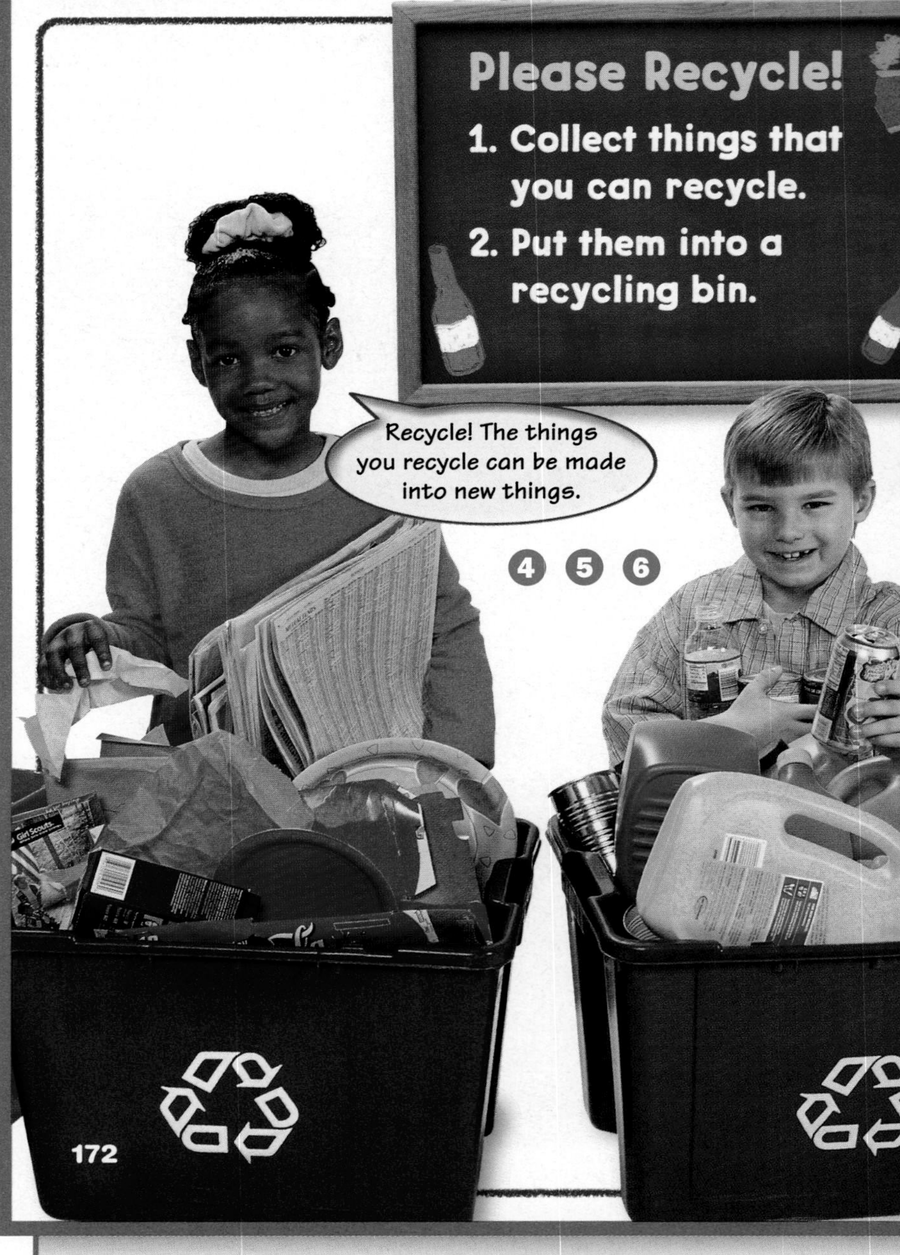

Practice and Extend

School Recycling

- Explain to children that all people in school can share a responsibility for recycling.
- Have children visit the administrative office staff to ask about recycling.
- Have children note any special bins or signs for recycling.
- Have custodial staff show children where recyclables are left to be picked up.

Here is what our class recycles. What can you recycle at school? What can you recycle at home? 7 8

What did you learn?

1. How do you show that you care about the Earth when you reduce, reuse, and recycle?
2. What is the **main idea** of this lesson?
3. **Think and Share** In your journal, write how you can reduce, reuse, and recycle each day.

173

SOCIAL STUDIES
Background

Possible Misconceptions

Tell children that recyclables are used to make many common household items, such as plastic drink containers. Explain, however, that recyclables can also be used to make many surprising things:

- glass to make part of a mixture to cover roads
- plastic to make carpets; park benches; bridges for people to cross; and soft, warm jackets

Workbook, p. 44

Caring for Our Resources
Write reduce, reuse, or recycle by each picture.
We brought our own bags!
reuse
Let's turn off the water.
reduce
We used to throw cans away!
recycle
Write an ending for this sentence.
I can reuse by
Answers will vary.

Also on Teacher Resources CD-ROM.

Page 173

7 **Why might you be considered a good citizen if you recycle?** Possible answer: It helps make sure that things made from natural resources are available for everybody. **Make Inferences**

SOCIAL STUDIES STRAND
Economics

Tell children that some states have bottle deposit laws. Explain that this means that people pay a deposit or extra money for beverage containers. They get money back from a store when they return used bottles and cans. Ask children if they think this plan gets people to recycle beverage containers more often. Have children support their answers. (Possible answers: Yes. People have an incentive to recycle—they get money back. No. People like to do all their recycling in one place.)

8 **Many cardboard juice containers have an aluminum foil lining. Do you think the containers can be recycled?** No—unless they are separated from the lining. **Apply Information**

3 Close and Assess

Start a word web on the board with "the 3 R's" in the center and three branches labeled "Recycle," "Reuse," and "Reduce." Have children take turns adding to the web with ideas from the lesson.

✓ What did you learn?

1. You help keep Earth from running out of natural resources.
2. You should save natural resources by reducing, reusing, and recycling.
3. **Think and Share** Children's journal entry should identify reasonable examples of reducing, reusing, and recycling.

Endangered Animals

Objectives

- Obtain information about a topic using maps and pictures.
- Identify ways that protecting natural resources helps animals.
- Respond to important problems with the Earth's natural resources.

1 Introduce and Motivate

Preview Explain that when all of a group of animals, such as the giant panda and the mountain gorilla, are endangered, that means they are all in danger of becoming extinct. Then explain that *extinct* means "died out" or "no longer existing." Tell them that dinosaurs are extinct. Point out that once there were many giant pandas and mountain gorillas. Now there are only a few. Let children know that these endangered animals need to be protected so they do not become extinct.

Warm Up To activate prior knowledge, tell children that most animals are used to living in a certain kind of place. When that place is destroyed or even damaged, the animal may become endangered. Ask children what would happen to fish in the ocean if poisons were dumped in its waters.

2 Teach and Discuss

Pages 174–175

Have children preview the map and pictures on pp. 174–175. Point out the animals shown in each circle.

Endangered Animals

Helping the Earth helps animals too. Some animals are endangered.

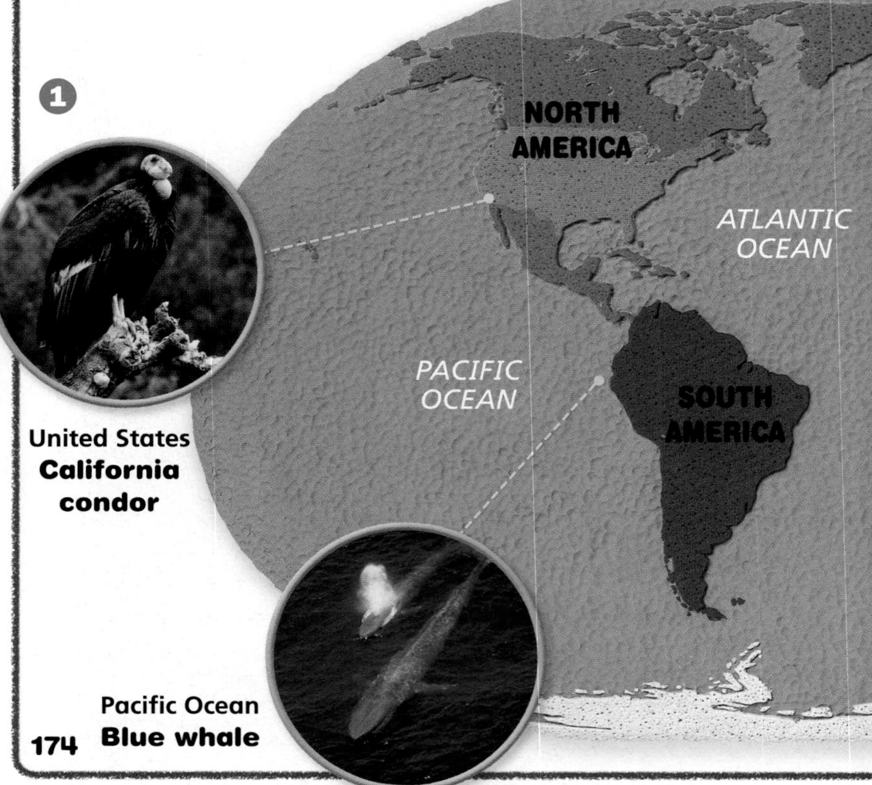

United States
California condor

Pacific Ocean
Blue whale

174

Practice and Extend

About Endangered Species

- The United States Interior Department can protect endangered plants and animals under the Endangered Species Act.
- Plants or animals listed under this act get strict protection. Many times this means protecting wildlife habitats from nearby development.
- In the United States, laws against poisoning or shooting endangered animals have helped prevent them from dying out. Some of these animals have grown in number since the laws were passed.
- Twenty nine different plants and animals, including the Miami blue butterfly and the Big Cypress fox squirrel were recently put on the Endangered Species list.

Endangered means that very few of these animals are living. Some day, some kinds of endangered animals might not be found on Earth any more. The pictures show some endangered animals.

For more information, go online to *the Atlas* at **www.sfsocialstudies.com.**

2

TIC OCEAN

OPE

ASIA

CA

INDIAN OCEAN

AUSTRALIA

ARCTICA

China
Giant panda

India
Tiger

Democratic Republic of the Congo
Mountain gorilla

175

1 What kinds of animals are in the circles? Condor or bird, whale, panda, tiger, gorilla
Analyze Pictures

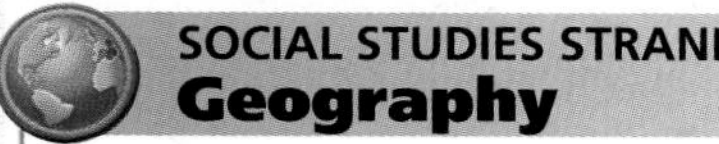

SOCIAL STUDIES STRAND
Geography

Explain that the animals shown in the circles live in the general part of the world where the lines point to on the map. Ask children what continent the giant panda lives on. (Asia)

Ongoing Assessment

If... children do not understand how to use the pictures and the map,	**then...** show them how to trace their finger along the dotted line from the giant panda to Asia.

Problem Solving

2 What might you do to let people know about endangered animals? Possible answer: Gather information about endangered animals. List options such as making a poster or sending e-mail. Ask other children to help make a poster.
Solve Problems

3 Close and Assess

Discuss with children how helping the Earth helps animals too. Explain that some animals are endangered because the place where they naturally live is getting smaller.

CURRICULUM CONNECTION
Science

Research an Endangered Animal

- Provide books and articles about the five endangered animals pictured on pp. 174–175.
- Have children draw pictures of one of the animals. Have children write a caption telling something about the animal.

WEB SITE
Technology

You may help children find out more about places on these pages by clicking on *Atlas* at **www.sfsocialstudies.com.**

Use with pages 170–175

Lesson 5 Wrap-Up

MEETING INDIVIDUAL NEEDS
Leveled Practice

Thrift Shop

Have children "set up" a thrift shop— a store where used clothes and miscellaneous items are sold to raise money for charity—on a bulletin board by "stocking" it with labeled drawings of clothing, toys, books, etc.

Easy Have children sort the items on the thrift shop bulletin board into categories, such as things to wear, to play with, and to read. **Reteach**

On-Level Have children price the items with sticky notes, and sell them to customers with play money. **Extend**

Challenge Have children record the purchases in a book and count up the "profits." Have children announce that the thrift shop "profits" will be donated to an organization that protects natural resources. **Enrich**

Hands-on Activities

CURRICULUM CONNECTION
Writing

Save Animals

Objective Demonstrate an understanding of lesson vocabulary.

Materials poster board, crayons or markers

Learning Style Visual

Individual

Time 20–25 minutes

1. Have children make a poster asking people to help save one of the endangered animals shown on pp. 174–175.

2. Have children include a title and a drawing on their poster.

3. Remind children to add the word *endangered* to their "My Word Book."

CURRICULUM CONNECTION
Literature

Blue Whales

Objective Read about blue whales and illustrate their size.

Materials picture book, paper, crayons

Learning Style Visual/Spatial

Group

Time 15–30 minutes

1. Explain to children that blue whales are the largest mammals to live on Earth.

2. Read *Big Blue Whale*, an informational text, by Nicola Davies to the class. Show the illustrations as you read.

3. In order to help children comprehend the large size of the blue whale, have children draw a picture of an elephant, a human being, or a dog next to a blue whale.

CURRICULUM CONNECTION
Drama

Mugs

Objective Use role-playing to show how to reuse things.

Learning Style Kinesthetic

Partners 

Time 15–20 minutes

Invite children to think about all the paper that would be saved if adults asked to have their coffee put in their personal durable mug instead of a paper cup.

1. Organize children in pairs, one to play the adult, the other to play the child.

2. Help teams prepare short skits of the child offering a mug to the adult drinking coffee from a paper cup. The adult takes the mug and agrees that it's a good idea.

Ending Unit 4

End with a Legend pages 176–177	Children will listen to and talk about a legend: "Johnny Appleseed."	
Unit 4 Review pages 178–181	Children will review unit vocabulary words and the unit skills of finding the main idea, reading a time line, and locating land and water on a globe and map. Children will answer questions about what they learned in the unit. Children will learn about several books about Earth.	Resources • Workbook, p. 45 ✓ • Assessment Book, pp. 13–16
Unit 4 Project page 182	Children will present a weather report. They will also be directed to a Web site where they can learn more about the weather.	Resource • Workbook, p. 46

Wrap-up

Activity

Postcard of a Place to Visit

Have children make a postcard about a beautiful location on Earth where they would like to visit. The location does not have to be named.

- On the front of the postcard, have children create a picture that includes a landform, body of water, or natural resource in the location. Have children write a caption describing the location.
- On the back of the postcard, ask children to write a short message telling about why they like the location.

Performance Assessment
You can use the activity on this page as a performance assessment.

✓ Assessment Scoring Guide

Postcards of a Place to Visit	
4	Shows geographic features clearly and with a sense of place; writes accurate caption and strongly reasoned message.
3	Shows geographic features clearly and with a sense of place; writes accurate caption but incomplete message.
2	Shows geographic features clearly and with a sense of place, but writes vague caption and incomplete message.
1	Shows geographic features clearly but does not provide a sense of place.

Johnny Appleseed

Objective

- Retell stories from selected folktales and legends.

1 Introduce and Motivate

Preview Tell children that apple trees are very common in the United States. In fact, they are grown in all 50 states. Ask children if they have ever seen an apple tree or apple orchard. Tell children that a legend is a story that has come down from the past that many people have believed. Remind children that a legend, unlike history, is not entirely true. A legend usually starts with something or someone real and then exaggerates. In this case, there really was a John Chapman and he sold apple trees. But the story grew far beyond what the real John Chapman did. Tell children that the legend of Johnny Appleseed explains how apple trees spread.

Warm Up Point to the pictures of Johnny Appleseed on pp. 176–177. Ask children what he is holding in the picture on p. 176 (apple seeds), doing in the picture at the bottom of p. 177 (scattering apple seeds), and holding in the picture on the side of p. 177 (apples). Point out that he isn't wearing shoes.

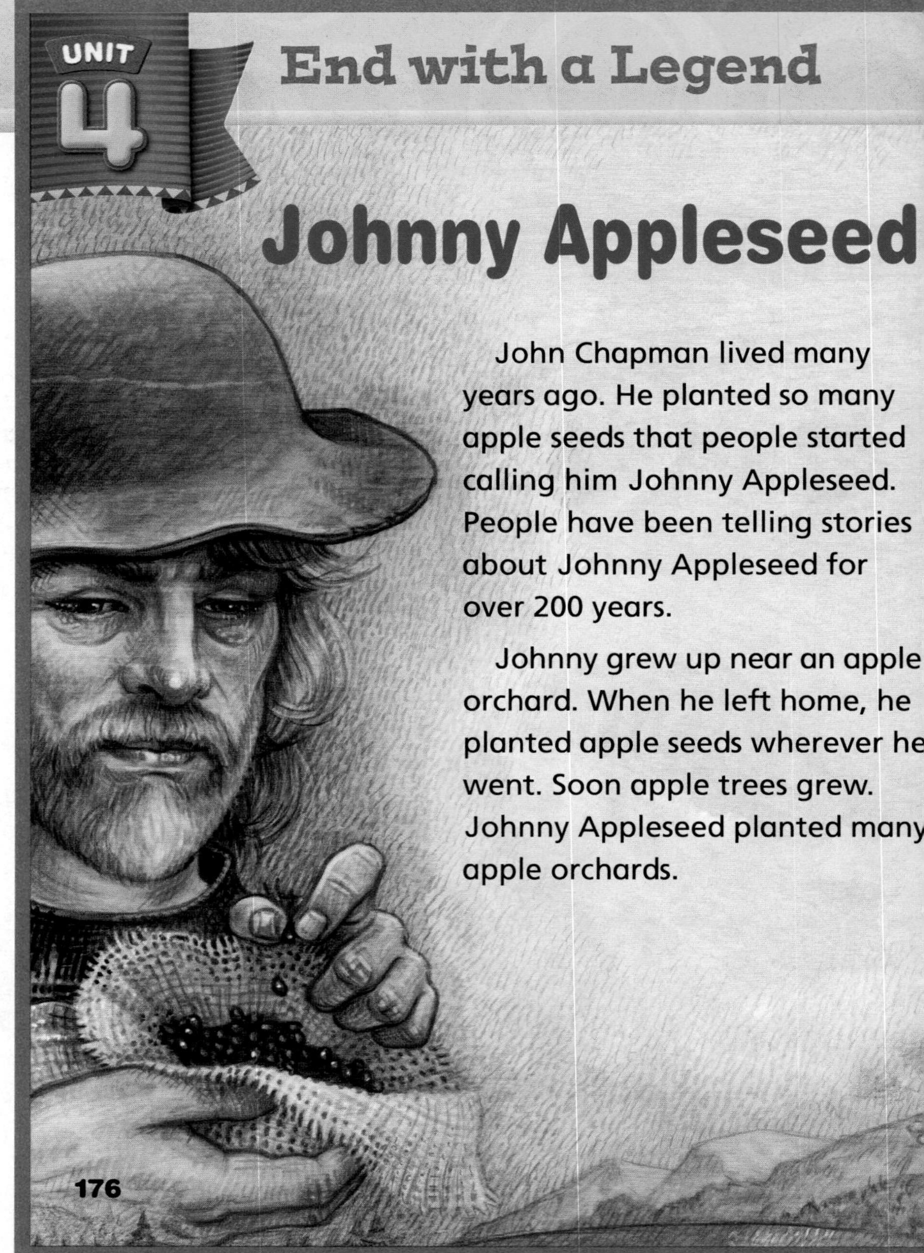

UNIT 4
End with a Legend
Johnny Appleseed
John Chapman lived many years ago. He planted so many apple seeds that people started calling him Johnny Appleseed. People have been telling stories about Johnny Appleseed for over 200 years.
Johnny grew up near an apple orchard. When he left home, he planted apple seeds wherever he went. Soon apple trees grew. Johnny Appleseed planted many apple orchards.
176

Practice and Extend

CURRICULUM CONNECTION
Reading

Books About Things That Grow

Read children other stories about things that grow, such as ***The Legend of The Bluebonnet*** by Tomie DePaola (Putnam Pub Group Juv, ISBN 0-399-20937-9, 1986), a tale about the origin of the state flower of Texas, and ***The Sunflower Garden*** by Janice May Udry (available in libraries), a story about a native American girl who started the first sunflower garden in her village. Have children retell the stories.

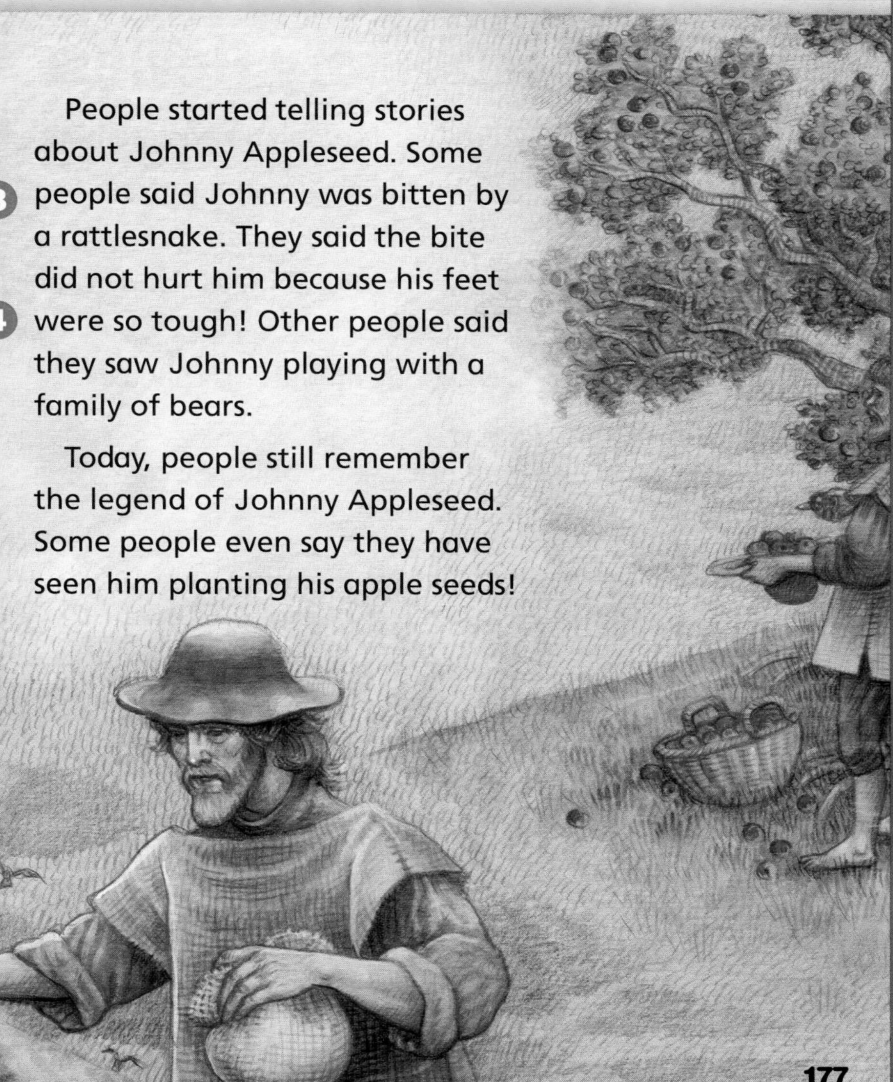

People started telling stories about Johnny Appleseed. Some
3 people said Johnny was bitten by a rattlesnake. They said the bite did not hurt him because his feet
4 were so tough! Other people said they saw Johnny playing with a family of bears.

Today, people still remember the legend of Johnny Appleseed. Some people even say they have seen him planting his apple seeds!

177

Practice and Extend

CURRICULUM CONNECTION
Drama

Jill and Johnny Appleseeds Dance

Have children retell the story of Johnny Appleseed in dance, accompanied by appropriate music, such as Aaron Copland's *Appalachian Spring*. Have several children—shoeless Jill and Johnny Appleseeds wearing wide-brim hats—dance around scattering confetti. The other children, who have been lying on the floor, slowly rise with their arms spread like branches, holding apples. The Jill and Johnny Appleseeds then dance around collecting the apples as they drop into their hat.

2 Teach and Discuss

Invite children to listen as you read the legend. Encourage them to picture in their minds the events.

1 **Why was Johnny Chapman given the name Johnny Appleseed?** Because he planted so many apple seeds **Analyze Information**

2 **What did Johnny grow up near?** An apple orchard **Apply information**

Ongoing Assessment

If... children do not understand what an orchard is,	**then...** explain that it is an area of land on which fruit trees are grown.

SOCIAL STUDIES STRAND
Economics

About 100 varieties of apples are grown for sale in the United States. Thirty-six states grow apples for sale. Most apples are handpicked in the fall.

3 **Why was the snake able to bite Johhny Appleseed's foot?** Because he walked barefoot **Analyze Pictures**

4 **Why might Johnny Appleseed be considered a good citizen?** Answers will vary but may include that by planting apple seeds he gave greatly to others. **Draw Conclusions**

3 Close and Assess

Have children retell the story of Johnny Appleseed in their own words.

Review

Resources

- Assessment Book, pp. 14–17
- Workbook, p. 45: Vocabulary Review

Vocabulary Review

1. natural resource
2. lake
3. river
4. mountain

Answers to Test Prep

1. history
2. weather

UNIT 4

Review

Vocabulary Review

natural resource
river
mountain
lake

Tell which word completes each sentence.

1. A useful thing that comes from the Earth is called a ______.
2. A body of water that has land around it is a ______.
3. A long body of water is called a ______.
4. The highest kind of land is a ______.

★ ★ ★ ★ ★ ★ ★ ★

TEST PREP Which word completes the sentence?

1. A story about people and places of the past is called ______.
   a. weather b. recycle
   c. history d. natural resource
2. Sunny is one kind of ______.
   a. mountain b. weather
   c. plain d. natural resource

178

Practice and Extend

Assessment Options

✓ Unit 4 Assessment

- Unit 4 Content Test: Use Assessment Book, pp. 14–15
- Unit 4 Skills Test: Use Assessment Book, pp. 16–17

Standardized Test Prep

- Unit 4 tests contain standardized test formats.

✓ Unit 4 Performance Assessment

- See p. 182 for information about using the Unit 4 Project as a means of performance assessment.
- A scoring guide for the Unit 4 Project is provided in the teacher's notes on p. 182.

Test Talk

- Test Talk Practice Book

Skills Review

Find the Main Idea

Read the following sentences.

Debby recycles each day. She saves empty cans. She saves paper after she writes or draws on it. She saves the newspaper her family reads each day. Debby and her family take the cans and paper to the recycling center in town.

What is the main idea?

a. empty cans **b.** going to town

c. recycling **d.** saving paper

Look for details to support your answer.

Locate Land and Water

Make a map and map key. Show land and water. Draw symbols on your map key. Label the symbols to show different types of land and water.

Practice and Extend

For more information, you can select the dictionary or encyclopedia from *Social Studies Library* at **www.sfsocialstudies.com.**

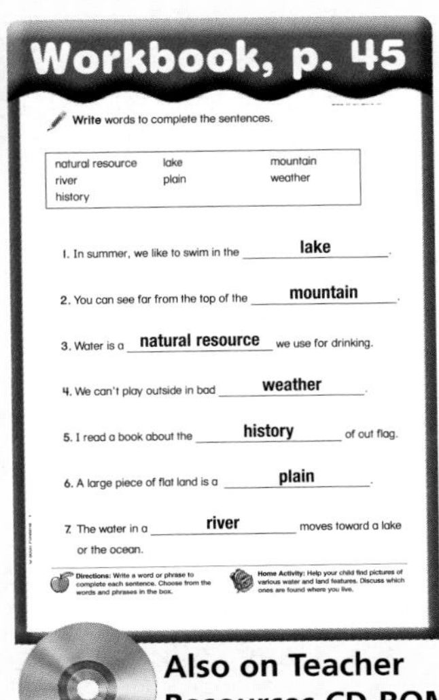

Workbook, p. 45

Write words to complete the sentences.

natural resource, lake, mountain, river, plain, weather, history

1. In summer, we like to swim in the **lake**.
2. You can see far from the top of the **mountain**.
3. Water is a **natural resource** we use for drinking.
4. We can't play outside in bad **weather**.
5. I read a book about the **history** of our flag.
6. A large piece of flat land is a **plain**.
7. The water in a **river** moves toward a lake or the ocean.

Also on Teacher Resources CD-ROM.

Skills Review

Find the Main Idea

Target Skill

- Remind children that the main idea is what the paragraph is about.
- Tell them that details support the main idea.

Use the following score guide.

✓ Assessment Scoring Guide

Find the Main Idea	
4	Selects the main idea.
3	Selects an important supporting detail that is close to the main idea.
2	Selects an important supporting idea that is far from the main idea.
1	Selects a detail that barely supports the main idea.

Locate Land and Water

Children's map key should contain symbols of land and water with labels; the map itself should contain the symbols in an arrangement that reasonably mirrors nature. Suggest that children create a map of a place in the community or beyond.

Use Information from the Text
Use the Skills Review question to model the Test Talk strategy.

Decide where you will look for the answer.
Have children make notes about details from the text that answer the question.

Use information from the text.
Have children check their notes, then ask themselves, "Do I have the right information?" Have children look back at the question and the text to make sure they have the right answer.

Review

continued

Skills Review

Read a Time Line

1. 5
2. Thursday
3. Debby read a book.

Skills on Your Own

- Children's time line should include a drawing of an activity for each day of the school week.

Use the following scoring guide.

✓ Assessment Scoring Guide

Read a Time Line	
4	Makes 5 boxes, names and correctly spells the 5 school days, shows school activities.
3	Makes 5 boxes, names and correctly spells the 5 school days, includes non-school activities.
2	Makes 5 boxes and names but incorrectly spells the 5 school days.
1	Makes 5 boxes but names non-school days.

Review

Study Skills

Read a Time Line

Debby drew a time line showing what she did each day after school. Use the time line to answer the questions.

1. How many days did Debby put in her time line?
2. Which day did Debby ride her bike?
3. What did Debby do on Tuesday?

Skills On Your Own

Draw a time line of five things that happened in school this week. Write each day of the week. Draw pictures that show what happened on each day.

180

Practice and Extend

Revisit the Unit Question

✓ Portfolio Assessment

- Have children look back at the list of ways we can care for our Earth, made on p. 135.
- Ask children to add ways to care for Earth, such as planting trees, that they learned about in this unit.
- Ask children ways they would like to help take care of Earth.
- Ask children to draw a picture of themself caring for Earth.
- Have children write a sentence describing their drawing.
- Have children add their list, drawing, and sentence to their Social Studies Portfolio.

What did you learn?

1. Describe two kinds of weather.
2. What are some natural resources that you need to live?
3. Name three ways people can care for the Earth.
4. **Write and Share** Write about natural resources in your community. Put the **main idea** in your first sentence. Write other sentences that tell how you can use the natural resources.

Read About Earth

Look for books like these in the library.

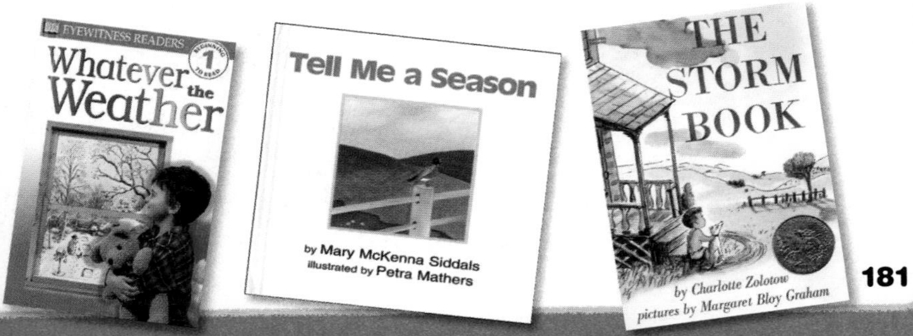

181

Practice and Extend

CURRICULUM CONNECTION
Literature

Books About Caring for Earth and About People Around the World

You may want to read and discuss with children the following books about the ways to care for Earth and about people around the world.

The Great Kapok Tree: A Tale of the Amazon Rain Forest by Lynne Cherry (Voyager Picture Book, ISBN 0-152-02614-2, 2000).

Ecoart!: Earth-Friendly Art & Craft Experiences for 3–9-year-olds by Laurie Carlson (Williamson Publishing, ISBN 0-913-58968-3, 1992).

Bob's Recycling Day by Annie Auerbach (Simon Spotlight, ISBN: 0-689-84379-8, 2001).

This Is the Way We Go to School by Edith Baer (Scholastic Trade, ISBN 0-590-43162-5, 1992).

What did you learn?

1. Answers will vary but may include sunny, rainy, and cold.
2. Answers will vary but may include land, water, air, trees, and oil.
3. Answers will vary but may include use less paper, plant trees, and reuse bags.
4. **Write and Share** Children's answers should accurately identify and describe natural resources in their community. The main idea should be in the first sentence. The supporting details should reflect ways to use natural resources.

Read About Our World

You may want to have these books available in the classroom. Read the books aloud for children; then invite them to browse through the books. Encourage them to tell why these books are good ones to include in this unit. They may also wish to review the books for classmates.

Whatever the Weather by Karen Wallace (DK, ISBN 0-789-44750-9, 1999) Looking out a window, William watches the weather change with the seasons. **Easy**

Tell Me a Season by Mary McKenna Siddals (Clarion Books, ISBN 0-395-71021-9, 1997) This book presents the change of seasons by describing and showing the changes that occur in one house and its surroundings. **On-Level**

The Storm Book by Charlotte Zolotow (HarperTrophy, ISBN 0-064-43194-0, 1989) This book depicts a fierce summer storm. **Challenge**

Unit 4 Project

Weather Report

Objective

- Identify and describe different kinds of weather.

Resource

- Workbook, p. 46

Materials

construction paper, scissors, crayons, string, cotton balls, glue, and other art supplies

Follow This Procedure

- Tell children that they are going to present a weather report to the class.
- Review with children the different kinds of weather.
- Have children work in groups of four or five. Tell them that one child in each group will be the weather reporter. The others will act out situations and show props appropriate for different kinds of weather.
- Have the children make props such as a sun for a sunny day, streamers for a windy day, an umbrella for a rainy day, or cotton for clouds. If possible, videotape the presentations.
- Direct each group to present a weather report.

✓ Assessment Scoring Guide

	Weather Report
4	Describes one type of weather with accurate vocabulary, precise details, and suitable props.
3	Describes one type of weather with mostly accurate vocabulary, some details, and suitable props.
2	Describes one type of weather with limited vocabulary, few details, and less elaborate props.
1	Describes one type of weather with limited details, incorrect vocabulary, and props.

Weather Report

Create a weather television program of your own.

1 **Choose** one kind of weather.

2 **Make** or draw something to show the weather you chose.

3 **Give** a television weather report. Show the class what you made that tells about the weather.

4 **Ask** students to tell you what they learned from your report.

Go to www.sfsocialstudies.com/activities to learn more about weather.

182

Practice and Extend

Hands-on Unit Project

✓ Performance Assessment

- The Unit Project can also be used as a performance assessment activity.
- Use the scoring guide to assess each group's work.

Children can launch the activity by clicking on *Grade 1, Unit 4* at **www.sfsocialstudies.com/activities.**

Workbook, p. 46

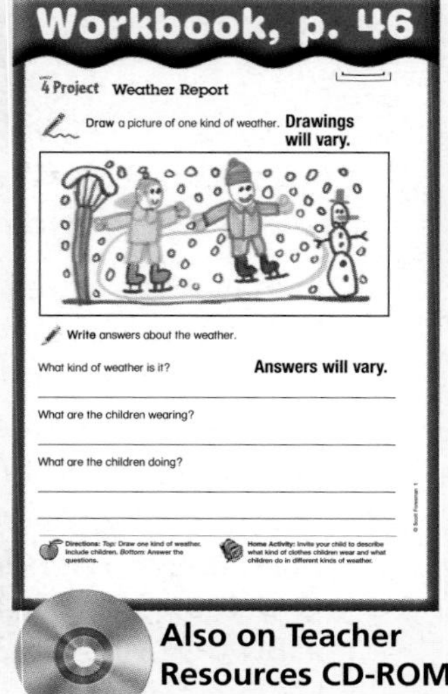

4 Project Weather Report
Draw a picture of one kind of weather. Drawings will vary.
Write answers about the weather.
What kind of weather is it? Answers will vary.
What are the children wearing?
What are the children doing?

Also on Teacher Resources CD-ROM.

★ Unit 5 ★

This Is Our Country

This Is Our Country

UNIT 5

Unit 5 Planning Guide

This Is Our Country

Begin with a Song pp. 184–185 **Vocabulary Preview** pp. 186–187

Target Skill **Reading Social Studies, Recall and Retell** pp. 188–189

Lesson Titles	Pacing	Main Ideas
Lesson 1 **Native Americans** pp. 190–191 **Chart and Graph Skills: Read a Diagram** pp. 192–193 **Smithsonian Institution: Native American Objects** pp. 194–195	3 days	• The first people to live in North America were Native Americans. • A diagram is a picture that shows the parts of something. • Native Americans made many of the things they used.
Lesson 2 **Early Travelers to America** pp. 196–199 **Map and Globe Skills: Use a History Map** pp. 200–201	2 days	• Christopher Columbus landed near North America in 1492. Later, the Pilgrims came from England to North America to be free. • A history map shows places or routes from the past.
Lesson 3 **The Colonies Become Free** pp. 202–205 **Biography: Benjamin Franklin** pp. 206–207	2 days	• The 13 colonies fought a war against England to be free. • Benjamin Franklin helped the colonies become free.
Lesson 4 **Symbols in Our Country** pp. 208–209 **Then and Now: Our Country's Flag** pp. 210–215	2 days	• Our national symbols include the Statue of Liberty, the bald eagle, and the Liberty Bell. • Our flag, a symbol of freedom, has undergone many changes.
Lesson 5 **We Celebrate Holidays** pp. 212–215 **Biography: Abraham Lincoln** pp. 216–217	2 days	• On national holidays, we honor important people or events in history. • Abraham Lincoln, our 16th President, led our country during a war between the states.
Lesson 6 **Choosing Our Country's Leaders** pp. 218–221 **Citizen Heroes: Honesty Eleanor Roosevelt** pp. 222–223	2 days	• Citizens of our country vote to choose their leaders. These leaders help make our laws. • Eleanor Roosevelt worked for equal rights for all people.

✓ **End with a Song** pp. 224–225 ✓ **Unit 5 Review** pp. 226–229 ✓ **Unit 5 Project** p. 230

✓ = Assessment Options

Vocabulary	Resources	Meeting Individual Needs
	• Workbook, pp. 49–51 • Every Student Learns Guide, pp. 82–85	• ESL Support, TE p. 192 • Leveled Practice, TE p. 195a
freedom	• Workbook, pp. 52–53 • Vocabulary Card: freedom • Every Student Learns Guide, pp. 86–89	• ESL Support, TE pp. 198 • Leveled Practice, TE p. 201a
colony	• Workbook, pp. 53–54 • Vocabulary Card: colony • Every Student Learns Guide, pp. 90–93	• ESL Support, TE p. 204 • Leveled Practice, TE p. 207a
	• Workbook, p. 55 • Every Student Learns Guide, pp. 94–97	• ESL Support, TE p. 210 • Leveled Practice, TE p. 211a
holiday **President**	• Workbook, p. 56 • Vocabulary Cards: holiday, President • Every Student Learns Guide, pp. 98–101	• ESL Support, TE p. 220 • Leveled Practice, TE p. 217a
citizen **vote** **capital**	• Workbook, p. 57 • Vocabulary Cards: citizen, vote, capital • Every Student Learns Guide, pp. 102–105	

Providing More Depth

Multimedia Library

- ***Flag* by William Crampton**
- ***The First Thanksgiving* by Jean Craighead George**
- **Songs and Music**
- **Video Field Trips**
- **Software**

Additional Resources

- Family Activities
- Vocabulary Cards
- Daily Activity Bank
- Social Studies Plus!
- Big Book Atlas
- Outline Maps
- Desk Maps

ADDITIONAL Technology

- AudioText
- TestWorks
- Teacher Resources CD-ROM
- Map Resources CD-ROM
- **www.sfsocialstudies.com**

To establish guidelines for children's safe and responsible use of the Internet, use the **Scott Foresman Internet Guide.**

Additional Internet Links

To find out more about:

- Pilgrims, visit **www.plimoth.org**

Key Internet Search Terms

- American flag
- maps

Unit 5 Objectives

Beginning of Unit 5

- **Obtain information using oral sources, such as music.** (pp. 184–185)
- **Determine the meanings of words.** (pp. 186–187)
- **Recall and retell event or ideas.** (pp. 188–189)
- **Express ideas based on oral and written sources.** (pp. 188–189)
- **Describe various customs of familiies.** (pp. 188–189)
- **Describe ways that families meet basic needs.** (pp. 188–189)

Lesson 1
Native Americans
pp. 190–191

- **Obtain information about a topic using a variety of visual sources, such as maps.**
- **Describe similarities and differences in ways families meet basic needs.**
- **Obtain information about a topic using a variety of visual sources, such as diagrams.** (pp. 192–193)
- **Identify the human characteristics of types of houses.** (pp. 192–193)
- **Obtain information about a topic using a variety of visual sources, such as pictures and artifacts.** (pp. 194–195)

Lesson 2
Early Travelers to America
pp. 196–199

- **Describe the origins of selected holidays.**
- **Cite reasons for observing holidays.**
- **Obtain information abut a topic using a variety of visual sources, such as maps.** (pp. 200–201)
- **Use cardinal directions on a map.** (pp. 200–201)

Lesson 3
The Colonies Become Free
pp. 202–205

- **Describe the origin of selected holidays and celebrations such as Independence Day.**
- **Describe the events associated with Independence Day.**
- **Explain how selected celebrations reflect an American love of freedom.**
- **Identify historic figures, such as Nathan Hale, who have exemplified good citizenship.**
- **Identify contributions of historic figures such as George Washington.**
- **Identify contributions of historical figures who have influenced the nation.** (pp. 206–207)
- **Identify historic figures who exemplified good citizenship.** (pp. 206–207)
- **Identify historical figures who have exhibited a love of inventiveness.** (pp. 206–207)

Lesson 4
Symbols in Our Country
pp. 208–209

- **Identify the motto of the United States.**
- **Explain selected national and state patriotic symbols such as the Liberty Bell and the Alamo.**
- **Identify symbols that represent the United States and what it stands for.**
- **Recognize the symbols that honor and foster patriotism in the United States by identifying the bald eagle, Washington Monument, and Statue of Liberty.**
- **Obtain information about a topic using a variety of visual sources such as pictures and graphics.**
- **Explain selected national patriotic symbol such as the United States flag.** (pp. 210–211)
- **Distinguish between past and present.** (pp. 210–211)
- **Explain how selected symbols reflect an American love of freedom.** (pp. 210–211)

Lesson 5
We Celebrate Holidays
pp. 212–215

- **Describe the origins of selected holidays and celebrations of the nation, such as Martin Luther King, Jr. Day and Veterans Day.**
- **Cite reasons for observing special days and holidays.**
- **Describe the lives of people commemorated by Presidents' Day.**
- **Identify contributions of historical figures, such as Abraham Lincoln, who have influenced the nation.** (pp. 216–217)
- **Describe the lives of people commemorated by Presidents' Day.** (pp. 216–217)

Lesson 6
Choosing Our Country's Leaders
pp. 218–221

- **Identify leaders in the state and nation.**
- **Describe the roles of public officials, including governor and president.**
- **Locate Washington, D.C., and the capital of your state on a United States map.**
- **Identify historic figures, such as Eleanor Roosevelt, who have exemplified good citizenship.** (pp. 222–223)
- **Identify characteristics of good citizenship such as a belief in justice, truth, equality, and responsibility for the common good.** (pp. 222–223)

End of Unit 5
pp. 224–230

- **Identify anthems and mottoes of the United States and individual states.** (pp. 224–225)
- **Identifies a historic event and understands that events occur in a sequence.** (p. 230)

Assessment Options

✓ Formal Assessment

- **What did you learn?** PE/TE pp. 191, 199, 205, 209, 215, 221
- **Unit Review,** PE/TE pp. 226–229
- **Unit 5 Test,** Assessment Book, pp. 17–20
- **TestWorks,** (test generator software)

✓ Informal Assessment

- **Teacher's Edition Questions,** throughout Lessons and Features
- **Close and Assess,** TE pp. 191, 199, 205, 209, 215, 221
- **Try it!** PE/TE pp. 193, 201
- **Think and Share,** PE/TE pp. 191, 199, 205, 207, 209, 215, 217, 221
- **Write and Share,** PE/TE p. 229
- **Honesty in Action,** PE/TE p. 223
- **Hands-on History,** PE/TE p. 211

Ongoing Assessment

Ongoing Assessment is found throughout the Teacher's Edition lessons using an **If...then** model.

If = students' observable behavior, **then =** reteaching and enrichment suggestions

✓ Portfolio Assessment

- **Portfolio Assessment,** TE pp. 183, 228
- **Leveled Practice,** TE pp. 195a, 201a, 207a, 211a, 217a, 223a
- **Workbook,** pp. 47–59
- **Unit Review: Skills on Your Own,** PE/TE p. 228
- **Curriculum Connection: Writing,** TE pp. 195a, 201a, 207a, 211a, 217a, 223, 223a

✓ Performance Assessment

- **Hands-on Unit Project** (Unit 5 Performance Assessment), PE/TE pp. 183, 228, 230
- **Internet Activity,** PE p. 230
- **Unit Review: Write and Share,** PE/TE p. 229
- **Scoring Guides,** TE pp. 224a, 227, 228, 230

Test Talk

Test-Taking Strategies

Understand the Question

- **Locate Key Words in the Question,** TE p. 214
- **Locate Key Words in the Text,** TE p. 199

Understand the Answer

- **Choose the Right Answer,** Test Talk Practice Book
- **Use Information from the Text,** TE p. 221
- **Use Information from Graphics,** TE pp. 193
- **Write Your Answer,** TE p. 203

For additional practice, use the Test Talk Practice Book.

Featured Strategy

Use Information from Graphics

Children will:

- Undertand the question and form a statement that begins "I need to find out..."
- Skim the graphics to find the right information to support their answer.

PE/TE p. 228, **TE** p. 193

Curriculum Connections

Integrating Your Day

The lessons, skills, and features of Unit 5 provide many opportunities to make connections between social studies and other areas of the elementary curriculum.

Social Studies

Reading

Make a Picture Glossary, TE p. 187

Reading Skill–Recall and Retell, PE/TE pp. 188–189, TE p. 190, TE p. 208

Native American Story, TE p. 195a

Reading Skill—Main Idea and Details, TE p. 196

Reading Skill—Categorize, TE p. 202, TE p. 218

One If by Land, Two If by Sea, TE p. 207a

Reading Skill—Analyze Pictures, TE p. 212

Writing

Native American Objects, TE p. 195a

Making Words from Freedom, TE p. 201a

Picturing Symbols, TE p. 211a

New Mottoes, TE p. 211a

Holiday Spirit, TE p. 217a

A Letter to Eleanor Roosevelt, TE p. 223

Stand Up and Be Counted, TE p. 223a

It's a Secret! TE p. 223a

Math

Native American Design, TE p. 194

Compare Land Areas, TE p. 200

Making Cents, TE p. 217a

Tallying the Votes, TE p. 223a

Literature

One If by Land, Two If by Sea, TE p. 207a

Books About Our Country's Past, TE p. 229

Science

Keeping Fit, TE p. 189

Cool Shades, TE p. 207

Art

My Home, TE p. 190a

Make a Diagram of the Classroom, TE p. 192

All Aboard! TE p. 196a

Sailing the Ocean Blue, TE p. 201a

Red, White, and Boom, TE p. 202a

Arranging the Stars, TE p. 211a

Holiday Spirit, TE p. 212a

A Medal for Your Service, TE p. 217a

Let's Take a Vote, TE p. 218a

Welcome to the U.S.! TE p. 224a

Music/Drama

I Love a Parade! TE, p. 185

Traditional Tunes, TE p. 195A

Thanksgiving at Plymouth, TE p. 201a

Signing the Declaration of Independence, TE p. 207a

Look for this symbol throughout the Teacher's Edition to find **Curriculum Connections.**

Professional Development

Improving History Instruction in the Social Studies Classroom

by Rita Geiger
Norman Oklahoma Public Schools

The two major concepts of social studies are *space* and *time*. Children develop these concepts slowly and systematically during the elementary school years. *Space* includes the immediate environment (such as home, school, neighborhood, and city), which children learn about through direct experience. The concept of space then extends to include the child's remote environment (that of the state, nation, and world), areas which are learned about largely through vicarious experiences. *Time* consists of the past, present, and future. Elementary children relate primarily to the present, and the effective elementary social studies teacher should focus mainly on present experiences in the immediate environment. However, the teacher can help children begin to understand the past, or "history," through a variety of strategies and activities.

Here is how you can help children begin to understand the past as you teach Scott Foresman Social Studies.

Use the two Read Together Biographies (pp. 206–207 and pp. 216–217) to explore the lives of historical figures such as Benjamin Franklin and Abraham Lincoln.

To help children begin to understand spatial concepts, use the history map on pp. 200–201. To help them understand chronological relationships, use the time line in Then and Now: Our Country's Flag (pp. 210–211).

ESL Support

by Jim Cummins, Ph. D.
University of Toronto

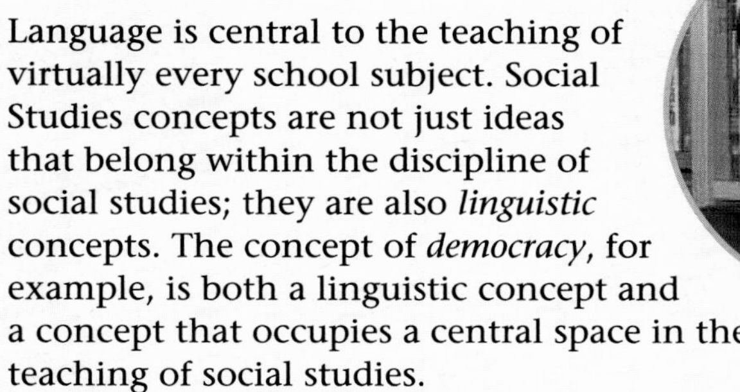

Language is central to the teaching of virtually every school subject. Social Studies concepts are not just ideas that belong within the discipline of social studies; they are also *linguistic* concepts. The concept of *democracy*, for example, is both a linguistic concept and a concept that occupies a central space in the teaching of social studies.

One important strategy in making the language of social studies comprehensible to ESL students involves activating and building their background knowledge. The more background knowledge we have, the more of the text we can understand.

Another way to support, or scaffold, students' learning is by modifying the input itself. Here are just a few ways to modify the presentation of academic content so students can more effectively access the meaning:

- Using visuals (pictures, photographs, real objects);
- Acting out through gestures and pantomime;
- Clarifying the language (paraphrasing ideas and explaining new concepts and words);
- Making personal and cultural connections.

The following examples in the Teacher's Edition will help you to enable ESL students to access content:

Focus on Meaning, TE p. 188

Questioning, TE p. 192

Telling About Cultural Traditions, TE p. 198

Understanding Bravery, TE p. 204

Interviewing and Retelling, TE p. 210

Telling About Holidays, TE p. 214

Interpret Maps, TE p. 220

Read Aloud

Yankee Doodle

words by Dr. Richard Shuckburgh

Traditional Song

Yankee Doodle went to town,
A-riding on a pony,
He stuck a feather in his cap
And called it macaroni!

Yankee Doodle, keep it up,
Yankee Doodle dandy;
Mind the music and the step,
And with the girls be handy!

Build Background

- Tell children that the words to "Yankee Doodle" were set to the tune of an English folk song. Ask them if they know any traditional songs with new words.

Read Alouds and Primary Sources

Read Alouds and Primary Sources contains additional selections to be used with Unit 5.

Bibliography

Cheyenne Again, by Eve Bunting and Irving Toddy (illustrator), (Clarion Books, ISBN 0-395-70364-6, 1995) **Easy**

First Thanksgiving Feast, The, by Joan Anderson and George Ancona (photographer), (Clarion Books, ISBN 0-395-51886-5, 1989) **Easy**

Hooray for the Fourth of July, by Wendy Watson (Houghton Mifflin, ISBN 0-618-04036-6, 2000) **Easy**

I Have Heard of a Land, by Joyce Carol Thomas and Floyd Cooper (illustrator), (Harpercollins, ISBN 0-064-43617-9, 2000) **Easy** ***ALA Notable, Coretta Scott King Honor Book, Notable Social Studies Book***

T Is for Texas, by Anne Bustard (Voyageur, ISBN 0-896-58113-6, 1989) **Easy**

To Be a Drum, by Evelyn Coleman and Aminah Brenda Lynn Robinson (illustrator), (Albert Whitman, ISBN 0-807-58007-4, 2000) **Easy**

Boston Coffee Party, The, by Doreen Rappaport and Emily Arnold McCully (illustrator), (HarperTrophy, ISBN 0-064-44141-5, 1990) **On-Level**

Sam the Minuteman, by Nathaniel Benchley and Arnold Lobel (illustrator), (Harper Trophy, ISBN 0-064-44107-5, 1987) **On-Level**

Star-Spangled Banner, The, by Francis Scott Key and Peter Spier (illustrator), (Yearling Books, ISBN 0-440-40697-8, 1992) **On-Level**

Flag We Love, The, by Pam Munoz Ryan and Ralph Masiello (illustrator), (Charlesbridge Publishing, ISBN 0-881-06844-6, 2000) **Challenge**

Story of the Statue of Liberty, The, by Betsy C. Maestro and Giulio Maestro (illustrator), (Mulberry Books, ISBN 0-688-08746-9, 1989) **Challenge**

History Workshop: Reconstructing the Past with Elementary Students, by Karen L. Jorgensen (Heinemann, ISBN 0-4350-8900-5, 1993) **Teacher Reference**

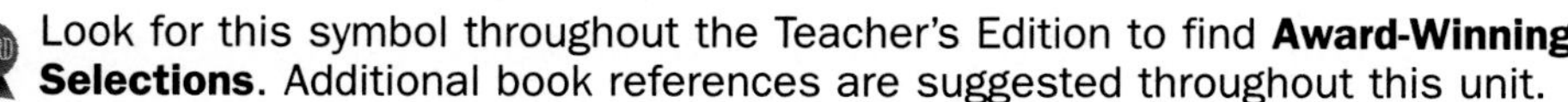

Look for this symbol throughout the Teacher's Edition to find **Award-Winning Selections**. Additional book references are suggested throughout this unit.

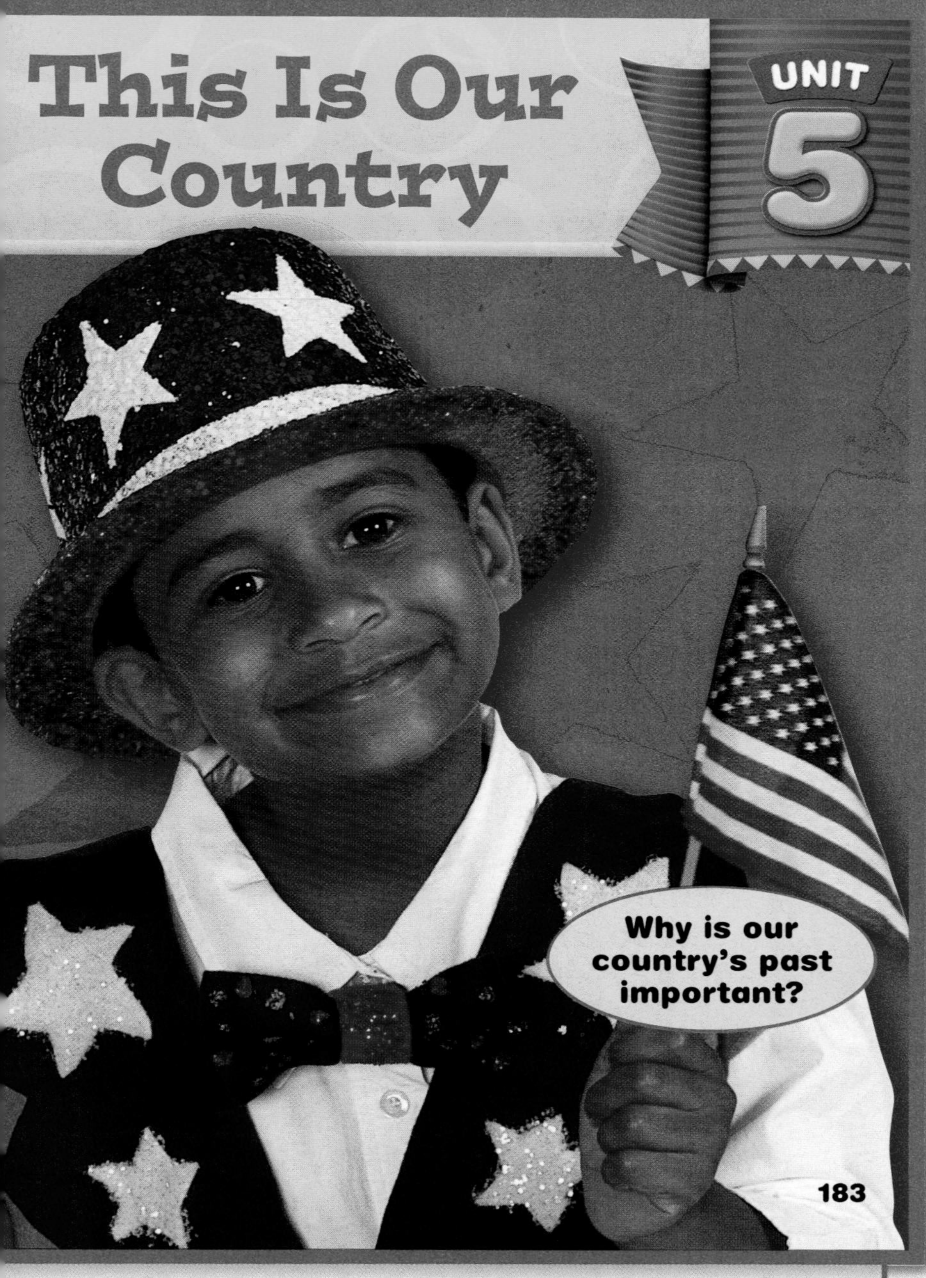

This Is Our Country
UNIT 5
Why is our country's past important?
183

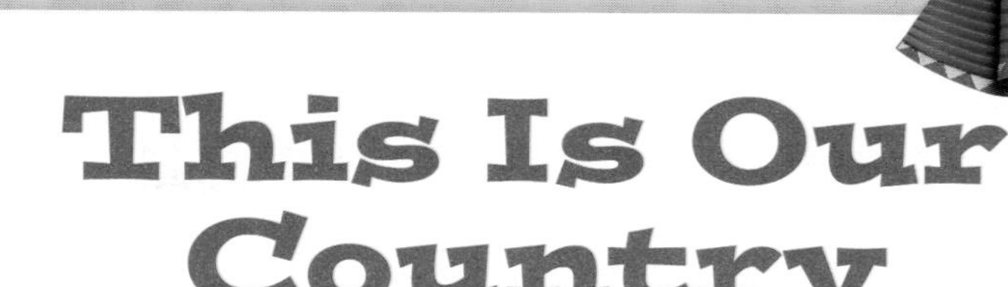

This Is Our Country

Unit Overview

In this unit children learn about people and events that have helped shape the history of the United States. They explore the origins of some of our national holidays and symbols, and they learn about the roles played by our leaders.

Introduce James

Read the unit title and then introduce the featured child for this unit as a first-grader named James. Talk about what holiday James might be celebrating. Explain that many holidays help us remember people and events from our country's past.

Unit Question

- Ask children the question on this page.
- Initiate a discussion of why our country's past is important.
- To activate prior knowledge, make a list on the board of children's ideas about why our country's past is important.

✓ **Portfolio Assessment** Keep a copy of this list for the Portfolio Assessment at the end of the unit on page 228.

Practice and Extend

Hands-on Unit Project

✓ **Unit 5 Performance Assessment**

- The Unit 5 Project, *History on Parade,* found on p. 230, is an ongoing performance assessment project to enrich children's learning throughout the unit.
- This project, which has children put on a history parade, may be started now or at any time during this unit of study.
- A performance assessment scoring guide is located on p. 230.

Holidays Are Special Days

Objective

- Obtain information using oral sources, such as music.

Resources

- *Songs and Music* CD "Holidays Are Special Days"
- Poster 9
- Social Studies Plus!

Introduce the Song

Preview Tell children that they will be singing a song about celebrating holidays. Focus attention on how the people in the picture are celebrating.

Warm Up To activate prior knowledge, ask children how their families celebrate special days, such as birthdays and anniversaries.

Sing the Song

- Have children sing the song "Holidays Are Special Days."
- Ask children to name things mentioned in the song that families may do when they get together on special days. (share food, have parades, have a celebration).
- Invite children to name any great people of our nation that they may know about.

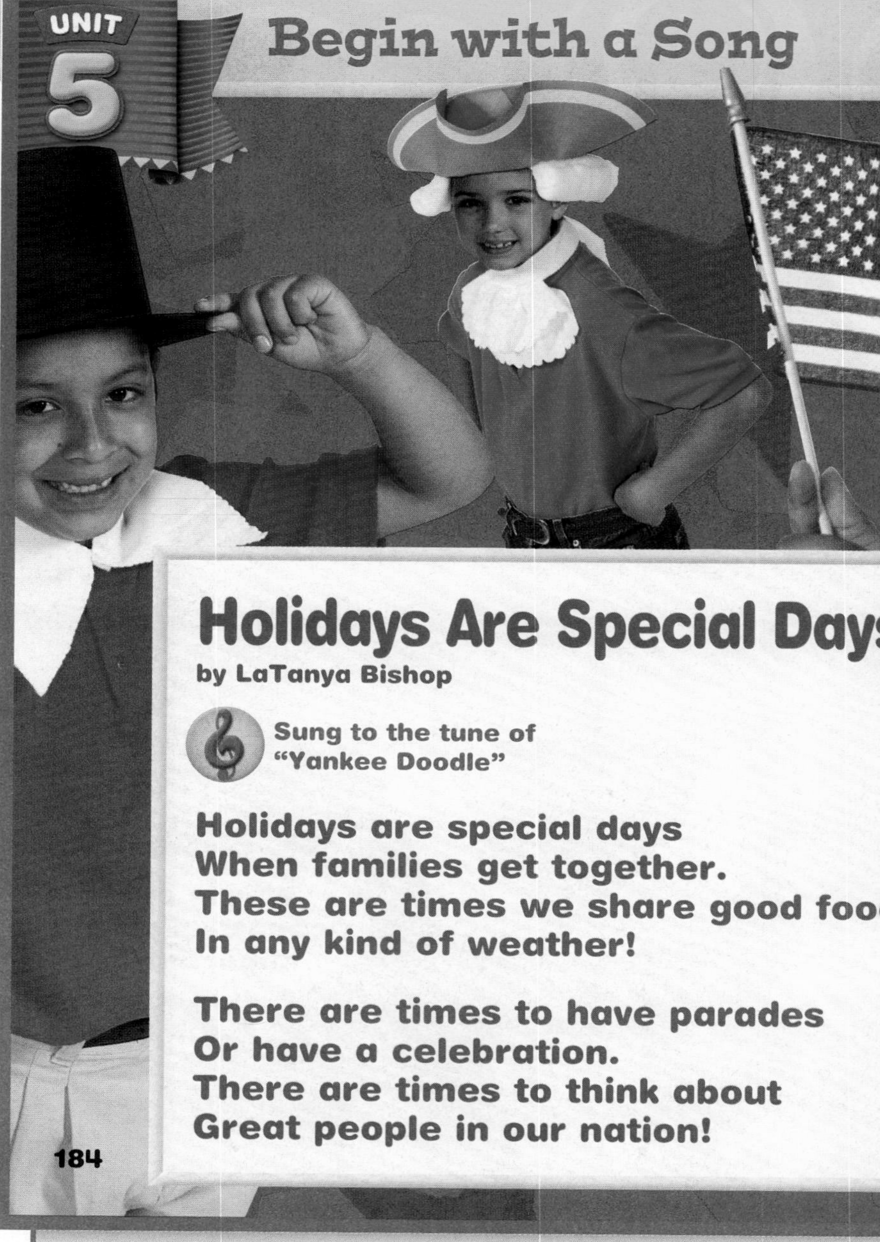

UNIT 5
Begin with a Song
Holidays Are Special Days
by LaTanya Bishop
Sung to the tune of "Yankee Doodle"
Holidays are special days
When families get together.
These are times we share good food
In any kind of weather!
There are times to have parades
Or have a celebration.
There are times to think about
Great people in our nation!
184

Practice and Extend

SOCIAL STUDIES Background

Possible Misconceptions

Children may not be aware that on some holidays we celebrate people and events in our nation's past. Tell children that on *their* birthdays, we celebrate the days on which they were born. Explain that on some holidays, we celebrate other people's birthdays. We also celebrate our *country's* birthday on July 4th.

AUDIO CD Technology

Play the *Songs and Music* CD to listen to "Holidays Are Special Days."

Talk About the Picture

Direct children's attention to the picture on these two pages. Ask children to name some things in the picture.

Point out to children that James is dressed like Uncle Sam. Uncle Sam stands for the United States government or people. Explain that most of the other children are dressed like people in our country's past.

1 **What is James holding?** The flag of the United States **Analyze Pictures**

Have children look at the girl and boy behind James on p. 185.

2 **Who are the girl and boy dressed like?** The girl is dressed like the Statue of Liberty. The boy is dressed like Abraham Lincoln.
Interpret National Symbols/Analyze Pictures

Have children look at the boy on the left on p. 184. Explain that he is dressed like some of the Pilgrims who came to North America long ago.

3 **What holiday do we celebrate that comes from the Pilgrims?** Thanksgiving
Analyze Pictures

Have children look at the boy on the right on p. 184. Explain that he is dressed like some of the people who fought for freedom against the English.

4 **What holiday do we celebrate that comes from the war against the English?**
Independence Day **Analyze Pictures**

CURRICULUM CONNECTION
Music/Drama

I Love a Parade!

- Tell children that they are going to be in a class parade. Assign each child a partner, and have partners line up.
- Distribute any rhythm instruments that may be available.
- Have children play and sing "Holidays Are Special Days" as they parade around the classroom.
- If children already know the words to "Yankee Doodle," they can sign this song, too, as they march around the room. Suggest that children without instruments pantomime the actions of the song as they march.

Vocabulary Preview

Objective

- Determine the meanings of words.

Resources

- Workbook, p. 47
- Vocabulary Cards
- Poster 10

Introduce the Vocabulary

Read aloud and point to each vocabulary word and the photograph illustrating it. Have volunteers give the meaning of the words. Then have children find several examples of vocabulary words in the illustration. Write these examples on the board.

Vocabulary Word	Illustrated Examples
vote	mayoral candidate, vote signs on car, man with sign for mayor
President	presidential truck
citizen	citizen of year, citizen with placard
capital	Washington D.C. sign on truck, state capital travel poster on building
holiday	4th of July banner, holiday sign in store window
freedom	symbols of freedom marchers, American flag on pole
colony	13 colonies exhibit on truck

SOCIAL STUDIES STRAND Citizenship

Listed below are some basic principles of history for young children. Direct your discussion of the illustration toward the development of these concepts.

- America in the past
- historic figures who shaped the nation
- historic figures who exemplify good citizenship
- origin of holidays that celebrate our nation and its leaders
- love of freedom
- patriotic symbolism of the flag
- voting
- role of public leaders
- places where laws are made

Vocabulary Preview

freedom

colony

holiday

President

186

Practice and Extend

SOCIAL STUDIES STRAND Citizenship

Let's Vote

- Explain to children that in the United States, people choose Presidents by voting for them.
- Discuss Presidents Washington and Lincoln with children.
- Distribute blank ballots, and have children vote for which President is their favorite.
- Collect the ballots, and have children help you count the votes. Declare the winner.

WEB SITE Technology

You can look up vocabulary words online. Click on *Social Studies Library* and select the dictionary at **www.sfsocialstudies.com.**

citizen

vote

capital

Talk About the Illustration

Allow children time to study the illustration. Encourage them to describe the parade from its front to its back.

1 **What symbols of freedom are shown in the parade?** The Liberty Bell, the Statue of Liberty, the American flag, the bald eagle, and Uncle Sam **Analyze Pictures**

2 **What holiday is being celebrated?** Fourth of July **Analyze Pictures**

Look Ahead

Tell children that they will learn more about each of these words as they study Unit 5.

You may want to revisit the picture with children to review the concepts and vocabulary in the unit.

3 **What Presidents are shown in the truck?** Abraham Lincoln and George Washington **Analyze Pictures**

CURRICULUM CONNECTION Reading

Make a Picture Glossary

Children can add the vocabulary for Unit 5 to "My Word Book." Words may be entered at the beginning of the unit or added as they are introduced in the specific lessons.

Workbook, p. 47

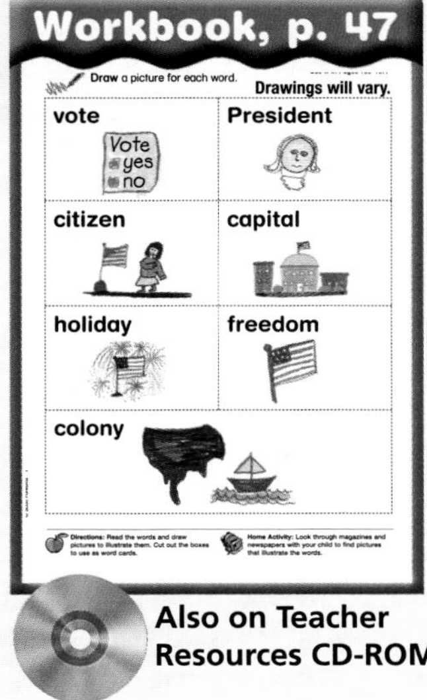
Draw a picture for each word. **Drawings will vary.**

vote	President
citizen	capital
holiday	freedom
colony	

Also on Teacher Resources CD-ROM.

James's Story

Recall and Retell

Objectives

- Recall and retell events or ideas.
- Express ideas based on oral and written sources.
- Describe various customs of families.
- Describe ways that families meet basic needs.

Resource

- Workbook, p. 48

About the Unit Target Skill

- The target reading skill for this unit is Recall and Retell. Children are introduced to the unit target skill here and are given an opportunity to practice it.

1 Introduce and Motivate

Preview Assess whether children understand the concepts of recall and retell by asking them first to recall important things that happen in a familiar story and then to retell the story to a classmate. If necessary, explain that *recall* means "remember," and that *retell* means "tell again."

Warm Up To activate prior knowledge, review with children the legend of Johnny Appleseed (pp. 176–177). Then help children make a list of important events from the story. Demonstrate how to use the list to retell the story.

James's Story

Recall and Retell

Hi! My name is James. I wrote a story about a Cheyenne Indian named Little Rabbit. Read my story to find out about Little Rabbit.

Little Rabbit

Long ago, there lived a boy named Little Rabbit. He liked to run races with his friends. He was very fast. He would win many of the races.

Little Rabbit was a Cheyenne. He lived on the Great Plains. Little Rabbit lived in a tepee with his family. When they moved from place to place, they folded the tepee up and carried it with them!

Little Rabbit's favorite time was when he was with his father. His father taught him many things. He taught Little Rabbit how to hunt for food with a bow and arrow. He also taught Little Rabbit how to ride a horse.

188

Practice and Extend

ACCESS CONTENT
ESL Support

Focus on Meaning Help children access the content of "Little Rabbit" by showing pictures of a tepee and a bow and arrow. Tell children that many Native Americans on the Great Plains lived in tepees.

Beginning Point to the picture of a tepee. Say *tepee*, and have children repeat after you. Repeat for the bow and arrow, making sure children distinguish the bow from the arrow.

Intermediate Ask children to identify the items pictured. Ask what a tepee is used for. (a home) Ask a volunteer to pantomome folding up a tepee and carrying it away. Ask another volunteer to pantomime using a bow and arrow.

Advanced Ask children to dictate captions for the two pictures. Encourage them to tell how each item is used.

You **recall** when you think about something you have read or heard. You **retell** when you put it into your own words. Think about the story James wrote. Tell the story in your own words.

A Cheyenne family

A Native American doll

Draw three pictures that show something you **recall** about Little Rabbit. Use your pictures to **retell** the story in your own words.

189

2 Teach and Discuss

Read pp. 188–189. Then tell children that they should first recall the important things in James's story. Read "Little Rabbit" again, asking children to follow along or to listen for important ideas. Then help them make a list of those ideas.

Little Rabbit was a fast runner.

He was a Cheyenne.

He lived with his family in a tepee.

His father taught him to hunt and to ride a horse.

Review the list with children. Have them use it to retell the story. Then cover the list, and ask a volunteer to retell the story.

Ongoing Assessment

If... children have difficulty recalling important ideas,	**then...** suggest that they draw or write to make notes that will help them to remember. Tell children that as they read in social studies, they should stop after each page or two and try to recall and retell the important ideas.

3 Close and Assess

Try it!

If you wish, remind children of the list of important events that you made after reading "Little Rabbit" so that they can refer to it as they draw their pictures. Have children work with partners to retell the story.

CURRICULUM CONNECTION Science

Keeping Fit

- Point out to children that running is good exercise. Tell them that people can keep fit and healthy by eating the right foods and by getting exercise.
- Have children find pictures of different ways people exercise to keep fit. Display the pictures on a bulletin board.
- Ask children what ways they exercise. Make a list on the board.

Workbook, p. 48

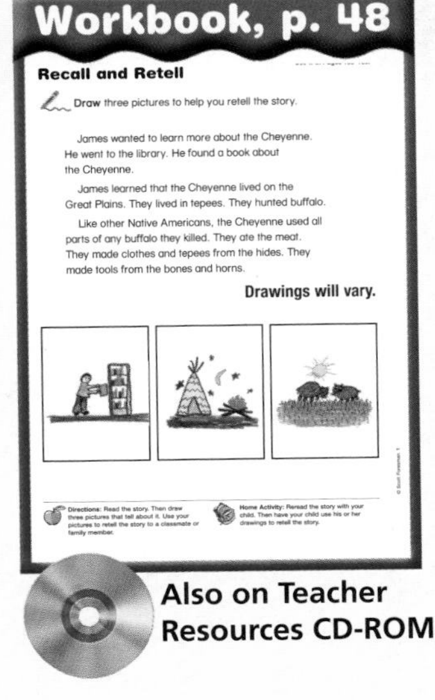

Recall and Retell

Draw three pictures to help you retell the story.

James wanted to learn more about the Cheyenne. He went to the library. He found a book about the Cheyenne.

James learned that the Cheyenne lived on the Great Plains. They lived in tepees. They hunted buffalo.

Like other Native Americans, the Cheyenne used all parts of any buffalo they killed. They ate the meat. They made clothes and tepees from the hides. They made tools from the bones and horns.

Drawings will vary.

Directions: Read the story. Then draw three pictures that tell about it. Use your pictures to retell the story to a classmate or family member.

Home Activity: Reread the story with your child. Then have your child use his or her drawings to retell the story.

Also on Teacher Resources CD-ROM.

Workbook Support

Use the following Workbook pages to support content and skills development as you teach Unit 5. You can also view and print Workbook pages from the Teacher Resources CD-ROM.

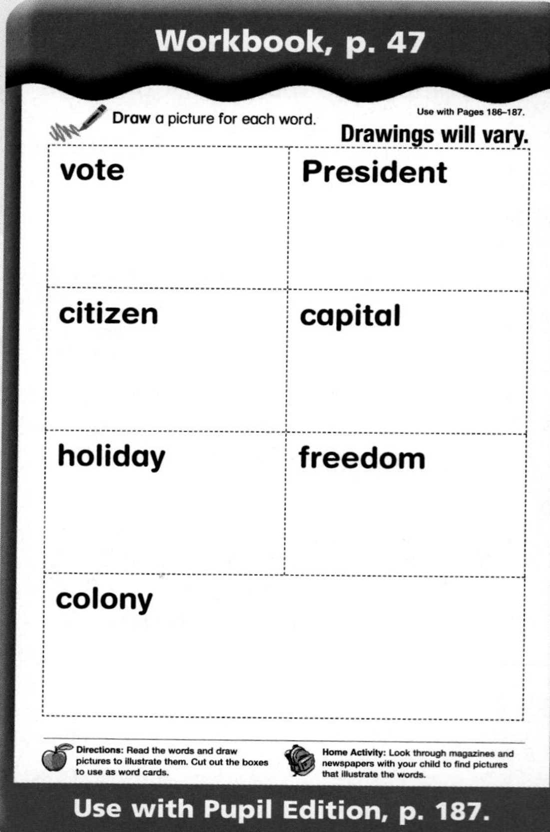

Workbook, p. 47

Use with Pages 186–187.

Draw a picture for each word.

Drawings will vary.

vote	President
citizen	capital
holiday	freedom
colony	

Directions: Read the words and draw pictures to illustrate them. Cut out the boxes to use as word cards.

Home Activity: Look through magazines and newspapers with your child to find pictures that illustrate the words.

Use with Pupil Edition, p. 187.

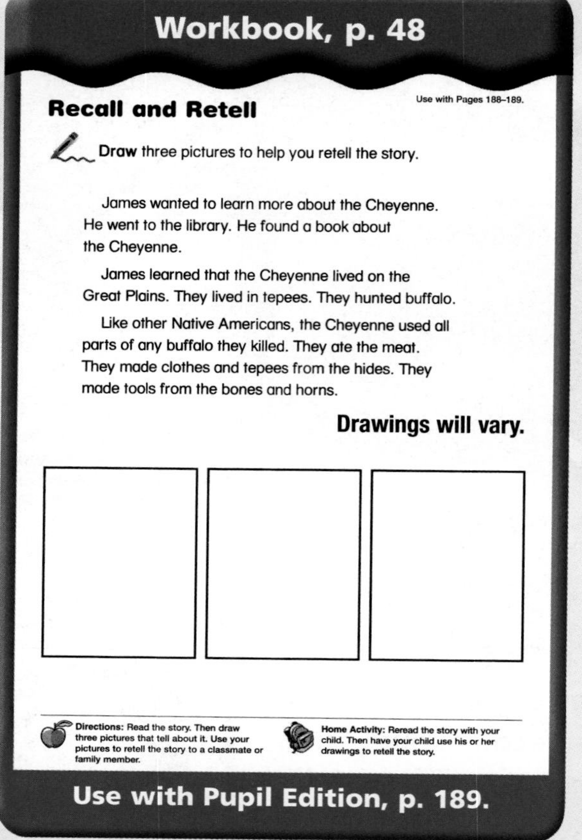

Workbook, p. 48

Use with Pages 188–189.

Recall and Retell

Draw three pictures to help you retell the story.

James wanted to learn more about the Cheyenne. He went to the library. He found a book about the Cheyenne.

James learned that the Cheyenne lived on the Great Plains. They lived in tepees. They hunted buffalo.

Like other Native Americans, the Cheyenne used all parts of any buffalo they killed. They ate the meat. They made clothes and tepees from the hides. They made tools from the bones and horns.

Drawings will vary.

Directions: Read the story. Then draw three pictures that tell about it. Use your pictures to retell the story to a classmate or family member.

Home Activity: Reread the story with your child. Then have your child use his or her drawings to retell the story.

Use with Pupil Edition, p. 189.

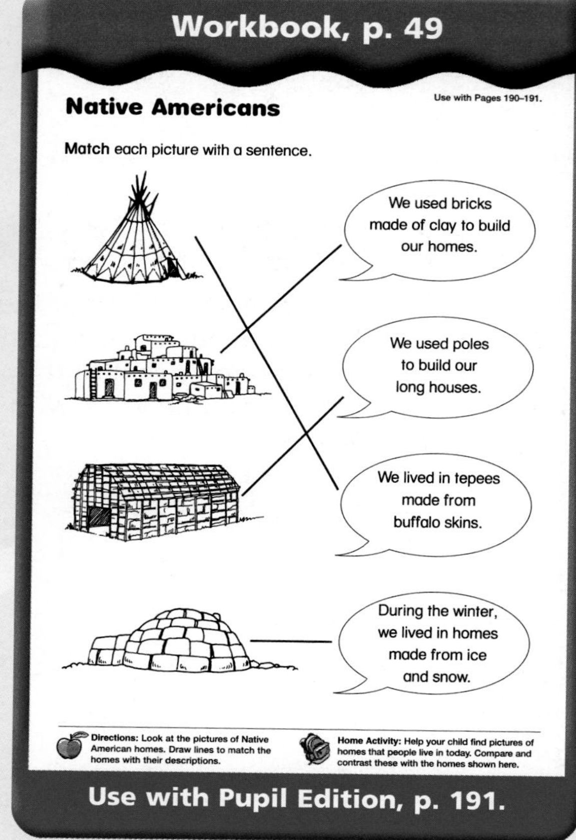

Workbook, p. 49

Use with Pages 190–191.

Native Americans

Match each picture with a sentence.

We used bricks made of clay to build our homes.

We used poles to build our long houses.

We lived in tepees made from buffalo skins.

During the winter, we lived in homes made from ice and snow.

Directions: Look at the pictures of Native American homes. Draw lines to match the homes with their descriptions.

Home Activity: Help your child find pictures of homes that people live in today. Compare and contrast these with the homes shown here.

Use with Pupil Edition, p. 191.

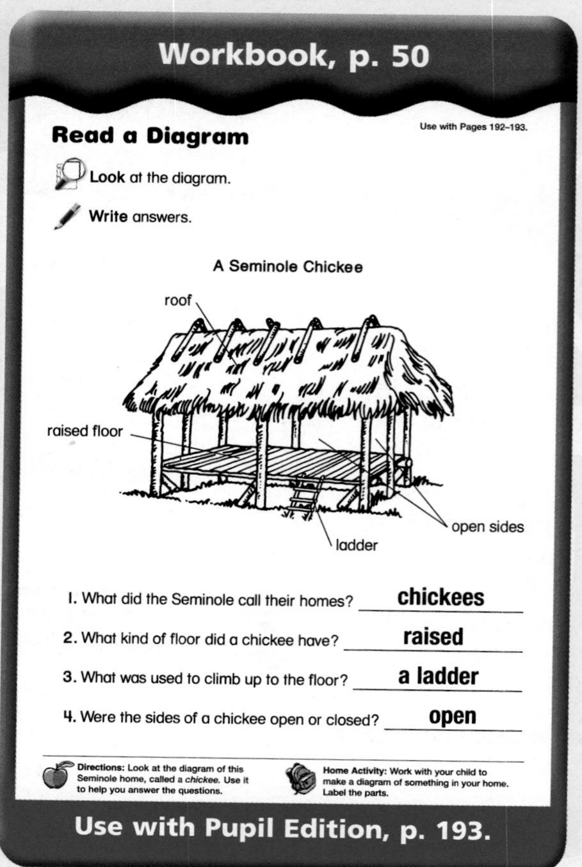

Workbook, p. 50

Use with Pages 192–193.

Read a Diagram

Look at the diagram.

Write answers.

A Seminole Chickee

roof

raised floor

open sides

ladder

1. What did the Seminole call their homes? **chickees**
2. What kind of floor did a chickee have? **raised**
3. What was used to climb up to the floor? **a ladder**
4. Were the sides of a chickee open or closed? **open**

Directions: Look at the diagram of this Seminole home, called a *chickee.* Use it to help you answer the questions.

Home Activity: Work with your child to make a diagram of something in your home. Label the parts.

Use with Pupil Edition, p. 193.

Workbook Support

Workbook, p. 51

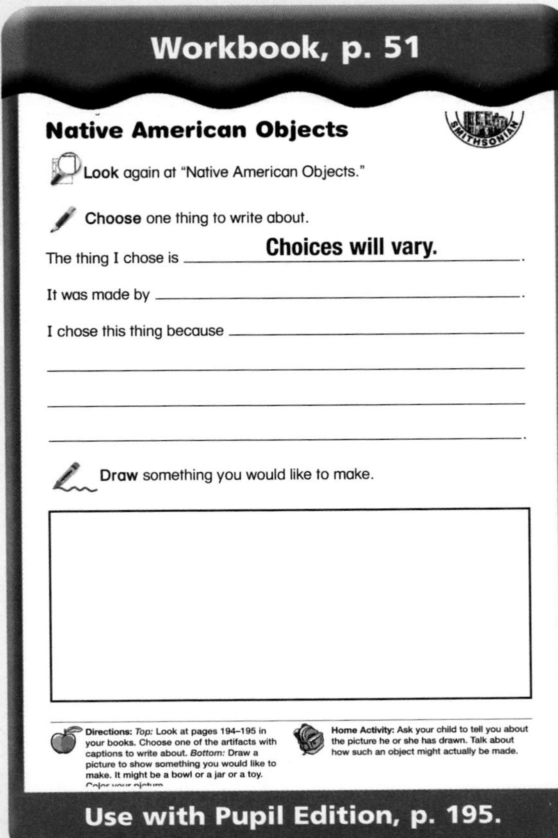

Native American Objects

Look again at "Native American Objects."

Choose one thing to write about.

The thing I chose is **Choices will vary.**

It was made by ________.

I chose this thing because ________

Draw something you would like to make.

Directions: *Top:* Look at pages 194–195 in your books. Choose one of the artifacts with captions to write about. *Bottom:* Draw a picture to show something you would like to make. It might be a bowl or a jar or a toy. Color your picture.

Home Activity: Ask your child to tell you about the picture he or she has drawn. Talk about how such an object might actually be made.

Use with Pupil Edition, p. 195.

Workbook, p. 52

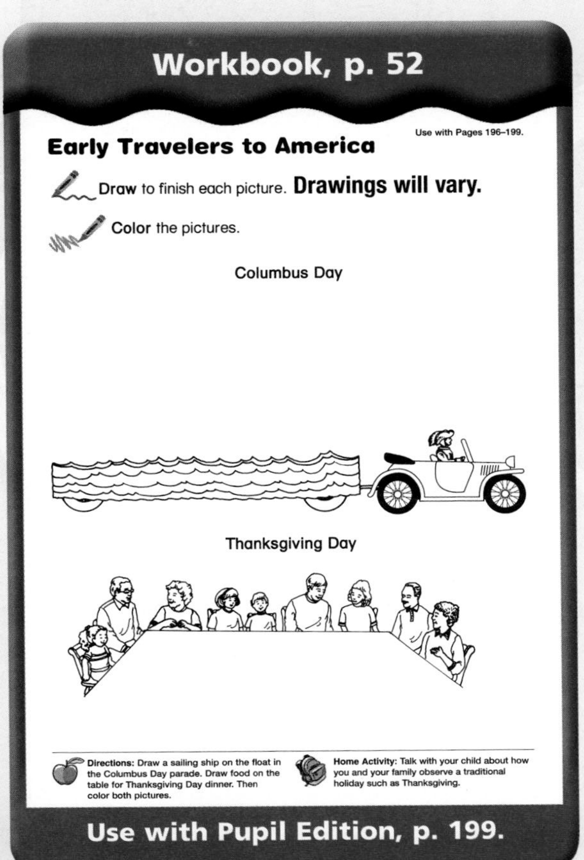

Early Travelers to America

Use with Pages 196–199.

Draw to finish each picture. **Drawings will vary.**

Color the pictures.

Columbus Day

Thanksgiving Day

Directions: Draw a sailing ship on the float in the Columbus Day parade. Draw food on the table for Thanksgiving Day dinner. Then color both pictures.

Home Activity: Talk with your child about how you and your family observe a traditional holiday such as Thanksgiving.

Use with Pupil Edition, p. 199.

Workbook, p. 53

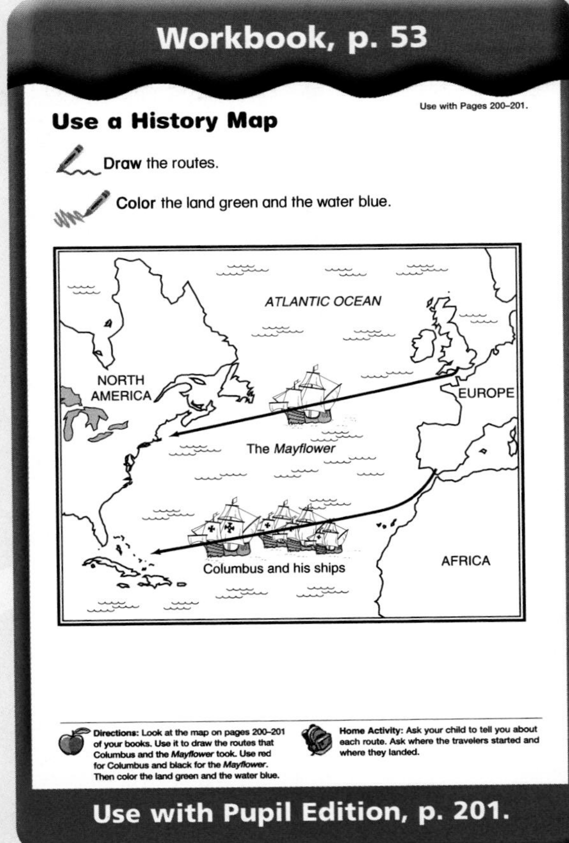

Use a History Map

Use with Pages 200–201.

Draw the routes.

Color the land green and the water blue.

Directions: Look at the map on pages 200–201 of your books. Use it to draw the routes that Columbus and the *Mayflower* took. Use red for Columbus and black for the *Mayflower*. Then color the land green and the water blue.

Home Activity: Ask your child to tell you about each route. Ask where the travelers started and where they landed.

Use with Pupil Edition, p. 201.

Workbook, p. 54

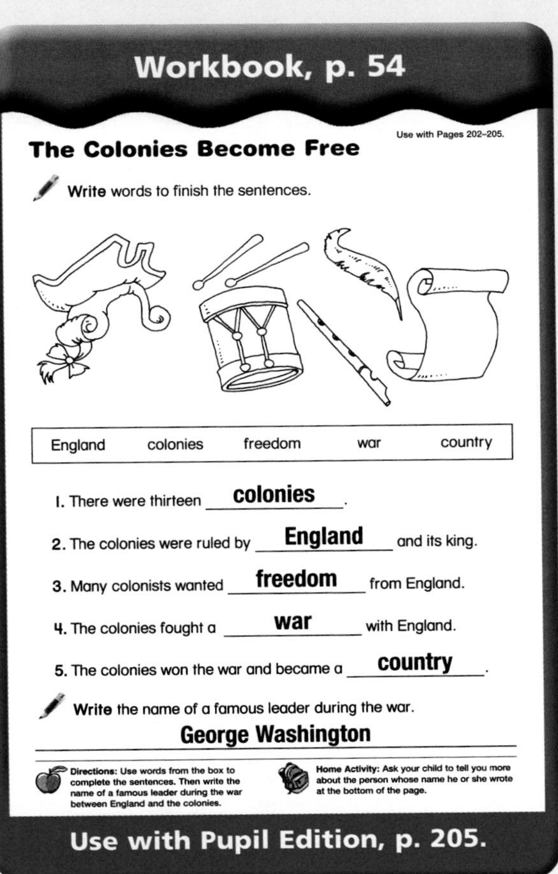

The Colonies Become Free

Use with Pages 202–205.

Write words to finish the sentences.

England	colonies	freedom	war	country

1. There were thirteen **colonies**.
2. The colonies were ruled by **England** and its king.
3. Many colonists wanted **freedom** from England.
4. The colonies fought a **war** with England.
5. The colonies won the war and became a **country**.

Write the name of a famous leader during the war.

George Washington

Directions: Use words from the box to complete the sentences. Then write the name of a famous leader during the war between England and the colonies.

Home Activity: Ask your child to tell you more about the person whose name he or she wrote at the bottom of the page.

Use with Pupil Edition, p. 205.

Workbook Support

Use the following Workbook pages to support content and skills development as you teach Unit 5. You can also view and print Workbook pages from the Teacher Resources CD-ROM.

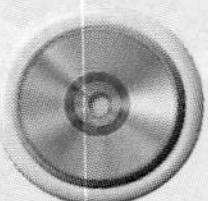

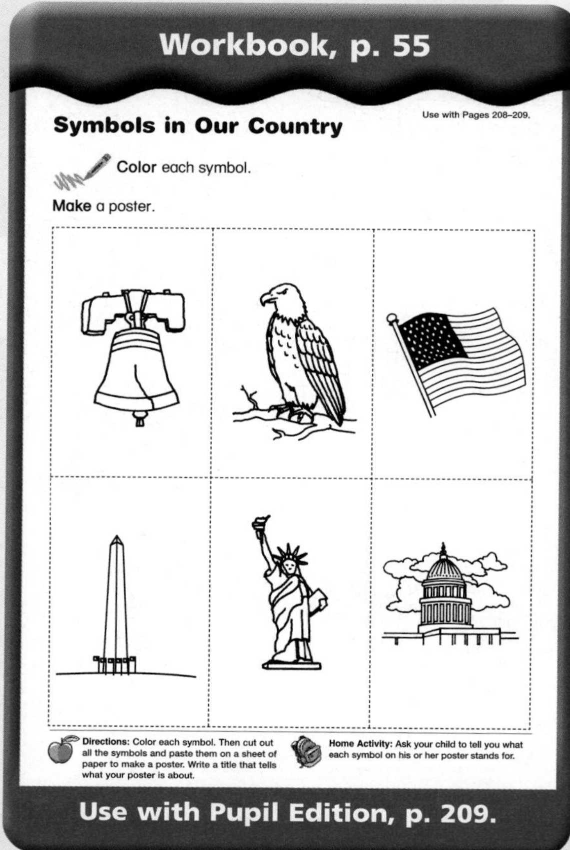

Workbook, p. 55

Symbols in Our Country

Use with Pages 208–209.

Color each symbol.

Make a poster.

Directions: Color each symbol. Then cut out all the symbols and paste them on a sheet of paper to make a poster. Write a title that tells what your poster is about.

Home Activity: Ask your child to tell you what each symbol on his or her poster stands for.

Use with Pupil Edition, p. 209.

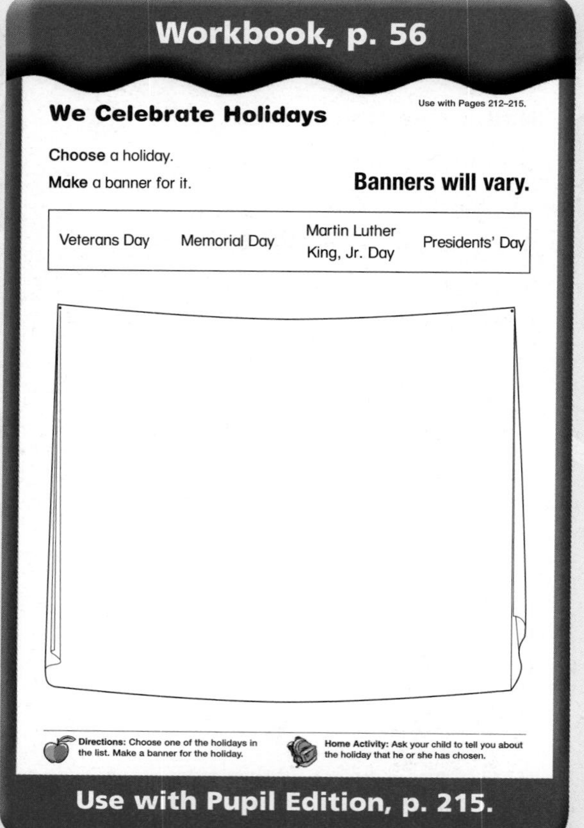

Workbook, p. 56

We Celebrate Holidays

Use with Pages 212–215.

Choose a holiday.

Make a banner for it.

Banners will vary.

Veterans Day	Memorial Day	Martin Luther King, Jr. Day	Presidents' Day

Directions: Choose one of the holidays in the list. Make a banner for the holiday.

Home Activity: Ask your child to tell you about the holiday that he or she has chosen.

Use with Pupil Edition, p. 215.

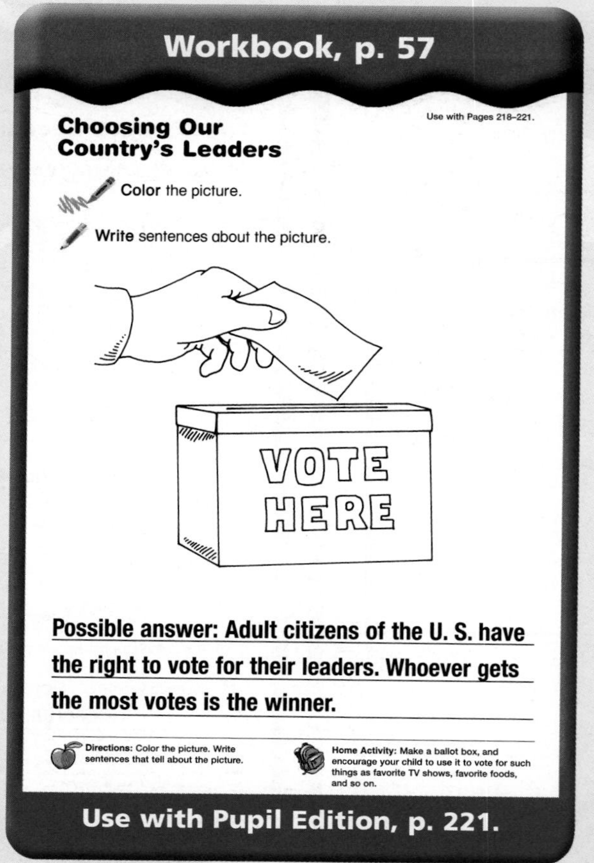

Workbook, p. 57

Choosing Our Country's Leaders

Use with Pages 218–221.

Color the picture.

Write sentences about the picture.

Possible answer: Adult citizens of the U. S. have the right to vote for their leaders. Whoever gets the most votes is the winner.

Directions: Color the picture. Write sentences that tell about the picture.

Home Activity: Make a ballot box, and encourage your child to use it to vote for such things as favorite TV shows, favorite foods, and so on.

Use with Pupil Edition, p. 221.

Workbook Support

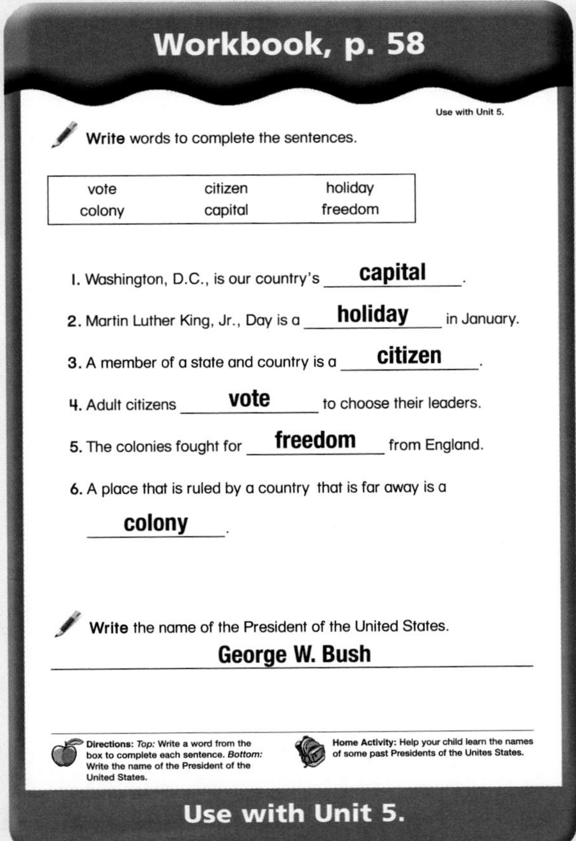

Workbook, p. 58

Use with Unit 5.

Write words to complete the sentences.

vote	citizen	holiday
colony	capital	freedom

1. Washington, D.C., is our country's **capital**.
2. Martin Luther King, Jr., Day is a **holiday** in January.
3. A member of a state and country is a **citizen**.
4. Adult citizens **vote** to choose their leaders.
5. The colonies fought for **freedom** from England.
6. A place that is ruled by a country that is far away is a **colony**.

Write the name of the President of the United States.

George W. Bush

Directions: *Top:* Write a word from the box to complete each sentence. *Bottom:* Write the name of the President of the United States.

Home Activity: Help your child learn the names of some past Presidents of the Unites States.

Use with Unit 5.

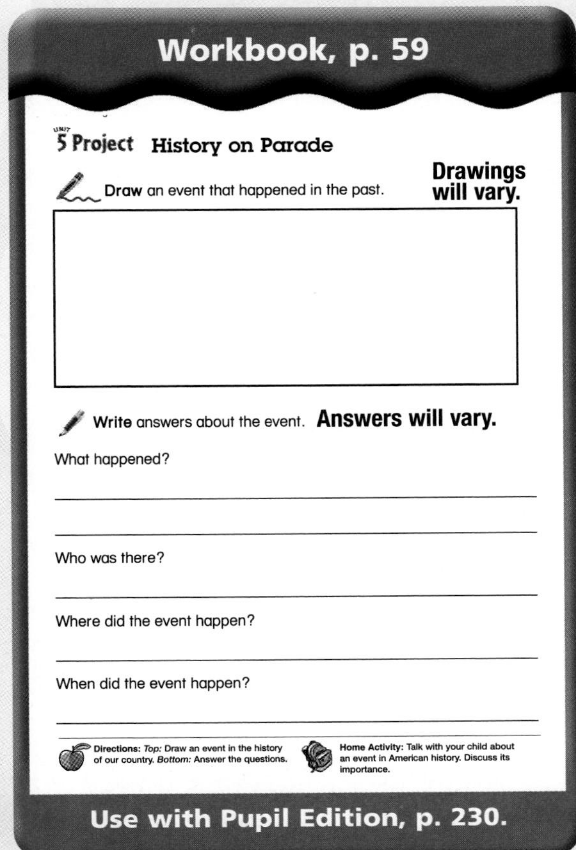

Workbook, p. 59

Unit 5 Project History on Parade

Draw an event that happened in the past. **Drawings will vary.**

Write answers about the event. **Answers will vary.**

What happened?

Who was there?

Where did the event happen?

When did the event happen?

Directions: *Top:* Draw an event in the history of our country. *Bottom:* Answer the questions.

Home Activity: Talk with your child about an event in American history. Discuss its importance.

Use with Pupil Edition, p. 230.

Assessment Support

Use the following Assessment Book pages and TestWorks to assess content and skills in Unit 5. You can also view and print Assessment Book pages from the Teacher Resources CD-ROM.

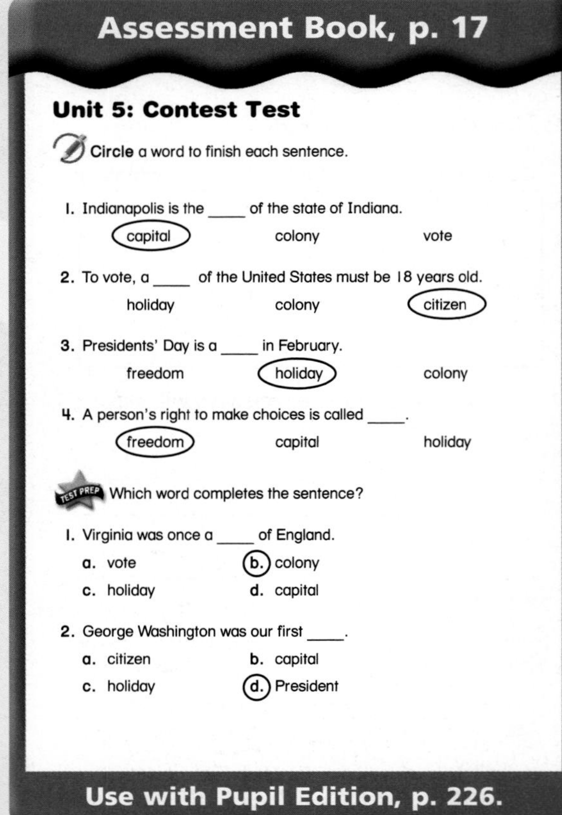

Assessment Book, p. 17

Unit 5: Contest Test

Circle a word to finish each sentence.

1. Indianapolis is the ____ of the state of Indiana.
   capital colony vote
2. To vote, a ____ of the United States must be 18 years old.
   holiday colony citizen
3. Presidents' Day is a ____ in February.
   freedom holiday colony
4. A person's right to make choices is called ____.
   freedom capital holiday

Which word completes the sentence?

1. Virginia was once a ____ of England.
   a. vote b. colony
   c. holiday d. capital
2. George Washington was our first ____.
   a. citizen b. capital
   c. holiday d. President

Use with Pupil Edition, p. 226.

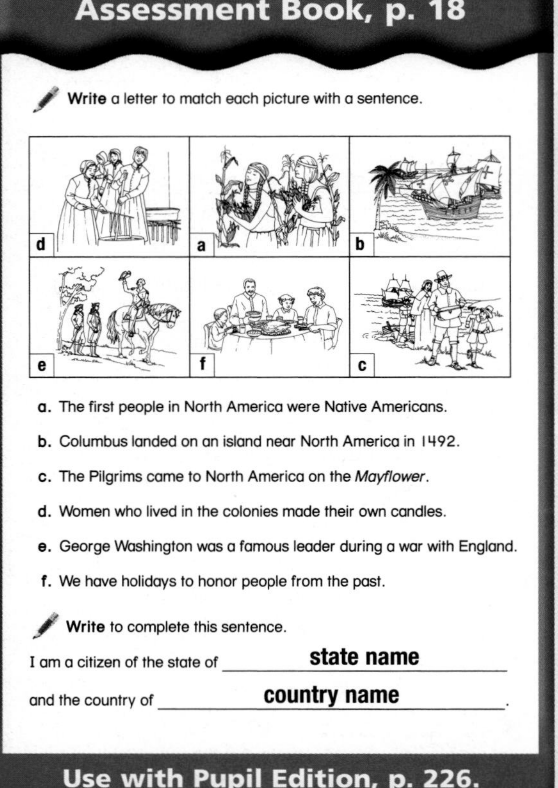

Assessment Book, p. 18

Write a letter to match each picture with a sentence.

a. The first people in North America were Native Americans.
b. Columbus landed on an island near North America in 1492.
c. The Pilgrims came to North America on the *Mayflower*.
d. Women who lived in the colonies made their own candles.
e. George Washington was a famous leader during a war with England.
f. We have holidays to honor people from the past.

Write to complete this sentence.

I am a citizen of the state of **state name**

and the country of **country name**.

Use with Pupil Edition, p. 226.

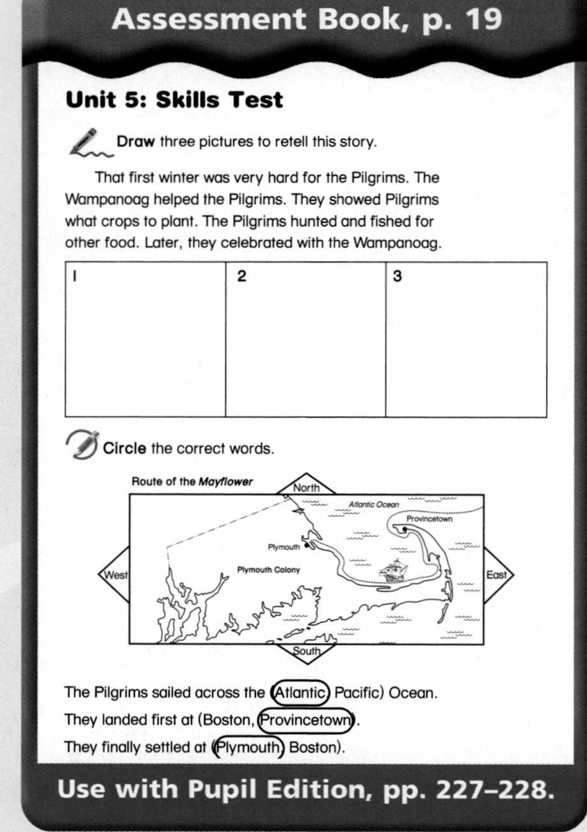

Assessment Book, p. 19

Unit 5: Skills Test

Draw three pictures to retell this story.

That first winter was very hard for the Pilgrims. The Wampanoag helped the Pilgrims. They showed Pilgrims what crops to plant. The Pilgrims hunted and fished for other food. Later, they celebrated with the Wampanoag.

1	2	3

Circle the correct words.

The Pilgrims sailed across the (Atlantic, Pacific) Ocean.
They landed first at (Boston, Provincetown).
They finally settled at (Plymouth, Boston).

Use with Pupil Edition, pp. 227–228.

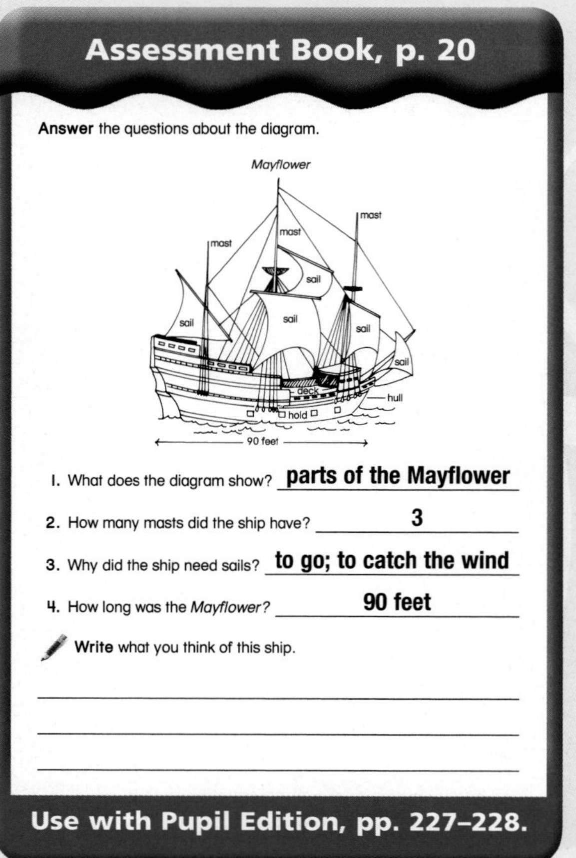

Assessment Book, p. 20

Answer the questions about the diagram.

1. What does the diagram show? **parts of the Mayflower**
2. How many masts did the ship have? **3**
3. Why did the ship need sails? **to go; to catch the wind**
4. How long was the *Mayflower*? **90 feet**

Write what you think of this ship.

____

____

____

Use with Pupil Edition, pp. 227–228.

Lesson 1 Overview

Native Americans **pages 190–191**	Children will learn about different groups of Native Americans and explore their diverse cultures and customs. 	Time 20 minutes Resources • Workbook, p. 49 • Every Student Learns Guide, pp. 82–85
Read a Diagram **pages 192–193**	Children will learn the meaning of the word *diagram* and gain knowledge about reading a diagram.	Time 15–20 minutes Resource • Workbook, p. 50
Smithsonian Institution: Native American Objects **pages 194–195**	Children will learn about the dress and tools of Native American groups.	Time 20 minutes Resource • Workbook, p. 51

Build Background

Activity

My Home

Time 15–20 minutes

Have children draw a picture of either the inside or outside of their home (for example, a house or apartment building). Invite students to label their picture "My Home." This activity will help children clarify similarities and differences between how they live and how Native Americans lived long ago.

If time is short, have children describe their home.

Read Aloud

People Then and Now

by Vanessa Gates

This much I know:
people long ago
were not like you and me,
I'm sure you'll agree.

They grew their own veggies
and lived in strange homes...
Wait a minute, if you please!
They needed food to eat
and a place to sleep.

Why I'm sure you'll agree
that's just like me!
This much I can say:
Long ago people
were like people today.

Native Americans

Objectives

- Obtain information about a topic using a variety of visual sources such as maps.
- Describe similarities and differences in ways families meet basic needs.

QUICK Teaching Plan

If time is short, discuss the map with students. Explain that long ago, like today, Native American groups lived in different parts of the United States.

- Have children look at the pictures of the different kinds of homes. Then have them describe the differences.

1 Introduce and Motivate

Preview Tell children that they will learn where different Native American groups lived long ago, what kinds of homes they built, what they ate, and how they got food.

Warm Up To activate prior knowledge, ask children what they know about how Native Americans lived long ago. Ask them if they think Native Americans lived in houses like ours today. Ask them whether they think Native Americans bought food at a grocery store or dined at a restaurant.

2 Teach and Discuss

Page 190

Identify James in the photograph. Invite volunteers to name the vegetables that James is holding (corn, squash).

Discuss with children the types of Native American homes shown. Explain that the Chinook lived in buildings calleds plank houses; the Pueblo lived in pueblos; the Lakota lived in tepees; the Wampanoag lived in wigwams.

Lesson 1

Native Americans

Many different groups of Native Americans lived in North America.

The first people to live in North America were Native Americans. We also call them American Indians.

Look at the map. It shows where some Native Americans lived long ago. Today, Native Americans still live in all parts of the United States.

1 2

190

Practice and Extend

READING SKILL
Recall and Retell

Target Skill

Analyze Pictures Tell children that they can use the pictures of Native American homes to help them recall and retell what they learned about Native Americans.

- Have children complete a word web by drawing the shapes of the Native American homes.

Some Native American groups hunted for their food. Other groups grew food such as corn, beans, and squash. Still others caught fish.

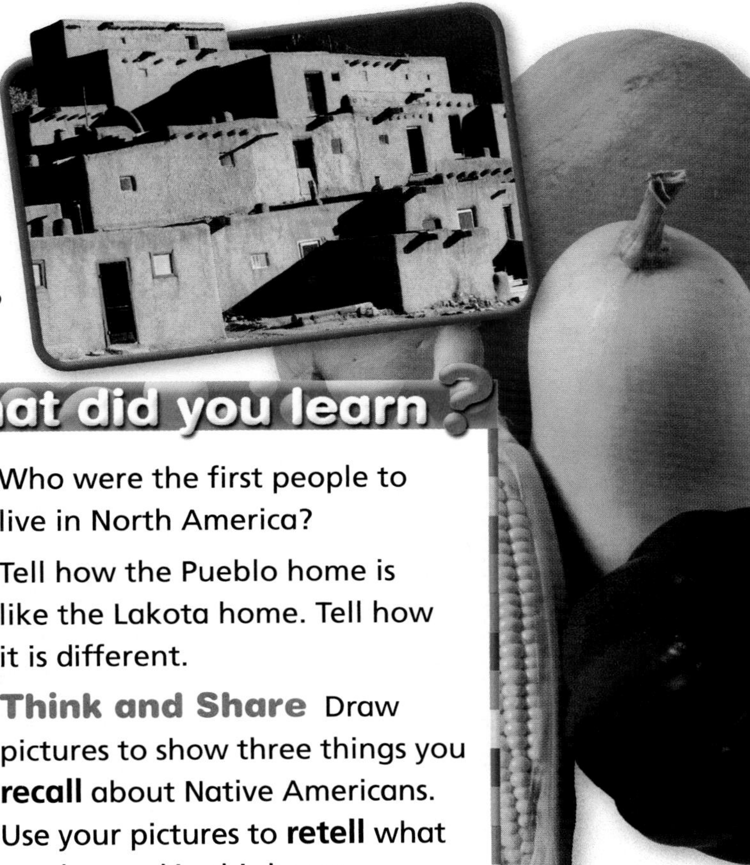

A Pueblo home

What did you learn?

1. Who were the first people to live in North America?
2. Tell how the Pueblo home is like the Lakota home. Tell how it is different.
3. **Think and Share** Draw pictures to show three things you **recall** about Native Americans. Use your pictures to **retell** what you learned in this lesson.

191

1 **Did the four groups of Native Americans live close to each other?** No. They lived in different parts of the United States. **Interpret Maps**

Ongoing Assessment

If... children cannot tell that the map represents a large area and that the groups lived far apart,	**then...** explain that there were many trails, rivers, plains, forests, or mountains separating the groups.

2 **How are Native American homes like our homes?** Answers may vary, but may include references to doors, windows, and roofs. **Compare and Contrast**

3 **What are some foods Native Americans ate?** Corn, beans, squash, fish **Recall and Retell**

4 **How did Native Americans get their food?** They hunted, fished, or grew food. **Recall and Retell**

3 Close and Assess

Have children form groups to discuss Native American homes. Then ask children to decide whether they would like to be Native Americans living long ago.

What did you learn?

1. Native Americans
2. Answers will vary but may include: Alike: Both have doors. Different: The Pueblo home has many doors. The Lakota home has one door.
3. **Think and Share** Answers should explain any three things students learned about any of the Native American groups.

FYI Social Studies Background

Native American Groups on the Map

Tell children that the Native American groups identified on the map may have called themselves other names, and, like people today, many of them moved from place to place.

Workbook, p. 49

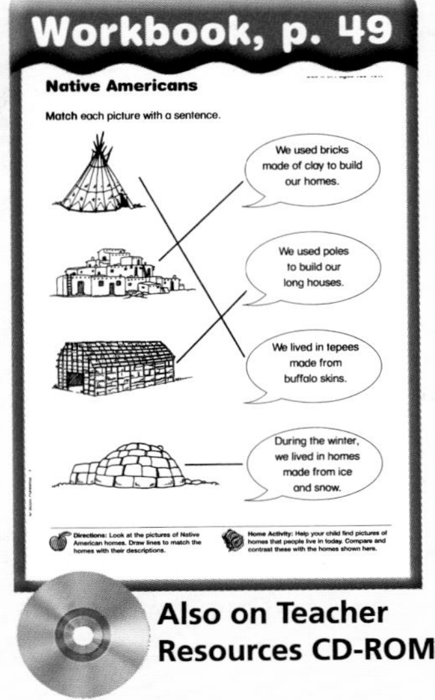

Native Americans

Match each picture with a sentence.

We used bricks made of clay to build our homes.

We used poles to build our long houses.

We lived in tepees made from buffalo skins.

During the winter, we lived in homes made from ice and snow.

Also on Teacher Resources CD-ROM.

Big Book/Pupil Book pp. 192–193
Chart and Graph Skills

Read a Diagram

Objectives

- Obtain information about a topic using a variety of visual sources such as diagrams.
- Identify the human characteristics of types of houses.

Skill Vocabulary

diagram a way to show the parts of something (p. 193)

1 Introduce and Motivate

Preview Explain that a diagram is a drawing that explains something. Draw a diagram of a bicycle. Label the wheels, seat, pedals, and handlebars.

Warm Up To activate prior knowledge ask students to remember the kinds of homes some Native Americans built (tepees, pueblos, wigwams, and plank houses). Explain that they will look at a diagram of one type of home, an earth lodge. Explain that using a diagram will help them understand the parts of the earth lodge.

Chart and Graph Skills

Read a Diagram

Native Americans lived in different types of homes. One type of Native American home was called an earth lodge. The picture below shows an earth lodge. Native Americans made fires inside earth lodges to cook and to keep warm. Smoke from the fire left the lodge through a hole in the roof.

192

Practice and Extend

ACCESS CONTENT
ESL Support

Questioning Have children ask and answer questions about the diagrams in the book and on the board.

Beginning Ask questions about the diagram using the word *where*. Example: *Where are the wheels?* Have children point to the part you ask about.

Intermediate Ask children what and where questions about the diagrams. Examples: *What is a roof?* and *Where is the roof?* Have children point to the part and answer verbally.

Advanced Have children take turns asking each other *what* and *where* questions about the diagrams. Have one child ask a question and another child answer by both pointing to the part and answering verbally.

For additional ESL Support, use Every Student Learns Guide, pp. 82–85.

CURRICULUM CONNECTION
Art

Make a Diagram of the Classroom

- Explain to children that often somebody makes a diagram of a house before the house can be built.
- Hand out an outline of the classroom. Explain that it is an outline of the classroom from above as it is viewed from the ceiling.
- Point to the location of the teacher's desk on the outline. Tell children to draw a small rectangle there. Then have children make *X*s to indicate the location of the door and windows.
- Have children label the locations of the door, windows, and desk.

Look at this diagram of an earth lodge. A **diagram** shows the parts of something. Name the parts of the earth lodge you see on the diagram.

1. What does a diagram show?
2. What part did Native Americans use to enter the earth lodge?
3. **On Your Own** Make a diagram that shows a room in your home. Label each part.

193

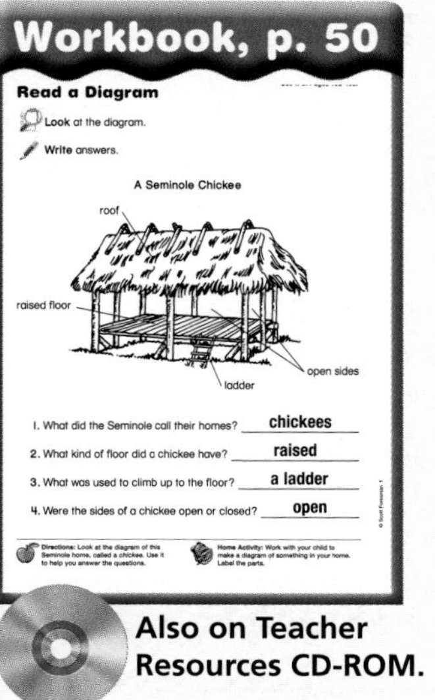

Workbook, p. 50

Read a Diagram

Look at the diagram.

Write answers.

A Seminole Chickee

1. What did the Seminole call their homes? chickees
2. What kind of floor did a chickee have? raised
3. What was used to climb up to the floor? a ladder
4. Were the sides of a chickee open or closed? open

Directions: Look at the diagram of this Seminole home, called a chickee. Use it to help you answer the questions.

Home Activity: Work with your child to make a diagram of something in your home. Label the parts.

Also on Teacher Resources CD-ROM.

2 Teach and Discuss

Read the introduction. Explain to children that today people might stay in a place called a lodge during special times of the year. For example, a family may vacation at a ski lodge in the winter. Have children look at the picture of the Native American earth lodge.

Point out the diagram. Explain to children that the picture shows both the inside and outside of an earth lodge. Say each part of the lodge and have children point to that part of the picture.

1 What type of Native American home is shown in the picture?
An earth lodge **Analyze pictures**

Test Talk

Use Information from Graphics

2 Why does the lodge have a hole in the roof?
It enables smoke from a fire to escape to the outside. Tell children to look at the diagram to figure out the right answer. **Make Inferences**

3 Close and Assess

Draw a diagram of a computer on the board with arrows pointing to the monitor, keyboard, and mouse. Have children name the parts. Then write them on the board.

Try it!

1. the parts of something
2. the entrance
3. **On Your Own** Diagrams will vary but should reflect the parts of a room at home.

Native American Objects

Objective

- Obtain information about a topic using a variety of visual sources such as pictures of artifacts.

Resource

- Workbook, p. 51

1 Introduce and Motivate

Preview Ask if children have ever modeled with clay. Ask if they have ever done any weaving. Encourage those who have to tell what materials they used and what they made.

Warm Up To activate prior knowledge, remind children that in Lesson 1, they learned about several Native American groups. Review the names Pueblo, Lakota, Wampanoag, and Chinook. Have children refer back to p. 190 to talk about the homes different Native Americans made. Tell children that they will now look at some other everyday things made by Native Americans.

Read the introduction with children. Ask a volunteer to read aloud what James says. Point out that all the things shown on pp. 194–195 were made by Native Americans.

2 Teach and Discuss

Focus children's attention on the larger objects. You may want to begin with the Aleut basket and move clockwise around the display. After reading each caption aloud for children, ask what materials they think were used to make the item. Also ask what the artifact may have been used for.

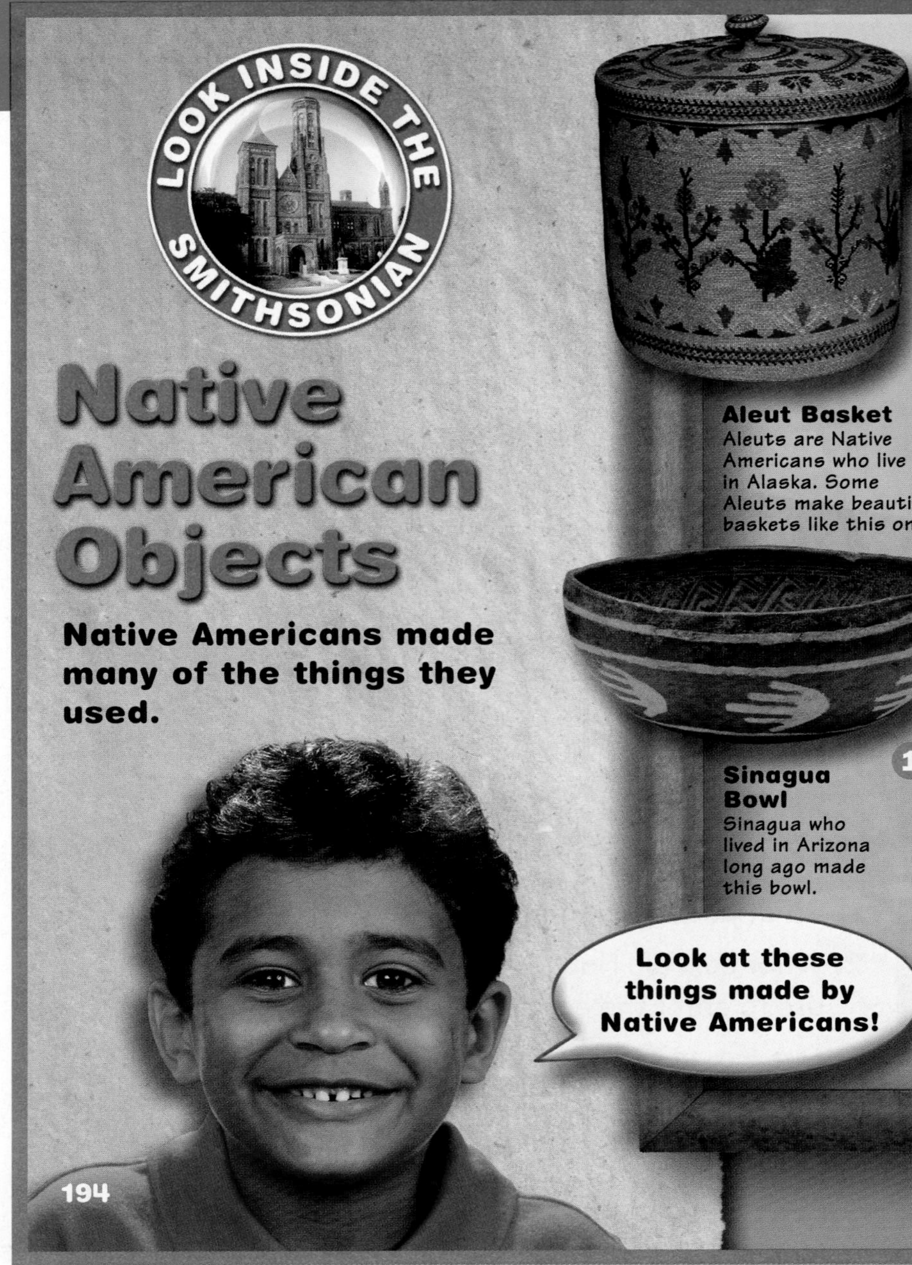

Look Inside the Smithsonian
Native American Objects
Native Americans made many of the things they used.
Aleut Basket
Aleuts are Native Americans who live in Alaska. Some Aleuts make beautifu
baskets like this one
Sinagua Bowl
Sinagua who lived in Arizona long ago made this bowl.
1
Look at these things made by Native Americans!
194

Practice and Extend

CURRICULUM CONNECTION
Math

Native American Design

- Show children samples of several geometric figures, including a circle, a square, a triangle, and a rectangle. Have children identify and describe the shapes.
- Ask children to find examples of geomeric shapes on the artifacts pictured on pp. 194–195.
- Have children use the shapes to draw their own designs. Or, have them cut out geometric shapes and paste them on construction paper to form abstract collages.

Toys
Toys such as this one were made by the Pueblo.
Gift Basket 2
This gift basket is covered with feathers and shells. It was made by the Pomo of California.
Native American Collection
3
1
Water Jar
Acoma Pueblo made this water jar. Acoma Pueblo live in New Mexico. The bird on the jar is a parrot.
Hopi Jar
This jar has a traditional Hopi design on it.

Artifacts are from the Smithsonian Institution. 195

You can visit the Smithsonian Institution online. Click on Smithsonian at **www.sfsocialstudies.com** or go to **www.si.edu.**

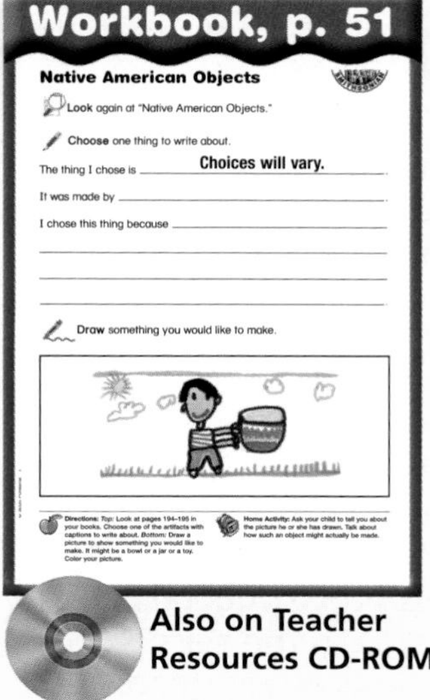

Also on Teacher Resources CD-ROM.

1 What do you think the jars and the bowl were used for? Possible answers: The jars may have been used to hold water. The bowl may have been for food. **Make Inferences**

2 Look at the gift basket made from feathers and shells. What does it tell you about the people who made it? Possible answers: Shells are found on the beach, so these Native Americans might have lived near the sea. They might have liked to give each other gifts too. **Make Inferencess**

3 Why do you think the Native Americans decorated so many of the things they made? Possible answer: They wanted to make the items beautiful. **Make Inferences**

Direct attention to the group of artifacts in the center of the display. Identify these for children, starting with the mask and moving clockwise around the display. Invite comments on the beauty of the design of the artifacts as you identify them.

- Haida (Northwest Coast) owl mask
- Columella beads
- Sikyatki (Southwest) bowl
- Mimbres (Southwest) bowl
- Acoma (Southwest) water jug
- Anasazi (Southwest) jar

3 Close and Assess

- Ask each child to choose an artifact that he or she thinks is especially interesting or beautiful. Encourage children to explain their choices.
- Point out that all the artifacts shown on pp. 194–195 were made by hand. Ask children to name some household tools and appliances that their families use. Ask if children think these things were also made by hand.
- Point out that when the Native Americans made some of the things shown on pp. 194–195, people did not know about electricity. Ask how children think Native Americans did such things as get water and prepare food. Talk about how today, we depend on electricity to get water and prepare food. Ask children to suggest other ways electricity has changed the ways people live.

Use with pages 190–195

Lesson 1 Wrap-Up

MEETING INDIVIDUAL NEEDS

Leveled Practice

Recall and Retell About Native Americans
Have children recall and retell what they learned about Native Americans.

Easy Have children draw a Native American home. Ask them to describe the home. **Reteach**

On-Level Have children draw a Native American home and make a label telling who lived there. **Extend**

Challenge Have children draw a Native American home, and make labels telling the parts of the home and who lived there. **Enrich**

Hands-on Activities

CURRICULUM CONNECTION
Writing

North American Objects

Objective Define and illustrate objects used by Native Americans.

Materials crayons

Learning Style Visual/Linguistic

Individual

Time 10–15 minutes

1. Help children distinguish among the words *basket* (a container made of twigs, grasses, etc. woven together), *jar* (a container of stone, baked clay, etc. with a mouth), and *bowl* (a hollow, rounded dish).

2. Have them draw one of these objects. Suggest they include a decoration like one on pp. 194–195. Then have them label the object.

CURRICULUM CONNECTION
Reading

Native American Story

Objective Act out a Native American story.

Materials picture book

Learning Style Verbal/Linguistic

Group

Time 15–30 minutes

1. Explain to children that many Native American groups have stories, or legends, that were passed down from earlier times to the present by parents to their children.

2. Read *How Jackrabbit Got His Very Long Ears* by Heather Irbinskas to the class. Show the illustrations as you read.

3. Have children act out important events of the story.

CURRICULUM CONNECTION
Music

Traditional Tunes

Objective Listen to traditional Native American songs.

Materials CD of Native American music

Learning Style Auditory/Verbal

Group

Time 15–20 minutes

1. Play one of the Native American songs from the CD *Traditional Voices: Historic Recordings of Traditional Native American Music*. Tell children which Native American group created the song.

2. Play more songs from Native American groups, and name the groups for children.

3. Ask children which song they liked best.

Lesson 2 Overview

Early Travelers to America **pages 196–199**	Children will gain knowledge about Christopher Columbus and the Pilgrims' life in America, and learn the meaning of the word *freedom*.	 Time 20–30 minutes Resources • Workbook, p. 52 • Vocabulary Card  freedom • Every Student Learns Guide, pp. 86–89
Use a History Map **pages 200–201**	Children will learn how to use a map that shows historic routes.	Time 15–20 minutes Resource • Workbook, p. 53

Build Background

Activity

All Aboard!

 **Time** 20 minutes

Provide children with an outline of a ship on construction paper. Ask children to imagine that they are taking a long sea voyage to a new land. Ask them to draw what they would take with them.

If time is short, have children brainstorm things they would take with them. Ideas may include food, family, pets, games, or books.

Activity

America

Samuel Francis Smith (1831)

My country, 'tis of thee,
Sweet land of liberty,
Of thee I sing;
Land where my fathers died,
Land of the Pilgrims' pride,
From ev'ry mountain-side,
Let freedom ring!

Early Travelers to America

Objectives

- Describe the origin of selected holidays.
- Cite reasons for observing holidays.

Vocabulary

freedom a person's right to make choices (p. 198)

QUICK Teaching Plan

If time is short, discuss Columbus's voyage with children. Use the illustration to show the voyage. Explain the origin of Columbus Day.

- Explain that the Pilgrims came to this land in search of freedom. Tell how the Wampanoag helped the Pilgrims, and how the Pilgrims and the Wampanoag celebrated their friendship.

1 Introduce and Motivate

Preview Display the Vocabulary Card **freedom**. Tell students that freedom means being allowed to choose things for yourself. Explain that many people come to the United States because they want more freedom. Here people have the freedom to elect public officials, express ideas, and practice their religion. They can also choose the job they want to do and the place where they want to live. Ask children what it would be like to live in a country where people didn't have these freedoms.

Warm Up To activate prior knowledge, ask children whether they have ever heard of Christopher Columbus. Tell children that he traveled from one side of the Atlantic Ocean to the other by ship. Ask volunteers to tell about when they were on a boat or a ship.

Tell children that a holiday is a day for pleasure, enjoyment, and remembering. On holidays, most people don't have to work. Then ask children about Thanksgiving. Ask them what people do on this holiday. Ask them what people eat. Then ask children if they know why we celebrate Thanksgiving.

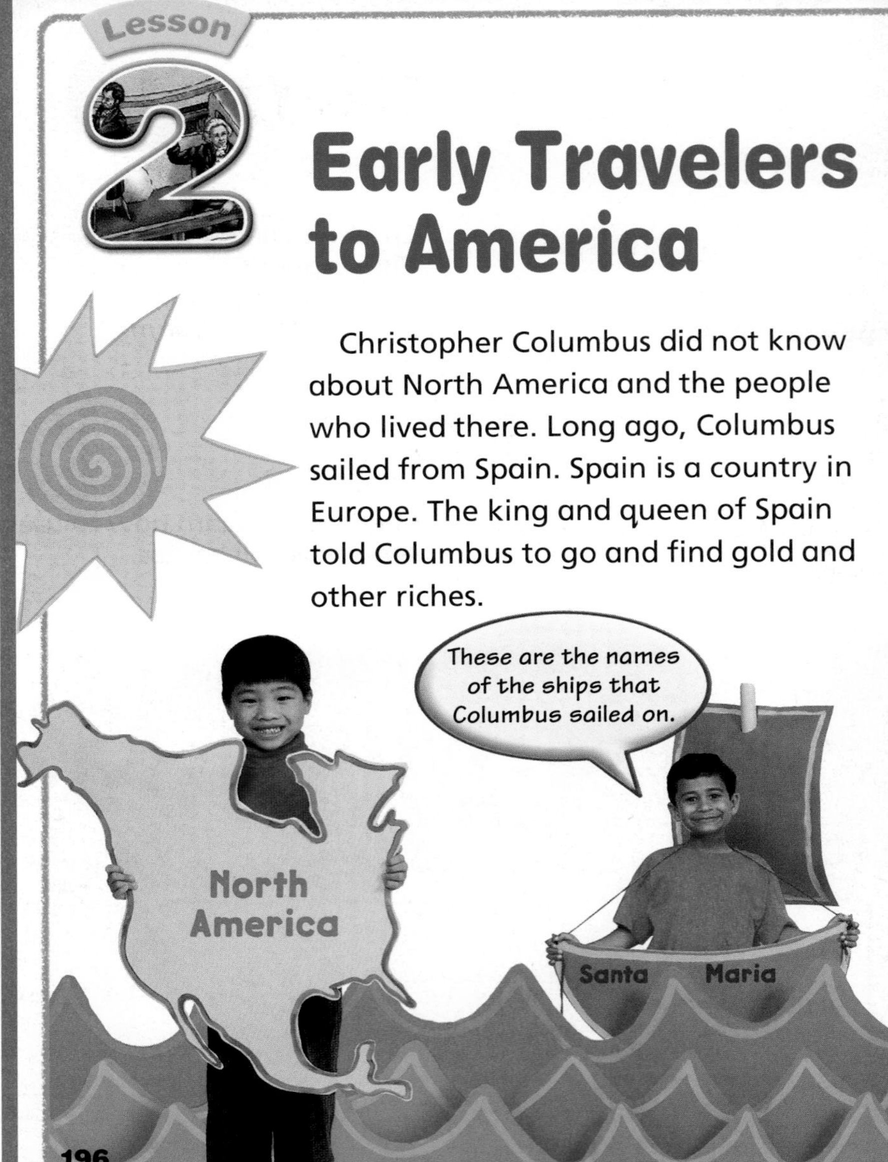

Lesson
Early Travelers to America
Christopher Columbus did not know about North America and the people who lived there. Long ago, Columbus sailed from Spain. Spain is a country in Europe. The king and queen of Spain told Columbus to go and find gold and other riches.
These are the names of the ships that Columbus sailed on.
North America
Santa Maria
196

Practice and Extend

READING SKILL Main Idea and Details

Tell children that pp. 196–197 are about Christopher Columbus's voyage to America. Ask children what information they learned about Christopher Columbus's voyage to America.

- Give children a copy of a web with a circle in the center and 3 spokes with circles on the end. Have them write *Columbus Sails to America* at the top of the page. Have them write *Columbus* in the center of the web.
- Have children complete the word web by writing one word of information about Christopher Columbus in each of three outer circles.

Columbus and his crew sailed for a long time. On October 12, 1492, they landed on an island near North America. The people who lived on this island were called the Taino. Columbus did not find gold. However, he did find people and a place that other people in Europe did not know about yet.

Every year, people remember the day Columbus landed on the island. The second Monday in October is Columbus Day.

Christopher Columbus

197

SOCIAL STUDIES Background

About the Taino

- The Taino (TY noh) belonged to the Arawak group of American Indians.
- Although Columbus saw that some Taino were wearing gold ornaments, he did not find the source of the gold.

WEB SITE Technology

You can look up vocabulary words online. Click on *Social Studies Library* and select the dictionary at **www.sfsocialstudies.com.**

2 Teach and Discuss

Page 196

Tell children that Christopher Columbus lived a long time ago. Then read pp. 196–197 with children.

Identify James in the picture. Invite volunteers to tell the name of the ship that James is inside. (*Santa Maria*) Then have them name the other ships. Identify the body of water (the waves) as the Atlantic Ocean. Have children follow Columbus's voyage by pointing to Spain, the Atlantic Ocean, and North America. Tell children that Columbus returned to Europe to tell others about the New World. Have children trace his route back to Spain.

Page 197

GEOGRAPHY
Movement

1 **Why did Christopher Columbus's voyage take a long time?** Answers may vary, but may include that Spain was across the Atlantic Ocean from North America and that long ago it took a long time to sail across the ocean. Draw Conclusions

2 **Did Christopher Columbus reach North America?** No. Christopher Columbus landed on a nearby island.
Make Inferences

3 **Even when October 12 is not on a Monday, why do you think Columbus Day is always celebrated on a Monday?** Celebrating on Monday enables people to extend their weekend.
Draw Conclusions

Lesson 2 continued

Page 198

Ask children to point to the picture of the ship. Tell them that the name on the ship reads *Mayflower*. Have them trace with their finger the ship's route from England on the right to North America on the left.

GEOGRAPHY Movement

4 How did the Pilgrims get from England to North America? They sailed on a ship called the *Mayflower*. **Recall and Retell**

5 Why did the Pilgrims go to North America? They wanted the freedom to practice their religion. **Apply Information**

Ongoing Assessment

If... children believe that the Pilgrims were the first Europeans to arrive on the mainland United States in 1620,	**then...** explain that in 1513 the Spanish landed on the Florida coast near present-day St. Augustine, Florida.

The Mayflower

Later, a group of people we call Pilgrims left England to come to **4** North America. They sailed on a ship called the *Mayflower*.

The Pilgrims wanted their freedom. **Freedom** is a person's right to make choices. The Pilgrims wanted the freedom to practice **5** their own religion.

198

Practice and Extend

FAST FACTS

Columbus thought he had reached land close to India, called the East Indies. He called the people from the island *Indians*. This name was then used for all native people in North and South America.

- Nobody knows for certain where Columbus first landed. Most experts believe it was in the present-day Bahamas. He also landed on present-day Cuba and Hispaniola (Haiti and the Dominican Republic).
- Columbus was not the first European to reach North America. Led by Leif Ericson, the Vikings, from an area of Europe called Scandinavia, set sail from Greenland and landed in North America in 1001—about 500 years before Columbus.

ESL — EXTEND LANGUAGE ESL Support

Telling About Cultural Traditions Have children tell about a holiday from their native culture during which they give thanks. If there is no comparable holiday to Thanksgiving, have children tell about another special day.

Beginning Have children use pictures, gestures, or a few words to tell about the holiday.

Intermediate Invite children to use words or sentences to tell about the holiday.

Advanced Encourage children to tell in sentences how and why people celebrate the holiday.

For additional ESL Support, use Every Student Learns Guide, pp. 86–89.

The Pilgrims built a village that they called Plymouth. Wampanoag Indians saved the Pilgrims by showing them how to grow corn and other plants. They also showed the Pilgrims how to fish.

The Pilgrims and the (6) Wampanoag celebrated. They were thankful. Today, people have a special day to give thanks. We call the day Thanksgiving.

What did you learn?

1. Why do we have Columbus Day and Thanksgiving?
2. Why is freedom important?
3. **Think and Share** Draw a picture of how Thanksgiving was celebrated long ago and how you celebrate it today. Tell how the pictures are alike and different.

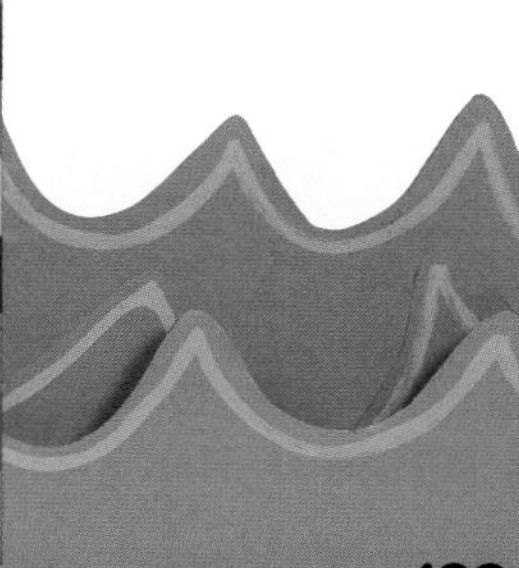

199

SOCIAL STUDIES Background

About the Pilgrims

- The Pilgrims' voyage to the United States in 1620 lasted 65 days. They were headed for Virginia but a storm drove them north to Massachusetts. Because they arrived in the winter, life was hard. Many of them died.
- In the spring, two Wampanoag (WAH puh NOH ag) Indians, Samoset and Squanto, taught the Pilgrims to plant corn and other crops. As a result, the first harvest was bountiful.

Workbook, p. 52

Early Travelers to America
Draw to finish each picture. Drawings will vary.
Color the pictures.
Columbus Day
Thanksgiving Day

Also on Teacher Resources CD-ROM.

Test Talk

Locate Key Words in the Text

(6) What did the Wampanoag show the Pilgrims how to grow? Corn and other plants
Have children locate key words in the text that match key words in the question.
Apply Information

(7) For what were the Pilgrims thankful? Answers will vary but may include freedom, food, and friendly neighbors. **Draw Conclusions**

3 Close and Assess

Have children discuss with a partner what they know about Christopher Columbus and the Pilgrims.

✓ What did you learn?

1. Answers will vary. These holidays remind us of the early settlers. They remind us of our freedom and why we should be thankful.
2. Answers will vary but may include: freedom is a person's right to make choices.
3. **Think and Share** To help children with their drawings, show children pictures of Pilgrims giving thanks and families in the present celebrating Thanksgiving. Suggest to children that they need only include two or three items (e.g., an ear of corn, a turkey, a Pilgrim's hat) in each drawing.

Use a History Map

Objectives

- Obtain information about a topic using a variety of visual sources such as maps.
- Use cardinal directions on a map.

1 Introduce and Motivate

Preview Ask children about the maps of the world they have seen. You may want to remind children of maps you have looked at as a class. Explain that they are going to look at a special kind of map called a history map. A history map shows places or things that happened in the past.

Warm Up To activate prior knowledge, ask children to remember the voyages of Christopher Columbus and the Pilgrims. Ask children to tell where Christopher Columbus's voyage started. (Spain) Ask children to tell the country from which the Pilgrims sailed. (England) Explain that the history map they will look at will show these places and the routes, or paths, that the ships took.

2 Teach and Discuss

Have children point to the part of the map that represents North America. Then have them point to England and Spain. Ask children to name the part of the map that is not land. (water) Ask them to tell how they know what parts of the map represent land. (They are labeled. They are a different color.) Have students trace with their finger the routes of the *Mayflower* and Columbus's ships.

1 Did the Pilgrims land north or south of Columbus? North **Interpret Maps**

Map and Globe Skills

Use a History Map

A history map shows places or routes from the past. Look at this map.

1 2

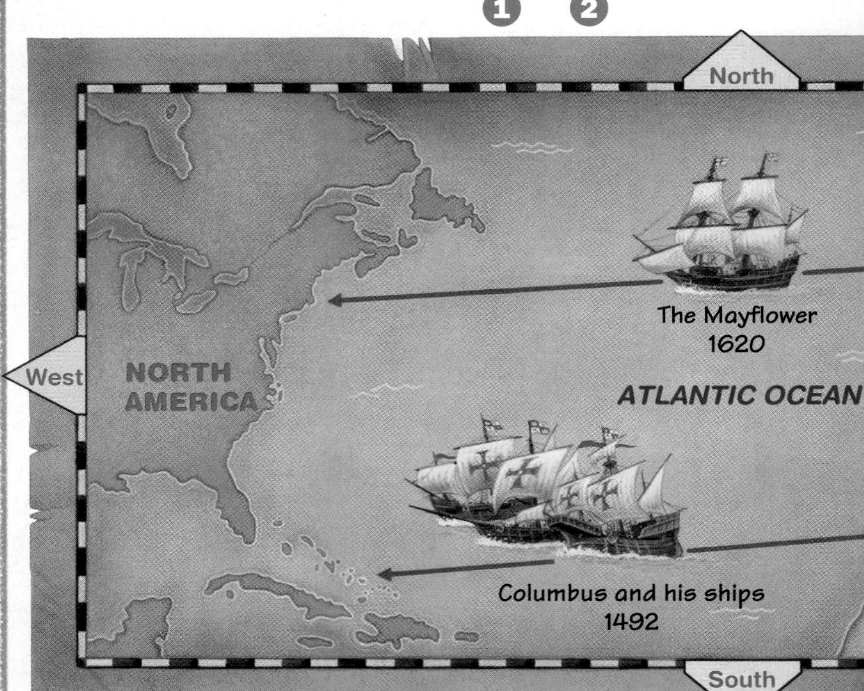

200

Practice and Extend

CURRICULUM CONNECTION
Math

Compare Land Areas

Have children compare the land size of countries and continents.

- Ask if Spain is larger than or smaller than Europe.
- Ask if North America is larger than or smaller than England.

Use your finger to follow the route Columbus took. Then follow the route the *Mayflower* took.

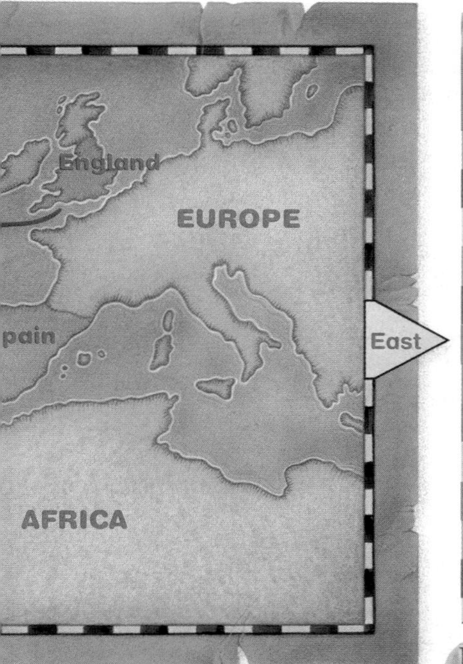

Try it!

1. Did Columbus sail east or west when he left Spain?
2. Name the ocean that the *Mayflower* sailed on.
3. **On Your Own** Write sentences telling what this history map shows.

For more information, go online to the *Atlas* at **www.sfsocialstudies.com.**

② Did the Pilgrim's sail from east to west or from west to east? East to west **Interpret Maps**

3 Close and Assess

Have children look at a globe to get a different representation of the locations shown on the map. Name the locations identified on the map and have children find them on the globe. Then have children trace from the area where Columbus landed back to Spain.

Try it!

1. Columbus sailed west after he left Spain.
2. The Mayflower sailed on the Atlantic Ocean.
3. **On Your Own** Sentences should tell about the people, place, and direction of the two voyages.

You may help children find out more by clicking on *Atlas* at **www.sfsocialstudies.com.**

Workbook, p. 53

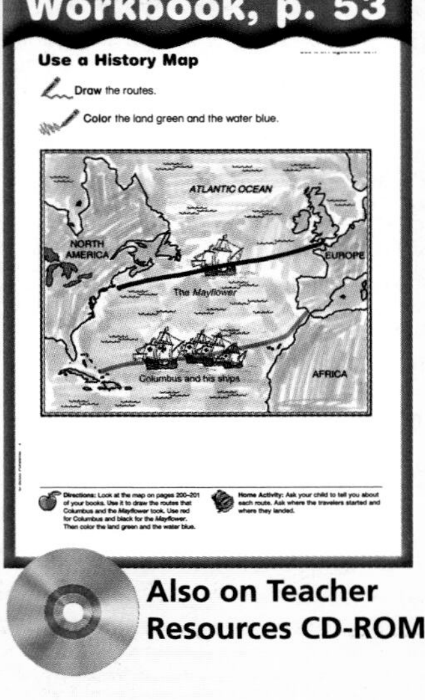
Use a History Map

Draw the routes.

Color the land green and the water blue.

Also on Teacher Resources CD-ROM.

Use with pages 196–201

Lesson 2 Wrap-Up

MEETING INDIVIDUAL NEEDS

Leveled Practice

Understand Steps in Instructions

Read *Cranberry Thanksgiving* by Wende and Harry Devlin to children. Help children understand that baking cranberry bread is a process with steps. Explain that a recipe is a list of both ingredients and instructions.

Easy Read the recipe for cranberry bread in the book. Have children call out the step numbers in the recipe as you read. **Reteach**

On-Level Have children read out loud the set of directions in the recipe for cranberry bread. **Extend**

Challenge Have children describe how they could help an adult with the steps for baking cranberry bread (e.g., by stirring the batter or washing cranberries). **Enrich**

Hands-on Activities

CURRICULUM CONNECTION

Writing

Making Words from Freedom

Objective Write words using the letters in *freedom*.

Materials paper, pencils

Learning Style Verbal-Linguistic

Individual

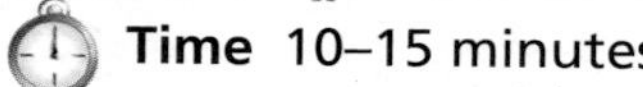

Time 10–15 minutes

freedom
do
free
me
red

1. Write the word *freedom* on the board. Remind children that the word *freedom* means a person's right to make choices.

2. Challenge children to write words that they can make with the letters in the word *freedom*. (*deer, do, fed, feed, free, freed, me, more, of, or, ore, red, rod, etc.*)

3. Remind children to add the vocabulary word *freedom* to their "My Word Book."

CURRICULUM CONNECTION

Drama

Celebration at Plymouth

Objective Dramatize the celebration between the Wampanoag and the Pilgrims.

Materials props, such as toy food

Learning Style Bodily/Kinesthetic Auditory/Verbal

Group

Time 20–30 minutes

1. Tell children that the Pilgrims and Wampanoag celebrated their friendship by playing games, running races, marching, and playing drums.

2. Have children dramatize a scene from the celebration, using actual or pretend items.

CURRICULUM CONNECTION

Art

Sailing the Ocean Blue

Objective Learn a poem and illustrate it.

Materials Construction paper and crayons

Learning Style Musical/Visual

Group

Time 15–20 minutes

1. Write the following rhyme on the board. *In fourteen hundred ninety-two, Columbus sailed the ocean blue.*

2. Have children copy the words at the top of a piece of construction paper.

3. Say the rhyme aloud. Have children repeat it with you until they have it memorized.

4. Have children draw a picture on their paper to accompany the words. Display the pictures in the classroom.

Lesson 3 Overview

The Colonies Become Free
pages 202–205

Children will gain knowledge about the colonies and how they became an independent nation and learn the meaning of the word *colony*.

 Time 20–30 minutes

Resources
- Workbook, p. 53
- Vocabulary Card colony
- Every Student Learns Guide, pp. 90–93

Benjamin Franklin
pages 206–207

Children will learn about Benjamin Franklin as a writer, inventor, and leader of America.

Time 15–20 minutes

Resource
- Workbook, p. 54

Build Background

Activity

Red, White, and Boom

 **Time** 20 minutes

Invite children to tell about the activities they do or see on Independence Day. Model the discussion by telling what events you attend, such as a picnic, parade, ball game, or fireworks display. Give each child a chance to speak. Then have children draw a picture of one of the activities.

If time is short, just have children discuss Independence Day activities.

Read Aloud

Time for Freedom

by Jason O'Donnell

More people followed the Pilgrims
To this land across the sea.

They came to live a better life
And for the chance to be free.

As time went on they knew
That freedom must be won.

They became a separate nation
After the long, brave fight was done.

Lesson 3 The Colonies Become Free

Objectives

- Describe the origins of selected holidays and celebrations such as Independence Day.
- Describe the events associated with Independence Day.
- Explain how selected celebrations reflect an American love of freedom.
- Identify historic figures such as Nathan Hale who have exemplified good citizenship.
- Identify contributions of historic figures such as George Washington.

Vocabulary

colony a place that is ruled by a country far away (p. 202)

QUICK Teaching Plan

If time is short, discuss the origin of Independence Day when the colonies declared that they were independent of England.

Lesson 3 The Colonies Become Free

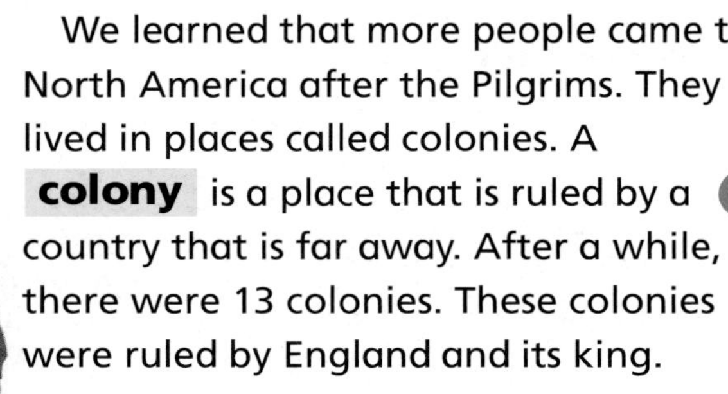

We learned that more people came to North America after the Pilgrims. They lived in places called colonies. A **colony** is a place that is ruled by a 1 country that is far away. After a while, there were 13 colonies. These colonies were ruled by England and its king.

2 Willamsburg was in the colony of Virginia.

202

1 Introduce and Motivate

Preview Display the Vocabulary Card **colony**. Tell children that many people came to America after the Pilgrims. They lived in areas called colonies that were ruled by England. Show children a map of the United States and point out the 13 states that were the 13 colonies (VA, NY, MA, CT, RI, NH, MD, NJ, NC, SC, PA, DE, and GA). Ask children how they think settlements in the colonies grew. (The colonists built homes, businesses, and farms. More colonists came. They had families. Some of the settlements expanded into towns and cities.)

Warm Up To activate prior knowledge, ask children what they know about George Washington. Children may know that he was the first President of the United States and that his face appears on the dollar bill and the state quarters. Explain that George Washington was a general in the army who helped lead the colonists in their fight for freedom from England's rule.

Practice and Extend

READING SKILL Categorize

Sorting Power to Rule

- After children have read p. 202, give them a graphic organizer with three stacked boxes connected by lines.
- Ask children to arrange the following words in order of who or what has the most power to rule: *England, colonists, colonies.* Explain that power to rule is the right to do something or to tell other people what to do.

WEB SITE Technology

You can look up vocabulary words online. Click on *Social Studies Library* and select the dictionary at **www.sfsocialstudies.com.**

Many colonists did not want to be
3 ruled by England. They did not want to follow England's laws. They wanted to be free. On July 4, 1776, a group of
4 leaders in the colonies agreed on an important paper called the Declaration of Independence. In the Declaration, they wrote that everyone had the right to be free. Today, we celebrate Independence Day on July 4.

SOCIAL STUDIES
Background

About the Declaration of Independence and Independence Day

- Thomas Jefferson wrote the Declaration of Independence with the help of Benjamin Franklin and John Adams.
- The Declaration of Independence states that a government should be based on popular consent, not the rule of a king.
- The Declaration of Independence was adopted on July 4, 1776. Americans have always celebrated this as America's birthday. However, the celebration of Independence Day only became commonplace after 1812. By the 1870s, the Fourth of July was the most important non-religious holiday in the country.

2 Teach and Discuss

Page 202

Ask children what James is holding.

C SOCIAL STUDIES STRAND
Culture

Tell children that in colonial times people used a quill for writing. A quill is a pen made from a large, stiff wing feather or tail feather of a bird.

1 **England was separated from its North American colonies by the Atlantic Ocean. Do you think England was close to America or far away?** Far away **Evaluate**

2 **How many original colonies were ruled by England?** Thirteen **Apply information**

Page 203

Test Talk

Write Your Answer

3 **What did many colonists want?** They wanted to be free. Ask children to reread their answer to make sure it is correct. **Apply Information**

4 **How did many leaders in the colonies clearly let everybody know that they wanted to be free?** They signed the Declaration of Independence. **Make Inferences**

continued

Page 204

5 How did George Washington help our country? Answers will vary but may include that he led colonial soldiers in many battles against English soldiers. **Apply Information**

Explain to children that *to regret* is to *be sorry*.

6 Why did Nathan Hale say he regretted that he could die only one time for his country? Possible answer: This was his way of expressing how proud he was to die for his country. **Make Inferences**

SOCIAL STUDIES STRAND
Citizenship

Point out to children that Nathan Hale is a model of good citizenship. Explain that a good citizen thinks not only of his or her rights but the rights of others. Tell children that Nathan Hale so much believed in his cause—the right of all Americans to be free—that he volunteered to spy on English soldiers in New York. Unfortunately, he was caught by them and hanged. He was only 21 years old. His bravery, however, inspired the colonists in their war against England.

5 The colonies fought a war with England to be free. The war lasted many years. George Washington was a famous leader in this war. He led many battles against English soldiers.

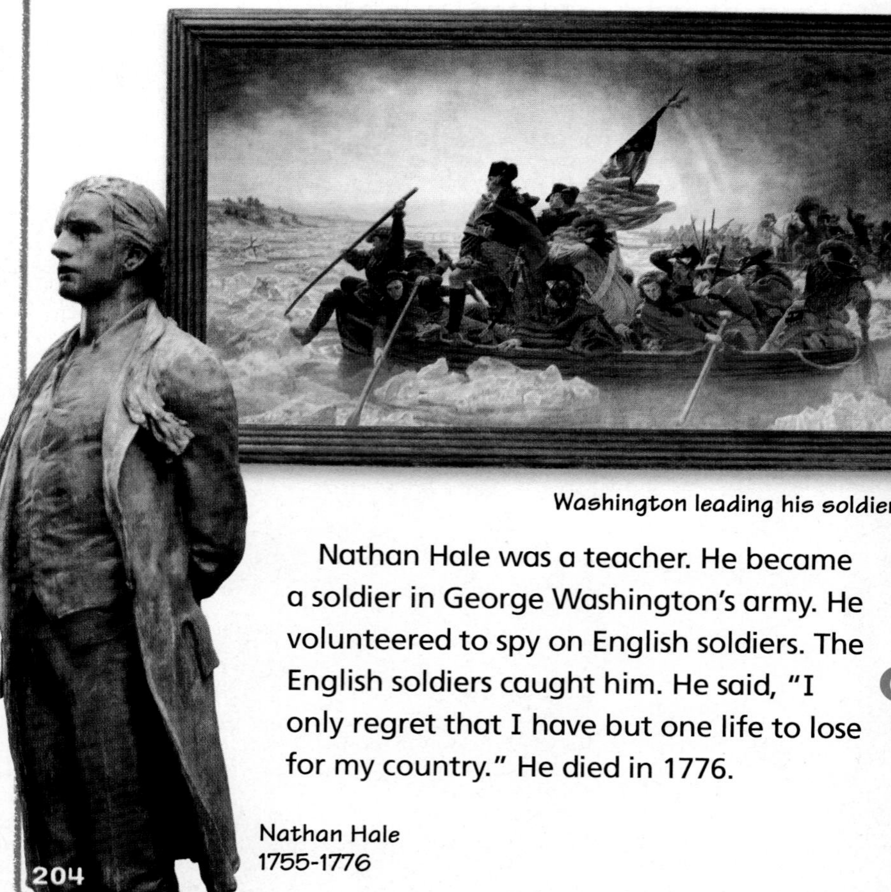

Washington leading his soldiers

Nathan Hale was a teacher. He became a soldier in George Washington's army. He volunteered to spy on English soldiers. The English soldiers caught him. He said, "I only regret that I have but one life to lose for my country." He died in 1776. 6

Nathan Hale
1755-1776

204

Practice and Extend

EXTEND LANGUAGE
ESL Support

Understanding Bravery To help children learn the meaning of the word *brave*, tell them that a brave person does the right thing even when it is hard or dangerous. Explain that Nathan Hale volunteered to go behind enemy lines to report on the movement of English soldiers. Have children draw a picture of many English soldiers represented by red stick figures with rifles, and Nathan Hale represented by a blue stick figure.

Beginning Ask children who is the brave colonist. Have them point to him.

Intermediate Have children write a title: "Nathan Hale Was Brave."

Advanced Have children write a title: "Nathan Hale Was Brave." Then ask them to tell why Nathan Hale was brave.

For additional ESL Support, use Every Student Learns Guide, pp. 90–93.

FYI

SOCIAL STUDIES
Background

Loyalists

- About 20 percent of the white population of the colonies opposed the War of Independence. These people were called "Loyalists." About 19,000 of them, armed by the English, even fought against fellow colonists in the war.

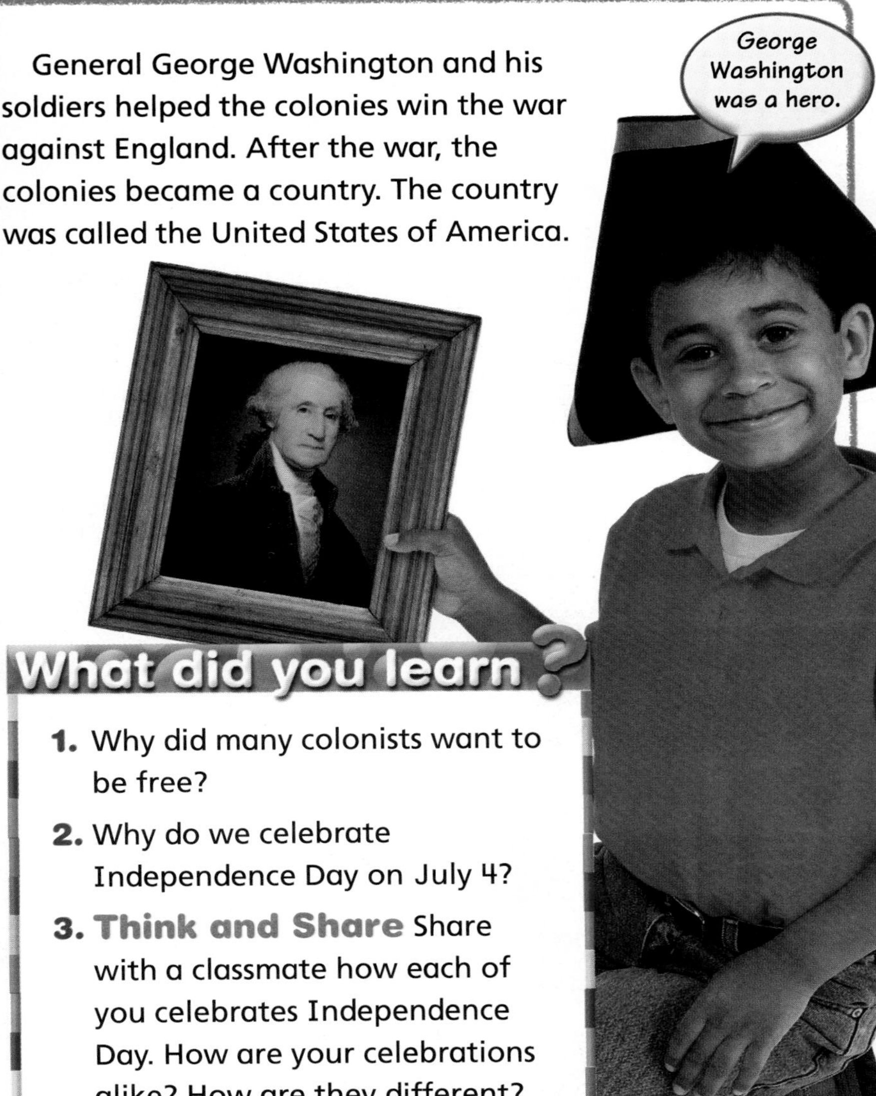
George Washington was a hero.

General George Washington and his soldiers helped the colonies win the war against England. After the war, the colonies became a country. The country was called the United States of America.

What did you learn?

1. Why did many colonists want to be free?
2. Why do we celebrate Independence Day on July 4?
3. **Think and Share** Share with a classmate how each of you celebrates Independence Day. How are your celebrations alike? How are they different?

205

FAST FACTS

- George Washington was President of the United States from 1789–1797.
- He is called the "Father of Our Country."
- His wife was named Martha. They had no children.
- He was an engineer before he became a soldier and a farmer after he was President.

Workbook, p. 54

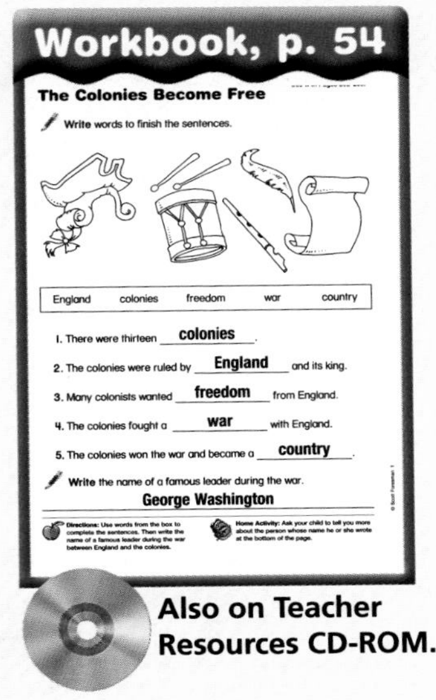

The Colonies Become Free

Write words to finish the sentences.

England colonies freedom war country

1. There were thirteen **colonies**.
2. The colonies were ruled by **England** and its king.
3. Many colonists wanted **freedom** from England.
4. The colonies fought a **war** with England.
5. The colonies won the war and became a **country**.

Write the name of a famous leader during the war.
George Washington

Also on Teacher Resources CD-ROM.

Page 205

Tell children that the war against England was fought from 1775 to 1783. Tell them that it was almost eight years.

7 The war lasted longer than you have been alive. Do you think the American Revolution was a long war? Answers will vary, but should reflect the concept of time. **Evaluate**

Explain that the war was very hard on the soldiers. They had to fight in harsh weather, such as snow and ice.

8 Why do you think the colonists were able to keep fighting for almost eight years? They strongly believed that they should be separate from England. **Make Inferences**

9 What is the difference between a colony and a country? Answers will vary but may include that a colony is a place far away from the country which controls it, and a country is a place in which people have their own government.

3 Close and Assess

Have children tell why the war against England was fought. Invite them to tell what they know about the Declaration of Independence. Then have pairs discuss one of the heroes they learned about.

✓ What did you learn?

1. They wanted to make rules for themselves.
2. Because that is the day leaders in the colonies agreed on the Declaration of Independence
3. **Think and Share** Children should give examples of activities they have participated in. Similarities and differences may include discussions of the people, food, and events.

Benjamin Franklin

Objectives

- Identify contributions of historical figures who have influenced the nation.
- Identify historic figures who exemplified good citizenship.
- Identify historical figures who have exhibited a love of inventiveness.

1 Introduce and Motivate

Preview Remind children that not all heroes are soldiers. Some, like Benjamin Franklin, are statespersons. A statesperson is somebody who is smart about the ways countries work. Tell children that Franklin needed glasses to read and to see in the distance. So he invented bifocals, special glasses for seeing both near and far.

Warm Up To activate prior knowledge, ask children to name some people they know who have helped their country. Have volunteers tell how the people named helped their country.

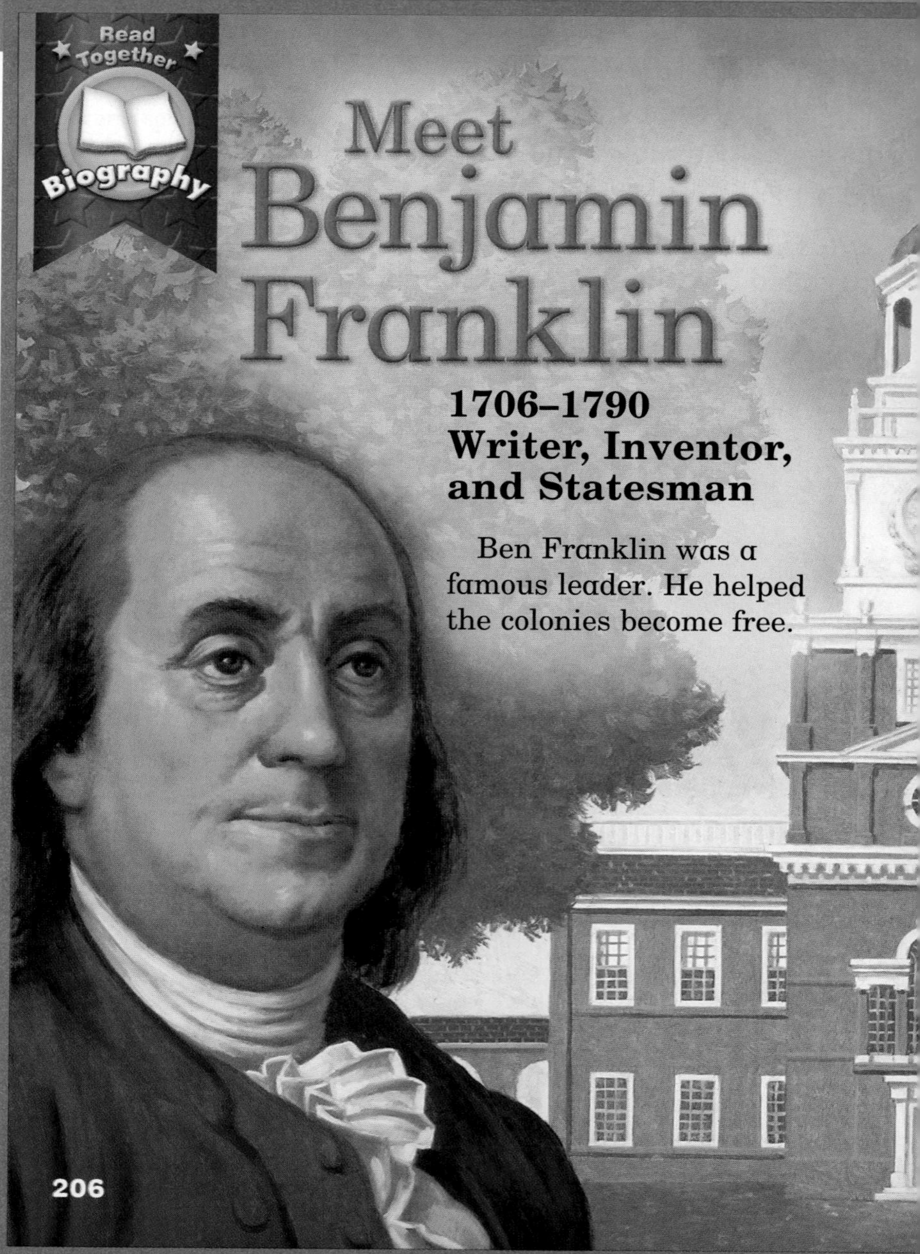

Read Together
Biography
Meet Benjamin Franklin
1706–1790
Writer, Inventor, and Statesman
Ben Franklin was a famous leader. He helped the colonies become free.
206

FYI SOCIAL STUDIES Background

Benjamin Franklin

- Born in Boston, Benjamin Franklin moved to Philadelphia, where he started a newspaper called the *Pennsylvania Gazette*. He wrote most of the articles for it. It was very successful and influential. He also printed books and pamphlets.
- When he became wealthy enough to retire from printing at 42 years old, his life was just beginning. He worked on his inventions; worked for public improvements, such as libraries and hospitals; and devoted himself to the concerns of our country.
- He was one of America's founding fathers.

FAST FACTS

- Benjamin Franklin was the 15th of 17 children.
- Seeking to prove that lightning was an electrical current, Franklin performed a famous experiment in 1752. He attached a metal key to a kite, which he flew during a storm. Lightning passed through the key, proving that lightning was electricity. Caution children not to perform this experiment at home.

You may help children find out more about Benjamin Franklin by clicking on *Meet the People* at **www.sfsocialstudies.com.**

Young Ben only went to school for about two years. However, he still wanted to learn. He learned math by himself. He loved to read. When he became older, he bought his own newspaper. It became very popular. **1**

Benjamin Franklin also wrote books. He wrote a book called *Poor Richard's Almanack*. It became very famous. **2**

Benjamin Franklin was an inventor too. He invented the rocking chair and a special type of eyeglasses. **3**

Benjamin Franklin wanted to help his country. He signed the Declaration of Independence. Later, he went to talk to the king of France. He asked the king to help the colonies become free. The king said he would. With France's help, America won its war against England.

Benjamin Franklin was born in Boston, Massachusetts.

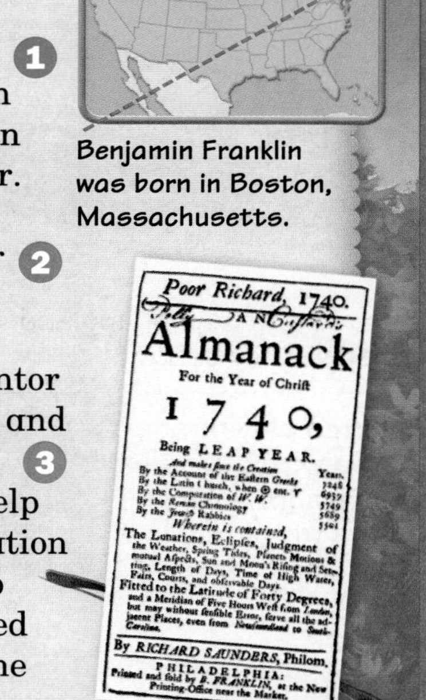

Poor Richard, 1740.

AN

Almanack

For the Year of Christ

1740,

Being LEAP YEAR.

Wherein is contained,

The Lunations, Eclipses, Judgment of the Weather, Spring Tides, Planets Motions & mutual Aspects, Sun and Moon's Rising and Setting, Length of Days, Time of High Water, Fairs, Courts, and observable Days.

Fitted to the Latitude of Forty Degrees, and a Meridian of Five Hours West from London, but may without sensible Error, serve all the adjacent Places, even from Newfoundland to South-Carolina.

By RICHARD SAUNDERS, Philom.

PHILADELPHIA:
Printed and sold by B. FRANKLIN, at the New Printing-Office near the Market.

Think and Share

Why is Benjamin Franklin an important person in our country's history?

For more information, go online to *Meet the People* at **www.sfsocialstudies.com**.

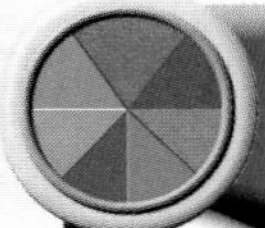

CURRICULUM CONNECTION
Science

Cool Shades

- Explain to children that people, animals, and plants need sunlight. Then explain that too much sun, however, can be harmful.
- Tell children that people around the world protect themselves from the sun in a variety of ways, from wearing wide-brim hats to carrying umbrellas. Tell children that sunglasses were invented to protect the eyes from the glare of the sun.
- Ask children to draw pictures of themselves wearing sunglasses with a bright sun overhead.
- Encourage children to fancifully decorate the sunglasses.

2 Teach and Discuss

1 How do you think young Ben learned math all by himself? Answers will vary but might include he read books that explained it. **Draw Conclusions**

Have children point to Boston on the map. Tell them that Boston was one of the first big cities in the United States. Then tell children that Benjamin Franklin moved to Philadelphia to start a printing business. Explain that an almanac is a book published each year that contains facts on many subjects.

Tell children that *Poor Richard's Almanac* included a collection of short sentences on the value of working hard, saving money, and leading a simple life. Many of the things Franklin wrote in the Almanac became famous. You may know his famous saying "Early to bed and early to rise, makes a man healthy, wealthy, and wise."

2 Do you think *Poor Richard's Almanack* included advice about using time wisely or stories about talking animals? Advice about going to sleep **Draw Conclusions**

3 Why might Franklin have decided to make a special type of glasses and a rocking chair? Answers might include: He could not see with the glasses he had; he wanted a chair that moved. **Generalize**

3 Close and Assess

Ask students to brainstorm aloud what they know about Ben Franklin. Then have them write a few sentences about him.

Think and Share

He helped the colonists win freedom. He asked France for help in the war. He helped write the Declaration of Independence. He invented things we still use today.

Use with pages 202–207

Lesson 3 Wrap-Up

MEETING INDIVIDUAL NEEDS

Leveled Practice

The Stamp Act

Tell children that the English enacted a law—the Stamp Act—to raise money for England. This act forced the colonists to buy stamps to put on the newspapers they bought.

Easy Have children playing the English make stamps with 10 cents written on the front. **Reteach**

On-Level Have children playing the colonists buy a stamp with play coins. Have them glue the stamp on a newspaper. Ask them to count what it would cost to buy stamps for 5 days. **Extend**

Challenge Have children stand on a wooden box and make a speech against putting stamps on newspapers because the money goes to the English. Suggest that their argument include how much money the English make in one day from the stamps. **Enrich**

Hands-on Activities

CURRICULUM CONNECTION

Writing

Far Away Places

Objective Demonstrate understanding of the lesson vocabulary.

Resources Vocabulary Card: **colony**

Materials crayons

Learning Style Visual

Individual

Time 10–15 minutes

1. Point out on a map the Atlantic Ocean, with the United States to the west and Europe to the east. Then point out the 13 American colonies and England.

2. Ask children to draw and label the ocean, the colonies, and England.

3. Remind children to add the vocabulary word *colony* to their "My Word Book."

CURRICULUM CONNECTION

Drama

Signing the Declaration of Independence

sObjective Dramatize the colonists signing the Declaration of Independence.

Materials props, including a piece of paper and a feather

Learning Style Verbal/Linguistic Bodily/Kinesthetic

Group

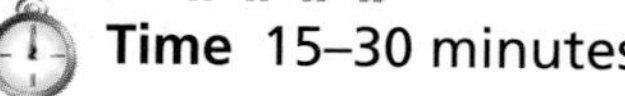

Time 15–30 minutes

1. Have students act out the colonial leaders discussing why they want to be free.

2. Have children conduct a "signing" of the Declaration of Independence using a feather to sign their names to the bottom of the document.

CURRICULUM CONNECTION

Reading

One If by Land, Two If by Sea

Objective Read a book about the American Revolution.

Materials picture book

Learning Style Auditory/Verbal

Group

Time 20–30 minutes

1. Read *The Midnight Ride of Paul Revere* by Longfellow, illustrated by Jeffrey Thompson, to the class. Tell children that this is the famous poem about Paul Revere, who rode a horse from Boston to Lexington, Massachusetts, warning people that the British were coming.

2. Use the illustrations to discuss the poem with students.

3. Ask students to tell about how Paul Revere exhibited good citizenship.

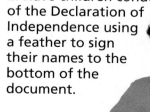

Lesson 4 Overview

Symbols in Our Country pages 208–209	Children will learn symbols in the United States and explore their meanings. 	Time 10–15 minutes Resources • Workbook, p. 55 • Every Student Learns Guide, pp. 94–97
Our Country's Flag pages 210–211	Children will learn about the history and meaning of the United States flag.	Time 10–15 minutes

Build Background

Activity

My Flag

Time 20 minutes

Point out the American flag in the classroom. Tell children that it stands for the United States. Give children construction paper showing the outline of a wavy flag flowing from the top of a pole. Have children decorate the flag to represent themselves. Ask children to include what is important to them. Have children tell about their flag when they have finished.

If time is short, discuss with children what they would include in a flag that stands for themselves.

Read Aloud

Monumental Riddle

by Shawna Morrison

I remind people of a person
who could not tell a lie.
I'm a monument
that stretches way into the sky.
Well, to tell you the truth,
I'm only 555 feet, 5 and $\frac{1}{8}$ inches tall.
But I think that's still pretty high
all and all.
What am I?

[Washington Monument]

Symbols in Our Country

Objectives

- Identify the motto of the United States.
- Explain selected national and state patriotic symbols such as the Liberty Bell and the Alamo.
- Identify symbols that represent the United States and what it stands for.
- Obtain information about a topic using a variety of visual sources such as pictures and graphics.

QUICK Teaching Plan

If time is short, point out each of the symbols and discuss the meaning and history of each.

1 Introduce and Motivate

Preview Have children look at the symbols in the lesson. Ask children whether they can identify any of them.

Warm Up To activate prior knowledge, ask children to name symbols and tell what they stand for, such as a heart (love). Tell children that our country and states also have symbols. Discuss with children how the Alamo is a symbol that stands not only for the courage of Texans but of all Americans.

2 Teach and Discuss

Page 208

As you discuss the symbols, be sure to point out that they are patriotic symbols: they honor those who helped build our country, and they foster appreciation for and loyalty to our nation and states. Symbols of our nation remind us to be patriotic. Explain that *patriotic* means "showing respect for and love of country."

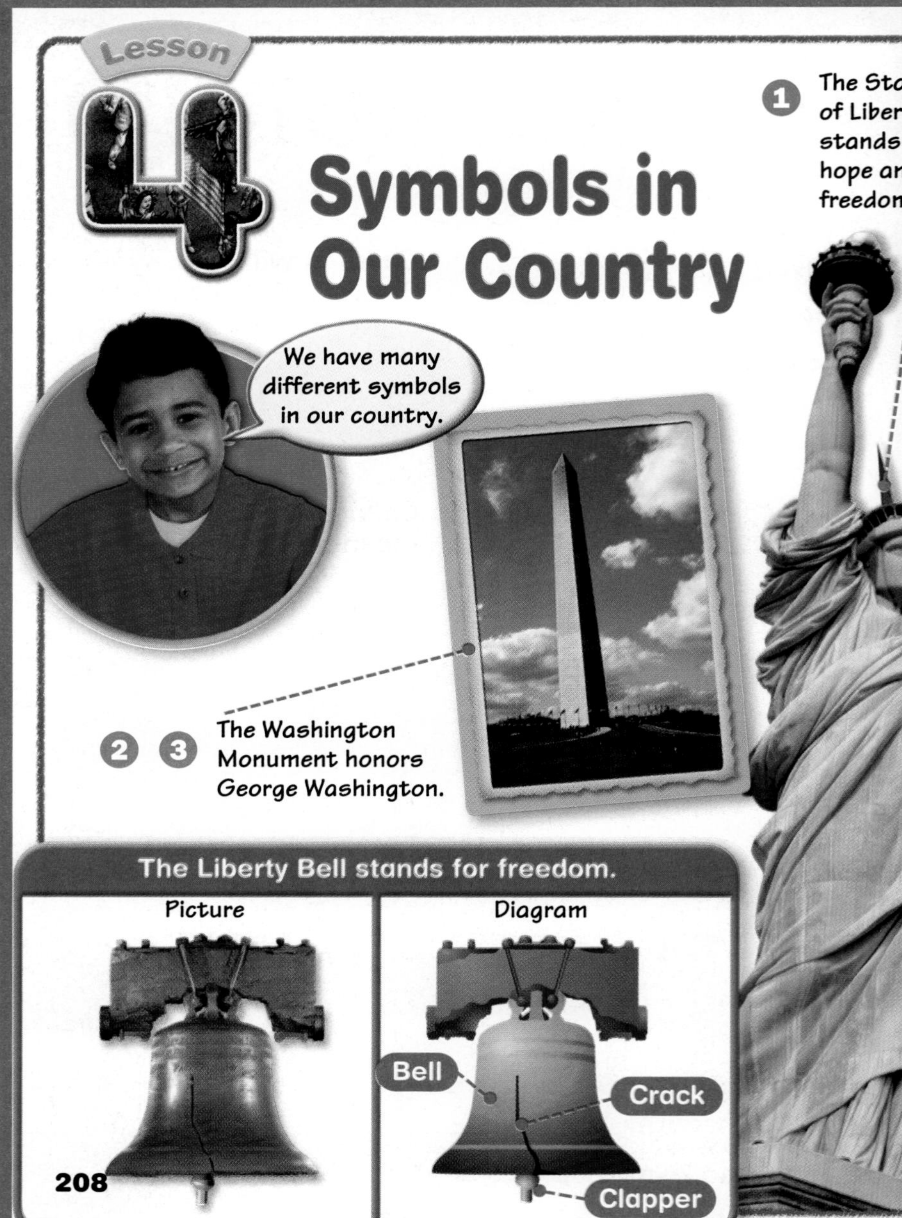
Lesson 4
Symbols in Our Country
We have many different symbols in our country.
1 The Statue of Liberty stands for hope and freedom.
2 3 The Washington Monument honors George Washington.
The Liberty Bell stands for freedom.
Picture
Diagram
Bell
Crack
Clapper
208

Practice and Extend

READING SKILL
Recall and Retell

- After children have read pages 208–211, give children a copy of a web with a center circle and four outer circles.
- Have children write *Our Country's Symbols* in the center circle.
- Have them write the names of the country's symbols in the outer circles. (Statue of Liberty, bald eagle, Liberty Bell, Washington Monument)
- Ask children to tell what they know about each symbol.

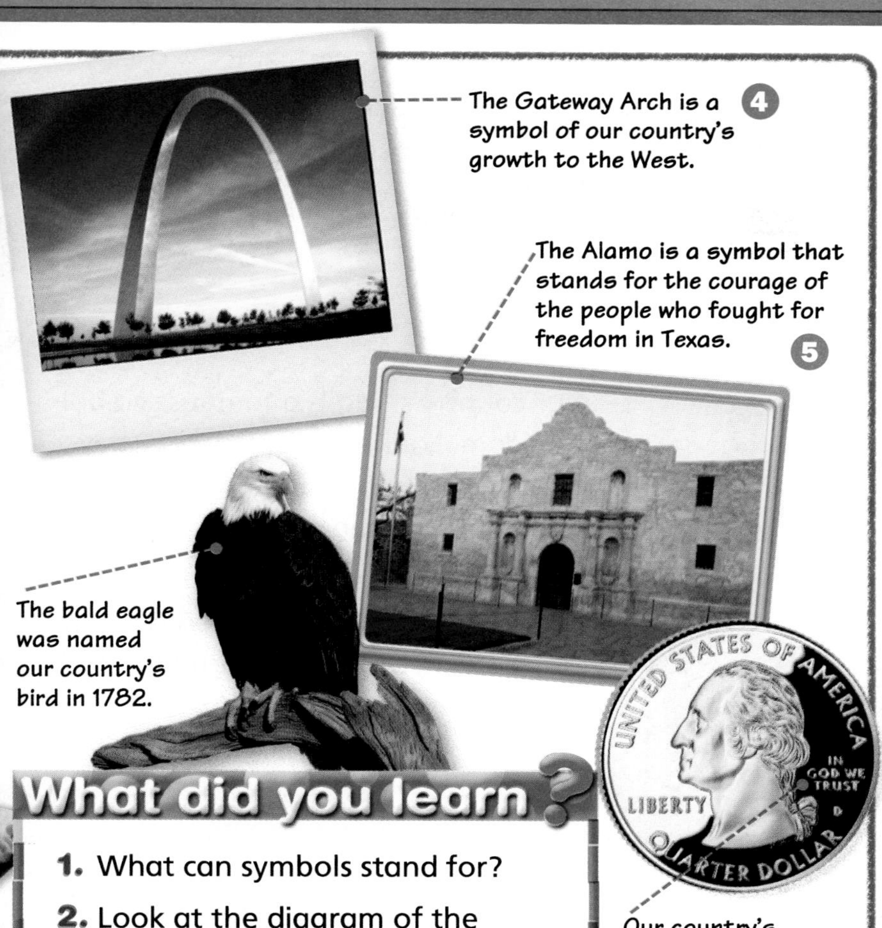

The Gateway Arch is a symbol of our country's growth to the West. 4
The Alamo is a symbol that stands for the courage of the people who fought for freedom in Texas. 5
The bald eagle was named our country's bird in 1782.
UNITED STATES OF AMERICA
LIBERTY
IN GOD WE TRUST
QUARTER DOLLAR

Our country's motto is "In God We Trust." A motto is a saying that people try to live by. Our country's motto stands for freedom and trust.

What did you learn?

1. What can symbols stand for?
2. Look at the diagram of the Liberty Bell. What part is inside the bell?
3. **Think and Share** Draw a new symbol for our country. Tell what your symbol stands for.

209

FYI SOCIAL STUDIES Background

About the Symbols

- The Statue of Liberty is on an island in New York Harbor.
- One of the meanings of *bald* is having white feathers on the head.
- The Liberty Bell was rung to signal the first public reading of the Declaration of Independence.
- The Washington Monument is 555 feet $5\frac{1}{8}$ inches tall.
- The Alamo is located in San Antonio, Texas.
- The Gateway Arch is in St. Louis, Missouri. The Mississippi River flows beside the arch.

Workbook, p. 55

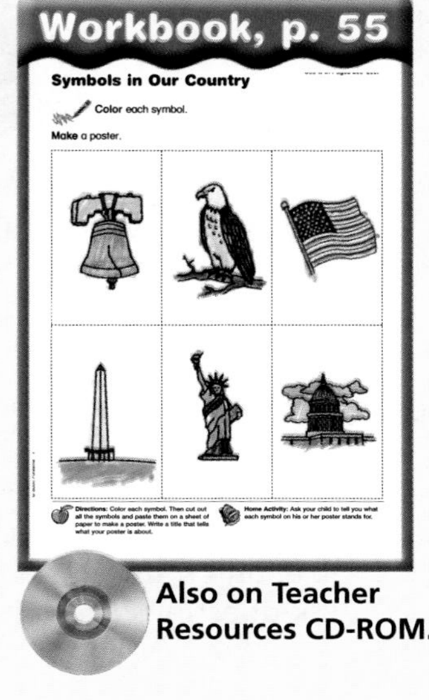

Symbols in Our Country
Color each symbol.
Make a poster.

Also on Teacher Resources CD-ROM.

1 **Why do you think the Statue of Liberty stands for hope and freedom?** Possible answer: People coming to the U.S. want freedom and feel hopeful. Draw Conclusions

2 **Why was a monument built for George Washington?** Answers will vary but may include: to honor him and to remind people of his great deeds. Interpret

3 **Who would you like to see a monument built for?** Answers will vary but may include leaders, citizen heroes, family members, or friends. Express Ideas

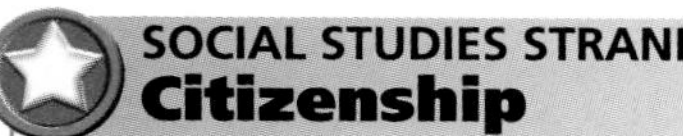

4 **Why do you think an arch is a symbol of the country's growth to the west?** Answers will vary but may include that it looks like a door to new places. Draw Conclusions

5 **What is the Alamo a symbol of?** The courage of the people who fought for freedom in Texas Recall and Retell

SOCIAL STUDIES STRAND
Citizenship

Ask children to identify the country's motto by pointing to it on the picture of the coin.

3 Close and Assess

Ask children to name some of the symbols of our country. Have them discuss with a partner what they know about these symbols.

✓ What did you learn?

1. Answers will vary but may include states, countries, and ideas, such as hope and freedom.
2. The clapper
3. **Think and Share** Answers will vary but children's symbols should stand for an ideal for the whole country, such as freedom or peace.

Living History

Our Country's Flag

Objectives

- Explain selected national patriotic symbols such as the United States flag.
- Distinguish between past and present.
- Explain how selected symbols reflect an American love of freedom.

1 Introduce and Motivate

Preview Point to the America flag in the classroom. Explain to children that a flag is not only a piece of cloth with a pattern on it but also a symbol. This flag is a symbol of our country.

Warm Up Recite and explain the Pledge of Allegiance. On a second reading, have children echo each line. Encourage children to be attentive and show their respect and thanks to the United States by standing, removing their hat, facing and looking at the flag, placing their right hand over their heart, and avoiding fidgeting.

Ask children if they have ever been to a sporting event where fans sang the national anthem. Sing the first line. Explain that the same patriotic behavior is expected for singing the anthem.

2 Teach and Discuss

Have children point to each flag along the time line. Tell children that these were American flags at different times. Have them note the different numbers of stars and stripes and arrangements of stars. Tell children what the stars and stripes stand for. Explain that the flag changed as new states were added to the country.

Have children point to the large flag. Tell them that this is what the flag looks like today. Have children discuss the differences between the present American flag and those of the past.

Living History

Our Country's Flag

Our country's flag is a famous symbol of freedom. Look at the pictures. They show some ways our flag has changed from the past to the present.

Today, the stripes stand for the number of states our country had when it became free. The 50 stars stand for each of our 50 states.

1

210

Practice and Extend

EXTEND LANGUAGE ESL Support

Interviewing and Retelling Have children interview family members to find out about a symbol of their native country, such as a flag. Ask children to make a drawing of the symbol and explain what it stands for.

Beginning Have children tell about the symbol. Ask questions to prompt for information, such as *What does the flag look like? Where is the statue located?*

Intermediate Have children tell what the symbol looks like, and if it is not a flag, where it is located. If necessary, ask questions to clarify, such as *What does the bird on the flag stand for?*

Advanced Without prompting, have children tell what the symbol is and what it stands for.

For additional ESL Support, use Every Student Learns Guide, pp. 94–97.

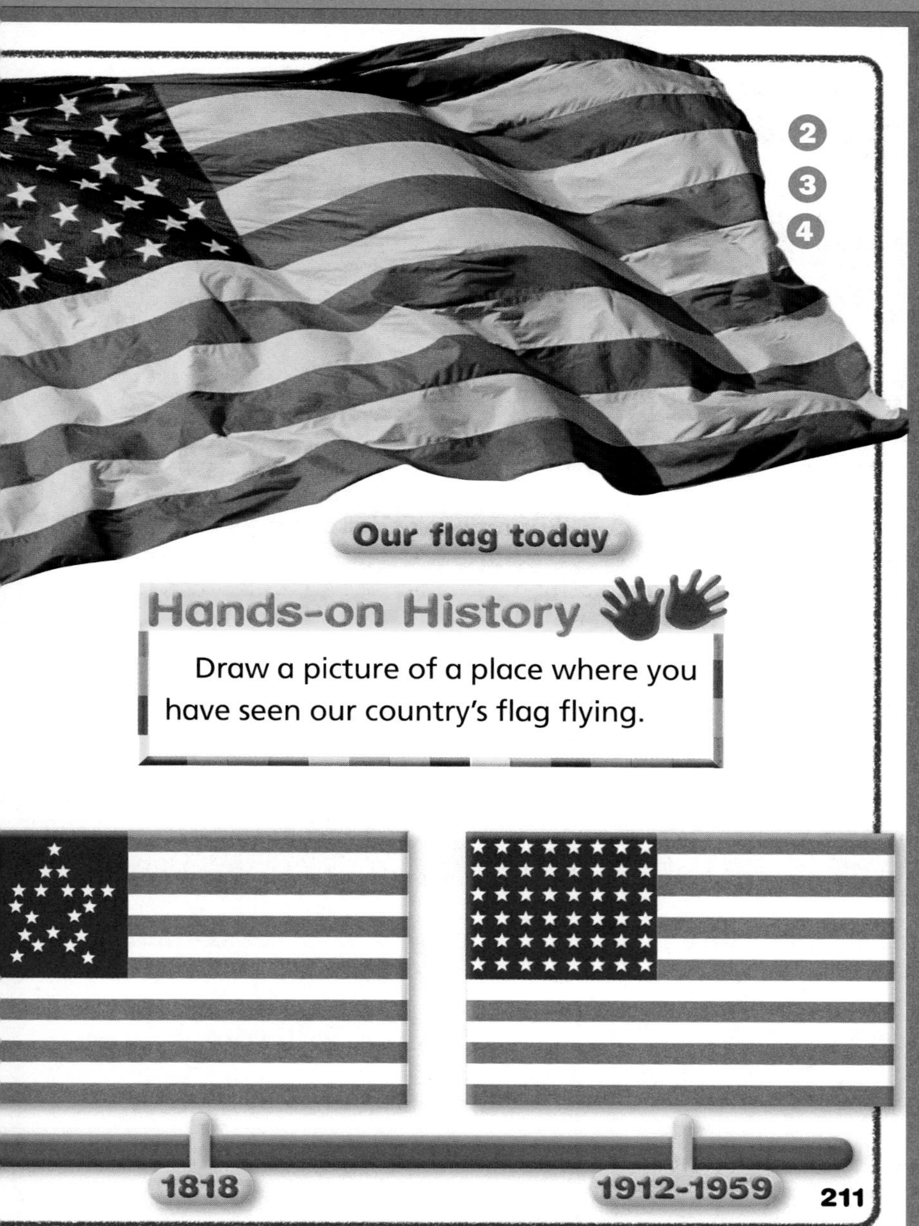

Our flag today

Hands-on History

Draw a picture of a place where you have seen our country's flag flying.

1818

1912-1959

211

SOCIAL STUDIES
Background

About the American Flag

- The American flag has changed many times in the history of our nation. The first flag to represent the United States had only 13 stars and 13 stripes. This is because at the time of the American Revolution the country consisted of 13 colonies.
- The 15-star, 15-stripe flag of 1795 was the only U.S. flag to have more than 13 stripes. This was the flag Francis Scott Key saw when he wrote the National Anthem.
- George Washington's original pencil sketch for the flag shows that he envisioned six-pointed stars. Some historians believe that it was Betsy Ross who convinced George Washington to go with the five-pointed star we now use.
- Flag Day is June 14. Many people fly a flag on that day to honor the United States flag.

1 **Count the stripes on the 1776 flag. How many are there? Why does it have this many stripes?** Thirteen; They represent the first 13 states. **Draw Conclusions**

2 **Look at the time line of flags. How was the 1795 flag alike and different from the 1776 flag?** Possible answers: Alike: same colors; Different: different number of stripes, 1795 flag had stars, 1776 flag did not **Compare and Contrast**

3 **Do you think the flag could change in the future?** Answers will vary but may include that the flag could change if another state joins the United States. **Draw Conclusions**

Show your state flag to children and discuss the symbolism. Recite the state pledge with children. Discuss its meaning.

4 **Besides each of the 50 states and our country, what else has a flag?** Answers will vary. Possible answers include: other countries, stores or restaurants, sports teams, the Olympic games, schools. **Apply Information**

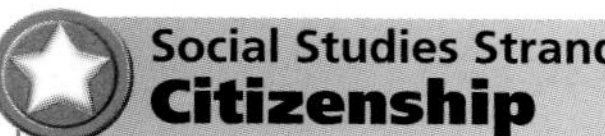

Social Studies Strand
Citizenship

Explain to children that during the war against England, there were many national and colonial flag designs. Some flags were decorated with stars and stripes, others, with a tree, an eagle, or a snake. All these flags reflected an American love of individualism, inventiveness, and freedom.

3 Close and Assess

Hands-on History

Have the class brainstorm places where children have seen the flag flying. Have children label the place on their drawing.

Use with pages 208–211

Lesson 4 Wrap-Up

MEETING INDIVIDUAL NEEDS

Leveled Practice

Viewing Symbols

To help children understand the use of American patriotic symbols, read selections and show illustrations from *The Children's Book of America* by William J. Bennett.

Easy Have children point to a picture of a symbol they learned in this lesson. Have them tell what the symbol means. **Reteach**

On-Level Have children look through the book to find three examples of symbols they learned in this lesson. Invite children to tell what the symbols mean or why each one is a symbol. **Extend**

Challenge Have children find illustrations of our country's symbols that have not been discussed. Have them tell what the symbols mean. **Enrich**

Hands-on Activities

CURRICULUM CONNECTION
Writing

Picturing Symbols

Objective Demonstrate understanding of the word *symbol*.

Materials paper, crayons, pictures of colonial flags

Learning Style Visual

Individual

Time 15–20 minutes

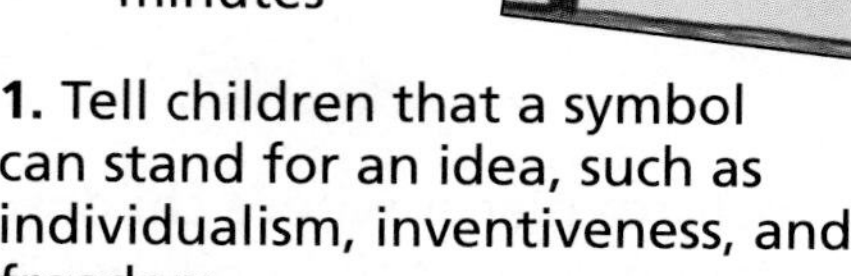

1. Tell children that a symbol can stand for an idea, such as individualism, inventiveness, and freedom.

2. Remind children that some flags represent freedom.

3. Show children pictures of some flags the colonies used during the war for independence.

4. Have children draw a flag one of the colonies might have flown during the war for independence. Have them write *Freedom* at the bottom of the drawing.

CURRICULUM CONNECTION
Math

Arranging the Stars

Objective Create arrangements for stars on the flag.

Materials paper, paper stars

Learning Style Logical/Mathematical/Visual/Spatial

Individual

Time 15–20 minutes

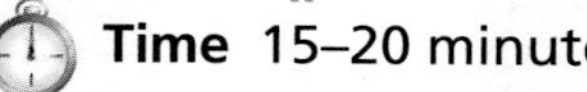

1. Assign children flags with the following years and number of stars: 1822—24 stars; 1848—30 stars; 1865—36 stars.

2. Tell them to arrange the stars in even rows, for example, 2 rows of 12 (for 24 stars), 3 rows of 10 (for 30 stars), and 4 rows of 9 (for 36 stars). Demonstrate with 28 stars (from the flag adopted in 1846).

CURRICULUM CONNECTION
Writing

New Mottoes

Objective Write a new motto.

Materials paper, pencils

Learning Style Interpersonal

Individual

Time 15–20 minutes

1. Remind children that a motto is often a short sentence that says what somebody believes.

2. Tell children that not only do countries and states have a motto, but so do people. For example, some people's motto is "Think before you speak."

3. Have children write their own motto. The motto could be for the class, the school, their family, or themselves.

Do my best

4. You might help children by having them complete the sentence: I believe in ______.

Lesson 5 Overview

We Celebrate Holidays **pages 212–215**	Children will learn about some of our country's holidays and explore why we celebrate them. 	Time 20–30 minutes Resources • Workbook, p. 56 • Vocabulary Cards holiday President • Every Student Learns Guide, pp. 98–101
Abraham Lincoln **pages 216–217**	Children will learn about Abraham Lincoln and the contributions he made to the country.	Time 15–20 minutes

Build Background

Activity

Holidays

 **Time** 20 minutes

Invite children to tell about special days in their home, such as birthdays or visits by grandparents. Explain to children that a holiday is a special day celebrated by all Americans at the same time, such as Valentine's Day, Mother's Day, and Halloween. Have children draw a picture of how they celebrate a holiday, and label the picture.

If time is short, talk with children about special days, including holidays. Invite children to share holidays they have experienced.

Read Aloud

Fourth of July

by Manuel DeSoto

Sure I like fireworks and parades
and picnics with hot dogs and lemonade.
But what I like best is saluting the flag.
It's never a drag
to honor the soldiers who fought bravely
to form a country
where we could
be free.

We Celebrate Holidays

Objectives

- Describe the origins of selected holidays and celebrations of the nation such as Martin Luther King, Jr. Day and Veterans Day.
- Cite reasons for observing special days and holidays.
- Describe the lives of people commemorated by Presidents' Day.

Vocabulary

holiday a special day celebrated to honor people or things that happened (p. 212)

President the leader of the United States (p. 215)

QUICK Teaching Plan

If time is short, discuss each holiday as you point out the illustrations of holiday celebrations.

- Tell children about Abraham Lincoln.

1 Introduce and Motivate

Preview Display the Vocabulary Card **holiday**. Invite a volunteer to tell the meaning. Ask children to name holidays they celebrate. Point to the illustrations and describe the holiday celebrations. Then display the Vocabulary Card **President**. Share with children the definition.

Warm Up To activate prior knowledge, have children look at the medals on p. 213. Explain that medals are given to soldiers as a reward for bravery or exceptional actions. Tell children that there are special holidays to honor the soldiers who have fought to keep us free. Then tell them that there are also holidays to honor other people who dedicated their lives to making our country better. Discuss with children how many customs and celebrations reflect an American love of individualism and inventiveness.

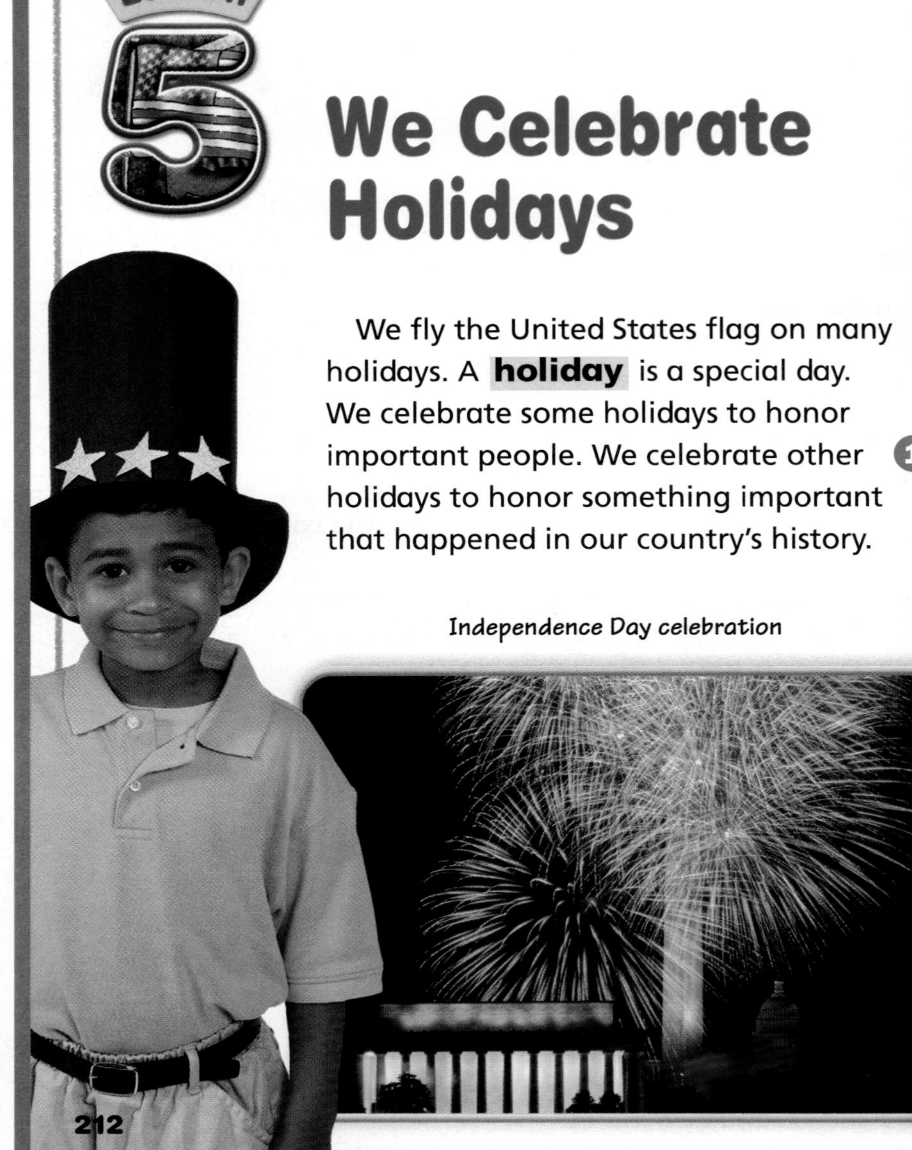

Lesson 5

We Celebrate Holidays

We fly the United States flag on many holidays. A **holiday** is a special day. We celebrate some holidays to honor important people. We celebrate other holidays to honor something important that happened in our country's history. 1

Independence Day celebration

212

Practice and Extend

READING SKILL Analyze Pictures

- After children look at the photographs on pp. 212–213, give children a web graphic organizer with an oval in the middle and three spokes with ovals.
- Have them write *Holidays* in the center oval.
- Have children complete the graphic organizer by writing a word or two in each circle describing the three holiday celebrations.

WEB SITE Technology

You can look up vocabulary words online. Click on *Social Studies Library* and select the dictionary at **www.sfsocialstudies.com.**

Memorial Day and Veterans Day are two holidays. On these days, Americans honor the people who fought in our country's wars.

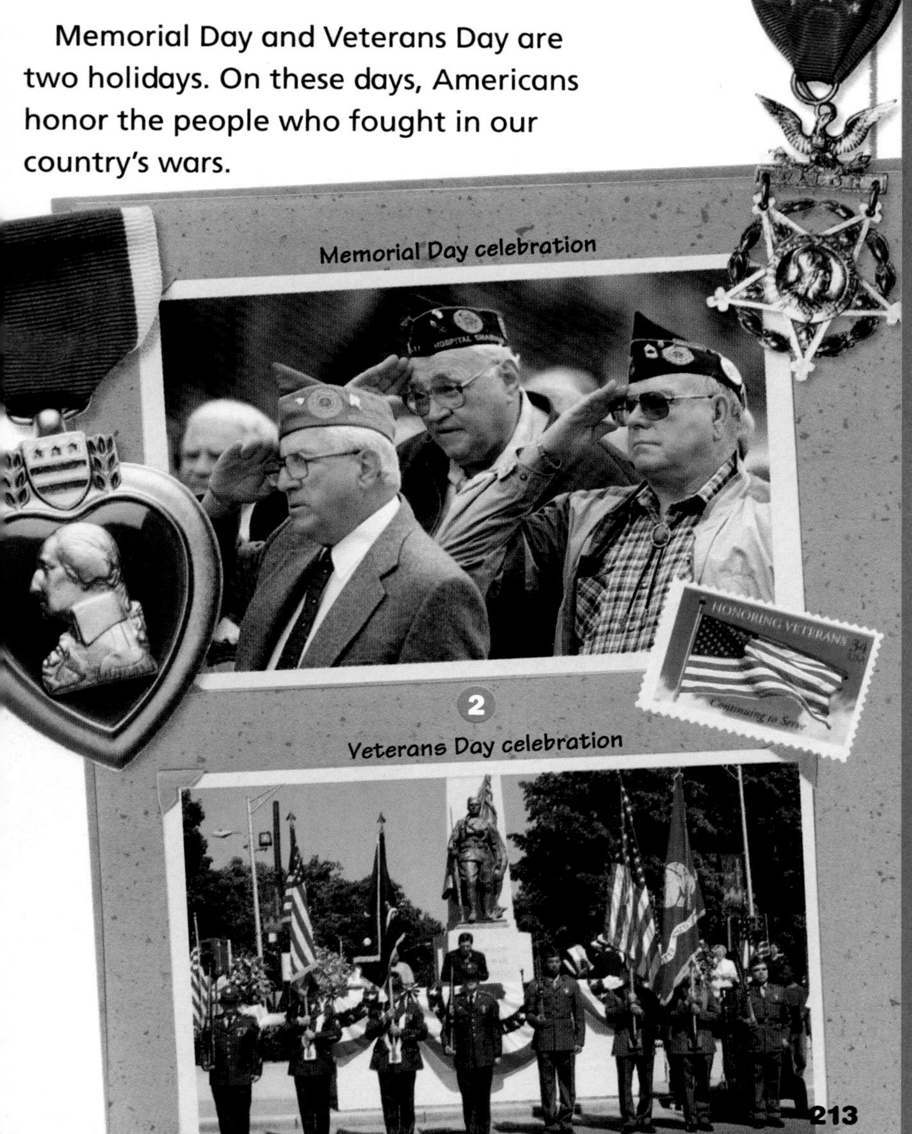

Memorial Day celebration

2 Veterans Day celebration

213

2 Teach and Discuss

Page 212

Point out the picture of the Independence Day celebration. Ask children what is shown in the sky. (fireworks)

1 **Why is a holiday a special day?** Answers will vary but may include that a holiday celebrates a person who influenced our country or an important event in our country's past. **Make Inferences**

Page 213

Explain to children that a veteran is someone who was a soldier. Explain that on Veterans Day in the United States, we honor those soldiers—both living and dead—who served in times of war. Explain that on Memorial Day we honor veterans who lost their lives fighting for our country.

2 **What are some holidays that are not shown?** Answers will vary but may include Columbus Day, Kwanzaa, New Year's Day, and Thanksgiving. **Apply Information**

FYI SOCIAL STUDIES Background

About Memorial Day and Veterans Day

- Memorial Day was first observed for soldiers killed in the Civil War.
- Most states observe Memorial Day on the last Monday in May.
- Memorial Day is marked by the laying of a wreath on the Tomb of the Unknown Soldier in Arlington National Cemetery (Virginia).
- Veterans Day was originally called Armistice Day and was set aside to celebrate the end of World War I. After the Korean War, it was designated as Veterans Day to honor soldiers of all U.S. wars.

continued

Page 214

SOCIAL STUDIES STRAND
History

Explain to children that once, in some states, African Americans had to sit at the back of the bus, were not allowed into restaurants for non-African Americans, and went to schools that were only for African Americans. In the 1950s and 1960s, Martin Luther King, Jr. led marches—sometimes at the risk to his life—to improve the lives of African Americans. His beautiful speeches inspired people from all backgrounds to work for change. He expressed a belief in equality for all people for the common good.

Test Talk

Locate Key Words in the Question

3 **What did Martin Luther King, Jr. believe?** He believed that all people should be treated equally. Have children find the key words in the question. Children should finish the statement "I need to find out what Dr. King believed." **Apply Information**

Have children look at picture of Dr. King giving a speech. Discuss the custom of reading or listening to parts of his speeches on Martin Luther King, Jr. Day.

4 **Why might people listen to a speech by Dr. King?** Possible answer: To help them become a better citizen. **Make Inferences**

Martin Luther King, Jr. Day is in January. On this holiday, we honor Martin Luther King, Jr.

Dr. King believed that all people should have the right to be treated fairly. He worked hard so that African 3 Americans would be treated with 4 respect. He wanted all Americans to be treated the same. His birthday was on January 15.

214

Practice and Extend

EXTEND LANGUAGE
ESL Support

Telling About Holidays To help children practice and extend their vocabulary, have them tell about a holiday in their native culture, such as Chinese New Year. Ask children if they know of a holiday similar to Memorial Day or Presidents' Day. Children may need to get information from family members.

Beginning Have children name the holiday in their native language and give a translation, if they can.

Intermediate Have children name the holiday and tell how it is celebrated.

Advanced Have children tell everything they know about a holiday. They can describe the way it is celebrated and its origin.

For additional ESL Support, use Every Student Learns Guide, pp. 98–101.

We celebrate Presidents' Day in February. The **President** is our country's leader. We honor George Washington and Abraham Lincoln on this holiday. Both of these Presidents were born in February.

George Washington was born in Virginia. He became a farmer. Later, he became our country's first President. We call him the "Father of our Country."

George Washington

Abraham Lincoln

What did you learn?

1. Why are Memorial Day and Veterans Day important holidays?
2. Why do we celebrate Martin Luther King, Jr. Day?
3. **Write and Share** Tell why we celebrate holidays.

215

FYI SOCIAL STUDIES Background

About Martin Luther King, Jr.

- Martin Luther King, Jr. was born in Atlanta, Georgia, on January 15, 1929.
- King worked with others to organize a bus boycott (1955–56) in Montgomery, Alabama, to protest racial segregation in public transportation.
- He was shot and killed on April 4, 1968.
- Since 1986, the third Monday in January has been designated a legal holiday for Martin Luther King, Jr.'s birthday.

Workbook, p. 56

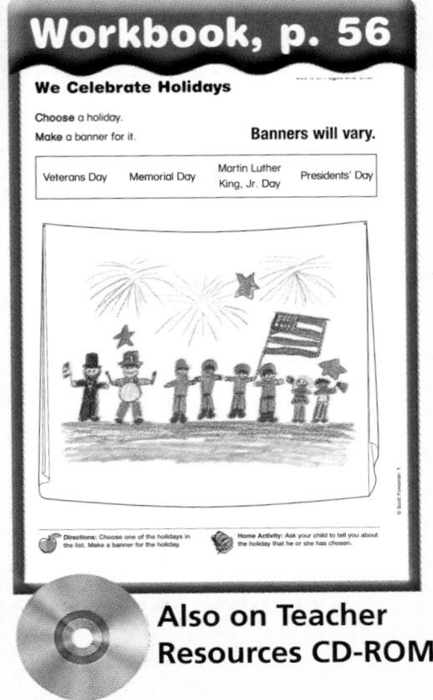

We Celebrate Holidays

Choose a holiday.
Make a banner for it.

Banners will vary.

Veterans Day	Memorial Day	Martin Luther King, Jr. Day	Presidents' Day

Also on Teacher Resources CD-ROM.

Page 215

5 What do we call our country's leader? The President **Apply information**

Ask children to recall what they learned about George Washington. (He was born in Virginia. He was a leader in the war against the English to make the colonies free. He was our first President. We call him the "Father of our Country.")

6 Why do you think we honor George Washington and Abraham Lincoln? Answers will vary but may include that they were great Presidents. **Express Ideas**

7 What good leaders do you know? Answers will vary. Students may say a family member or coach. **Why is this person a good leader?** Answers will vary but might include that the person knows how to be in charge. **Express Ideas**

3 Close and Assess

Ask children to write the names of the holidays they learned about. Pair students and invite them to interview each other to find out how they celebrate different holidays.

✓ What did you learn?

1. They honor people who fought in wars.
2. Answers will vary but may include that we honor him for speaking up so that all people would be treated fairly.
3. **Think and Share** We celebrate holidays to honor important people or to honor something important that happened in our country's history.

Abraham Lincoln

Objectives

- Identify contributions of historical figures such as Abraham Lincoln who have influenced the nation.
- Describe the lives of people commemorated by Presidents' Day.

1 Introduce and Motivate

Preview Ask children to look at the illustrations on pages 216–217. Invite students to share what they can tell about Abraham Lincoln from the pictures. (He had a beard. He wore a top hat. He lived in a log cabin.) With miniature toy logs, show children how a log cabin is built.

Warm Up Ask children to think about someone else they read about who had only a little schooling. (Ben Franklin) Invite children to discuss whether they think they could teach themselves to read, write, and do math or if they would need help at school.

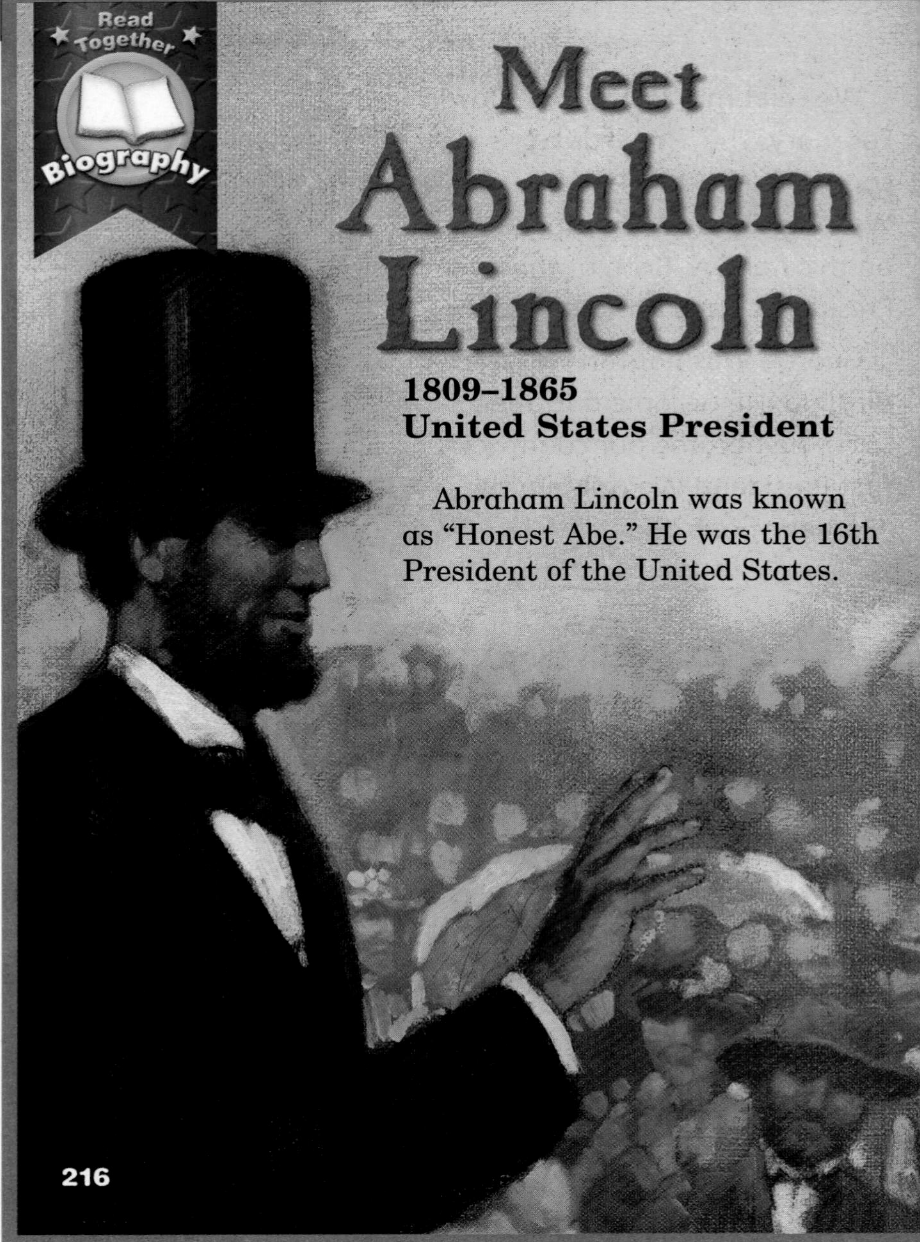

Read Together
Biography
Meet Abraham Lincoln
1809–1865
United States President
Abraham Lincoln was known as "Honest Abe." He was the 16th President of the United States.
216

Practice and Extend

SOCIAL STUDIES Background

About Abraham Lincoln

- Abraham Lincoln was born in a backwoods log cabin in Kentucky.
- His entire schooling amounted to no more than one year's attendance. However, he had a great love of learning. He walked miles just to borrow a book.
- During the Civil War he gave a famous speech, the "Gettysburg Address," to dedicate a battlefield.
- Although Lincoln played a large part in getting the Thirteenth Amendment, making slavery illegal, passed, he did not live to see it approved.
- Lincoln was shot and killed on April 14, 1865.
- Lincoln's face is one of four carved into Mount Rushmore, a 60-ft. high mountain and national monument in South Dakota.

Young Abe's family was very poor. He was not sent to school very often.
1 However, he taught himself many different things. He liked to read books and tell stories. People liked
2 listening to him. They thought he was a good speaker. Abraham Lincoln worked hard and became a lawyer. Later he became President of the United States.

Abraham Lincoln was born near Hodgenville, Kentucky.

Abraham Lincoln was the leader of our country during a war between the states. The states were fighting for many reasons. One reason was because some states wanted African
3 Americans to be free. Other states did not. Abraham Lincoln worked to keep our country together. He helped free African Americans.

Lincoln's hat

Lincoln's home when he was a boy

Think and Share

Why is Abraham Lincoln remembered as one of our greatest Presidents?

For more information, go online to *Meet the People* at **www.sfsocialstudies.com.**

2 Teach and Discuss

1 **If you could spend time teaching yourself something, what would it be?** Answers will vary but might include cooking, dancing, and things about dinosaurs. **Express Ideas**

2 **What do you think makes a good storyteller?** Answers will vary but may include someone who uses noises and voices or who tells funny stories, scary stories, and so on. **Express Ideas**

SOCIAL STUDIES STRAND
Geography

Explain that, before the Civil War, many African Americans were slaves. Slaves are people who, like a house or land, a bicycle or a doll, are owned by another person. Although slaves were given shelter, clothes, food, and tools, they worked hard but received no pay. Sometimes they were treated cruelly, but the worst thing was that they were not free. Many people in northern states opposed slavery. Many people in southern states supported it. When many southern states withdrew from the United States, Lincoln led the war to keep the country together, and he helped end slavery.

3 **Why did the states fight in a war when Lincoln was President?** Answers will vary but may include that some states wanted African Americans to be free, and other states did not. **Generalize**

3 Close and Assess

Ask children to tell one good quality they think Lincoln had. Then have them write a sentence or two about his life.

Think and Share

Answers will vary but may include that Lincoln worked to keep our country together, and helped free African Americans.

SOCIAL STUDIES
Background

Lincoln on the Map

- Show children a map of the United States.
- Show the states that Lincoln's family lived in. He moved from Kentucky to Indiana and then to Illinois, eventually settling in Springfield. Later he moved to Washington, D.C., when he became President.
- Point out to children the states that withdrew from the United States because they supported slavery. (TX, LA, MS, AL, GA, FL, SC, AR, TN, NC, and VA)

WEB SITE
Technology

You may help children find out more about Abraham Lincoln by clicking on *Meet the People* at **www.sfsocialstudies.com.**

Use with pages 212–217

Lesson 5 Wrap-Up

MEETING INDIVIDUAL NEEDS

Leveled Practice

Telling About a Holiday

Read books in the Holiday Histories series by Mir Tamim Ansary: *Memorial Day, Veterans Day, Martin Luther King Jr. Day and Presidents' Day*. Have students choose one holiday to tell about.

Easy Have children draw a picture that shows people celebrating the holiday today. Have students tell about their picture. **Reteach**

On-Level Have children create a three-page picture book with captions of people celebrating the holiday. Help students do research on the Internet or at the library if they would like to learn more information. **Extend**

Challenge Have children direct a two-act play. The first act shows the origin of the holiday. The second act shows how people celebrate the holiday today. **Enrich**

Hands-on Activities

CURRICULUM CONNECTION

Writing

Holiday Spirit

Objective Demonstrate understanding of the vocabulary words.

Resources Vocabulary Cards: **holiday, President**

Materials paper, pencils

Learning Style Verbal-Linguistic

Individual

Time 10 minutes

1. Write the following holidays on the board: Independence Day, Thanksgiving, Columbus Day.
2. Ask children what each holiday is for (celebrates the signing of the Declaration of Independence, is a day of thanks, celebrates the day Columbus landed near North America).
3. Remind children to add the vocabulary words *holiday* and *President* to their "My Word Book."

Presidents
George Washington
Abraham Lincoln
George W. Bush

CURRICULUM CONNECTION

Art

A Medal for Your Service

Objective Design a medal as a prize for someone.

Materials paper, crayons, ribbon, glue

Learning Style Visual

Individual

Time 10–15 minutes

1. Have children look at the medals again in their textbook on page 213. Remind them that soldiers received the medals for acting bravely.
2. Invite children to design their own medal. Suggest that they can make rubbings from coins if they prefer. Help children paste their design to the ribbon.
3. Ask children to announce who they will award their medal to.

CURRICULUM CONNECTION

Math

Making Cents

Objective Add the values of American coins.

Materials pennies and quarters

Learning Style Logical/Mathematical

Pairs

Time 10 minutes

1. Give each pair of children 10 pennies and 1 quarter.
2. Present pairs with math problems using the faces that appear on the coins. Ask: *How many cents is one Washington and one Lincoln?* or, *Is one Washington greater than or less than one Lincoln?*
3. You may want to extend the lesson by adding nickels, explaining that the face on the nickel belongs to another President, Thomas Jefferson.

Lesson 6 Overview

Choosing Our Country's Leaders **pages 218–221**	Children will learn how citizens vote for leaders. They will explore what state and country leaders do and where they work. They will also learn the meaning of the words *citizen, vote*, and *capital*. 	 Time 20–30 minutes Resources • Workbook, p. 57 • Vocabulary Cards citizen vote capital • Every Student Learns Guide, pp. 102–105
Eleanor Roosevelt **pages 222–223**	Children will learn about Eleanor Roosevelt and explore her contributions to our country.	Time 15–20 minutes

Build Background

Activity

Vote for a Place

 **Time** 20 minutes

Tell children that people can not only vote for leaders but also other choices, such as things to do or places to go. Have children suggest four places they would like to visit for a field trip, such as a zoo, science museum, or aquarium. List the places on the board. Name each place and ask children to raise their hand to vote for the place they would most like to visit. Remind children to vote only once. When the class has finished voting, add the votes and circle the place with the most votes. Then have children draw a picture of the place.

If time is short, talk with children about voting. Ask for examples of things they might vote on, such as student of the week or a field trip.

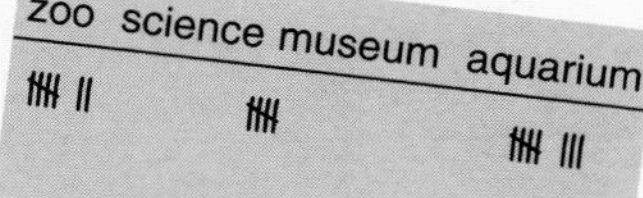

Read Aloud

Let's Take a Vote

by Ravi Iyer

Pancakes, blueberry muffins, eggs.
Make up your mind. Don't make me beg.
Milk and honey with fruit afloat.
We must decide on breakfast.
Let's take a vote.

Rabbit, dog, ferret, cat.
Lizard, snake, vampire bat.
What will our class pet be?
Take a vote and we shall see.

Baseball, kickball, soccer, tag. What game
should we play? Give me a name.
Go down the list, raise your hands high.
Oh, no! Tell me that it's not a tie.

Lesson

Choosing Our Country's Leaders

Objectives

- Identify leaders in the state and nation.
- Describe the roles of public officials including governor and president.
- Locate Washington, D.C. and the capital of your state on a United States map.

Vocabulary

citizen a member of a state and country (p. 218)

vote a choice that gets counted (p. 218)

capital the city where important leaders of a state or country live and work (p. 220)

QUICK Teaching Plan

If time is short, discuss what a citizen and voting are.

- Point out your state capital and Washington, D.C., on a map.

1 Introduce and Motivate

Preview Display the Vocabulary Card **citizen**. Discuss the definition. Then display the Vocabulary Card **vote**. Have children look at the pictures on pages 218–219. Explain that the man standing in the foreground on p. 218 is about to sign his name in preparation for voting, and James and his mother on p. 219 are surrounded by buttons and signs encouraging people to vote. Finally, display the Vocabulary Card **capital**. Discuss the definition. Invite a volunteer to tell the capital of your state.

Warm Up To activate prior knowledge, ask children to name the Presidents that they have learned about. (George Washington, Abraham Lincoln) Tell them that in the United States citizens vote for President. Then explain that voting is a fair way for a group to make a choice or a decision. Ask children if they have ever voted for a person or on a question that needed to be decided.

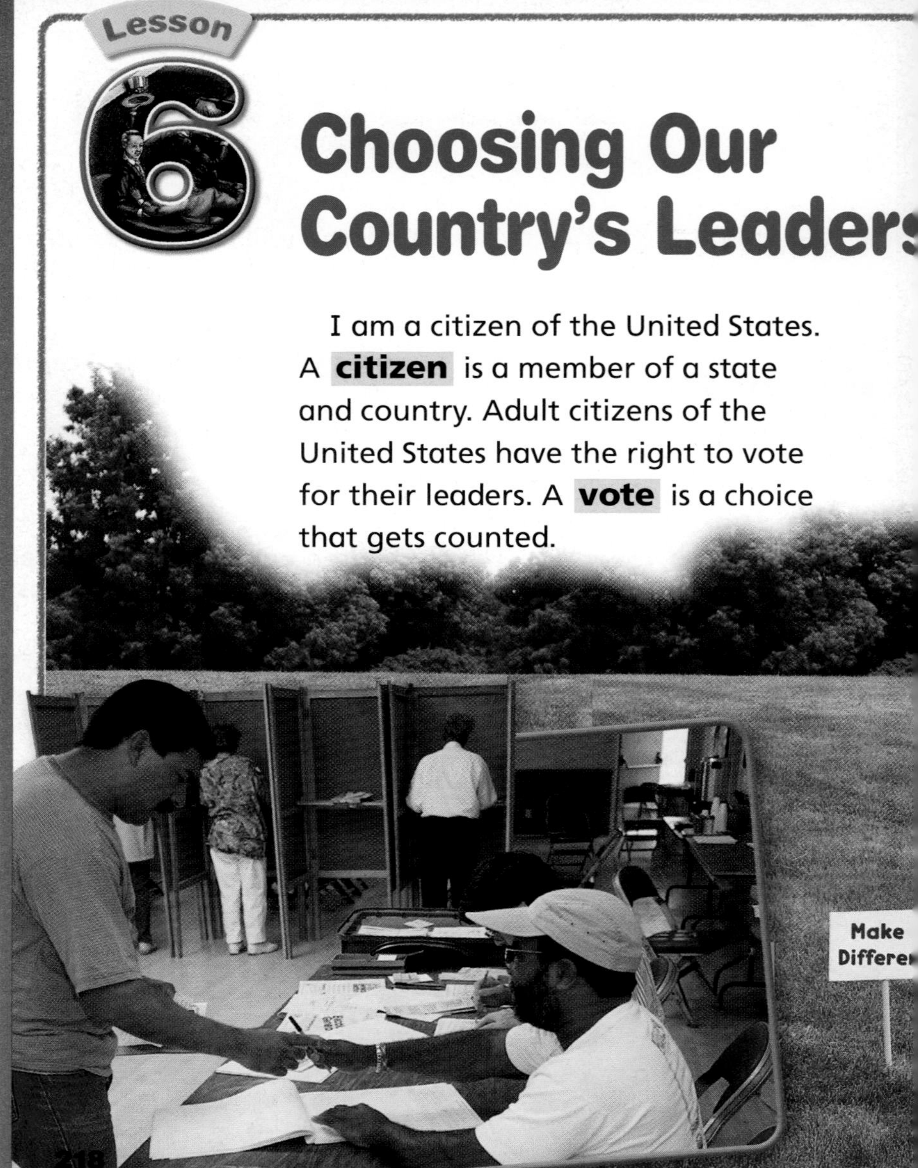

Lesson 6

Choosing Our Country's Leaders

I am a citizen of the United States. A **citizen** is a member of a state and country. Adult citizens of the United States have the right to vote for their leaders. A **vote** is a choice that gets counted.

218

Practice and Extend

READING SKILL Categorize

- After children have read pp. 218–221, give them a two-column chart entitled "Government Leader." The chart has three rows entitled "Nation," "State," and "City."
- Tell children that they will be completing a "Government Leader" chart. Explain that a government leader is a person who has an important position in the national, state, or city government.
- Help children complete the chart.

Each citizen votes one time. When the voting is finished, each vote is counted. Whoever gets the most votes, wins.

219

FAST FACTS

- In 1870, the Fifteenth Amendment to the Constitution was adopted to protect the voting rights of African Americans.
- In 1920, women won the right to vote when the Nineteenth Amendment was added to the Constitution.
- In 1924, Native Americans were declared citizens by Congress.
- The Civil Rights Act of 1965 finally brought an end to violations against the rights of African Americans to vote.

WEB SITE
Technology

You can look up vocabulary words online. Click on *Social Studies Library* and select the dictionary at **www.sfsocialstudies.com.**

2 Teach and Discuss

Explain that although citizens have the right to vote, they do not have to vote. That is why some buttons and signs encourage people to vote for a particular leader while others encourage people to simply vote.

Page 218

1 **Why do people display posters to encourage people to vote?** Answers will vary but should reflect that people want to encourage other people to make a difference in their community, state, or nation.
Draw Conclusions

2 **Who are some leaders that citizens vote for?** Answers will vary but may include President, governor, and mayor. **Apply Information**

Page 219

Problem Solving

3 **What would you do if you were asked to vote for people you knew nothing about?** Possible answer: Get information about them in order to learn about their points of view.
Solve Problems

Lesson 6 continued

Page 220

Tell children that the picture shows the Indiana State House, the building where the governor of Indiana works.

4 Who works in the Indiana State House besides the governor? State leaders who make laws **Making Inferences**

Ongoing Assessment

If... children do not understand how the governor and lawmakers work together,

then... explain that the lawmakers pass laws that regulate and guide daily life in Indiana and the governor puts the laws into action.

SOCIAL STUDIES STRAND Government

Explain to children that government is a group of people in charge of a country, state, city, or other place. A governor governs—or leads—the state government. The primary responsibility of state government is to serve the needs of the people of the state.

Explain to children that a seal is a design stamped on a letter or document to show ownership or authority.

5 What do you see in the scene on the seal of the state of Indiana? A woodsman, buffalo, trees, hills, and a setting sun **Analyze Pictures**

Every state has a leader called a governor. Citizens of each state vote for their governor. The governor works with other state leaders to help make laws for their state.

Each state has a capital. A **capital** is the city where important leaders of a state or country live and work. What is your state's capital? Find it on a map. 4

5

The governor of Indiana works in Indianapolis.

220

Practice and Extend

ESL ACCESS CONTENT ESL Support

Interpret Maps Have children draw an outline of your state and make a small star to indicate the location of the capital.

Beginning Model pointing to the state and capital while identifying them. Have children point to the state and capital and repeat the words.

Intermediate Ask children to label the outline of the state and the star indicating the capital.

Advanced Ask children to label the outline of the state and the star indicating the capital. Then have children write a caption for their map: The governor of [your state] works in [your capital].

For additional ESL Support, use Every Student Learns Guide, pp. 102–105.

Our country also has a capital. It is called Washington, D.C. The President of the United States lives and works in our country's capital.

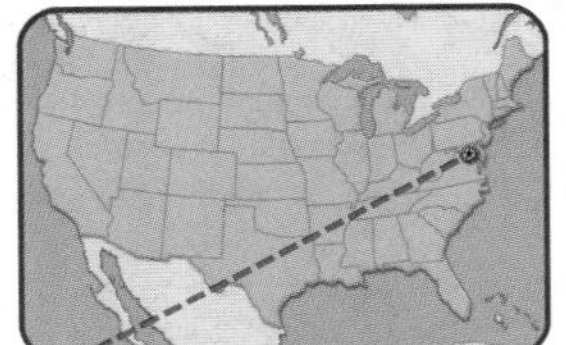

Washington D.C. is the capital of the United States.

The President works with other leaders in our country to help make our country's laws. The President also works with other leaders around the world. Citizens vote for President every four years in our country.

What did you learn?

1. How does a person's vote help decide who will be leader?
2. Who is the leader of our state? Who is the leader of our country?
3. **Think and Share** **Recall** three things you learned about the President of the United States. **Retell** what you learned.

221

FYI SOCIAL STUDIES Background

About the President of the United States

- The President must be a natural-born citizen—somebody who is either born in the United States or born outside the United States to United States citizens.
- The President must be at least 35 years old.
- No person can be elected President more than twice.

Workbook, p. 57

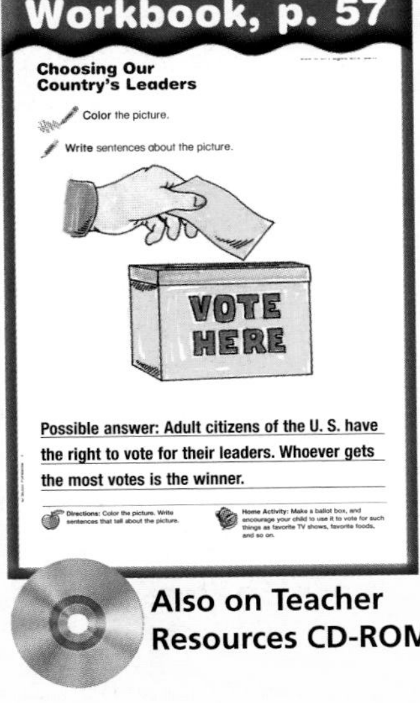

Choosing Our Country's Leaders

Color the picture.

Write sentences about the picture.

Possible answer: Adult citizens of the U. S. have the right to vote for their leaders. Whoever gets the most votes is the winner.

Also on Teacher Resources CD-ROM.

Page 221

Explain to children that a bill—a plan for a new law—may originate with Congress or the President. Once the bill is approved by Congress, it goes to the President. Only when the President signs the bill does it become the law of the land.

Test Talk

Use Information from the Text

6 Why is the President of the United States an important person? Answers will vary but may include that as the leader of the nation he helps make laws for the country and works with leaders around the world. Have children find the details from the text to support their answer.
Express Ideas

Ask children to tell who the President of our country is. Have children locate Washington, D.C., on a map of the United States.

7 After the President wins the election, how long does he or she keep the job? Four years
Apply Information

3 Close and Assess

Ask children to tell why people vote. (to make choices) Pair children and have them discuss the importance of voting.

What did you learn?

1. Every vote counts. The person who gets the most votes becomes the leader.
2. Children should name the governor of your state and President by their names.
3. **Think and Share** Children's answers should reflect what they learned about the President of the United States.

CITIZEN HEROES

Eleanor Roosevelt

Objectives

- Identify historic figures such as Eleanor Roosevelt who have exemplified good citizenship.
- Identify characteristics of good citizenship such as a belief in justice, truth, equality, and responsibility for the common good.

1 Introduce and Motivate

Preview Ask children to tell what the wife of the President of the United States is called. (First Lady) Tell children that they are going to learn about a woman who was First Lady a long time ago. Have children look at pictures of her.

Warm Up To activate prior knowledge, ask children what they learned about good citizens. Ask children what some of these good citizens did. Explain to children that Eleanor Roosevelt was a good citizen because she believed that people should be treated fairly. Ask children to name other people they learned about who wanted people to be treated fairly. (Martin Luther King, Jr., Abraham Lincoln)

CITIZEN HEROES

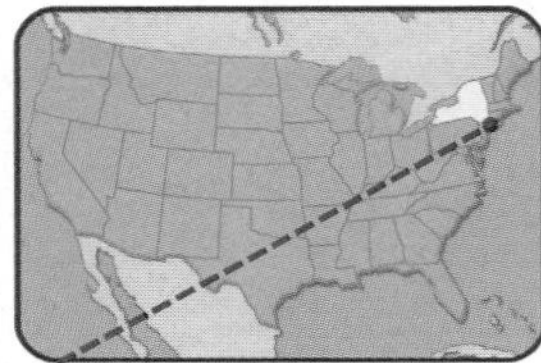

Eleanor Roosevelt was born in New York City, New York.

Eleanor Roosevelt

When Eleanor was young, she was very shy. When she grew older, she became more comfortable around people. She married a man named Franklin Roosevelt. He became our 32nd President.

Eleanor Roosevelt saw that there were problems in our country. She told people the truth about what she saw. She helped the poor. She worked hard to get equal rights for all people.

Young Eleanor

222

Practice and Extend

FYI SOCIAL STUDIES **Background**

About Eleanor Roosevelt

- Eleanor Roosevelt helped her husband Franklin, the President, who was disabled by a disease called polio. She went on tours and reported back to him what people were saying and what condition the country was in. She became his "eyes and ears."
- Each day she wrote a newspaper column called "My Day." She wrote honestly in this column.
- She was particularly interested in helping people who were needy.
- Because she believed that all people should be treated fairly, she helped write the *Universal Declaration of Human Rights* in 1948. This document said that all people had a right not to be unfairly punished, unfairly hurt, or unfairly put in jail. The document was read by people all over the world.

Eleanor Roosevelt wrote many books and newspaper articles. She was honest. She would say ❶ and write what she thought.

Eleanor Roosevelt traveled around the world many times. ❷ She visited many countries. She met many of the world's leaders.

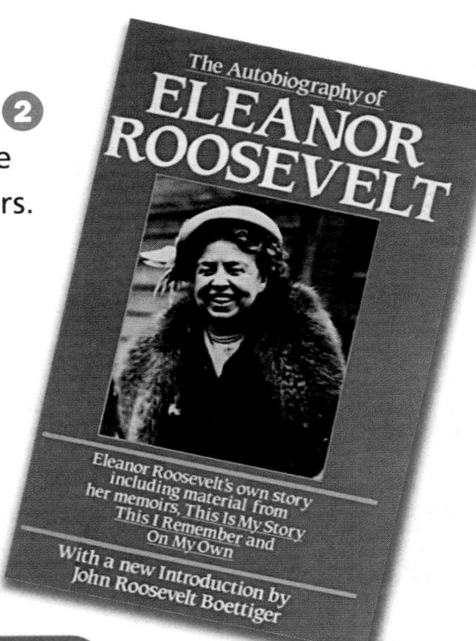

The Autobiography of
ELEANOR ROOSEVELT
Eleanor Roosevelt's own story including material from her memoirs, This Is My Story, This I Remember and On My Own
With a new Introduction by John Roosevelt Boettiger

How do you think Eleanor Roosevelt's honesty was helpful to others?

223

CURRICULUM CONNECTION Writing

A Letter to Eleanor Roosevelt

- Tell children that Eleanor Roosevelt received many letters from children.
- Have children imagine that Eleanor Roosevelt is the First Lady. Have them write a letter pointing out a problem that needs her attention.
- Suggest that children begin the letter by telling Eleanor Roosevelt good things they have read about her.

2 Teach and Discuss

Tell children that Eleanor Roosevelt worked hard to get equal rights not only for people in America but around the world. Explain that equal rights are fair requests, like the right to speak freely.

❶ **How did Eleanor Roosevelt know that there were problems in our country?** Answers may vary but could include that she saw problems when she traveled or she read about them in newspapers or letters. **Hypothesize**

❷ **Why do you think Eleanor Roosevelt is a citizen hero?** She was honest. She helped poor people. She worked so that all people would be treated fairly. **Draw Conclusions**

3 Close and Assess

Ask children to tell about the life of Eleanor Roosevelt. Then have children write one sentence to tell why she was a good citizen.

She expressed her honest opinions and wrote about injustice. She helped the poor and worked for equal rights for all people.

Use with pages 218–223

Lesson 6 Wrap-Up

MEETING INDIVIDUAL NEEDS
Leveled Practice

Making Rules
Have children suggest rules for the class. Write their rules on the board. Have them vote for the very best rule.

Easy Have children suggest at least one rule. **Reteach**

On-Level Have children suggest rules. Then have them tell how the rules will help the class. **Extend**

Challenge Have two teams debate the rules, presenting different views. **Enrich**

Hands-on Activities

CURRICULUM CONNECTION
Writing

Stand Up and Be Counted

Objective Demonstrate understanding of the vocabulary words.

Resources Vocabulary Cards: **vote, citizen, capital**

Materials cards

Learning Style Auditory/Verbal

Group

Time 10–15 minutes

1. Divide children into groups of four. Give each child in a group a card with a different vocabulary word.

2. Say the definition of one of the words. Ask children holding the word card that matches the definition to stand up and show their card. Repeat with the other two words.

3. Remind children to add the vocabulary words to their "My Word Book."

CURRICULUM CONNECTION
Math

Tallying the Votes

Objective Count the number of votes candidates receive.

Materials tally sheets, pencils

Learning Style Mathematical/Logical

Group

Time 5–10 minutes

1. Fill in a tally sheet to look like the results of a vote for "Funniest Animal." Make the results close.

2. Hand out the filled-in tally sheets.

3. Have groups count the number of tally marks for each candidate.

4. The group that accurately counts up the tallies first is the winner.

5. Extend the exercise by adding new "votes" to the original tally.

CURRICULUM CONNECTION
Writing

It's a Secret!

Objective Vote with secret ballots.

Materials paper, pencils, shoe box

Learning Style Visual

Individual

Time 10–15 minutes

1. Ask children for three suggestions for the fruit that should be served at a pretend picnic. Write the results on the board with small squares before the names. Have children copy the names and squares on paper ballots.

2. Have children make a check in the box of the fruit they choose. Tell them to fold their secret ballot and slip it into the shoe box slot. Tally the results on the board.

apples ☐
bananas ☐
grapes ☐

3. Have children draw a picture of the winner.

Ending Unit 5

End with a Song **pages 224–225**	Children will listen to and sing our national anthem: "The Star-Spangled Banner" by Francis Scott Key.	Resource • ***Songs and Music*** **CD**
Unit 5 Review **pages 226–229**	Children will review unit vocabulary words and the unit skills of recall and retell, using a history map and reading a diagram. Children will answer questions about what they learned in the unit. Children will learn about several books about the history of our country.	Resources • Workbook, pp. 58–59 • Assessment Book, pp. 17–20
Unit 5 Project **page 230**	Children will have a history parade. They will also be directed to a web site where they can learn more about our country's history.	

Wrap-up

Activity

Welcome to America!

Have children make posters to welcome visitors. Ask them to include at least one picture of what it's like to live in America and at least one national symbol, such as the Statue of Liberty.

- Have children cut out appropriate pictures from magazines or draw pictures themselves. They should arrange their pictures to form a collage and then paste them into place on large sheets of oaktag.
- Help children write titles for their posters. Remind them to spell all the words correctly, and to print neatly.
- Display children's posters prominently in your classroom.

Performance Assessment

You can use the activity on this page as a performance assessment.

✓ **Assessment Scoring Guide**

Make a Poster About America	
4	Includes an appropriate title, one or more pictures that depict life in America, and a national symbol. Contains no errors in spelling.
3	Includes the first three required elements but contains errors in spelling.
2	Includes two of the four required elements.
1	Includes only one of the required elements.

The Star-Spangled Banner

Objective

- Identify anthems and mottoes of the United States and individual states.

1 Introduce and Motivate

Preview Point to and read the title of the song. Tell children that this song—"The Star-Spangled Banner"—is the national anthem of the United States. Read the songwriter's name, and then ask children what they think the words *star-spangled banner* refer to. (the U.S. flag) Have children point to the flag in the picture. Tell children that states also have songs. For example, the state song of Texas is "Texas, Our Texas" and the state song of Indiana is "On the Banks of the Wabash, Far Away." Discuss your state song.

2 Teach and Discuss

You may want to read the words to "The Star-Spangled Banner" with children before singing it. Explain any words or phrases children may not understand, such as *twilight's last gleaming* and *perilous fight*. (See Background below.)

❶ **Why do some people hold their hands over their hearts as they sing our national anthem?** To show their respect for the flag **Hypothesize**

❷ **Why do you think people stand when our national anthem is played or sung?** To show respect **Hypothesize**

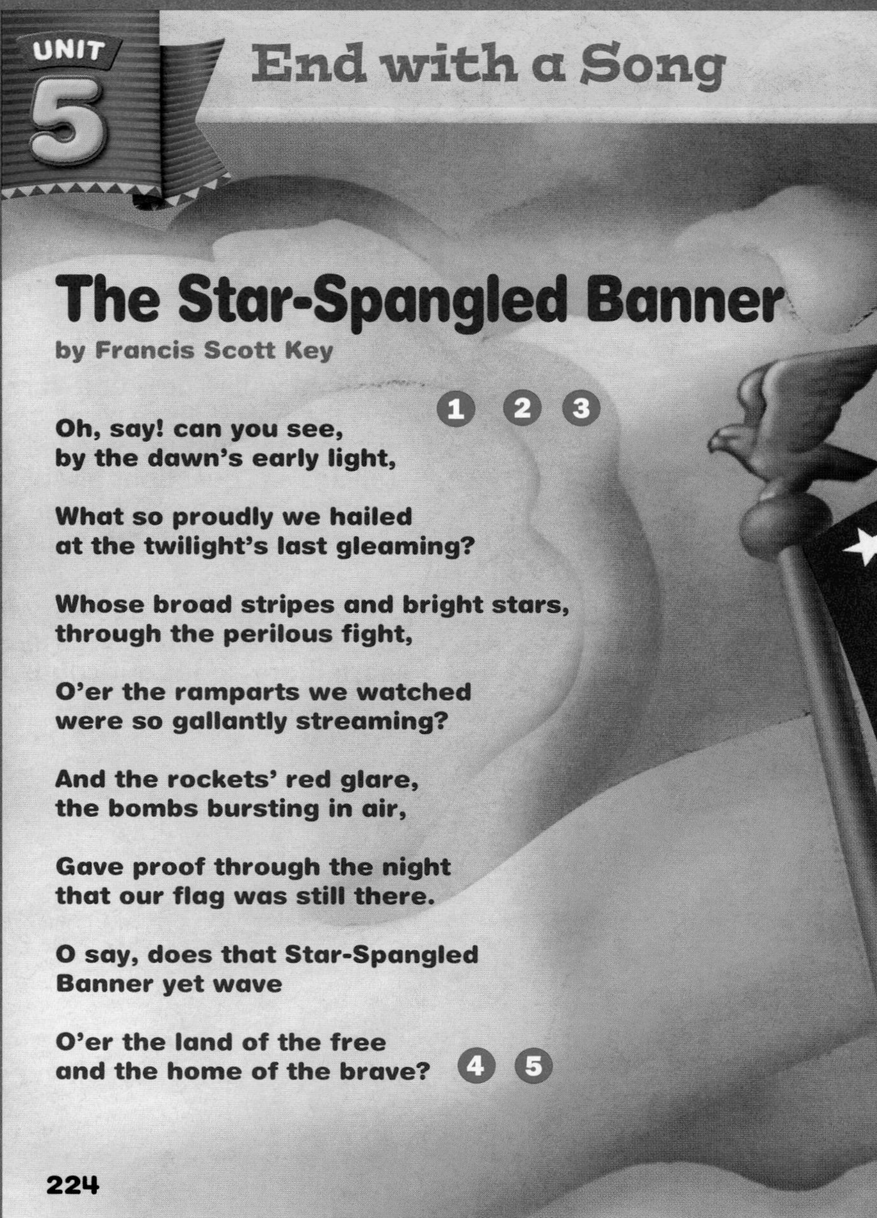

UNIT 5

End with a Song

The Star-Spangled Banner

by Francis Scott Key

❶ ❷ ❸

Oh, say! can you see,
by the dawn's early light,

What so proudly we hailed
at the twilight's last gleaming?

Whose broad stripes and bright stars,
through the perilous fight,

O'er the ramparts we watched
were so gallantly streaming?

And the rockets' red glare,
the bombs bursting in air,

Gave proof through the night
that our flag was still there.

O say, does that Star-Spangled
Banner yet wave

O'er the land of the free
and the home of the brave? ❹ ❺

224

Practice and Extend

SOCIAL STUDIES
Background

The Writing of the National Anthem

- Francis Scott Key composed the words of the anthem during the War of 1812, which was fought between the United States and England. The melody was borrowed from another song: "To Anacreon in Heaven."
- Key wrote the song as he watched the bombardment of Fort McHenry from aboard a troop ship in Baltimore Harbor.
- The bombardment lasted all day and almost all night. At dawn, Key saw that the American flag was still flying at Fort McHenry. He was so moved that he pulled a letter or envelope from his pocket and used it to write the now-famous words.
- The anthem has four verses; only the first verse is shown here.

3 When have you heard our national anthem played or sung? Possible answer: Before a sporting event begins **Apply Information**

4 What is a motto? Possible answer: A word or short sentence that tells what a nation, state, group, or person believes or stands for

SOCIAL STUDIES STRAND

Citizenship

Tell children that the official motto of the United States is *In God We Trust*. Write these words on the board, using all capital letters. Then distribute pennies or other U.S. coins to children. Ask them to find these same words on the coins. Ask children why they think these words appear on the coins.

Tell children that states also have mottoes. For example, the motto of Texas is "Friendship" and the motto of Indiana is "The Crossroads of America." Discuss your state motto and what it means.

5 Why do you think it is important for the United States to have a national anthem and a motto? Possible answer: To have a song and a saying that sums up the beliefs and feelings most people share about their country

3 Close and Assess

- Have children stand and place their hands over their hearts as you sing the national anthem or play it on the *Songs and Music* CD.
- Display the words to the first verse of the national anthem on chart paper. Have children stand and sing the song along with you as you point to the words.

Review

Resources

- Assessment Book, pp. 17–20
- Workbook, p. 58: Vocabulary Review

Vocabulary Review

1. President
2. capital
3. vote
4. holiday

Answers to Test Prep

1. c. freedom
2. a. citizen

UNIT 5

Review

Vocabulary Review

vote
holiday
President
capital

Match each word to a picture.

1. 

2. 

3. 

4. 

★ ★ ★ ★ ★ ★ ★ ★

Which word completes the sentence?

1. The Pilgrims came to North America for ________.

   a. a holiday **b.** riches
   c. freedom **d.** gold

2. A member of a state and country is called a _______.

   a. citizen **b.** capital
   c. holiday **d.** vote

Practice and Extend

Assessment Options

✓ Unit 5 Assessment

- Unit 5 Content Test: Use Assessment Book, pp. 17–18
- Unit 5 Skills Test: Use Assessment Book, pp. 19–20

Standardized Test Prep

- Unit 5 tests contain standardized test formats.

✓ Unit 5 Performance Assessment

- See p. 230 for information about using the Unit 5 Project as a means of performance assessment.
- A scoring guide for the Unit 5 Project is provided in the teacher's notes on p. 230.

Test Talk

- Test Talk Practice Book

Skills Review

Recall and Retell

Make a list of what you learned about Nathan Hale. Read your list. Then put the list away. Try to **recall** what the list said and **retell** what you remember to a friend.

★ ★ ★ ★ ★ ★ ★ ★

Use a History Map

Ben Franklin traveled to France in 1776. Look at the map to answer these questions.

1. Which direction did Ben Franklin travel to France?
2. What ocean did he travel across?
3. What continent is south of France?

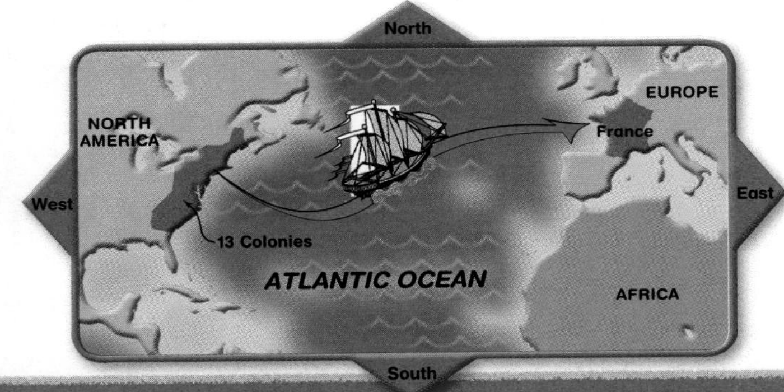

227

For more information, you can select the dictionary or encyclopedia from *Social Studies Library* at **www.sfsocialstudies.com.**

Workbook, p. 58

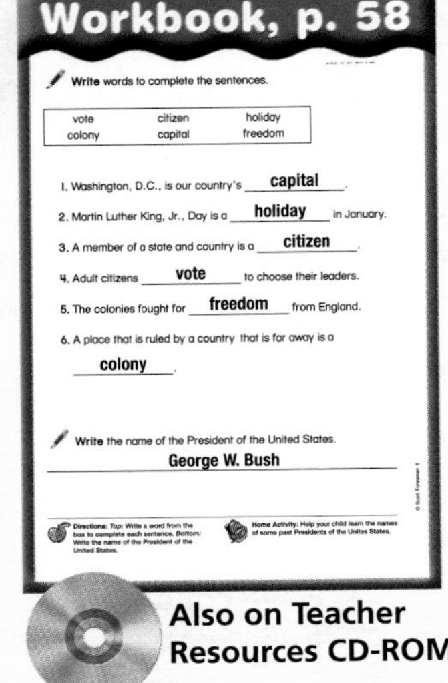

Write words to complete the sentences.

vote	citizen	holiday
colony	capital	freedom

1. Washington, D.C., is our country's capital.
2. Martin Luther King, Jr., Day is a holiday in January.
3. A member of a state and country is a citizen.
4. Adult citizens vote to choose their leaders.
5. The colonies fought for freedom from England.
6. A place that is ruled by a country that is far away is a colony.

Write the name of the President of the United States.
George W. Bush

Also on Teacher Resources CD-ROM.

Skills Review

Recall and Retell

Target Skill

- Children's lists may include these facts:

  Nathan Hale was a teacher.

  He was a soldier in George Washington's army.

  He spied on the English but was caught.

  He is a hero who died for his country.

✓ Assessment Scoring Guide

Picture Clues	
4	Recalls and tells 3–4 facts about Nathan Hale, especially those that relate to his heroism.
3	Recalls and tells 2–3 facts about Nathan Hale, especially those that relate to his heroism.
2	Recalls and tells 1–2 facts about Nathan Hale, especially those that relate to his heroism.
1	Recalls and tells a fact about Nathan Hale but not one that relates to his heroism.

Using a History Map

1. east
2. Atlantic Ocean
3. Africa

Review

continued

Skills Review

Read a Diagram

1. Possible answers include: torch, crown, and lookout.
2. Crown
3. Lookout

Test Talk

Use Information from Graphics
Use Read a Diagram, Question 2, to model the Test Talk strategy.

Understand the question.
Children should ask themselves "What label points to the part on the statue's head?"

Use information from graphics.
Ask children to skim the diagram to find the right information to support their answer.

Skills on Your Own

- Children's diagrams should include labels for all the parts and name the President: Abraham Lincoln.
- President Lincoln is on the front of the penny.

Use the following scoring guide.

✔ Assessment Scoring Guide

	Draw a Diagram
4	Diagram includes all the parts as well as the name of the President.
3	Diagram includes most of the parts as well as the name of the President.
2	Diagram includes only some of the parts or is missing the name of the President.
1	Diagram includes some of the parts or the name of the President—but not both.

Review

Study Skills

Read a Diagram

Look at the diagram of the Statue of Liberty. Answer the questions.

Test Talk
Use the diagram to help you find the answer.

1. What parts are outside the statue?
2. What part is on the statue's head?
3. Where can you stand to look down at the ground?

Skills On Your Own

Draw a diagram of the front of a penny. Label the parts. What President of the United States is pictured on the penny?

228

Practice and Extend

Revisit the Unit Question

✔ Portfolio Assessment

- Have children look back at the list of reasons why our country's past is important, made on p. 183.
- Discuss with children the importance of freedom in America's past.
- Ask children to identify some of the historical events that express America's love of freedom.
- Ask children to draw a picture of our country's past.
- Have children write a sentence describing the drawing.
- Have children add their list, drawing, and sentence to their Social Studies Portfolio.

What did you learn?

1. Tell what the United States flag and the Liberty Bell stand for.
2. Name three important Americans we honor with a holiday.
3. What does a governor do?
4. **Write and Share** Write about some of the reasons why you are proud to be an American or living in the United States.

Read About Our Country

Look for books like these in the library.

229

CURRICULUM CONNECTION
Literature

Books About Our Country's Past

Children might enjoy reading these books about our country's past.

Ox-Cart Man, by Donald Hall and Barbara Cooney (illustrator) (Puffin, ISBN 0-140-50441-9, 1983) Follow the life of a farm family in the early days of our country. **Easy** Caldecott Medal, 1980

Dakota Dugout, by Ann Warren Turner and Ronald Himler (illustrator) (Aladdin, ISBN 0-689-71296-0, 1989) Describes life on the prairie for the pioneer families of the mid-19th century through the eyes of a woman who lived there. **On-Level** ALA Notable Book

Peppe the Lamplighter, by Elisa Bartone and Ted Lewin (illustrator) (Mulberry Books, ISBN 0-688-15469-7, 1997) A boy in New York's Little Italy is happy to find work lighting street lamps when the lamplighter returns to Italy. **Challenge** Caldecott Honor Book, 1994

What did you learn?

1. Both the United States flag and the Liberty Bell stand for freedom.
2. Three important Americans we honor with a holiday are President George Washington, President Abraham Lincoln, and Martin Luther King, Jr.
3. A governor leads a state.
4. **Write and Share** Children's answers should reflect pride in the fact that the laws of United States promote justice, truth, equality, and responsibility for the common good.

Read About Our Country

You may want to have these books available in the classroom. Read the books aloud for children; then invite them to browse through the books. Encourage them to tell why these books are good ones to include in this unit. They may also wish to review the books for classmates.

George, the Drummer Boy, by Nathaniel Benchley and Don Bolognese (illustrator) (HarperCollins Children's Books, ISBN 0-060-20501-6, 1977) This book presents the beginning events of the American Revolution from an unusual viewpoint: that of an English drummer boy. The book not only provides information about the war from both sides but also in a personal way, which helps young readers become engaged. **Easy**

Picture Book of Eleanor Roosevelt, A, by David A. Adler and Robert Casilla (illustrator) (Holiday House, ISBN 0-823-40856-6, 1991) This book is a brief account of Eleanor Roosevelt's life told in simple sentences and colorful illustrations. It chronicles the unfolding of Roosevelt's strong-mindedness and presents her accomplishments. **On-Level**

Across the Wide Dark Sea: The Mayflower Journey, by Jean Van Leeuwen and Thomas B. Allen (illustrator) (Dial Books for Young Readers, ISBN 0-803-71166-2, 1995) This book tells the story of sailing to America and building a settlement. Told from the viewpoint of a young boy, it describes the Pilgrims' voyage, their first harsh winter, and the help they received from American Indians, and evokes the hopeful voyages of all immigrants to America. **Challenge**

Unit 5 Project

History on Parade

Objective

- Identifies a historic event and understands that events occur in a sequence.

Resource

- Workbook, p. 59

Materials

construction paper, posterboard, scissors, crayons, paint, glue, cotton balls

Follow This Procedure

- Tell children that they are going to put on a history parade. Each child will make a drawing or object that shows something that happened in history. The event they show may be related to a person or a group of people.

- Explain that they will choose an event or a person and create a prop or costume; examples include a Pilgrim's hat for the first Thanksgiving; a ship for Christopher Columbus arriving in the New World; a drawing of an early U.S. flag or the Liberty Bell; construction paper stovepipe hat for Abe Lincoln.

- Direct children to make their props. Give each child an index card with the event's date. Help children determine the correct sequence. Once the props are completed, instruct children to line up in order and ask them to tell about their event.

- Hold a classroom parade. Consider holding the parade elsewhere in the school as well.

✓ Assessment Scoring Guide

	History on Parade
4	Describes a historic event correctly, creates an object that accurately illustrates the event, and demonstrates correct sequence of all events.
3	Describes a historic event somewhat correctly, creates an object that illustrates the event, and demonstrates correct sequence of most events.
2	Describes a historic event with some incorrect details, creates an object that somewhat illustrates the event, and demonstrates correct sequence of few of the events.
1	Describes a historic event incorrectly, does not create an object that illustrates the event, and demonstrates sequence of events inaccurately.

Unit 5 Project

History on Parade

Have a history parade.

1. **Choose** something that happened in the past.
2. **Draw** or make an object that shows what happened.
3. **Tell** what happened.
4. **Line** up in order of when things happened. The first event should be first in line. The last event should be last. Walk around your classroom on parade.

Internet Activity

Go to www.sfsocialstudies.com/activities to learn more about events in American history.

Practice and Extend

✓ Performance Assessment

- The Unit Project can also be used as a performance assessment activity.
- Use the scoring guide to assess each group's work.

Children can launch the activity by clicking on *Grade 1, Unit 5* at **www.sfsocialstudies.com/activities.**

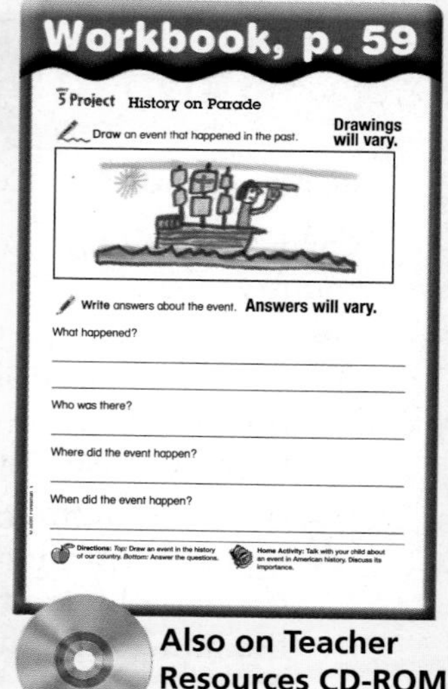

Workbook, p. 59

5 Project History on Parade

Draw an event that happened in the past. **Drawings will vary.**

Write answers about the event. **Answers will vary.**

What happened?

Who was there?

Where did the event happen?

When did the event happen?

Directions: *Top:* Draw an event in the history of our country. *Bottom:* Answer the questions.

Home Activity: Talk with your child about an event in American history. Discuss its importance.

Also on Teacher Resources CD-ROM.

★ Unit 6 ★

Our Country, Our World

Our Country, Our World

UNIT 6

UNIT 6

Unit 6 Planning Guide

Our Country, Our World

Begin with a Song pp. 232–233 **Vocabulary Preview** pp. 234–235

Target Skill **Reading Social Studies, Predict** pp. 236–237

Lesson Titles	Pacing	Main Ideas
Lesson 1 **Visiting the Market** pp. 238–239 **Make a Decision** pp. 240–241	2 days	• A market is a place where goods are sold and services are provided. • Making a decision is a process that requires many steps.
Lesson 2 **How Things Have Changed** pp. 242–243 **Citizen Heroes: Respect Joseph Bruchac** pp. 244–245	2 days	• Technological advances, such as computers and scanners, have changed the way people live and work. • Joseph Bruchac, Native American writer, shows respect by recording the traditional stories told by elders.
Lesson 3 **Inventors and Inventions** pp. 246–249 DK **Telephones** pp. 250–251	2 days	• Many inventions help people communicate. These include the printing press; the telephone, invented by Alexander Graham Bell; and the phonograph, invented by Thomas Alva Edison. • The telephone has gone through many changes since it was first invented.
Lesson 4 **How Travel Has Changed** pp. 252–253 **Chart and Graph Skills: Read a Bar Graph** pp. 254–255 **Biography: Mae Jemison** pp. 256–257	3 days	• Land transportation has changed greatly over time. • A bar graph helps people compare groups. • Mae Jemison was the first African American woman to travel into space.
Lesson 5 **Life Around the World** pp. 258–261 **Biography: Laurence Yep** pp. 262–263 **Here and There: It Is Time to Leave** pp. 264–265	3 days	• Children around the world are alike and different. • Laurence Yep, a Chinese American writer, writes about the Chinese American way of life. • There are many sayings around the world for leave taking.

✓ **End with a Folktale** pp. 266–267 ✓ **Unit 6 Review** pp. 268–271 ✓ **Unit 6 Project** p. 272

✓ = Assessment Options

Vocabulary	Resources	Meeting Individual Needs
market	• Workbook, pp. 62–63 • Vocabulary Card: market • Every Student Learns Guide, pp. 106–109	• ESL Support, TE p. 240 • Leveled Practice, TE p. 241a
	• Workbook, p. 64 • Every Student Learns Guide, pp. 110–113	• ESL Support, TE p. 243 • Leveled Practice, TE p. 245a
communicate **invention** **inventor**	• Workbook, p. 65 • Vocabulary Cards: communicate, invention, inventor • Every Student Learns Guide, pp. 114–117	• ESL Support, TE p. 248 • Leveled Practice, TE p. 251a
	• Workbook, pp. 66–67 • Every Student Learns Guide, pp. 118–121	• ESL Support, TE p. 257 • Leveled Practice, TE p. 257a
world	• Workbook, p. 68 • Vocabulary Card: world • Every Student Learns Guide, pp. 122–125	• ESL Support, TE p. 260 • Leveled Practice, TE p. 265a

Providing More Depth

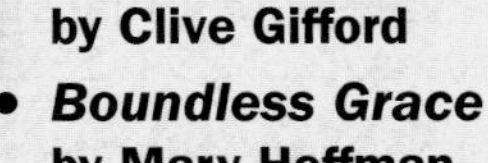

Scott Foresman DK Multimedia Library

-  ***Media and Communication*** **by Clive Gifford**
- ***Boundless Grace*** **by Mary Hoffman**
- **Songs and Music**
- **Video Field Trips**
- **Software**

Additional Resources

- Family Activities
- Vocabulary Cards
- Daily Activity Bank
- Social Studies Plus!
- Big Book Atlas
- Outline Maps
- Desk Maps

ADDITIONAL Technology

- AudioText
- TestWorks
- Teacher Resources CD-ROM
- Map Resources CD-ROM
- **www.sfsocialstudies.com**

To establish guidelines for children's safe and responsible use of the Internet, use the **Scott Foresman Internet Guide.**

Additional Internet Links

To find out more about:

- views of space from Earth, visit **www.nasa.gov**
- views of Earth's land features from space, visit **http://earth.jsc.nasa.gov/**

Key Internet Search Terms

- inventors
- inventions

Unit 6 Objectives

Beginning of Unit 6

- **Obtain information about a topic using a variety of oral sources such as songs.** (pp. 232–233)
- **Determine the meanings of words.**
- **Obtain information about a topic using a variety of visual sources such as pictures.** (pp. 234–235)
- **Recognize words that help make a prediction.**
- **Analyze pictures and text to make a prediction.**
- **Make a prediction based on information given.** (pp. 236–237)

Lesson 1
Visiting the Market
pp. 238–239

- **Identify the role of markets in the exchange of goods and services.**
- **Use a decision-making process to identify a situation that requires a decision, gather information, identify options, predict consequences, and take action to implement a decision.** (pp. 240–241)

Lesson 2
How Things Have Changed
pp. 242–243

- **Describe how household tools and appliances have changed.**
- **Describe how technology has changed recreation.**
- **Describe how technology has changed the way people work.**
- **Identify people who exemplify good citizenship and exhibit a love of individualism.** (pp. 244–245)

Lesson 3
Inventors and Inventions
pp. 246–249

- **Describe how technology has changed communication.**
- **Identify historic figures such as Alexander Graham Bell and Thomas Edison who have exhibited a love of inventiveness.**
- **Obtain information about a topic using a variety of visual sources, such as pictures.** (pp. 250–251)
- **Describe how technology has changed communication.** (pp. 250–251)

Lesson 4
How Travel Has Changed
pp. 252–253

- **Describe how technology has changed transportation.**
- **Obtain information about a topic using a variety of visual sources, such as pictures.** (pp. 254–255)
- **Create visual and written material, including graphs.** (pp. 254–255)
- **Identify people who exhibit a love of individualism.** (pp. 256–257)

Lesson 5
Life Around the World
pp. 258–261

- **Compare housing, clothes, and foods from different parts of the world.**
- **Identify people who exhibit a love of individualism.** (pp. 262–263)
- **Show what people around the world say when they leave.** (pp. 264–265)

End of Unit 6

- **Retell stories from selected folktales and legends such as Aesop's fables.** (pp. 266–267)
- **Create visual and written material including pictures, maps, time lines, and graphs.** (pp. 270–271)
- **Understand how machines benefit daily life.** (p. 272)

Assessment Options

✓ Formal Assessment

- **What did you learn?** PE/TE pp. 239, 243, 249, 253, 261
- **Unit Review,** PE/TE pp. 268–271
- **Unit 6 Tests,** Assessment Book pp. 21–24
- **TestWorks,** (test generator software)

✓ Informal Assessment

- **Teacher's Edition Questions,** throughout Lessons and Features
- **Close and Assess,** TE pp. 239, 243, 249, 253, 261
- **Try it!** PE/TE pp. 237, 241, 255,
- **Think and Share,** PE/TE pp. 243, 249, 253, 257, 261, 263
- **Respect in Action,** PE/TE p. 245

Ongoing Assessment

Ongoing Assessment is found throughout the Teacher's Edition lessons using an **If...then** model.

If = students' observable behavior,

then = reteaching and enrichment suggestions

✓ Portfolio Assessment

- **Portfolio Assessment,** TE pp. 231, 270
- **Leveled Practice,** TE pp. 234, 241a, 245a, 251a, 257a, 265a
- **Workbook Pages,** pp. 00-00
- **Unit Review: Skills on Your Own,** PE/TE p. 270
- **Curriculum Connection: Writing,** TE pp. 241a, 245a, 251a, 257a, 265a

✓ Performance Assessment

- **Hands-on Unit Project** (Unit 6 Performance Assessment) PE/TE pp. 231, 268, 272
- **Internet Activity,** PE p. 272
- **Unit Review: Write and Share,** PE/TE p. 271
- **Scoring Guides,** TE pp. 266a, 269, 270, 272

Test Talk

Test-Taking Strategies

Understand the Question

- **Locate Key Words in the Question,** TE p. 259
- **Locate Key Words in the Text,** TE p. 244

Understand the Answer

- **Choose the Right Answer, Test Talk Practice Book**
- **Use Information from the Text,** TE p. 249
- **Use Information from Graphics,** TE p. 255
- **Write Your Answer,** TE pp. 241, 271

For additional practice, use the Test Talk Practice Book.

Featured Strategy

Write Your Answer

Children will:

– Make sure their answer is correct.

– Make sure their answer is complete.

– Make sure their answer is focused.

PE/TE p. 271, **TE** p. 241

Curriculum Connections

Integrating Your Day

The lessons, skills, and features of Unit 6 provide many opportunities to make connections between social studies and other areas of the elementary curriculum.

Social Studies

Reading

Reading Skill—Predict, PE/TE pp. 236–237, TE p. 238, TE p. 246

Reading Skill—Categorize, TE p. 242

The Storyteller's Craft, TE p. 245

Things Change, TE p. 245a

Reading Skill—Sequence, TE p. 252

Reading Skill—Compare and Contrast, TE p. 258

Writing

To Market Again, Rhyme Time, TE p. 241a

Computers of the Future, TE p. 245a

Related Words, TE p. 251a

A-Mazin'! TE p. 257a

Asia Puzzle, TE p. 265a

Math

Calculating Telephone Numbers, TE p. 251

Measurement, TE p. 254

Literature

Books by Laurence Yep, TE p. 263

Aesop's Fables, TE p. 267

Books About Our Country Our World, TE p. 271

Music/Drama

Up, Up, and Away! TE, p. 233

Singing at the Corner Grocery Store, TE p. 241a

Performing Change, TE p. 245a

I've Been Working on the Railroad, TE p. 246a

Telephone Etiquette, TE p. 250

All Riiiight! TE p. 251a

Transportation Songs, TE p. 257a

The Sound of Music, TE p. 265

Science

Find Locations on a Globe, TE p. 237

Vote for Scientific Tools, TE p. 241

Zoom Rockets, TE p. 257a

Looking at the World, TE p. 265a

Art

My Times, TE p. 242a

Bar Code, TE p. 245a

Business Cards, TE p. 251a

Find Pictures of Communication, TE p. 251a

Modes of Transport, TE p. 252a

Create Pictures Showing the World, TE p. 265a

Look for this symbol throughout the Teacher's Edition to find **Curriculum Connections.**

Professional Development

Real World Knowledge and Authentic Assessment

by James B. Kracht
Texas A&M University

Curriculum, instruction, and assessment are the three critical elements of any teaching-learning system. Assessment provides information about how well students have achieved the goals set forth in the curriculum. Educators have devised a variety of new assessment tools that can help to reveal why students sometimes fail and whether or not students have mastered complex curriculum standards. These tools include alternative assessment, authentic assessment, portfolio, performance task, and rubric.

Throughout Unit 6, Scott Foresman Social Studies provides a variety of ways to assess children's learning. Examples include:

- *analytical questions throughout the lesson*
- *ongoing assessment features in lessons*
- *end of the unit performance, skills, and portfolio assessments, which include rubric assessment charts, pp. 266a–272*
- *Unit 6 Project, p. 272, "Future World," requires children to make a model of a machine people might use in the future, to create a commercial telling why the machine should be used, and to ask classmates for feedback. This task involves children in applying their knowledge (of how technology affects daily life) to produce a product and performance.*

ESL Support

by Jim Cummins, Ph. D.
University of Toronto

Academic language proficiency does not automatically develop on the basis either of students' conversational fluency in English or their knowledge of discrete language skills taught by means of direct instruction in school. Students should be encouraged to become *language detectives* who investigate the mysteries of language. When we explore English and Spanish Social Studies vocabulary students who know Spanish or some other Romance language are given opportunities to shine in the classroom. They have prior knowledge in the form of their first language (L1) that is directly relevant to being a successful linguistic detective.

The following examples in the Teacher's Edition will help you to enable ESL children to extend language:

- **Focus on Meaning** on p. 236 helps English Language Learners learn that to predict is to *tell* what will happen *before* it happens.
- **Watching Television** on p. 243 has children performing activities which reinforce the meaning of *vision* in the word *television.*

Read Aloud

Ring around the World
by Annette Wynne

Ring around the world,
Taking hands together,
All across the temperate
And the torrid weather.

Past the royal palm trees,
By the ocean sand,
Make a ring around the world
Taking each other's hand.

In the valleys, on the hill,
Over the prairie spaces,
There's a ring around the world
Made of children's friendly faces.

Build Background

- Ask children to tell about family members who live or have lived in places outside the United States.
- Ask children about they ways they might communicate with people around the world.

Read Alouds and Primary Sources

Read Alouds and Primary Sources contain additional selections to be used with Unit 6.

Bibliography

Market Day: A Story Told With Folk Art, by Lois Ehlert (Harcourt Brace, ISBN 0-152-02158-2, 2000) **Easy**

On Market Street, by Arnold Lobel and Anita Lobel (Illustrator) (Greenwillow, ISBN 0-688-80309-1, 1981) Alphabet book about a child who goes to Market Street to buy one item for each letter of the alphabet. Each merchant is made out of materials that he or she is selling. **Easy**

Saturday Market, by Patricia Grossman and Enrique O. Sanchez (Illustrator) (Lothrop Lee & Shepard, ISBN 0-688-12176-4, 1994) **Easy**

Alexander Graham Bell: A Photo-Illustrated Biography, by Greg Linder (Bridgestone Books, ISBN 0-736-80202-9, 1999) **On-Level**

Great Ball Game: A Muskogee Story, The, by Joseph Bruchac and Susan L. Roth (Illustrator) (Dial Books for Young Readers, ISBN 0-803-71539-0, 1994) **On-Level**

I Spy a Freight Train: Transportation in Art, by Lucy Micklethwait (Greenwillow, ISBN 0-688-14700-3, 1996) **On-Level**

Market, by Ted Lewin (Lothrop Lee & Shepard, ISBN 0-688-12161-6, 1996) **On-Level**

Picture Book of Thomas Alva Edison, A, by David A. Adler, John Wallner (Illustrator), Alexandra Wallner (Illustrator) (Holiday House, ISBN 0-823-41246-6, 1996) Book that chronicles the life of Thomas Alva Edison from the mishaps of his youth to his great accomplishments. **On-Level**

Dragon Prince: A Chinese Beauty and the Beast Tale, The, by Laurence Yep and Kam Mak (Illustrator) (Harpercollins Juvenile Books, ISBN 0-060-24381-3, 1997) **Challenge**

Mae Jemison: The First African American Woman Astronaut, by Liza N. Burby (Powerkids Press, ISBN 0-823-95027-1, 1998) **Challenge**

Wake Up, World!: A Day in the Life of Children Around the World, by Beatrice Hollyer (Henry Holt &Company, ISBN 0-805-06293-9, 1999) Book that chronicles a typical day in the life of children from eight countries around the world. **Challenge**

Keepsakes : Using Family Stories in Elementary Classroom, by Linda Winston (Heinemann, ISBN 0-435-07235-8, 1997) **Teacher Reference**

Look for this symbol throughout the Teacher's Edition to find **Award-Winning Selections**. Additional book references are found throughout this unit.

Our Country,
Our World
UNIT
6
Where in the world would you like to visit?
231

Our Country, Our World

Unit Overview

In this unit children learn about the market, decision-making, technology, and inventions. They also learn about life around the world.

Introduce Kay

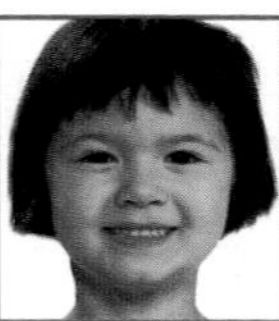

Read the unit title and then introduce the featured child for this unit as a first grader named Kay. Ask what is on the suitcase in the picture. (Airport stickers and tags from around the world)

Unit Question

- Ask children the question on this page.
- Initiate a discussion of how children learned about the places they would like to visit.
- To activate prior knowledge, make a list on the board of places in the world where children would like to visit.

✓ **Portfolio Assessment** Keep a copy of this list for the Portfolio Assessment at the end of the unit on page 270.

Practice and Extend

Hands-on Unit Project

✓ Unit 6 Performance Assessment

The Unit 6 Project, Invent a Machine of the Future, found on p. 272, is an ongoing performance assessment project to enrich children's learning throughout the unit.

- This project, which has children making a model and giving a commercial, may be started now or at any time during this unit of study.
- A performance assessment scoring guide is located on p. 272.

Explore with Me!

Objective

- Obtain information about a topic using a variety of oral sources such as songs.

Resources

- *Songs and Music* CD "Explore with Me!"
- Poster 11
- Social Studies Plus!

Introduce the Song

Preview Tell children that they will be singing a song about exploring the world. Show children photographs of places around the world. Ask if they can identify any of the places.

Warm Up To activate prior knowledge, ask children what they might experience if they traveled to a faraway place. (You try new foods, see new things, and meet new people.) Then ask what it is like to welcome somebody home from a trip.

Sing the Song

- Have children sing the song "Explore with Me!"
- Ask children to identify the kinds of transportation named in the song.
- Ask children to tell about a place people have told them that they visited.

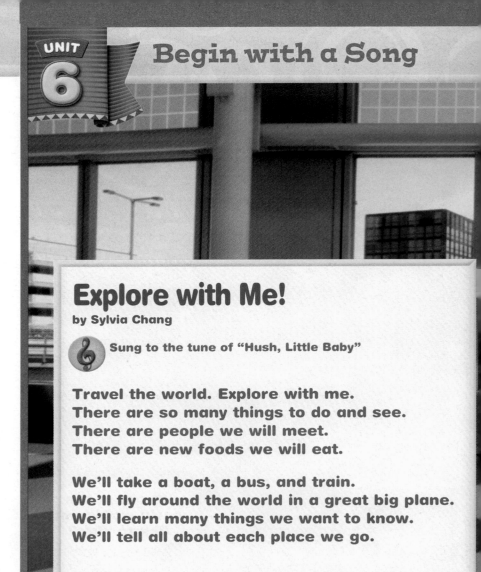

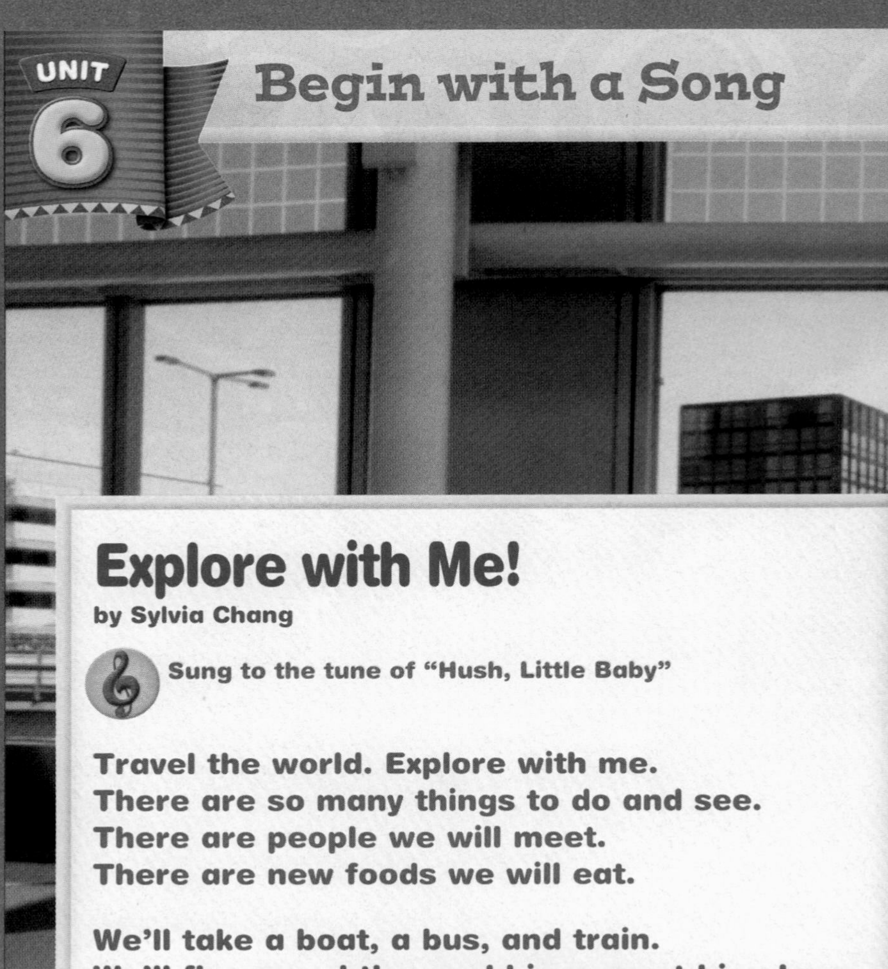

UNIT 6
Begin with a Song
Explore with Me!
by Sylvia Chang
Sung to the tune of "Hush, Little Baby"
Travel the world. Explore with me.
There are so many things to do and see.
There are people we will meet.
There are new foods we will eat.
We'll take a boat, a bus, and train.
We'll fly around the world in a great big plane.
We'll learn many things we want to know.
We'll tell all about each place we go.
232

Practice and Extend

SOCIAL STUDIES Background

Possible Misconceptions

Children may not be aware that people travel in different ways depending on where they are going. Tell children that if they are going to a nearby store, they might walk or take a bus. If they are going to another country, such as France or Japan, they might take a ship or an airplane.

AUDIO CD Technology

Play the CD, *Songs and Music*, to listen to the song "Explore with Me!"

Talk About the Picture

Direct children's attention to the picture on these two pages.

1 **Where is Kay?** At an airport **What clues tell you where she is?** Answers may include the airplane and suitcases. Analyze Pictures

2 **What is Kay doing?** She is hugging someone. **Why?** She may be saying goodbye or hello. That person may be leaving or arriving. Analyze Pictures

Up, Up, and Away!

- Tell children that they are going on a pretend class trip in an airplane. Line up chairs in pairs and have the passengers take their seats.
- Ask for a volunteer to be the pilot. Have the pilot sit at the head of the plane.
- Have children sing "Explore with Me!" as they fly toward their destination.
- Suggest that the pilot pantomime the tipping of the plane's wings and that all the passengers lean accordingly.

Vocabulary Preview

Objectives

- Determine the meanings of words
- Obtain information about a topic using a variety of visual sources such as pictures.

Resources

- Workbook, p. 60
- Vocabulary Cards
- Poster 12

Introduce the Vocabulary

Read aloud and point to each vocabulary word and the photograph illustrating it. Have volunteers give the meanings of the words. Then have children find examples of culture vocabulary words in the picture. Write these examples on the board.

Vocabulary Word	Illustrated Examples
market	food market, arts and crafts
communicate	boy talking on telephone, girl giving directions
invention	round machine with wheels, radio, telephone, computer, electric light bulb, automobile
inventor	Alexander Graham Bell, Thomas Alva Edison, Henry Ford, Amanda Jones
world	foods from many countries, “Food Market” banner

SOCIAL STUDIES STRAND
Culture

Listed below are some basic principles of culture for young children. Direct most of your discussion of the picture towards the development of these concepts.

- different kinds of markets
- goods and services
- technology that has changed work, home, and recreation
- inventions that help people communicate
- changes in land transportation
- similarities and differences between people around the world

UNIT 6

Vocabulary Preview

market

communicate

invention

234

Practice and Extend

MEETING INDIVIDUAL NEEDS
Leveled Practice

Visit a School Fair

Invite children to take a look at the areas with inventions and arts and crafts in the picture (p. 234).

Easy Randomly name some of the inventions and arts and crafts, identifying them as inventions or arts and crafts. Have children repeat the words after you. **Reteach**

On-Level Have one partner randomly name some of the inventions and arts and crafts and the other partner identify them as inventions or arts and crafts. Have partners reverse roles. **Extend**

Challenge Have children list some of the inventions and arts and crafts. Then have them compare and contrast the inventions and the drawings. (Alike: Children created them. Different: Many of the inventions are machines. They have a practical use. The drawings are things made to look beautiful.) **Enrich**

inventor

world

235

WEB SITE
Technology

You can look up vocabulary words online. Click on *Social Studies Library* and select the dictionary at **www.sfsocialstudies.com.**

Workbook, p. 60

Draw a picture for each word.
Drawings will vary.

communicate
inventor
invention
market
world

Also on Teacher Resources CD-ROM.

Talk About the Picture

Allow children time to study the picture. The picture shows a school fair with food from around the world, an arts and crafts market, inventions, and ways to communicate. Encourage children to identify and describe these parts of the picture.

Have children look at the boy in the upper left on p. 234.

1 **How is the boy communicating?** By telephone **Analyze Pictures**

Have children look at the famous inventions on the table at the top of p. 234 and the posters of their inventors on the wall. Explain that the woman in the poster on the right is Amanda Jones. She invented the vacuum method of canning. Canning is a common method of food preservation in America. Part of the air is removed in the can in order to reduce the growth of bacteria.

2 **Who are the other inventors? Connect them to the inventions on the table.** Alexander Graham Bell (telephone), Thomas Alva Edison (electric light bulb), and Henry Ford (automobile) **Analyze Pictures**

Look Ahead

Tell children they will learn more about each of the vocabulary words as they study Unit 6.

You may want to revisit the picture with children to review the concepts and vocabulary in the unit.

Have children look at the table on the lower left of p. 234 with things invented by children.

3 **Which invention is for transportation?** The round machine with wheels **Make Inferences**

Look at tables with foods from around the world on p. 235.

4 **What countries does the food come from?** Mali, China, Greece, and Mexico. **Analyze Information**

Kay's Grandparents

Predict

Objectives

- Recognize words that help make a prediction
- Analyze pictures and text to make a prediction.
- Make a prediction based on information given.

Resource

- Workbook, p. 61

About the Unit Target Skill

- The target reading skill for this unit is Predict.
- Children are introduced to the unit target skill here and are given an opportunity to practice it.
- Further opportunities to practice predicting are found throughout Unit 6.

1 Introduce and Motivate

Preview Assess whether children understand the concept of predicting by telling them *Tomorrow I will walk from my home to the grocery store. If it rains on the way, I will ....* Ask them to predict what you might do if it suddenly rains. (Run to the store, stand in a doorway, ask somebody for a ride, return home for an umbrella, etc.) Explain that to *predict* means to tell what you think may happen next.

Warm Up To activate prior knowledge, point to and identify the things from around the world shown on pp. 236–237. Then list them on the board. Tell children that they are going to vote for the thing they would most like to have. Ask them to write down what thing they predict will receive the most votes. Take a vote. Tally the results on the board. Have children display their predictions.

Reading Social Studie

Kay's Grandparents

Predict

Hi. My name is Kay. My grandparents just arrived for a visit. They have travelec to many countries. They brought me gifts from some of the countries. They brought me a fan from Japan. They also brought me clothes and other gifts from Mexico and stuffed animals from Australia.

236

Practice and Extend

EXTEND LANGUAGE
ESL Support

Focus on Meaning Discuss the meaning of the word *predict* with children. Explain that to *predict* is to tell what will happen before it happens. Tell children that they can check the accuracy of their prediction in the future.

Beginning Have children draw a picture of what the weather might be tomorrow, and orally complete the sentence *I predict* ___ to tell what the weather might be.

Intermediate Have children draw a picture of what the weather might be tomorrow and write a caption that completes the sentence *I predict* ___.

Advanced Have children make a "Tomorrow's Weather" chart with two heads: "What I Predict" and "What Actually Happened." Have them fill in the first column daily for a week, completing the sentence *I predict* ___. Then have them fill in the second column the following day.

Now I want to give my grandparents a gift. I can draw a picture for them. I can make a card. I can give them flowers.

It is time to predict. **Predict** means to tell what you think will happen next. What do you think I will give my grandparents?

I decided to draw them a picture of myself. They said they liked it very much. Did I do what you thought I would do?

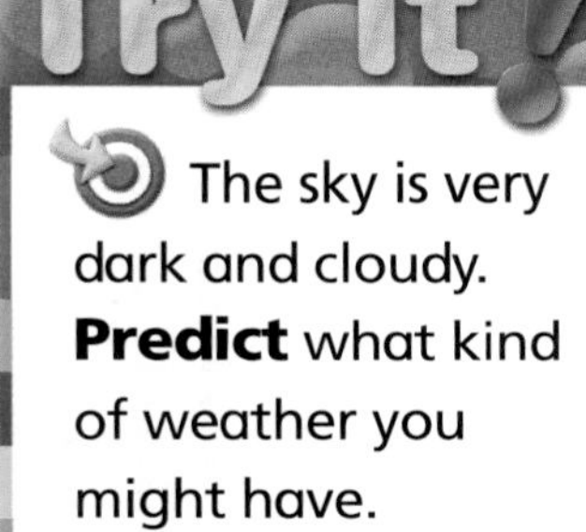

Try it!

The sky is very dark and cloudy. **Predict** what kind of weather you might have.

237

2 Teach and Discuss

Look at the picture on p. 236.

Discuss with children some of the gifts Kay's grandparents gave her. Then discuss the different things Kay can give her grandparents. Talk about the picture Kay made for her grandparents.

3 Close and Assess

Try it!

Have children draw pictures of their prediction. You may first want to discuss with them what often happens after a sky turns dark and cloudy. (It rains.)

SOCIAL STUDIES STRAND Geography

Find Locations on a Globe

Revisit the meaning of cardinal directions.

Have children find the United States, Japan, Mexico, and Australia on a globe. First have them locate their home state in the United States. Then have them locate the other countries by tracing the route and saying aloud the cardinal directions.

Workbook, p. 61

Predict

Write what you predict will happen.

Juan and his family are in Mexico City. They are visiting Juan's grandparents. This is the first time that Juan has been in Mexico.

His grandfather has taken Juan to Chapultepec Park. It is the biggest park in Mexico City! There is a zoo in the park.

What will Juan do?

Juan will go to the zoo.

Juan has fun at the park. His grandfather has a good time too. Juan asks if he can buy something to take home. He wants to remember this day!

What will Juan buy?

Juan will buy a balloon.

Directions: Read each part of the story. Write what you predict Juan will do. Then write what you predict he will buy.

Home Activity: While watching a TV show with your child, take advantage of commercial breaks to share predictions about what will happen in the show.

Also on Teacher Resources CD-ROM.

Workbook Support

Use the following Workbook pages to support content and skills development as you teach Unit 6. You can also view and print Workbook pages from the Teacher Resources CD-ROM.

Workbook, p. 60

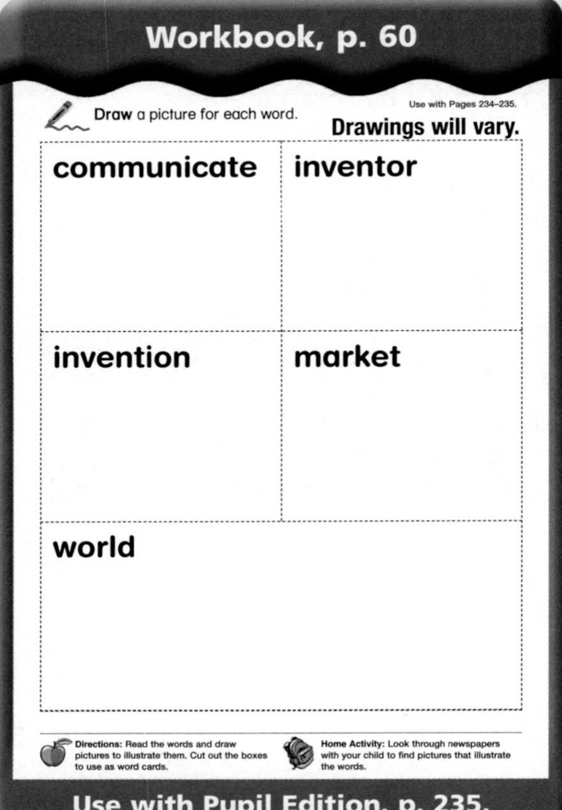

Use with Pages 234–235.

Draw a picture for each word. **Drawings will vary.**

communicate	inventor
invention	market
world	

Directions: Read the words and draw pictures to illustrate them. Cut out the boxes to use as word cards.

Home Activity: Look through newspapers with your child to find pictures that illustrate the words.

Use with Pupil Edition, p. 235.

Workbook, p. 61

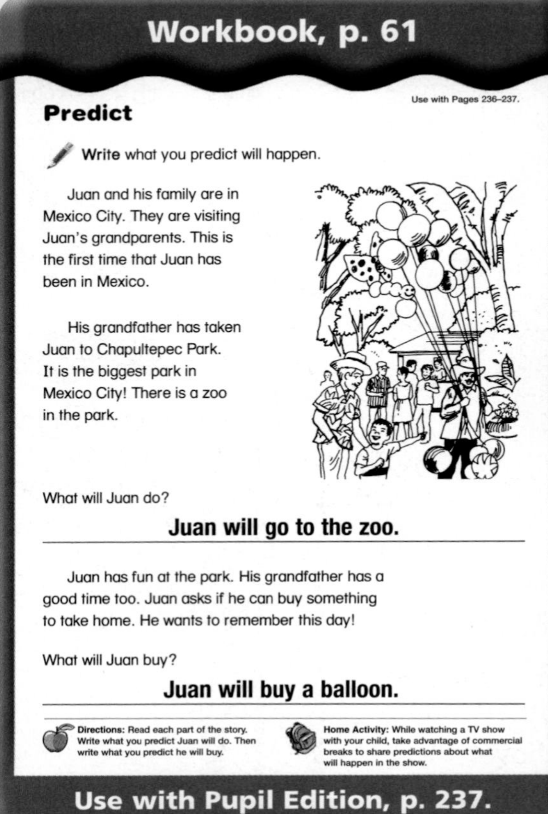

Use with Pages 236–237.

Predict

Write what you predict will happen.

Juan and his family are in Mexico City. They are visiting Juan's grandparents. This is the first time that Juan has been in Mexico.

His grandfather has taken Juan to Chapultepec Park. It is the biggest park in Mexico City! There is a zoo in the park.

What will Juan do?

Juan will go to the zoo.

Juan has fun at the park. His grandfather has a good time too. Juan asks if he can buy something to take home. He wants to remember this day!

What will Juan buy?

Juan will buy a balloon.

Directions: Read each part of the story. Write what you predict Juan will do. Then write what you predict he will buy.

Home Activity: While watching a TV show with your child, take advantage of commercial breaks to share predictions about what will happen in the show.

Use with Pupil Edition, p. 237.

Workbook, p. 62

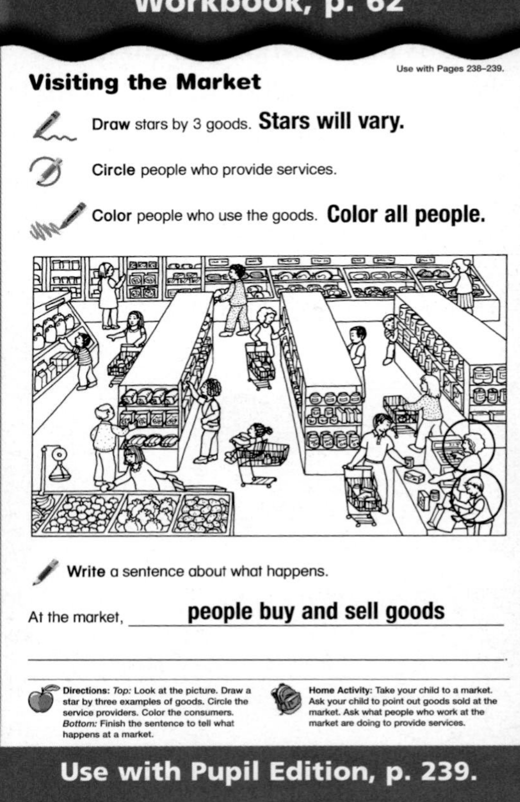

Use with Pages 238–239.

Visiting the Market

Draw stars by 3 goods. **Stars will vary.**

Circle people who provide services.

Color people who use the goods. **Color all people.**

Write a sentence about what happens.

At the market, **people buy and sell goods**

Directions: *Top:* Look at the picture. Draw a star by three examples of goods. Circle the service providers. Color the consumers. *Bottom:* Finish the sentence to tell what happens at a market.

Home Activity: Take your child to a market. Ask your child to point out goods sold at the market. Ask what people who work at the market are doing to provide services.

Use with Pupil Edition, p. 239.

Workbook, p. 63

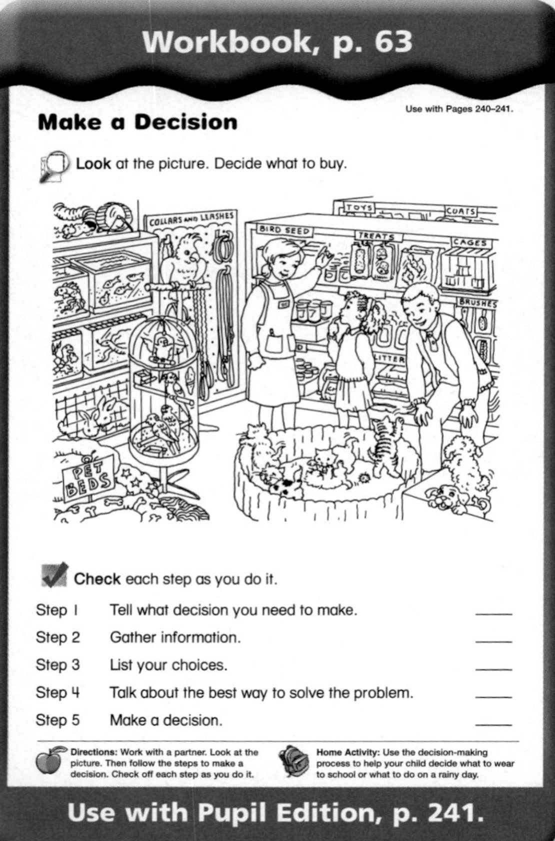

Use with Pages 240–241.

Make a Decision

Look at the picture. Decide what to buy.

Check each step as you do it.

Step 1 Tell what decision you need to make. ____

Step 2 Gather information. ____

Step 3 List your choices. ____

Step 4 Talk about the best way to solve the problem. ____

Step 5 Make a decision. ____

Directions: Work with a partner. Look at the picture. Then follow the steps to make a decision. Check off each step as you do it.

Home Activity: Use the decision-making process to help your child decide what to wear to school or what to do on a rainy day.

Use with Pupil Edition, p. 241.

Workbook, p. 64

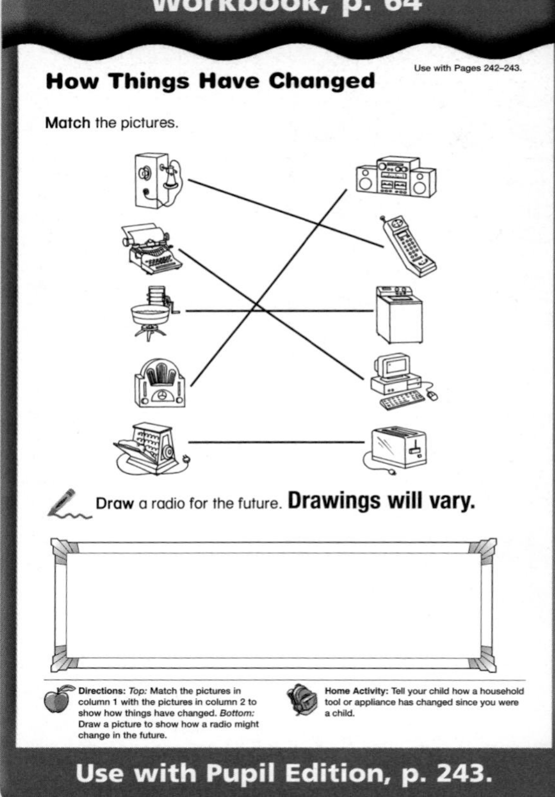

Use with Pages 242–243.

How Things Have Changed

Match the pictures.

Draw a radio for the future. **Drawings will vary.**

Directions: *Top:* Match the pictures in column 1 with the pictures in column 2 to show how things have changed. *Bottom:* Draw a picture to show how a radio might change in the future.

Home Activity: Tell your child how a household tool or appliance has changed since you were a child.

Use with Pupil Edition, p. 243.

Workbook, p. 65

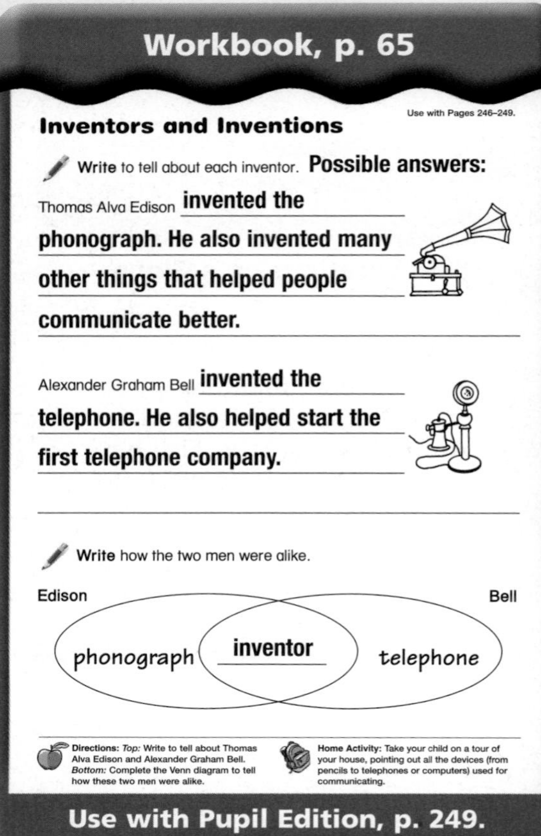

Use with Pages 246–249.

Inventors and Inventions

Write to tell about each inventor. **Possible answers:**

Thomas Alva Edison **invented the phonograph. He also invented many other things that helped people communicate better.**

Alexander Graham Bell **invented the telephone. He also helped start the first telephone company.**

Write how the two men were alike.

Directions: *Top:* Write to tell about Thomas Alva Edison and Alexander Graham Bell. *Bottom:* Complete the Venn diagram to tell how these two men were alike.

Home Activity: Take your child on a tour of your house, pointing out all the devices (from pencils to telephones or computers) used for communicating.

Use with Pupil Edition, p. 249.

Workbook Support

Workbook, p. 66

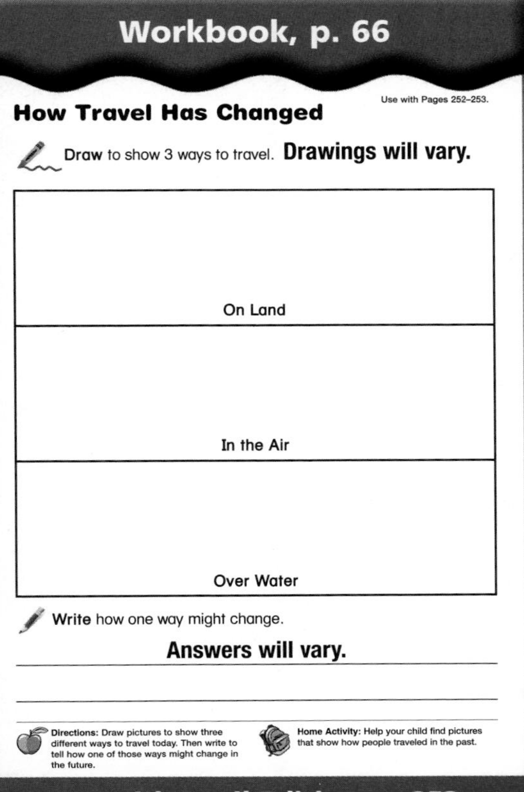

How Travel Has Changed

Use with Pages 252–253.

Draw to show 3 ways to travel. **Drawings will vary.**

On Land

In the Air

Over Water

Write how one way might change.

Answers will vary.

Directions: Draw pictures to show three different ways to travel today. Then write to tell how one of those ways might change in the future.

Home Activity: Help your child find pictures that show how people traveled in the past.

Use with Pupil Edition, p. 253.

Workbook, p. 67

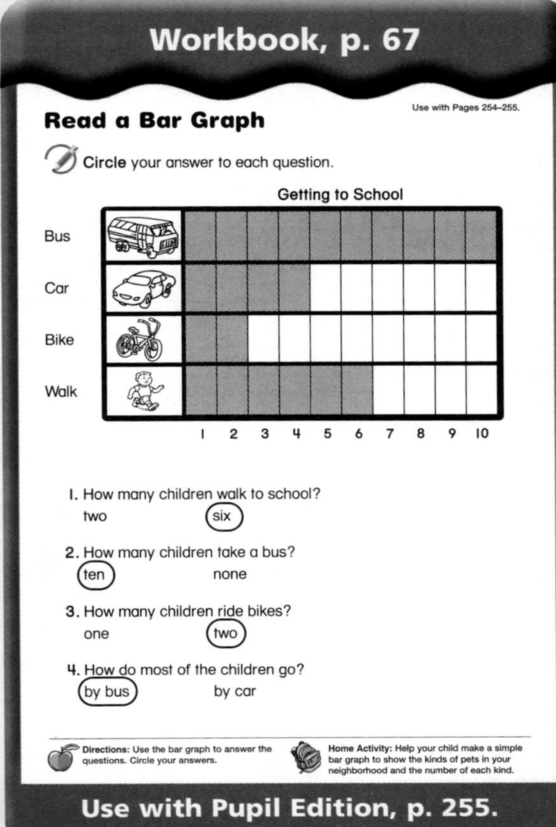

Read a Bar Graph

Use with Pages 254–255.

Circle your answer to each question.

1. How many children walk to school?
   two (six)
2. How many children take a bus?
   (ten) none
3. How many children ride bikes?
   one (two)
4. How do most of the children go?
   (by bus) by car

Directions: Use the bar graph to answer the questions. Circle your answers.

Home Activity: Help your child make a simple bar graph to show the kinds of pets in your neighborhood and the number of each kind.

Use with Pupil Edition, p. 255.

Workbook, p. 68

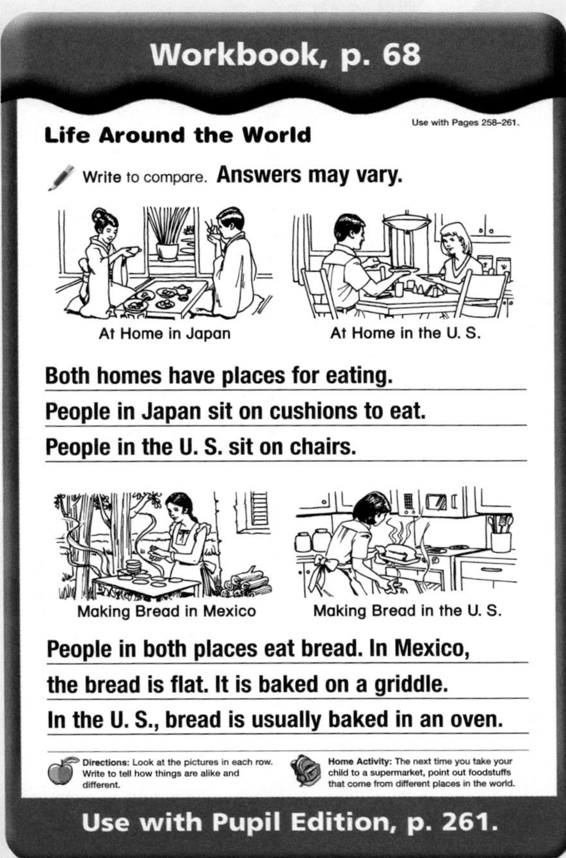

Life Around the World

Use with Pages 258–261.

Write to compare. **Answers may vary.**

At Home in Japan

At Home in the U. S.

Both homes have places for eating.

People in Japan sit on cushions to eat.

People in the U. S. sit on chairs.

Making Bread in Mexico

Making Bread in the U. S.

People in both places eat bread. In Mexico, the bread is flat. It is baked on a griddle. In the U. S., bread is usually baked in an oven.

Directions: Look at the pictures in each row. Write to tell how things are alike and different.

Home Activity: The next time you take your child to a supermarket, point out foodstuffs that come from different places in the world.

Use with Pupil Edition, p. 261.

Workbook, p. 69

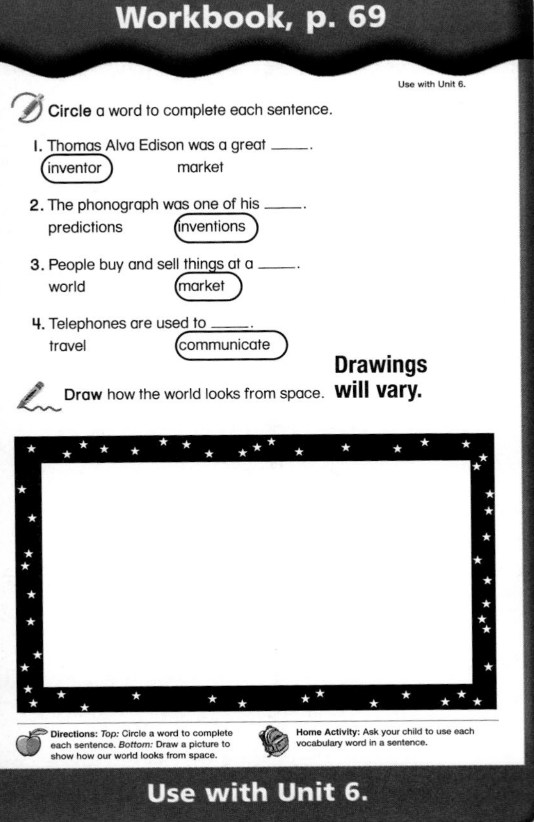

Use with Unit 6.

Circle a word to complete each sentence.

1. Thomas Alva Edison was a great ____.
   (inventor) market
2. The phonograph was one of his ____.
   predictions (inventions)
3. People buy and sell things at a ____.
   world (market)
4. Telephones are used to ____.
   travel (communicate)

Draw how the world looks from space. **Drawings will vary.**

Directions: *Top:* Circle a word to complete each sentence. *Bottom:* Draw a picture to show how our world looks from space.

Home Activity: Ask your child to use each vocabulary word in a sentence.

Use with Unit 6.

Workbook, p. 70

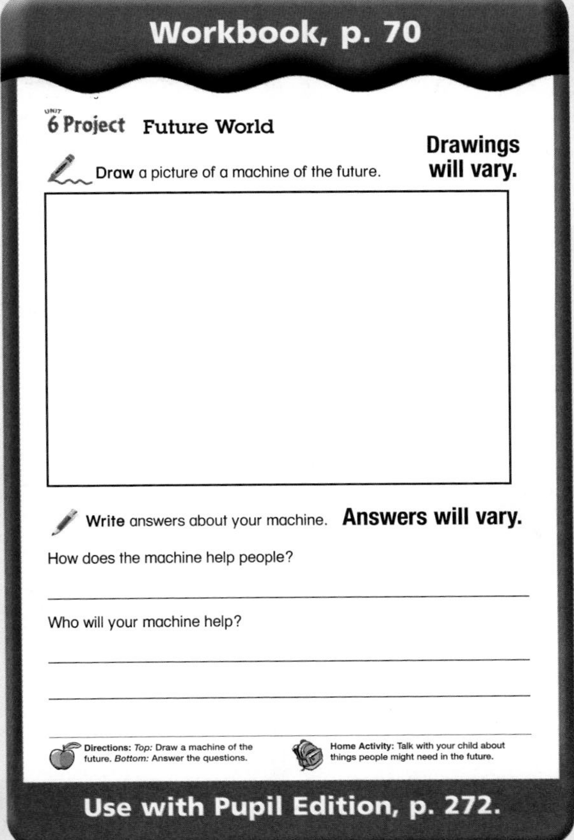

Unit 6 Project **Future World**

Draw a picture of a machine of the future. **Drawings will vary.**

Write answers about your machine. **Answers will vary.**

How does the machine help people?

Who will your machine help?

Directions: *Top:* Draw a machine of the future. *Bottom:* Answer the questions.

Home Activity: Talk with your child about things people might need in the future.

Use with Pupil Edition, p. 272.

Assessment Support

Use the following Assessment Book pages and TestWorks to assess content and skills in Unit 6. You can also view and print Assessment Book pages from the Teacher Resources CD-ROM.

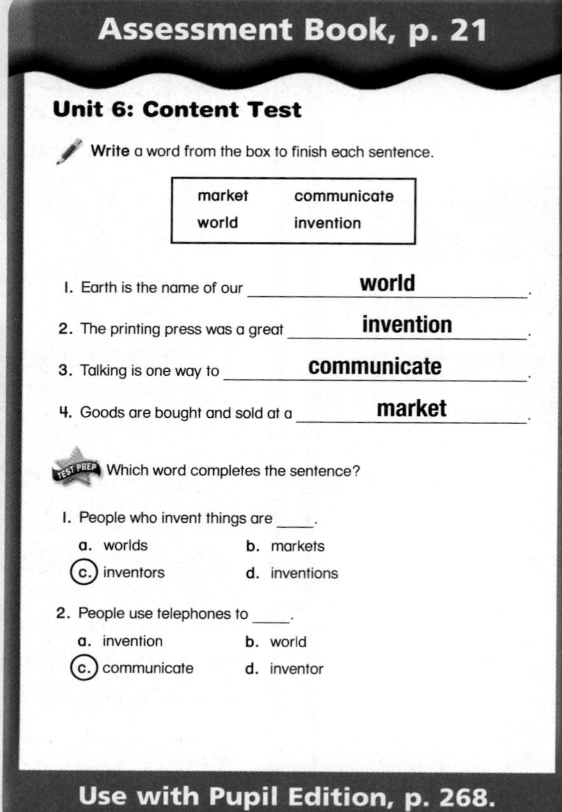

Assessment Book, p. 21

Unit 6: Content Test

Write a word from the box to finish each sentence.

market	communicate
world	invention

1. Earth is the name of our ___world___.
2. The printing press was a great ___invention___.
3. Talking is one way to ___communicate___.
4. Goods are bought and sold at a ___market___.

Which word completes the sentence?

1. People who invent things are ____.
   a. worlds b. markets (c.) inventors d. inventions
2. People use telephones to ____.
   a. invention b. world (c.) communicate d. inventor

Use with Pupil Edition, p. 268.

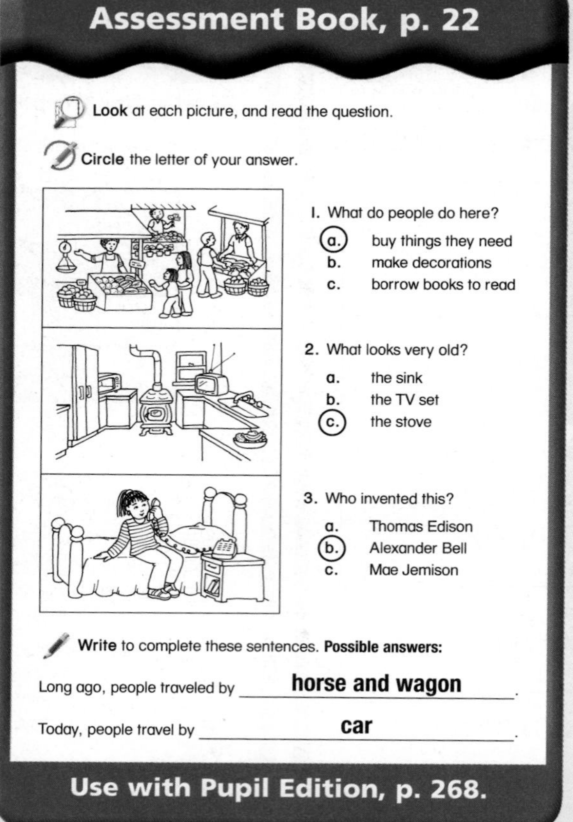

Assessment Book, p. 22

Look at each picture, and read the question.

Circle the letter of your answer.

1. What do people do here?
   (a.) buy things they need
   b. make decorations
   c. borrow books to read
2. What looks very old?
   a. the sink
   b. the TV set
   (c.) the stove
3. Who invented this?
   a. Thomas Edison
   (b.) Alexander Bell
   c. Mae Jemison

Write to complete these sentences. **Possible answers:**

Long ago, people traveled by ___horse and wagon___.

Today, people travel by ___car___.

Use with Pupil Edition, p. 268.

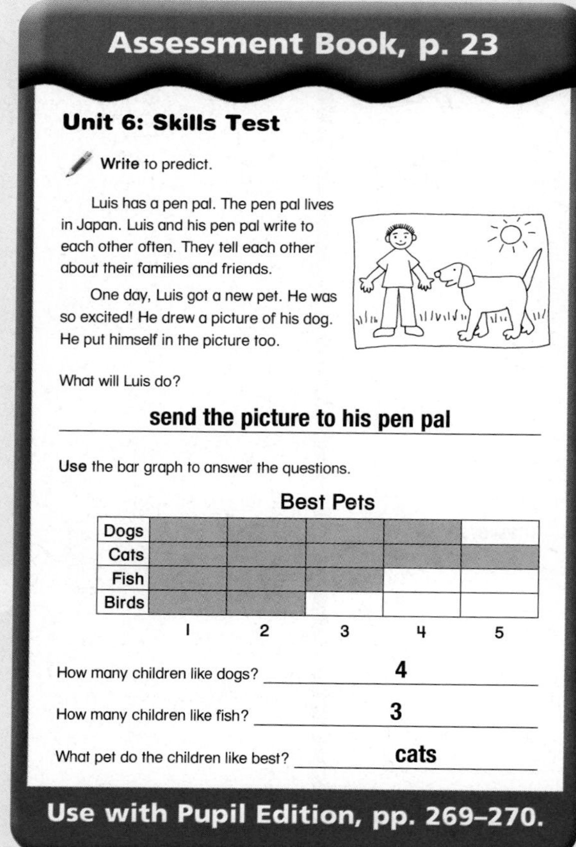

Assessment Book, p. 23

Unit 6: Skills Test

Write to predict.

Luis has a pen pal. The pen pal lives in Japan. Luis and his pen pal write to each other often. They tell each other about their families and friends.

One day, Luis got a new pet. He was so excited! He drew a picture of his dog. He put himself in the picture too.

What will Luis do?

___send the picture to his pen pal___

Use the bar graph to answer the questions.

Best Pets

Dogs, Cats, Fish, Birds; 1, 2, 3, 4, 5

How many children like dogs? ___4___

How many children like fish? ___3___

What pet do the children like best? ___cats___

Use with Pupil Edition, pp. 269–270.

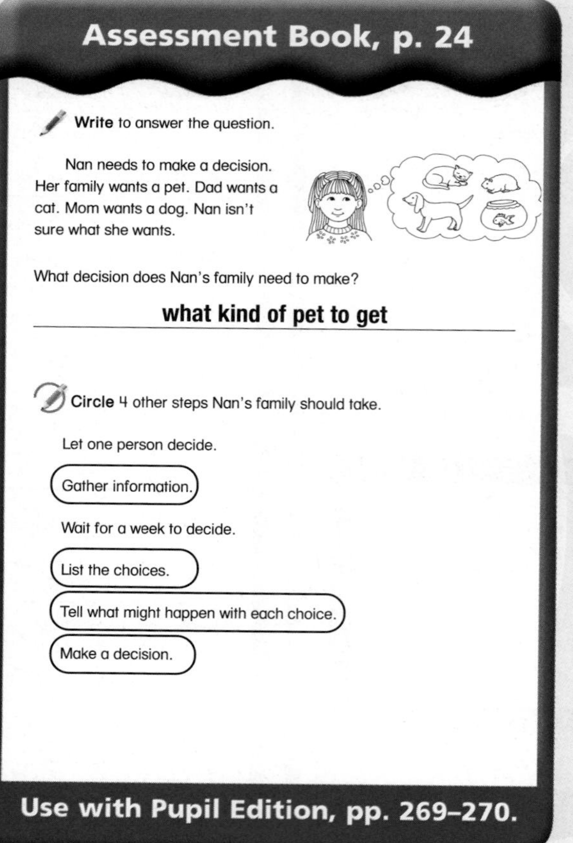

Assessment Book, p. 24

Write to answer the question.

Nan needs to make a decision. Her family wants a pet. Dad wants a cat. Mom wants a dog. Nan isn't sure what she wants.

What decision does Nan's family need to make?

___what kind of pet to get___

Circle 4 other steps Nan's family should take.

Let one person decide.

(Gather information.)

Wait for a week to decide.

(List the choices.)

(Tell what might happen with each choice.)

(Make a decision.)

Use with Pupil Edition, pp. 269–270.

Lesson 1 Overview

Visiting the Market **pages 238–239**	Children will learn about the role of markets in providing goods and services.	 Time 10–15 minutes Resources • Workbook, p. 62 • Vocabulary Card **market** • Every Student Learns Guide, pp. 106–109
Make a Decision **Pages 240–241**	Children will learn and use the steps in decision making.	Time 10–15 minutes Resource • Workbook, p. 63

Build Background

Activity

Market Day

 **Time** 20 minutes

Describe a market to children. Then have them create a fruit market in the classroom, using fruit, signs, paper bags, and paper money. Invite some children to sell the fruit and others to buy it.

- Have the sellers prepare signs with the prices of their fruits.
- After the buyers have bought fruit, have children exchange roles.

If time is short, have children describe a market where goods are sold. Ask them to draw a picture of items for sale.

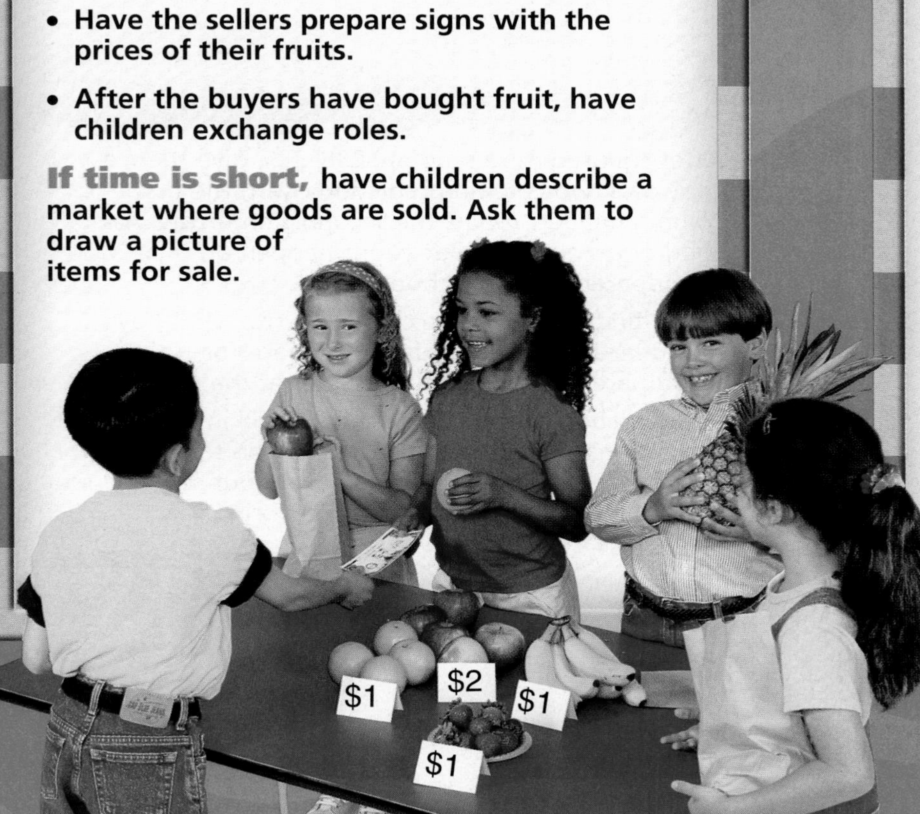

Read Aloud

To Market

nursery rhyme

To market, to market
To buy a fat pig,
Home again, home again,
Jiggety jig,
To market, to market
To buy a fat hog,
Home again, home again,
Jiggety jog,
To market, to market
To buy a plum bun,
Home again, home again,
Market is done.

Lesson 1 Visiting the Market

Objective

- Identify the role of markets in the exchange of goods and services.

Vocabulary

market a place where goods are sold (p. 238)

QUICK Teaching Plan

If time is short, discuss the meaning of the word *market*. Explain that goods and services are provided at a market.

- Remind children that goods are things that are grown or made. Tell them that goods are usually bought and sold. Ask children for examples of household goods.
- Remind children that services are jobs in which people help others. Ask them the ways that a waiter in a restaurant provides a service.

1 Introduce and Motivate

Preview Display the Vocabulary Card **market** and ask children to tell things a family needs. Make a list of the things on the board. Then ask children to tell where these goods can be bought. Tell children that they will be learning about a place where people buy food.

Warm Up To activate prior knowledge, ask children to tell if they have ever sold goods (for example, lemonade or cookies). Ask children to identify the goods in the pictures on pp. 238–239.

2 Teach and Discuss

Page 238–239

① **How do people pay for goods at the market?** With money Draw Conclusions

Lesson 1 Visiting the Market

Tomorrow is Grandparents Day at my school! Many grandparents will come to visit. They will bring special foods to our cl

My grandparents and I went to the market to buy the food we will bring. A **market** is a place where goods are sold.

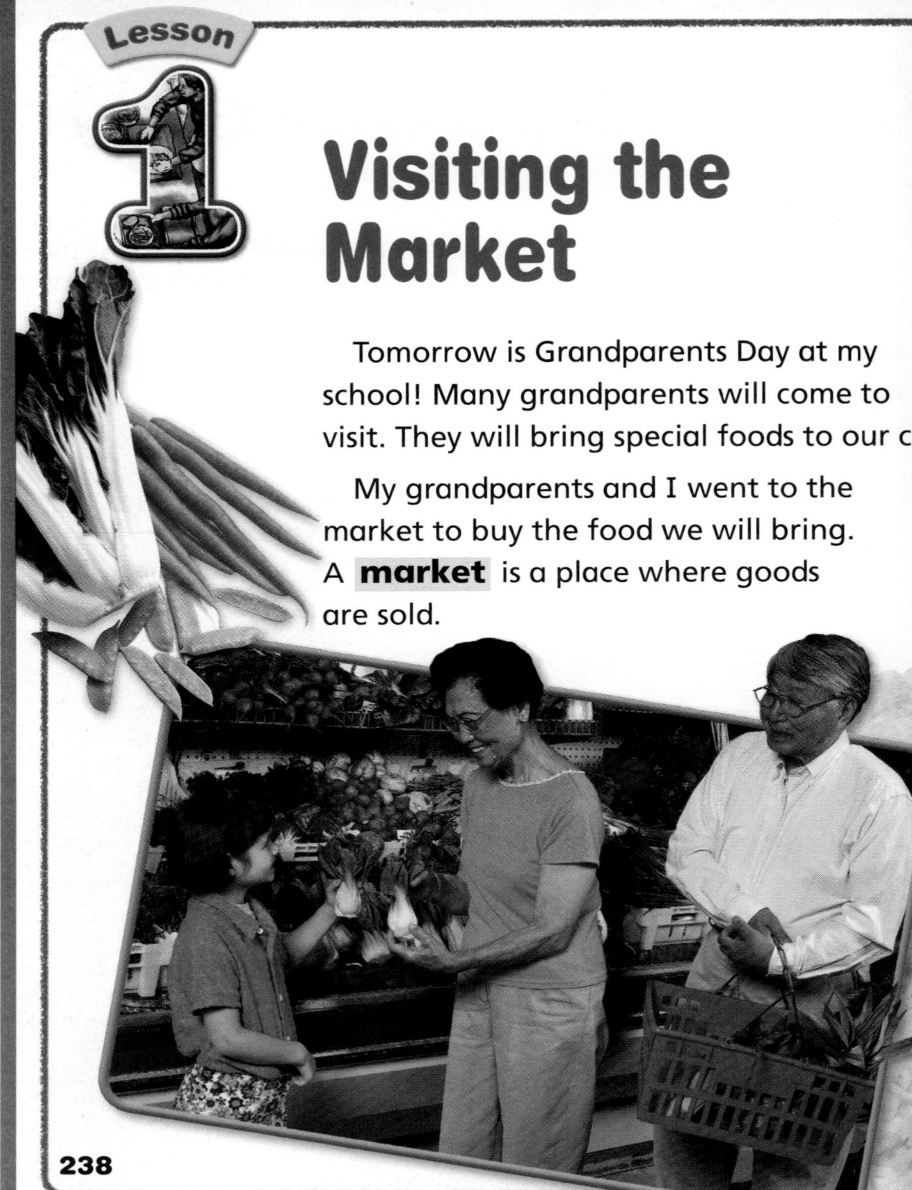

Practice and Extend

READING SKILL Predict

Target Skill

- After children have read pp. 238–239, give them a copy of a two-column prediction chart, the first column headed *Today*, the second, *Tomorrow*. Ask children to predict what might happen on Grandparents Day in school.
- In the first column, have children write what Kay's grandparents will do today to prepare for Grandparents Day. (Buy vegetables at the market)
- In the second column, have children fill in their predictions about what the class will do tomorrow for Grandparents Day. (Answers will vary but may include eat the food that the grandparents bring.)

The food we are bringing is made with vegetables. We picked out the vegetables we wanted.

People who work at the market provide services. One worker weighed the vegetables and wrote how much they cost on the bag. 1 2 3

What did you learn?

1. What goods did Kay and her grandparents buy?
2. What service did they use?
3. Kay and her grandparents chose their groceries. They took the groceries to the front of the store. **Predict** what may happen next.

239

SOCIAL STUDIES
Background

Possible Misconceptions

- Some children may not understand that a grocery store or supermarket is only one kind of market. Crafts, clothing, or electronics can also be sold in a market.

WEB SITE
Technology

You can look up vocabulary words online. Click on *Social Studies Library* and selecting the dictionary at **www.sfsocialstudies.com.**

Workbook, p. 62

Visiting the Market

Draw stars by 3 goods. **Stars will vary.**

Circle people who provide services.

Color people who use the goods. **Color all people.**

Write a sentence about what happens.

At the market, **people buy and sell goods**

Directions: *Top:* Look at the picture. Draw a star by three examples of goods. Circle the service providers. Color the consumers. *Bottom:* Finish the sentence to tell what happens at a market.

Home Activity: Take your child to a market. Ask your child to point out goods sold at the market. Ask what people who work at the market are doing to provide services.

Also on Teacher Resources CD-ROM.

SOCIAL STUDIES STRAND
Economics

Explain to children that people depend on one another for goods and services. Usually the goods and services are provided for payment in money. Sometimes, however, people trade goods, such as food, and services rather than pay for them. This exchange is called bartering. Ask children if they have ever traded things.

2 **Why do sellers need a market?** Answers will vary but should reflect that sellers need a place to sell their goods. **Apply Information**

Decision Making

3 **What would you do if you wanted to buy your grandparents two flowers but you only had money for one? Support your choice.** Answers will vary but should reflect that children have to make a choice. Possible answers: Save money and buy the two flowers later so each grandparent has one. Buy one flower that they can share so they have the flower for Grandparents Day. **Make Decisions**

3 Close and Assess

Ask children to tell what people do at the market. (Buy and sell goods; provide services) Have partners discuss a market they have visited with their family. Ask them to tell what goods were available, what steps were taken in the purchase of an item, and what services were provided.

What did you learn?

1. Kay and her grandparents bought vegetables.
2. Someone at the store weighed the vegetables and wrote the cost on the bag.
3. Possible answer: The grandparents will pay for the groceries.

Make a Decision

Objective

- Use a decision-making process to identify a situation that requires a decision, gather information, identify options, predict consequences, and take action to implement a decision.

1 Introduce and Motivate

Preview Ask children to look at the illustrations on pages 240–241. Explain that these are numbered steps in making decisions about decorations for Grandparents Day. Explain that the scenes in the thought balloons do not show what is actually happening. They are thoughts that show what might happen.

Warm Up To activate prior knowledge, ask children what things they would need to make decisions about for a birthday party (guests, food, decorations, fun activities).

Thinking Skills

Make a Decision

Kay's class had to decide how to
1 decorate their classroom for Grandparents Day. Here are the steps they followed to make their decision.
2

Step 1 Tell what decision you need to make.

How should we decorate?

Step 2 Gather informatio

How many decorations do we already have?

3 **Step 3** List your choices.

How Should We Decorate?
1. Make name tags.
2. Put up streamers.
3. Put welcome signs by the door.
4. Put up balloons.

240

Practice and Extend

ACCESS CONTENT ESL Support

Analyze Pictures Help children create an invitation to a classroom Grandparents Day party. Write the following on the board: "Dear family member,/ You are invited to Grandparents Day Party on ____________./ I hope you will come./ Love,/____________"

Beginning Have children copy the invitation. Help children complete it. Then have them create an illustration for it.

Intermediate Have children copy the invitation and then fill in the blanks on their own. Then have them create an illustration for the invitation.

Advanced Have children copy the invitation, add one or two sentences, and fill in the blanks. Then have them illustrate the invitation.

For additional ESL Support, use Every Student Learns Guide pp. 106–109.

Grandparents might like name tags.

Step 4 Tell what might happen with each choice.

Step 5 Make a decision.

Kay's class could pick two different ways to decorate. They voted. Most of the children voted for welcome signs and balloons. They could not wait to decorate!

Welcome to our class

1. Why did Kay's class have to make a decision?
2. If you were in Kay's class, how would you vote?
3. **On Your Own** Tell or write about a decision you and your class made.

2 Teach and Discuss

1. **About what do Kay and her classmates have to make a decision?** How to decorate the classroom for Grandparents Day **Express Ideas**

2. **What information do Kay and her classmates need to gather?** They need to know how many decorations they already have. **Analyze Information**

3. **How is making a list helpful in making a decision?** Possible answer: A list helps you remember all the choices. **Interpret Charts**

4. **What decoration do they think the grandparents will like?** Name tags **Analyze Information**

Write Your Answer

5. **What decorations did Kay's class vote for? Write your answer.** Welcome signs and balloons. Tell children to use details from the text to support their written answer. Remind them that their answer should be complete as well as correct. **Analyze Information**

CURRICULUM CONNECTION Science

Vote for Scientific Tools

Explain to children that tools have improved the work of scientists. Have children decide what scientific tool to use in a classroom activity.

- Have children find out what tools are available in school.
- Have children list the tools, such as magnet, clock, globe, magnifying glass.
- Have children discuss the kinds of activities they would do with each tool.
- Have children vote for the scientific tool to use.

Workbook, p. 63

Make a Decision

Look at the picture. Decide what to buy.

Check each step as you do it.

Step 1 Tell what decision you need to make.
Step 2 Gather information.
Step 3 List your choices.
Step 4 Talk about the best way to solve the problem.
Step 5 Make a decision.

Also on Teacher Resources CD-ROM.

3 Close and Assess

Ask children to tell the steps used when making a decision. Have groups make a decision about plans for a class party.

Try it!

1. They had to find ways to decorate the classroom. Then they had to pick the two best decorations.
2. Answers will vary, but may include balloons and streamers because they are the most colorful.
3. **On Your Own** Students should tell or write about the steps they went through to make the class decision.

Use with pages 238–241

Lesson 1 Wrap-Up

MEETING INDIVIDUAL NEEDS

Leveled Practice

Market Day

Ask children to select items, such as necklaces, toy trucks, or videos, to sell at a market. Have them draw pictures of their items and display them in their "booth" in the classroom market.

Easy Have children label their pictures. **Reteach**

On-Level Have children use their pictures to create a poster for their goods. Tell them to include words describing their goods. **Extend**

Challenge Have children write a flyer for the market, listing what goods and services are offered. **Enrich**

Hands-on Activities

CURRICULUM CONNECTION

Writing

To Market Again

Objective Demonstrate understanding of the lesson vocabulary through reading literature.

Resource Vocabulary Card: **market**

Materials story about a market

Learning Style Auditory/Verbal

Group

 **Time** 10–15 minutes

1. Read aloud *To Market, To Market* by Anne Miranda.

2. Ask children what is real about the story and what is not real.

3. Then have them draw one of the vegetables the woman buys for soup.

4. Display the Vocabulary Card and have children add the word *market* to their "My Word Book."

CURRICULUM CONNECTION

Music

Singing at the Corner Grocery Store

Objective Sing about the items found in a grocery store.

Materials *The Corner Grocery Store & Other Songs* by Raffi (Uni/Rounder, 1992)

Learning Style Musical

Group

 **Time** 10–15 minutes

1. Play the song "The Corner Grocery Store."

2. Play the song again and have children sing along with the song.

3. Encourage children to make up verses for other items found at the grocery store.

4. Have them add the verses to "My Word Book."

CURRICULUM CONNECTION

Writing

Rhyme Time

Objective Write a poem that rhymes.

Materials paper, pencils

Learning Style Auditory

Partners

 **Time** 10–15 minutes

1. Read the nursery rhyme *To Market* again.

2. Ask children to identify the words that rhyme. *(pig/jig, hog/jog, bun/done)*

3. Have partners list words that rhyme with one of those rhymes and write them down. *(big, fig, dig, wig; frog, clog, log; fun, begun, none, run, son, sun, ton, one, won)*

big
fig
dig
wig

4. Have partners write a two-line poem using two of their rhyming words.

Lesson 2 Overview

How Things Have Changed pages 242-243	Children will explore how technology changes the way people live and work.	Time 10–15 minutes Resources • Workbook, p. 64 • Every Student Learns Guide, pp. 110–113
Joseph Bruchac Pages 244-245	Children will learn about Joseph Bruchac.	Time 10–15 minutes

Build Background

Activity

My Times

Time 20 minutes

Show children pictures of the way people lived long ago and in the recent past, such as a person reading by candlelight or cooling off with a fan blowing on a block of ice. Have children create a collage from magazine photographs of a modern family in a living room or kitchen. Ask children to discuss how household tools and appliances have changed the way people live.

If time is short, show children pictures of the way people lived long ago and in the recent past, and have children tell about how life is different today. Prompt them by asking about how people enjoy music and eating.

Read Aloud

Phone Home

by Emily Kurtz

Off to the bedroom
to tell my sister
how much
I miss her!
But she's gabbing
on her cell phone.

Off to the kitchen
to tell my mom I'll assist her!
But she's gabbing
with—you guessed it—my sister
on her cell phone.

I suppose if I don't want to be alone,
I'll have to get a cell phone
of my own.

How Things Have Changed

Objectives

- Describe how household tools and appliances have changed.
- Describe how technology has changed recreation.
- Describe how technology has changed the way people work.

QUICK Teaching Plan

If time is short, discuss how technology has changed at work and home.

- Discuss how the objects in the chart on p. 243 have changed.

1 Introduce and Motivate

Preview Ask children to read aloud what Kay's grandmother says on p. 242. Show children the bar code on various products. Explain that the scanner "reads" the bars to add up the cost of the items. Then explain that in some places, items are still labeled with the price, which the cashier adds up by punching numbered buttons on a cash register.

Warm Up To activate prior knowledge, ask children to read aloud what Kay's grandfather says on p. 242. Ask children how they would use a computer to type their name and print it. Then show children a typewriter. Have them type their name on it. Ask what the differences are between the computer and the typewriter.

2 Teach and Discuss

Page 242

1 **How have computers changed the way people work?** Answers will vary, but may include that they make rewriting and saving stories easier. **Analyze Information**

How Things Have Changed

We learned many interesting things from the grandparents who visited our class. They told us how work has changed. We learned how some things at home have changed too.

1
I used a typewriter. Now people use computers!
2
I used to punch buttons at the store. Now I scan.

242

Practice and Extend

READING SKILL Categorize

Make a Then and Now Chart

- After children have read pp. 242–243, help them brainstorm a list of things that were commonly used in the past and a list of things that are commonly used now. Remind children that many things that were commonly used in the past are still used today.
- Give children squares of paper. Ask them to draw pictures of the things on the lists.
- Have children make a two-column chart with "Then" and "Now" heading the columns.
- Have children complete the chart by pasting their drawings in the appropriate columns. Remind them to keep related things in the same rows.

My class made a chart to show other ways things have changed. How do you think things might change in the future? 4

What did you learn?

1. Tell two ways work has changed.
2. How has something you do for fun changed?
3. **Think and Share** Think of something you use at home. **Predict** how it might change in the future. Draw a picture and write or tell about it.

243

EXTEND LANGUAGE
ESL Support

Watching Television Explain to children how new machines and devices influence people's lives. Write the word *television* on the board. Circle *vision*. Explain that it means the act of seeing.

Beginning Have children brainstorm why people watch TV.

Intermediate Have children orally complete the sentence *People watch TV because ___.* Create a word web with their suggestions.

Advanced Have children tell what people did before TV.

For additional ESL Support, use Every Student Learns Guide, pp. 110–113.

Workbook, p. 64

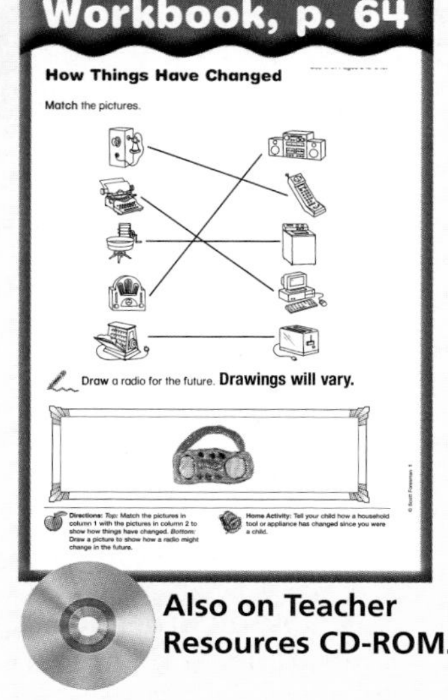

How Things Have Changed
Match the pictures.
Draw a radio for the future. Drawings will vary.

Also on Teacher Resources CD-ROM.

2 **How have store scanners changed the way people work?** Answers will vary, but may include that they make adding the costs of items faster and more accurate. **Analyze Information**

Page 243

Discuss how each household tool or appliance in the chart has changed the way families live. Then discuss how the technology in the chart has changed recreation.

3 **Do all people use the latest things?** Answers will vary but should reflect that not all people use the latest technology. For example, some people might wash dishes by hand. **Analyze Information**

Have children interview their grandparents to find out about recreation when they were children. Then discuss with children how technology has changed recreation from the time when their grandparents were children.

4 **Do you think the way people have fun has changed?** Answers will vary, but may include that some activities, such as playing computer games, are new, while others, such as playing outdoor sports, are the same. **Hypothesize**

3 Close and Assess

Ask children to tell about technology that has changed the way they live. Invite children to make a list with a partner of things that have changed.

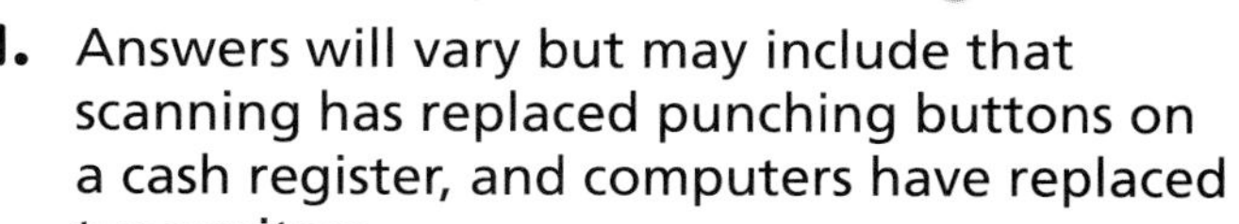

1. Answers will vary but may include that scanning has replaced punching buttons on a cash register, and computers have replaced typewriters.
2. Answers will vary but may include people used to listen to records and now they listen to CDs.
3. **Think and Share** Pictures and descriptions should reflect how something might look in the future.

CITIZEN HEROES

Joseph Bruchac

Objective

- Identify people who exemplify good citizenship and exhibit a love of individualism.

1 Introduce and Motivate

Preview Tell children that Joseph Bruchac is a Native American who writes down Native American stories. Have them look at the picture on the bottom of p. 245. Explain that Bruchac is signing his name in a book. The signature of a person, called an autograph, is valued by the person purchasing the book. Ask children to read the titles of Bruchac's two books shown on pp. 244–245.

Warm Up To activate prior knowledge, ask children to remember what they learned about Native Americans. (Children might remember that they were the first people to live in America and that some hunted for food while others grew food.) Explain to children that many Native Americans, like other peoples around the world, use storytelling as a way to pass along information from parents to children.

2 Teach and Discuss

Explain that the word *respect* means to show consideration for someone or something.

Test Talk

Locate Key Words in the Text

1 What can we learn to respect through many Native American stories? Each other and the Earth. Have children locate the key words (*respect* and *stories*) in the text that match the key words in the question. **Analyze Information**

CITIZEN HEROES

Joseph Bruchac

Joseph Bruchac was born in Saratoga Springs, New York.

Joseph lived with his grandparents when he was young. Joseph's grandfather was an Abenaki Indian.

Joseph became interested in the stories told by Native American, or American Indian, elders. Many of the stories told how we should respect each other and the Earth. 1

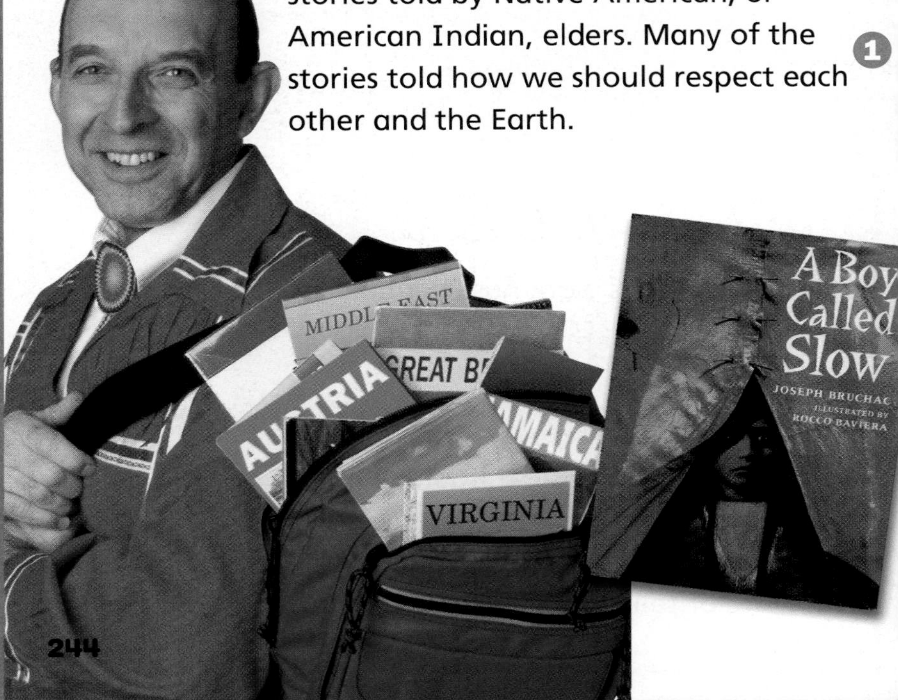

244

Practice and Extend

SOCIAL STUDIES Background

About Joseph Bruchac

- Young Joseph would follow his grandfather everywhere. His grandfather showed him how to walk in the woods quietly and to fish.
- Joseph started to write poems when he was in second grade. He liked to read stories about animals.
- Joseph Bruchac showed his love of individualism by writing down the stories told by Native American elders.
- Joseph Bruchac has written more than 50 books for adults and children. His poems, articles, and stories have appeared in more than 500 publications.
- The homelands of the Abenaki (AB uhr NAK ee) tribe were in Maine, New Hampshire, and Vermont.

Today, Joseph Bruchac is a writer. He still listens to stories told by Native American elders. He tells these stories in ❷ many of his books and poems. He also sings songs. Many of the songs tell Native American stories.

Joseph Bruchac respects Native American stories. He thinks it is a good idea to share these stories. He thinks people can learn a lot from them. ❸❹

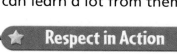

Respect in Action

How does Joseph Bruchac show that he respects Native American stories?

Joseph Bruchac signing one of his books

245

❷ **Where does Joseph Bruchac get some of his stories from?** He listens to Native American elders. **Apply Information**

SOCIAL STUDIES STRAND
Culture

Explain that many Native American stories are about overcoming fear, being helpful, showing respect, and making friends. Tell children that these traditional stories may help them learn to deal with these issues.

❸ **Why does Joseph Bruchac write down the stories he hears?** He wants to share the ways of Native American peoples. He believes other people can learn from them. **Analyze Information**

❹ **What are some ways you can tell a story?** Answers will vary but may include writing a book or poem, singing a song, or speaking to a group. **Apply Information**

3 Close and Assess

Ask children to tell what they learned about Joseph Bruchac. Ask them to discuss with a partner people they respect and how they show their respect.

Respect in Action

Joseph Bruchac listens to stories told by elders and shares them through stories, poems, and songs.

CURRICULUM CONNECTION
Reading

The Storyteller's Craft

Read and discuss any of the following children's books by Joseph Bruchac to children.

- ***How Chipmunk Got His Stripes: A Tale of Bragging and Teasing,*** by Joseph Bruchac, James Bruchac (illustrator), Jose Aruego (illustrator), and Ariane Dewey (illustrator) (Dial Books for Young Readers, ISBN 0-803-72404-7, 2001) **Easy**
- ***Many Nations,*** by Joseph Bruchac (Econo-Clad Books, ISBN 0-613-11838-3, 1999), International Reading Teacher's Choice Award **On-Level**
- ***Thirteen Moons on Turtle's Back: A Native American Year of Moons,*** by Joseph Bruchac and Thomas Locker (Illustrator) (Philomel Books, ISBN 0-399-22141-7, 1992) **On-Level**
- ***Earth Under Sky Bear's Feet: Native American Poems of the Land, The,*** by Joseph Bruchac (Econo-Clad Books, ISBN 0-613-10503-6, 1999) **Challenge**

Use with pages 242–245

Lesson 2 Wrap-Up

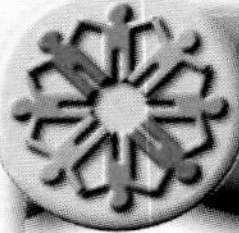

MEETING INDIVIDUAL NEEDS

Leveled Practice

Performing Change

Assign groups an object that has changed work, recreation, or tasks in the home. Have groups present performances that show how the object has changed daily life.

Easy Assign groups an object such as a washing machine. Help them dramatize how people washed clothes before the washing machine and how people wash clothes in a washing machine. **Reteach**

On-Level Assign groups an object such as a car. Help them dramatize how people traveled before the car and how people travel in a car. Have the group explain how the object has changed people's lives. **Extend**

Challenge Assign groups an object such as a television. Help them dramatize how people were entertained before television and how people watch television. Have the group explain how the object has changed communication and recreation. **Enrich**

Hands-on Activities

CURRICULUM CONNECTION

Writing

Computers of the Future

Objective To understand the word *change*.

Materials drawings of computers, crayons

Learning Style Spatial

Individual

 **Time** 10–15 minutes

1. Provide children with simple drawings of a computer on large paper. Tell children to make the computer friendlier for the future.
2. Give children suggestions, such as propping a hat on top or decorating areas with stars or stripes.
3. Have children add a sentence about how the computer will change in the future and then show their picture.

CURRICULUM CONNECTION

Art

Bar Code

Objective Make a bar code.

Materials paper, crayons

Learning Style Spatial

Individual

 **Time** 10–15 minutes

1. Explain to children that a bar code is a band of thick and thin black bars on a white background, printed on items for sale in a store. Tell that these bars are scanned by a computer that lists the price (and other information) about the item. Remind children of the bar codes they saw earlier.
2. Have children draw the back of a cereal box. Tell them to draw a bar code on the lower right side of the box.
3. You may want to display their drawings on the bulletin board.

CURRICULUM CONNECTION

Reading

Things Change

Objective Tell about changes between the past and present.

Materials paper, crayons, book

Learning Style Visual/Linguistic

Group

 **Time** 10–15 minutes

1. Read with children *When I Was Young in the Mountains* by Cynthia Rylant.
2. Discuss the story with children. Then divide them into groups and have them name the household items (such as the oil lamp, candle, old black stove) and activities (such as pumping water from a well) that have changed since the time of the story. Then have children tell what has replaced the items and activities.
3. Have children draw a picture of one thing from the story that has changed.

Lesson 3 Overview

Inventors and Inventions

pages 246–249

Children will learn about inventions that have helped people to communicate better and the inventors who made them.

Time 20–30 minutes

Resources

- Workbook, p. 65
- Vocabulary Cards
  communicate invention
  inventor
- Every Student Learns Guide, pp. 114–117

Telephones

Pages 250–251

Children will explore the development of the telephone.

Time 15–20 minutes

Build Background

Activity

Playing Telephone

Time 15 minutes

Have children play the game *Telephone*. Ask children to sit in a large circle. Start a message around the circle by whispering to the first child Alexander Graham Bell's first words spoken over a telephone: "Mr. Watson, come here. I want you!" Have each child whisper the message to the next child. When the message gets around the circle, have the last child say it out loud. Repeat the original message. Discuss with children the reliability of passing information by word of mouth.

If time is short, discuss the telephone as a way for people to communicate with each other.

Read Aloud

I've Been Working on the Railroad

by Bill Basham

I've been working on the
railroad
All the livelong day.
I've been working on the
railroad
Just to pass the time away.

Can't you hear the whistle
blowing?
Rise up so early in the morn.
Can't you hear the captain
shouting?
Dinah, blow your horn.

Lesson 3 Inventors and Inventions

Objectives

- Describe how technology has changed communication.
- Identify historic figures such as Alexander Graham Bell and Thomas Edison who have exhibited a love of inventiveness.

Vocabulary

communicate to give and get information (p. 246)

invention something new (p. 246)

inventor someone who makes or invents something (p. 247)

QUICK Teaching Plan

If time is short, discuss the meaning of the word *communicate*. Discuss different inventions that people have used to communicate.

- Tell children who Alexander Graham Bell and Thomas Edison were and describe their inventions.

1 Introduce and Motivate

Preview Display the Vocabulary Card **communicate**. Ask children to name things that people use to give and receive information. Tell children that people not only communicate information but also thoughts and feelings. Then display the Vocabulary Cards **invention** and **inventor**. Explain that an invention is something made for the first time and an inventor is the person who makes the invention.

Warm Up To activate prior knowledge, ask children to recall inventions that they have already learned about. Remind children that they learned about Benjamin Franklin who invented the rocking chair. Explain that they will learn about inventions that help people communicate. Discuss how Americans have customs and celebrations that reflect their love of individualism and inventiveness.

Lesson 3 Inventors and Inventions

Telling stories and singing songs are two ways to communicate. You **communicate** when you give and get information. 1

An **invention** is something new. Many inventions have helped people communicate. The printing press and the telephone are two important inventions people have used to communicate. 2 3

246

Practice and Extend

READING SKILL Predict

- Tell children that in this lesson they will learn about inventions that help people communicate better.
- Distribute a prediction chart. Ask children to predict what three inventions they might learn about that help people communicate better. Have them write their predictions in the "My Prediction" column.
- After children have read pp. 246–249, tell them to complete the chart by filling in the "What I Actually Learned" column.

WEB SITE Technology

You can look up vocabulary words online. Click on *Social Studies Library* and select the dictionary at **www.sfsocialstudies.com.**

Long ago, there were no machines to copy the pages of a book. Books had to be copied by hand. This took a long time. Then an inventor made a machine called the printing press. An **inventor** is someone who makes or invents something new.

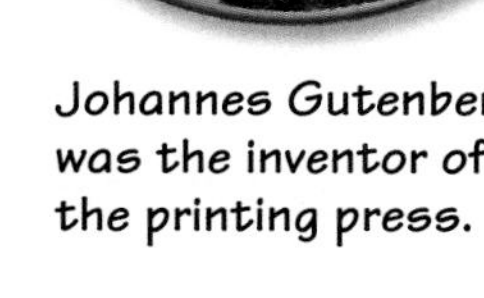

Johannes Gutenberg was the inventor of the printing press.

People could use the printing press to make many copies of a page. Books and newspapers could be made more quickly. People in many places around the world were able to get information from the books and newspapers.

First printing press

247

2 Teach and Discuss

Page 246

1 When two people are together, what do they use besides words to communicate? Answers will vary but may include talking, making sounds, using facial expressions, and making gestures. **Analyze Information**

C SOCIAL STUDIES STRAND
Culture

"Talking" drums is one kind of communication that people have used. People in African villages sent messages by beating drums. This practice is still used today by some people in parts of Africa.

2 What inventions are used to communicate besides the printing press and the telephone? Possible answers: The computer, radio, and television **Make Inferences**

3 With whom do you communicate? What do you communicate? Answers will vary. Children may say that they communicate with their family, friends, and teacher about a variety of things. **Apply Information**

Page 247

4 What way of bookmaking did the printing press replace? Copying a book by hand **Analyze Information**

C SOCIAL STUDIES STRAND
Culture

Tell children that the printing press used metal type that was manually arranged, letter by letter, to form pages of text. This type was inked and pressed onto paper—hence the name *printing press*.

5 How did the invention of the printing press increase the spread of information? Possible answer: More books could easily be made, so more people could read them. **Hypothesize**

FYI SOCIAL STUDIES
Background

Other Inventors and Inventions

- There were many women inventors. Mary Anderson invented windshield wipers; Beulah Henry, a clock for teaching children time; Margaret Knight, a machine to make square-bottomed paper bags; Grace Hopper, a computer program that could understand the English language and translate it into computer code.
- There were also many African American inventors. Elijah McCoy invented a lubricator for steam engines. Benjamin Banneker constructed the first wooden clock in America. Garrett Morgan invented the yellow caution light.
- Other inventions that have helped us to communicate: telegraph (1837), typewriter (1867), television (circa 1925), and cellular telephone (1979).

continued

Page 248

6 **What had to be put in place before people miles away from each other could talk by telephone?** Wires between the telephones **Make inferences**

✓ Ongoing Assessment

If...	then...
If... children do not understand that wires were needed to connect telephones,	**then...** explain that until recently telephone messages were usually sent over wires by means of electricity.

7 **How do you think people far away from each other communicated before the telephone was invented?** Answers will vary but may include by letter or telegraph. **Hypothesize**

A man named Alexander Graham Bell invented the telephone. With a telephone, people did not have to be in the same room to talk to each other. They could use the telephone to talk to 6 someone miles away. The telephone 7 helped change the way people communicate.

Alexander Graham Bell

1847–1922

Alexander Graham Bell taught at a school for the deaf. He helped start the first telephone company called Bell Telephone Company.

Thomas Alva Edison

1847–1931

Thomas Edison made more than 1,000 inventions. Many of his inventions helped people communicate better. He also invented many other things, such as the light bulb we use today

248

Practice and Extend

ACCESS CONTENT ESL Support

Inventions Remind children that some inventions help people communicate better. Display pictures with labels of the following: leaf, telephone, flower, radio, dog, printing press, rock. Read the labels aloud as you point to the pictures.

Beginning As you reread the labels, one at a time, ask children if and why the object is an invention.

Intermediate Have children choose an invention. Then have children tell how the invention helps people communicate.

Advanced Have children choose two inventions. Then have children help create a Venn diagram comparing each way of communication.

For additional ESL Support, use Every Student Learns Guide, pp. 114–117.

SOCIAL STUDIES Background

About Alexander Graham Bell

- Alexander Graham Bell was born in 1847 in Edinburgh, Scotland.
- Influenced by his father, who invented "visible speech" (a way to help the deaf position their vocal organs to make sound), he studied sound.
- He wanted to invent a machine that would transmit sound electronically. In 1876, he was granted a patent for his "electrical speech machine," which we now call a telephone.
- Bell helped found the National Geographic Society, the world's largest nonprofit scientific and educational organization.

Thomas Alva Edison was a famous inventor. One of his inventions was the phonograph. This was the first time people could hear recorded sounds. What do you use to hear recorded sounds?

Today, people around the world communicate in many ways. We even have machines that let people on Earth talk to astronauts in space!

1. Why are Edison and Bell such important inventors?
2. How did Alexander Graham Bell change the way people communicate?
3. **Think and Share** Recall and retell what you learned about Thomas Alva Edison.

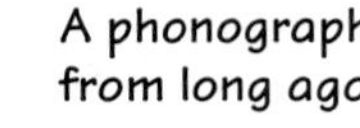

A phonograph from long ago

249

Page 249

8 How do you think people listened to music before Thomas Edison invented the phonograph? They listened to live performances. **Apply Information**

Use Information from the Text

9 How are the activities of Bell and Edison alike and different? Answers will vary but may include the following. Alike: Both made inventions, the telephone and the phonograph, that send sound to help people communicate. Different: Bell sent sound live. Edison sent recorded sound. Have children look back at the text to make sure they have the right information. **Compare and Contrast**

10 Why do you think astronauts need to communicate from space? Possible answer: To get instructions from people on Earth **Analyze Information**

3 Close and Assess

Ask children to tell what the word *invention* means. Have them discuss with a partner the inventions that help people communicate.

✓ **What did you learn?**

1. Edison and Bell helped people to communicate better.
2. Alexander Graham Bell made it possible for people who are far away from each other to talk.
3. **Think and Share** Answers will vary but should include that Edison invented the phonograph.

Social Studies Background

About Thomas Edison

- Thomas Edison set up a small chemical laboratory in the cellar of his home when he was only 10 years old.
- Edison invented a transmitter that vastly increased the range of Alexander Graham Bell's telephone.
- Edison received more than 1,000 patents.
- Edison helped form the Edison Electric Light Company. In 1882, the company completed the first permanent, commercial power station.

Workbook, p. 65

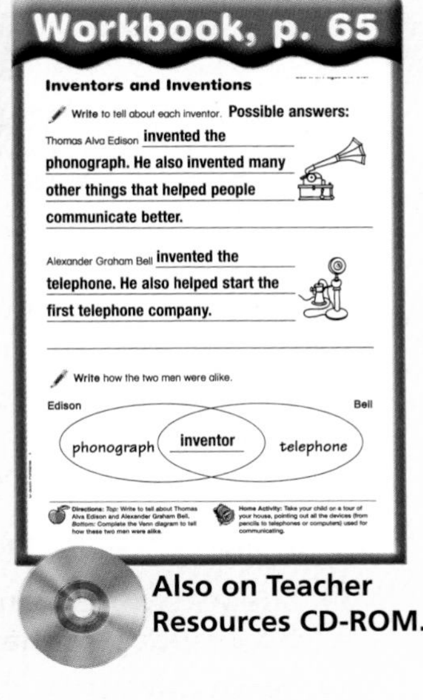

Inventors and Inventions

Write to tell about each inventor. Possible answers:

Thomas Alva Edison invented the phonograph. He also invented many other things that helped people communicate better.

Alexander Graham Bell invented the telephone. He also helped start the first telephone company.

Write how the two men were alike.

Edison | Bell

phonograph | inventor | telephone

Also on Teacher Resources CD-ROM.

Telephones

Objectives

- Obtain information about a topic using a variety of visual sources, such as pictures.
- Describe how technology has changed communication.

1 Introduce and Motivate

Preview Ask children to look at the illustrations on pp. 250–251. Ask children to tell whether they have ever seen any telephones that look like those pictured.

Warm Up To activate prior knowledge, have children look carefully at the pictures. Have them tell what features are the same on these telephones as on telephones of today. (a speaking part and a listening part)

COMMUNICATION

Telephones

Alexander Graham Bell makes a telephone call.

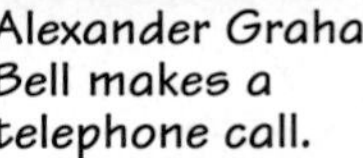

Alexander Graham Bell invented the telephone in 1876. How do telephones help people? 1

Bell's "Box telephone" of 1876–1877 had a combined mouthpiece and earpiece. 2

In early years, an operator took your number and the number you wanted. Then the operator connected the call.

This wall phone of 1879 was invented by Thomas Edison.

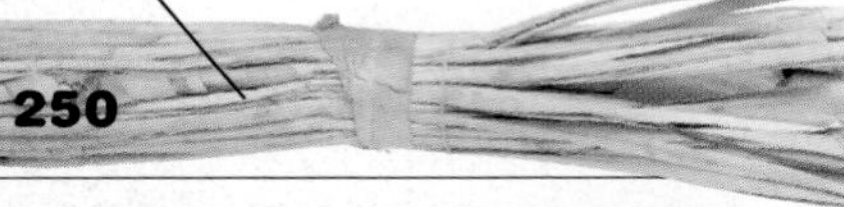

The first telephone wires were copper with a glass covering. 3

250

Practice and Extend

CURRICULUM CONNECTION

Drama

Telephone Etiquette Teach children proper telephone manners and telephone safety.

- Bring in two telephones that are not connected. Show children how the phones work.
- Teach children proper phone etiquette. Model a polite way to answer a phone (cordially say "hello"), to ask for a person ("May I speak to LaJeanne, please?"), and to end a conversation. ("It was nice to talk to you.") Have children practice these skills with a partner.
- Suggest to children that they ask older family members how much information they should disclose to a caller.
- Teach children to dial *911* for an emergency. Emphasize that this number is for emergencies only.

By 1885, the mouthpiece and earpiece were combined to form a handset.
Earpiece
"Cradle" telephones like this one were popular by the 1890s. This phone is from 1937.
Hook for earpiece
piece
Mouthpiece
4 5 Numbered dial
251

2 Teach and Discuss

Ask children to remember how people communicated over long distances before the invention of the telephone. (by letter or telegraph) Explain to children that it took a while for most homes to get telephone service.

1 **How do you think people's lives changed after they got telephones in their homes?** Answers will vary but might include that they didn't write as many letters and they spent more time on the phone and less time doing other activities. **Hypothesize**

Have children follow along as you read the text. Ask them to point to each picture as you tell about it.

2 **How did people use a "box telephone?"** They spoke and listened through the same piece. **Analyze Pictures**

3 **What were the first telephone wires made of?** Copper **Analyze Information**

4 **How did the invention of the dial on the phone change the way people used the telephone?** It allowed people to make their own connections without an operator. **Cause and Effect**

5 **How are our phones today different from the ones pictured?** They are smaller, lighter, portable, and (most) have buttons not dials. **Compare and Contrast**

CURRICULUM CONNECTION
Math

Calculating Telephone Numbers

- Have children write down phone numbers as a result of math problems. For example, say: "The first number is 20 minus 11." Do this for seven numbers.
- Make sure children put the numbers in groups of three, then groups of four, separated by a hyphen.

3 Close and Assess

Ask children to describe how phones have changed from when they were first invented.

Use with pages 246–251

Lesson 3 Wrap-Up

MEETING INDIVIDUAL NEEDS

Leveled Practice

Find Pictures of Communication

Have children find pictures in magazines or newspapers that show people communicating. Have children pay close attention to any technologies people are using in the pictures. Have children make a collage of their pictures.

Easy Have each child tell about one of his or her pictures. Write down the topics on chart paper as children tell about each. Invite volunteers to share a second picture after everyone has had a turn. Display the list in the classroom. **Reteach**

On-Level Have children pantomime one of the pictures, for example, talking on the telephone or reading a book. Have the class guess how he or she is communicating. **Extend**

Challenge Have children write about some of the pictures they collected. Have them write a sentence for each picture that tells how it stands for communication. **Enrich**

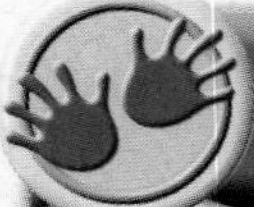

Hands-on Activities

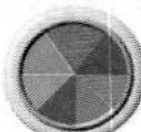

CURRICULUM CONNECTION
Writing

Related Words

Objective Demonstrate understanding of the lesson vocabulary.

Materials paper, pencils

Resources Vocabulary Cards **invention, inventor, communicate**

Learning Style Verbal/Linguistic

Individual

Time 10–15 minutes

1. Tell children that the word *invent* means to make something new. Explain that adding a syllable to the end of *invent* would change its meaning.

2. Ask children to write two words from the lesson that are related to *invent.*

3. Remind children to add *invention* and *inventor* as well as *communicate* to their "My Word Book."

CURRICULUM CONNECTION
Art

Business Cards

Objective Print multiple copies.

Materials rubber stamp, letters and shapes, ink pad, card-size pieces of paper

Learning Style Visual/Bodily/Kinesthetic

Individual

Time 45 minutes

1. Help children print three "business cards" using a rubber stamp. Explain to them that a rubber stamp works like a printing press.

2. Have children set their name in a rubber stamp. Help children make sure that the letters are right side up and facing in the right direction.

3. Ink the rubber stamp for children. Have them print their name on three "business cards."

4. Invite children to decorate their cards with stars or other shapes.

CURRICULUM CONNECTION
Drama

All Riiiight!

Objective Communicate using non-verbal means.

Learning Style Auditory/Visual/Bodily/Kinesthetic

Partners

Time 45 minutes

1. Remind children that people can communicate not only without inventions but without words.

2. First, have partners tell words that indicate assent (*yes, okay*) and congratulations or celebration (*all right!, way to go!, yes!*).

3. Then have partners show nonverbal ways of displaying assent (thumbs-up, nodding, OK sign) and congratulations or celebration (handshake, high five, upraised arms).

Lesson 4 Overview

Lesson	Description	Time and Resources
How Travel Has Changed pages 252–253	Children will explore how land transportation in the United States has changed from horse and wagon to the modern automobile. 	Time 10–15 minutes Resources • Workbook, p. 66 • Every Student Learns Guide, pp. 118–121
Read a Bar Graph pages 254–255	Children will learn how to interpret a bar graph.	Time 10–15 minutes Resource • Workbook, p. 67
Mae Jemison pages 256–257	Children will explore the life of Mae Jemison, the first African American woman in space.	Time 10–15 minutes

Build Background

Activity

Modes of Transport

 **Time** 20 minutes

Have children look through magazines to find pictures of things people use to get from one place to another. Have children create a collage with the pictures. Challenge children not to cut out any duplicate types of transportation. Possible types of transportation include: airplane, helicopter, and spaceship; car, truck, bus, motorcycle; train, subway, trolley; ship, submarine, boat; bicycle, skates, skateboard; horse, camel, elephant.

If time is short, ask children to brainstorm ways that people get from one place to another.

Read Aloud

Over Land

by Allison Rowe

Giddy-up, giddy-up,
I travel by horse.
Hold tight to the reins.
Don't fall off, of course.

Swish, swish,
I travel by bike.
Pedal hard and then glide.
It's coasting I like.

Vroom, vroom,
I travel by car.
Looking out the window,
I see near and far.

Don't care how I go,
Old or new,
As long as I
return to you.

Lesson 4

How Travel Has Changed

Objective

- Describe how technology has changed transportation.

QUICK Teaching Plan

If time is short, discuss the different modes of transportation over land.

- Explain that transportation has changed as new things were invented, such as the engine.
- Discuss how many forms of transportation are used to carry goods from place to place.

1 Introduce and Motivate

Preview Ask children to look at the time line and name the ways people travel that are shown. Ask them to tell which ways they have used to travel.

Warm Up To activate prior knowledge, remind children how inventions (printing press, telephone, phonograph) have changed the way people communicate. Tell children that there have also been inventions that changed the way people get from place to place. Explain that the wheel itself was a new invention once. Ask children what means people use to travel with and without wheels.

2 Teach and Discuss

Pages 252–253

Explain to children that the time line shows a period of time in order from earliest to latest. Discuss each picture. Explain that the horse pulls the wagon. Tell children that another way to say this is: *the horse provides the power for the wagon to move.*

1 What provides the power for a bicycle to move? Pushing on the pedals makes the wheels turn. **Make Inferences**

2 What provides the power for a car to move? Gas makes the engine run. **Make Inferences**

Lesson 4

How Travel Has Changed

Horse and Wagon

1

Bicycle

The way people communicate has changed. The way people travel has also changed. The time line shows some ways transportation on land has changed from the past to the present.

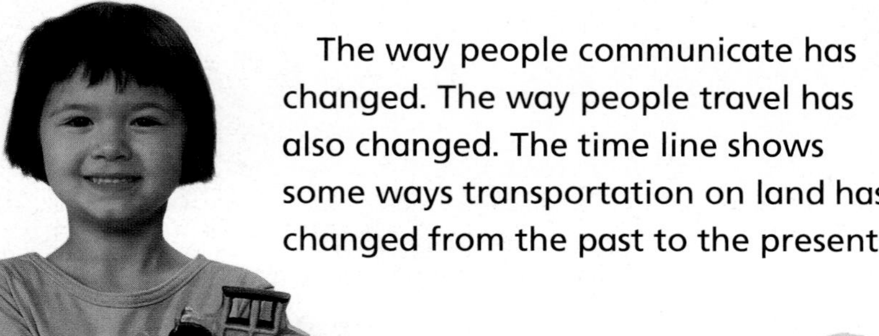

252

Practice and Extend

READING SKILL
Sequence

Creating a Time Line Have children complete a time line for different types of transportation.

- After children have read pp. 252–253, give them a time line with *First, Next,* and *Last* marked off below the line.
- Write the following words on the board: *airplane, spaceship, glider*. Discuss with children these modes of air transportation.
- Ask children to think about which way of air travel came first, next, and last. Then have them draw pictures of the modes of transportation over the appropriate times.

Old Model T Car

Car of Today

What did you learn?

1. How has the way we travel on land changed?
2. Name other ways people can travel on land.
3. **Think and Share** **Predict** how people might drive in the future. Draw a picture and tell about it.

253

SOCIAL STUDIES Background

Facts About Transportation

- Besides horses, animals that transport goods are oxen, which pull carts; dogs, which pull sleds; and mules, which carry bags.
- Wheels were solid wood until about 2000 B.C., when spokes were invented to make the wheels lighter and faster.
- The first self-propelled bicycle was invented in 1839 by Kirkpatrick Macmillan in Scotland.

Workbook, p. 66

How Travel Has Changed
Draw to show 3 ways to travel. Drawings will vary.
On Land
In the Air
Over Water
Write how one way might change.
Answers will vary.

Also on Teacher Resources CD-ROM.

3 Which way of travel came first, the bicycle or the Model T car? Bicycle *Interpret Time Lines*

Ongoing Assessment

If... children cannot tell which way of travel came before or after another,	**then...** explain that a time line works from left to right. Have children trace the time line from the left (beginning) to the right (end) with their finger.

4 How are the ways to travel shown on the time line alike? Answers will vary but may include that they all move on land. *Compare and Contrast*

SOCIAL STUDIES STRAND
Economics

Explain that many forms of transportation, such as trucks, trains, and ships, are used to carry goods from one place to another. Ask children to tell what kinds of goods a truck might carry. (Possible answers: food, clothing, furniture, appliances, electronics, and other things sold in stores.)

3 Close and Assess

Ask children to list ways people travel over ice and snow. Have partners draw a picture of two people traveling over ice or snow, one using a motorized means of transportation, the other using a non-motorized means of transportation.

What did you learn?

1. Answers will vary but may include that many people now use cars that move at fast speeds. As a consequence, travel takes less time.
2. Camel; horse; truck, bus, motorcycle, skateboard, skates, scooter; train; sled
3. **Think and Share** Drawings and oral descriptions should reflect how people might drive in the future. Suggest that children explain what powers their means of transportation.

Read a Bar Graph

Objectives

- Obtain information about a topic using a variety of visual sources, such as pictures.
- Create visual and written material, including graphs.

Vocabulary

bar graph a way to compare groups (p. 254)

1 Introduce and Motivate

Preview Ask children to look at the bar graph on p. 254. Tell them that it compares the quantity of things using bars of different lengths. The more there is of a thing, the longer the bar.

Warm Up To activate prior knowledge, ask children to name the places where things travel. (on land, under ground, in the air, in space, on water, under water) Ask children to name where the things on the side of the bar graph travel.

Chart and Graph Skills

Read a Bar Graph

A **bar graph** helps you compare groups. Look at this bar graph. The title is at the top of the graph. The pictures on the side of the graph show how Kay's class thinks children will travel to school in the future. 1 2 3

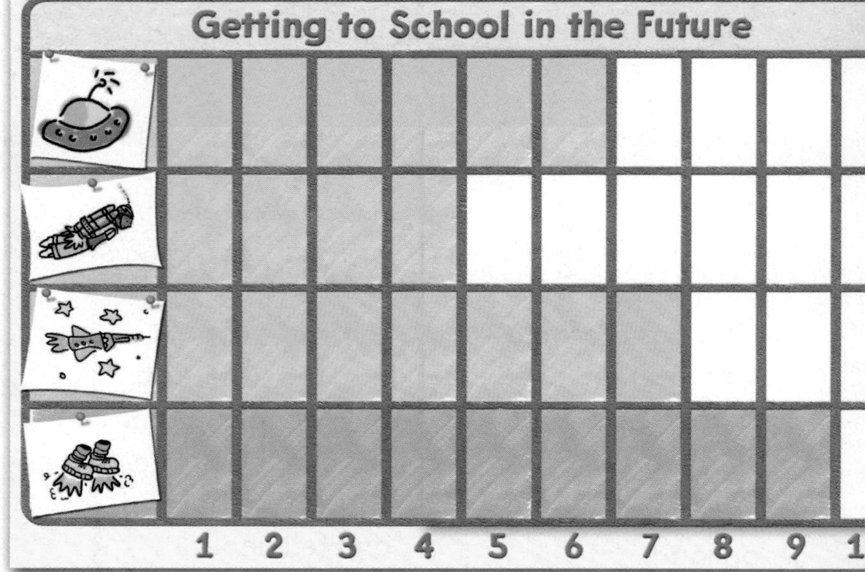

254

Practice and Extend

CURRICULUM CONNECTION
Math

Measurement

- Have children "travel" from one starting point to three destinations in the room, such as from the front desk to the board, the window, and the door.
- Help children measure the three distances.
- Write the destinations and the distances on the board.
- Ask children which are the longest and shortest distances.
- Help children create a bar graph comparing the distances they traveled.

Use your finger to follow the bar next to the rocket. Find the number at the bottom of the graph. It shows that seven children think people will travel to school by rocket in the future.

Try it!

1. What is the title of the bar graph?
2. How does Kay's class think most children will travel to school in the future?
3. **On Your Own** Make a bar graph with your class of favorite ways to travel. **Predict** what most of your class will choose.

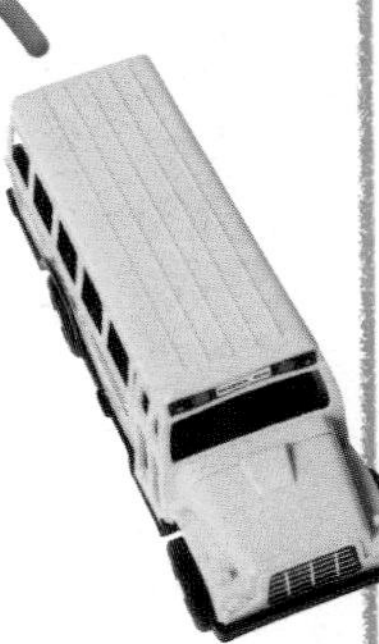

255

Workbook, p. 67

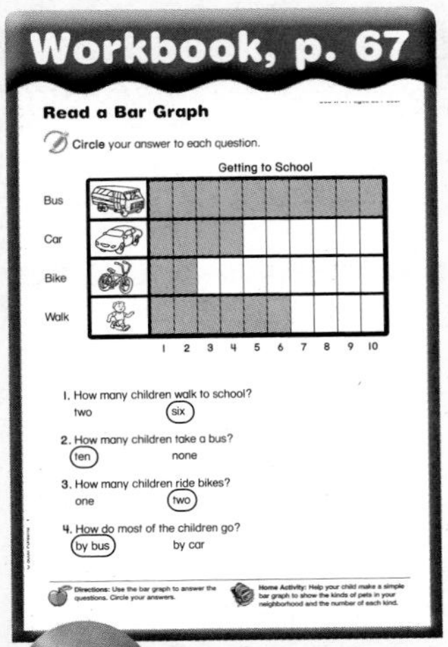

Read a Bar Graph

Circle your answer to each question.

Getting to School

Bus
Car
Bike
Walk

1 2 3 4 5 6 7 8 9 10

1. How many children walk to school? two (six)
2. How many children take a bus? (ten) none
3. How many children ride bikes? one (two)
4. How do most of the children go? (by bus) by car

Also on Teacher Resources CD-ROM.

2 Teach and Discuss

Explain to children that the bar graph shows the number of children in Kay's class who chose a way of travel that they think will be used by children in the future.

Test Talk

Use Information from Graphics

1 How many children chose the power pack machine? Four; Tell children to use information from the graph to support their answer. Interpret Graphs

2 Did more children in Kay's class think children in the future will travel by round machine or jet shoes? Jet shoes Interpret Graphs

3 What way of travel did the fewest number of children choose? Power pack Interpret Graphs

3 Close and Assess

Have children vote on their favorite way to travel: bicycle, skateboard, skates, or scooter. Have partners create bar graphs showing the results.

Try it!

1. "Getting to School in the Future" is the title of the bar graph.
2. Kay's class thinks that most children in the future will travel to school using jet shoes.
3. **On Your Own** Make sure the bar graphs include a title, pictures of ways to travel on the side, and numbers of children along the bottom. Ask children to double check that they have accurately representated the results of the vote.

Mae Jemison

Objective

- Identify people who exhibit a love of individualism.

1 Introduce and Motivate

Preview Write each of the words used to describe Mae Jemison on the board: *doctor, scientist, educator, astronaut.* Help children define each word. (Doctor: a person who treats people who are sick or injured. Scientist: a person who is an expert in studying living things, what things are made of, heat and magnetism, and so on. Educator: a teacher or a specialist in education. Astronaut: a person who travels in space.)

Warm Up To activate prior knowledge, point to the picture of the space ship on p. 256. Explain that this is the space shuttle taking off. Point to the picture of Mae Jamison on the same page. Explain that she is wearing a space suit and holding a helmet. Help children identify some of the patches on the space suit: American flag, wings (the insignia of the United States Air Force), and NASA.

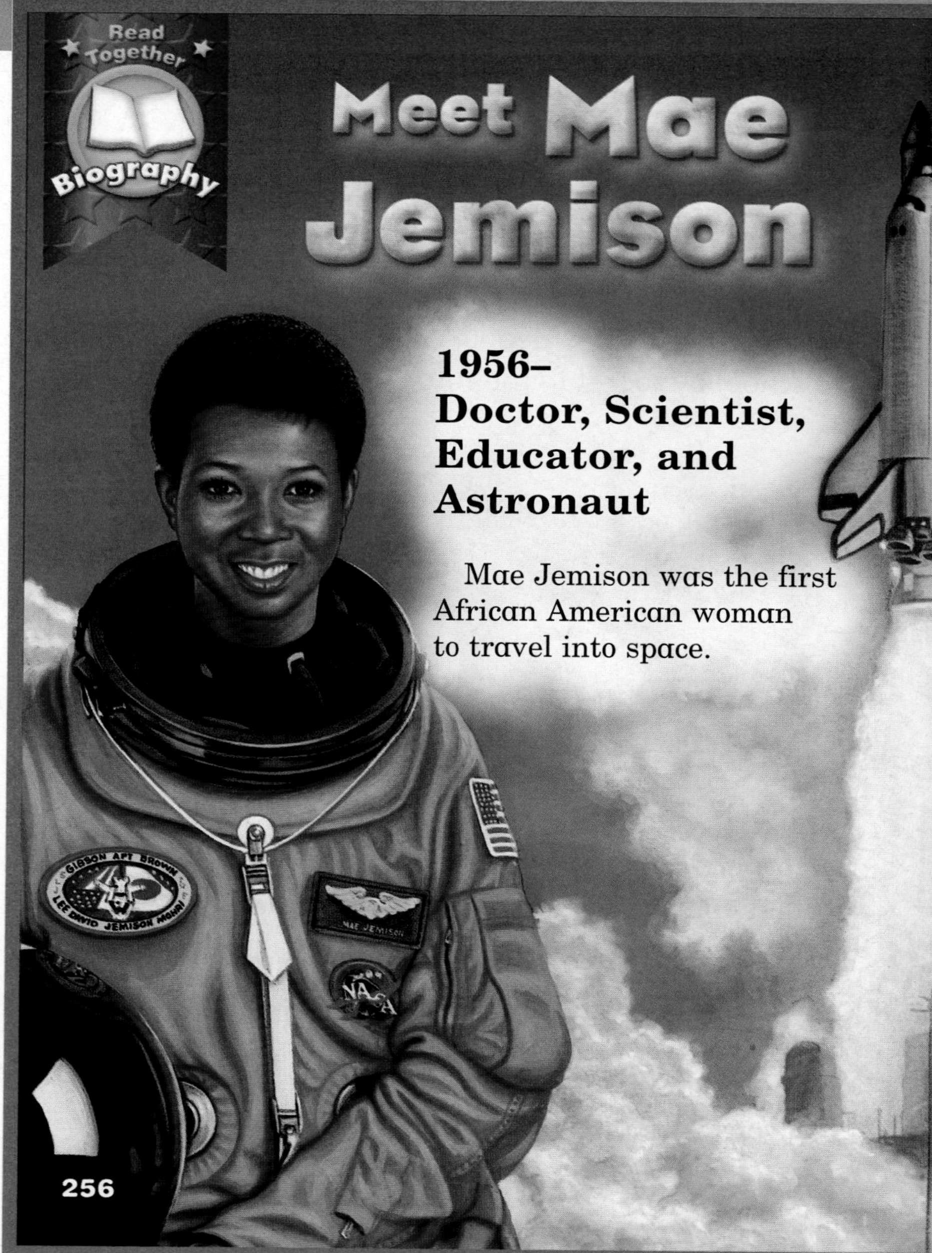

Read Together
Biography
Meet Mae Jemison
1956–
Doctor, Scientist, Educator, and Astronaut
Mae Jemison was the first African American woman to travel into space.
256

Practice and Extend

SOCIAL STUDIES Background

About Mae Jemison

- Mae Jemison's parents encouraged her to do her best. She was an excellent student. She earned degrees in chemical engineering and medicine.
- After receiving her *Doctor of Medicine* degree, she went to Africa to provide medical care for the Peace Corps crew and U.S. Embassy workers.
- Mae Jemison was one of 15 astronaut candidates selected from 2000 applicants. She flew on one mission into space in 1992. She worked for NASA for more than five years.
- She now works on projects to help developing countries have more technology. Her group is called the Jemison Group, Inc.

WEB SITE Technology

You may help children find out more about Mae Jemison by clicking on *Meet the People* at **www.sfsocialstudies.com.**

Mae liked science when she was a child. She grew up to become a doctor and scientist. Mae Jemison traveled many places around the world. She helped to care for the people living in each place. 1

Mae Jemison was born in Decatur, Alabama.

Later, Mae Jemison joined the NASA Space Program. She was the science mission specialist on the space shuttle *Endeavor*. In space, she helped do many experiments. Some of these experiments looked at how being in space affected people and animals. 2

Mae Jemison working in space

After she left NASA, Mae Jemison started a group that works on many different projects. The group started a science camp for children. The camp is called 3 The Earth We Share. At the camp, children from around the world learn about science.

Think and Share

Think about something that interests you. Tell what jobs you might do using your interest.

For more information, go online to *Meet the People* at **www.sfsocialstudies.com.**

ACCESS CONTENT ESL Support

Biography Explain to children that social studies includes biographies of people, like Mae Jamison, who have influenced the community or nation. Remind them that a biography is a true story of a person's life.

Beginning Ask children to talk about what they see in the illustration and photo of Mae Jamison.

Intermediate Ask children to tell three events, in sequence, of Mae Jamison's life.

Advanced Ask children to tell about Mae Jamison's life, in sequence, and tell how she influenced the nation.

For additional ESL Support, use Every Student Learns Guide, pp. 118–121.

2 Teach and Discuss

1 **What did Mae Jemison grow up to become?** Both a doctor and scientist. **Apply Information**

GEOGRAPHY Location

Explain to children that NASA stands for National Aeronautics and Space Administration. NASA studies and explores science and space. Two of its major facilities are the John F. Kennedy Space Center in Merritt Island, Florida, and the Lyndon B. Johnson Space Center in Houston, Texas. Help children find Merritt Island and Houston on a map.

2 **What experiments did Mae Jemison perform in space for the NASA Space Program?** Experiments that looked at how being in space affected people and animals **Analyze Information**

Explain to children that an ordinary person may show his or her love of individualism by standing out from others.

3 **How does Mae Jemison stand out from other people?** Answers will vary but may include: She is a doctor and a scientist. She was an astronaut. She likes to help children from around the world learn about science. **Make Inferences**

3 Close and Assess

Ask children to tell about Mae Jemison's accomplishments. Invite them to write a short paragraph telling why people admire her.

Think and Share

Children's responses should reflect jobs using their interest.

Use with pages 252–257

Lesson 4 Wrap-Up

MEETING INDIVIDUAL NEEDS
Leveled Practice

I Go With My Family . . .
Read children the book *I Go with My Family to Grandma's* by Riki Levinson, which is widely available in libraries. Show the illustrations of the different ways of traveling used to get to Grandma's house in New York City.

Easy Have children name the ways of traveling used in the story. (bicycle, trolley, horse and wagon, train, car, ferry) Have them tell whether people still commonly use these ways of traveling in the United States. **Reteach**

On-Level Assign groups one of the illustrations showing ways to travel. Have groups discuss what it would be like to travel in the way shown. Have them tell whether people still commonly use this way of traveling in the United States. **Extend**

Challenge Have children select one of the illustrations showing ways to travel. Ask them to imagine that they are the storyteller and to tell about their travels. Have them describe what the ride feels like, what they see, and where they are going. **Enrich**

Hands-on Activities

CURRICULUM CONNECTION
Writing

A Mazin'!

Objective Demonstrate understanding of the lesson vocabulary.

Materials Pencils

Learning Style Verbal/Linguistic

Individual

Time 10–15 minutes

1. Explain to children that the word *travel* means to go from one place to another.

2. Distribute copies of a maze. Have children take a trip through the maze from home to the park.

3. Explain to children that some of the roads go to the park, but others are dead ends. Tell them that they cannot cross any lines as they travel.

CURRICULUM CONNECTION
Science

Zoom Rockets

Objective Create a picture showing travel in the future.

Materials paper, crayons

Learning Style Visual

Individual

Time 10–15 minutes

1. Have children draw a picture of people flying with backpack rockets. Tell children that these rockets enable people to fly among tree tops or over houses, but no higher.

2. Encourage children to create a name for their backpack rocket and share it with the class.

CURRICULUM CONNECTION
Music

Transportation Songs

Objective Demonstrate understanding of ways to travel by analyzing songs.

Materials Paper, pencils, words to songs if not known

Learning Style Auditory/Verbal/Musical

Group

Time 10–15 minutes

1. Sing transportation songs with children: "She'll Be Coming Round the Mountain," "I've Been Working on the Railroad," "Row, Row, Row Your Boat," "The Wheels on the Bus."

2. Have children identify and discuss the way of travel in each song.

3. Have children draw one of the ways of traveling that are illustrated in the songs.

Lesson 5 Overview

Life Around the World **pages 258–261**	Children will learn about the world and explore how its people are alike and different.	Time 15–20 minutes Resources • Workbook, p. 68 • Vocabulary Card **world** • Every Student Learns Guide, pp. 122–125
Laurence Yep **pages 262–263**	Children will learn about Laurence Yep, a Chinese American who writes about the Chinese American way of life.	Time 10–15 minutes
It Is Time to Leave **pages 264–265**	Children will learn what people in other countries say when they part.	Time 10–15 minutes

Build Background

Activity

Highlight the World

Time 30 minutes

Show children on a globe where the four children from around the world live. Locate their countries and continents. (Carlitos—Argentina—South America; Mónika—Hungary—Europe; Esta—Tanzania—Africa; Daisuke—Japan—Asia) Place stickies with the first letter of the four children's names to their continents. As you point to a letter, say the name and have children repeat it.

If time is short, locate the four countries and continents on a globe.

Read Aloud

Couplet

by Robert Louis Stevenson

The world is so full
  of a number of things,
I'm sure we should all
  be as happy as kings.

Lesson 5 Life Around the World

Objective

- Compare housing, clothes, and foods from different parts of the world.

Vocabulary

world a name for Earth and everything on it (p. 258)

QUICK Teaching Plan

If time is short, discuss the meaning of the word *world*

- Discuss with children how the clothing, food, and homes of children around the world are alike and different than theirs.
- Have children find the places in the lesson on a globe.

1 Introduce and Motivate

Preview Display the Vocabulary Card **world** to children. Tell them that a ship can sail around the world. Ask them what countries they would like to sail to and why.

Warm Up To activate prior knowledge, ask children to point to ocean and land areas on the picture of the world on pp. 258–259.

2 Teach and Discuss

Pages 258

1 Where do you think the picture of the world was taken from? It was probably taken from a space satellite or a space shuttle.
Make Inferences

Lesson 5 Life Around the World

The world looks different from way up in space.

From space, Dr. Jemison could look down at the world. The **world** is a name for Earth and everything on it. Look at the picture. It shows how the world looks from space. 1

258

Practice and Extend

READING SKILL Compare and Contrast

- Discuss with children how the children shown on pp. 258–261 are alike and different from them.
- Give children a copy of a Venn diagram.
- Have children pick one of the children they learn about and compare and contrast what the child eats or wears with what they eat or wear.
- Have children fill in the diagram with the information.

From space, everything on the world might look like it is the same. When you are closer, you can see how people around the world are alike and different. Look at the pictures of children around the world. How is the clothing they wear like what you wear? How is it different? 3

My name is Mónika. I live in Hungary. 2

My name is Carlitos. I live in Argentina.

My name is Esta. I live in Tanzania.

My name is Daisuke. I live in Japan.

259

SOCIAL STUDIES STRAND

Geography

As you read the captions to children, have them repeat the names and countries. (Daisuke is pronounced Dye SOO keh, Tanzania, (TAN zuh NEE uh or tan ZAN ee uh). Show children where the children of the world live. Locate their countries on a globe. Point out the continents where the countries are located. (Argentina—South America; Hungary—Europe; Tanzania—Africa; Japan—Asia) Invite children to find other countries on the continents.

2 **What country does Mónika live in?** Hungary **Which child lives in Argentina?** Carlitos **Which child lives in Africa?** Esta **Which continent does Daisuke live on?** Asia
Apply Information/Interpret Maps

Test Talk

Locate Key Words in the Question

3 **What ways can people be alike and different besides clothing?** Answers may vary, but might include: food, homes, customs (e.g., celebrations), work, transportation. Tell children that key words such as *alike* and *different* tell them to look for similarities and contrasts.
Compare and Contrast

SOCIAL STUDIES

Background

About Our World

- More than two-thirds of Earth's surface is made up of water. The rest is land.
- Earth has four oceans. They are (from largest to smallest) the Pacific, Atlantic, Indian, and Arctic.
- The world's largest country in area is Russia.

WEB SITE

Technology

You can look up vocabulary words online. Click on *Social Studies Library* and select the dictionary at **www.sfsocial studies.com.**

continued

Pages 260–261

Discuss the chart with children. As you point to a box, have children point to it. Help children describe ways the children from around the world are alike and different. Encourage children to describe ways that are not in the chart, such as language, climate, and age. Use the DK book *Children Like Me* or other books to aid the discussion.

4 **What is one food that Mónika eats?** Meat and vegetable soup **Analyze Pictures**

5 **How is Esta's food different from Daisuke's?** Esta eats beans. Daisuke eats rice cakes wrapped in seaweed. **Analyze Pictures**

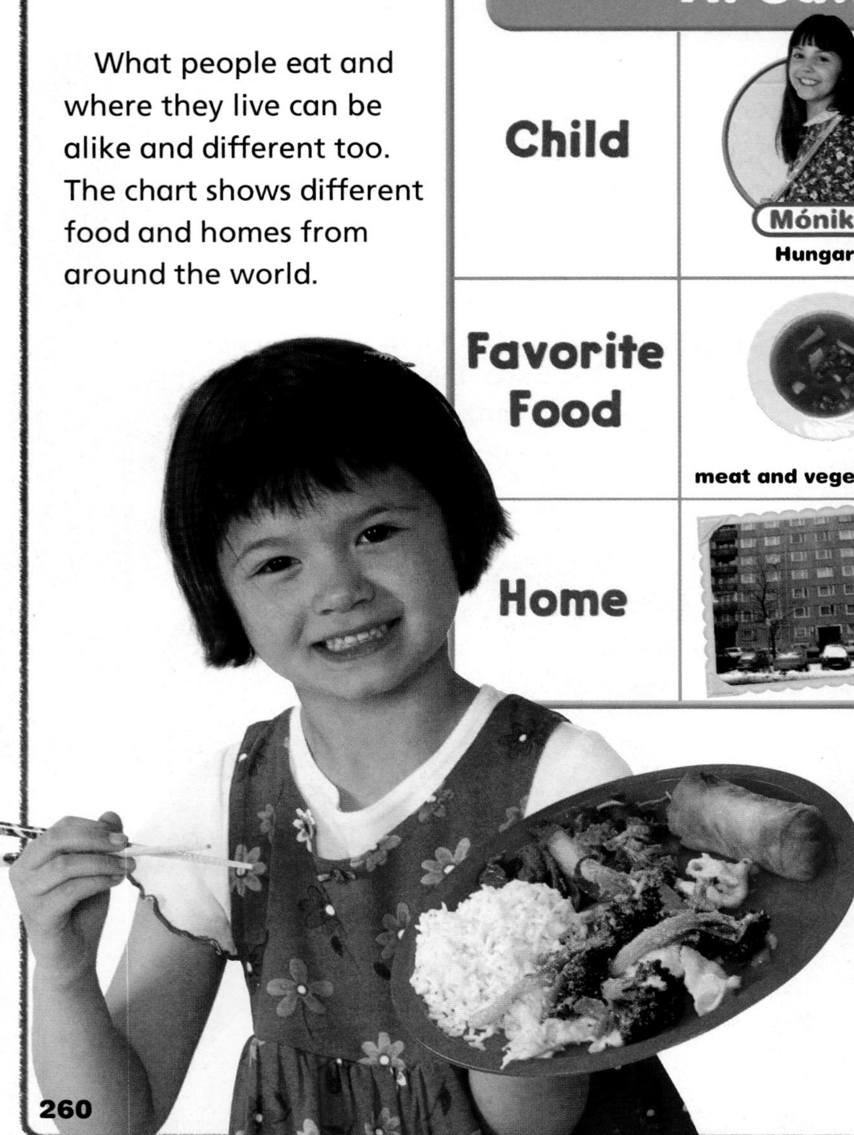

Around
What people eat and where they live can be alike and different too. The chart shows different food and homes from around the world.
Child
Mónika
Hungary
Favorite Food
meat and vegetab
Home
260

Practice and Extend

Telling About Dinner Discuss with children the steps involved in eating dinner: shopping for food, preparing it, serving it, and cleaning up. Emphasize the interactions between family members in this process. Invite children to describe the process in their native country. If necessary, have them interview a family member to find out more.

Beginning Have children draw one of the steps done in their native country. Ask them to describe what they draw.

Intermediate Have children work in pairs or groups to mime the process done in their native country.

Advanced Have children describe eating dinner in their native country. Then ask them to tell how the experience is alike and different from eating dinner where they live now.

For additional ESL Support, use Every Student Learns Guide, p. 122–125.

he World

Carlitos
Argentina

Esta
Tanzania

Daisuke
Japan

sausage

5
beans

6
rice cakes wrapped in seaweed

What did you learn?

1. How are homes around the world alike and different?
2. What does Carlitos eat? How is it different from what Mónika eats?
3. **Think and Share** How are these children like you?

261

Problem Solving

6 Imagine that one of the children from around the world is coming to visit you. You want to bake cookies for the child but do not know how. What can you do? Answers will vary, but should include most of the problem-solving steps. Identify the problem: How to bake cookies. With the help of a family member, find recipes and research ingredients available in the kitchen, such as butter, eggs, sugar, and flour. Choose a recipe that uses available ingredients. Solve the problem by asking a family member to help you bake the cookies. **Solve Problems**

3 Close and Assess

Ask children to make a drawing of themselves with the children from around the world.

✓ What did you learn?

1. Accept all reasonable answers
2. Carlitos eats sausage. Sausage is chopped meat mixed with spices. Sausage is shaped like a tube. Soup is a liquid that is made by boiling meat, fish, or vegetables in water or stock.
3. **Think and Share** Answers will vary, but should reflect what children learned about the clothing, food, and homes of the children around the world.

FYI Social Studies Background

About Tanzania

- Tanzania is located in eastern Africa on the Indian Ocean.
- Elephants, giraffes, lions, zebras, and other wild animals live in Tanzania's vast Serengeti National Park and other areas. Hunting is prohibited or limited in these places.
- Mount Kilimanjaro, Africa's highest mountain (19,340 feet), is in Tanzania.

Workbook, p. 68

Life Around the World

Write to compare. Answers may vary.

At Home in Japan — At Home in the U. S.

Both homes have places for eating.
People in Japan sit on cushions to eat.
People in the U. S. sit on chairs.

Making Bread in Mexico — Making Bread in the U. S.

People in both places eat bread. In Mexico,
the bread is flat. It is baked on a griddle.
In the U. S., bread is usually baked in an oven.

Also on Teacher Resources CD-ROM.

Laurence Yep

Objective

- Identify people who exhibit a love of individualism.

1 Introduce and Motivate

Preview Tell children that Laurence Yep is a writer who is Chinese American. His father was born in China, but Laurence was born in America. Have children look at the background in the picture on p. 262. Point out the pyramidal tower built over the Cathay House. Then point out the streetcar. Explain that it is a "bus" on rails that provides public transportation along streets. Tell children that the tower and streetcar indicate the location is Chinatown in San Francisco, California.

Warm Up To activate prior knowledge, ask children to remember what they learned about Joseph Bruchac (He writes books for children about Native Americans).

2 Teach and Discuss

Page 263

Have children locate China on a globe. Ask them what continent China is on. (Asia) Have students trace with their finger a line from China to San Francisco.

1 Why do you think many Chinese people settled in San Francisco, California, when they came to the United States? It was the first stop in America, across the Pacific Ocean from China.
Draw Conclusions

2 Why do you think where Laurence Yep lived is called Chinatown? Many Chinese live there. They speak the Chinese language.
Make Inferences

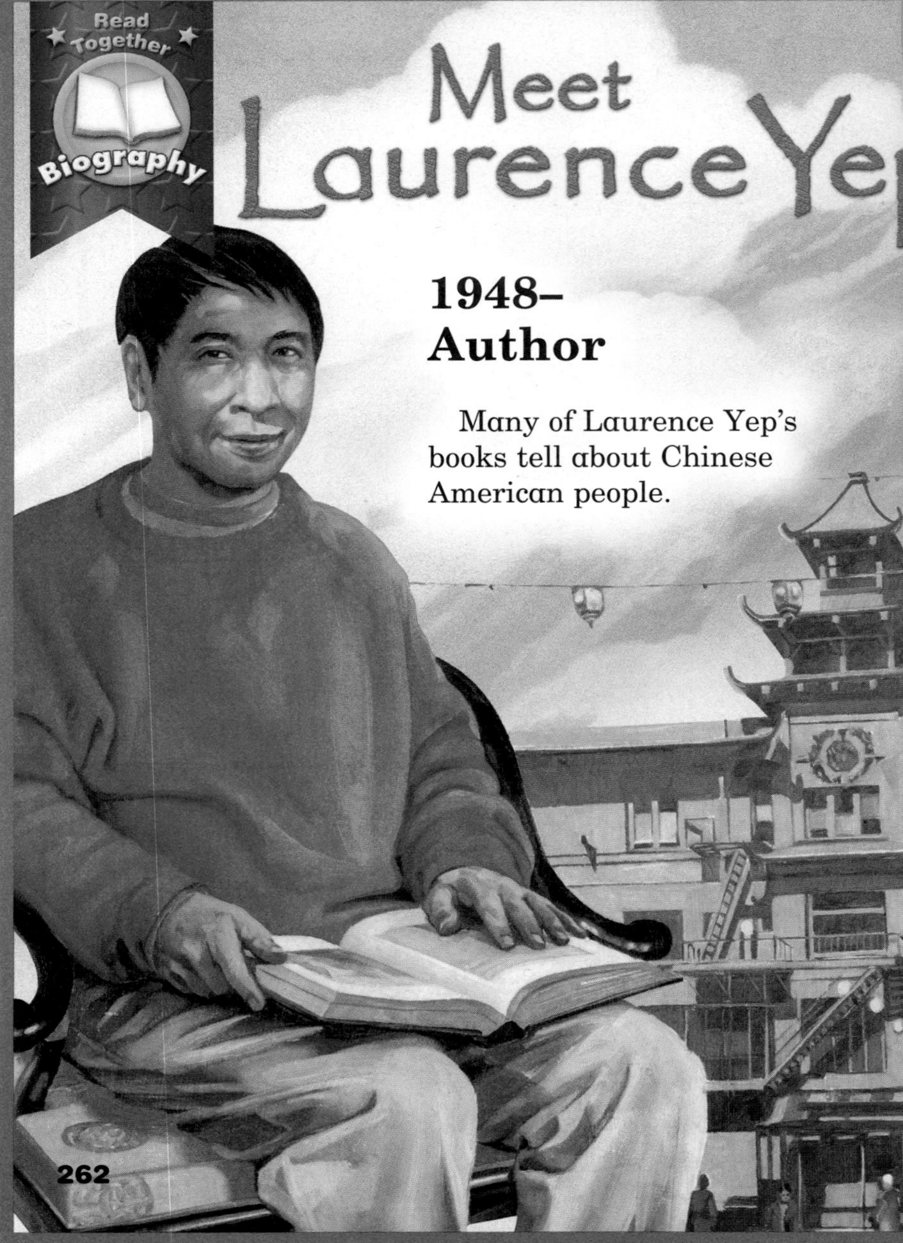

Read Together
Biography
Meet Laurence Yep
1948–
Author
Many of Laurence Yep's books tell about Chinese American people.
262

Practice and Extend

FYI SOCIAL STUDIES Background

About Laurence Yep

- Laurence Yep's father and mother ran a grocery in San Francisco.
- Laurence Yep sold his first story to a science fiction magazine when he was 18. The magazine paid him one cent for each word.
- *Dragon's Gate* is a historical work of fiction about a 14-year-old Chinese boy who comes to America after the Gold Rush. He works on the railroad.
- *Dragonwings* is the story of a young Chinese immigrant who comes to California in the early 1900's. He works with family members in a laundry.
- The Newbery Medal is awarded annually to the author of the most distinguished American book for children by the Association for Library Service to Children, a division of the American Library Association.

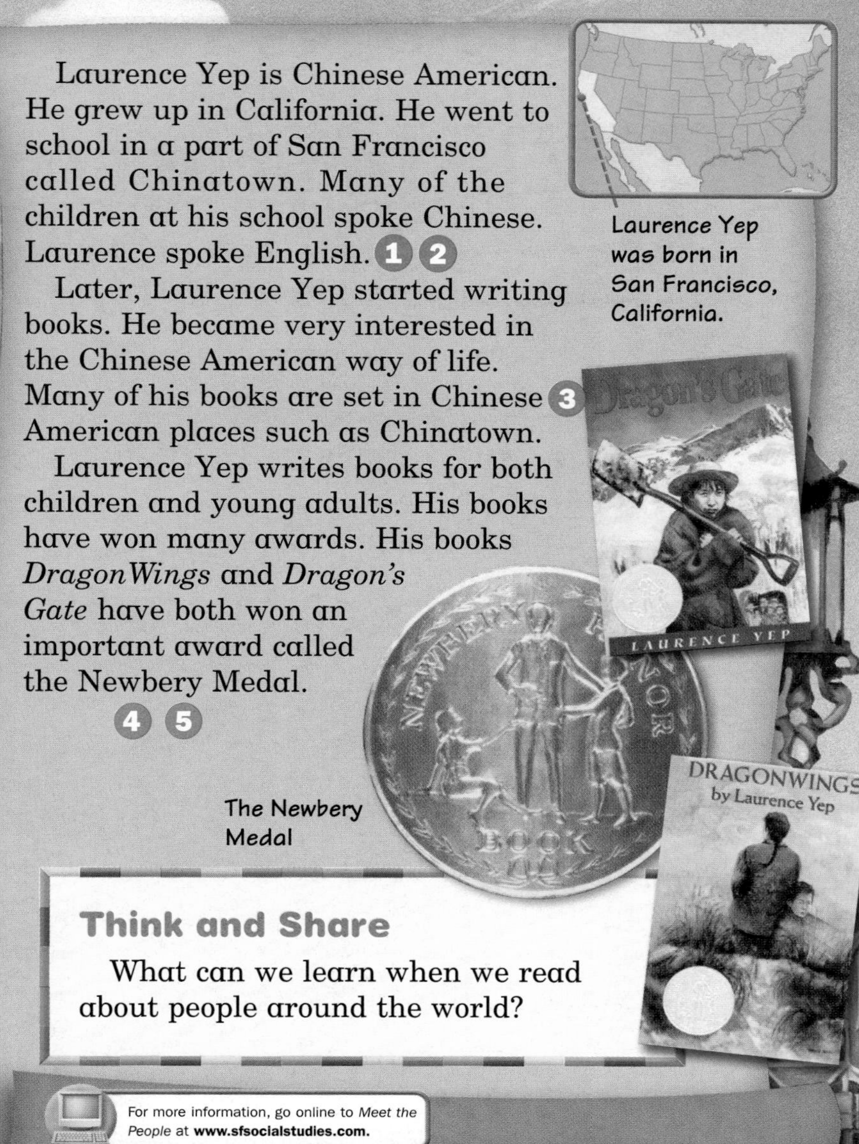

Laurence Yep is Chinese American. He grew up in California. He went to school in a part of San Francisco called Chinatown. Many of the children at his school spoke Chinese. Laurence spoke English. 1 2

Later, Laurence Yep started writing books. He became very interested in the Chinese American way of life. Many of his books are set in Chinese American places such as Chinatown. 3

Laurence Yep writes books for both children and young adults. His books have won many awards. His books *DragonWings* and *Dragon's Gate* have both won an important award called the Newbery Medal. 4 5

Laurence Yep was born in San Francisco, California.

The Newbery Medal

Think and Share

What can we learn when we read about people around the world?

For more information, go online to *Meet the People* at **www.sfsocialstudies.com.**

263

3 What shows Laurence Yep's love of individualism and sets him apart from other writers? Answers will vary, but may include that he writes about the Chinese American way of life. **Express Ideas**

4 How are Joseph Bruchac and Laurence Yep alike and different? Answers will vary but may include the following. Alike: They were both born in the United States and that they both write about their heritage. Different: Joseph Bruchac often writes down stories that others tell him. Laurence Yep often creates his own stories. Bruchac writes about Native Americans, Yep about Chinese Americans. **Compare and Contrast**

5 What important award has two of Laurence Yep's books won? The Newbery Medal **Recall and Retell**

3 Close and Assess

Ask children to tell what they know about Laurence Yep. Ask partners to discuss the way of life of their parents and grandparents.

Think and Share

Answers will vary but may include that we can learn about the way of life of people around the world.

CURRICULUM CONNECTION Literature

Books by Laurence Yep

Laurence Yep has written many books for young readers. Read aloud and discuss any of the following picture books.

- ***Tiger Woman,*** by Laurence Yep and Robert Roth (Illustrator) Bridgewater Books, ISBN 0-816-73464-X, 1995) **Easy**
- ***Junior Thunder Lord, The,*** by Laurence Yep and Robert Van Nutt (Illustrator) (Bridgewater Books, ISBN 0-816-73454-2, 1994) **On-Level**
- ***Man Who Tricked a Ghost, The,*** by Laurence Yep (Econo-Clad Books, ISBN 0-785-78614-7, 1999) **Challenge**

WEB SITE Technology

You may help children find out more about Laurence Yep by clicking on *Meet the People* at **www.social studies.com.**

It Is Time to Leave

Objective

- Show what people around the world say when they leave.

1 Introduce and Motivate

Preview Have children look at the photographs of the children and the speech balloons on pp. 264–265. Ask children to guess what the children from around the world are saying. (They might be saying a form of "hello" or "good-bye.")

Warm Up To activate prior knowledge, ask children to tell ways to say good-bye in English or other languages. (Examples are *bye, see ya, so long, ciao,* and *aloha*.)

2 Teach and Discuss

As you pronounce the sayings for children, have them repeat the sayings. (See pronunciations at the right.)

Put a saying on one side of a flash card and the name of the country where it is spoken on the other side. Have partners learn the saying and the country by using the flash card.

① **Why do we say something when we leave another person?** Answers will vary, but may include that it is polite and that it makes parting less sad. **Express Ideas**

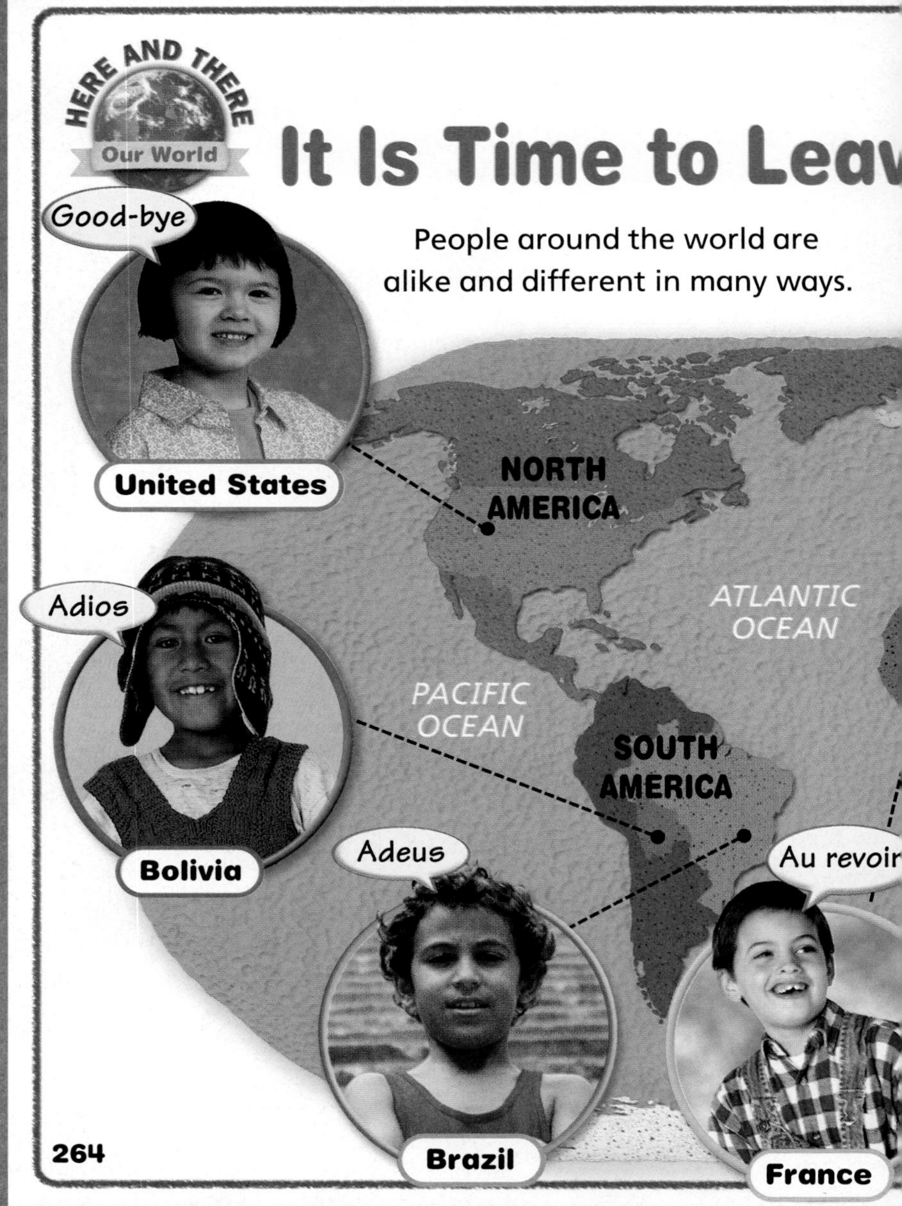

Practice and Extend

SOCIAL STUDIES Background

Pronunciation of Words Meaning "Good-bye"

- **Adiós** /ah dee OSE/ Bolivia.
- **Adeus** /ah DAY us/ Brazil.
- **Au revoir** /o ruh VWAHR/ France.
- **Sai an jima** /SA uhn JOO muh/ Nigeria.
- **Sayonara** /SY uh NAHR uh/ Japan.
- **Arrivederla** /ah ree vuh DAYR la/ Italy.

WEB SITE Technology

You may help children find out more about these pages by clicking on *Atlas* at **www.sfsocial studies.com.**

In many countries, people have a saying when they leave another person. 1 2

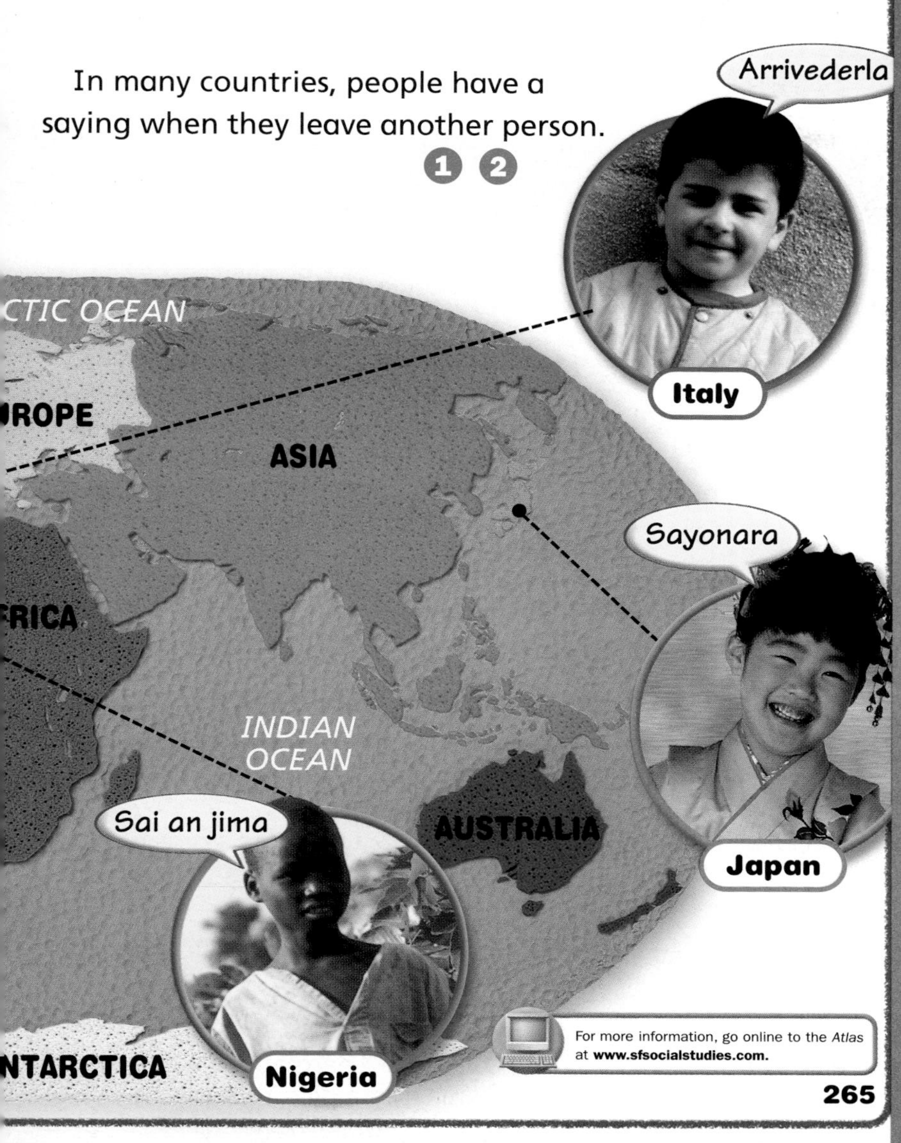

2 How might people say good-bye without using words? They might wave, hug, kiss, shake hands, or slap hands. **Apply Information**

3 Close and Assess

Ask children to tell how saying words to people who are leaving shows that people around the world are alike and different. (Alike: They say words when they leave people. Different: They use different words.)

CURRICULUM CONNECTION
Music

The Sound of Music

Have children listen to the song "So Long, Farewell" from *The Sound of Music* soundtrack. Teach them the words to the chorus: *So Long, Farewell, Auf Wiedersehen, Good-by,* and have them sing along when you play the song again.

FAST FACTS

- Each of the more than 250 ethnic groups in Nigeria has its own language.
- Although English is the official language of Nigeria, the three most widely used languages are those of the Hausa, Yoruba, and Igbo, the three largest ethnic groups.
- *Sai an jima* is the way the Hausa people of northern Nigeria say good-bye.

Use with pages 258–265

Lesson 5 Wrap-Up

MEETING INDIVIDUAL NEEDS
Leveled Practice

Create Pictures Showing the World

Have children draw pictures showing what it is like to live in different places around the world.

Easy Have children draw a picture of the home of one of the children from around the world. **Reteach**

On-Level Have children draw two pictures: a home of one of the children from around the world and one of their home. Have children compare the homes. **Extend**

Challenge Have children draw two pictures: a home of one of the children from around the world and one of their home. Have children write sentences comparing and contrasting the homes. **Enrich**

Hands-on Activities

CURRICULUM CONNECTION
Writing

Asia Puzzle

Objective Demonstrate understanding of the lesson vocabulary.

Materials puzzle

Learning Style Verbal/Linguistic

Individual

Time 15 minutes

1. Display the Vocabulary Card *world*.
2. Tell children that four countries in Asia are China, Vietnam, India, and Japan. Write the names on the board.
3. Distribute the puzzle to children. Tell them to use the names of the countries to complete the puzzle. Explain that some letters have already been filled in.
4. Remind children to add their lesson vocabulary word to their "My Word Book."

CURRICULUM CONNECTION
Science

Looking at the World

Objective View pictures of Earth from space.

Materials computer with Internet connection

Learning Style Visual

Group

Time 15 minutes

1. Help children view current pictures of Earth from space on the Internet.
2. Use the photo gallery at the National Space Science Data Center **(http://nssdc.gsfc.nasa.gov/)** to help children identify continents and approximate locations of cities and countries.
3. Use the Johnson Space Center's Web site **(http://earth.jsc.nasa.gov/)** to help children identify land and water features.

SOCIAL STUDIES STRAND
Geography

Work Around the World

Objective Learn about a country by making a picture book.

Materials paper, crayons, pencils, reference material, such as the book *Children Just Like Me*

Learning Style Verbal/Linguistic

Group

Time 30 minutes

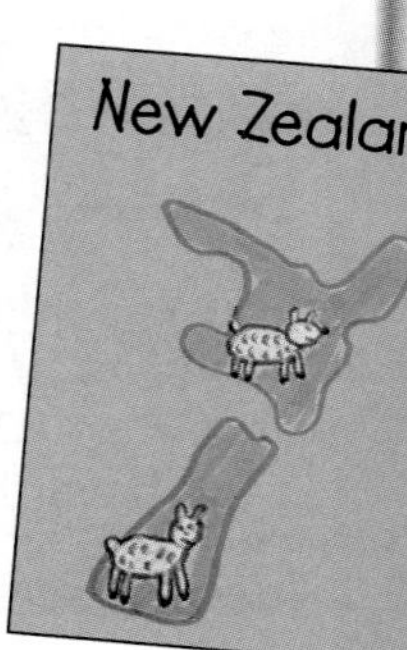

1. Have groups create a two-page picture book about work around the world.
2. Help groups find information about work in a country.
3. Have groups fold a large sheet of paper to make two pages. Have them write the information at the bottom of each page.
4. Have groups illustrate each page and design a cover with the name of the country.

Ending Unit 6

End with a Folktale pages 266–267	Children will listen to and talk about a folktale: "The Farmer's Little Girl" adapted from Aesop.	
Unit 6 Review pages 268–271	Children will review unit vocabulary words and the unit skills of making a prediction, making a decision, using a bar graph, and making a bar graph. Children will answer questions about what they learned in the unit. Children will learn about several books about our world. 	Resources • Workbook, p. 69 ✓• Assessment Book, pp. 21–24
Unit 6 Project page 272	Children will invent a machine of the future. They will also be directed to a Web site where they can learn more about our world.	Resource • Workbook, p. 70

Wrap-up

Activity

Welcome to the USA!

Have children make posters to welcome visitors from other countries. Suggest that their posters show activities of what it is like to live in this country—and at least one national symbol, such as the Statue of Liberty.

- Have children cut out pictures from magazines showing people at work, home, or play. Have them draw the national symbol. Then have them make a collage with the pictures and paste them into place on a large sheet of oaktag.
- Help children write a title for their poster. Remind them to spell all the words correctly and to print neatly.
- Display children's posters in the classroom.

Performance Assessment
You can use the activity on this page as a performance assessment.

✓ Assessment Scoring Guide

Make Posters About the USA	
4	Includes one or more pictures that depict life in America, a national symbol, and an appropriate title. Contains no errors in spelling or grammar.
3	Includes all three required elements but contains errors in spelling and/or grammar.
2	Includes two of three required elements.
1	Includes only one of the required elements.

The Farmer's Little Girl

Objective

- Retell stories from selected folktales and legends such as Aesop's fables.

1 Introduce and Motivate

Preview Explain to children that a folktale is a story handed down by word of mouth by the common people. Further explain that a fable is a kind of folktale that teaches a lesson. Have children look at the picture on the bottom of p. 266. Explain that the girl is stirring and beating milk in a container, called a churn, to form butter.

Warm Up Explain to children that *moral* means the lesson in the right thing to do taught by the story. Discuss two morals: "Haste makes waste" and "Don't count your chickens before they hatch."

2 Teach and Discuss

Read the fable "The Farmer's Little Girl." Discuss with children what happens in the story. Then have children recall and retell it. Explain that the moral of this story is that you should concentrate on the task at hand.

1 **What was the girl doing while she was milking the cow?** Thinking about buying new clothes **Analyze Information**

2 **Predict what will happen after you read that the girl was thinking about other things as she carried the bucket of milk on her head.** Answers will vary but may include that she's going to drop the bucket. **Predict**

UNIT 6
End with a Folktale

The Farmer's Little Girl

Adapted from Aesop

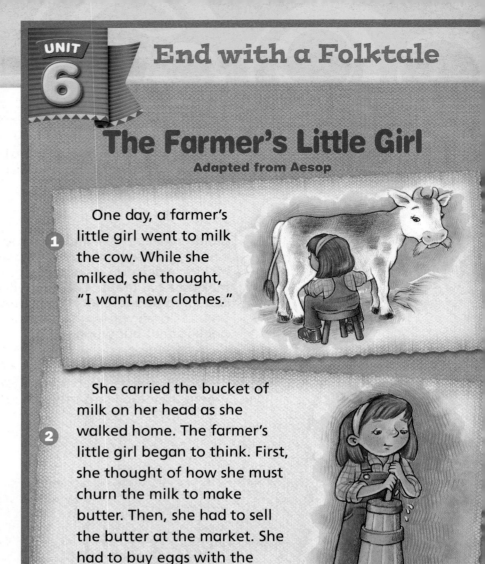

1 One day, a farmer's little girl went to milk the cow. While she milked, she thought, "I want new clothes."

2 She carried the bucket of milk on her head as she walked home. The farmer's little girl began to think. First, she thought of how she must churn the milk to make butter. Then, she had to sell the butter at the market. She had to buy eggs with the money she made.

Practice and Extend

SOCIAL STUDIES
Background

Moral of the Story

Discuss with children the meaning of the following morals of Aesop's fables.

- Little by little does the trick.
- One good turn deserves another.
- Necessity is the mother of invention.
- Whatever you do, do with all your might.
- Appearances are deceptive.
- An ounce of prevention is worth a pound of cure.
- People are known by the company they keep.

3 After that, she had to feed the chickens that hatched from the eggs. Later, she had to take the chickens to market. Finally, she could buy new clothes!

4 She could not wait. She began to run. She could not hold on to the bucket. It fell off her head! All of the milk spilled out.

Moral: Sometimes when you hurry, you only get farther behind.

267

SOCIAL STUDIES STRAND

Economics

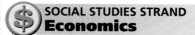

Discuss with children the ways people exchange goods and services at a market. Ask children to identify the steps a family must take to buy clothes, such as working to earn money for goods and making choices about what goods to buy.

3 **Identify examples of goods in the story.** Answers may include butter, eggs, chickens, and clothes.

4 **What do you think the girl could have done to prevent spilling the milk?** Answers will vary but may include that she could have paid more attention to carrying the bucket.

3 Close and Assess

- Have children tell the meaning of the story in their own words.
- Have children change the ending of the story.

CURRICULUM CONNECTION

Literature

Aesop's Fables

Children might enjoy reading more of Aesop's fables.

- Go online at **AesopFables.org** to find a collection of Aesop's fables. Read fables with children.
- Discuss with children the moral of the stories. Ask children to retell the stories in their own words.
- Then have children illustrate their favorite fable.

Children might also enjoy reading these books of Aesop's fables: ***Aesop for Children, The,*** by Mio Winter and Milo Winter (Photographer) (Scholastic Trade, ISBN 0-590-47977-6, 1994) **Easy**; ***Aesop's Fables,*** by Aesop and Jerry Pinkney (Illustrator) (Seastar Pub Co, ISBN 1-587-17000-0, 2000) **On-Level**; ***Aesop's Fables,*** by Aesop and Fritz Kredel (Illustrator) (Price Stern Sloan Pub, ISBN 0-448-06003-5, 1977) **Challenge**

Review

Resources

- Assessment Book, pp. 21–24
- Workbook, p. 69: Vocabulary Review

Vocabulary Review

1. inventor
2. market
3. world

Answers to Test Prep

1. c. communicate
2. b. invention

UNIT 6

Review

Vocabulary Review

world
inventor
market

Tell which word completes each sentence.

1. Thomas Edison was a famous _______.
2. A place to buy goods is called a _______.
3. The Earth and everything on it is called the _______.

★ ★ ★ ★ ★ ★ ★ ★

Which word completes the sentence?

1. You give and get information when you _______.
   a. market **b.** inventor
   c. communicate **d.** world
2. The telephone was an important _______.
   a. inventor **b.** invention
   c. market **d.** world

268

Practice and Extend

Assessment Options

✓ Unit 6 Assessment

- Unit 6 Content Test: Use Assessment Book, pp. 21–22
- Unit 6 Skills Test: Use Assessment Book, pp. 22–24

Standardized Test Prep

- Unit 6 tests contain standardized test formats.

✓ Unit 6 Performance Assessment

- See p. 272 for information about using the Unit 6 Project as a means of performance assessment.
- A scoring guide for the Unit 6 Project is provided in the teacher's notes on p. 272.

Test Talk

- Test Talk Practice Book

Skills Review

Predict

In your class, vote for your favorite pet. **Predict** which pet will get the most votes.

★ ★ ★ ★ ★ ★ ★ ★

Make a Decision

Suppose your class has to decide where to go on a field trip. How would you decide where to go? Use the steps below to make your decision. Draw a picture to show each step.

1. Tell what decision you need to make.
2. Gather information.
3. List your choices.
4. Tell what might happen with each choice.
5. Make a decision.

269

For more information, you can select the dictionary or encyclopedia from *Social Studies Library* at **www.sfsocialstudies.com.**

Workbook, p. 69

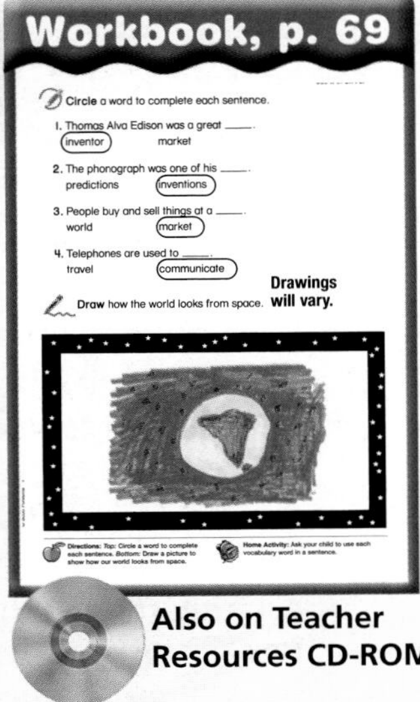

Also on Teacher Resources CD-ROM.

Skills Review

Predict

Children's answers should reflect that predicting means telling what they think will happen next.

- Tell children that what they predict will happen is not necessarily what they wish will happen.
- Remind children that a prediction can never be certain.

Use the following scoring guide.

✓ Assessment Scoring Guide

Predict the Pet That Gets the Most Votes	
4	Understands voting is an expression of a wish and predicting is telling what will happen, and makes a reasonable prediction.
3	Understands voting and predicting but makes an unreasonable prediction.
2	Understands predicting but not voting and makes an unreasonable prediction.
1	Understands voting but not predicting.

Make a Decision

Children's drawings should reflect the steps. Tell children they may use the photographs on pp. 240–241 as a model.

Skills Review

Read a Bar Graph

1. 10

2. Pink

3. Blue

Skills on Your Own

- Children's bar graph should be in the correct format, accurately reflect how the friends travel to school, and have all words spelled correctly.

Use the following scoring guide.

✓ Assessment Scoring Guide

Use a Bar Graph	
4	Format, results, and spelling are completely correct.
3	Format and results are completely correct but not spelling.
2	Format is completely correct but not results and spelling.
1	Format, results, and spelling are only partially correct.

Review

Skills Review

Read a Bar Graph

Kay asked her friends to name their favorite color. Read her bar graph to answer the questions.

1. How many friends did Kay ask?

2. What color did the most people like?

3. What color did three people like?

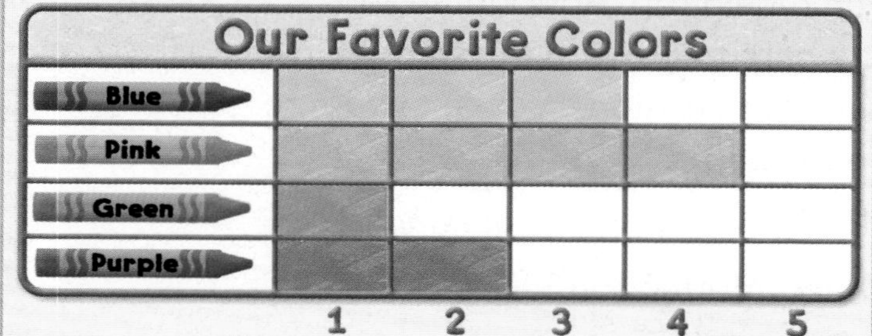

Skills On Your Own

Make a bar graph that shows how you and some friends travel to school. Ask your friends how they get to school. Write the ways they get to school on the left. Write numbers on the bottom. Fill in the bar to show how many travel in each way.

270

Practice and Extend

Revisit the Unit Question

✓ Portfolio Assessment

- Have children look back at the list of places made on p. 231.
- Have children list details about a place in the world they would like to visit.
- Ask children to underline countries around the world they learned about in this unit.
- Ask children to draw a picture of the place they would like to visit.
- Ask children to write a sentence about why they want to visit this place.
- Have children add their list, drawings, and sentences to their Social Studies Portfolio.

What did you learn?

1. What goods and services can you get in a market?
2. Name two inventors who helped change the way people communicate.
3. Name three ways people can be alike and different.
4. **Write and Share** Write about how one thing people use at home has changed.

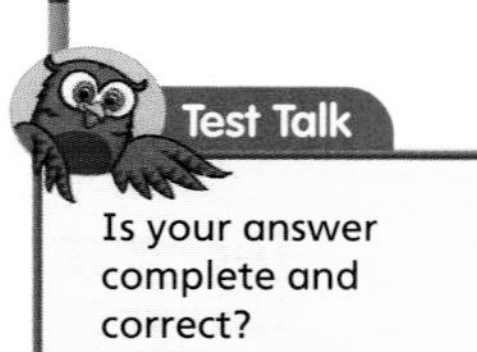

Test Talk
Is your answer complete and correct?

Read About Our World

Look for books like these in the library.

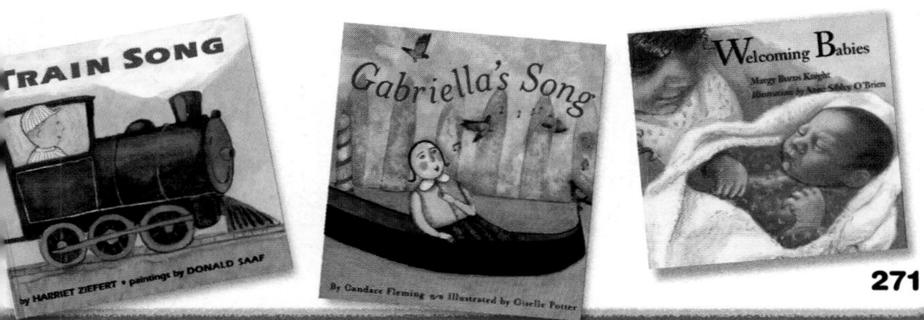

271

What did you learn?

1. You can get goods such as food, clothing, toys, and school supplies, and get services such as aiding you find goods and putting goods in a bag for you.
2. Alexander Graham Bell and Thomas Alva Edison
3. Answers will vary but may include that what people wear, what they eat, and where they live can be alike and different.
4. Answers will vary but may include household tools, devices, and appliances.

Test Talk

Write Your Answer
Use *What did you learn?* to model the Test Talk strategy.

Make sure the answer is correct.
Children should make sure their written answer has only correct details.

Make sure the answer is complete.
Have children include numerous details in their written answer.

For additional practice, use the Test Talk Practice Book.

Read About Our World

You may want to have these books available in the classroom. Read the books aloud for children; then invite them to browse through the books.

Train Song, by Diane Siebert (Harper Trophy, ISBN 0-785-71735-8, 1990) This book poetically evokes the sound and rhythm of moving trains. **Easy** ***Notable Children's Trade Book in Social Studies***

Gabriella's Song, by Candace Fleming (Atheneum, ISBN 0-689-80973-5, 1997) This book is the story of a happy child, Gabriella, who composes a song inspired by Venice. **On-Level** ***Parents' Choice Silver Honor***

Welcoming Babies, by Margy Burns Knight and Anne Sibley O'Brien (illustrator) (Tilbury House Publishers, ISBN 0-884-48123-9, 1994) This book shows how babies are welcomed into a different cultures. **Challenge**

CURRICULUM CONNECTION
Literature

Books About Our Country, Our World

You may want to read and discuss with children the following books about cultures around the world and the ways technology as changed the ways we live today.

Travel and Transport Then and Now, by Alistair Smith, Ruth Russell (designer) and Adrienne Salgado, (illustrator) (Usborne Pub Ltd, ISBN 0-746-03102-5, 2000) **Easy**

Abuela's Weave, by Omar S. Castaneda and Enrique O. Sanchez (illustrator) (Lee & Low Books, ISBN 1-880-00020-2, 1995) **On-Level**

Madlenka, by Peter Sis (Frances Foster Books, ISBN 0-374-39969-7, 2000) **On-Level**

Imaginative Inventions: The Who, What, Where, When, and Why, of Roller Skates, Potato Chips, Marbles, and Pie (and More!), by Charise Mericle Harper (Little, Brown &Co., ISBN 0-316-34725-6, 2001) **Challenge**

Unit 6 Project

Future World

Objective

- Understand how machines benefit daily life.

Resource

- Workbook, p. 70

Materials

shoe boxes, paper, crayons, scissors, glue, string, cardboard tubes, egg cartons, and other common objects

Follow This Procedure

- Tell children that machines help make work easier. Ask them to think of different kinds of machines people use every day. Write their answers on the board.
- Discuss how each of the machines listed on the board makes work easier.
- Ask children to invent a machine they think people might use in the future.
- Review with children the information that a commercial gives a consumer, such as the product name, what the product does, its price, its benefits and advantages, and where it can be bought.
- Have children create a TV commercial to tell about their inventions.

✓ **Assessment Scoring Guide**

	Future World
4	Creates a detailed model of a machine of the future and describes its benefits clearly and thoroughly.
3	Creates a detailed model of a machine of the future but does not describe its benefits fully.
2	Creates a model of a machine of the future and somewhat describes its benefits.
1	Creates an incomplete model of a machine of the future and cannot describe its benefits.

Future World

Invent a machine of the future.

1. **Think** of a machine people might use in the future.
2. **Make** a model of your machine.
3. **Give** a commercial. Tell why people should use your machine.
4. **Ask** your classmates if they would or wouldn't use your machine and why.

Internet Activity

Go to www.sfsocialstudies.com/activities to learn more about inventions.

Practice and Extend

✓ **Unit 6 Performance Assessment**

- The Unit Project can also be used as a performance assessment activity.
- Use the scoring guide to assess each group's work.

Children can launch the activity by clicking on *Grade 1, Unit 6* at **www.sfsocialstudies.com/activities.**

Workbook, p. 70

6 Project Future World

Draw a picture of a machine of the future. **Drawings will vary.**

Write answers about your machine. **Answers will vary.**

How does the machine help people?

Who will your machine help?

Also on Teacher Resources CD-ROM.

Reference Guide

Table of Contents

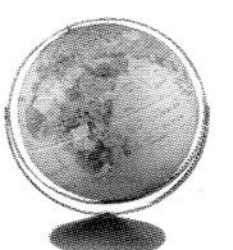

Atlas
- Photograph of the Earth R2
- Photograph of North America R3
- Map of the World R4
- Map of the United States of America R6
- Map of Our Fifty States R8

Geography Terms R10

Picture Glossary R12

Index R24

Credits R28

Atlas

Photograph of the Earth

Atlas

Photograph of North America

Atlas

Map of the World

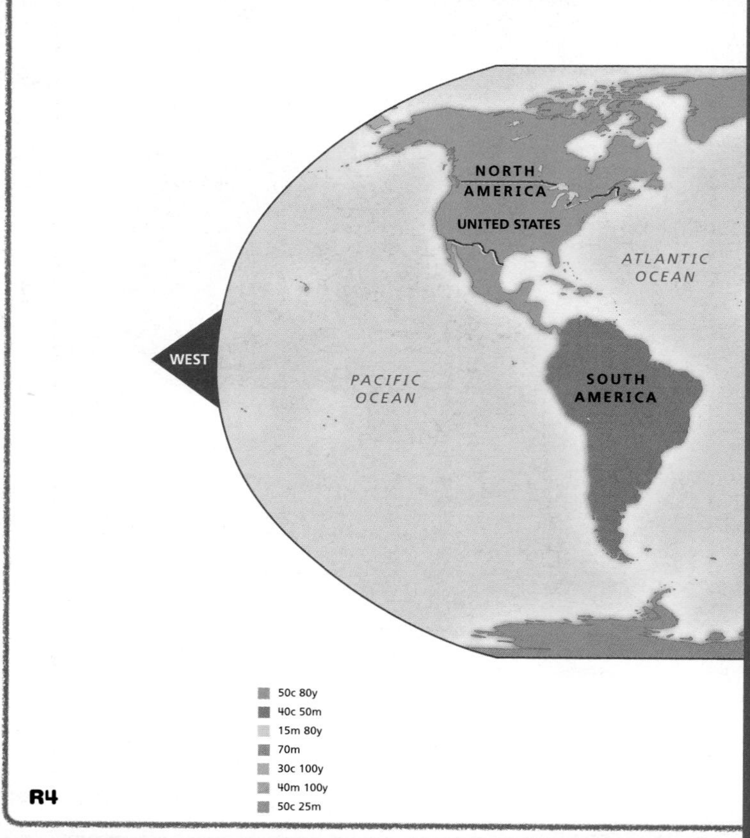

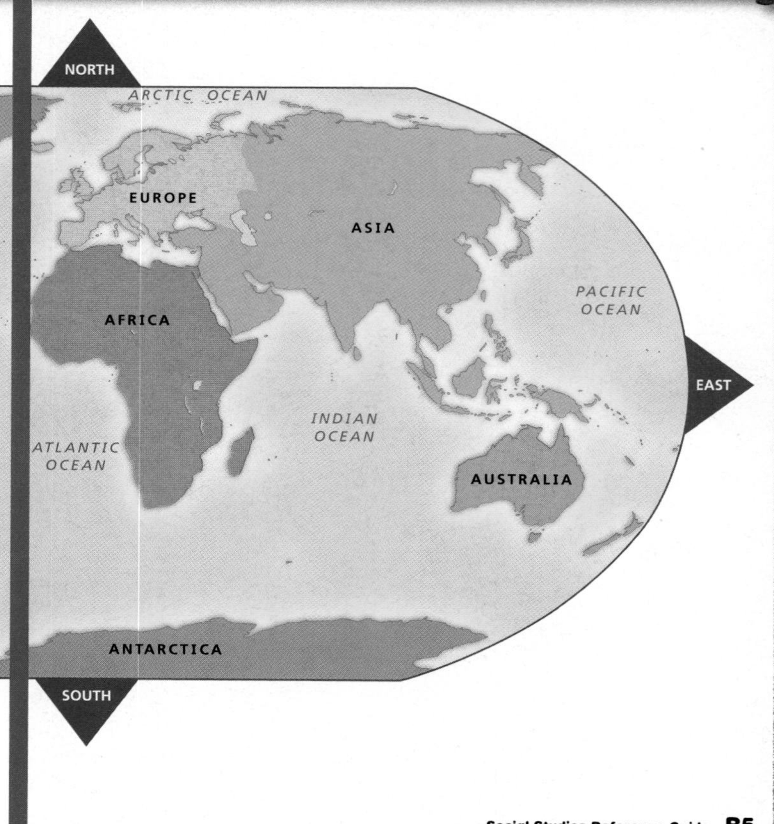

50c 80y
40c 50m
15m 80y
70m
30c 100y
40m 100y
50c 25m

Atlas

Map of the United States of America

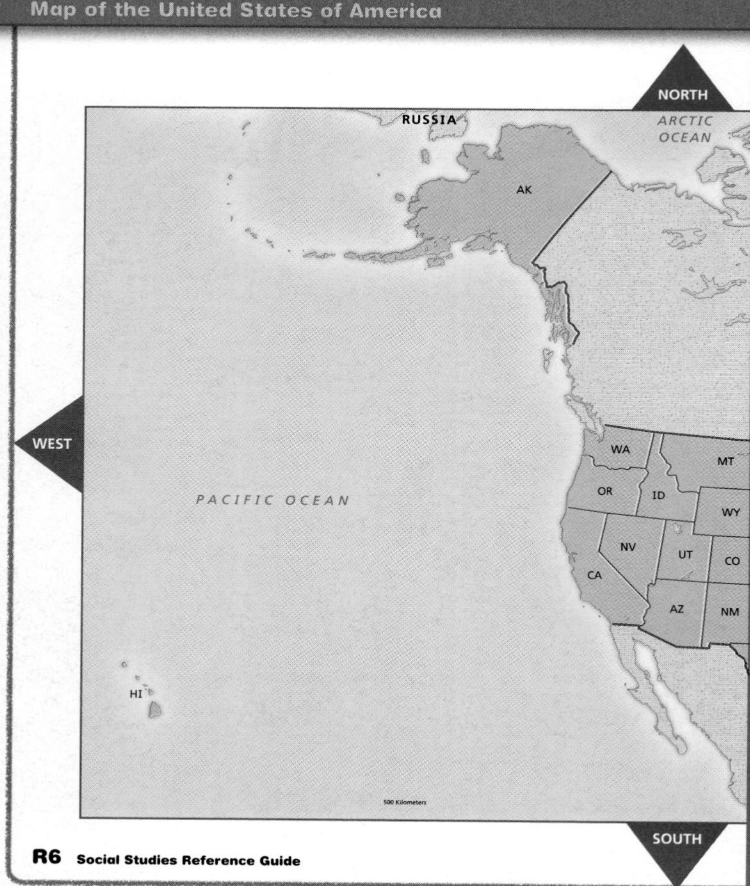

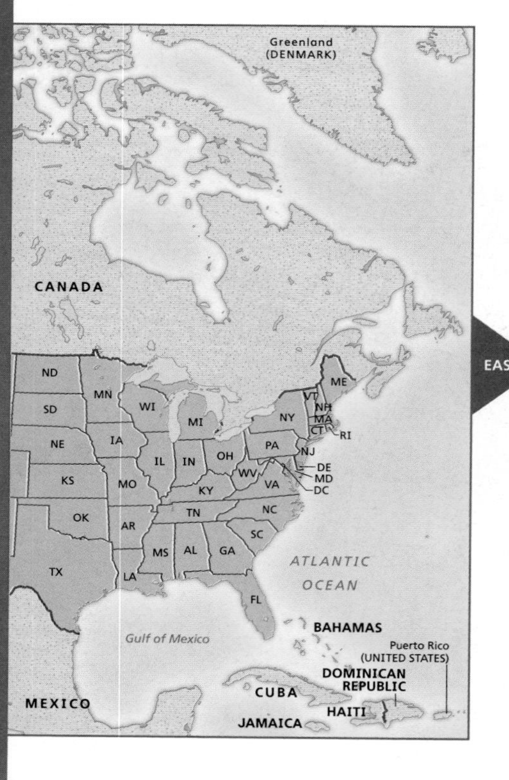

State or area	Abbreviation
Alabama	AL
Alaska	AK
Arizona	AZ
Arkansas	AR
California	CA
Colorado	CO
Connecticut	CT
Delaware	DE
District of Columbia	DC
Florida	FL
Georgia	GA
Hawaii	HI
Idaho	ID
Illinois	IL
Indiana	IN
Iowa	IA
Kansas	KS
Kentucky	KY
Louisiana	LA
Maine	ME
Maryland	MD
Massachusetts	MA
Michigan	MI
Minnesota	MN
Mississippi	MS
Missouri	MO
Montana	MT
Nebraska	NE
Nevada	NV
New Hampshire	NH
New Jersey	NJ
New Mexico	NM
New York	NY
North Carolina	NC
North Dakota	ND
Ohio	OH
Oklahoma	OK
Oregon	OR
Pennsylvania	PA
Rhode Island	RI
South Carolina	SC
South Dakota	SD
Tennessee	TN
Texas	TX
Utah	UT
Vermont	VT
Virginia	VA
Washington	WA
West Virginia	WV
Wisconsin	WI
Wyoming	WY

Atlas

Map of Our Fifty States

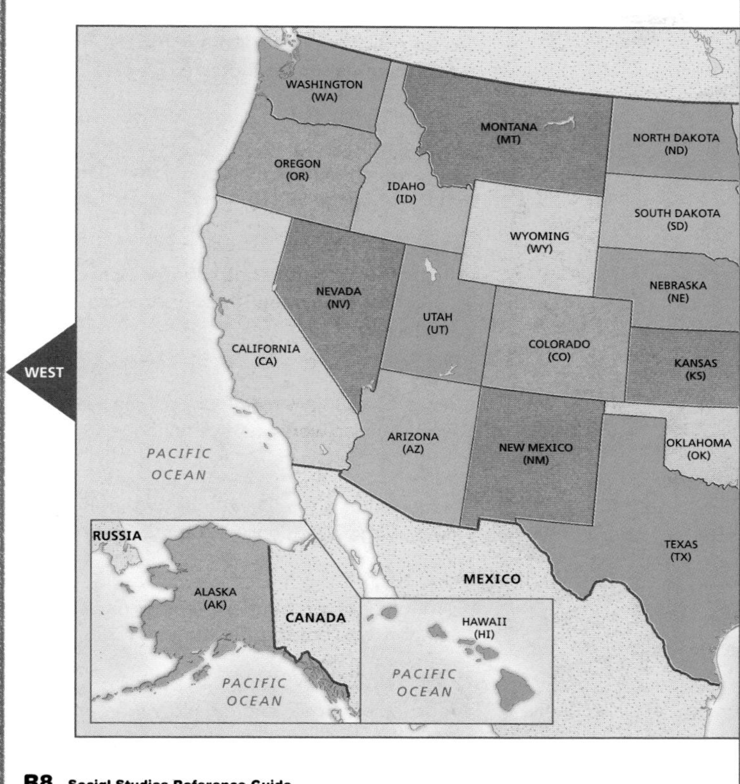

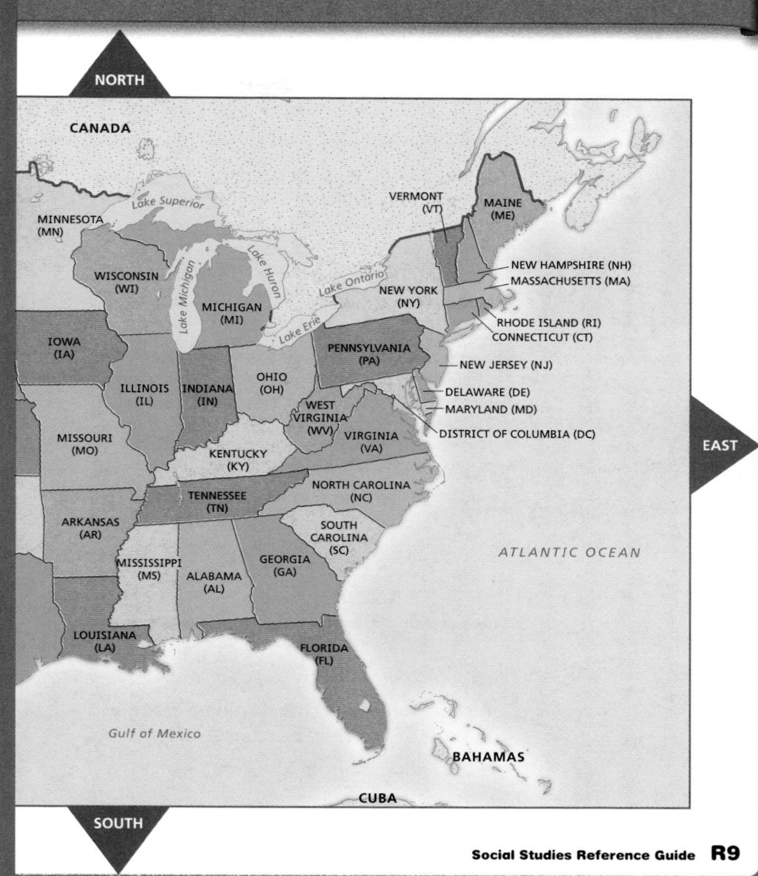

Geography Terms

forest
large area of land where many trees grow

hill
rounded land higher than the land around it

island
land with water all around it

lake
large body of water with land all or nearly all around it

mountain
highest land on Earth

ocean
a very large body of salt water

plain
very large area of flat land

river
large stream of water leading to a lake, another river, or ocean

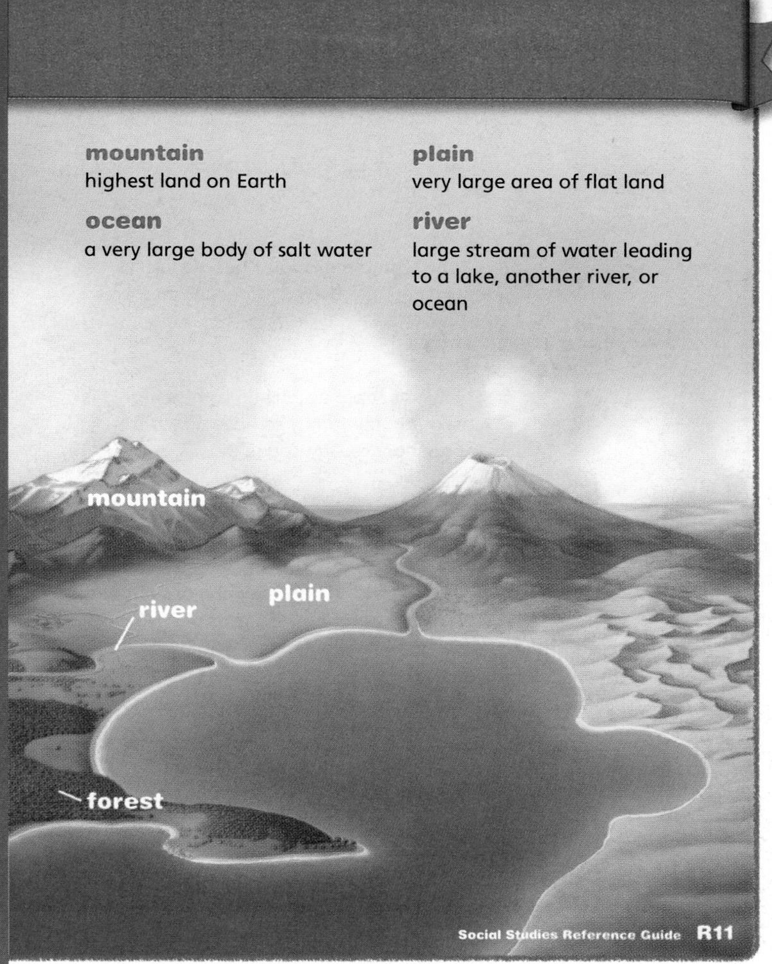

Picture Glossary

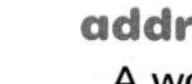

address
A way to find a home or another building. My **address** is 9 Green Street. (page 50)

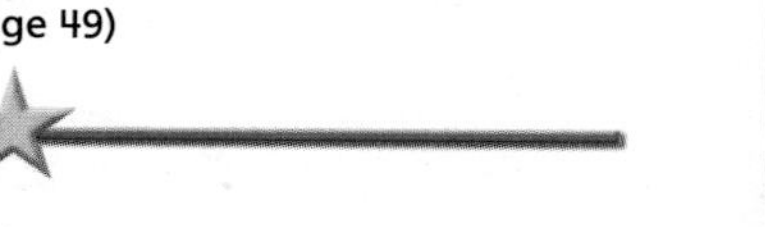

alike
How things are the same. These houses look **alike.** (page 49)

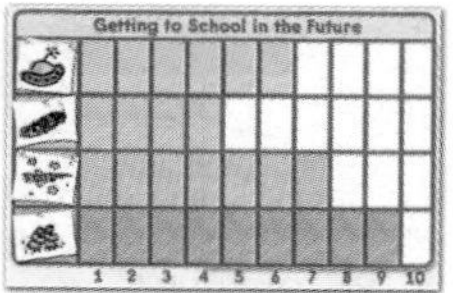

bar graph
A picture that shows how many or how much. This **bar graph** shows how children might get to school in the future. (page 254)

calendar
A chart that shows the days, weeks, and months of the year. I circled Presidents' Day on the **calendar.** (page 20)

capital
The city where important leaders of a state or country live and work. Washington D.C., is the **capital** of the United States. (page 220)

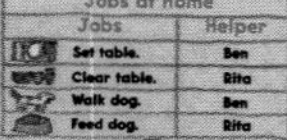

chart
A way to show things using words and pictures. This **chart** shows the jobs we have at home. (page 98)

citizen
A member of a state and country. I am a **citizen** of the United States of America. (page 218)

city
A big community where many people live and work. My dad works in the **city**. (page 56)

colony
A place that is ruled by a country that is far away. Virginia was once a **colony**. (page 202)

communicate
Give and get information. People can use a telephone to **communicate.** (page 246)

community
A group of people and the place where they live. I live in a big **community** with many neighborhoods. (page 56)

Picture Glossary

continent
A very large piece of land. South America is a **continent.** (page 76)

country
A land where a group of people live. My **country** is the United States of America. (page 16)

custom
The way people usually do something. It is a **custom** in my family to have a picnic on Independence Day. (page 62)

diagram
A drawing that shows the parts of something. This **diagram** shows the parts of a Native American earth lodge. (page 193)

different
How things are not the same. Many **different** kinds of homes are in my neighborhood. (page 49)

directions
North, south, east and west. The **directions** on a map helped us find the park. (page 60)

Earth
The planet on which we live. My class takes care of the **Earth** by recycling. (page 140)

endangered
A plant or animal of which very few are living. The mountain gorilla is **endangered.** (page 175)

farm
Land people use to raise crops or animals. My family raises corn on our **farm**. (page 57)

flag
A symbol that stands for a country. The American flag is a **symbol** of our country. (page 16)

freedom
A person's right to make choices. Many people come to the United States in search of **freedom**. (page 198)

Picture Glossary

globe
A round model of the earth. A **globe** shows the earth's land and water. (page 154)

goods
Things that are grown or made. A farmer grows **goods** such as fruits and vegetables. (page 108)

group
A number of persons or things. I like to play with a **group** of friends. (page 9)

hill
Land that is higher than the land around it. We climbed to the top of the **hill.** (page 150)

history
The story of people and places from the past. I like reading about our country's **history.** (page 164)

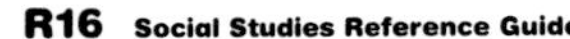

holiday
A special day. Independence Day is a **holiday.** (page 212)

invention
Something new. The telephone was an important **invention.** (page 246)

inventor
Someone who makes or invents something new. Alexander Graham Bell was a famous **inventor**. (page 247)

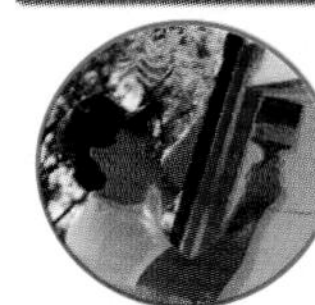

job
The work people do. My neighbor's **job** is to paint houses. (page 94)

lake
A large body of water that has land either totally or almost totally around it. A **lake** is smaller than an ocean. (page 152)

Picture Glossary

law
A rule that people must obey. It is a **law** that cars must stop at stop signs. (page 70)

leader
Someone who helps people decide what to do. The **leader** of a community is called a mayor.

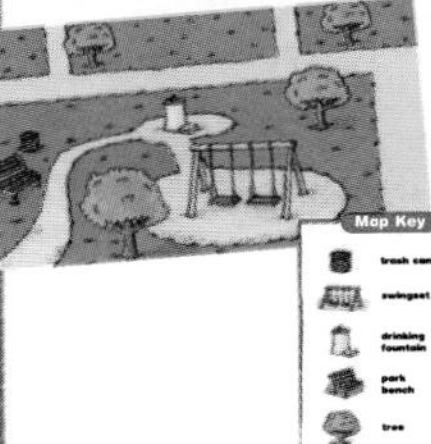

map
A drawing of a place. This is a **map** of my neighborhood park. (page 54)

map key
Tells what the symbols on a map mean. Look at the **map key** to help you read the map. (page 55)

market
A place where goods are sold. We buy fruit at the **market.** (page 238)

money
Coins or bills that people use to buy goods. I used my **money** to buy a book. (page 104)

mountain
The highest kind of land. The **mountain** has snow on the top. (page 150)

natural resource
A useful thing that comes from nature. Water is a **natural resource.** (page 156)

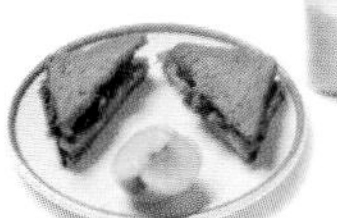

needs
Things people must have to live. Food is one of our **needs.** (page 100)

neighborhood
A place where people live, work, and play. I live in a busy **neighborhood.** (page 52)

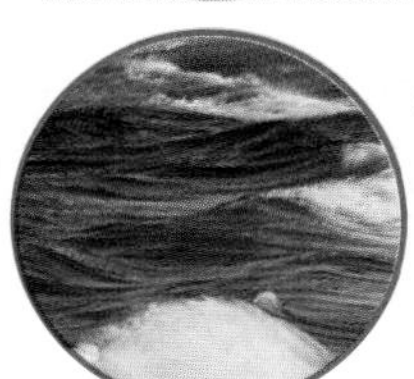

ocean
A very large body of salt water. The Atlantic **Ocean** is east of the United States. (page 76)

Picture Glossary

plain
A large, mostly flat piece of land. People sometimes grow fruits and vegetables on a **plain.** (page 151)

President
Our country's leader. The **President** of the United States makes many important decisions. (page 215)

recycle
A process where things can be made into new things. I **recycle** cans at home. (page 172)

reduce
To use less of something. I **reduce** the amount of paper I use by writing on both sides. (page 171)

reuse
To use something again. I will **reuse** this shoe box. (page 171)

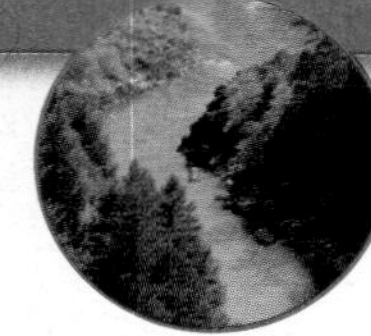

river
A long body of water which usually moves toward a lake or the ocean. We traveled down the **river** in a boat. (page 153)

route
A way to get from one place to another. Every day I use the same **route** to get from my home to my school. (page 120)

rule
Something that tells us what to do and what not to do. One **rule** we have at home is to make our beds every morning. (page 22)

school
The place where we learn. I learn about math in **school.** (page 6)

service
A job a person does to help others. As a firefighter, my mom provides a **service** to our neighborhood. (page 109)

Picture Glossary

state
A part of a country. Florida is a **state** in our country. (page 75)

symbol
A picture that stands for a real thing. The picture shows a **symbol** for a tree. (page 54)

time line
A chart that shows the order in which things happen. The **time line** shows it will be windy on Wednesday. (page 146)

tools
Things that are used to help people do work. My parents use different kinds of **tools.** (108)

town
A small community. Our **town** has only one grocery store. (page 57)

transportation
A car, bus, or other way that people and goods move from place to place. A school bus is a kind of **transportation** that takes me to school. (page 124)

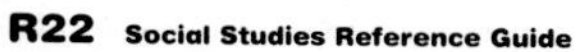

volunteer
A person who works for free. My neighbor is a **volunteer** in my community. (page 110)

vote
A choice that gets counted. Citizens of the United States **vote** for a new President every four years. (page 218)

wants
Things we would like to have. Some of my **wants** are new toys and books. (page 101)

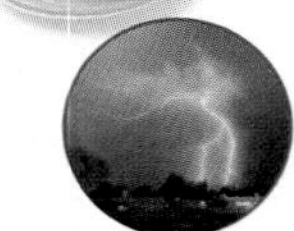

weather
How it is outside at a certain place and time. The **weather** is rainy. (page 142)

world
A name for Earth and everything on it. The picture shows how the **world** looks from space. (page 258)

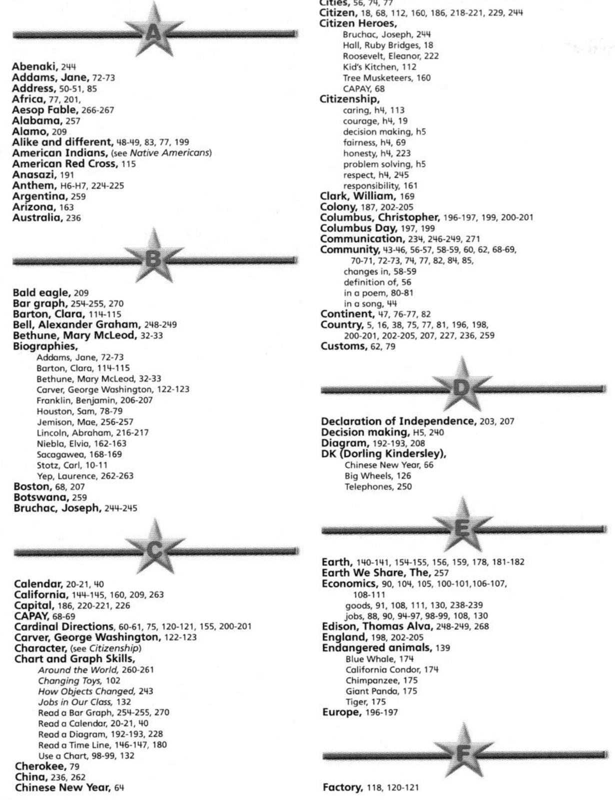

Index

A

Abenaki, 244
Addams, Jane, 72-73
Address, 50-51, 85
Africa, 77, 201,
Aesop Fable, 266-267
Alabama, 257
Alamo, 209
Alike and different, 48-49, 83, 77, 199
American Indians, (see *Native Americans*)
American Red Cross, 115
Anasazi, 191
Anthem, H6-H7, 224-225
Argentina, 259
Arizona, 163
Australia, 236

B

Bald eagle, 209
Bar graph, 254-255, 270
Barton, Clara, 114-115
Bell, Alexander Graham, 248-249
Bethune, Mary McLeod, 32-33
Biographies,
  Addams, Jane, 72-73
  Barton, Clara, 114-115
  Bethune, Mary McLeod, 32-33
  Carver, George Washington, 122-123
  Franklin, Benjamin, 206-207
  Houston, Sam, 78-79
  Jemison, Mae, 256-257
  Lincoln, Abraham, 216-217
  Niebla, Elvia, 162-163
  Sacagawea, 168-169
  Stotz, Carl, 10-11
  Yep, Laurence, 262-263
Boston, 68, 207
Botswana, 259
Bruchac, Joseph, 244-245

C

Calendar, 20-21, 40
California, 144-145, 160, 209, 263
Capital, 186, 220-221, 226
CAPAY, 68-69
Cardinal Directions, 60-61, 75, 120-121, 155, 200-201
Carver, George Washington, 122-123
Character, (see *Citizenship*)
Chart and Graph Skills,
  Around the World, 260-261
  Changing Toys, 102
  How Objects Changed, 243
  Jobs in Our Class, 132
  Read a Bar Graph, 254-255, 270
  Read a Calendar, 20-21, 40
  Read a Diagram, 192-193, 228
  Read a Time Line, 146-147, 180
  Use a Chart, 98-99, 132
Cherokee, 79
China, 236, 262
Chinese New Year, 64
Cities, 56, 74, 77
Citizen, 18, 68, 112, 160, 186, 218-221, 229, 244
Citizen Heroes,
  Bruchac, Joseph, 244
  Hall, Ruby Bridges, 18
  Roosevelt, Eleanor, 222
  Kid's Kitchen, 112
  Tree Musketeers, 160
  CAPAY, 68
Citizenship,
  caring, h4, 113
  courage, h4, 19
  decision making, h5
  fairness, h4, 69
  honesty, h4, 223
  problem solving, h5
  respect, h4, 245
  responsibility, 161
Clark, William, 169
Colony, 187, 202-205
Columbus, Christopher, 196-197, 199, 200-201
Columbus Day, 197, 199
Communication, 234, 246-249, 271
Community, 43-46, 56-57, 58-59, 60, 62, 68-69, 70-71, 72-73, 74, 77, 82, 84, 85,
  changes in, 58-59
  definition of, 56
  in a poem, 80-81
  in a song, 44
Continent, 47, 76-77, 82
Country, 5, 16, 38, 75, 77, 81, 196, 198, 200-201, 202-205, 207, 227, 236, 259
Customs, 62, 79

D

Declaration of Independence, 203, 207
Decision making, H5, 240
Diagram, 192-193, 208
DK (Dorling Kindersley),
  Chinese New Year, 66
  Big Wheels, 126
  Telephones, 250

E

Earth, 140-141, 154-155, 156, 159, 178, 181-182
Earth We Share, The, 257
Economics, 90, 104, 105, 100-101,106-107, 108-111
  goods, 91, 108, 111, 130, 238-239
  jobs, 88, 90, 94-97, 98-99, 108, 130
Edison, Thomas Alva, 248-249, 268
England, 198, 202-205
Endangered animals, 139
  Blue Whale, 174
  California Condor, 174
  Chimpanzee, 175
  Giant Panda, 175
  Tiger, 175
Europe, 196-197

F

Factory, 118, 120-121

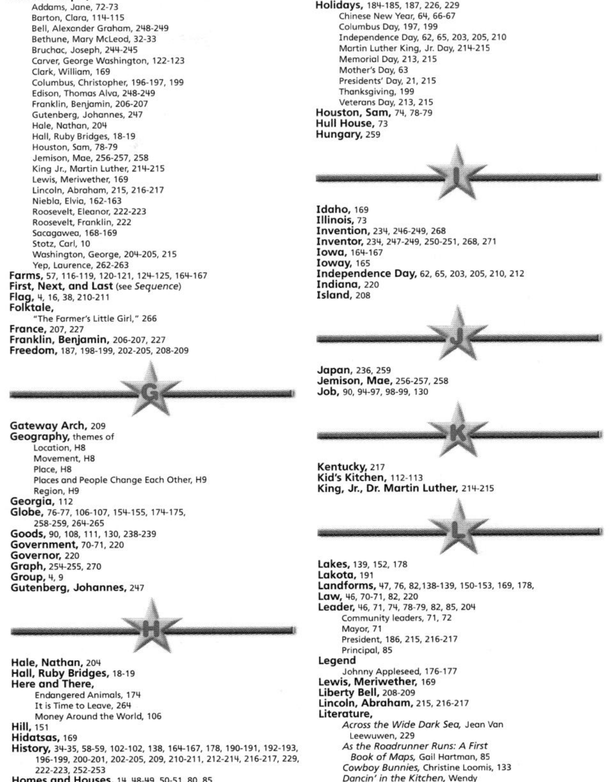

Famous People,
  Addams, Jane, 72-73
  Barton, Clara, 114-115
  Bell, Alexander Graham, 248-249
  Bethune, Mary McLeod, 32-33
  Bruchac, Joseph, 244-245
  Carver, George Washington, 122-123
  Clark, William, 169
  Columbus, Christopher, 196-197, 199
  Edison, Thomas Alva, 248-249
  Franklin, Benjamin, 206-207
  Gutenberg, Johannes, 247
  Hale, Nathan, 204
  Hall, Ruby Bridges, 18-19
  Houston, Sam, 78-79
  Jemison, Mae, 256-257, 258
  King Jr., Martin Luther, 214-215
  Lewis, Meriwether, 169
  Lincoln, Abraham, 215, 216-217
  Niebla, Elvia, 162-163
  Roosevelt, Eleanor, 222-223
  Roosevelt, Franklin, 222
  Sacagawea, 168-169
  Stotz, Carl, 10
  Washington, George, 204-205, 215
  Yep, Laurence, 262-263
Farms, 57, 116-119, 120-121, 124-125, 164-167
First, Next, and Last (see *Sequence*)
Flag, 4, 16, 38, 210-211
Folktale,
  "The Farmer's Little Girl," 266
France, 207, 227
Franklin, Benjamin, 206-207, 227
Freedom, 187, 198-199, 202-205, 208-209

G

Gateway Arch, 209
Geography, themes of
  Location, H8
  Movement, H8
  Place, H8
  Places and People Change Each Other, H9
  Region, H9
Georgia, 112
Globe, 76-77, 106-107, 154-155, 174-175, 258-259, 264-265
Goods, 90, 108, 111, 130, 238-239
Government, 70-71, 220
Governor, 220
Graph, 254-255, 270
Group, 4, 9
Gutenberg, Johannes, 247

H

Hale, Nathan, 204
Hall, Ruby Bridges, 18-19
Here and There,
  Endangered Animals, 174
  It is Time to Leave, 264
  Money Around the World, 106
Hill, 151
Hidatsas, 169
History, 34-35, 58-59, 102-102, 138, 164-167, 178, 190-191, 192-193, 196-199, 200-201, 202-205, 209, 210-211, 212-214, 216-217, 229, 222-223, 252-253
Homes and Houses, 14, 48-49, 50-51, 80, 85
  Native American Lodge, 193, 260-261
Holidays, 184-185, 187, 226, 229
  Chinese New Year, 64, 66-67
  Columbus Day, 197, 199
  Independence Day, 62, 65, 203, 205, 210
  Martin Luther King, Jr. Day, 214-215
  Memorial Day, 213, 215
  Mother's Day, 63
  Presidents' Day, 21, 215
  Thanksgiving, 199
  Veterans Day, 213, 215
Houston, Sam, 74, 78-79
Hull House, 73
Hungary, 259

I

Idaho, 169
Illinois, 73
Invention, 234, 246-249, 268
Inventor, 234, 247-249, 250-251, 268, 271
Iowa, 164-167
Ioway, 165
Independence Day, 62, 65, 203, 205, 210, 212
Indiana, 220
Island, 208

J

Japan, 236, 259
Jemison, Mae, 256-257, 258
Job, 90, 94-97, 98-99, 130

K

Kentucky, 217
Kid's Kitchen, 112-113
King, Jr., Dr. Martin Luther, 214-215

L

Lakes, 139, 152, 178
Lakota, 191
Landforms, 47, 76, 82,138-139, 150-153, 169, 178,
Law, 46, 70-71, 82, 220
Leader, 46, 71, 74, 78-79, 82, 85, 204
  Community leaders, 71, 72
  Mayor, 71
  President, 186, 215, 216-217
  Principal, 85
Legend
  Johnny Appleseed, 176-177
Lewis, Meriwether, 169
Liberty Bell, 208-209
Lincoln, Abraham, 215, 216-217
Literature,
  Across the Wide Dark Sea, Jean Van Leewuwen, 229
  As the Roadrunner Runs: A First Book of Maps, Gail Hartman, 85
  Cowboy Bunnies, Christine Loomis, 133
  Dancin' in the Kitchen, Wendy

Index

  Gelsanliter and Frank Christian, 133
  Gabriella's Song, Candace Fleming, 271
  George the Drummer Boy, Nathaniel Benchley, 229
  Long Ago and Today: A Home Album, Peter and Connie Roop, 85
  Mary McLeod Bethune, Eloise Greenfield, 41
  Picture Book of Eleanor Roosevelt, David Adler, 229
  School from A to Z, Bobbie Kalman, 41
  Storm Book, The, Charlotte, Zolotow, 181
  Tell Me a Season, Mary McKenna Siddals, 85
  Train Song, Diane Siebert, 271
  Weed is a Flower: The Life of George Washington Carver, A, Aliki, 133
  Welcoming Babies, Mary Burns Knight, 271
  Whatever the Weather, Karen Wallace, 181
  Where I Live, Frances Wolfe, 85
  Yoko, Rosemary Wells, 41
Louisiana, 18

M

Main idea, 140-141, 145, 159, 173, 179, 181
Maps,
  of addresses, 51
  locate land and water, 154-155
  follow a route, 120-121, 131
  use a history map, 200-201, 227
  make a map of land and water, 179
  map symbols, 54-55, 83
  Native American Homes, 191
  of United States, 75
  use a map key, 54-55, 83,
  use four directions, 60-61, 84
Map and Globe Skills,
  Follow a Route, 120-121, 131
  Locate Land and Water, 154-155, 179
  Use Four Directions, 60-61, 84
  Use a History Map, 200-201, 227
  Use a Map Key, 54-55, 83
Map and Globe Skills Review, H10-H14
Market, 235, 238-239, 268, 271
Martin Luther King Jr. Day, 214-215
Massachusetts, 68, 115, 207
Mayflower, 198, 200
Mayor, 71, 82, 85
Memorial Day, 213, 215
Mexico, 79, 163, 236
Michigan, 144-145
Missouri, 123, 209
Money, 104-105, 106-107, 228
Mother's Day, 63
Motto, H6-H7, 209
Mountains, 139, 150-151, 153, 169, 178
Muir, John, 159
Music (see *songs*)

N

NASA Space Program, 257
Native Americans, 79, 165-166, 168-169, 190-191, 192-193, 194-195, 197, 199, 244-245
Natural resource, 138, 156-159, 163, 170-173, 178, 181
Needs, 91, 100, 130
Neighborhood, 46, 50-53, 80, 82
New York, 222, 244
Newbury Award, 263
Niebla, Elvia, 162-163
Nobel Peace Prize, 73
North Dakota, 169
North America, 76, 197-198, 200, 208

O

Ocean, 47, 76, 82, 152
  Arctic, 77
  Atlantic, 76
  Indian, 77
  Pacific, 76, 152

P

Peanuts, 116-119, 122-123
Pennsylvania, 11, 208
Picture clues, 6-7, 9, 27, 31, 39
Pilgrims, 198-199, 226, 229
Plains, 151, 153
Pledge of Allegiance, H6-H7, 16-17
Pledge to Texas Flag, H6-H7
Plymouth, 199
Poems,
  "One Great Big Community," 80
  "School Today," 36
  "Work Day," 128
Poor Richard's Almanack, 207
Predict, 236-237, 239, 243, 253, 255, 269
President, 186, 215, 216-217, 221, 226, 228
Presidents' Day, 21, 215
Principal, 25, 85
Problem solving, H5, 26-27, 39
Projects
  Follow Me!, 42
  News for All, 86
  Jobs in Your Community, 134
  Weather Report, 182
  History on Parade, 230
Public officials (see *Governor, Mayor, and President*)

R

Reading Skills,
  Alike and Different, 48-49, 77, 83, 199
  Main Idea, 140-141, 145, 159, 173,179, 181
  Predict, 236-237, 239, 243, 253, 255, 269
  Put Things in Order, 92-93, 95, 97, 117-119, 131
  Recall and Retell, 188-189, 221, 227, 249, 261
  Use Picture Clues, 6-7, 9, 27, 31, 39
Recall and Retell, 188-189, 221, 227, 249, 261
Recycle, Reduce, Reuse, 136-137, 170-173
Reviews, 38-41, 82-85, 130-133, 178-181, 226-229, 286-271
Rivers, 153, 169
Roosevelt, Eleanor, 222-223
Roosevelt, Franklin, 222
Routes, 120-121, 131
Rules, 5, 22-25, 38, 70-71

S

Sacagawea, 168-169
Saratoga Springs, New York, 244
School, 4, 6-7, 14-17, 18-19, 34-35, 36-38
  cleaning up a, 26-27
  definition of, 6
  how it changed over time, 28-31
  in a poem, 36-37
  in a song, 1-3
  jobs at, 96
  rules, 22-25
Smithsonian,
  Play Ball!, 12-13
  Weather and Fun, 148-149
  Native American Objects, 195-194
Sequence, 92-93, 95, 97, 117-119, 131
Services, 90, 109, 111, 130, 239
Shoshone, 168, 169
Songs,
  "Explore with Me," 232
  "Holidays are Special Days," 184
  "Lots of Jobs," 88
  "Show You Care," 136
  "The Star-Spangled Banner," 224
  "This Is My Community," 44
  "We Go to School," 2
South Carolina, 33
Spain, 196, 201
Star-Spangled Banner, 224-225
States, 47, 75, 77, 81, 82, 85
Statue of Liberty, 208, 228
Stotz, Carl, 10-11
Symbols, map, 54-55, 83
Symbols, national, 230
  American flag, 4, 16, 38, 210-211
  Bald Eagle, 208
  Liberty Bell, 208
  Statue of Liberty, 208, 228
Symbols, state
  Alamo, 209
  Gateway Arch, 209

T

Taino, 197
Tanzania, 259
Technology, 242-243, 246-248, 252-253
Tennessee, 79
Texas, 75, 78-79, 82
  Alamo, 209
  State flag, 79
Thanksgiving, 199
Then and Now,
  Changing Toys, 102
  How a Community Changed, 58
  Our Country's Flag, 210
  Things We Use, 34
Thinking Skills,
  Make a Decision, 240, 269
  Problem on the Playground, 26
Time,
  past, present, and future, 34-35, 58-59, 102-103, 147, 183, 164-167, 190, 201, 210-211, 249, 252
  yesterday, today, and tomorrow, 142-145, 199, 203, 253-255
Time line, 146-147, 166, 180, 210-211, 252-253
Tools, 91, 108
Town, 57, 71, 77
Transportation, 91, 124-125, 126-127, 130, 252-253, 254-255, 271
Tree Musketeers, 160-161

U

United States, 16, 75-76, 78-79, 205, 206, 218, 221
  American Revolution, 204
  capital of, 221
  Declaration of Independence, 203
  flag of, 211
  government of (see Government)
  history of (see History)
  holidays in (see Holidays)
  map of, 75
  Pledge of Allegiance to, H6-H7, 16-17
  President of, 186, 215, 216-217, 221, 226, 228
  states in, 47, 73, 75, 77, 78-79, 81, 82, 85, 144-145, 160, 163, 208, 209, 263
  symbols of, 208, 228, 230

V

Veteran's Day, 40, 213, 215
Virginia, 79, 202
Volunteer, 90, 110-111, 112-113, 114-115, 130
Voting, 186, 218-221, 226, 227, 229

W

Wampanoag, 199
Wants, 91, 101, 130
Washington, D. C., 221
Washington, George, 204-205, 208, 215
Washington Monument, 208
Weather, 138, 142-145, 146-147, 148-149, 163, 181, 236
Work, 87-89, 92, 93, 108-111
  in a song, 88
  in a poem, 128-129
  jobs, 88, 90, 94-97, 98-99
  tools, 91, 108, 111, 133
World, 234, 258-261, 268
Writing, 7, 11, 17, 21, 25, 27, 31, 35, 38-41, 49, 53, 55, 57, 59, 61, 65, 71, 77, 79, 82-85, 89, 91, 93, 99, 101, 103, 105, 111, 115, 119, 121, 123, 125, 130-134, 141, 145, 147, 153, 155, 159, 163, 167, 169, 173, 178-182, 189, 191, 193, 199, 201, 205, 207, 209, 215, 217, 219, 221, 237, 239, 241, 243, 249, 253, 255, 257, 261, 263, 271

Y

Yep, Laurence, 262-263

Credits

Illustrations

4, 17, 138 Susan Simon; 4, 46 Tom Barrett; 10, 11 Robert Gunn; 20, 32 Keith Batchelor; 36 Reggie Holladay; 46 Linda Howard Bittner; 54 Donna Catanese; 62 Robert Krugle; 78 Mitchell Heinze; 80 Susan Tolonen; 83 David Brion; 84, 157 Steven Boswick; 114 Laurie Harden; 116 Eileen Mueller Neill; 122 Stacey Schuett; 155, 190 Amy Vangsgard; 176 Richard Stergulz; 179 Yvonne Gilbert; 200 Doug Knutson; 206 Ann Barrow; 216 Bill & Debbie Farnsworth; 224 Darryl Ligasan; 227 Steven Mach; 227 Mark Stein; 228 Rose Mary Berlin; 266 Loretta Lustig; 266 Karen Stormer Brooks

Photographs

Unit 1: 4 (TL) Frank Siteman/Index Stock Imagery, (CL) David Young-Wolff/PhotoEdit; 5 (CR) Tom Prettyman/PhotoEdit; 8 (BC) CMCD/PhotoDisc, (BR) PhotoDisc; 9 (Bkgd) Mark E. Gibson/Visuals Unlimited; 11 (CL) SuperStock; 18 (BL, BR) AP/Wide World; 19 (C) AP/Wide World; 25 (T) Daemmrich Photography, (CR) Bob Daemmrich/Stock Boston, (CL) Stone; 26 (B) Tony Freeman/PhotoEdit; 27 (TR, CR) Tony Freeman/PhotoEdit; 29 (T) Popperfoto/Archive Photos, (B) Frank Siteman/Index Stock Imagery; 30 (BC) Jeffry W. Myers/Stock Boston, (T) Fox Photos/Hulton Getty Picture Collection/Stone; 31 (Bkgd) PhotoLink/PhotoDisc; 33 (CR, BL) Corbis-Bettmann, (BR) Corbis; 38 (TL) Frank Siteman/Index Stock Imagery, (BL) Tom Prettyman/PhotoEdit; 39 (TR) Laura Dwight/PhotoEdit, (C) Michael Newman/PhotoEdit, (CL) Gregg Mancuso/Stock Boston; **Unit 2:** 44 (C) Ellis Vener; 46 (TL) Michael Newman/PhotoEdit, (TC) SuperStock, (BL) Paul Conklin/PhotoEdit, (BC) David Hiller/PhotoDisc; 47 (TR) SuperStock, (CR) A & L Sinibaldi/Stone; 48 (BL) Daemmrich Photography, (BR) Amy C. Etra/PhotoEdit; 49 (BL) Felicia Martinez/PhotoEdit, (CL) PhotoEdit; 50 (CL) Daemmrich Photography; 52 (B) Michael S. Yamashita/Corbis-Bettmann, (C) Michael Newman/PhotoEdit; 56 (B) SuperStock; 57 (T) Michele Burgess/Stock Boston, (C) Chuck Pefley 1997/Stock Boston; 58 (B) Courtesy of the Houston Public Library/UT at San Antonio; 59 (C) Jim Olive Photography; 64 (C) Kevin Fleming/Corbis-Bettmann; 66 Barnabas and Anabel Kindersley/© Dorling Kindersley; 67 Barnabas and Anabel Kindersley/© Dorling Kindersley; 70 (BL) David Hiller/PhotoDisc, (BR) Hisham F. Ibrahim/PhotoDisc, (BC) Mark C. Burnett/Stock Boston, (CR) Robert Brenner/PhotoEdit; 73 (CR) AP/Wide World; 74 (BC) Ellis Vener; 79 (BR) Richard Cummins/Viesti Collection, Inc., (CR) Corbis-Bettmann; **Unit 3:** 90 Joe Sohm/Image Works; 90 (T) PhotoDisc; 91 (TC, BC) PhotoDisc; 102 (BL) PhotoDisc; 103 (TL) Siede Preis/PhotoDisc, (CR) Courtesy Action Products International, Inc.; 111 (L) Richard Pasley/Stock Boston (C), Michael Newman/PhotoeEdit, (R) Michael Newman/PhotoeEdit; 112 Courtesy, Pam Woolery; 117 Runk/Schoenberger/Grant Heilman Photography (C) Grant Heilman/Grant Heilman Photography (B) © David Frazier Photo Library; 118 (T) © David R. Frazier Photo Library © Grant Heilman/Grant Heilman Photography (B) Larry Lefever/Grant Heilman Photography; 123 (C) Spencer Ainsley/Index Stock Imagery, (CR) Hulton/Archive Photos; 124 (BL) PhotoDisc; 124 (TL, CL, BL) Corbis, (BR) Spencer Ainsley/Image Works; 126 (C) © Dorling Kindersley, (B) Stephen Oliver/© Dorling Kindersley, (CL) © Dave Hopkins; 127 (T, C) Stephen Oliver/© Dorling Kindersley, (TR, CL, BR) © Dave Hopkins; **Unit 4:** 136 (Bkgd) Lee Rentz/Bruce Coleman Inc.; 138 (TL) Kent Wood/Photo Researchers, Inc., (CL) Wolfgang Kaehler, (BL) Georg Gerster/Photo Researchers, Inc.; 139 Peter Weimann/Animals Animals/Earth Scenes, (BR) Andy Levin/Photo Researchers, Inc., (TR) Charlie Ott/Photo Researchers, Inc., (C) D. Robert Franz/Bruce Coleman Inc., (TR) Pat O'Hara/Corbis; 143 (TR) Nick Daly/Stone, (C) Randy Wells/Stone, (TL) Joseph Nettis 1989/Stock Boston; 148 Smithsonian Institution; 149 Smithsonian Institution; 150 (BL) Georg Gerster/Photo Researchers, Inc., (BC) Lee Rentz/Bruce Coleman Inc.; 151 (T) Josef Beck/FPG International LLC, (B) Georg Gerster/Photo Researchers, Inc.; 152 (TC) George Lepp/Corbis, (BC) Wolfgang Kaehler; 153 (TC) Myrleen Ferguson Cate/PhotoEdit; 156 (BC) Michael Gadomski/Animals Animals/Earth Scenes; 158 (TR) Emma Lee/Life File/PhotoDisc; 163 Living History Farms; 164 (Bkgd) Living History Farms; 166 (BL) Culver Pictures Inc., (BC) Living History Farms, (BR) Michael Gadomski/Animals Animals/Earth Scenes, (Bkgd) F. Schussler/PhotoLink/PhotoDisc; 174 (CL) Tom McHugh/Photo Researchers, Inc., (BC) Phillip Colla Photography; 175 (TR) Lynn M. Stone/Bruce Coleman Inc., (CR) E. Hanumantha Rao/Photo Researchers, Inc.; **Unit 5:** 186 (CL) Joseph Sohm; ChromoSohm Inc./Corbis, (TL) David & Peter Turnley/Corbis, (BL) Museum of the City of New York/Corbis; 187 (CL) Bob Daemmrich/Daemmrich Photography; 192 (BR) Corbis-Bettmann; 197 (TR) The Granger Collection, New York; 199 (TR) Bettmann/Corbis; 202 Francis G. Mayer/Corbis; 203 (BC) The Granger Collection, New York; 204 (C) Bettmann/Corbis, (BL) Lee Snider/Corbis; 207 (CR) Bettmann Archive/Corbis, (BR) Courtesy of the Historical and Interpretive Collections of the Franklin Institute; 208 (R)Gail Mooney/Corbis, (B)Bill Ross/Corbis; 209 (CL) W. Perry Conway/Corbis, (CR) D. Boone/Corbis, (TL) Kelly-Mooney Photography/Corbis, (BR) Obverse ©; 212 Kevin Fleming/Corbis; 213 (BC) Rhoda Sidney/PhotoEdit, (CL, C) Bettmann Archive/Corbis, (TR) Benn/Corbis; 214 (BC) Flip Schulke/Corbis; 217 (BR) Morton Beebe/Corbis; 218 (C) David Young-Wolff/PhotoEdit; 220 (CL) Mark Burnett/Stock Boston, (BC) Cathlyn Melloan/Stone; 221 (CR) The Granger Collection, New York; 222 (CR) Courtesy of FDR Library, Hyde Park, NY; 223 (BL) AP/Wide World; 226 (TC) Library of Congress; **Unit 6:** 232 (TL) Adrain Carroll/Corbis; 235 (TR) PhotoDisc; 243 (BC) Schenectady Museum; Hall of Electrical History Foundation/Corbis, (TR, C, TC) PhotoDisc; 244 (CL) Courtesy, Lee & Low Books; 248 Library of Congress; 258 (BC) PhotoDisc; 259 Barnabas and Anabel Kindersley/© Dorling Kindersley; 260 Anabel and Barnabas Kindersley/© Dorling Kindersley; 261 Anabel and Barnabas Kindersley/© Dorling Kindersley

Front and End Matter

H4 (TC) ©Comstock Inc.; EM Leland Klanderman; EM1 Leland Klanderman

"Ring Around the World" by Annette Wayne from *Story and Verse for Children* selected and edited by Miriam Blanton Huber, Ph.D. Reprinted by permission. "Water" by Hilda Conkling. Reprinted by permission.

Teacher Resources

Facing Fear: Helping Students Cope with Tragic Events

Together, we can save a life

As much as we would like to protect our children, we cannot shield them from personal or community tragedies. We can, however, help them to be prepared for unforeseen dangerous events and to learn about facing and moving beyond their fears, sadness, and related concerns.

Common Responses to Trauma and Disaster

Children experience many common reactions after a trauma. These include reexperiencing the event (for example, flashbacks), avoidance and numbing of feelings, increased agitation, and changes in functioning. These reactions may be manifested in clingy behaviors, mood changes, increased anxieties, increased startle responses (for example, more jumpy with noises), physical complaints, and regressive behavior. Increased aggressive behaviors may also be seen. When the trauma or disaster is human-made, such as a terrorist event, children may react with hurtful talk, behaviors, or play. All of these reactions are normal responses and will, in general, dissipate with time. However, should these persist or increase over time, a referral to a mental health professional might be considered. Similarly, should these reactions result in a danger to self or others, immediate action is warranted.

Issues of Safety, Security, and Trust

In the aftermath of terrorism or other tragic events, very young children can feel overwhelmed with concerns of safety, security, and trust. They are often unsure where to turn for help. When the safety of their world is threatened, they may feel insecure and fearful. As a result, they may be more anxious and frightened. Children may be more clingy with teachers as well as with parents. This may be due to worry about their own safety as well as the safety of those important to them. Abandonment is a major childhood fear, so children need frequent reassurance they will be cared for and will not be left behind. This message may need to be repeated many times each day. By returning to a regular classroom routine, teachers can help to reinforce a sense of security in young children.

Children's increased fear may also encompass a worry that the trauma will reoccur. Because children this age have not developed a complete sense of time, exposure to replays of the trauma or disaster via television may lead them to believe that the event is happening again and again. This reexposure can result in increasing worry and fear. Limiting this exposure, as well as exposure to adult conversations about the event, may reduce the stress in children.

Expressing Thoughts and Feelings

Young children may have difficulty putting their thoughts and feelings into words. In order to express these, they may act out ideas through play. Teachers may see play that attempts to recreate the event. Children may repeatedly erect buildings with blocks only to knock them down. Children may pretend to be rescue workers or to be rescued. Children may also become more aggressive or destructive in their play as they act out feelings of anger about what has happened. Teachers may see a direct link to the event (for example, buildings being destroyed) or behaviors seemingly unrelated to the event (such as a game of tag on the playground). Children this age may talk incessantly about the event. To these repetitions, children may gradually add new bits of knowledge that they gain from others. At times, as young children try to make the story "fit" into their concept of the world around them, the repetitions may come to include misinformation or misperceptions of the event. Questions related to the trauma may be equally repetitive. Teachers may answer a child's question only to have the same question repeated within a few minutes. Having the same answer will increase the child's sense of security and help the child process the trauma.

Children this age may have difficulty understanding the results of the event. For example, very young children have magical thinking as well as the belief in the reversibility of loss. Therefore, they may believe that those killed in a disaster will return or that buildings can be easily rebuilt. Children may have many questions and discussions about death and dying. They do not have a mature grasp of the irreversibility of death.

Identifying Factors to Predict Children at Greatest Risk

Changes in behavior are likely after young children experience a trauma or disaster. One indicator of increased distress may be more whining and irritable behaviors. Young children may have more angry outbursts or temper tantrums, even over seemingly minor events. They may also be more defiant in their behaviors. The opposite may also be seen; some children will become more withdrawn and less engaged in classroom activities.

Children may show a change in functioning. They may have toileting accidents. A return to baby talk is not unusual. Sleep may be disrupted after a trauma, so children may be less rested, which can also produce more irritability. Children may want more help with schoolwork. Not only does this demonstrate increased stress, it also addresses the need for an increased sense of safety and security by having the teacher provide one-on-one attention. At times, children may have problems with attention and concentration on new work presented, which may require multiple presentations of the material. *(continued on the following page)*

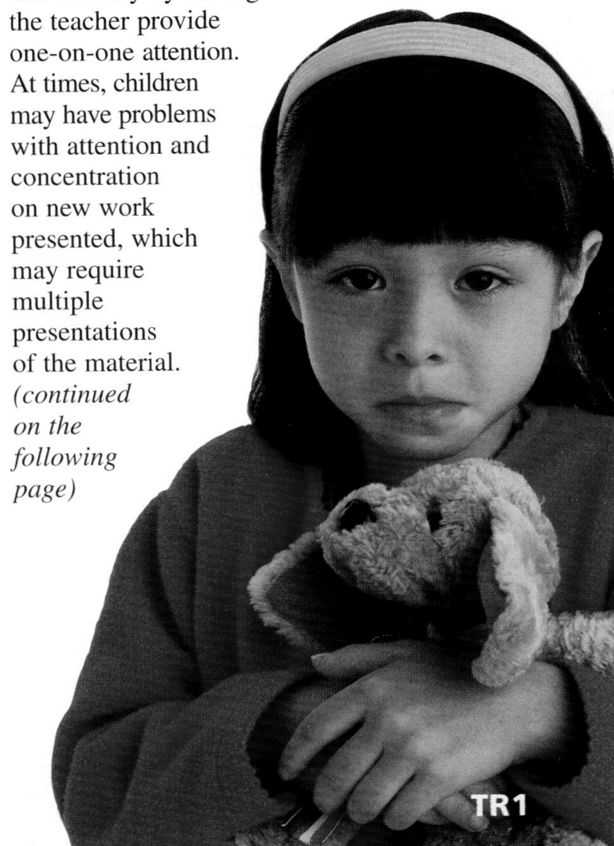

(continued from p. TR1)

Moving Forward in Spite of Life-Affecting Events

Frightening events, such as the terrorist attacks in the United States on September 11, 2001, the Oklahoma City bombing in 1995, earthquakes, tornadoes, and hurricanes here and in other countries, massive transportation accidents, and war or armed conflict or other military action, impact us all. Events that are caused by human beings can be particularly frightening and raise unique concerns. Terrorist actions and other violent acts are designed to instill fear in individuals and communities, if not countries. Because they happen without warning, there is no time to prepare. This unpredictability leaves us witha heightened sense of vulnerability and anxieties that the event could be repeated again, anywhere. With increased media coverage, even those not directly impacted can be significantly affected by an event. Images make us feel closer to the victims, and we may perceive ourselves as victims of the actions as well. The questions that arise from disasters of human design are difficult, if not impossible, to answer. We want answers to "Why?" and "How could they?" and are often left frustrated by the lack of satisfying responses. This frustration also gives rise to intense feelings of anger. The anger toward the perpetrators may be uncomfortable and difficult to express in productive ways. As adults struggle with reactions and feelings in the aftermath of a terrorist action or tragic event, children are similarly searching for how to best handle their feelings. At all ages, they take cues from adults around them (parents, teachers, and community and national leaders).

Children need to know that their reactions and feelings to such events are normal. They need to recognize that others feel very similarly. Most important, children need to know that they will begin to feel better with time and that it is acceptable to enjoy friends, family, and activities. They need to know that there are things they can do to help themselves move forward in a positive way.

Activities to Help Children Address Fears

The following activities are designed to help you help your students address their fears and move beyond them.

- **What Happened**—Divide a piece of poster board into five areas. In each area, draw a symbol for one of the senses. As you discuss a trauma/disaster, record what children saw with their eyes, felt inside, heard with their ears, smelled with their nose, and tasted in their mouth.
- **Searching for a Sense of Safety**—Help children list people they can count on and places they can go for safety in an emergency. Remind children that it is important for them to know their address, phone number, name (first and last), and parents' names (first and last) to give to helpers in order to reunite them with their families.
- **Naming Feelings**—Help children share ideas and feelings with each other by having them draw a picture of a feeling they or other children may have had after a trauma or disaster. Remind them that feelings may vary and that there are no rights and wrongs.
- **Dealing with Feelings**—Distribute strips of paper and ask children to write down or draw some feelings they would like to get rid of. Then tape each strip to the string of a balloon and release the balloon outdoors. Discuss with children how letting go of the balloon might help them let go of bad feelings.
- **Finding Hidden Treasures**—On yellow or gold paper, duplicate coins to serve as "treasure coins." Distribute to children and have them write or draw a good thing, feeling, activity, or person they have in their life. Remind children to use both sides of the coin and to use as many treasure coins as they would like. Invite children to share their treasures. You may also wish to make a treasure chest to store the coins.

Books for Young Readers

Smoky Night Bunting, Eve. Illus. by David Diaz. Harcourt Brace, 1999. Children who witness the Los Angeles riots experience dangerous times.

A Terrible Thing Happened: A story for children who have witnessed violence or trauma Holmes, Margaret, and Sasha J. Mudloff. Illus. by Cary Pillo and Thomas Payne. American Psychological Association, 2000. Children explore conscious and subconscious feelings they might have after a traumatic event.

Thunder Cake Polacco, Patricia. Paper Star, 1997. A young girl overcomes her fear of thunderstorms as she helps her grandmother make a cake.

Pip's Magic Stoll, Ellen. Voyager Picture Book, 1999. A young salamander tries to find the wizard who will help him overcome his fear of the dark.

My Many Colored Days Seuss, Dr. Illus. by Lou Fancher and Steve Johnson. Knopf, 1996. Children explore a colorful book about feelings and emotions.

American Red Cross

Information on American Red Cross *Facing Fear: Helping Young People Deal with Terrorism and Tragic Events*

The American Red Cross *Facing Fear* curriculum contains lesson plans for teachers and includes hands-on or interactive activities for the classroom that will help students and their families prepare for disastrous situations and equip them with tools to sort out their feelings and fears.

For further information or to obtain copies of the *Facing Fear* curriculum materials, or the curriculum materials that focus on natural disaster preparedness, called *Masters of Disaster*™, contact your local American Red Cross chapter. Visit **http://www.redcross.org** to find your nearest Red Cross chapter, and visit **www.redcross.org/disaster/masters** for specific information on the curriculum. American Red Cross products are available exclusively from local Red Cross chapters in the United States.

With permission, parts above were adapted from Healing After Trauma Skills, *Robin H. Gurwitch and Anne K. Messenbaugh, University of Oklahoma Health Sciences Center.*

Cause and Effect

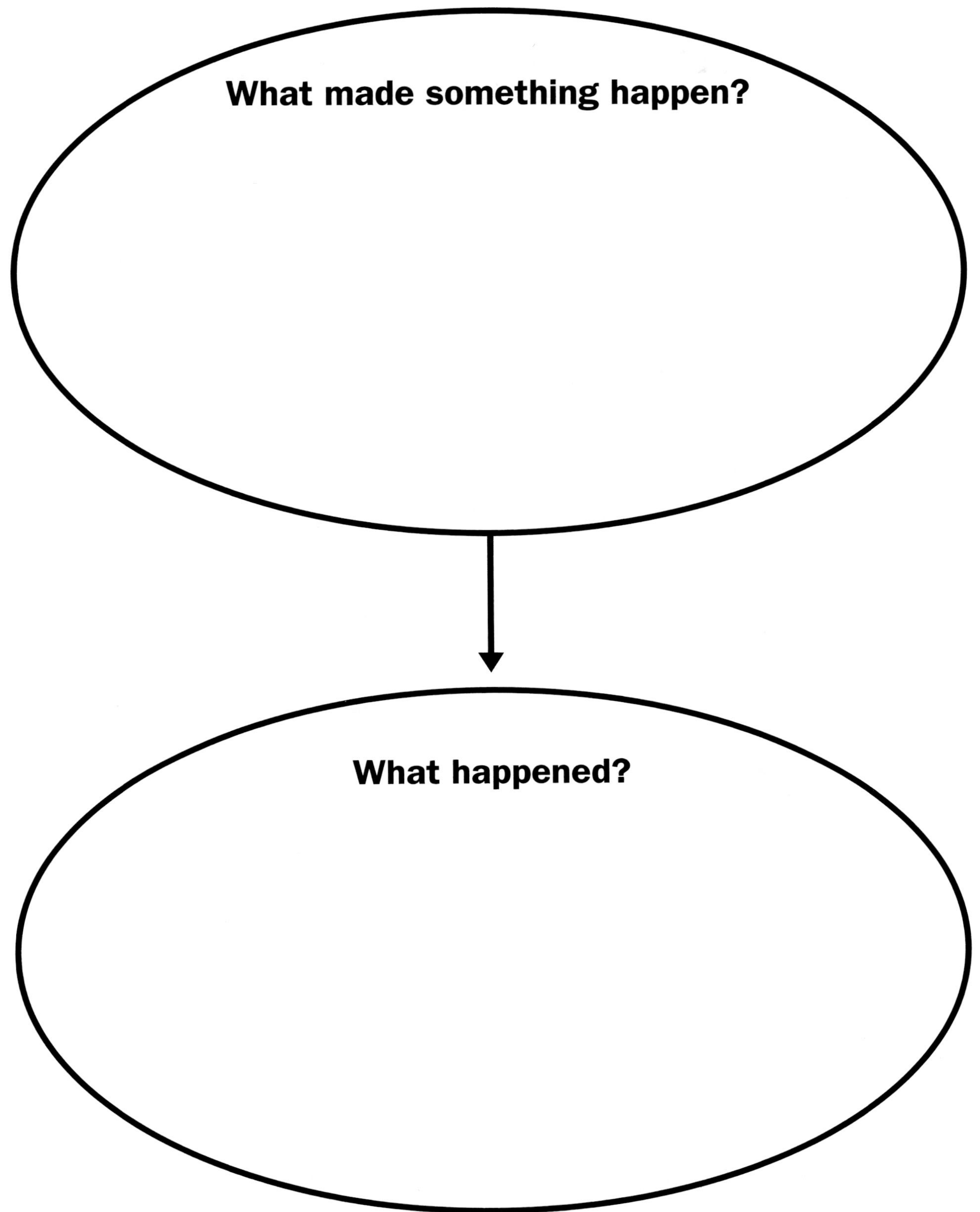
What made something happen?
What happened?

Cause and Effect

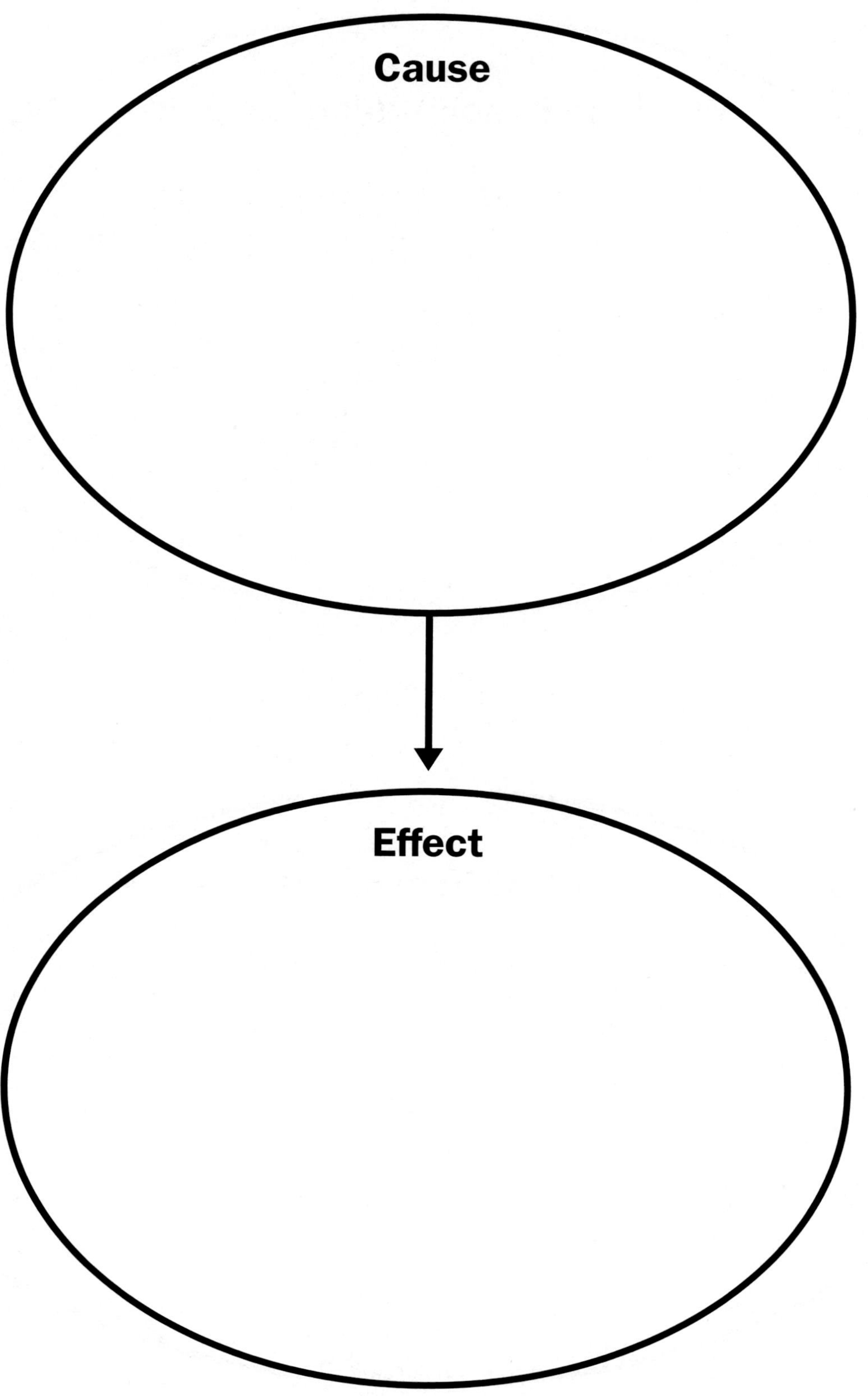

Compare and Contrast (Venn Diagram)

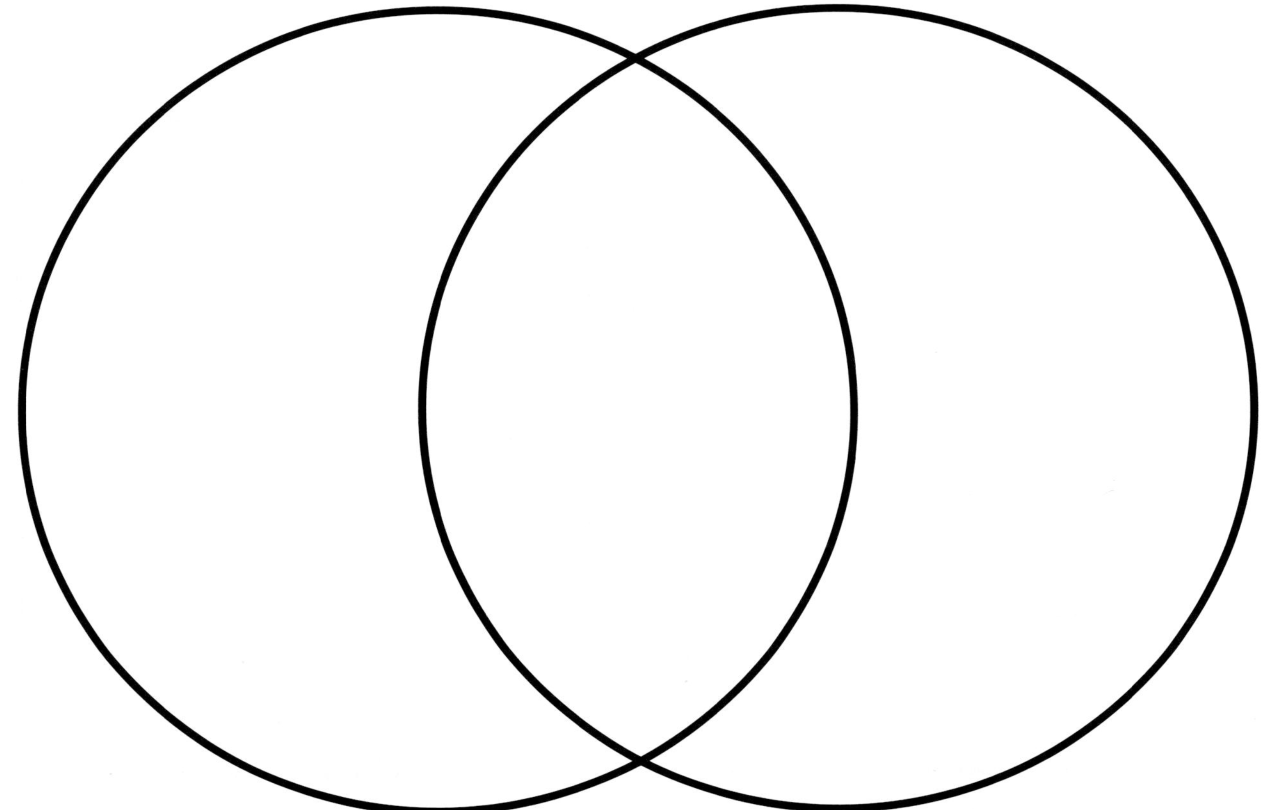

Compare and Contrast

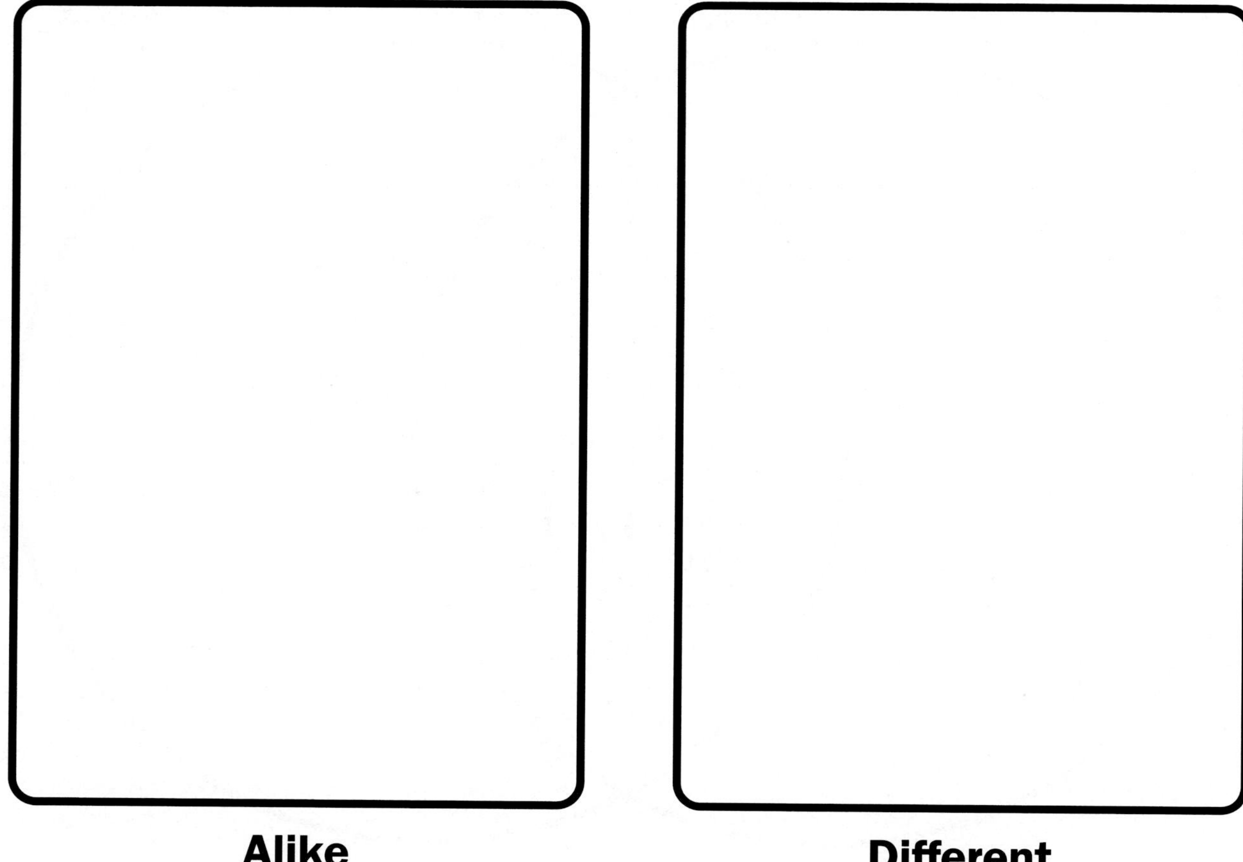

Main Idea and Details

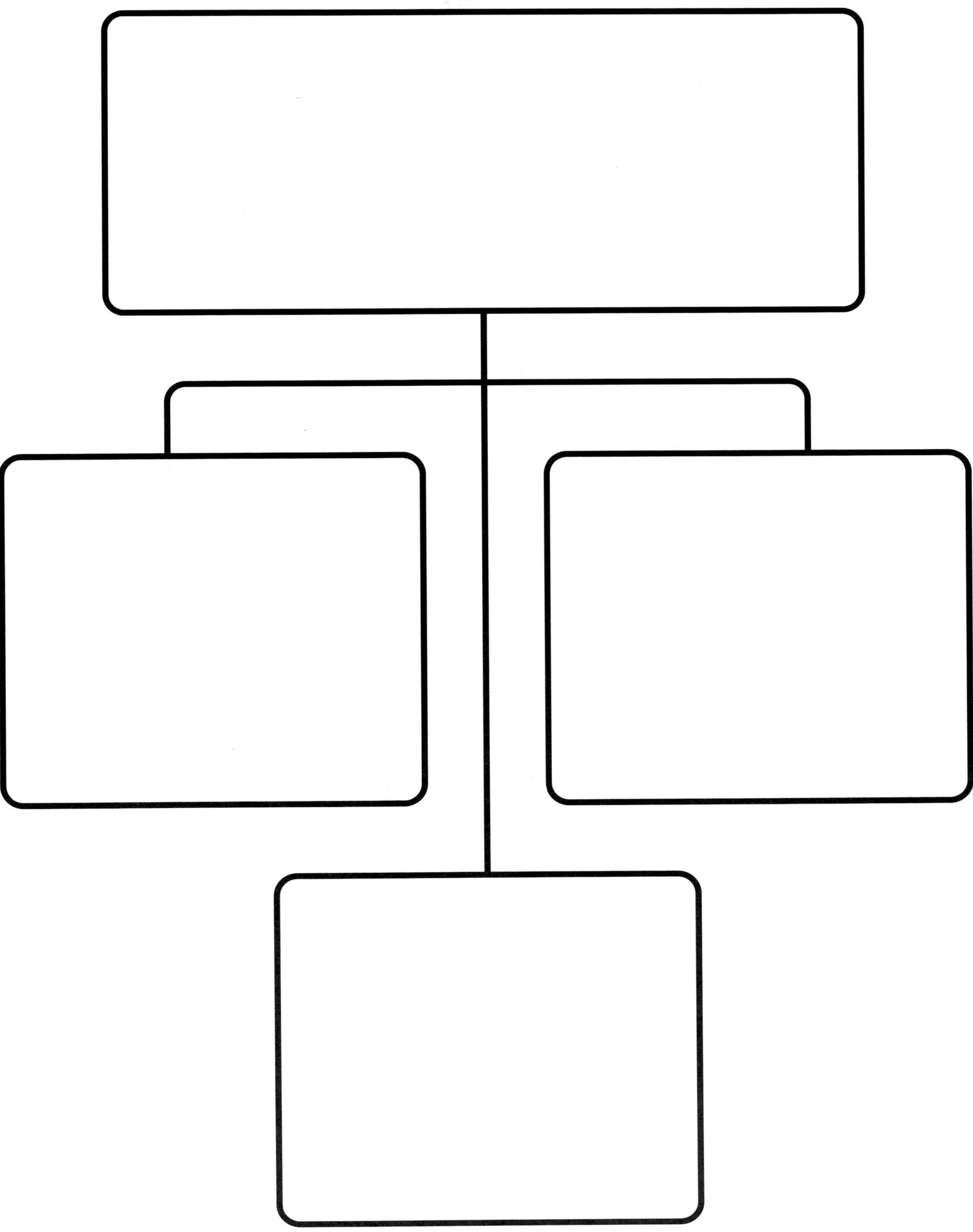

Predict

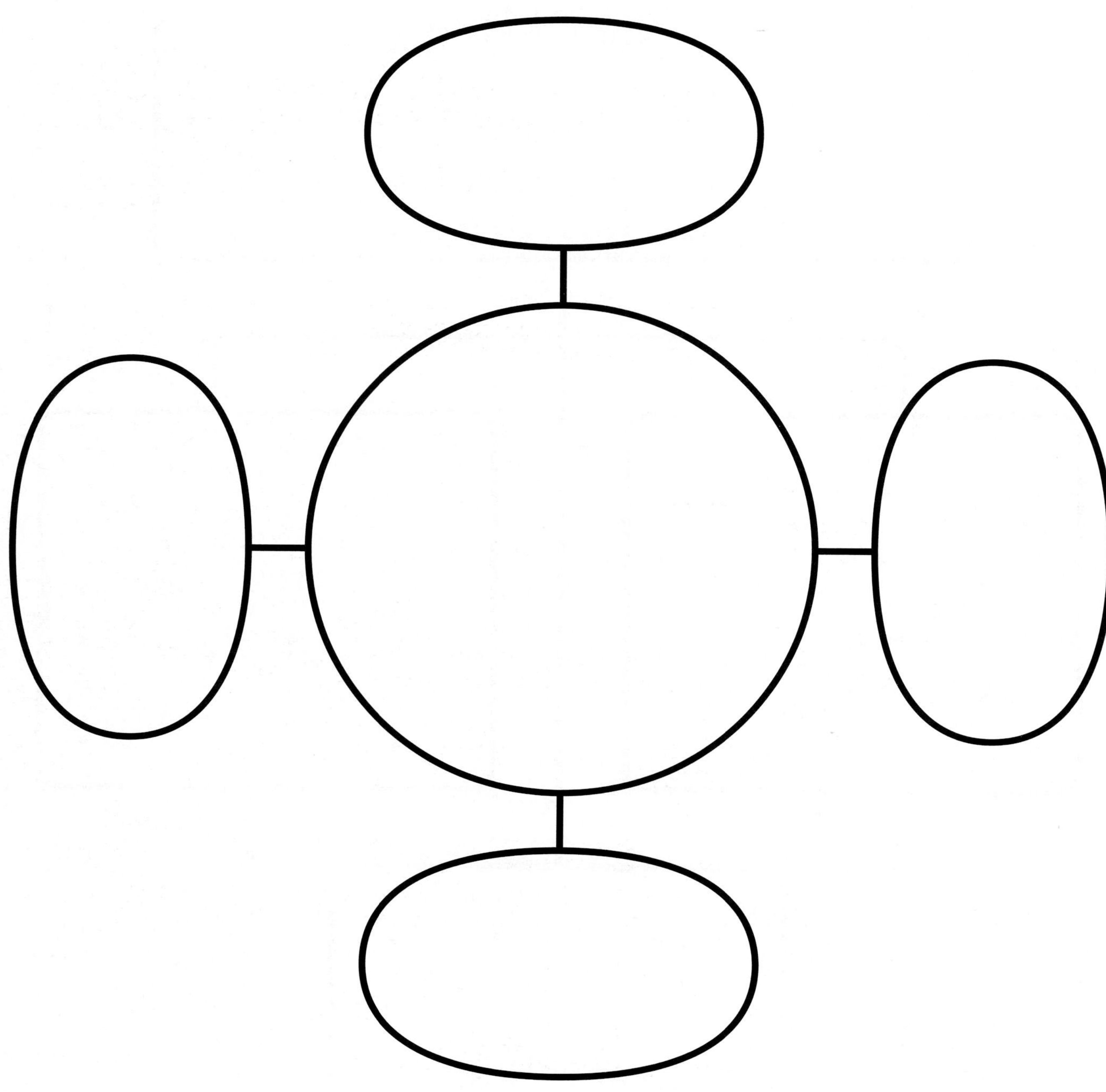

Predict

Graphic Organizers

Recall and Retell

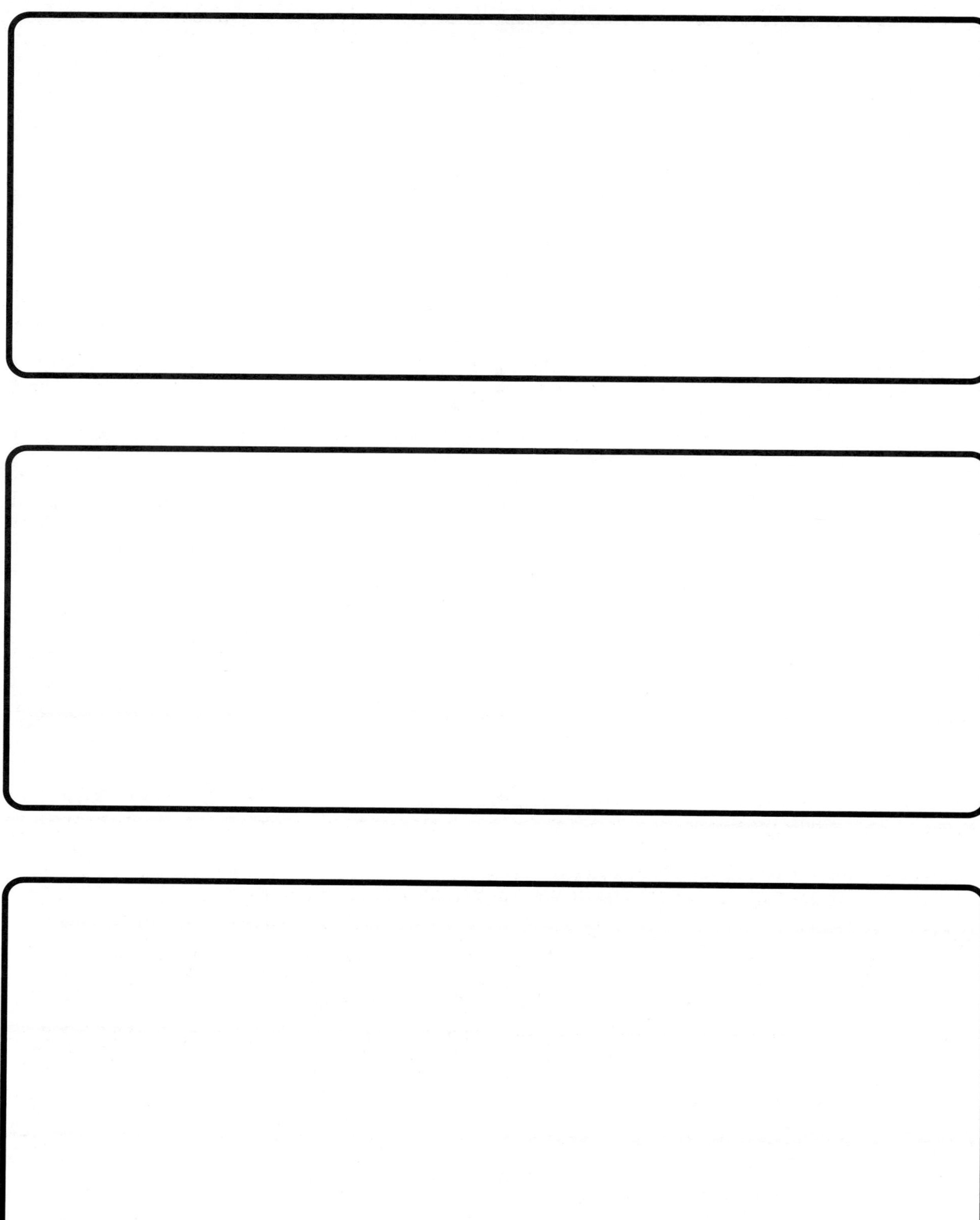

Sequence

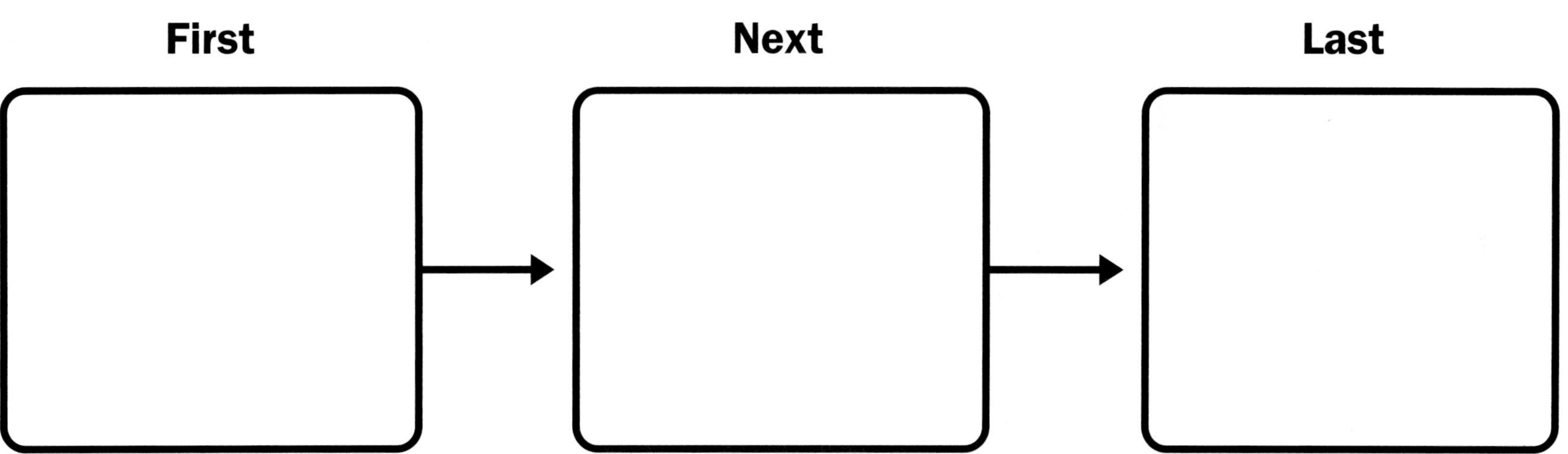

Use a Decision-Making Process

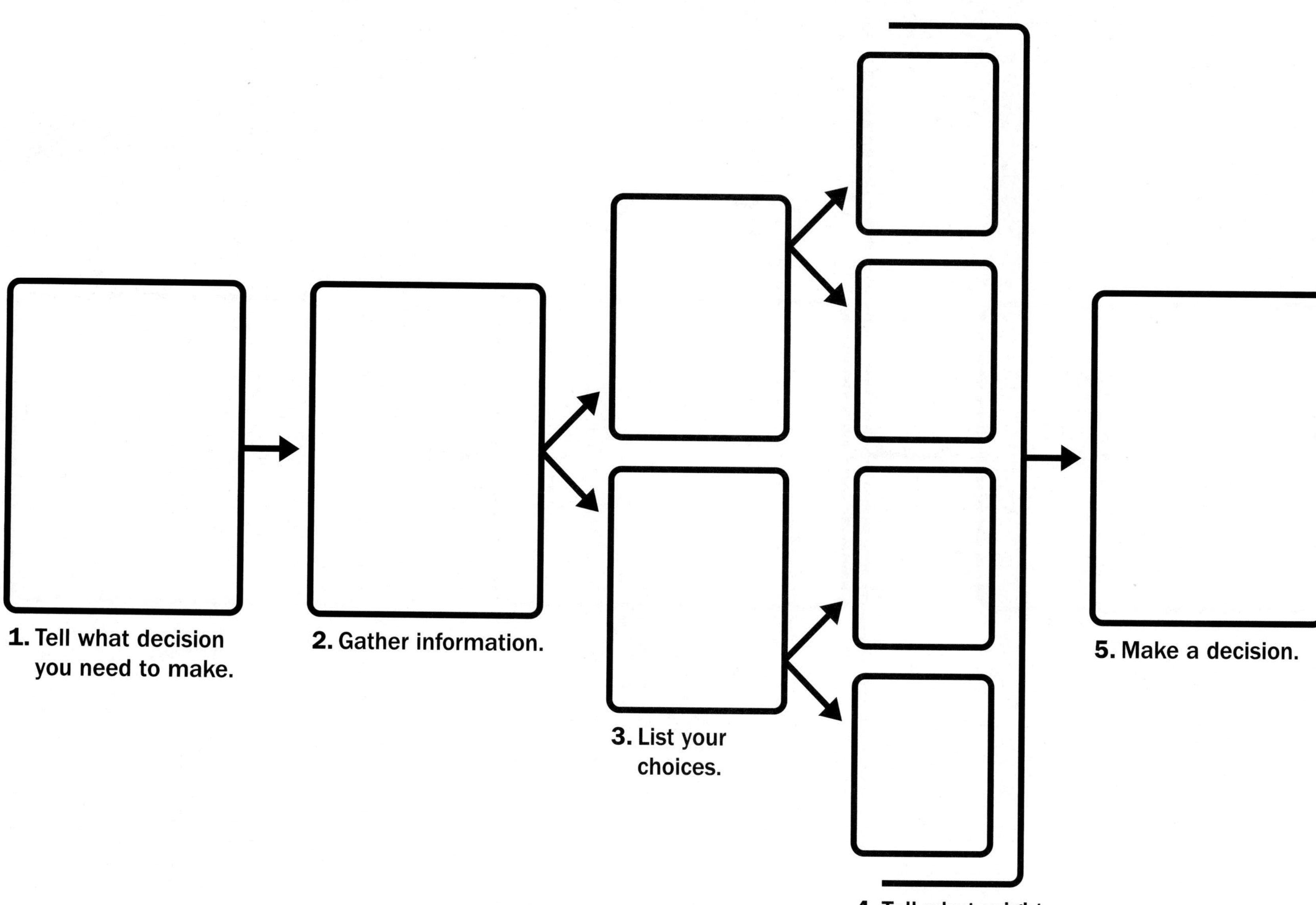

1. Tell what decision you need to make.
2. Gather information.
3. List your choices.
4. Tell what might happen with each choice.
5. Make a decision.

Use a Problem-Solving Process

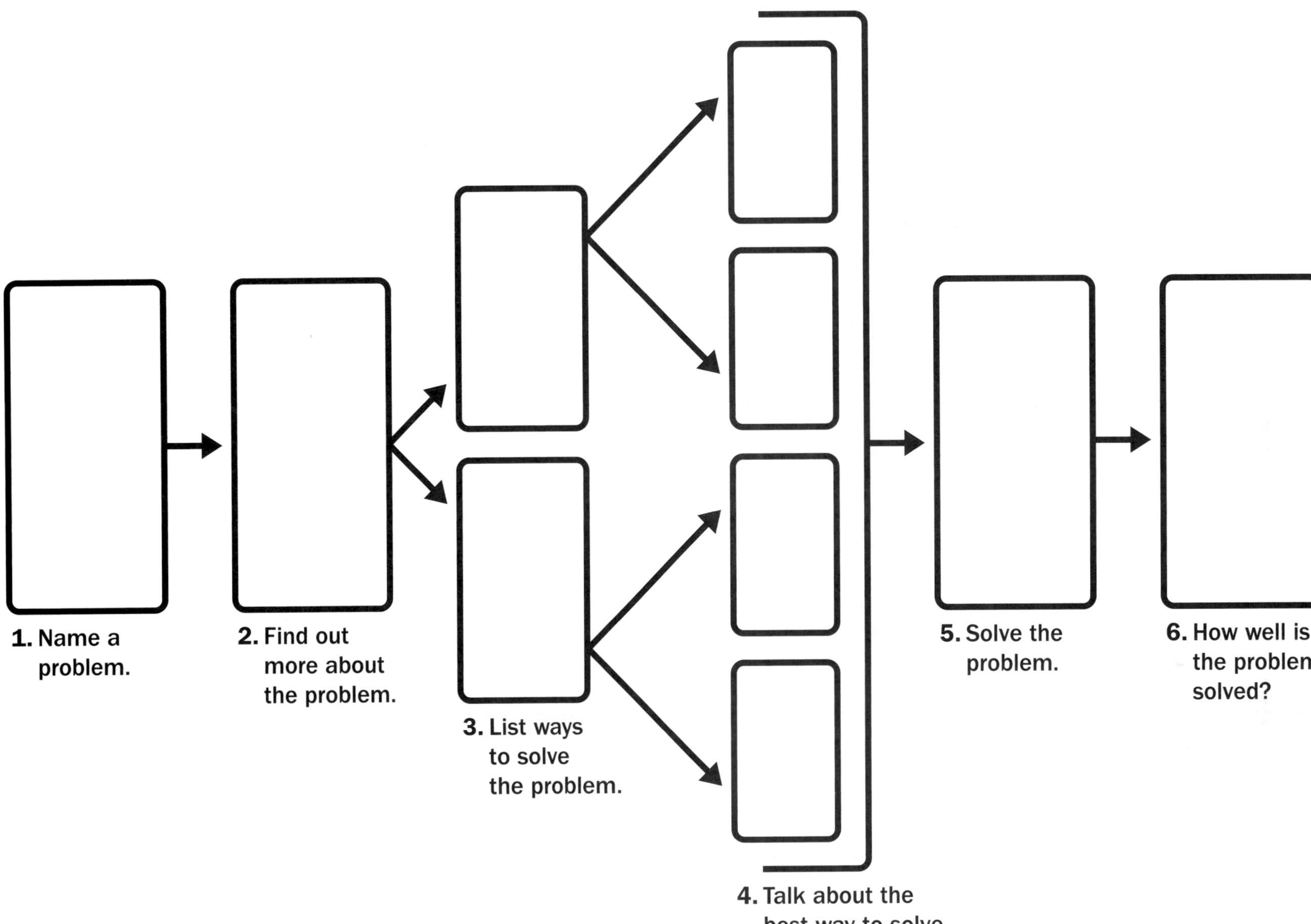
1. Name a problem.
2. Find out more about the problem.
3. List ways to solve the problem.
4. Talk about the best way to solve the problem.
5. Solve the problem.
6. How well is the problem solved?

K-W-L Chart

Topic ______________________________

What We **K**now	What We **W**ant to Know	What We **L**earned

K-W-L Interactive Reading Strategy was developed and is reprinted by permission of Donna Ogle, National-Louis University, Evanston, Illinois.

Unit 1

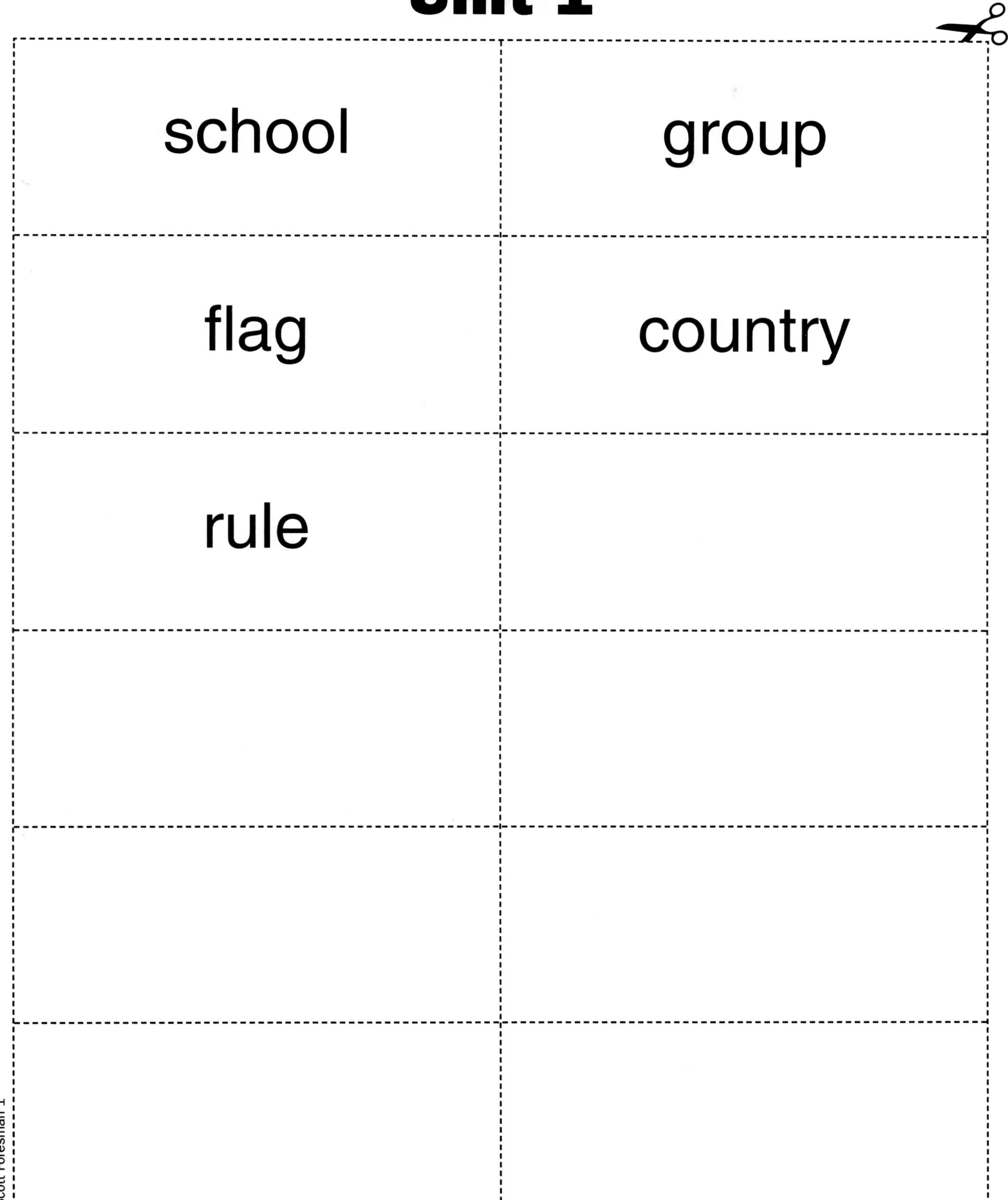

school	group
flag	country
rule	

Vocabulary Words

Unit 2

neighborhood	community
law	leader
state	continent
ocean	

Unit 3

job	needs
wants	tools
goods	service
volunteer	transportation

Vocabulary Words

Unit 4

weather	mountain
plain	lake
river	natural resource
history	

Unit 5

freedom	colony
holiday	President
citizen	vote
capital	

Vocabulary Words

Unit 6

market	communicate
invention	inventor
world	

Dear Family:

Here is what we're learning in Social Studies!

Unit 1 Main Ideas

- ★ A school is a place where people learn.
- ★ In school, people sometimes work together in a group.
- ★ A group is made up of people or things.
- ★ A country is a land where a group of people live.
- ★ The flag of the United States stands for our country.
- ★ A rule tells what to do and what not to do.
- ★ Rules help keep us safe. They also help us treat everyone fairly.

Talk Together

Discuss school with your child. Ask him or her to tell about the teacher, the principal, or other school helpers. Help your child compare and contrast his or her school with the schools he or she learns about in class.

★ Activity ★

Help your child share things he or she does at school.

- ✔ Help your child make a list of things he or she does at school each day.
- ✔ Use a calendar for the current month.
- ✔ Help your child record any special events at school on the calendar.
- ✔ Each day have your child tell you the date and draw a picture of something that he or she did at school that day.

Fast Facts

In 1647, Massachusetts passed a law that required the building of public schools. Every town that had 50 families had to build a school for the children. Usually the school was a wooden building with one large room.

Thank you for supporting your child's Social Studies education!

Family Activities

Estimada familia:

¡Esto es lo que estamos aprendiendo en estudios sociales!

Unidad 1 Ideas principales

★ Una escuela es un lugar donde las personas aprenden.

★ En la escuela, la gente a veces trabaja en grupo.

★ Un grupo se compone de personas o cosas.

★ Un país es la tierra donde vive un grupo de personas.

★ La bandera de los Estados Unidos representa a nuestro país.

★ Una regla establece lo que se debe y no se debe hacer.

★ Las reglas nos ayudan a mantenernos fuera de peligro. También nos ayudan a tratar a los demás de una manera justa.

Para conversar

Hable de la escuela con su niño o niña. Pídale que le hable sobre su maestro o maestra, el director o la directora u otras personas que ayudan en la escuela. Ayúdele a comparar y contrastar su escuela con las escuelas que ha estudiado en clase.

★ Actividad ★

Use un calendario del mes actual.

✔ Ayude a su niño o niña a anotar los eventos especiales de la escuela en el calendario.

✔ Use un calendario del mes en curso.

✔ Ayude a su niño o niña a apuntar eventos especiales de la escuela en el calendario.

✔ Pida a su niño o niña que todos los días le diga la fecha y que dibuje algo que hizo en la escuela ese día.

Datos curiosos

En 1647, en Massachusetts se aprobó una ley que requería la construcción de escuelas públicas. Todos los pueblos con 50 familias tenían que construir una escuela para sus niños. Por lo regular la escuela era un edificio de madera con una sola habitación grande.

¡Gracias por ayudar a su niño o niña con su educación de estudios sociales!

Dear Family:

Here is what we're learning in Social Studies!

Unit 2 Main Ideas

- ★ A neighborhood is a place where people live, work, and play.
- ★ Many homes in a neighborhood have an address with a number and a street name.
- ★ A community is a group of people and the place where they live.
- ★ People in a community can share many different customs.
- ★ A law is a rule that people must obey.
- ★ Laws help keep communities safe and clean.
- ★ A leader helps people decide what to do.
- ★ A state is part of a country.
- ★ A continent is a very large piece of land.
- ★ An ocean is a very large body of salt water.

Talk Together

Ask your child to tell about your neighborhood. Talk about the homes and people in your neighborhood. Draw a small circle inside a large circle. Help your child understand that your neighborhood is part of a community just like the small circle is part of the large circle. Talk about the community where you and your child live.

★ Activity ★

Help your child explore your neighborhood.

- ✔ Take a walk through your neighborhood and help your child name the people and places you see.
- ✔ Ask your child to tell about new buildings or changes you see.

Family Activities

Fast Facts

California has more people than any other state in the United States. Alaska is the largest state in size. Rhode Island has the fewest people and the smallest size of all the states.

Thank you for supporting your child's Social Studies education!

Estimada familia:

¡Esto es lo que estamos aprendiendo en estudios sociales!

Unidad 2 Ideas principales

- ★ Un vecindario es un lugar donde la gente vive, trabaja y juega.
- ★ Muchas de las residencias de un vecindario tienen una dirección con un número y un nombre de calle.
- ★ Una comunidad es un grupo de personas y el lugar donde viven.
- ★ Los habitantes de una comunidad pueden compartir muchas costumbres diferentes.
- ★ Una ley es una regla que las personas deben obedecer.
- ★ Las leyes ayudan a mantener las comunidades limpias y seguras.
- ★ Un líder ayuda a la gente a decidir qué hacer.
- ★ Un estado es una parte de un país.
- ★ Un continente es una extensión de tierra muy grande.
- ★ Un océano es una extensión de agua salada muy grande.

Para conversar

Pida a su niño o niña que le hable de su vecindario. Hable con su niño o niña de las residencias y personas de su vecindario. Tracen un círculo pequeño dentro de un círculo grande. Ayude a su niño o niña a entender que su vecindario es parte de una comunidad del mismo modo que el círculo pequeño es parte del círculo grande. Hablen sobre la comunidad donde usted y su niño o niña viven.

★ Actividad ★

Ayude a su niño o niña a explorar su vecindario.

- ✔ Den un paseo por el vecindario y ayude a su niño o niña a nombrar las personas y lugares que ven.
- ✔ Pida a su niño o niña que le hable de los nuevos edificios o cambios que vean.

Datos curiosos

California es el estado que más habitantes tiene de los Estados Unidos. Alaska es el estado más grande. Rhode Island es el estado más pequeño y con menos habitantes.

¡Gracias por ayudar a su niño o niña con su educación de estudios sociales!

Dear Family:

Here is what we're learning in Social Studies!

Unit 3 Main Ideas

★ A job is the work people do.

★ Needs are things people must have to live. Wants are things people would like to have.

★ Most people work to make money.

★ People can spend or save the money they have.

★ Some workers use tools to grow or make goods.

★ Some workers have service jobs. Some people are volunteers.

★ Transportation moves people and goods from place to place.

Talk Together

Ask your child to tell you about the jobs he or she read about at school. Have your child explain why he or she would or would not like to do each job.

★ Activity ★

Help your child learn about different jobs.

✔ Write the names of jobs on small pieces of paper.

✔ Put the papers in a bag.

✔ Have your child take a paper from the bag, name the job, and tell something about it.

✔ Take turns drawing papers.

Five of the fastest-growing jobs in the early 2000s are:

- *computer engineers—people who design or fix computers or computer software*
- *computer support specialists—people who help you when you have a problem with a computer or computer software*
- *systems analysts—people who study the way something is done on a computer and help find ways to make it better*
- *database administrators—people who work with the information on computer software*
- *desktop publishing specialists—people who use computers to make printed materials*

Thank you for supporting your child's Social Studies education!

Family Activities

Estimada familia

¡Esto es lo que estamos aprendiendo en estudios sociales!

Unidad 3 Ideas principales

- ★ Un empleo es el trabajo que tiene una persona.
- ★ Las necesidades son cosas que la gente debe tener para poder vivir. Los deseos son cosas que a la gente le gustaría tener.
- ★ La mayoría de la gente trabaja para ganar dinero.
- ★ Las personas pueden gastar o ahorrar el dinero que tienen.
- ★ Algunos trabajadores usan herramientas para cultivar, críar o fabricar cosas.
- ★ Algunos trabajadores tienen empleos de servicio. Algunas personas son trabajadores voluntarios.
- ★ El transporte permite llevar personas y mercancías de un lugar a otro.

Para conversar

Pida a su niño o niña que le hable de los empleos sobre los que ha leído en la escuela. Pídale que le explique por qué le gustaría o no tener esos empleos.

★ Actividad ★

Ayude a su niño o niña a explorar el mundo del trabajo.

- ✔ Escriba los nombres de empleos en pequeños pedazos de papel.
- ✔ Ponga los papelitos en una bolsa.
- ✔ Pida a su niño o niña que saque un papelito de la bolsa, lea el nombre del empleo y diga algo sobre éste.
- ✔ Túrnense sacando papelitos.

Datos curiosos

Cinco de los empleos de mayor crecimiento a principios del siglo XXI son:

- *Ingenieros de computadoras—personas que diseñan o arreglan computadoras o software para computadoras*
- *Especialistas de apoyo técnico—personas que ayudan a resolver problemas con una computadora o software de computadora*
- *Analistas de sistemas—personas que estudian la forma en que se hace algo en una computadora y ayudan a encontrar formas de mejorarlo*
- *Administradores de bases de datos—personas que trabajan con la información de software de computadora*
- *Especialistas en autoedición—personas que usan computadoras para hacer materiales impresos*

¡Gracias por ayudar a su niño o niña con su educación de estudios sociales!

Dear Family:

Here is what we're learning in Social Studies!

Unit 4 Main Ideas

★ The weather is how it is outside at a certain place and time.

★ Places on Earth can have different kinds of weather.

★ Earth has different landforms such as mountains, plains, lakes, and rivers.

★ A natural resource is a useful thing that comes from nature.

★ History tells the story of people and places from the past.

★ Follow the 3 R's to reduce, reuse, and recycle natural resources.

Talk Together

Ask your child to tell you things he or she has learned about the Earth and its mountains, lakes, rivers, and plains. Then have him or her describe the weather for the day.

★ Activity ★

Help your child chart the weather.

✔ Make a weather chart for a week.

✔ Draw seven boxes on a sheet of paper and label the days of the week.

✔ Have your child draw a picture to show the weather for each day.

Fast Facts

The highest mountain in the United States is Mount McKinley in Alaska. The lowest place is a desert called Death Valley in California. The deepest lake in the United States is Crater Lake in Oregon. It is located in an inactive volcano. There is an island called Wizard Island in the middle of Crater Lake.

Thank you for supporting your child's Social Studies education!

Family Activities

Estimada familia:

¡Esto es lo que estamos aprendiendo en estudios sociales!

Unidad 4 Ideas principales

- ★ El tiempo es cómo está el clima de un cierto lugar y momento.
- ★ Los lugares de la Tierra pueden tener distintas clases de clima.
- ★ La Tierra tiene accidentes geográficos como montañas, llanuras, lagos y ríos.
- ★ Un recurso natural es una cosa útil que proviene de la naturaleza.
- ★ La historia trata de personas y lugares del pasado.
- ★ Siga las 3 R, para reducir, reutilizar y reciclar recursos naturales.

Para conversar

Pida a su niño o niña que le cuente cosas que haya aprendido sobre la Tierra y sus montañas, lagos, ríos y llanuras. Después pídale que describa el tiempo que hace ese día.

★ Actividad ★

Ayude a su niño o niña a llevar en registro del tiempo que hace.

- ✔ Haga una tabla del clima de una semana.
- ✔ Dibuje siete cuadros en una hoja de papel y escriba los días de la semana.
- ✔ Pida a su niño o niña que haga un dibujo del clima de cada día.

Datos curiosos

La montaña más alta de los Estados Unidos es el monte McKinley de Alaska. El lugar más bajo es un desierto llamado el Valle de la Muerte en California. El lago más profundo de los Estados Unidos es el lago Cráter en Oregón. Está ubicado en un volcán inactivo. Hay una isla llamada Wizard en el medio del lago Cráter.

¡Gracias por ayudar a su niño o niña con su educación de estudios sociales!

Dear Family:

Here is what we're learning in Social Studies!

Unit 5 Main Ideas

- ★ Native Americans were the first people to live in North America.
- ★ Christopher Columbus landed near North America in 1492.
- ★ The Pilgrims came to North America because they wanted the freedom to practice their own religion.
- ★ The Pilgrims lived in colonies. Colonies are places that are ruled by a country that is far away.
- ★ A holiday is a special day when we honor an important person or event.
- ★ The President is our country's leader.
- ★ A capital is a city where important leaders of a state or country live and work.
- ★ A citizen is a member of a state and country.
- ★ Adult citizens in the United States have a right to vote.

Talk Together

Have your child tell you about the first people to live in North America. Then ask your child about Columbus, the Pilgrims, and the early leaders of our country. Name various holidays and have your child tell why we celebrate each holiday.

★ Activity ★

Help your child learn about our country's flag.

- ✔ Use pieces of paper or strips of cloth to make a flag.
- ✔ Help your child make the 13 red and white stripes and the blue section with the 50 stars.
- ✔ You may want to make a flag that has only 13 stars for the original 13 colonies.

Fast Facts

The first capital of the United States was Philadelphia, Pennsylvania. In 1800, Washington, D.C., became the nation's capital. The city was named after George Washington.

Thank you for supporting your child's Social Studies education!

Family Activities

Estimada familia:

¡Esto es lo que estamos aprendiendo en estudios sociales!

Unidad 5 Ideas principales

★ Los indígenas norteamericanos fueron los primeros habitantes de América del Norte.

★ Cristóbal Colón desembarcó cerca de América del Norte en 1492.

★ Los peregrinos llegaron a América del Norte porque querían tener la libertad de practicar su propia religión.

★ Las colonias son lugares gobernados por otro país.

★ Un día festivo es un día especial en el que honramos a una persona o suceso importante.

★ El presidente es una líder de los Estados Unidos.

★ Una capital es una ciudad donde viven y trabajan los líderes importantes de un estado o país.

★ Un ciudadano pertenece a un estado y a un país.

★ Los ciudadanos adultos de los Estados Unidos tienen el derecho a votar.

Para conversar

Pida a su niño o niña que hable sobre los primeros habitantes de América del Norte. Luego pregúntele sobre Colón, los peregrinos y los primeros líderes de los Estados Unidos. Nombre varios días festivos y pida a su niño o niña que le diga por qué se celebra cada día.

★ Actividad ★

Ayude a su niño o niña a aprender cosas sobre la bandera de nuestro país.

✔ Use pedazos de papel o tiras de tela para hacer la bandera de los Estados Unidos.

✔ Ayude a su niño o niña a hacer las 13 franjas rojas y blancas y la sección azul con las 50 estrellas.

✔ Quizás prefieran hacer una bandera con sólo 13 estrellas por las 13 colonias originales.

Datos curiosos

La primera capital de los Estados Unidos fue Filadelfia, Pennsylvania. En 1800, Washington, D.C., se convirtió en la capital de la nación. La ciudad fue nombrada en honor a George Washington.

¡Gracias por ayudar a su niño o niña con su educación de estudios sociales!

Dear Family:

Here is what we're learning in Social Studies!

Unit 6 Main Ideas

- ★ The world is a name for Earth and everything on it.
- ★ A market is a place where goods are sold.
- ★ People who work at a market provide services.
- ★ You communicate when you give and get information.
- ★ An invention is something new.
- ★ An inventor is someone who makes or invents something new.

Talk Together

Ask your child to tell you who invented the printing press and who invented the telephone. Then ask your child who invented the light bulb we use today. Encourage your child to tell about one of the people in the lessons and the important things he or she did.

★ Activity ★

Help your child explore the world.

- ✔ Look at a newspaper with your child.
- ✔ Point to pictures or read aloud the headlines about events around the world.
- ✔ Talk about what is happening and where it is happening.

Fast Facts

The fax machine was invented by Alexander Bain of Scotland more than 150 years ago. Long before fax machines were used in homes and most businesses, they were used by police departments and newspapers.

Thank you for supporting your child's Social Studies education!

Estimada familia:

¡Esto es lo que estamos aprendiendo en estudios sociales!

Unidad 6 Ideas principales

- ★ El mundo es otro nombre para la Tierra y todo lo que hay en ella.
- ★ Un mercado es un lugar donde se vende mercancía.
- ★ La gente que trabaja en un mercado provee servicios.
- ★ Nos comunicamos cuando damos y recibimos información.
- ★ Un invento es algo que no existía antes.
- ★ Un inventor es alguien que hace o inventa algo nuevo.

Para conversar

Pida a su niño o niña que le diga quién invéntó la prensa y quién invéntó el teléfono. Pregunte a su niño o niña quién inventó la bombilla de luz que usamos hoy. Anime a su niño o niña que hable sobre una de las personas que estudió en clase y de las cosas importantes que él o ella hizo.

★ Actividad ★

Ayude a su niño o niña a explorar el mundo.

- ✔ Hojee el periódico con su niño o niña.
- ✔ Señale fotos o lea en voz alta los titulares sobre sucesos mundiales.
- ✔ Hablen de lo que está pasando y dónde está pasando.

Datos curiosos

La máquina de fax fue inventada por Alexander Bain de Escocia hace más de 150 años. Mucho antes de que las máquinas de fax se usaran en el hogar y en muchos negocios, se usaban en departamentos de la policía y en los periódicos.

¡Gracias por ayudar a su niño o niña con su educación de estudios sociales!

ESSENTIAL KNOWLEDGE	K	1	2	3	4	5	6
History							
Understand human influence in shaping communities, states, and nations	★	★	★	★	★	★	★
Contributions of ordinary people	★	★	★	★	★	★	★
Historic figures and their lives		★	★	★	★	★	★
Understand the origins and significance of customs, holidays, celebrations, and landmarks in the community, state, nation, and world	★	★	★	★	★	★	★
Understand the concepts of time and chronology	★	★	★	★	★	★	★
Order of events	★	★	★	★	★	★	★
Past, present, future	★	★	★	★	★	★	★
Political, economic, and social change	★	★	★	★	★	★	★
Cause and effect		★	★	★	★	★	★
Understand how various sources provide information			★	★	★	★	★
Primary sources			★	★	★	★	★
Secondary sources			★	★	★	★	★
Understand how human needs, ideas, issues, and events influence past and present	★	★	★	★	★	★	★
Exploration, colonization, and settlement	★	★	★	★	★	★	★
Conflict and revolution	★	★	★	★	★	★	★
Immigration			★	★	★	★	★
Growth and expansion			★	★	★	★	★
Understand that the past influences the present	★	★	★	★	★	★	★
Connecting past and present	★	★	★	★	★	★	★
Comparing past and present	★	★	★	★	★	★	★
Geography							
Understand concept of location	★	★	★	★	★	★	★
Relative and exact	★	★	★	★	★	★	★
Factors influencing location		★	★	★	★	★	★
Understand concept of place	★	★	★	★	★	★	★
Landforms, bodies of water, vegetation, animal life	★	★	★	★	★	★	★
Climate, weather, and seasonal patterns	★	★	★	★	★	★	★
Understand human-environment interactions	★	★	★	★	★	★	★
Natural resources and land use	★	★	★	★	★	★	★
Human features (housing, roads)	★	★	★	★	★	★	★
Human adaptations to and modifications of their environments		★	★	★	★	★	★
Understand the concept of movement	★	★	★	★	★	★	★
Movement of ideas through cultural sharing	★	★	★	★	★	★	★
Colonization, immigration, settlement patterns (people)		★	★	★	★	★	★
Physical characteristics affect trade (products)			★	★	★	★	★
Physical characteristics affect human activities (culture)			★	★	★	★	★
Understand concept of region		★	★	★	★	★	★
Physical characteristics		★	★	★	★	★	★
Political characteristics			★	★	★	★	★

ESSENTIAL KNOWLEDGE	K	1	2	3	4	5	6
Population characteristics			★	★	★	★	★
Economic characteristics			★	★	★	★	★
Time zones					★	★	★
Understand and use geographic tools to collect, analyze, and interpret information	★	★	★	★	★	★	★
Maps and globes	★	★	★	★	★	★	★
Comparison of world regions and countries		★	★	★	★	★	★
Read, interpret, and construct charts, maps, and diagrams		★	★	★	★	★	★

Economics

ESSENTIAL KNOWLEDGE	K	1	2	3	4	5	6
Understand how scarcity of resources leads to economic choice	★	★	★	★	★	★	★
Basic human needs and wants	★	★	★	★	★	★	★
Goods and services	★	★	★	★	★	★	★
Production, distribution, and consumption	★	★	★	★	★	★	★
Work and income	★	★	★	★	★	★	★
Saving and spending	★	★	★	★	★	★	★
Opportunity cost	★	★	★	★	★	★	★
Understand markets and price	★	★	★	★	★	★	★
Exchange of goods and services	★	★	★	★	★	★	★
Impact of mass production and specialization			★	★	★	★	★
Supply and demand				★	★	★	★
Competition				★	★	★	★
Economic interdependence				★	★	★	★
Imports, exports, and trade				★	★	★	★
Understand economic patterns and systems	★	★	★	★	★	★	★
Effects of transportation and communication	★	★	★	★	★	★	★
Free enterprise			★	★	★	★	★
Entrepreneurship			★	★	★	★	★

Government

ESSENTIAL KNOWLEDGE	K	1	2	3	4	5	6
Understand the purposes of government	★	★	★	★	★	★	★
Promotion of the common good	★	★	★	★	★	★	★
Order and security			★	★	★	★	★
Distribution of services			★	★	★	★	★
Protection of individual rights and freedoms			★	★	★	★	★
Understand the structure of government	★	★	★	★	★	★	★
Purpose of rules and laws	★	★	★	★	★	★	★
Roles and responsibilities of authority figures and public officials	★	★	★	★	★	★	★
Levels of government (local, state, and national)		★	★	★	★	★	★
Government services		★	★	★	★	★	★
Branches of government			★	★	★	★	★
Government documents			★	★	★	★	★
Political parties						★	★
Understand the functions of government	★	★	★	★	★	★	★

ESSENTIAL KNOWLEDGE	K	1	2	3	4	5	6
Making, amending, and removing laws	★	★	★	★	★	★	★
Enforcing laws		★	★	★	★	★	★
Financing of services			★	★	★	★	★
Understand types of governments		★	★	★	★	★	★
Citizenship							
Understand good citizenship	★	★	★	★	★	★	★
Historic figures and ordinary people	★	★	★	★	★	★	★
Citizenship traits (caring, respect, responsibility, fairness, honesty, courage)	★	★	★	★	★	★	★
Working for the common good	★	★	★	★	★	★	★
Believing in truth and justice	★	★	★	★	★	★	★
Treating all people equally	★	★	★	★	★	★	★
Solving problems	★	★	★	★	★	★	★
Making decisions	★	★	★	★	★	★	★
Understand state and national identities	★	★	★	★	★	★	★
Flags, symbols, anthems, pledges	★	★	★	★	★	★	★
Customs and celebrations	★	★	★	★	★	★	★
Mottoes		★	★	★	★	★	★
Understand the freedoms, rights, and responsibilities of citizens		★	★	★	★	★	★
Individual freedoms (choosing your associates, choosing where you live)		★	★	★	★	★	★
Economic freedoms (choosing your own work, owning property)		★	★	★	★	★	★
Political freedoms (joining a political party, running for office, purpose of and need for free elections)		★	★	★	★	★	★
Rights (free speech, voting rights, freedom of religion, equal protection and opportunity under the law)		★	★	★	★	★	★
Responsibilities/ participating, voting		★	★	★	★	★	★
Responsibilities/ keeping informed			★	★	★	★	★
Understand democratic principles		★	★	★	★	★	★
Due process and equal protection under the law				★	★	★	★
Majority rule with minority respect				★	★	★	★
Government by law				★	★	★	★
Culture							
Understand social groups and institutions	★	★	★	★	★	★	★
Family and community	★	★	★	★	★	★	★
Education	★	★	★	★	★	★	★
Religion		★	★	★	★	★	★
Politics			★	★	★	★	★
Understand similarities and differences among people	★	★	★	★	★	★	★
Culture and culture region	★	★	★	★	★	★	★
Language	★	★	★	★	★	★	★
Customs, holidays, and traditions	★	★	★	★	★	★	★
Similarities among diverse groups	★	★	★	★	★	★	★
Contributions of diverse groups	★	★	★	★	★	★	★

Scope and Sequence

ESSENTIAL KNOWLEDGE	K	1	2	3	4	5	6
Understand how the arts express cultural heritage	★	★	★	★	★	★	★
Literature	★	★	★	★	★	★	★
Music, drama, dance	★	★	★	★	★	★	★
Role of writers and artists		★	★	★	★	★	★
Art			★	★	★	★	★
Architecture			★	★	★	★	★
Science, Technology, and Society							
Understand how technology has affected life	★	★	★	★	★	★	★
Tools and appliances	★	★	★	★	★	★	★
Communication	★	★	★	★	★	★	★
Transportation	★	★	★	★	★	★	★
Recreation	★	★	★	★	★	★	★
Work, education, and learning	★	★	★	★	★	★	★
Medicine				★	★	★	★
Understand the significance of the inventions or creations of people in technology	★	★	★	★	★	★	★
Understand the changes brought about by scientific discoveries and technological inventions	★	★	★	★	★	★	★
Predict how future discoveries and innovations could affect life in the United States	★	★	★	★	★	★	★

ESSENTIAL SKILLS	K	1	2	3	4	5	6
Map and Globe Skills							
Understand directions		★	★	★	★	★	★
Cardinal directions		★	★	★	★	★	★
Intermediate directions			★	★	★	★	★
Understand globes	★	★	★	★	★	★	★
Purpose of globe	★	★	★	★	★	★	★
Equator			★	★	★	★	★
Hemispheres				★	★	★	★
Poles				★	★	★	★
Prime meridian/International Date Line				★	★	★	★
Arctic and Antarctic Circles				★	★	★	★
Latitude and longitude				★	★	★	★
Understand, use, and create maps	★	★	★	★	★	★	★
Location of cities, states, countries, continents, oceans	★	★	★	★	★	★	★
Comparison of map with photograph	★	★	★	★	★	★	★
Comparison of map with globe	★	★	★	★	★	★	★
Locator map		★	★	★	★	★	★
Routes and mental mapping		★	★	★	★	★	★
Grids			★	★	★	★	★
Inset maps				★	★	★	★

ESSENTIAL SKILLS	K	1	2	3	4	5	6
Map projections						★	★
Understand and use map symbols	★	★	★	★	★	★	★
Landforms and bodies of water	★	★	★	★	★	★	★
Symbols	★	★	★	★	★	★	★
Key and legend		★	★	★	★	★	★
Direction symbols and compass rose		★	★	★	★	★	★
Borders			★	★	★	★	★
Scale and distance				★	★	★	★
Lines of latitude and longitude					★	★	★
Elevation tints					★	★	★
Understand and use special purpose maps		★	★	★	★	★	★
Historical map		★	★	★	★	★	★
Political map		★	★	★	★	★	★
Physical map			★	★	★	★	★
Climate map				★	★	★	★
Product and resource map				★	★	★	★
Transportation map					★	★	★
Distribution map					★	★	★
Precipitation map					★	★	★
Elevation map					★	★	★
Population map					★	★	★
Population density map					★	★	★
Understand time zones					★	★	★
Understand cartograms							★
Chart and Graph Skills							
Understand charts and graphs	★	★	★	★	★	★	★
Charts	★	★	★	★	★	★	★
Diagrams	★	★	★	★	★	★	★
Calendars and time lines	★	★	★	★	★	★	★
Bar graphs	★	★	★	★	★	★	★
Pie (circle) graphs				★	★	★	★
Line graphs				★	★	★	★
Climographs						★	★
Critical Thinking Skills							
Problem solving	★	★	★	★	★	★	★
Identify a problem	★	★	★	★	★	★	★
Gather information	★	★	★	★	★	★	★
List and consider options	★	★	★	★	★	★	★
Consider advantages and disadvantages	★	★	★	★	★	★	★
Choose and implement a solution	★	★	★	★	★	★	★
Evaluate the effectiveness of a solution	★	★	★	★	★	★	★

Scope and Sequence

ESSENTIAL SKILLS	K	1	2	3	4	5	6
Decision making	★	★	★	★	★	★	★
Identify a situation that requires a decision	★	★	★	★	★	★	★
Gather information	★	★	★	★	★	★	★
Consider the options	★	★	★	★	★	★	★
Predict the consequences	★	★	★	★	★	★	★
Take action	★	★	★	★	★	★	★
Analysis of information	★	★	★	★	★	★	★
Sequence	★	★	★	★	★	★	★
Categorize and classify	★	★	★	★	★	★	★
Compare and contrast	★	★	★	★	★	★	★
Identify main ideas and details	★	★	★	★	★	★	★
Predict		★	★	★	★	★	★
Identify cause-and-effect relationships			★	★	★	★	★
Summarize				★	★	★	★
Generalize				★	★	★	★
Make inferences and draw conclusions				★	★	★	★
Identify different points of view and frames of reference (detection of bias)				★	★	★	★
Fact and opinion				★	★	★	★
Evaluation of arguments and sources				★	★	★	★

Research Skills

	K	1	2	3	4	5	6
Tables and charts	★	★	★	★	★	★	★
Time lines	★	★	★	★	★	★	★
Bar graphs	★	★	★	★	★	★	★
Diagrams		★	★	★	★	★	★
Pie (circle) graphs				★	★	★	★
Line graphs				★	★	★	★
Flowcharts						★	★
Primary and secondary sources	★	★	★	★	★	★	★
Audio and video recordings	★	★	★	★	★	★	★
Art	★	★	★	★	★	★	★
Photographs	★	★	★	★	★	★	★
Biographies, autobiographies, and oral histories	★	★	★	★	★	★	★
Internet	★	★	★	★	★	★	★
Computer software	★	★	★	★	★	★	★
Artifacts and historical records		★	★	★	★	★	★
Atlases and gazetteers		★	★	★	★	★	★
News sources and current events		★	★	★	★	★	★
Speeches				★	★	★	★
Encyclopedias				★	★	★	★
Dictionaries and thesauruses				★	★	★	★
Almanacs				★	★	★	★

ESSENTIAL SKILLS	K	1	2	3	4	5	6
Political cartoons						★	★
Use appropriate math skills to interpret maps and graphs		★	★	★	★	★	★
Reading Skills							
Vocabulary	★	★	★	★	★	★	★
Context clues (synonym, antonym, definition)	★	★	★	★	★	★	★
Abbreviations and acronyms		★	★	★	★	★	★
Classification and categorization of words		★	★	★	★	★	★
Multiple meanings		★	★	★	★	★	★
Dictionary and glossary			★	★	★	★	★
Gazetteer				★	★	★	★
Comprehension	★	★	★	★	★	★	★
Order	★	★	★	★	★	★	★
Picture clues	★	★	★	★	★	★	★
Sequence	★	★	★	★	★	★	★
Compare and contrast	★	★	★	★	★	★	★
Use of visuals (pictures, maps, time lines, graphs, charts, models, graphic organizers)	★	★	★	★	★	★	★
Recall and retell	★	★	★	★	★	★	★
Main idea and details		★	★	★	★	★	★
Picture analysis		★	★	★	★	★	★
Prediction		★	★	★	★	★	★
Understand and use graphic and typographical features (boldface, headings, captions, phonetic respellings)		★	★	★	★	★	★
Summarize a chapter or section		★	★	★	★	★	★
Context clues			★	★	★	★	★
Understand and use book parts (table of contents, glossary, atlas, gazetteer, index, bibliography, appendices)			★	★	★	★	★
Scan for specific facts or ideas				★	★	★	★
Understand and use textbook study features (prereading questions, preview and focus statements, summary statements, postreading questions)				★	★	★	★
Make outlines				★	★	★	★
Cause and effect				★	★	★	★
Drawing conclusions				★	★	★	★
Summarize				★	★	★	★
Understand characteristics of text types (autobiography, biography, essay, expository, historical fiction, informational, journal/diary, legend, letter, narrative, poetry, speech)				★	★	★	★
Generalize					★	★	★
Take notes					★	★	★
Speaking and Listening							
Understand and use speaking and listening skills	★	★	★	★	★	★	★
Dramatization	★	★	★	★	★	★	★
Song	★	★	★	★	★	★	★
Poems	★	★	★	★	★	★	★

Scope and Sequence

ESSENTIAL SKILLS	K	1	2	3	4	5	6
Stories	★	★	★	★	★	★	★
Oral directions	★	★	★	★	★	★	★
Interviews		★	★	★	★	★	★
Debates				★	★	★	★
Use standard grammar and sentence structure				★	★	★	★
Oral reports						★	★
Writing Skills							
Understand forms of writing	★	★	★	★	★	★	★
Descriptive	★	★	★	★	★	★	★
Narrative	★	★	★	★	★	★	★
Expository		★	★	★	★	★	★
Persuasive				★	★	★	★
Understand and use writing skills and processes	★	★	★	★	★	★	★
Lists	★	★	★	★	★	★	★
Captions and labels	★	★	★	★	★	★	★
Use standard grammar, spelling, sentence structure, and punctuation	★	★	★	★	★	★	★
Report		★	★	★	★	★	★
Letter		★	★	★	★	★	★
Collect, organize, and record information		★	★	★	★	★	★
Identify and use reliable sources		★	★	★	★	★	★
Use multimedia tools		★	★	★	★	★	★
Journal/diary			★	★	★	★	★
Essay				★	★	★	★
Research paper				★	★	★	★
Summary				★	★	★	★
News report and feature story				★	★	★	★
Editorials and opinion articles				★	★	★	★
Biography and autobiography						★	★
Speech						★	★
Bibliography						★	★
Historical fiction						★	★
Legend						★	★

Unit 1 Bibliography

Froggy Goes to School, by Jonathan London and Frank Remkiewicz (illustrator), (Puffin, ISBN 0-14-056247-8, 1998) **Easy**

My First Day of School, by Patrick K. Hallinan (Hambleton-Hill; ISBN 1-57102-154-X, 2000) **Easy**

My Teacher Sleeps in School, by Leatie Weiss and Ellen Weiss (illustrator), (Econo-Clad Books, ISBN 0-808-57413-2, 1999) **Easy**

AWARD *Owen*, by Kevin Henkes (Greenwillow, ISBN 0-688-11449-0, 1993) **Easy** ***Caldecott Honor Book, 1994***

School from A to Z, by Bobbie Kalman (Crabtree Publishing, ISBN 0-86505-418-5, 1999) **Easy**

See You Tomorrow, Charles, by Miriam Cohen and Lillian Hoban (illustrator), (Bantam Books, ISBN 0-440-41151-3, 1997) **Easy**

Double Trouble in Walla Walla, by Andrew Clements and Sal Murdocca (illustrator), (Millbrook Press, ISBN 0-7613-0275-1, 1997) **On-Level**

AWARD *Lilly's Purple Plastic Purse*, by Kevin Henkes (Greenwillow, ISBN 0-688-12897-1, 1996) **On-Level** ***ALA Notable Book, 1997***

No Good in Art, by Miriam Cohen and Lillian Hoban (illustrator), (Morrow, ISBN 0-688-84234-8, 1980) **On-Level**

Rex and Lilly Schooltime, by Laurene Krasny Brown and Marc Brown (illustrator), (Little Brown, ISBN 0-316-10920-7, 1997) **On-Level**

When Jo Louis Won the Title, by Belinda Rochelle and Larry Johnson (illustrator), (Houghton Mifflin, ISBN 0-395-81657-2, 1996) **On-Level**

Yoko, by Rosemary Wells (Hyperion Press, ISBN 0-7868-0395-9, 1998) **On-Level**

Marianthe's Story: Painted Words, Spoken Memories, by Aliki (Greenwillow, ISBN 0-688-15661-4, 1998) **Challenge**

Mary McLeod Bethune, by Eloise Greenfield (Harper Trophy, ISBN 0-064-46168-8, 1994) **Challenge**

More Than Anything Else, by Marie Bradby and Chris Soentpiet (illustrator), (Orchard Books, ISBN 0-531-09464-2, 1995) **Challenge**

Nobody's Mother Is in Second Grade, by Robin Pulver and G. Brian Karas (illustrator), (Dial Books for Young Readers, ISBN 0-8037-1210-3, 1992) **Challenge**

Story of Ruby Bridges, The, by Robert Coles (Scholastic, ISBN 0-590-57281-4, 1995) **Challenge**

AWARD *Toll-Bridge Troll, The*, by Patricia Rae Wolff and Kimberly Bulcken Root (illustrator), (Voyager Picture Book, ISBN 0-152-02105-1, 2000) **Challenge** ***ALA Notable Book, 1996***

AWARD *Virgie Goes to School with Us Boys*, by Elizabeth Fitzgerald Howard and E. B. Lewis (illustrator), (Simon & Schuster, ISBN 0-689-80076-2, 2000) **Challenge** ***ALA Notable Book, 2001***

Bringing History Home, by M. Gail Hickey (Allyn & Bacon, ISBN 0-205-28169-9, 1998) **Teacher Reference**

Hands Around the World, by Susan Milord (Williamson, ISBN 0-913-58965-9, 1992) **Teacher Reference**

Through My Eyes, by Ruby Bridges (Scholastic, ISBN 0-590-18923-9, 1999) **Teacher Reference**

AWARD Look for this symbol throughout the Teacher's Edition to find **Award-Winning Selections**.

Unit 2 Bibliography

Carpenters, by Vicky Franchino (Compass Point Books, ISBN 0-756-50006-0, 2000) **Easy**

Fire Fighters, by Lucia Raatma (Compass Point Books, ISBN 0-756-50009-5, 2000) **Easy**

Letter Carriers, by Alice K. Flanagan (Compass Point Books, ISBN 0-756-50010-9, 2000) **Easy**

Mayors, by Alice K. Flanagan (Compass Point Books, ISBN 0-756-50064-8, 2001) **Easy**

My Town, by Rebecca Treays (EDC, ISBN 0-746-03079-7, 1998) **Easy** ***Notable Social Studies Book, 1999***

Officer Buckle and Gloria, by Peggy Rathmann (Putnam, ISBN 0-399-22616-8, 1995) **Easy** ***Caldecott Medal 1996***

Police Officers, by Alice K. Flanagan (Compass Point Books, ISBN 0-756-50011-7, 2000) **Easy**

As the Roadrunner Runs: A First Book of Maps, by Gail Hartman (Bradbury, ISBN 0-02-743092-8, 1994) **On-Level**

Aurora Means Dawn, by Scott Russell Sanders and Jill Kastner (illustrator), (Aladdin, ISBN 0-689-81907-2, 1998) **On-Level**

City Mouse—Country Mouse and Two More Mouse Tales from Aesop by John C. Wallner (illustrator), (Scholastic, ISBN 0-590-41155-1, 1987) **On-Level**

Home Album, A, by Peter and Connie Roop (Heineman, ISBN 1-57572-602-5, 1998) **On-Level**

How to Make an Apple Pie and See the World, by Marjorie Priceman (Alfred A. Knopf, ISBN 0-673-61098-5, 1994) **On-Level**

Little House, The, by Virginia Lee Burton (Turtleback, ISBN 0-606-01531-0, 1969) ***Caldecott Medal, 1943*** **On-Level**

Me on the Map, by Joan Sweeney and Annette Cable (illustrator), (Dragonfly, ISBN 0-517-88557-3, 1998) **On-Level**

My New York, by Kathy Jakobsen (Little Brown, ISBN 0-316-45653-5) **On-Level**

Philharmonic Gets Dressed, The, by Karla Kuskin (HarperCollins, ISBN 0-06-443124-X, 1986) **On-Level**

Raising Yoder's Barn, by Jane Yolen and Bernie Fuchs (illustrator), (Little Brown, ISBN 0-316-96887-0, 1998) **On-Level**

Uptown, by Bryan Collier (Henry Holt, ISBN 0-805-05721-8, 2000) **On-Level** ***Coretta Scott King Award***

Wee Sing Around the World, by Pamela Conn Beall and Susan Hagen Nipp (Penguin Putnam, ISBN 0-8431-3740-1) **On-Level**

Where I Live, by Christopher Wormell (Dial, ISBN 0-8037-2056-4,1996) **On-Level**

Journey, The, by Sarah Stewart and David Small (illustrator), (Farrar Straus & Giroux, ISBN 0-374-33905-8, 2001) **Challenge**

Miss Rumphius, by Barbara Cooney (Viking, ISBN 0-140-50539-3, 1985) **Challenge** ***Notable Social Studies Book***

New Coat for Anna, A, by Harriet Ziefert and Anita Lobel (illustrator), (Econo-Clad Books, ISBN 0-833-51245-5, 1999) **Challenge**

Smoky Night, by Eve Bunting and David Diaz (illustrator), (Harcourt Brace, ISBN 0-152-01884-0, 1999) **Challenge** ***Caldecott Medal***

Urban Roosts: Where Birds Nest in the City, by Barbara Bash (Little Brown, ISBN 0-316-08312-7, 1992) **Challenge**

Window, by Jeannie Baker (Greenwillow, ISBN 0-688-08918-6, 1991) **Challenge**

Mapmaking with Children, by David Sobel (Heinemann, ISBN 0-325-00042-5, 1998) **Teacher Reference**

Look for this symbol throughout the Teacher's Edition to find **Award-Winning Selections.**

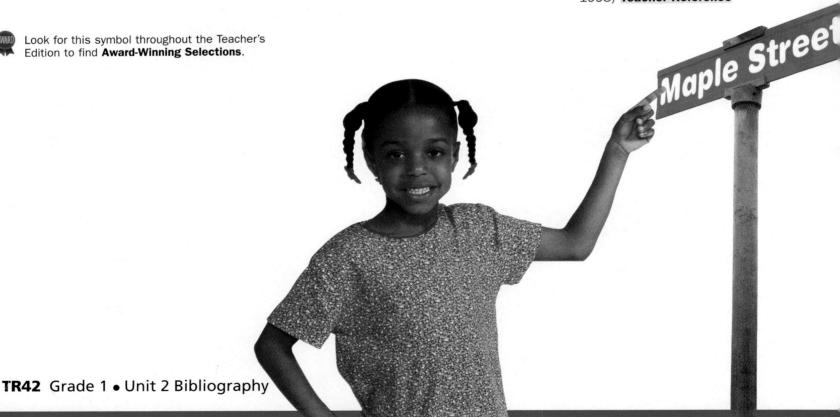

Unit 3 Bibliography

Career Day, by Anne F. Rockwell (HarperCollins Children's Book Group, ISBN 0-06-027565-0, 2000) **Easy**

Cowboy Bunnies, by Christine Loomis (Putnam, ISBN 0-399-22625-7, 1997) **Easy**

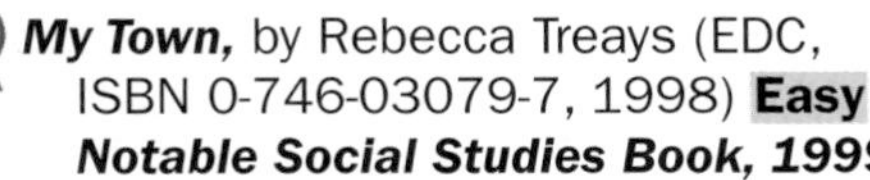

My Town, by Rebecca Treays (EDC, ISBN 0-746-03079-7, 1998) **Easy** ***Notable Social Studies Book, 1999***

Sam and the Lucky Money, by Karen Chinn (Lee and Low, ISBN 1-880-00013-X, 1995) **Easy**

3 Pigs Garage, by Peter Lippman (Workman Publishing International Ltd., ISBN 0-7611-1361-4, 1998) **Easy**

Trucks That Build, by Lars Klove (Simon & Schuster, ISBN 0-68-98176-22, 1999) **Easy**

Buzby, by Julia Hoban and John Himmelman (illustrator), (Harper Audio, ISBN 0-694-70044-4, 1996) **On-Level**

Dancin' in the Kitchen, by Wendy Gelsanliter and Frank Christian (Putnam, ISBN 0-399-23035-1, 1998) **On-Level**

Dream Jar, The, by Bonnie Pryor (Morrow, ISBN 0-688-13062-3, 1996) **On-Level**

Jamal's Busy Day, by Wade Hudson and George Ford (illustrator), (Just Us Books, ISBN 0-940975-21-1, 1991) **On-Level**

Little Red Hen (Makes a Pizza), The, by Philemon Sturges (Dutton, ISBN 0-525-45953-7, 1999) **On-Level**

Night Worker, The, by Katie Banks and Georg Hallensleben (illustrator), (Farrar Straus & Giroux, ISBN 0-374-35520-7, 2000) **On-Level** ***2001 Charlotte Zolotow Award, An ALA Notable Children's Book***

Tight Times, by Barbara Shook Hazen and Trina Shart Hyman (illustrator), (Viking, ISBN 0-140-504427-7, 1983) **On-Level**

Window Music, by Anastasia Sven (Viking, ISBN 0-670-87287-3, 1998) **On-Level**

Work Song, by Gary Paulsen (Harcourt Brace, ISBN 0-152-00980-9, 1997) **On-Level**

Animal Rescue: The Best Job There Is, by Susan E. Goodman (Simon & Schuster, ISBN 0-689-81794-0, 2000) **Challenge**

Boy Who Loved to Draw, Benjamin West, The, by Barbara Brenner (Houghton Mifflin, ISBN 0-395-85050-0, 1999) **Challenge** ***Notable Social Studies Trade Book, 2000***

Magic School Bus Gets Programmed, by Joanna Cole (Scholastic Books, ISBN 0-590-18731-7, 1999) **Challenge**

Mama & Papa Have a Store, by Amelia Lau Carling (Dial Books for Young Readers, ISBN 0-8037-2044-0, 1998) **Challenge** ***Pura Belpré Honor, 2000***

Weed Is a Flower: The Life of George Washington Carver, A, by Aliki (Aladdin, ISBN 0-671-66490-5, 1988) **Challenge**

Steven Caney's Kids' America, by Steven Caney (Workman, ISBN 0-911-10480-1, 1978) **Teacher Reference**

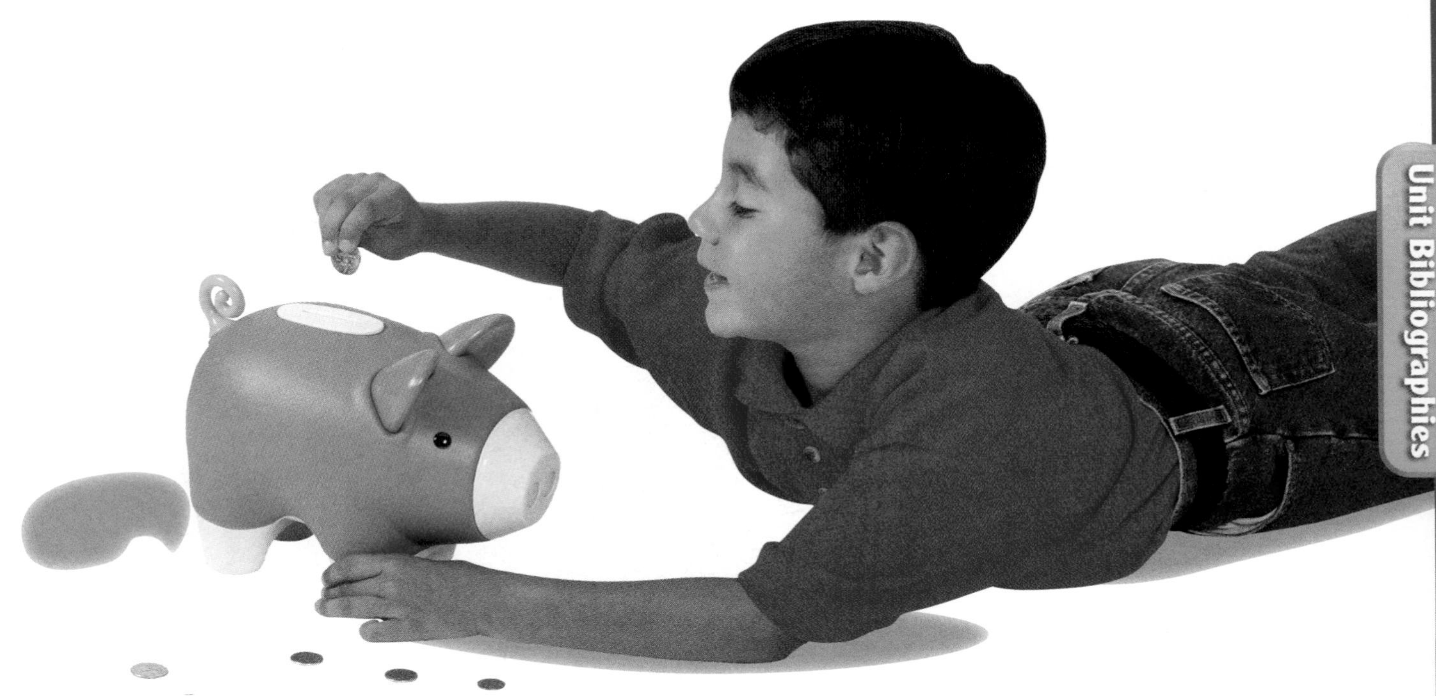

Look for this symbol throughout the Teacher's Edition to find **Award-Winning Selections**.

Unit 4 Bibliography

Big Blue Whale, by Nicola Davies and Nick Maland (illustrator), (Candlewick, ISBN 1-564-402895-X, 1997) **Easy**

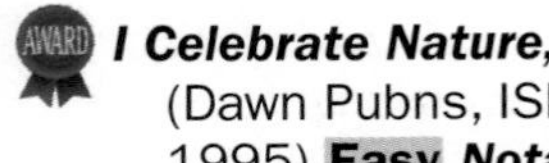

I Celebrate Nature, by Diane Iverson (Dawn Pubns, ISBN 1-883-22000-9, 1995) **Easy** ***Notable Social Studies Book***

I Took a Walk, by Henry Cole (Greenwillow, ISBN 0-688-15115-9, 1998) **Easy**

Morning, Noon, and Night, by Jean Craighead George and Wendell Minor (illustrator), (HarperCollins, ISBN 0-060-23628-0, 1999) **Easy**

This Is the Way We Go to School, by Edith Baer (Scholastic Trade, ISBN 0-590-43162-5, 1992) **Easy**

Whatever the Weather, by Karen Wallace (DK, ISBN 0-789-44750-9, 1999) **Easy**

Backyard, by Donald M. Silver and Patricia J. Wynne (illustrator), (McGraw-Hill, ISBN 0-070-57930-X, 1997) **On-Level**

Birdsong, by Audrey Wood and Robert Florczak (illustrator), (Voyager, ISBN 0-152-02419-0, 2001) **On-Level** ***Notable Social Studies Book***

Bob's Recycling Day, by Annie Auerbach (Simon Spotlight, ISBN: 0-689-84379-8, 2001) **On-Level**

Ecoart!: Earth-Friendly Art & Craft Experiences for 3–9-Year-Olds, by Laurie Carlson (Williamson Publishing, ISBN 0-913-58968-3, 1992) **On-Level**

Great Kapok Tree: A Tale of the Amazon Rain Forest, The, by Lynne Cherry (Voyager Picture Book, ISBN 0-152-02614-2, 2000) **On-Level**

Legend of the Bluebonnet, The, by Tomie DePaola (Putnam Pub Group Juv, ISBN 0-399-20937-9, 1986) **On-Level**

Picture Book of Sacagawea, A, by David A. Adler and Dan Brown (illustrator), (Holiday House, ISBN 0-823-41485-X, 2000) **On-Level**

Tell Me a Season, by Mary McKenna Siddals (Clarion Books, ISBN 0-395-71021-9, 1997) **On-Level**

Where Once There Was a Wood, by Denise Fleming (Henry Holt, ISBN 0-805-06482-6, 2000) **On-Level** ***Notable Social Studies Book***

Storm Book, The, by Charlotte Zolotow (HarperTrophy, ISBN 0-064-43194-0, 1989) **Challenge**

Sunflower Garden, by Janice May Udry (Harvey House, ISBN 0-817-84471-6, 1969) **Challenge**

Turtle Bay, by Saviour Pirotta and Nilesh Mistry (illustrator), (Farrar Straus & Giroux, ISBN 0-374-37888-6, 1997) **Challenge** ***Notable Social Studies Book***

Where Does the Garbage Go?, by Paul Showers and Randy and Paul Chewning (illustrators), (HarperCollins, ISBN 0-064-45114-3, 1994) **Challenge**

Mapmaking with Children: Sense of Place Education for the Elementary Years, by David Sobel (Heinemann, ISBN 0-325-00042-5, 1998) **Teacher Reference**

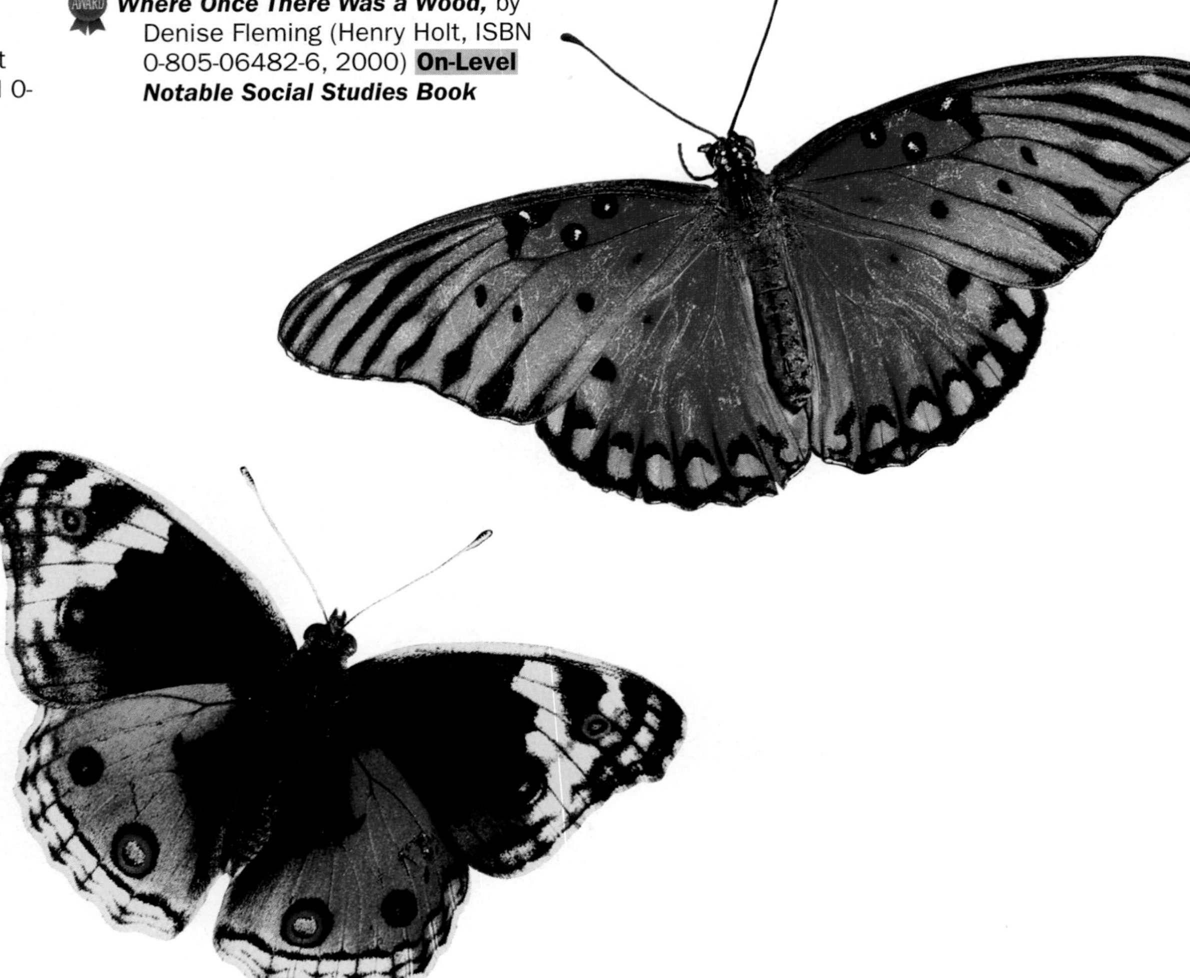

Look for this symbol throughout the Teacher's Edition to find **Award-Winning Selections**.

Unit 5 Bibliography

Cheyenne Again, by Eve Bunting and Irving Toddy (illustrator), (Clarion Books, ISBN 0-395-70364-6, 1995) **Easy**

First Thanksgiving Feast, by Joan Anderson and George Ancona (photographer), (Clarion Books, ISBN 0-395-51886-5, 1989) **Easy**

George, the Drummer Boy, by Nathaniel Benchley and Don Bolognese (illustrator), (HarperCollins Children's Books, ISBN 0-060-20501-6, 1977) **Easy**

Hooray for the Fourth of July, by Wendy Watson (Houghton Mifflin, ISBN 0-618-04036-6, 2000) **Easy**

I Have Heard of a Land, by Joyce Carol Thomas and Floyd Cooper (illustrator), (HarperCollins, ISBN 0-0644-3617-9, 2000) **Easy** ***ALA Notable, Coretta Scott King Honor Book, Notable Social Studies Book***

Ox-Cart Man, by Donald Hall and Barbara Cooney (illustrator), (Puffin, ISBN 0-140-50441-9, 1983) **Easy** ***Caldecott Medal, 1980***

T Is for Texas, by Anne Bustard (Voyageur, ISBN 0-896-58113-6, 1989) **Easy**

To Be a Drum, by Evelyn Coleman and Aminah Brenda Lynn Robinson (illustrator), (Albert Whitman, ISBN 0-807-58007-4, 2000) **Easy**

Working Cotton, by Sherley Anne Williams and Carole Byard (illustrator), (Voyager, ISBN 0-152-01482-9, 1997) **Easy** ***Caldecott Honor Award, Coretta Scott King Honor Book***

Boston Coffee Party, The, by Doreen Rappaport and Emily Arnold McCully (illustrator), (HarperTrophy, ISBN 0-064-44141-5, 1990) **On-Level**

Dakota Dugout, by Ann Warren Turner and Ronald Himler (illustrator), (Aladdin, ISBN 0-689-71296-0, 1989) **On-Level** ***ALA Notable Book***

Grandfather's Journey, by Allen Say (Houghton Mifflin, ISBN 0-395-57035-2, 1993) **On-Level** ***Caldecott Medal***

How Jackrabbit Got His Very Long Ears, by Heather Irbinskas and Kenneth J. Spengler (illustrator), (Rising Moon, ISBN 0-873-58566-6), 1994) **On-Level**

Midnight Ride of Paul Revere, The, by Henry Wordsworth Longfellow and Jeffery Thompson (illustrator), (National Geographic Society, ISBN 0-792-27674-4, 2000) **On-Level**

Picture Book of Eleanor Roosevelt, A, by David A. Adler and Robert Casilla (illustrator), (Holiday House, ISBN 0-823-40856-6, 1991) **On-Level**

Sam the Minuteman, by Nathaniel Benchley and Arnold Lobel (illustrator), (HarperTrophy, ISBN 0-064-44107-5, 1987) **On-Level**

Star-Spangled Banner, Francis Scott Key and Peter Spier (illustrator), (Yearling Books, ISBN 0-440-40697-8, 1992) **On-Level**

Across the Wide Dark Sea: The Mayflower Journey, by Jean Van Leeuwen and Thomas B. Allen (illustrator), (Dial Books for Young Readers, ISBN 0-803-71166-2, 1995) **Challenge**

Buffalo Days, by Diane Hoyt-Goldsmith and Lawrence Migdale (illustrator), (Holiday House, ISBN 0-823-41327-6, 1997) **Challenge** ***Carter G. Woodson Award***

Flag We Love, The, by Pam Munoz Ryan and Ralph Masiello (illustrator), (Charlesbridge Publishing, ISBN 0-881-06844-6, 2000) **Challenge**

Peppe the Lamplighter, by Elisa Bartone and Ted Lewin (illustrator), (Mulberry Books, ISBN 0-688-15469-7, 1997) **Challenge** ***Caldecott Honor Book, 1994***

Story of the Statue of Liberty, by Betsy C. Maestro and Giulio Maestro (illustrator), (Mulberry Books, ISBN 0-688-08746-9, 1989) **Challenge**

History Workshop: Reconstructing the Past with Elementary Students, by Karen L. Jorgensen (Heinemann, ISBN 0-435-08900-5, 1993) **Teacher Reference**

Look for this symbol throughout the Teacher's Edition to find **Award-Winning Selections**.

Unit Bibliographies

Unit 6 Bibliography

How Chipmunk Got His Stripes: A Tale of Bragging and Teasing, by Joseph Bruchac, James Bruchac (illustrator), Jose Aruego (illustrator), and Ariane Dewey (illustrator). (Dial Books for Young Readers, ISBN 0-803-72404-7, 2001) **Easy**

Market Day: A Story Told With Folk Art, by Lois Ehlert (Harcourt Brace, ISBN 0-152-02158-2, 2000) **Easy**

On Market Street, by Arnold Lobel and Anita Lobel (Illustrator) (Greenwillow, ISBN 0-688-80309-1, 1981) **Easy**

Saturday Market, by Patricia Grossman and Enrique O. Sanchez (Illustrator) (Lothrop Lee & Shepard, ISBN 0-688-12176-4, 1994) **Easy**

Tiger Woman, by Laurence Yep and Robert Roth (illustrator). Bridgewater Books; ISBN: 0-816-73464-X, 1995) **Easy**

Train Song, by Diane Siebert (Harper Trophy, ISBN 0-785-71735-8, 1990) **Easy** ***Notable Children's Trade Book in Social Studies***

Travel and Transport Then and Now, by Alistair Smith, Ruth Russell (designer) and Adrienne Salgado, (illustrator), (Usborne Pub Ltd, ISBN 0-746-03102-5, 2000) **Easy**

Abuela's Weave, by Omar S. Castaneda and Enrique O. Sanchez (illustrator), (Lee & Low Books, ISBN 1-880-00020-2, 1995) **On-Level**

Alexander Graham Bell: A Photo-Illustrated Biography, by Greg Linder (Bridgestone Books, ISBN 0-736-80202-9, 1999) **On-Level**

Gabriella's Song, by Candace Fleming (Atheneum, ISBN 0-689-80973-5, 1997) **On-Level** ***Parents' Choice Silver Honor***

Great Ball Game: A Muskogee Story, The, by Joseph Bruchac and Susan L. Roth (Illustrator) (Dial Books for Young Readers, ISBN 0-803-71539-0, 1994) **On-Level**

I Spy a Freight Train: Transportation in Art, by Lucy Micklethwait (Greenwillow, ISBN 0-688-14700-3, 1996) **On-Level**

Junior Thunder Lord, The, by Laurence Yep and Robert Van Nutt (illustrator) (Bridgewater Books, ISBN 0-816-73454-2, 1994) **On-Level**

Madlenka, by Peter Sis (Frances Foster Books, ISBN 0-374-39969-7, 2000) **On-Level**

Many Nations, by Joseph Bruchac (Econo-Clad Books, ISBN 0-603-11838-3, 1999) **On-Level** ***International Reading Teacher's Choice Award***

Market, by Ted Lewin (Lothrop Lee & Shepard, ISBN 0-688-12161-6, 1996) **On-Level**

Picture Book of Thomas Alva Edison, A, by David A. Adler, John Wallner (Illustrator), Alexandra Wallner (Illustrator) (Holiday House, ISBN 0-823-41246-6, 1996) **On-Level**

Thirteen Moons on Turtle's Back: A Native American Year of Moons, by Joseph Bruchac and Thomas Locke (illustrator) (Philomel Books, ISBN 0-399-22141-7, 1992) **On-Level**

Dragon Prince: A Chinese Beauty and the Beast Tale, The, by Laurence Yep and Kam Mak (illustrator) (HarperCollins Juvenile Books, ISBN 0-060-24381-3, 1997) **Challenge**

Earth Under Sky Bear's Feet: Native American Poems of the Land, The, by Joseph Bruchac (Econo-Clad Books, ISBN 0-613-10503-6, 1999) **Challenge**

Imaginative Inventions: The Who, What, Where, When, and Why, of Roller Skates, Potato Chips, Marbles, and Pie (and More!), by Charise Mericle Harper (Little, Brown & Co., ISBN 0-316-34725-6, 2001) **Challenge**

Mae Jemison: The First African American Woman Astronaut, by Liza N. Burby (Powerkids Press, ISBN 0-823-95027-1, 1998) **Challenge**

Wake Up, World!: A Day in the Life of Children Around the World, by Beatrice Hollyer (Henry Holt & Company, ISBN 0-805-06293-9, 1999) **Challenge**

Welcoming Babies, by Margy Burns Knight and Anne Sibley O'Brien (illustrator) (Tilbury House Publishers, ISBN 0-884-48123-9, 1994) **Challenge**

Keepsakes: Using Family Stories in Elementary Classroom, by Linda Winston (Heinemann, ISBN 0-435-07235-8, 1997) **Teacher Reference**

Look for this symbol throughout the Teacher's Edition to find **Award-Winning Selections**.

Index

Activate Prior Knowledge (*see* ESL Support)
American Red Cross, TR1–TR2
Analyze Information (*see* Reading Skills)
Analyze Pictures (*see* Reading Skills)
Apply Information (*see* Reading Skills)

Art
- **Curriculum Connection,** 1f, 3, 13a, 43f, 47, 51, 64, 75, 87f, 135f, 155, 155a, 183f, 192, 201a, 217a, 231f, 245a, 251a

Assessment
- **Formal,** 1e, 43e, 87e, 135e, 183e, 231e
- **Informal,** 1e, 43e, 87e, 135e, 183e, 231e
- **Lesson Reviews,** 9, 17, 21, 25, 31, 53, 57, 65, 71, 77, 97, 101, 105, 111, 119, 125, 145, 153, 159, 167, 173, 191, 199, 205, 209, 215, 221, 239, 243, 249, 253, 261
- **Ongoing,** SF11, 1e, 7, 24, 29, 33, 43e, 49, 53, 61, 87e, 93, 97, 105, 110, 118, 135e, 141, 143, 151, 154, 158, 163, 165, 171, 172, 175, 183e, 189, 191, 198, 215, 220, 231e, 248, 253
- **Performance,** 1e, 1, 36a, 38, 42, 43e, 43, 80a, 82, 87e, 87, 128a, 130, 134, 135e, 135, 176a, 178, 182, 183e, 183, 224a, 226, 231e, 231, 266a, 268, 272
- **Portfolio,** 1e, 1, 40, 43e, 43, 87e, 87, 132, 135e, 135, 180, 183e, 183, 228, 231e, 231, 270
- **Scoring Guides (Rubrics),** 36a, 39, 40, 80a, 83, 84, 128a, 131, 132, 134, 176a, 179, 180, 182, 224a, 227, 228, 266a, 269, 270, 272
- **Support,** 7c, 49c, 93c, 142c, 189c, 237c
- **TestWorks CD-ROM,** 1c, 43c, 87c, 135c, 183c, 231c
- **Unit Reviews,** SF11, 38–41, 82–85, 130–133, 178–181, 226–229, 268–271

Atlas
- **Big Book Atlas,** 1c, 43c, 87c, 135c, 183c, 231c
- **Social Studies Reference Guide Atlas,** R2–R9

AudioText (*see* Technology)
Auditory Learning (*see* Meeting Individual Needs, Learning Styles)
Authors, SF2, 1g, 43g, 87g, 135g, 183g, 231g

Background
- **Addams, Jane, and Hull House,** 72
- **Addresses,** 52
- **American flag,** 211
- **American Indians,** 191
- **Barton, Clara,** 114
- **Bell, Alexander Graham,** 248
- **Bethune, Mary McLeod,** 32
- **Bruchac, Joseph,** 244
- **CAPAY (Coalition for Asian Pacific American Youth),** 68
- **Caring for Our Earth,** 137
- **Carver, George Washington,** 122
- **Chinese New Year,** 66
- **Communities,** 44
- **Declaration of Independence,** 203
- **Earth,** 259
- **Edison, Thomas,** 249
- **Endangered Animals,** 174
- **Essential Elements of Geography,** H8
- **Exploration and Travel,** 232
- **Farming,** 167
- **Franklin, Benjamin,** 206
- **Group Behavior,** 9
- **Holidays,** 184
- **Houston, Sam,** 78
- **Houston, Texas,** 58
- **Independence Day,** 203
- **Inventors and Inventions,** 247
- **Jemison, Mae,** 256
- **Kid's Kitchen,** 112
- **Kinds of Jobs,** 109
- **King, Martin Luther, Jr.,** 214
- **Lincoln, Abraham,** 216
- **Loyalists,** 204
- **Markets,** 239
- **Memorial Day,** 213
- **Money,** 106
- **Moral of the Story,** 266
- **Mother's Day,** 63
- **Muir, John,** 159
- **National Anthem,** 224
- **National/Political Symbols,** 209
- **Native Americans,** 166, 191
- **Oceans,** 152
- **Pilgrims,** 199
- **President of the United States,** 221
- **Pronunciation of Words Meaning "Good-bye,"** 264
- **Racial Segregation,** 18–19
- **Recycling,** 137, 173
- **Roosevelt, Eleanor,** 222
- **Rules,** 24
- **Sacagawea,** 168
- **Stereotypes,** 88
- **Stotz, Carl,** 10
- **Taino,** 197
- **Tanzania,** 261
- **Toys in History,** 102
- **Transportation,** 125, 253
- **Tree Musketeers,** 160
- **Trucks,** 126
- **Veterans Day,** 213
- **Wants vs. Needs,** 101
- **Water Supply,** 165
- **Work at Home,** 95
- **Yep, Laurence,** 262

Bibliography
- **Grade-level,** TR41–TR46
- **Unit-level,** 1h, 43h, 87h, 135h, 183h, 231h

Biography
- **Addams, Jane,** 72–73
- **Barton, Clara,** 114–115
- **Bethune, Mary McLeod,** 32–33
- **Carver, George Washington,** 122–123
- **Franklin, Benjamin,** 206–207
- **Houston, Sam,** 78–79
- **Jemison, Mae,** 256–257
- **Lincoln, Abraham,** 216–217
- **Niebla, Elvia,** 162–163
- **Sacagawea,** 168–169
- **Stotz, Carl,** 10–11
- **Yep, Laurence,** 262–263

Build Background, 1h, 8a, 14a, 28a, 43h, 50a, 56a, 62a, 70a, 74a, 87h, 94a, 100a, 104a, 108a, 116a, 124a, 135h, 142a, 150a, 156a, 164a, 170a, 183h, 190a, 196a, 202a, 208a, 212a, 218a, 231h, 238a, 242a, 246a, 252a, 258a (*see also* ESL Support, Build Background)
Building Citizenship Skills (*see* Citizenship)

Categorize/Classify (*see* Reading Skills)
Cause and Effect (*see* Reading Skills)
Character (*see* Citizenship)

Chart and Graph Skills
- **Read a Bar Graph,** 254–255
- **Read a Calendar,** 20–21
- **Read a Time Line,** 146–147
- **Use a Chart,** 98–99

Citizen Heroes
- **Caring,** 112–113
- **Courage,** 18–19
- **Fairness,** 68–69
- **Honesty,** 222–223
- **Respect,** 244–245
- **Responsibility,** 160–161

Citizenship
- **Building Citizenship Skills,** H4–H5
- **Decision Making,** H5, 71, 105, 239
- **Problem Solving,** H5, 26, 27, 39, 69, 72, 113, 175, 219, 261

Index

Social Studies Strand, 4, 16, 19, 21a, 27a, 69, 73, 73a, 113, 159, 161, 172, 186, 204, 209, 211, 225

Compare and Contrast (*see* Reading Skills)

Critical Thinking
- **Decision Making,** 71, 105, 239, 240–241
- **Problem Solving,** 26–27, 39, 69, 72, 113, 175, 219, 261

Culture
- **Social Studies Strand,** 35a, 64, 67, 107, 169, 203, 245, 247

Curriculum Connections (*see* Art; Drama; Geography; Literature; Mathematics; Music; Reading; Science; Writing)

DK (Dorling Kindersley), SF8, 66–67, 126–127, 250–251
Decision Making, H5, 71, 105, 144, 239, 240–241 (*see also* Critical Thinking)
Diagram, 192–193, 208, 228

Discovery Channel School
- **Discovery Channel School,** SF9, H2–H3
- **Unit Projects,** H2–H3, 42, 43, 86, 87, 134, 135, 182, 183, 230, 231, 272
- **Videos,** 49h, 231h

Drama
- **Curriculum Connection,** 1f, 13a, 43f, 55a, 69a, 87f, 99a, 113, 115a, 118, 135f, 149a, 169, 175a, 177, 183f, 185, 185a, 201a, 207a, 231f, 233, 250, 251a

Draw Conclusions (*see* Reading Skills)

ESL Support
- **ESL Support,** SF7, 1g, 6, 15, 23, 29, 43g, 110
- **Access Content,** 15, 29, 48, 92, 96, 101, 118, 151, 154, 156, 171, 188, 192, 220, 240, 248, 257, 260
- **Activate Prior Knowledge,** 140, 151, 152
- **Build Background,** 61, 64, 105, 157, 166
- **Extend Language,** 23, 52, 59, 76, 144, 162, 198, 204, 210, 214, 236, 243, 265
- **Professional Development** (Dr. Jim Cummins), 1g, 43g, 87g, 135g, 183g, 231g

Economics
- **Social Studies Strand,** 23, 35a, 77, 80, 90, 96, 107a, 127a, 151, 157, 158, 171, 173, 217, 239, 253, 267

English Language Learners (*see* ESL Support)
Enrich Activities (*see* Meeting Individual Needs, Leveled Practice—Easy, On-Level, Challenge Activities)
Evaluate (*see* Reading Skills)
Express Ideas (*see* Reading Skills)
Extend Activities (*see* Meeting Individual Needs, Leveled Practice—Easy, On-Level, Challenge Activities)
Extend Language (*see* ESL Support)

Facing Fear: Helping Students Cope with Tragic Events, TR1–TR2
Family Activities (in English and Spanish), TR21–TR32
Fast Facts, 2, 34, 76, 119, 158, 198, 205, 206, 215, 219

Generalize (*see* Reading Skills)

Geography
- **Building Geography Skills,** H10–H11, H12–H13, H14
- **Social Studies Strand,** 29, 46, 55, 55a, 75, 76, 79, 107, 120, 145, 149a, 155a, 169a, 175, 217, 259, 265a
- **Themes of Geography,** H8–H9, 27, 51, 59, 75, 144, 197, 198, 257

Government
- **Social Studies Strand,** 27a, 73a, 163, 172, 220

Graphic Organizers
- **Graphic Organizers,** 50, 56, 62, 74, 94, 142, 190, 196, 208, 218, 238, 242, 252
- **Teacher Resources Tab Section,** TR3–TR14

Hands-on Unit Project (Discovery Channel School), H2–H3, 1, 42, 43, 86, 87, 134, 135, 182, 183, 230, 231, 272
Here and There, 106–107, 174–175, 264–265

History
- **Social Studies Strand,** 30, 58, 79, 79a, 125, 169a, 186, 214

Holidays, 20, 21, 63, 64, 66–67, 184–185, 196–197, 198, 199, 202–203, 212–213, 214–215 (*see also* Social Studies Plus!)
Hypothesize (*see* Reading Skills)

Individual Learning (*see* Meeting Individual Needs, Learning Styles)
Internet (*see* Technology)
Interpret Charts, Chart and Graph Skills (*see* Reading Skills)
Interpret Graphs, Chart and Graph Skills (*see* Reading Skills)
Interpret Maps, Map and Globe Skills (*see* Reading Skills)
Interpret Time Lines (*see* Reading Skills)

Kinesthetic Learning (*see* Meeting Individual Needs, Learning Styles)

Language Arts (*see* Reading; Writing)
Learning Styles (*see* Meeting Individual Needs, Learning Styles)
Leveled Practice—Easy, On-Level, Challenge Activities (*see* Meeting Individual Needs, Leveled Practice)

Literature
- **Bibliography,** 1h, 43h, 87h, 135h, 183h, 231h
- **Curriculum Connection,** 1f, 12, 19, 37, 43f, 57, 61a, 79a, 87f, 111, 127a, 135f, 183f, 225, 231f, 263, 267
- **End with a Folktale,** ***The Farmer's Little Girl,*** 266–267
- **End with a Legend,** ***Johnny Appleseed,*** 176–177
- **End with a Poem,**
  - **"One Great Big Community,"** 80–81
  - **"School Today,"** 36–37
  - **"Work Day,"** 128–129
- **Trade Books,** 1c, 1h, 43c, 43h, 87c, 87h, 135c, 135h, 183c, 183h, 231c, 231h

Logical Learning (*see* Meeting Individual Needs, Learning Styles)

Main Idea, 140–141, 145, 159, 173, 179, 181
Main Idea and Details (*see* Reading Skills)
Make Decisions (*see* Reading Skills)
Make Inferences (*see* Reading Skills)
MapQuest, SF4
Maps, 51, 54–55, 60–61, 75, 83, 84, 120–121, 131, 154–155, 179, 191, 200–201, 227

Map and Globe Skills
- **Follow a Route,** 120–121, 131
- **Locate Land and Water,** 154–155, 179
- **Use a History Map,** 200–201, 227
- **Use a Map Key,** 54–55, 83
- **Use Four Directions,** 60–61, 84

Map and Globe Skills Review, H10–H14
Map Resources CD-ROM, 1c, 43c, 87c, 135c, 183c, 231c

Mathematics
- **Curriculum Connection,** 1f, 7, 21a, 35a, 43f, 61a, 87f, 93, 98, 103a, 107, 107a, 135f, 163a, 183f, 200, 211a, 217a, 223a, 231f, 251, 254

Meeting Individual Needs, Learning Styles
- **Auditory,** 30
- **Kinesthetic,** 30

Meeting Individual Needs, Leveled Practice
- **Easy, On-Level, Challenge Activities,** SF7, 4, 13a, 16, 21a, 27a, 35, 35a, 46, 55a, 61a, 69a, 73, 73a, 79a, 90, 99a, 103a, 107a, 115a, 127a, 149a, 155a, 163a, 169a, 175a, 195a, 201a, 207a, 211a, 217a, 223a, 241a, 245a, 251a, 257a, 265a

Multimedia Library, 1c, 43c, 87c, 135c, 183c, 231c

Music
- **"America, the Beautiful,"** H7
- **Begin with a Song,**
  - **"Explore with Me,"** 232–233
  - **"Holidays are Special Days,"** 184–185
  - **"Lots of Jobs,"** 88–89
  - **"Show You Care,"** 136–137
  - **"This is My Community,"** 44–45
  - **"We Go to School,"** 2–3
- **Curriculum Connection,** 1f, 13a, 36, 43f, 69a, 87f, 89, 96, 135f, 183f, 185, 195a, 231f, 233, 241a, 257a, 265
- **End with a Song,**
  - **"The Star Spangled Banner,"** 224–225

Musical Learning (*see* Meeting Individual Needs, Learning Styles)
Sing Aloud, 246a
***Songs and Music* CD,** 1c, 2, 43c, 44, 87c, 88, 135c, 136, 183c, 184, 231c, 232

Objectives
- **Lesson Objectives,** 50, 54, 56, 58, 60, 62, 66, 70, 74, 80, 94, 104, 108, 140, 142, 146, 150, 156, 164, 170, 174, 190, 192, 196, 202, 206, 210, 212, 216, 218, 238, 240, 242, 244, 246, 250, 252, 258, 262
- **Unit Objectives,** 1d, 43d, 87d, 135d, 136, 183d, 186, 231d, 232, 234, 236, 266, 270

Pacing, 1b, 43b, 87b, 135b, 183b, 231b
Patriotism, H6–H7, 14, 16–17, 204, 208, 209, 210, 213, 224 (*see also* Citizenship)
Picture Clues (*see* Reading Skills)

Planning Guides
- **Unit Planning Guides,** 1b–1c, 43b–43c, 87b–87c, 135b–135c, 183b–183c, 231b–231c

Pledge of Allegiance, H6, 16, 17
Poems, 8a, 14a, 22a, 28a, 36, 50a, 56a, 70a, 74a, 80, 94a, 100a, 104a, 108a, 116a, 128, 124a, 142a, 150a, 156a, 170a, 190a, 202a, 208a, 212a, 218a, 238a, 242a, 252a, 258a
Point of View (*see* Reading Skills)
Predict (*see* Reading Skills)
Problem Solving, 27, 39, 69, 113, 175, 219, 261 (*see also* Critical Thinking)
Professional Development, 1g, 43g, 87g, 135g, 183g, 231g
Projects (*see* Discovery Channel School, Unit Projects)

Quick Teaching Plan, SF5, 8, 14, 22, 28, 50, 56, 62, 70, 74, 94, 100, 104, 108, 116, 124, 142, 150, 156, 164, 170, 190, 196, 202, 208, 212, 218, 238, 242, 246, 252, 258

Read Aloud, 1h, 8a, 14a, 22a, 28a, 43h, 50a, 56a, 62a, 70a, 74a, 87h, 94a, 100a, 104a, 108a, 116a, 124a, 135h, 142a, 150a, 156a, 164a, 170a, 183h, 190a, 196a, 202a, 208a, 212a, 218a, 231h, 238a, 242a, 252a, 258a

Reading
- **Curriculum Connection,** 1f, 11, 20, 43f, 54, 79a, 81, 87f, 91, 99a, 115a, 128, 129, 135f, 175a, 176, 183f, 187, 195a, 207a, 231f, 235, 245, 245a

Reading Skills
- **Analyze Information,** 103, 105, 112, 121, 127, 160, 161, 163, 176, 241, 242, 243, 244, 245, 247, 251, 257, 266
- **Analyze Pictures,** 5, 9, 27, 28, 29, 34, 35, 45, 47, 57, 58, 63, 67, 71, 89, 103, 106, 107, 109, 110, 124, 125, 126, 127, 137, 143, 147, 166, 172, 175, 190, 199, 212, 233, 237, 251, 260
- **Apply Information,** 9, 11, 15, 24, 25, 29, 34, 59, 63, 64, 69, 71, 91, 95, 96, 97, 109, 110, 123, 143, 153, 157, 158, 165, 169, 172, 173, 198, 199, 203, 204, 211, 213, 219, 221, 225, 239, 245, 247, 249, 257, 259, 265
- **Categorize/Classify**, 22, 24, 92, 104, 141, 202, 218
- **Cause and Effect,** 11, 18, 23, 33, 35, 63, 70, 115, 123, 158, 163, 171, 251
- **Compare and Contrast,** 9, 12, 13, 19, 21, 23, 28, 29, 30, 35, 36, 47, 48, 50, 52, 56, 57, 59, 62, 66, 74, 75, 80, 89, 91, 95, 100, 103, 107, 147, 150, 152, 153, 191, 242, 249, 251, 253, 258, 259, 263
- **Context Clues,** 171
- **Draw Conclusions,** 5, 13, 16, 17, 19, 33, 51, 66, 100, 101, 103, 104, 109, 113, 115, 125, 143, 160, 165, 197, 199, 207, 211, 219, 223, 262
- **Evaluate,** 17, 23, 69, 119, 203, 205
- **Express Ideas,** 25, 30, 63, 73, 209, 215, 217, 221, 241, 263, 264
- **Generalize,** 68, 71, 207, 217
- **Hypothesize,** 5, 25, 29, 30, 31, 223, 224, 243, 247, 248, 251
- **Interpret Charts,** 21, 98, 241
- **Interpret Graphs,** 255
- **Interpret Maps,** 51, 55, 60, 61, 75, 76, 77, 121, 155, 169, 191, 200, 201, 259
- **Interpret Time Lines,** 147, 166, 211, 253
- **Main Idea and Details,** 15, 17, 33, 36, 45, 55, 63, 65, 72, 81, 102, 106, 108, 113, 115, 119, 127, 140, 142, 144, 156, 161, 168, 170, 171, 179, 196

Make Decisions, 105, 239, 269
Make Inferences, 3, 15, 17, 18, 27, 31, 33, 34, 36, 45, 52, 53, 59, 63, 67, 73, 75, 79, 80, 95, 96, 97, 99, 101, 103, 104, 115, 117, 118, 126, 127, 128, 144, 147, 157, 159, 163, 165, 166, 169, 171, 173, 176, 193, 197, 203, 205, 213, 220, 247, 248, 252, 257, 258, 262
Picture Clues, 6, 8, 28, 39, 110
Point of View, 17, 23, 68
Predict, 13, 23, 59, 91, 236, 238, 246, 266, 269
Recall and Retell, 51, 64, 68, 75, 79, 151, 188, 190, 198, 208, 227
Sequence, 14, 15, 20, 26, 92, 94, 116, 117, 118, 123, 131, 164, 166, 167, 252
Solve Problems, 26, 72, 113, 175, 219, 261

Recall and Retell (*see* Reading Skills)
Research and Writing Skills, 11, 21, 27, 31, 79, 111, 119, 125, 145, 189, 201, 221, 257
Reteach Activities (*see* Meeting Individual Needs, Leveled Practice—Easy, On-Level, Challenge Activities)
Rubrics (*see* Assessment, Scoring Guides [Rubrics])

Science
Curriculum Connection, 1f, 16, 26, 43f, 49, 60, 61a, 87f, 117, 127, 135f, 141, 143, 146, 163, 163a, 175, 183f, 189, 207, 231f, 237, 241, 257a, 265a
Science/Technology, Social Studies Strand, 17, 24, 57, 141, 143

Scope and Sequence, TR33–TR40
Skills (*see* Chart and Graph Skills; Map and Globe Skills; Reading Skills; Research and Writing Skills; Thinking Skills)
Smithsonian Institution, SF8, 12–13, 148–149, 190a, 194–195
Social Learning (*see* Meeting Individual Needs, Learning Styles)
Social Studies Strand (*see* Citizenship; Culture; Economics; Geography; Government; History; Science; Technology; Writing)
Sociology (*see* Culture)
Solve Problems (*see* Reading Skills)
Songs (*see* Music)
Standardized Test Prep, SF11, 38, 82, 130, 178, 226, 268 (*see also* Test Talk)
Summarize (*see* Reading Skills)

Symbols
Alamo, 209
American flag, 16, 208
Bald eagle, 208, 209
Gateway Arch, 209
Liberty Bell, 208, 209
Statue of Liberty, 208, 209
Washington Monument, 208, 209

Technology
Additional Internet Links, 1c, 43c, 87c, 135c, 183c, 231c
AudioText, SF7, 1c, 43c, 87c, 135c, 183c, 231c
Key Internet Search Terms, 1c, 43c, 87c, 135c, 183c, 231c
***Songs and Music* CD,** 1c, 2, 43c, 44, 87c, 88, 135c, 136, 183c, 184, 231c, 232
Teacher Resources CD-ROM, 1c, 5, 7, 9, 17, 21, 25, 27, 31, 39, 43c, 47, 49, 49c, 53, 55, 57, 61, 65, 71, 77, 83, 87c, 91, 93, 93a, 97, 99, 101, 105, 111, 119, 121, 125, 131, 135c, 141, 145, 147, 153, 155, 159, 167, 173, 179, 183c, 187, 189, 191, 193, 199, 201, 205, 209, 215, 221, 227, 231c, 235, 237, 241, 243, 249, 253, 255, 261, 269
Video Field Trips, 1c, 43c, 87c, 135c, 183c, 231c
Web Site (www.sfsocialstudies.com), SF9, 1c, 2, 5, 8, 10, 13, 16, 22, 33, 39, 42, 43c, 51, 56, 70, 72, 75, 78, 83, 87c, 91, 95, 100, 106, 109, 114, 123, 124, 131, 134, 143, 146, 150, 155, 156, 163, 164, 166, 169, 175, 179, 186, 197, 201, 202, 206, 212, 217, 219, 227, 235, 239, 246, 256, 258, 259, 263, 269

Test Prep (*see* Standardized Test Prep)

Test Talk
Choose the Right Answer, 1e, 43e, 87e, 130, 135e, 183e, 231e
Locate Key Words in the Question, 1e, 41, 43e, 52, 87e, 95, 135e, 152, 183e, 214, 231e, 259
Locate Key Words in the Text, 1e, 11, 43e, 85, 87e, 102, 135e, 172, 179, 183e, 199, 231e, 244
Use Information from Graphics, 1e, 21, 43e, 47, 87e, 91, 135e, 166, 183e, 193, 228, 231e, 255
Use Information from the Text, 1e, 19, 43e, 66, 87e, 107, 135e, 144, 179, 183e, 221, 231e, 249
Write Your Answer, 1e, 31, 43e, 53, 87e, 93, 135e, 161, 183e, 203, 231e, 241, 271

TestWorks CD-ROM, 1c, 43c, 87c, 135c, 183c, 231c
Then and Now, SF5, 34–35, 58–59, 102–103, 210–211
Thinking Skills (*see* Decision Making; Problem Solving)
Tolerance, 43g, 50, 64, 68–69, 222–223

Unit Project (*see* Discovery Channel School, Unit Projects)
Unit Review, 38–41, 82–85, 130–133, 178–181, 226–229, 268–271

Verbal Learning, 13a, 21a, 35a, 55a, 69a, 73a, 79a, 99a, 103a, 107a, 115a, 127a, 149a, 155a, 163a, 169a, 195a, 201a, 207a, 217a, 223a, 241a, 251a, 257a, 265a (*see also* Meeting Individual Needs, Learning Styles)
Visual Learning, 13a, 21a, 55a, 61a, 69a, 79a, 99a, 103a, 107a, 115a, 127a, 155a, 163a, 169a, 175a, 195a, 201a, 207a, 211a, 217a, 223a, 245a, 251a, 257a, 265a (*see also* Meeting Individual Needs, Learning Styles)

Vocabulary
Lesson Vocabulary, 6, 8, 14, 18, 20, 22, 34, 36, 50, 54, 56, 60, 70, 74, 94, 98, 100, 108, 120, 124, 142, 146, 150, 156, 164, 174, 192, 196, 202, 212, 218, 238, 246, 254, 258
Picture Glossary, R12–R19
Preview, SF6, 4–5, 46–47, 90–91, 138–139, 186–187, 234–235
Vocabulary Words, TR15–TR20

Washington, George, 205, 215

Workbook

Workbook Support, 5, 7a–7b, 36a, 39, 47, 49, 49a–49b, 53, 55, 57, 61, 65, 71, 77, 83, 91, 93, 93a–93b, 97, 99, 100a, 101, 105, 111, 119, 121, 125, 131, 141, 141a–141b, 145, 147, 150a, 153, 155, 156a, 159, 164a, 167, 170a, 173, 179, 187, 189, 189a–189b, 191, 193, 199, 201, 205, 209, 215, 221, 227, 235, 237, 237a–237b, 238a, 241, 242a, 243, 246a, 249, 252a, 253, 255, 261, 269

Writing

Curriculum Connection, 1f, 5, 13a, 21a, 27a, 33, 43f, 45, 55a, 69a, 73a, 87f, 99a, 103, 103a, 115, 115a, 127a, 135f, 136, 149a, 155a, 163a, 169a, 175a, 183f, 195a, 201a, 207a, 211a, 217a, 223, 223a, 231f, 241a, 245a, 251a, 257a, 258a, 265a

Index

Credits

Illustrations

1 Kate Flanagan; **Unit 1:** 1D Benrei Huang; 1H, 21A Matt Straub; 8 Janet Skiles; 11 Ginna Magee; 12 Mike Dammer; 19 George Barile; **Unit 2:** 43B Susan Tolonen; 43H, 50A, 56A, 62A Matt Straub; **Unit 4:** 135D Yvonne Gilbert; 182 Janet Skiles; **Unit 5:** 183D Darryl Ligasan; 183H Matt Straub; **Unit 6:** 231H Matt Straub

Photographs

Every effort has been made to secure permission and provide appropriate credit for photographic material. The publisher deeply regrets any omission and pledges to correct errors called to their attention in subsequent editions.

Unless otherwise acknowledged, all photographs are the property of Scott Foresman, a division of Pearson Education.

Unit 1: 13A PhotoDisc; 28A Johnston; Francis Benjamin/Corbis-Bettmann; **Unit 2:** 61A Ron Slenzak/Corbis-Bettmann; 62A PhotoDisc; 70A PhotoDisc; 74A PhotoDisc; 100A PhotoDisc; **Unit 3:** 108A (BL, BR) PhotoDisc, (BC) Eyewire, Inc.; 115A (T, BR) PhotoDisc, (C, B) Eyewire, Inc.; 116A PhotoDisc; 123A PhotoDisc; 142A V.C.L./Paul Viant/FPG International LLC; **Unit 4:** 150A (BL) Joel W. Rogers/Corbis-Bettmann, (BC) Dave Jacobs/Stone, (BR) PhotoDisc; 156A Joel W. Rogers/Corbis-Bettmann; 164A PhotoDisc; 170A Richard Cummins/Corbis-Bettmann; **Unit 5:** 195A Lindsay Hebberd/Corbis-Bettmann; 202A Bettmann/Corbis; 208A Eyewire, Inc.; **Unit 6:** 265A PhotoDisc; **Teacher Resources:** TR40 SuperStock; TR43 The Granger Collection, New York

Notes

Notes

Notes